Dictionary of Literary Biography • Volume Fourteen

British Novelists Since 1960

Part 2: H-Z

Dictionary of Literary Biography

1: *The American Renaissance in New England*, edited by Joel Myerson (1978)

2: *American Novelists Since World War II*, edited by Jeffrey Helterman and Richard Layman (1978)

3: *Antebellum Writers in New York and the South*, edited by Joel Myerson (1979)

4: *American Writers in Paris, 1920-1939*, edited by Karen Lane Rood (1980)

5: *American Poets Since World War II*, 2 volumes, edited by Donald J. Greiner (1980)

6: *American Novelists Since World War II*, Second Series, edited by James E. Kibler, Jr. (1980)

7: *Twentieth-Century American Dramatists*, 2 volumes, edited by John MacNicholas (1981)

8: *Twentieth-Century American Science-Fiction Writers*, 2 volumes, edited by David Cowart and Thomas L. Wymer (1981)

9: *American Novelists, 1910-1945*, 3 volumes, edited by James J. Martine (1981)

10: *Modern British Dramatists, 1900-1945*, 2 volumes, edited by Stanley Weintraub (1982)

11: *American Humorists, 1800-1950*, 2 volumes, edited by Stanley Trachtenberg (1982)

12: *American Realists and Naturalists*, edited by Donald Pizer and Earl N. Harbert (1982)

13: *British Dramatists Since World War II*, 2 volumes, edited by Stanley Weintraub (1982)

14: *British Novelists Since 1960*, 2 volumes, edited by Jay L. Halio (1983)

Yearbook: 1980, edited by Karen L. Rood, Jean W. Ross, and Richard Ziegfeld (1981)

Yearbook: 1981, edited by Karen L. Rood, Jean W. Ross, and Richard Ziegfeld (1982)

Documentary Series, volume 1, edited by Margaret A. Van Antwerp (1982)

Documentary Series, volume 2, edited by Margaret A. Van Antwerp (1982)

Documentary Series, volume 3, edited by Mary Bruccoli (1983)

Dictionary of Literary Biography • Volume Fourteen

British Novelists
Since 1960

Part 2: H-Z

Edited by Jay L. Halio
University of Delaware

A Bruccoli Clark Book
Gale Research Company • Book Tower • Detroit, Michigan 48226
1983

Manufactured by Braun-Brumfield, Inc.
Ann Arbor, Michigan
Printed in the United States of America

Copyright © 1983
GALE RESEARCH COMPANY

Library of Congress Cataloging in Publication Data

Main entry under title:

British novelists since 1960.

    (Dictionary of literary biography; v. 14)
    "A Bruccoli Clark Book."
    Contents: pt. 2. H-Z
    1. English fiction—20th century—Bio-bibliography.
    2. Novelists, English—20th century—Biography—Dictionaries. I. Halio, Jay. L. II. Series.
PR881.B73   823'.914'09 [B]   82-2977
ISBN 0-8103-0927-0 (pt. 2)   AACR2

For L. Leon Campbell

Contents

Part 1

Foreword..xi

Preface...xix

Permissions and Acknowledgments..................xxi

Brian W. Aldiss (1925-)............................3
  Colin Greenland

Keith Alldritt (1935-)...............................18
  Malcolm Page

A. Alvarez (1929-)...................................22
  Sibyl L. Severance

Martin Amis (1949-)................................29
  Marla Levy

Paul Bailey (1937-)..................................33
  Thomas J. Cousineau

Beryl Bainbridge (1933-)..........................38
  Barbara C. Millard

J. G. Ballard (1930-)................................50
  John Fletcher

John Banville (1945-)...............................58
  George O'Brien

A. L. Barker (1918-)................................63
  Kim Heine

Stan Barstow (1928-)...............................69
  Elizabeth Allen

Nina Bawden (1925-)...............................77
  Gerda Seaman

David Benedictus (1938-)..........................86
  T. Winnifrith

John Berger (1926-)..................................91
  G. M. Hyde

Caroline Blackwood (1931-)......................98
  Priscilla Martin

Dirk Bogarde (1921-)...............................103
  Frank Crotzer

Malcolm Bradbury (1932-)........................108
  Melvin J. Friedman

Melvyn Bragg (1939-).............................117
  Peter Conradi

Christine Brooke-Rose (1926-)..................124
  Morton P. Levitt

Jeremy Brooks (1926-).............................130
  Georgia L. Lambert

Brigid Brophy (1929-)..............................137
  S. J. Newman

Christy Brown (1932-1981)..........................147
  Cathleen Donnelly

George Mackay Brown (1921-)..................150
  Thomas J. Starr

Anthony Burgess (1917-)..........................159
  Geoffrey Aggeler

Alan Burns (1929-)..................................187
  David W. Madden

A. S. Byatt (1929-)..................................194
  Caryn McTighe Musil

Angela Carter (1940-)..............................205
  Lorna Sage

Juanita Casey (1925-)..............................213
  Fleda Brown Jackson

David Caute (1936-)................................219
  Gerald Steel

Gerda Charles (1914-)..............................224
  Priscilla Martin

Barry Cole (1936-)..................................230
  Theresa M. Peter

Isabel Colegate (1931-)............................235
  Sarah Turvey

Lionel Davidson (1922-)...........................244
  Rosemarie Mroz

Margaret Thomson Davis (1926-)...............249
  Patrick Lyons

Margaret Drabble (1939-)..........................256
  Barbara C. Millard

Maureen Duffy (1933-).............................273
  Gerald Werson

Contents

Janice Elliot (1931-).................................282
  Virginia Briggs

J. G. Farrell (1935-1979) 288
  T. Winnifrith

Elaine Feinstein (1930-) 292
  Peter Conradi

Eva Figes (1932-) 298
  Peter Conradi

Penelope Fitzgerald (1916-) 302
  Catherine Wells Cole

John Fowles (1926-) 309
  Ellen Pifer

Michael Frayn 336
  Malcolm Page

Jane Gardam (1928-) 342
  Patricia Craig

Penelope Gilliatt (1932-) 349
  Thomas O. Calhoun

Jacky Gillott (1939-1980)........................356
  June Sturrock

Giles Gordon (1940-) 362
  Randall Stevenson

Contributors...373

Part 2

Permissions and Acknowledgments.....................xi

Clifford Hanley (1922-) 377
  Sheila G. Hearn

Catherine Heath (1924-) 381
  Gerard Werson

Aidan Higgins (1927-) 389
  Bill Grantham

Susan Hill (1942-) 394
  Catherine Wells Cole

Helen Hodgman (1945-) 401
  Malcolm Page

Desmond Hogan (1950-) 405
  Susan Matthews

David Holbrook (1923-) 410
  John Fletcher

David Hughes (1930-) 415
  Elizabeth Holly Snyder and Jay L. Halio

Jim Hunter (1939-) 420
  Susan Matthews

Dan Jacobson (1929-) 427
  Anne Fisher

Robin Jenkins (1912-) 433
  Glenda Norquay

B. S. Johnson (1933-1973).......................438
  Morton P. Levitt

Jennifer Johnston (1930-) 445
  Fleda Brown Jackson

Gabriel Josipovici (1940-) 452
  Linda Canon and Jay L. Halio

Maurice Leitch (1933-) 458
  Gordon Henderson

Penelope Lively (1933-) 463
  Jane Langton

David Lodge (1935-) 469
  Dennis Jackson

Colin MacInnes (1914-1976)......................481
  Harriet Blodgett

Elizabeth Mavor (1927-) 489
  Teresa Valbuena and Jay L. Halio

Ian McEwan (1948-) 495
  John Fletcher

John McGahern (1934-) 501
  Patricia Boyle Haberstroh

William McIlvanney (1936-) 508
  Cairns Craig

Stanley Middleton (1919-) 511
  June Sturrock

Julian Mitchell (1935-) 518
  Simon Edwards

Michael Moorcock (1939-) 524
  Colin Greenland

Nicholas Mosley (1923-) 535
  Peter Lewis

Helen Muir (1937-) 542
  Amanda M. Weir

Iris Murdoch (1919-) 546
  John Fletcher

John Noone (1936-) 562
  Gordon Henderson

Robert Nye (1939-) 564
   Elizabeth Allen

Edna O'Brien (1932-) 572
   Patricia Boyle Haberstroh

Julia O'Faolain (1932-) 580
   Mary Rose Callaghan

James Plunkett (1920-) 584
   Gordon Henderson

David Pownall (1938-) 592
   Malcolm Page

Christopher Priest (1943-) 598
   John Fletcher

Barbara Pym (1913-1980) 604
   Paul Binding

Ann Quin (1936-1973) 608
   Judith Mackrell

Frederic Raphael (1931-) 614
   John P. Kent

Piers Paul Read (1941-) 622
   Philip Flynn

Bernice Rubens (1928-) 632
   Judith Vincent

Paul Scott (1920-1978)............................638
   Margaret B. Lewis

Tom Sharpe (1928-) 646
   Simon Edwards

Robert Shaw (1927-1978)...........................654
   Malcolm Page

Penelope Shuttle (1947-) 661
   Kathleen Fullbrook

Alan Sillitoe (1928-) 666
   Catherine Smith

Andrew Sinclair (1935-) 675
   Judith Vincent

Anthony Storey (1928-) 681
   Jay L. Halio

David Storey (1933-) 689
   Dennis Jackson

Emma Tennant (1937-) 708
   Georgia L. Lambert

Rosemary Tonks (1932-) 715
   Michelle Poirier and Jay L. Halio

Rose Tremain (1943-) 721
   Simon Edwards

William Trevor (1928-) 723
   Paul Binding and Jay L. Halio

Elizabeth Troop (1931-) 730
   Simon Edwards

Frank Tuohy (1925-) 736
   Lindsey Tucker

Auberon Waugh (1939-) 745
   Joan Grumman and Anne Kowalewski

Fay Weldon (1931-) 750
   Harriet Blodgett

Paul West (1930-) 760
   Brian McLaughlin

Raymond Williams (1921-) 768
   René J. A. Weis

A. N. Wilson (1950-) 776
   Alan Hollinghurst

Colin Wilson (1931-) 780
   John A. Weigel

Appendix I: "You've Never Had It So Good" Gusted by "Winds of Change": British Fiction in the 1950s, 1960s, and After 789
   John Fletcher

Appendix II: Books for Further Reading........797

Contributors..803

Cumulative Index.....................................805

Permissions

The following people and institutions generously permitted the reproduction of photographs and other illustrative materials: John Goldblatt, p. 390; Jerry Bauer, pp. 395, 445, 482, 496, 501, 508, 511, 518, 524, 535, 542, 546, 598, 623, 639, 646, 666, 676, 682, 690, 745, 751, 777; Mark Gerson, pp. 410, 439, 572, 581, 632, 654, 724, 736; Caroline Forbes, p. 421; Fay Godwin's Photo Files, pp. 427, 459, 564; Richard Mewton, p. 464; Paul Morby, p. 470; Sophie Fallows, p. 559; Rebecca Nye, p. 568; A. Thompson, p. 592; Andrew Whittock, p. 605; Nobby Clark, p. 615; McFarlin Library, University of Tulsa, p. 644; David Sillitoe, p. 673; Jane Bown, *Observer* Newspapers, p. 709; Laurie Asprey, p. 721; Clive Barda, p. 731; Lufti Ozkok, p. 768.

Acknowledgments

This book was produced by BC Research.

Karen L. Rood is senior editor for the *Dictionary of Literary Biography* series. Sally Johns was the in-house editor.

The production staff included Judith S. Baughman, Mary Betts, Joseph Caldwell, Patricia Coate, Angela Dixon, Lynn Felder, Joyce Fowler, Robert H. Griffin, Nancy L. Houghton, Sharon K. Kirkland, Cynthia D. Lybrand, Alice A. Parsons, Joycelyn R. Smith, Robin A. Sumner, Carol J. Wilson, and Lynne C. Zeigler.

Charles L. Wentworth was photo editor. Walter W. Ross and Anne Dixon did the library research with the assistance of the staff at the Thomas Cooper Library of the University of South Carolina: Michael Freeman, Gary Geer, Alexander M. Gilchrist, W. Michael Havener, David Lincove, Donna Nance, Harriet B. Oglesbee, Jean Rhyne, Paula Swope, Jane Thesing, Ellen Tillett, and Beth S. Woodard.

Special thanks are due to Anne Cleary, Anne-Marie Ehrlich, Georgia L. Lambert, Mary O'Toole, Bernard Oldsey, and Eleanor Leishman. Assistance with the photographic copy work for this volume was given by Colorsep Graphics of Columbia, South Carolina, and Pat Crawford of Imagery, Columbia, South Carolina.

Dictionary of Literary Biography • Volume Fourteen

British Novelists
Since 1960

Part 2: H-Z

Dictionary of Literary Biography

Clifford Hanley
(28 October 1922-   )

Sheila G. Hearn
University of Edinburgh

BOOKS: *Dancing in the Streets* (London: Hutchinson, 1958);
Love From Everybody (London: Hutchinson, 1959); republished as *Don't Bother to Knock* (London: Brown, Watson, 1961);
The Taste of Too Much (London: Hutchinson, 1960);
The System, as Henry Calvin (London: Hutchinson, 1962);
It's Different Abroad, as Calvin (London: Hutchinson, 1963; New York: Harper & Row, 1963);
Nothing but the Best (London: Hutchinson, 1964); republished as *Second Time Round* (Boston: Houghton Mifflin, 1964);
A Skinfull of Scotch (London: Hutchinson, 1965; Boston: Houghton Mifflin, 1965);
The Italian Gadget, as Calvin (London: Hutchinson, 1966);
The Hot Month (London: Hutchinson, 1967; Boston: Houghton Mifflin, 1967);
The DNA Business, as Calvin (London: Hutchinson, 1967);
A Nice Friendly Town, as Calvin (London: Hutchinson, 1967);
Miranda Must Die, as Calvin (London: Hutchinson, 1968);
The Red-Haired Bitch (London: Hutchinson, 1969; Boston: Houghton Mifflin, 1969);
The Chosen Instrument, as Calvin (London: Hutchinson, 1969);
Boka Lives, as Calvin (New York: Harper & Row, 1969);
The Poison Chasers, as Calvin (London: Hutchinson, 1971);

Clifford Hanley

Take Two Popes, as Calvin (London: Hutchinson, 1972);

The Burns Country (Newport, R. I.: J. Arthur Dent, 1975);

Prissy (London: Collins, 1978);

The Biggest Fish in the World (Edinburgh: Chambers, 1979);

The Scots (London: David & Charles, 1980; New York: Times Books, 1980);

The Spirit of Scotland (Edinburgh: B.B.C. Scotland, 1980).

The division of Clifford Hanley's books into two categories—those written under his own name and those attributed to a pseudonym—immediately suggests his conformity with a major cliche of modern Scottish literary criticism: that Scottish writers are the victims of a series of particularly deep historical divisions in their society and its culture, and that this inheritance results in their reflection and embodiment, in literary terms, of the varieties of national schizophrenia. But the choice of "Henry Calvin" as that pseudonym, with its reference to the religious reformation, often held to be the origin and original of those many divisions, is so explicit as to constitute a joke against the critics; and the joke is heightened by the fact that the interesting division in Hanley's work is not between the novels and the thrillers—although they are published under different names—but between the fiction, which may use Scotland as a scenic backdrop and, consequently, mention distinctively Scottish themes only in passing, and the rest of his writing, which is obsessed with Scotland and the notion of Scottishness. Unfortunately, what denies this divide is that in neither category does Hanley achieve the highest significance, since in both cases he fails to make the transition from an almost embarrassed awareness to an analysis of his themes.

Hanley was born in Glasgow's Gallowgate, one of nine children of Henry and Martha Griffiths Hanley. In his autobiography, *Dancing in the Streets* (1958), he points out how typical his family background was of the west of Scotland: his paternal grandfather had migrated from Dublin around the turn of the century, and his maternal grandmother was from Tiree in the Inner Hebrides, so that the Hanleys represented the ethnic and religious composition of the city's population.

Dancing in the Streets is an immensely entertaining account of his working-class childhood in the tenements of the Gallowgate, and later in one of the housing estates built between Shettleston and Tollcross in an attempt to ease the pressure on the inner city. Hanley emphasizes throughout: the imaginative and verbal richness he found in Glasgow: for example, he records the dialogue accompanying his youthful adventures quite naturalistically. But he seems to have been untroubled by the social proscription of some varieties of Scots: "We spoke the King's English without any difficulty at school, a decent grammatical informal Scots in the house, and gutter-Glasgow in the streets, and we never mixed the three or used the wrong one except as a joke. There was nothing wrong with people who spoke school English all the time, but they were a little cut off from real life, or suffering from harmless pretentiousness, or maybe just foreigners who didn't know." Although he ignores the class implications of Scotland's linguistic complexities, the practice of switching register clearly encouraged a sensitivity to dialogue, and this has stood him in good stead even when dealing with the English-speaking characters who largely populate his fiction; but it may perhaps have also contributed to some elements of carelessness and glibness in the quality of his prose.

While still at school, Hanley, again with some typicality, discarded his family's Conservatism as easily as he seems to have given up their Christianity, and became a socialist. He was an active member of the Independent Labour Party, and I.L.P. pacifism led him to be exempted as a conscientious objector from military service. During the war he worked as a reporter for a local news agency, but he also developed his interest in staging amateur plays and shows, and success with a radio comedy series established him as an entertainer as well as a journalist. One aspect of this side of his career has been his writing of song lyrics, the most famous of which must be "Scotland the Brave." Composed in the mid-1950s, this is the most extreme example of his complicity with the tradition of Scottish tartanry which he often sends up in his books on Scotland but which he has never brought himself to attack or reject outright. The ludicrous stereotype of the kilt-bedecked Scot temporarily laying aside his bagpipes to deliver himself of cliched, sententious statements between excessive gulps of the whiskey of which he begrudges the price—an image most widely propagated through the music-hall career of Sir Harry Lauder—continues to dominate consciousness of the nation both within and outside Scotland, and Hanley's ambivalent exploitation of the system is not an amusing side-issue but a charge bearing crucial importance in Scottish cultural politics.

The success of *Dancing in the Streets* (especially

in the United States) and payment for the film rights of his second book, *Love From Everybody* (1959), enabled him to become a full-time writer, but he has continued to be a prolific columnist and media personality as well. He and his wife, Anna, have three children: Clifford, born in 1948; Jane born in 1951; and Joanna, born in 1958.

Love From Everybody is the comic story of the complications faced by a young Edinburgh travel agent when several of the foreign girls to whom he has given keys to his flat arrive unexpectedly during the hectic weeks of the International Festival. Dated most by its sexual prudery, the book was clearly hovering on the brink of the "swinging sixties": apart from a curious fascination which leads to broken fingernails being mentioned from novel to novel in descriptions of intimate encounters, the sexual mores portrayed in Hanley's fiction have kept pace with changes in public attitudes over the last two decades, never being in advance of middle-of-the-road opinion.

In *The Taste of Too Much* (1960) a group of Scottish teenagers are episodically observed during their last year at school. They emerge as ordinary, respectable upper-working-class kids, more troubled by school exams than anything else, and really rather dull. Experiencing the usual agonies of adolescence, they react undramatically and, above all, sensibly. The development of the chief character, Peter Haddow, is marked by his success in turning an interfering aunt out of the family home, but he is untouched and untroubled by the larger issues of social aspirations and religious intolerance which Hanley raises but fails to investigate. The ethos of the novel seems based on that sentimental faith in the basic goodness of ordinary Scottish folk—whatever their "pawky" humor and lovable eccentricities—which was the foundation of the nineteenth-century school of Scottish kailyard novelists such as J. M. Barrie, Ian McLaren, and S. R. Crockett. Critical opinion may have turned from their parochial concerns—unable to contend with any issue beyond the realm of the "cabbage-patch" from which their name derives—and values, but their popular persistence, as reflected in novels such as Hanley's, is unremitting.

The protagonist of *Nothing but the Best* (1964) appears more interesting: the self-made Tom Fletcher, whose wife has recently died, finds his directorship of English Brothers under threat in the takeover of the small office furniture manufacturers by a larger conglomerate. But the problems of his social rise, his bereavement, and his relationship with his son are shelved rather than solved through

the meeting with the unconvincing Gladys Appleby and the sudden, unexamined decision to start his own business. The optimistic conclusion seems a disappointingly simplistic response to the potential of the initial situation.

Similarly, *The Hot Month* (1967) begins with some promise. The Boag family is about to depart for a holiday in the Highland village of Ochie, and Stacey, an aspiring novelist in search of a style, has some difficulty in articulating her more refined awareness of the importance of diurnal reality: " 'Children . . . Land Rover,' she scribbled, in the bastard mixture that remained from her shorthand lessons. 'Significant? Charged with et cetera. 3 lives . . . hovering on the brink of et cetera.' She was irritated by her lack of fluency, but to hell, she thought, you always manage to find something to put in place of the et ceteras. It's part of the agony. She crossed out the last et cetera and wrote ' agony ' in its place. It looked silly. She stared hard at the children as if she might be able to dissolve them into words if she stared hard enough. Nothing happened at all. They went on being human beings." But Stacey and her reflections on the writing of fiction seem to disappear toward the middle of the book (although she is brought back nearer the end to mark the revolt of a henpecked husband). The novel's chief concern is to chart the domestic squabbles of the Boags against a background of predict-

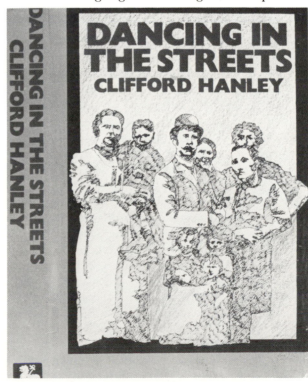

Dust jacket for Hanley's first book, an autobiography

ably and unnaturally representative Highlanders, such as the republican garage mechanic, the operatically inclined policeman, the chinless wonders of the local aristocracy, and the obliging girl who runs the village store. Again, the result is superficial and disappointing, and the kailyard sentiment is only just held below the surface.

Hanley's interest in Stacey's element of artistic self-consciousness is expanded in *The Red-Haired Bitch* (1969), his only novel to involve any stylistic experimentation as he switches between present and past tenses. This device occasionally gives the narrative additional pace, but it is not handled originally and gradually becomes mechanistic and contrived. The novel concerns the staging of a play originally intended to debunk the sentimental popular view of Mary Queen of Scots which is turned by a commercially minded theater manager into a musical romance that merely reinforces the accepted image. Serious themes such as the role of the Scottish theater in the perpetuation of cultural stereotypes as an alternative to bankruptcy are not thoroughly explored: Hanley seems to dodge the issue by making the bellicose, self-obsessed playwright a far less sympathetic character than the theater manager, and by switching the focus of the novel to the domestic rebellion of the composer Johnny McGill.

Prissy (1978), on the other hand, seems to become more interesting toward the middle of the book, at the point when the fourteen-year-old daughter of the British Prime Minister decides to pass up the chance of escaping from her kidnappers in order to ensure that they are suitably punished for the injuries done to her bodyguard. Hanley appears to be willfully turning his back on potentially interesting material as he concentrates on the working out of the details of her revenge and turns Prissy into a simple moral monstrosity.

Hanley claims to have adopted his pseudonym in order to escape from the expectation, following *Dancing in the Streets*, that his thrillers would deal exlusively with Glasgow. He contends that all the "Calvin" books are moralities: "the goodies are good and the baddies are evil." But the goodies are also dull, the baddies often turn out to be merely petty criminals, and both sides act with a degree of incompetence that simply—and infuriatingly—delays the action. These are serious handicaps in novels purporting to be thrillers. *The System* (1962), *The DNA Business* (1967), and *A Nice Friendly Town* (1967) are quite unmemorable; *The Italian Gadget* (1966) fails to establish any tension by the absurdity of its premise that all Italians are closet Machiavel-

lians prepared to act with duplicity for the flimsiest of motives; and *Miranda Must Die* (1968), a variation of the theme of the blessed fool, collapses because the girl in question is made merely irritating. *The Chosen Instrument* (1969) and *The Poison Chasers* (1971) concern the adventures of two road engineers, first in a local revolution on the vaguely South American island of Tatra, then in the discovery of an unknown missile station in the Scottish Highlands. *Take Two Popes* (1972) contains one idea, that the use of a double to improve Papal security may simply result in confusion. The police officer's abandonment of his shrewish wife is reminiscent of similar resolutions in *The Hot Month* and *The Red-Haired Bitch*. Only *It's Different Abroad* (1963), which again works on the family tensions exposed during a holiday, has a heroine of some intelligence; but once more the book suffers from the mundane treatment of the villains and the predictable resolution of the plot.

A Skinfull of Scotch (1965) and *The Scots* (1980) are catalogues of the cardinal elements in the neo-kailyard stereotype of the Scot, such as whiskey, tartan, the rivalry of Glasgow and Edinburgh, Hogmanay ceremonies, and the poetry of Robert Burns. Superficially amusing, they fail to recognize the seriousness of their subjects, and coming some forty years after their exposure in Hugh MacDiarmid's *A Drunk Man Looks at the Thistle* (1926), these books constitute a dangerous perpetuation of long-redundant myths.

For some time Hanley wrote for documentary films, one of which, *Seawards the Great Ships* (1960), won the Oscar for Best Foreign Documentary. He is the author of one serious drama, "The Durable Element" (unpublished), and has collaborated with Ian Gourlay on three Christmas shows for Glasgow's Citizens Theatre ("Saturmacnalia," "Oh for an Island," and "Dick McWhittie") and "Oh Glorious Jubilee" for the Royal Gala Opening of the Leeds Playhouse in 1971 (all unpublished). He has acted as Scottish Chairman of International PEN, as Scottish Chairman of the Writers Guild of Great Britain, and as a member of the Scottish Arts Council. He was the Scottish Arts Council's exchange program Writer in Residence at York University, Toronto, in 1979-1980. He continues to work as a newspaper columnist, has recorded his own television series, and has recently completed a novel, "Another Street, Another Dance," based on the material of *Dancing in the Streets*.

Screenplay:
Seawards the Great Ships, Films of Scotland, 1960.

Catherine Heath

(17 November 1924-   )

Gerard Werson

BOOKS: *Stone Walls* (London: Cape, 1973);
The Vulture (London: Cape, 1974);
Joseph and the Goths (London: Cape, 1975);
Lady on the Burning Deck (London: Cape, 1978; New
York: Taplinger, 1979).

Catherine Heath was born 17 November 1924 in London to Dutch immigrants Samuel and Anna de Boer Hirsch. Her father, a Jew from Rotterdam, worked as an accountant, and her mother, a Lutheran from Friesland, had taken a university degree in economics. Heath was educated at a state school, Hendon County Grammar School, and she graduated with honors from St. Hilda's College, Oxford, in 1946. After graduation she·lectured for two years at University College, Cardiff, Wales, and during 1949-1952 she taught on a part-time basis at both Oxford and Cambridge. In 1947 she married Dennis Frederick Heath, and in that year they moved to Cambridge. In addition to her teaching she worked briefly as a free-lance journalist. During 1952-1963 she raised her family, an adopted son and daughter (Anthony David and Anne Lindsay), before resuming teaching in a London suburb at Carshalton College of Further Education. "My students are very tactful," she observes. "The fact that I write books never gets mentioned." In 1977 she divorced her husband but continued to live in Carshalton. She is a regular communicant of the Church of England at her parish church.

Heath's publications include, to date, four novels, poetry, and a radio play broadcast by the BBC. She is completing a new novel entitled "Behaving Badly." Her work has been widely and warmly reviewed and she is consolidating a growing reputation as an important writer who is bringing her own distinctive gifts to the genre of English social comedy. Heath wanted to be a writer from a very early age, "from three or four years old." Her university education impeded this desire, she acknowledges, causing her to construct the syllogism: "Writers are gods: I'm not a god: therefore, I'm not a writer." Yet her academic training encouraged her to write, she now feels, with "precision and craftsmanship." She admits to being something

of a "purist, a pedant," and for her exactitude of language is important: "language mustn't be used casually or in a slipshod way. I love the correct use of the semi-colon." Heath was brought up, she remarks, in a profoundly religious home with Dutch Lutheran and Jewish influences. Her explanation of why she chose to write fiction in her forties is religious, she comments, in a medieval sense: "In your forties death becomes possible. I wanted to write a book, to justify my own existence. Then publication came. And then reviews. By that time I'd already written my second novel." She has little interest in the formalist school of writing about writing, forever preoccupied with itself, and acknowledges few specific influences on her own fiction. She admires Iris Murdoch's "enormous story-telling gift, a marvellous energy that's given

Catherine Heath

me the courage to make new things happen." Heath also values the instruction she received at Oxford from the distinguished critic Dame Helen Gardner.

Running through Heath's work are elements that can be traced, in part, to biographical origins: an inability to accept without questioning the hypocrisies of conventional middle-class English life and also an ability to retain an open mind; a sense of constant movement and an opposition of city life to rural retreat; an acute unease and tension; an emphasis on the roles of women in contemporary society; and a religious faith which is not tempered with customary English agnosticism. It is significant that in Heath's first novel, *Stone Walls* (1973), one of the few men to whom Martha positively responds is a dark-skinned foreigner whose voice has an "upward lilt of delight" and whose "unconcealed, unselfconscious way [Martha finds] so attractive, so restful." He is contrasted with an Englishman whom she meets at a party, whom she finds intellectually alert, smart, and null. In *The Vulture* (1974), the settled peace and security of a large house on the estate of Wittenden is suddenly disturbed for the narrator by her chance recollection: "At the very beginning of the war I had seen a picture of the public degradation in a Vienna park of a Jewish doctor and his wife, an elderly couple in their sixties, bewildered and unbelieving before a row of taunting faces." Heath cannot tolerate the existence of inherited wealth, which guarantees the survival of the conservative English system, because it has not been earned. Her work-in-progress, "Behaving Badly," refers to the face of an English intellectual, "a mixture of shrewdness, self-indulgence, and indefensible innocence," and the narrator questions the attitudes of middle-class youth: "Where did it come from, this assumption that they at least would survive the unemployment and violence and betrayal of the world about her?"

Heath's own professional career and her divorce have both, perhaps, given depth to the portraits of women who are central in her work. Heroines in her successive novels have become, she comments, more demanding. She adds that the change achieved through female emancipation has been "inadequate, limited." From the annual enrollment of forty-five girls at her coeducational school, Heath was the only one to enter the sixth form and to go on to university. "We identified ourselves," she states, "in 'mother and wife' terms. . . . I cannot identify with young women who don't want children." Throughout Heath's fiction women are, almost without exception, associated with a constant sense of emotional and physical insecurity: young and middle-aged, they share a need to seek refuge with people or with places. The conclusions of her novels leave her principal female characters resigned rather than contented—sensibly, they know better than to persistently seek happiness.

Heath's novels reflect, in a manner that is rare in postwar English fiction, the changing nature of our society and the consequent tensions arising from it. The central question to which she persistently addresses herself is this: recent changes in manners and morals have given many of us, notably city dwellers, a new freedom in which to experiment with our lives, but what is the price we are paying for this gain in self-knowledge? Heath implies that happiness and contentment rarely result from our loss of the old sustaining certainties, but she is careful to add that these certainties had value only when they rested on the good and the right. She also points out, with considerable tragicomic force, that because we are living now we have no alternative but to take part in the experiment. Heath shares, to an extent, the mordant wit of Philip Larkin's "Annus Mirabilis," a poem set in 1963 that describes the "Permissive Society": "Then all at once the quarrel sank: / Everyone felt the same, / And every life became / A brilliant breaking of the bank, / A quite unlosable game." If everybody can win prizes, Heath might object, there is little point in entering the competition; what is the point of playing? Larkin often cannot resist the tug of nihilism. Heath resists it partly on the grounds of her religious faith and partly, perhaps, because the novel form itself generally demands an intricate and lengthy exposition of our ambiguous motives, unlike a short poem. (This is not to suggest that the impulse to "write off" humankind is totally absent from Heath's novels.)

One of the ironies suffusing these novels is that Heath's passion for grammatical rules accompanies a frequent willingness to breach social conventions within her own carefully constructed narratives. She remarks that she does not enjoy reading Gothic fiction and fantasy because "they're too easy. It's important to have rules. If anything can happen, what's the point?" She excepts Mervyn Peake's *Gormenghast* (1951) and claims it as one of the inspirations of *Stone Walls*, but she points out that Peake constructed for his readers a universe of rules. This desire, this need for rules in Heath's novels, is accompanied by a latent violence that is sometimes openly expressed by her characters in words and deeds. Even in our fast changing times, Heath insists, the rules exist, and we know when we have transgressed. However, without the Absolutes of

God and the Four Last Things, the novelist whose imagination operates vividly within a moral framework can only point out, perhaps firmly, that we have overstepped the line. Heath, a sophisticated moralist, is forced into the serio-comic position of saying that our recognition of our transgression matters, but it seems almost as if the rueful recognition is sufficient: how can she tell us to go away and sin no more when neither she nor her reader is certain of the status of the transgression?

This vital question is not raised to suggest that Heath's fiction lacks its own kind of certitude. It is riddled with the quality that the English literary critic and psychologist D. W. Harding detected in Jane Austen and termed "regulated hatred," a dislike of philistinism, of pretense, and of unkindness, that erupts into the reader's consciousness. In an obvious sense, all of English social comedy written during the past 150 years is a footnote to Jane Austen, yet Heath is unable to depend upon Austen's secure moral convictions that were based on an unquestioned social and economic class structure. Heath is vividly aware of this contradiction in her work: an accepted mode, a fine grammatical style emphasizing the value of rules clashes with her reluctance to accept the status quo and her open preoccupations with sex and money. She is keen to expose the chief hypocrisies prevalent in English society, the assertions that we are all equal now and that we live in an open and fair-minded society. In Heath's bourgeois comedies, influenced by Evelyn Waugh and Nancy Mitford, content clashes with style and almost forces a disjunction between what is said and the way in which it is expressed. Her sense of comic timing, her irony, and also her habitual unease spring from this opposition.

When *Stone Walls* was published in 1973, it received enthusiastic reviews, most of which drew attention to its "cool observation," a quality that some reviewers complacently noted as "very English." The book tells the story of Martha Lang, the custodian of Tilbrook House in Somerset. Her fiance, Henry Rossiter, the wealthy owner of the great house, has gone abroad on a long trip and Martha remains as housekeeper. During his long absence, aided by members of the staff, she supervises the unpacking, classification, and cataloguing of the vast, indiscriminate purchases of antiques Rossiter periodically sends home: "they had become the purpose for which the house existed." He also sends Martha infrequent conventional letters of regard and, sometimes, a choice present, which is either (she is unable to decide) a "proof of love, or a casual gift to an old friend." Fearing rejection, she is

unable to post to him her letters of open emotional rage and appeal and feels herself becoming a fragile labeled object. Tilbrook receives its "monstrous flood" of things, and, as in the estate of Xanadu in *Citizen Kane*, they exist to illustrate the egoism of their owner. Laughter in Tilbrook, as the gardener's boy William notes, is "the result of strain, an escape from tension." Martha is undefeated by the vanloads of crates and packing cases until, unexpectedly, an entire Bavarian summer house arrives. She revolts and decides upon a move to London, a new job, a new flat, and even, perhaps, an affair. Her move to London is described in a sparkling chapter depicting a party given by friends in Hampstead (their "beautiful room" is characteristically contrasted with their "grandmother's cluttered and ugly front parlour, never used except for company"). Martha's assorted and aging friends are unable to dance to the music of time, but as Ruth, whom Martha has not seen for ten or fifteen years, "stood there, black hair, white skin, white dress clinging to her body, it seemed as if time's power might after all be limited." Heath cannot, however, permit this pleasing untruth (even with its qualifications "seemed," "might") to pass uncorrected: Ruth dyes her hair and her husband has suffered two heart attacks.

The structure of *Stone Walls* moves the reader with a graceful rhythm between London and Tilbrook, gently mocking Martha's inability to choose. She makes a life for herself (though she rejects the phrase as a cliche), moves into a small flat, and finds a clerical job at a foreign embassy. Life often appears to her to be "shoddiness, grime," yet she appreciates the anonymity of the great city. This pleasant sensation of a lack of identity is disturbed when Martha meets by chance the curator of Tilbrook, Patrick Burton, in the National Gallery. Her loving description of a Stubbs painting, redolent of its eighteenth-century certainties, is contrasted with Burton's increasing insanity, Martha's own insecurity, and the wilderness of surrounding London. In a deft comic episode Martha tentatively begins an affair and throws herself upon her new friend to whom she is attracted, Mehdevi, with a "surge of uncertainty and relief." But they are interrupted by a ring at the door and a policeman informs them of Burton's death. Responding both to this announcement and to her inner doubts—and also to a letter from William's mother, desiring her son's reinstatement at Tilbrook—Martha returns to the great house. Comforted by its luxurious certainties and by the beauty of the surrounding country, she finds the courage to dismiss her insupportable companion, Ida; the narrator comments: "Only Ida had escaped." Martha has chosen to return to her stone walls within which she can acknowledge ties of loyalty and also cherish her own isolation. The novel's closing paragraph reminds the reader, *vanitas vanitatum*: "Outside twilight gathered, and upstairs, in a small closet off Lady Dorothy's room, a line of dust from an unsuspected infestation of furniture beetle trickled silently to the floor."

In Heath's first novel the pattern of the right and the unattainable good is matched against a threatening disorder. This characteristic and invisible signature is written throughout her work. In Heath's fiction the good is not identified with the large private estate and it is rarely associated with a warm domesticity. Stone walls protect those inside and keep outsiders out. The enchanted garden is an emblem of insecurity, sunlight, and private wealth: F. Hodgson Burnett's *The Secret Garden* is one of Heath's favorite novels. Internal evidence dates the setting of *Stone Walls* as no earlier than 1963, yet the estate of Tilbrook belongs to the past. Life outside its walls has changed, as William, unlike his mother, recognizes, but the private wealth enabling the estate to function continues. This wealth, the expression of neither subtle discrimination nor joy in conspicuous consumption, is often, in Heath's fiction, touched with the surreal. The Rossiters are "model employers," the narrator carefully stresses, but the feudal system that operates unchanged within the stone walls permits the head gardener to behave toward his boys with meanness and cruelty. The eccentric occupants of Tilbrook revolve around the determined, calm figure of Martha Lang (the name is perhaps an amalgam of martyr and languish), and their conversations during their meals together are recorded with an accurate ear for the lack of warmth and emotional directness peculiar to professional middle-class life. In this fine novel, constructed and decorated with skill, contrasting themes and paradoxes and an entertaining variety of characterization are rendered in a lively and graceful prose.

The Vulture, published in 1974, is, by comparison with Heath's first novel, an interesting but minor achievement. It lacks the subtlety and the rich and acute observation that characterize her best work, but it displays her accuracy of eye and ear, her narrative gift, and her felicities of style. *The Vulture* describes the unwilling move of Rosemary Barton, a middle-aged woman with grown-up children, to a small Kent village. She and her husband, who are both near retirement, have hitherto lived in a smart London suburb. Rosemary has devoted much of her time to good causes and worked for local voluntary organizations. She is unable to adjust to her new life in her country cottage, which is crowded with unpacked objects. She resorts to a village cafe, the Copper Kettle, a "chintzy cafe with its air of faded gentility" that has seized her imagination. Here the pattern of prewar English life has continued, with apparent serenity, ignoring the abrupt change and decay that have siezed the cities of Britain. John Barton is absent on an extended business trip abroad; in his absence Rosemary remembers her marriage as a "quirk of chance. . . . I could not remember what it was like to be in love." She retreats to the warm, bright cafe set in the "order and harmony" of the village square. Surrounded by rural gentry, Rosemary lives vicariously, ashamed as she "secretly and avidly watched the women who gathered there, envying them their ease, their self-assurance, their unspoken knowledge (but what knowledge? that was what I coveted). . . . As I had wondered as a girl if I were a nymphomaniac, so I wondered now if I were a snob." The narrator understands the cause of her fascination: "These women lived in a world I had believed past. Their every gesture spoke to it—of security, of traditional ways, of an absence of fear."

A chance meeting with Lady Weston, the owner of Wittenden House, increases Rosemary's range of acquaintances in the village. Hovering over the novel, however, is the shadow of the tame vulture glimpsed in the opening pages: "Imagine not knowing it was here," Rosemary speculates, seeing the vulture in the sunny English landscape, "not knowing, and strolling down for a country walk one evening, and looking up and seeing *that* watching one. . . ." The vulture is personified by Vicky, the nineteen-year-old alcoholic friend of Rosemary's son Giles, yet the equation is not glib: the bird of prey also illustrates the contentious relationship between mother and son, Rosemary's admirable but bloodthirsty need to find good causes to support, and her own insecurity. The powerful theme of *The Vulture*—that in our country retreat we cannot escape from ourselves into a present tense that appears, comfortably, to be the historic past—steers the narrative forward with a compelling energy. Even within the garden of Wittenden House, Rosemary knowingly manipulates her view of things, rather as Martha reinterprets Henry's letters. Only through this manipulation, this "favourite game," can Rosemary accept her "materialistic middle-age," her "milk-and-water self," and turn aside from "our own hard century."

The Vulture is marred by the absence of careful

qualification and paradox that fuel Heath's best work and by the presence of a didacticism that is, at times, over-explicit. The characterization is also lacking in resonance: Vicky, with her bounced checks and her petty thefts and her irresponsibility, is an accurately itemized catalogue rather than a rounded character, and John Barton is drawn with insufficient conviction. Heath's ear for dialogue does not serve her well in her description of the confrontations between mother and son: there is an element of caricature here, a glibness, diluting the tension that ought to depend partly upon what is unstated and partly upon what must be dragged to the surface. The narrator's deliberately understated description of Rosemary's discovery of her son's homosexuality is inadequately explored rather than tactfully turned aside. Throughout *The Vulture* a lack of chiaroscuro lessens the effects. The brilliancy of dialogue evident throughout *Joseph and the Goths* and "Behaving Badly" causes the reader to wonder if Heath is at ease narrating in the first person singular: *The Vulture* and *Lady on the Burning Deck*, both of which are in this mode, lack something of the ironic distancing that, in the genre of social comedy, lends enchantment.

Joseph and the Goths, published in 1975, is perhaps Heath's most successful novel to date. It repeats themes explored in her previous work: the opposition of town and country, the present versus the recent past, the predicament of the wife and husband isolated in marriage, and the need that all her characters share for dreams that can be accepted as firm realities. Here Heath's power of observation is operating in a wider, more ambitious framework, and her gift for social satire is evident in her acute eye and ear for the pretensions and the achievements of the professional middle class. The reader's enjoyment increases whenever Heath's Christian accuracy gets the better of her Christian charity. Through her creation of Joseph Hocking, the solitary old survivor of the deserted village of Ayton, she also succeeds in objectifying her central theme of the insecurity of the inner self facing up to external danger.

Ayton has become the weekend residence of alien commuters. Joseph is unable to accept the newcomers as vandals, for they are, in their patient way, determined conservationists. So, in a dim recollection of a history lesson, he christens them Goths. His principal enemies are his landlords, Eddie and Rosie Markham, who live in the cottage next door. Joseph has other weekend neighbors who provoke him with their effrontery and their lack of roots and attachments to his village. The

valiant defender of the old ways, Joseph attempts—with some success—a guerrilla campaign to unsettle and unnerve the Goths, but they continue to misunderstand and patronize him in their fair-minded, obtuse way. Joseph recognizes (as do all of Heath's characters, except the young) that time is running out. He must strike soon. A chance encounter enables him to enlist the support of a young man, Tony, and his girl friend, Sue, members of a gang of motorbikers. The subtle and plausible characterization of this awkward old man, unable to adjust to the changing world, is poised against a delicate description of Eddie, who reassures and renews himself in his weekend retreats, and Rosie, who fears the insecurity of the weekly disruption. The Markhams are locked into a faded, worn marriage charged with misunderstanding and tenderness and exasperation. The changing nature of their relationship (it remains intact, yet in an important sense, in the novel's conclusion, it retires into disintegration) is matched against Joseph's terrifying single-mindedness. The liberal, honest Markhams are unable to persuade Joseph to move further down the terrace of cottages they own, thereby extending their own property. They cannot force themselves to exercise their legal rights and compel Joseph to move. Therefore, in order to be comfortable, they secretly desire his death. Heath is adept at describing the agonies of choice experienced by the good bourgeoisie.

Minor characters in *Joseph and the Goths* are drawn with sure, exact strokes that give depth to the narrative. A vivid comic sensibility is evident throughout. In an episode of marked skill, Joseph is linked with the brief sexual liaison between Eddie and Sue: in a passage that economically combines both farce and subtlety of observation, the episode mingles contempt, desire, derision, Eddie's need to renovate (his own self-esteem and Joseph's guttering), and a short-lived sense of affinity between the two men.

Assisted by the vandals who do not understand what he is seeking to preserve, Joseph triumphs briefly during an evening in which he loses touch with reality and embarks upon destruction. Order is restored (in the context of Heath's fiction this phrase is generally ironic, if not subversive) and Joseph's death is misinterpreted by the Goths, though significantly it is understood by the guardians of Order, the police (who tactfully remain silent). The Goths plan to erect a monument to commemorate Joseph: "Really the whole affair was almost a blessing. Many of the Ayton residents had by now almost perfected their own houses and gar-

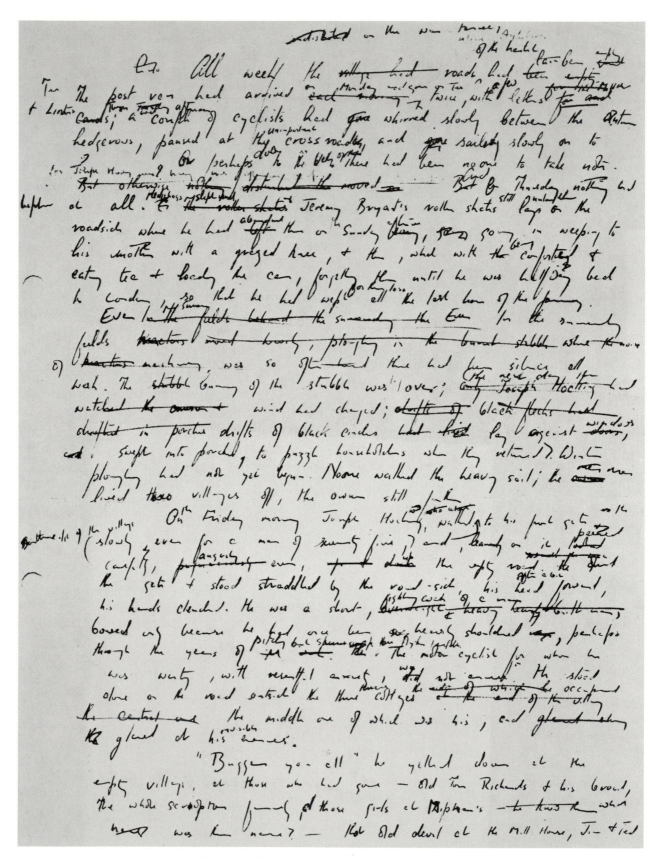

First page of the manuscript for Joseph and the Goths

dens; they were not at all sorry to be presented with this new field for their endeavours." Yet in a wry and brilliant conclusion, one of Joseph's slow-burning guerrilla actions finally explodes and he achieves, posthumously, a real triumph: he embarasses the bourgeoisie. He blocked the cesspit near the homes of the newcomers and he waited, in vain during his lifetime, for their consequent embarassment, incredulous at the Goths' apparent lack of bodily functions. But after Joseph's death, during a long and labored speech given to the Ayton Conservation Society by his landlord, Eddie Markham, the cesspit finally overflows and bad smells mingle with polite society. They turn up their noses, as they did to Joseph himself: this enforced honesty is his real memorial. This conclusion in itself qualifies, in a curious way, the recognition that Eddie experiences when he is himself rescued from death: "Eddie resigned himself to the fact that to the totality of hate one could but oppose, tentatively, the imperfections of attempted love." In a rather similar way, a vision of secure life is both celebrated and mocked in Rosie's thoughts: "An image of neatly uniformed children drifting home from school had risen in her mind. Plane trees shadowed the quiet Finchley streets. Trains ran; miners sang in their chapel choirs; violence had ended with the defeat of the Nazis; people had been . . . predictable."

The didactic themes animating this major novel exist simultaneously with and are indivisible from its broad acute comedy, its tenderness, and its skillful construction. In *Joseph and the Goths* the reader notes a rich, complex blend of humor that is a development in Heath's fiction, and a corresponding widening and deepening evidence of her range. But the power of this novel (and of *Stone Walls*) springs from its compression. Heath needs her sense of style to control her material, to make palatable to her readers her constant temptation to preach. The discreet understatement that made autumnal eighteenth-century music within *Stone Walls* is not absent from *Joseph and the Goths*, but here the poignant solitary figure of Martha is, in the persona of Joseph, associated with the luminous everyday objects, the glowing solidity of a Flemish interior. Joseph is mad, yet in the integrity of his honesty and the accuracy of his perceptions he is not, as is Martha, associated with the surreal. He is subsumed in the wider social context of his village in which he belongs and through which he is forced to wander, a robust, despairing ghost.

In *Lady on the Burning Deck*, published in 1978, Heath attempts to explore the predicament of a middle-aged woman who is living (perhaps it is more correct to observe that she is surviving) in the complex world of contemporary London. Reviewing the novel in the *Washington Post*, Clara Claiborne Park drew attention to the broad comedy "suffused with a rueful tenderness that shadows what might otherwise be a mere summer afternoon's romp." The verbal elegance and visual fun of *Joseph and the Goths*, which has affinities with several plays by Peter Nichols, concentrates on the nature of "feminine life" in a style suggesting the influence of Fay Weldon. *Lady on the Burning Deck* sparkles throughout with the high spirits that cause the parents of irrepressibly fizzy children to warn them, "if you're not careful you'll soon be in tears." The baffled middle-aged characters in Heath's novels often resemble alert children who are mystified by the alien world in which they find themselves. Dr. Elias, the librarian of Tilbrook in *Stone Walls*, is described as a "patient observer" in a "strange world." This theme of disorientation, of the self struggling to make sense of a present and future that cannot be guaranteed by the self's reference to the past, is directly expressed and openly explored in *Lady on the Burning Deck*.

The narrator and central character, Frances, is a middle-aged widow who has a lover (Wednesday nights only), Nathaniel, the Chairman of the Matthew Berwick Society, who is not her type—"He is not the kind of man one would marry. . . . He is not the kind of man my husband would have brought home." She is the curator of Berwick's carefully preserved house, where "Everything is still, ordered, tranquil, a little dusty": the kitchen in her apartment is "all scarlet and white and stainless steel" and, Frances adds, is "slightly out-of-date." She draws strength from the house, which is occupied by squatters during the course of the novel, and particularly from a rosewood table in the drawing room, which she lovingly polishes. After the squatters have left, Frances is appalled by the damage done to the table, but this is not merely a contrast between past craftsmanship and present vandalism: the table's surface has acted as a mirror and when it is scratched it spoils both her capacity for pretense and her self-regard. The theme of the present versus the recent past is conveyed through the descriptions of the six children belonging to Frances and her two closest friends from childhood, Ruth and Jenny.

The contrast drawn between past and present is, in Heath's work, never a clear indication of approval or of condemnation: her inability to make such a judgment is one of her strongest motivations. The brilliant concluding sentence of this novel's opening paragraph lauds the "real life" of the recent past: "a friend of mine then, just back from Lodz, tells me that the neighbours who had looted her childhood home (ah, now I remember, it was to revisit her childhood home) had invited her into coffee and that it had been brought in (on a silver tray once belonging to her parents) by a maid. It had been brought in, she said, I assure you, by a maid. In a black dress, with a white muslin and lace apron. So think about that for a while." The children of this feminine triangle (and the novel is in this respect rather too neat) are as full of enthusiasm for their various beliefs as "nineteenth-century tractarians." The narrative voice of Frances regrets, "My frivolity is a recurring distress to my children. My seriousness equally perturbs them, revealing as it so often does the moral failures of prejudice or elitism or latent authoritarianism. I do my best to learn." When the narrator's daughter runs away from her college with one of her tutors, Frances in her distress questions her daughter's friend, who regards Frances with incomprehension: "Who are these people, her eyes ask, who think they have a contract with God that life will keep its expected pattern? And what does it all matter?"

A sly and accurate comic sense is evident throughout *Lady on the Burning Deck*. When Frances goes to enlist the support of her son, who is illegally squatting, she notes one of the squatters' many slogans: "Do your own thing. Find your own squat. THIS IS OURS." The policeman standing outside, to whom Frances refuses to give her identity, remarks: "Nice young people they seem, some of them. You'd be surprised." The distinctive humor of this very funny novel is provided by the apparent competence of the fluent narrative voice that succeeds in confronting this now inexplicable pattern of living: not solving the problems that it presents but in its steady loquacity demonstrating a determination to look it in the eye, to see the thing through. Perhaps it is this playfulness, gleaming with a defeated sophistication that refuses to retreat into tragedy, allied with the theme of parent-child relationships, narrated through the insistent open voice of the individual conscience, that gives the prose a Jewish quality (also strongly present in "Behaving Badly"). The humor also depends on Heath's subversive conservatism which upsets the customary expectations of her readers: age gives in to youth, a respectable woman tells lies to a policeman, the articulate and energetic son (who is homosexual) can only be applauded for his determination to stand and fight the good fight. The narrative voice also frequently lacks the quiet decorum generally associated with the female English novelist: there are suggestions here of a Woody Allen monologue and perhaps the wisecracks of Groucho Marx, or the extrovert larks of Lily Tomlin and the tone of voice used by Gloria Nagy in *Virgin Kisses*.

This slightly lunatic freedom of narrative voice apparently released from constraints is a new development in Heath's fiction, and the gain is accompanied by her acute sense of social context. The tone of voice here—and this is what makes it amusing—is calculating yet at the same time unable to exercise control. What is not present in this successful novel is Heath's pointedness, an elegant economy effectively registering complex observation through marked indirection. When this quality appears, as in the witty observation that the narrator's son "praises only the items in the house which have nothing to do with its true nature" (he praises the umbrella stand, a 1920s addition: Frances refers to her "1920s soul"), the narrative increases in significance. Heath cannot afford to be discursive: her style demands the order she suspects to be illusory.

What value, Heath is forced to question, can rapid change hold for us, in itself, without indebtedness to the secure continuity of the past? This theme, evident throughout in her treatment of individual character and of social context, distinguishes her from her contemporary Barbara Pym, a novelist whose work is superficially similar to Heath's. The pressure under which Heath writes give her novels a contemporaneity, a sense of wit and comic timing, and a constant questioning. These pressures, when shaped with Heath's power of construction, generally make the work of most of her contemporaries appear trivial by comparison. Unlike many writers in her chosen genre, Heath also advances and develops—rapidly. Her work-in-progress, "Behaving Badly," a remarkable chamber opera of voices, marks a new stage in her technique. Joseph's answer to Heath's central question is to deliberately throw a lighted match into the petrol-soaked home of the newcomers; Martha knowingly immolates herself within stone walls: Rosemary welcomes the vulture who needs her; Frances dances on the burning deck, directing her glances of "longing" and of "passion" not to a man or woman but to the past, to the "stable houses" and to the "sober unsurprising souls." The conclusion of "Behaving Badly" indicates, for the first time in Heath's fiction, the possibility of a happy ending. But it has been bought, literally: the woman who would rather behave badly than retire sells her flat in order to buy a beautiful young man whom she desires. He is homosexual. Armed with the bleak knowledge that their romance might be short-lived and disastrous, she is able to hope for happiness. The flower of the heroine's desire spreads its petals, surprisingly, in the cold climate.

Few novelists working in this genre during the past thirty years, with the outstanding exception of Muriel Spark (interestingly, Spark is a Jewish convert to Catholicism), have communicated directly and pungently with their audience: Catherine Heath is among these few distinguished writers. Yet the comparison with Spark's glittering mastery of style raises the difficulty that the reader is infrequently disconcerted during his reading of Heath's work by an almost fatal redundancy, a repetition, an over-emphatic stress. It is as if (and it would be characteristic) this novelist does not trust her audience sufficiently. But acknowledging the chaos of much of contemporary life, we, the audience, require the order—even though we do not believe in it—of a complete harmony. The reader who discovers such faults in Heath's best work resembles, perhaps, the Hapsburg Emperor Joseph, who remarked to the composer at the premiere of *Entfuhrung aus dem Serail*, "Too fine for our ears, and a terrible lot of notes, my dear Mozart."

Heath's fiction is remarkable for its elegant description of suffering, both real and imagined; for its apparently detached ironic statement of conflict, lack of fullfilment, and remorse; and for its comic perception of our struggle to survive. *Vanitas vanitatum:* in the context of her fiction the scriptural allusion is both joke and epitaph.

Radio Script:

Scorpio Male Seeks Libran Mate, Radio 4, BBC, 9 February 1979.

Other:

"Hysterectomy," in *New Poetry 3* (London: Arts Council of Great Britain, 1977).

Aidan Higgins

(3 March 1927-)

Bill Grantham

BOOKS: *Felo De Se* (London: Calder, 1960); republished as *Killachter Meadow* (New York: Grove, 1961); republished as *Asylum and Other Stories* (London: Calder, 1978; Dallas: Riverrun Press, 1978);

Langrishe, Go Down (London: Calder, 1966; New York: Grove, 1966);

Images of Africa: Diary (1956-60) (London: Calder & Boyars, 1971);

Balcony Of Europe (London: Calder & Boyars, 1972; New York: Delacorte, 1972);

Scenes From A Receding Past (London: Calder, 1977; Dallas: Riverrun Press, 1977).

For some Irish writers, their motherland is still the sow that devours her farrow. The formal issues of modernism, so at odds with the curious religious and social balances of Irish society, still remain as issues for those who, even in the latter portion of the twentieth century, leave home only to evoke images and ideas of Ireland in all they write. Educated at James Joyce's Clongowes, protege of Samuel Beckett, Aidan Higgins maintains a line and style of writing most of his countrymen have chosen to abandon.

Aidan Higgins was born in Celbridge, County Kildare, a place that recurs in his novels, to Bartholomew Joseph and Lilian Ann Boyd Higgins. He received his early education at Celbridge Convent and Kilashee Preparatory School before going on to Clongowes Wood College, a private boys boarding school run by the Society of Jesus and portrayed in James Joyce's *A Portrait of the Artist as a Young Man*. Like Joyce, he felt no love for the place, and his experiences there are alluded to in *Scenes From A Receding Past* (1977). Leaving school, he worked as a copywriter in the Domas Advertising Agency in Dublin. During a two-week hospital stay due to scarlet fever he began his first serious writing, although he did not have anything published at that time.

The early influences on Higgins's literary career were from the triumvirate of Irish modernist novelists: Joyce, Brian O'Nolan (known also by his pen names, Myles na Gopaleen and Flann O'Brien), and Samuel Beckett. *A Portrait of the Artist as a Young Man* was read at Clongowes, O'Nolan's *At Swim-Two-Birds* came from the local library and circulated in the family, and Beckett's *More Pricks Than Kicks*, encountered in the early 1950s, came together to provide much of the shape for Higgins's subsequent work.

In 1955, having moved to London and worked in several laboring jobs, Higgins married a South African, Jill Damaris Anders. They had three sons—Carl in 1958, Julien in 1961, and Elwin in 1965. In 1956 he joined John Wright's Marionette Company as a puppet operator and toured Europe and Southern Africa for two years, after which he settled in Johannesburg as a scriptwriter for Filmlets, an advertising company. His diary of these years, *Images of Africa* (1971), vividly details the supremacist psychosis as the Sharpeville massacre approaches. During this time he entered into correspondence with Samuel Beckett, whose work had been such a strong influence on him. Beckett was encouraging and indeed helpful, recommending Higgins to his London publisher John Calder. In 1959 Higgins's short story "Lebensraum" won second place in a competition run by the London *Observer*, and the following year Calder published it with other stories under the title *Felo De Se*. The next year Grove Press published the collection under the title *Killachter Meadow*, another story in the book.

This first volume, which won the Somin Trust Award in 1963, revealed many of Higgins's strongest characteristics, notably the austere syntax and meticulous narrative that imply a kind of Germanic poise. His publisher saw an affinity with Djuna Barnes. The comparison carries force, particularly in the light of Barnes's techniques: the making of the past into part of the weave of the narrative of the present; the relationship between elemental savagery and the obscure object of desire; above all, the use of an English language which is dislocated from the Anglo-Saxon traditions of story-narrative and character and more in affinity with the English of the translator: a "Continental" English. All these elements may be found in *Felo De Se*; this collection looked forward in a quite direct way to Higgins's first novel, *Langrishe, Go Down* (1966), which was based on the story "Killachter Meadow."

Langrishe, Go Down centers on the affair in 1932 between Imogen Langrishe, a spinster from a declining line of the Irish landed middle class, and Otto Beck, a German research student. Framing this episode are two sections, one set in 1937, the other in 1938, filled with the deaths and obsessions of the Langrishe family—(Imogen and her three sisters). While the action is confined to a debilitated section of Ireland and its culture, the dramatic sweep encompasses the vast upheavals on the European scene during the time covered by the book. Otto, a former student of philosophers Husserl and Heidegger, sees with anxiety the rise of National Socialism at home, while even dying Ireland is infected with this alien, essentially pan-European virus as daubings appear on walls in support of the local Fascist leader O'Duffy. The final scenes of the novel juxtapose the vividly detailed squalor of Otto's rooms after six years of decay and neglect, the death of Imogen's sister Helen after a long and wasting illness, and the Anschluss.

Higgins's most typical (and most successful) device in *Langrishe, Go Down* is his depiction of localized, personal events being held in suspension by outside matters which at once appear beyond the reach of the characters of the story and yet hold them completely in thrall. It is not the technique of the historical novel: the characters are neither participants in nor victims of the great consequences of

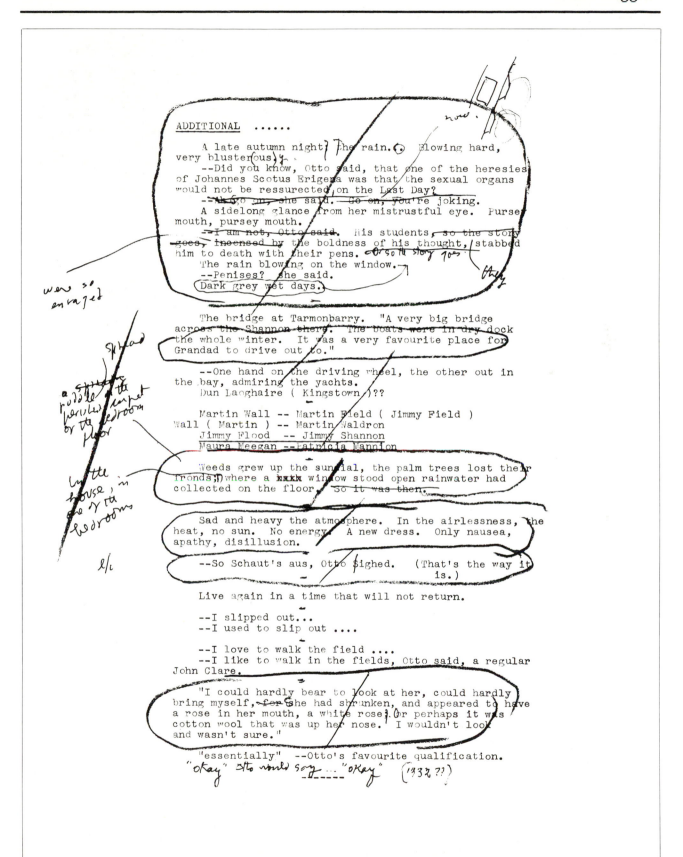

ADDITIONAL ......

A late autumn night. The rain. Blowing hard, very blusterous.

--Did you know, Otto said, that one of the heresies of Johannes Scotus Erigena was that the sexual organs would not be ressurected on the Last Day?

--Ah go on, she said. Go on, you're joking.

A sidelong glance from her mistrustful eye. Pursey mouth, pursey mouth.

--I am not, Otto said. His students, so the story goes, incensed by the boldness of his thought, stabbed him to death with their pens.

The rain blowing on the window.

--Penises? she said.

Dark grey wet days.

The bridge at Tarmonbarry. "A very big bridge across the Shannon there. The boats were in dry dock the whole winter. It was a very favourite place for Grandad to drive out to."

--One hand on the driving wheel, the other out in the bay, admiring the yachts.
Dun Laoghaire (Kingstown)??

Martin Wall -- Martin Field (Jimmy Field)
Wall (Martin) -- Martin Waldron
Jimmy Flood -- Jimmy Shannon
Maura Meegan -- Patricia Mannion

Weeds grew up the sundial, the palm trees lost their fronds, where a kxxxx window stood open rainwater had collected on the floor. So it was then.

Sad and heavy the atmosphere. In the airlessness, the heat, no sun. No energy. A new dress. Only nausea, apathy, disillusion.

--So Schaut's aus, Otto sighed. (That's the way it is.)

Live again in a time that will not return.

--I slipped out...
--I used to slip out ....

--I love to walk the field ....
--I like to walk in the fields, Otto said, a regular John Clare.

"I could hardly bear to look at her, could hardly bring myself, for she had shrunken, and appeared to have a rose in her mouth, a white rose. Or perhaps it was cotton wool that was up her nose. I wouldn't look and wasn't sure."

"essentially" --Otto's favourite qualification.

Work sheet for Langrishe, Go Down

significant moments. Instead, it is essentially a psychological technique whereby the most diverse temporal, personal, and political strands are seen to share a common psychopathology. It is here that the affinities with Djuna Barnes's employment of Jungian themes—racial memory and universal archetypes in particular—can be most clearly seen. Nevertheless, the scale of the narrative eschews any appeal to epic modes of presentation. The invitation is not to see the central characters as emblems or ciphers, but as symptoms—particular manifestations of certain configurations of ideas and moments from which can be generalized the nature of the novel's background and the forces working through it. Through this amalgamation of two common but usually separate narrative functions—the local working on the global, and the global working on the local—Higgins maintains a tight control over his material. Without this, the novel might easily have collapsed under its own weight.

Part of the force of *Langrishe, Go Down* lies in its treatment of the family as a kind of collective neurosis, imprisoning its members inextricably in a welter of obsessions and delusions. In an interview with Bill Grantham, Higgins has pointed out that the sisters in the novel were based on his own brothers. The action is partly in Celbridge, his childhood home. It is probably not helpful to attempt to unravel the web of family relationships referentially when so little is explicated in the surface text of the novel. What this connection does direct attention to, however, is twofold. First and most obviously, it provides a formal link to the autobiographical technique of the two following novels. Secondly, and perhaps more importantly, it highlights a key narrative technique in Higgins's work. The fictive expression of the guiding authorial presence in the later novels may be seen less as Higgins's expressing his own life than as a particular idea of it. The creation of a psychopathology for his narrative is not only peculiar to *Langrishe, Go Down*: in the more explicit autobiography of the subsequent novels, Higgins promotes not simply himself, but a complex map of potentials and frustrations, contextualized by his surroundings, but also contextualizing them. *Langrishe, Go Down* warns us that not only can fiction veil autobiography, but that autobiography can veil fiction.

Langrishe, Go Down remains the best regarded of Higgins's novels to date and has been translated into eleven languages. It received particularly good reviews for a first novel by critics on both sides of the Atlantic who noted its graceful deployment of a mass of fine detail as well as its debt to the Irish modernist and postmodernist novel traditions. It was a cowinner of the James Tait Black Memorial Prize in 1967, as well as being shortlisted for the *Guardian* Fiction Prize. In 1978, the playwright Harold Pinter took a screenplay he had written of the novel and adapted it for BBC television. The highly acclaimed production included Pinter himself as Shannon, Jeremy Irons as Otto Beck, and Judi Dench as Imogen.

Following the success of *Langrishe, Go Down*, Higgins was, in 1969, awarded a German Academic Scholarship which he took up in Berlin. This was followed by the Award of the Irish Academy of Letters in 1970. In addition, he received support from the Arts Council of Great Britain while preparing his second novel, *Balcony of Europe*, which appeared in 1972.

At the center of this book is an Irish painter, Dan Ruttle, modeled on Higgins himself. While living in Spain in 1962 and 1963 with his New Zealand-born wife, Olivia, Ruttle embarks on an affair with Charlotte Bayless, the American wife of a friend. Forming the backdrop is a panorama of grotesques and misfits, all distillations of aspects of the European societies rent asunder by the war and finding it impossible to put back together what has been lost. The novel is generically connected with such antecedents as Hemingway's *The Sun Also Rises*, but it exploits the anachronism of its 1960s setting. Taking cafes and bars (such as the Balcony of Europe of the novel's title), visiting Americans, and itinerant artists from the cosmopolitan Europe of the prewar novel and placing them in a more modern period at once fragments explicit formal connections and forges them. This temporal dislocation generates sets of tensions which can resolve themselves only into torpor or collapse.

The technique of *Balcony of Europe*, while related to that of *Langrishe, Go Down*, is also a development away from it. The action is more diverse and peopled with more characters, the focus seems less tight, and the pace is, by comparison, relaxed. The painful tautness of the world of Imogen Langrishe is replaced by a kind of ease. What is consistent between the two novels is the double-edged causality which persists: characters generate their own environment which in turn regenerates them. *Balcony of Europe* dwells in details: for instance, a careful listing of individuals' figures of speech is given—a conscious debt to Flann O'Brien—songs, noises, small thoughts, passing feelings. By blending meticulous observation with events which rarely seem to hint at the types of catastrophes which always lie on the fringes of *Langrishe, Go Down*, Higgins manages to produce a work again similar to a historical novel, but not quite in that category. History itself is the issue here—its status, its theory, its influence. At the end of *Balcony of Europe* Higgins lists some "rejected epigraphs." Among them are two of particular interest in these contexts. One is from W. B. Yeats:

> I begin to see things double—doubled in history, world history, personal history.

The second is from a historian, H. A. L. Fisher:

> Purity of race does not exist. Europe is a continent of energetic mongrels.

Balcony of Europe is peopled by just such energetic mongrels, simultaneously making history and being controlled by it.

After a six-year wait for a second Higgins novel, many critics regarded *Balcony of Europe* as something of a disappointment. This was not a universal view, however, and the novel made the shortlist for the Booker-McConnell Prize, the premier fiction award in the non-American English-speaking world.

Higgins's third novel, *Scenes From A Receding Past* (1977), was a long time in preparation, an extract from the work in progress having appeared in the *Dublin Magazine* as early as 1971, before the publication of *Balcony of Europe*. As the title implies, the book continues the development to an explicitly autobiographical fiction. Dan Ruttle appears again, first as a child, then as an adult in London in the post-*Balcony of Europe* period. The family and the schools, the jobs and travels, are like Higgins's own. Where smoke screens exist in the text, they are lifted in an author's note at the beginning of the book, which explains, for instance, that the New Zealand home of Olivia Ruttle is really in South Africa (the home of Higgins's wife). The novel passes from the earliest recollections of infanthood, through the fears and strangeness of childhood and advancing sexuality in adolescence, to uncertain adulthood in Ireland and then England. It is constructed primarily through use of a montage effect: events and moments blend with newspaper reports, scorecards from cricket matches, and other ephemera from Ruttle's life.

Scenes From A Receding Past is the most problematic of Higgins's three novels. In it, some of the characteristics of his style become writ large, almost overblown. The balance between detail and sweep, so carefully maintained in *Langrishe, Go Down*, seems lost beneath a welter of suggestions and hints at resonance, which often do not quite cohere. But it is also something of a working out, a culmination of some of the issues that the author raised as Higgins / Ruttle (and, as has been seen, in the quasi-autobiographical dimension of *Langrishe, Go Down*). The darkness at the end of the first novel seems fully located in a time and a culture which no longer exists. The end of *Scenes From A Receding Past* internalizes this bleakness and cannot leave it behind in the old Ireland. Even with the caveats about undue association of Higgins the novelist with any projections which may appear in the novels, the close of this novel raises issues in the development of his art that cannot be ignored:

> Long ago I was this, was that, twisting and turning, incredulous, baffled, believing nothing, believing all. Now I am, what? I feel frightened, sometimes, but may be just tired. I feel depressed quite often, but may be just hungry.
>> All but blind
>> In his chambered hole
>> Gropes for worms . . .

Clearly no novel by a living, working novelist can be viewed as a culmination or summing up, even of work up to date. However, Ruttle's lack of a sense of direction at the end of *Scenes From A Receding Past* is, at the very least, reflexive with the form of the novel, which seems sometimes to debate with itself out loud and look for the breakthrough in style and content that it never quite achieves. The critical reception was generally muted, but also disappointed, as if sensing that an important novelist was ill at ease with his chosen form. The American Irish Foundation, however, gave Higgins its 1977 Literary Award when *Scenes From A Receding Past* was published.

Aidan Higgins now lives in a suburb of North London. Since the publication of his latest novel, he has written for BBC radio, including some plays and a documentary on Brian O'Nolan. His 1977 anthology of short stories for a British book club reads almost like a manifesto: no easy or obvious choices from Britain, Ireland or America, but much from Yeats, Isak Dinesen, Djuna Barnes, Beckett, and Richard Brautigan. He is currently working on his fourth novel, in epistolary form, provisionally titled "Bornholm Night Ferry." Admirers of Higgins's work will be looking for an assimilation of the best features of his style, already noted, with some sort of break from the prison of home which has afflicted so many Irish exiles. He has reached the middle of his career as a novelist of a wide and deserved reputation of whom much is expected, but who still waits to break through into the smaller circle of the greatly praised. It should not be beyond him.

Other:

A Century of Short Stories, edited by Higgins (London: Cape, 1977);

Carl, Julien, and Elwin Higgins, *Colossal Gongorr and the Turkes of Mars*, edited by Higgins (London: Cape, 1979).

Susan Hill
(5 February 1942-   )

Catherine Wells Cole

BOOKS: *The Enclosure* (London: Hutchinson, 1961);

Do Me A Favour (London: Hutchinson, 1963);

Gentleman and Ladies (London: Hamilton, 1968; New York: Walker, 1969);

A Change for the Better (London: Hamilton, 1969);

I'm the King of the Castle (London: Hamilton, 1970; New York: Viking, 1970);

The Albatross and Other Stories (London: Hamilton, 1971; New York: Saturday Review Press, 1975);

Strange Meeting (London: Hamilton, 1971; New York: Saturday Review Press, 1972);

The Custodians (London: Covent Garden Press, 1972);

The Bird of Night (London: Hamilton, 1972; New York: Saturday Review Press, 1972);

A Bit of Singing and Dancing, and Other Stories (London: Hamilton, 1973);

In the Springtime of the Year (London: Hamilton, 1974; New York: Saturday Review Press, 1974);

The Cold Country and Other Plays for Radio (London: BBC Publications, 1975);

The Magic Apple-Tree (London: Hamilton, 1982).

Although her output has diminished since the early 1970s, Susan Hill remains a significant figure in the English literary scene. Her novels sell solidly and attract considerable critical attention; she has won several literary prizes. Conventionally structured and precisely crafted, her works characteristically explore states of isolation, loss, and detachment.

Susan Hill was born in 1942 to R. H. and Doris Hill in Scarborough, a seaside resort on the east coast of England, elegant rather than boisterous and long past its heyday. She loved its old-world, genteel atmosphere, which much resembles that of Royal Leamington Spa, where she lived during the 1970s. Several of her novels are set in similarly quiet, faded resorts. After attending grammar schools in Scarborough and in Coventry, she read English at King's College, London University, graduating with an honors degree in 1963. For the next five years she reviewed books for the *Coventry Evening Telegraph*; since 1969 she has been a full-time writer, literary journalist, and broadcaster. In 1975 she married Shakespeare scholar Stanley Wells; they have one daughter and now live in Oxfordshire.

Hill has said that she prefers to forget her first two novels—they have often been overlooked by critics and reviewers. *The Enclosure* (1961) was actually written when she was sixteen and still at school; *Do Me A Favour* (1963) was written when she was an undergraduate at London University. She says that no one who read them would have imagined that she would ever write any more novels, and they do not resemble her later work to any marked extent. They are nonetheless interesting, if only for their exploration of areas of experience which rarely appear in her subsequent novels.

In *The Enclosure* Hill tracks the collapse of a marriage. A novelist in her mid-forties with one undergraduate son by a former husband, Virginia Stirling is now married to Guy, a theater director. They live near London. Their relationship flourishes while he is successful, but, when his company goes bankrupt, Virginia feels her hitherto unassailable love for him ebbing away. She finds herself pregnant; they move to Lancashire where Guy gets a job in a repertory company; the baby is stillborn; Guy returns to London, and Virginia

Susan Hill

chooses isolation in the North, enclosed and absorbed in her writing. The plot offers considerable potential for color and incident, but the treatment is flat and calm, almost to the point of tedium. This dispassionate balance is something Hill later uses with more deliberation and technical assurance. Much of *The Enclosure*'s potential for realistic surface texture (the theater, Virginia's being pregnant at forty-five, their financial worries) is dissipated in ways that are simply beyond the author's control (again, Hill was only sixteen). The context of Virginia's life is unconvincing, and, although the gap in age and experience between author and central character is no greater than what Hill attempts later with considerable success, it results in some rather priggish telling-off: "Virginia never tried to realize that the fact that she was unhappy was basically her fault. . . . A little friendliness, more understanding, towards Guy might have helped her a great deal in finding more happiness, even if not that of intense love." In fact, it is Virginia's isolation throughout

the novel, despite Hill's attempts to provide her with a convincing social life, which points to the later novels. Although Virginia's selfishness still provokes her author's overt disapproval at the end of the novel, she has reached a situation where Hill appears to feel comfortable with her as she sits alone at her desk writing, observed only by the small child from the flat below.

Do Me a Favour is about Monica Bristow, at twenty-two a successful novelist and dramatist living in London. Her central relationship is with Dan, a journalist, although the novel attempts to deal more fully with a larger cast of characters than *The Enclosure*. At times this effort is relatively successful, as in the glimpses of Dan's sister, caught in an unfulfilling marriage with a Cambridge don. But other characters suffer from a lack of attention; for example, Victor, Monica's friend, who betrays his socialist ideals when the "working class musical" he has written is a commercial hit. Similarly underrealized is the suicide of Peter Goosens, a colleague of Dan's, whose wife leaves him because of his lack of ambition. The chill detachment with which Hill later treats shocking events is missing here: Peter's death is treated so casually that it is almost insignificant. *Do Me A Favour* frequently achieves monotony rather than understatement; the overall effect is of imprecision in Hill's style. Perhaps also her own experience is too similar to Monica's for her to feel imaginatively free. Although Monica as a writer is given more attention in *Do Me A Favour* than Virginia, as a writer, received in *The Enclosure*, this fact is presented with no special insight: "she had a quick, lively talent which made her style witty and profound, at the same time attractive both to public and critics."

The ups and downs of an emotional relationship between a man and a woman are central to Hill's first two novels. It is perhaps fair to say that they are both remarkable by virtue of her youth, rather than for any insights they provide into such relationships or into the social conditions (job, money, friends) which determine lives. *The Enclosure* attracted some critical attention, which focused chiefly on the author's youth; *Do Me a Favour* provoked little favorable critical comment. In a 26 November 1972 interview in the *Observer*, Hill said it "sank under a bombardment of appalling reviews." After five years working on the *Coventry Evening Telegraph*, during which time she published no novels, Hill directed her talents of clarity, precision, and balance to less mainstream areas of experience.

Gentleman and Ladies (1968) portrays a much smaller world. It is set in the village of Haverstock, where the ladies of the title live, all of them aging and aware of mortality. Hill focuses on one of them at her bedroom window, looking out "upon an unjust world, upon undeserved sadness, upon concatenation of ill-luck, upon the at least equal odds of sickness, spinsterhood and narrow horizons." Largely, this is what the novel deals with, though it is not all as gloomy as this quotation might imply. The gentleman of the title, Hubert Gaily, a fifty-four-year-old bachelor living with his mother, is eventually able to marry Florence Ames; through Florence's widowed friend Dorothea Shottery, he and his mother become part of the life of the village. Yet, although Hubert is treated as a positive force in the novel, he is also, as the outsider, its least convincing figure. He is urban, working class: he is present, by accident, at the funeral of Miss Faith Lavender, which opens the novel. Afterward the ladies discuss him; Isabel Lavender has noticed that he wore boots. This indication of class difference is an example of the kind of observation for which Hill has been much praised. Yet it is also faintly anachronistic (even though the novel, like much of Hill's work, is not precisely located in time). But there is just enough fudging of the realities of Hubert and his grim old mother, Ada (who takes her new daughter-in-law solidly to her heart), to weaken this part of the novel.

The most successfully drawn characters are those on whom the outside world hardly ever impinges. The remaining Lavender sisters, Kathleen and Isabel, find the balance of their lives impossible to regain without Faith: Isabel's behavior becomes gradually stranger until she is seriously deranged. Her death, which happens at a ladies' coffee morning, is touched with the grotesque; but it is also extremely convenient for the long-suffering Kathleen, who can now go to live with Dorothea. The ease with which such problems are solved is perhaps the least satisfactory aspect of this novel: it certainly is clear-eyed and unsentimental about the business of aging and dying, but death is not always the worst thing that can happen to people. The unsympathetic Alida Thorne, unmarried at sixty-one, looks after her bedridden mother, Eleanor. Eleanor's mind is sharp, but she prefers to live in her memory, and this tension between past and present is something Hill creates, here and in other novels, extremely well. Alida's hypochondria and selfishness finally drive Eleanor into an old people's home; but here, against expectations, she thrives and begins to enjoy life fully again. Her eventual decline and death are caused by a revitalized Alida's offer to have her home for a holiday. Despite the inevitable deaths and illnesses of a novel about the elderly, and, despite the sharpness of its observations and its lightly ironic style, *Gentleman and Ladies* is perhaps too cozy, the world Hill has created too unrealistically safe. *Gentleman and Ladies* was well received by reviewers, who admired its tautness and its precise observation. In a June 1974 article in *Books and Bookmen*, James Brockway commented that, "for all its deft compassion," it possessed already the two main ingredients of Hill's subject matter, "Cruelty and Death."

Gentleman and Ladies was adapted as a radio play by Hill in 1970 and, as *Miss Lavender is Dead*, was one of the first of a long series of her plays to be produced by the B.B.C., some taken from her novels, others on original themes. Although few of her plays are technically very adventurous, they do make skillful use of the medium, particularly in their characters' frequent awareness of forces outside themselves. David Wade, writing on "Radio Writers" in *Contemporary Dramatists*, says that each of Hill's plays says "far more than can be accounted for by its not very eventful story-line. There is something cool and deep about Miss Hill's work. Like a river under trees."

Her next novel, *A Change for the Better* (1969), is bleaker. Set in Westbourne, a faded seaside resort, it is, like *Gentleman and Ladies*, curiously anachronistic in its examination of social manners. It is a world of private hotels, paid companions, and a desperately genteel concern with keeping up appearances. The central figure is Deirdre Fount, who keeps a small drapery shop with her mother, Mrs. Winifred Oddicott. Both women are generally referred to, as are most of the characters, by their full names. This practice can, in Hill's later novels, degenerate into a mannerism, but the meaningless formality is well matched here to the stiff emptiness of people's lives. Hill's style, formal and precise, conveys the blankness of Deirdre's life: "dear God, I am thirty-nine years old already and that is almost forty. I am nine years divorced, albeit most decently, and I have an eleven-year-old son. I count the packets of pins. I am my mother's daughter. Is this to be all?"

Deirdre's decisive effort to free herself from her mother comes when she decides to take her son, James, away for a holiday by themselves. James, however, prefers to go on holiday with a school friend, and Deirdre finally sees that he is as distant from her as she is from her own mother: "He would rather be with strangers, she thought, and that is what my mother says of me." She spends a holiday alone in an environment very similar to that of Westbourne; the novel suggests that there is nowhere for her to escape to and thus turns its own rather dated quality into an advantage: there is no "real" world outside. The taut writing and stylized dialogue build up Westbourne as a metaphor for all stifled and barren life. Some characters will survive: James will, and so will Mrs. Flora Carpenter, who (freed by widowhood from being a doormat) moves out of the stuffy Prince of Wales Hotel to a modern flat on the seafront. But the title's implications are only ironic for Deirdre, who remains in the drapery shop even after the deah of Mrs. Oddicott: "I do feel that it is what my mother would have wanted."

A Change for the Better added to Hill's critical reputation. Jonathan Raban in *London Magazine*, calling the novel a "rueful comedy of manners," drew particular attention to its precise use of language: "This sort of debased operatic style . . . brings a whole decaying scene to life." The novelist

Pamela Hansford Johnson named it as her book of the year in a *Daily Telegraph* survey; this selection is symptomatic of Hill's appeal to an older generation of writers and critics.

The social isolation of Westbourne and many of its inhabitants works best as metaphor: that of Hill's next novel, *I'm the King of the Castle* (1970), is essential for its action to be convincing. Edmund Hooper, a schoolboy, lives with his widowered father in Warings, a dark, gloomy house on the outskirts of a small village. The relationship between father and son is an uneasy one; Edmund is a strange, secretive child, but he is attached to the house and especially to the Red Room, where there are collections of moths in glass cases. Mr. Joseph Hooper (as in *A Change for the Better*, adults' names are given in full; the boys are usually referred to by second names only, a formality still observed in some English schools and which here conveys the stiff, formal relationships of the novel) decides to engage a housekeeper, the widowed Mrs. Helena Kingshaw, whose son, Charles, is the same age as Edmund. Edmund does not want them to come; he must be king of the castle:

> "It is my house," he thought, "it is private, I got here first. Nobody should come here."
>
> Still, he would not give anything of himself away, the other boy could be ignored, or evaded, or warned off. It depended on what he was like. All sorts of things could be done.

Charles is, in fact, a natural victim, and the novel is an account of the reign of terror that Edmund inflicts on him. The house becomes intolerable to Charles, especially the Red Room—he has a horror of moths. The sadism with which Edmund plays on all Charles's weaknesses is completely convincing—though less so is the degree of isolation from which Charles suffers. The novel takes place during the summer holidays, and almost until the end the two boys have no other companions. Mr. Hooper and Mrs. Kingshaw are attracted to each other, and she, eager to remarry, attempts to smooth over friction between the two boys and completely fails to see what is going on.

Charles, like Deirdre Fount, longs to escape from an intolerable situation and is at the same time afraid to do so. When he does at last run away, Edmund follows him and they get lost in Hang Wood. This is the first of Hill's novels to contrast the

Dust jacket for Hill's 1970 novel, winner of the Somerset Maugham Award

natural world with man-made environments: the point of the contrast here is that, although the wood is a terrifying place, it is in many ways safer than Warings and its refined torments. During the night the boys spend in the open, Charles is less afraid and feels that the balance of the relationship has shifted, but, once they are brought back to the house, Edmund reasserts himself. Finally, unable to bear the thought of his mother's marrying Mr. Hooper and thus of his always having to live with Edmund, Charles returns to the wood and drowns himself. Like all Charles's sufferings, this is conveyed in a manner that is scrupulously dispassionate.

I'm the King of the Castle's view of childhood invites comparison with William Golding's *Lord of the Flies*, but the comparison must be to the detriment of the former. The novel is weakened by its particularity, by the evident care Hill takes to isolate these two boys in every way. And such an obsessively narrow central relationship does become at times a matter for literary ingenuity rather than anything else, as Edmund devises fresh miseries for Charles. Although *I'm the King of the Castle* has been largely

successful (it won the Somerset Maugham Award in 1971), working on small areas of experience in a style that is quiet, deliberate, and precise can at times make Hill's novels appear slightly thin and overstretched. James Brockway concedes that the novel's artifice is a shade too evident but admires Hill's dispassionate handling of the awfulness of life; he calls the book a "horror story of hatred and fear and mental cruelty."

Hill is frequently at her best in the short story. Her next book, *The Albatross and Other Stories* (1971), won the John Llewelyn Rhys Memorial Prize. The title story is novella length and deals with Duncan Pike, slow in the head, who lives with his invalid mother in a bleak fishing town. For him, the sea offers escape, but he is also terrified of it; he panics when Ted Flint, his hero, offers to take him out in his boat. "I could go" becomes "I could have gone." Duncan reaches a crisis when Ted is drowned; he pushes his drugged mother's wheelchair into the sea and sets fire to their cottage, but escape is still illusory. He finds himself at a barn some miles inland and retreats inside, curled up in the dark until he is found: "So this was where he had wanted to be, then. This place. He felt no surprise." The view from inside Duncan's head is well sustained for the narrative's ninety-two pages, and the wintry seaside setting is fittingly bleak. But even here, there is some apparently detached observation which at times distracts. At one moment, when Duncan is working, "A gust of wind blew the door of the toolshed open suddenly, and there was the winter sky, bleached and grey as a gull's back." It is not clear that Duncan is capable of such consoling perceptions of nature. As with similar moments in all her novels, there is a feeling of a closely-observed background which has no real relationship to, or control over, characters' lives. Hill has said of Thomas Hardy's use of landscape that it is not always metaphorical but can be "a remarkable and arresting visual image which will lead us into a fascinating human story." Sometimes she appears to manipulate background (urban, rural, or domestic) so that the story exists in a sort of limbo.

Hill's sixth novel, *Strange Meeting* (1971), is firmly located in time, during World War I. It is told largely from the point of view of John Hilliard, a young officer returning to the trenches after a convalescent stay at home in England. His feelings of horror and terror, and his inability to communicate them, are assuaged by the loving friendship he establishes with a new officer, David Barton. In the closing winter offensive, Barton is killed.

The futility of war is conveyed in Hill's characteristically precise, hard-edged prose. World War I is a perfect model of a senseless, alien world in which love and concern can be expressed only at a personal level, and the extent of Hilliard's need for Barton makes some sense in this context. The complete lack of sympathy from his own family, their failure to understand anything of what he suffers, is less plausible. Even his sister, Beth, to whom he had been very close in childhood, is a stranger to him. Hilliard's emotional isolation in the novel is gained at the expense of some credibility, and David Barton, too, is somewhat less than believable. No one dislikes Barton; he is outgoing, attractive, perfectly at ease. His family (heard only through their letters) are equally open and friendly, and the novel is finally optimistic in that they will clearly take Hilliard to their hearts. Through knowing Barton he has become more free, more communicative; Barton also changes, his fundamental optimism tempered by the realities of this war. To the end, however, he is almost too good to live, and his characterization remains a flaw in an otherwise impressive novel. *Strange Meeting* was less well received by reviewers.

Writing in *Books and Bookmen*, Diane Leclercq perceived a lack of connection between the central characters—"if they convince, it is as young men of the '70's"—and the portrayal of the war itself—"vivid but televisual." Despite the claim of its title, she found *Strange Meeting* "rather more Rupert Brooke than Wilfred Owen."

In *The Bird of Night* (1972) Hill again turns her back on contemporary issues to consider a relationship that can only exist because of its unusualness and because of one of the characters' craving for solitude. It is one of the most skillfully crafted of her novels (it won the Whitbread Literary Award for fiction in 1972), and its careful construction sustains the reader's interest throughout. The narrative is presented by Harvey Lawson, partly in the present, as an old man, partly in the past, by means of his journals. He recreates and remembers his life with Francis Croft, the most brilliant poet of his generation, and his care for Francis in his attacks of insanity. In many ways the relationship is an extension of the one between Hilliard and Barton; Harvey is steady and rather withdrawn, Francis is brilliantly charismatic. Hill takes an artistic risk in making Francis a poet, and this characterization at times falls into doomed genius cliches. She has the same problem as with David Barton: that of conveying convincingly dazzling personal charm and warmth. The antithesis, Francis's madness, uses her matter-of-factness to better advantage, and certain moments are genuinely horrific. Francis, however glamorous, is not the character of the greatest interest. The novel is really concerned with Harvey, with his memory, with the loyalty to Francis's privacy that makes Harvey, finally, burn his journals to keep them from "those arrogant, salacious young men" who want to make literary capital from them.

The book is moving in its portrayal of Harvey's present loneliness—his being looked after by a housekeeper, walking slowly down to the sea when he can, feeling the cold. Yet life with Francis seems hardly to have been more attractive, and it is only gradually revealed that there was anything in it for Harvey. He is happy with Francis, even through his worst attacks, because Francis is totally dependent on him: "I saw that I needed to have someone entirely dependent on me, and it surprised me, because I had always assumed that I was solitary by nature." Later, asked by a doctor why he has given up his job and his own life to look after Francis, he replies simply, "Because I love him." Certainly the dependence is well established in the novel, but there are few normal good times between the two men, and this is perhaps a case where Hill's customary reticence about sexuality detracts from the novel as a whole. She has said that the imagination is more erotic than words on a page can be, but *The Bird of Night* suffers from the absence of even the suggestion of this element in Harvey's love for Francis. It is, however, on the whole, one of her most successfully sustained novels.

The critic Michele Murray sums up Hill's achievement in *The Bird of Night* in terms which relate also to much of her other writing: "It is a thoroughly *created* piece of work, a novel wrought of language, carefully designed to tell a story drawn, not from the surface of the author's life or fragments of her autobiography, but from the heart of the imagination."

In the Springtime of the Year (1974) appears to have a more obvious link with the surface of Hill's life than any of her earlier novels. It shows a young woman, Ruth Bryce, living through the months and seasons following the death of her husband, Ben, a farm laborer. The novel concentrates almost exclusively on the central figure of Ruth, with the formlessness of her grief counterpointed by the regularity of seasonal change; it is Hill's most pastoral and most heartfelt work. Before writing the book, she had mourned the death of a man whom she loved and whom she would have married.

Ruth, naturally, has periods of intense grief, and the novel largely succeeds in communicating this intensity in language that is controlled, even understated. Ruth wants to be completely alone, and the novel respects her wish in ways that diminish its own credibility. Her adoring father does not come to see her when Ben dies; there is a gulf between her and all the other villagers, with the exception of Ben's younger brother, Jo; she earns money by taking in sewing and so does not have to go out and meet people at work. She does not have to worry about rent, as the cottage she lives in was left to her by her Godmother Fry. The unreality of fairy tale clings to the novel, and, though it draws much of its strength from the archetypal movement from death to renewal, it is less convincing about people than it is about landscape. Neither Ben nor Jo is a convincing member of the working-class family which produced them (a discrepancy which is mentioned but remains unresolved). Dora Bryce, huddled over her fire, weeping noisily, is hard to accept as the mother of two sons who "had the same clear grasp of the truth that lay beneath the surface of things, [who] saw, as [Ruth] had only glimpsed once or twice, the whole pattern. They had the gift of angels."

Like David Barton in *Strange Meeting*, Ben is regarded as exceptional by everyone who knows him, but in both novels this is something which readers are told rather than shown. Hill rarely seems to achieve the extremely difficult object of realizing her vibrant characters nearly as convincingly as she realizes their victims, their lovers, or their observers. Ben dies when a tree he is felling crushes him, and his death has a profound impact on Potter, the man who finds him: "It was death and—and life. I'd never doubt that now. Never. It was inside me and all around. And him. A change . . . Some great change."

Like Hill herself, Ruth is sustained by religious belief. Some moments are quite moving—such as Easter morning, when the graves, decorated with flowers the evening before, look "as though all the people had indeed truly risen and were dancing in the sunshine." It is perhaps part of Hill's intention that the idyllic inevitability of the novel's natural background should diminish the pain of Ruth's loss, but this grief remains somehow diluted by its removal from everyday actuality. Margaret Atwood in the *New York Times Book Review* has compared *In the Springtime of the Year* to a handmade quilt, in that it is traditional, well-stitched, and moves slowly toward completion. The same might be said of Hill's writing in general: its strengths and weaknesses are both conveyed by the comparison.

Susan Hill has produced no new work of fiction since her marriage and the subsequent birth of her daughter, although she is still prominent as a critic, broadcaster, and reviewer. Her most recently published book is *The Magic Apple-Tree* (1982), an evocation of the seasons and customs of the Oxfordshire countryside where she now lives.

Other:

The Distracted Preacher and Other Tales by Thomas Hardy, edited by Hill (Harmondsworth, U.K.: Penguin, 1979).

Helen Hodgman

(27 April 1945-   )

Malcolm Page
Simon Fraser University

BOOKS: *Blue Skies* (London: Duckworth, 1976);
Jack and Jill (London: Duckworth, 1978).

Helen Hodgman, the only child of John and
Martha Willes, spent the first year of her life in
London. When her father returned from army service and resumed his job as a gas fitter, the family
moved to Colchester, Essex. When she was five they
moved again to the nearby village of Kelvedon. She
was educated at the Anglican village elementary
school and at Colchester High School for Girls. In
1958, when she was thirteen, the family moved to
Hobart, Tasmania; at that time Hobart was experiencing a boom in building, and her father was
provided work as a Rotary Club adoptee. She left

school at fifteen to work as a bank teller but soon felt
that she needed more education. She served for a
year as a junior teacher, enabling her to enter the
Teachers' College in Hobart for a two-year course
qualifying her for elementary school teaching.
After completing the course, she married Roger
Hodgman, and a daughter, Meredith, was born in
1965. She opened an art gallery with a friend in
1967, introducing major contemporary Australian
artists to Hobart. She returned to London in 1971,
followed the next year by her husband, who became
director of the E15 Acting School, and they lived in
Ladbroke Grove. She had many short-term jobs in
London, among them domestic cleaner, clerk in a
betting shop, market researcher, and demonstrator

Helen Hodgman

of kitchen equipment in Harrods.

Although Hodgman had long seen herself as a writer, it was not until 1975 that she actually wrote her first novel. *Blue Skies*, written in six months, was quickly accepted for publication in 1976 by Duckworth, a publishing company specializing in short novels.

The title of *Blue Skies* is ironic: Hodgman loathes the lovely beach suburb of Hobart which provides her setting, and she cannot forget that the aborigines were driven out and destroyed to make its development possible. The anonymous narrator is a bored housewife: the "numberless days . . . when the clock always said three o'clock in the afternoon" grow tedious. A good-natured, shadowy husband rarely comes home. As Julian Barnes points out in the *New Statesman*, "The vacuous expanses of placid, pointless marriage are well-drawn—togetherness being a visit to the supermarket or a weekend drive." There are also a baby daughter (of whom she is not overly fond) and a mortgage—but life is less normal than first appears.

The narrator sleeps and wakes at the wrong times, a psychosomatic protest at this way of life. Her quest for consolation gives her two lovers. Jonathan, whom she meets on Tuesdays, is a restaurant manager whose attitudes lay him open to "charges of 'pouffery,' the Australian crime against the sanctity of mateship." Accused of indecency, he is beaten up and obliged to leave town—she calmly records: "Tuesdays had done a bunk." Ben, an artist, her Thursday's man, wears womens' clothes and may sleep with his sister. Eventually he is arrested on a drug charge. The narrator's depressions increase, despite the doctor's antidepressant pills and lovemaking with a third lover, a coach driver. Growing delusions produce aborigine ghosts. Irritated by her talkative neighbor, she murders her with an electric lawn mower, a death the police accept as an accident.

On a down-to-earth level, Hodgman is writing of the boredom of being a housewife and of Australian intolerance of nonconformists. Nick Totten in the *Spectator* rightly grasped that Hodgman was after more original and profound themes: "Time looms over the novel as a great enemy, to be harried and reduced by sleep, sex, or simple blankness. . . . Everyone in *Blue Skies* is sleep-walking; when they wake up, perhaps they will turn out to be in a Beckett narrative."

John Mellors in the *Listener* disliked the book: "It was a mistake to let her narrator show only two facets of her character, the selfish and the scatty. . . . What is lacking is the sense that the author cares

Dust jacket for Hodgman's second novel, praised for its "tough and tidy" style

about what happens to her creatures." Susannah Clapp in the *Times Literary Supplement* explained what she found wrong with the work: "The possibilities for interest that she provides are too many and too various. Characters appear, are confounded by their disasters, and exit without further trace. . . . An anxiety to make every moment tell leads to over-tricky phrasing and hectic scene-painting." On the other hand, Lorna Sage in the *Observer* cautiously pronounced this "cool immoral tale" to be "a promising beginning." Nick Totten praised "its precise yet undramatic style: a light which, in illuminating only the immediately relevant, implies a whole landscape." Rosalind Wade wrote enthusiastically in *Contemporary Review*: "Hodgman describes babies, dramatic scenery and cloud effects quite brilliantly. She is taut and economical in conveying character with the minimum of dialogue—so economical that she deprives herself of sufficient elbow room to develop a theme."

Hodgman's second novel, *Jack and Jill* (1978), took longer to write than the first, involving some research in 1930s Australian newspapers to achieve the sense of the period. Hodgman finds this book somewhat less satisfactory than her first book, partly because the long time span covered prevents it from having as neat a form. Completed in the late summer of 1977, *Jack and Jill* tells the story of Jill from the day her mother dies in the late 1920s (when Jill is a toddler) through to about 1970. She grows up on a poor, isolated, interior farm with her father, Douggie. During her childhood Jack arrives:

> He presented himself at their door one dinner-time, when the homely stench of singed mutton-chop hung over the air.... His nose twitched appreciatively; his flat, incurious eyes took everything in.... He was also young, strong and altogether eager to make good. He had set out from Melbourne, of all places, to find proper man's work.

So Jack becomes the hired hand. He takes the young Jill on a trip to the city, then teaches her to drive, eventually seducing her. Jill goes to the University of Sydney while Jack joins the army during the war. He returns in a wheelchair, "dessicated by starvation, crippled by torture and crushed legs" in a Japanese prisoner-of-war camp. Jill visits England, on her return accepting Jack's marriage proposal. They go to live on the farm where she grew up, her father having died in the meantime. Jill becomes successful as the author of books about a boy, Barnaby. An admirer of these books, Raelene, visits to help Jill with the housework, and she sleeps with Jack. Raelene leaves, and Jack spends some time on his own with Hildy, a wandering homosexual filmmaker. Jill meanwhile decides to give up writing and spend her time working the farm. Jack rejoins Jill, they survive a bushfire, and Raelene comes back, pregnant. Jill decides to take on the baby as the one she never had, and Raelene accepts a one-way ticket to San Francisco in exchange.

Although *Jack and Jill* covers a long period of time, the book is very short. The narrative is bald: there is some sense of allegory, or broader meaning, but Hodgman never so much as hints at what this is, merely presenting some selected facts about her four characters. The book is assertively Australian with its numerous references to waratahs and stringybark, abo kids and 'roo shooting, Banjo Paterson and Hans Heysen prints, the Manly ferry and Rushcutters Bay. The style is showy, powerful, and immediate: "his long toes chalky with moonlit dust." Most marked are the distasteful and the grotesque: Hodgman frequently writes of "scabby dogs" and cutting up snakes, of "septic eye-sockets and missing teeth," while "the high spot" of young Jill's week "was when they combed the contents of her bottle-brush head—burrs and buzzies, various creepy-crawlies dislodged from the greenery as she tripped past—out on to an old copy of the *Sydney Morning Herald* and burned the result."

Reviewers searched somewhat wildly to place the book: Marigold Johnson in the *Times Literary Supplement* tried "Australia's answer to Beryl Bainbridge." The style was "tough and tidy"; Hodgman "seldom allows herself the luxury of analysing the behaviour of the protagonists, of deflecting her pen from an effectively cryptic narrative." Johnson also remarked: "Her slyly contrived inference as to the superior guts and gumption will not go unnoticed in a male-dominated society." Peter Kemp in the *Listener* noted the "mannered, perky callousness," continuing: "Sentimentality provides the punchbag; it is the kind of book in which a character who gets a lump in the throat is soon going to get one on the head. . . . The novel gleefully resounds with the noise of people being brought down to earth with a bump. Miss Hodgman's favourite trick in the jolting line is to juxtapose the nice and the nasty."

Jeremy Treglown in the *New Statesman*, noticing Jill's writing at the end of the novel, "Jack shall have Jill / Nought shall go ill," claimed that "Hodgman is aiming at Shakespearean comedy." He found much to praise: Douggie's "limitations are beautifully sent up. . . . Hodgman does the farm very well, too, with its dust and snakes and sheep suffering from nodule worm." He concludes, however, that "neither the details nor the plotting quite hold up the irrevocably—and, in a way, rather promisingly—unravelled middle."

Mary Hope in the *Spectator*, finding the book "perfectly observed," had unqualified praise: "Difficult to categorise the charm and verve of such a wild creation, but Miss Hodgman's way with the Australian language makes Barry Humphries pale by comparison. Strange and mad as the story is, it's sheer delight from beginning to end. The sane perversity of human relationship is blown sky-high. . . . Hodgman is a winner." While Johnson's placing was as an "odd and somehow chilling little novella," Julia O'Faolain in the *Observer* concluded: "Hodgman chooses pithiness too often. . . . Half-stunned by a plethora of punch-lines, I was left wondering whether a three-dimensional novel might be smothering somewhere inside the smart corseting of this pert little yarn." Peter Kemp identified a different fault: "The trouble is, [the characters] are just synthetic fabrications, so, for all its energy, the exercise seems finally not much more meaningful than bludgeoning a kapok kangaroo." *Jack and Jill* received the Somerset Maugham Award. Hodgman's two novels were published later in Australia, where they have been well received.

Roger Hodgman was appointed director of the Vancouver Playhouse Theatre School in 1977, and the family moved to Vancouver, British Columbia. Later separated from her husband, Helen Hodgman worked as a ticket seller at a movie theater and then for a North Vancouver arts center, Presentation House, chiefly as editor of its newspaper. She plans to return to live in Sydney, Australia, in January 1983.

Hodgman's first play, *Oh Mother, Is It Worth It?*, grew, she says, "from personal experience, fantasy, discussion, and conversations overheard." The New Play Center, Vancouver, staged it in April 1981 as part of the Du Maurier Festival of New One-act Plays. Hodgman worked closely throughout rehearsals with the director. In the play an unnamed mother and daughter interact in very short scenes. Daughter crawls on with pacifier, soon piles up bricks (only to have them scattered by tidy would-be Supermom), becomes a schoolgirl, piano student, teenager, and bride. The mother is a kind of clown, showing off to the audience, while the daughter is more a suffering human. When Daughter is married with a daughter of her own (represented by a dummy which has previously served as Husband), she turns to attack Mother's blunders in child rearing. Mother has fed her daughter saws, aphorisms, incomplete information, and contradictions: be pretty to attract men and then mistrust them. Two

daring but rather awkward stylistic shifts follow to end the play: the pair sit at a table and read in turn from a book, *This-Is-Your-Life* fashion, in artfully literary language; then Mother lies down (and perhaps dies) and Daughter walks out. Hodgman leaves her audience aware of the necessity and the difficulty of coming to terms with what one generation has done to the next.

Hodgman sees herself more as novelist than dramatist, and she is working on a third novel, as yet untitled, set in London: an excerpt was published in *A Room of One's Own*, a Vancouver feminist quarterly, in fall 1982. She will also write the screenplay for *Blue Skies*: plans are advancing in Australia to make it into a film. She also intends to write a study of Tasmanian aborigines.

Hodgman's favorite author is Graham Greene, and his influence can perhaps be seen in her eye and ear for vivid and unsettling descriptions of place. A closer parallel for her two novels is the Southern gothic of Carson McCullers and Flannery O'Connor. (Hodgman did not read O'Connor until 1979—after her own two books had been written— and she was much impressed.) Hodgman's talents include a jagged, spiky style and an original, distinctive view of the quirks and savagery of human behavior. Her sharp and individual eye turns from Australia to England in the forthcoming book.

Play:
Oh Mother, Is It Worth It?, Vancouver, New Play Center, Waterfront Theater, 16 April 1981.

Periodical Publication:
"From an Untitled Novel," *A Room of One's Own* (Vancouver, B.C.), 7, Nos. 1-2 (1982): 2-14.

Desmond Hogan
(10 December 1950-   )

Susan Matthews
St. Anne's College, Oxford

BOOKS: *The Ikon-Maker* (Dublin: Irish Writers' Co-operative, 1976; London: Writers & Readers, 1979; New York, Braziller, 1980);
The Diamonds at the Bottom of the Sea (London: Hamilton, 1979; New York: Braziller, 1979);
The Leaves on Grey (London: Hamilton, 1979; New York, Braziller, 1980);
Children of Lir: Stories from Ireland (London: Hamilton, 1981; New York, Braziller, 1981).

Stories from Ireland, the subtitle of Desmond Hogan's 1981 collection of short stories, *Children of Lir*, describes his writing as a whole in two distinct senses. The traditional voice of Irish storytellers reappears in Hogan's narratives, providing a distinctive lyricism that links the varied Irish characters whose memories form his stories and novels. Yet almost all of Hogan's stories were written out-

Desmond Hogan

side Ireland; they are stories *from* Ireland, not simply *of* Ireland, often telling of travel and of escape from a confined society.

Desmond Hogan was born and educated in Ballinasloe, County Galway. His father owned a drapery shop, and Desmond was the second in William and Christina Connolly Hogan's family of five sons. After attending the local convent primary school, he moved in 1964 to the Catholic secondary school. He began writing at the age of nine, at first inventing plays to perform with friends during the school holidays to an audience of local children in sheds and gardens around the town. His themes were Dracula stories, religious apparitions, and Irish fairy tales. At secondary school he began to write short stories, encouraged not by the traditional teaching of the school but by his private reading: D. H. Lawrence, F. Scott Fitzgerald, Carson McCullers, Boris Pasternak, and Katharine Mansfield. Hogan describes his adolescence as lonely but filled by fantasy and dreams. Many of his stories written at that time and later take up this theme of the imaginative life of the solitary and the apparently lonely. From his reading, as well as from the films that he saw on trips to Dublin, he created a fantasy world which was woven into the prosaic and limited life of rural Ireland. In "The Mourning Thief," a story from his 1981 collection, *Children of Lir: Stories from Ireland*, he describes a son returning to Ireland to visit his dying father: "Adolescence returned with a sudden start: the gold flurry of snow as the train in which he was travelling sped towards Dublin, the films about Russian winters. Irish winters became Russian winters in turn, and half Liam's memories of adolescence were of the fantasised presence of Russia. Ikons, candles, streets agleam with snow."

By 1969, when Hogan arrived at University College, Dublin, to study English and philosophy, two of his stories had already appeared in *Irish Press*, which published many young Irish writers; and in 1971, when he was only twenty, Hogan won the Hennessy Award for one of his stories. Nevertheless, at university in Dublin, he felt provincial, strongly aware of his country background. University College had already passed through its year of student unrest in 1968, the year before he arrived, and the preoccupations of the students from privileged, middle-class backgrounds were ones with which Hogan felt little sympathy, even though, while he was a student in Dublin, his life became superficially that of a privileged student. In an interview in 1978, Hogan described student life: "All those young people talking about Beckett and Camus and debating suicide. The children of the affluent. Privileged in society. And that's all we could do." For three years he stopped writing, losing confidence in his ability. But his reading continued; Malcolm Lowry and Hart Crane were two of his discoveries during this time. In 1979 Hogan wrote about Dublin student life in his novel *The Leaves on Grey*. He draws on his own experience but also distances it by setting the novel in the 1950s in order to gain a historical perspective. At the same time, the 1950s were close enough for him to be able to draw on his own childhood memories.

Hogan stayed on at University College for an additional year after taking his B.A., during which time he earned an M.A. degree. Then, in the summer of 1974, he set off from Ireland, hitchhiking across Europe. He began writing again once he had left Ireland and continued after his return to Dublin, where he taught English for six months in a vocational school. For the first time he came into close contact with the poverty and deprivation of the lives of many Dublin working-class children. Several short stories appeared in Irish journals such as the *Irish Press*, *Dublin Magazine*, and *Transatlantic Review*, and some (but not all) were included in his 1979 collection of short stories *The Diamonds at the Bottom of the Sea*. One story grew and became Hogan's first novel, *The Ikon-Maker*, which was written in 1974 and published two years later.

Like many of Hogan's stories, *The Ikon-Maker* takes the point of view of a woman, in this case a mother, Susan, left behind in Ballinasloe when her son travels to London and later to Europe. Each of the characters feels the smallness and claustrophobia of the Irish rural community: the men leave, and even Susan sees the narrowness of the community after the loss of her son and her own visit to London in search of him. Yet in London she also realizes her Irishness, and returning to Ireland she feels, for a time, fully herself: "She was going back to Ireland. But not as a country-woman. For years she'd camouflaged herself as one . . . and if she'd spent her life listening to curlews and watching the rainbowside of the sky it was because all the time, inside, she was performing her own private

part in history, rejecting Ireland, the evil of conformity by outwardly accepting it. . . ."

Hogan draws parallels between the private emotions of the characters and the troubles of contemporary Ireland. Both Susan and her son, Diarmaid, are haunted by images of violence: the mother by memories of the war years in London and by television reports from Northern Ireland, and the son by the suicide of a schoolfriend many years before. Susan's sense that the guilt of violence is a shared responsibility introduces a theme that Hogan develops in later stories. She blames herself for the death of her son's friend "because in a sense she'd interned Diarmaid in that school. There he'd taken up a hopeless cause. The cause of that boy." *The Ikon-Maker* holds the reader's attention through the intensity with which Hogan portrays the feelings of the mother, Susan. And where the themes and ideas of the book are expressed roughly or naively, this technique is often appropriate to the characters of mother and son. It is Hogan's sympathy for his characters that causes both the strengths and weaknesses of the novel. Published first in Ireland, the book found an English publisher only in 1979. In a review of Hogan's later stories, Michael Coady wrote: "In spite of a certain gaucherie of style, I found that his novel, *The Ikon-Maker* refused to be put down."

From January 1975 to the summer of 1977, Hogan worked with a children's theater company, the Children's T-Company, performing plays in Dublin and elsewhere, in schools and in streets. In 1978 he described how this experience contrasted with the solitariness of his adolescence: "I found myself riding about on a bicycle, giving readings in convents, acting on the streets, talking with Unionists in Belfast. I had to relate socially. I was given a communal sense, a sense of relationship with the country I lived in and the political system of which I was a part." During this time he had two lunchtime plays performed at the Peacock Theatre, part of the Abbey Theatre in Dublin: in 1975, *A Short Walk to the Sea* ran for two weeks, and, the following year, *Sanctified Distances* for three weeks.

Hogan had already traveled once to California in 1976 to visit friends, but in 1977 he won an American literary prize (the Rooney Prize, given by the Pittsburgh Steelers) and with this money he traveled again. Leaving Ireland in October 1977, he visited California again, as well as Egypt and Greece, in the course of the next two years. From January 1978 to the summer of 1979 he worked as a substitute teacher in London.

In 1979 his first short-story collection, *The*

Diamonds at the Bottom of the Sea, was published. The book contains stories written over a period of ten years (including, for instance, "Blow-Ball," written while Hogan was still at school). The seventeen stories, most very short, cover a wide range of settings and characters; some are set in provincial Ireland, others in Dublin, and several describe the Irish abroad. The pace at which the narrative swoops over passing years and between changing scenes brings the order of memory and symbol to the subjective narratives of the varied characters. "The Bombs" describes how a young man from Dublin gradually rediscovers innocence in California. "The Last Time" is narrated by an Irishwoman, married and living in Clapham, who searches back in her memory and on in her reading to find the image of a boy she had known in her home town who opened the narrow confines of her life by his knowledge of books and films. He remains for her an image of glamour and aspiration: "in Chelsea library I began reading books by Russian authors. . . . I began reading books by Russian authors. . . . I never reached him; I just entertained him like as a child in the West of Ireland I had held a picture of Claudette Colbert under my pillow to remind me of glamour." The myths that pattern many of the stories are ones of metamorphosis and escape. Several stories describe the limiting morality of Irish society. In "Jimmy" (which was written first as a radio play and was subsequently rewritten as a short story) a middle-aged man returns to Ireland after years abroad, having been forced into exile by the scandal of a suspected homosexual affair. To his sister, Emily, who is now reunited with him, he becomes a symbol of all that modern Ireland rejects: "Emily often watched him, knowing that like De Valera he represented something of Ireland. But an element other than pain, fear, loneliness. He was the artist. He was the one foregone and left out in a rush to be acceptable."

The Diamonds at the Bottom of the Sea was received more favorably by critics in England than in Ireland. Janice Elliot, writing in the *Sunday Telegraph*, said: "It is not merely Mr. Hogan's sympathy for every condition, but the quality of his writing that is extraordinary. A spare lyricism. An avoidance of all the stylistic traps of Irishness. Vigour without rush. Sentiment without whimsy." But Matthew Coady, reviewing Hogan's collection for the *Irish Times*, was highly critical: "On almost every page, alas, there is evidence of an unforgivable and inexplicable carelessness in the craft of words. . . . Quite a number of the stories here read like somnambulistic first drafts, felt intuitively on the

Dust jacket for Hogan's second novel, which questions the values upon which the Irish Republic was founded

nerve-ends and written quickly, with the mind, as it were, switched off. Dialogue is often perfunctory and unconvincing and the story seemingly without disciplined direction." Both these criticisms and the praise which Hogan's stories have won can be explained in part by the way in which he works. Rather than cutting and altering a first draft, Hogan revises by writing a complete second version, hence both the roughness and the freshness which characterize his final text.

Only a week after publication, *The Diamonds at the Bottom of the Sea* had to be withdrawn when one of the stories became the subject of a writ for libel, originating in Ireland. Hogan lost the case, and the collection was reissued several months later without the offending story, "The Dehillys," in which a small boy sees a policeman beating his wife. However, in 1979 the volume won the John Llewelyn Rhys Memorial Prize, and the money from this award enabled Hogan to stay on in England and to concentrate on writing.

The Leaves on Grey, published in 1979, is Hogan's second novel, but it is the first book he planned as a novel rather than the form that he writes most naturally, the short story. A first draft of over four hundred pages was rewritten in its present, far shorter form. The novel explores, in more detail than before, Hogan's theme of the limitations of contemporary Ireland. Sean McMahon, a conventional and successful middle-aged lawyer, narrates the story; he looks back to his childhood in a rural setting in the brief opening section, and in the central section of the book he describes his time as a student at University College, Dublin, in the 1950s. An epilogue, set in 1972, draws the loosely organized fragments and images of the narrative together. But it is not the narrator who dominates the story, for he does not identify himself until well into the book and then only as if by accident. His story is dominated by others: by Liam, the friend of his childhood and of his student days, and above all by the memory of Liam's mother, the Russian born Mrs. Keneally. Through Liam and his mother, Hogan describes the qualities of poetic imagination, glamour, romantic aspiration, and quiet, contemplative withdrawal. Mrs. Keneally kills herself in the aftermath of a love affair that shocks the small town: "Nuns could have killed themselves. Their heroine had confused them. What about the train of gifts from convent to Keneally home, the honey, the marmalade, the cakes, had they led to sin?" Through Mrs. Keneally and other characters, Hogan also questions the values on which the Irish Republic was founded: "Ireland was officially declared a republic that Easter. Little boys in white shirts and long white trousers banged triangles as they marched about the town and Mrs. Keneally said, looking out a window, 'Vive la république. Long live a bloody eyesore.' " Hogan also describes the disillusion of others of her generation: "A young man he'd accompanied arch socialists and romantics to fight on the streets of Dublin in 1916 . . . .But he'd seen bridges crash, ignorant men take over and smother a nation. . . ." The greyness of Ireland is everywhere; yet in the vivid images of the narrative, the clothes, books, parties, and characters that the narrator recalls, the brightness of the leaves of the title is also conveyed: "There was nothing, but nothing, to recommend this retarded island and yet we . . . danced a fine dance, wore bow-ties, cravats to advertise a vice. It should have been Paris, should have been Berlin but being Dublin the experience was none the worse for that, just that the ensemble of lavatories smelled worse, and the skies implored just too much rain." The narrator's voice becomes generalized to record the more vivid and committed lives that cross his own, the bright but transient leaves against the greyness of conformity.

The short and concentrated narrative succeeds in conveying lyrically Hogan's account of the creation of contemporary Ireland. Writing in the *Times*, Myrna Blumberg said: "Desmond Hogan establishes himself among the best novelists with *The Leaves on Grey*. He has a lot to say, which he does with elegance and maturity. . . ."

Since writing *The Leaves on Grey*, Hogan has continued to live in London, supporting himself solely by his writing. In 1980 he adapted his first novel, *The Ikon-Maker*, into a play which was taken by a touring company around England and performed in London at the Gate Theatre for a run of four weeks in January 1981. A second collection of short stories, *Children of Lir*, was also published in 1981. At the end of *The Leaves on Grey*, Liam thinks of one of his mother's friends, a maker of stained glass: "I recall one window she made, depicting the story of the Children of Lir, swans rising from human bodies. . . . And those swans will always represent to me the grief of Ireland, the human spirit freeing itself from human form, the pain of a nation, distilling itself into tenderness." Many of the stories in *Children of Lir* develop this theme, though often the myth finds a less hopeful conclusion. In "The Mourning Thief" a son returns to Ireland to the deathbed of his father. To the son, the violence of contemporary Ireland is a direct result of the violence out of which the Republic was born. The father had fought in 1916, but "Liam was against violence, pure and simple. Nothing could convince him that 1916 was right. Nothing could convince him it was different from now, old women, young children, being blown to bits in Belfast." In "The Sojourner" Jackie and Moira, living in London, feel that their Irishness implicates them in the guilt of Mountbatten's murder: "The guilt was a shared one Jackie thought, a handed down one. Everyone's hands were dipped in blood; blood of intolerance. . . . So Jackie and Moira assumed responsibility for the deaths of the Earl Mountbatten, the Dowager Lady Brabourne and the two children killed with them." In two stories, "Protestant Boy" and "Cats," Hogan traces the effect of a friendship between Catholic and Protestant. In *Children of Lir*, Hogan's distinctive style and voice persist, but the stories show a new intensity of focus. The sharply idiosyncratic images and the colorful portraits of Irish characters are gathered together into an explicit meditation on the causes and effects of violence. As Janice Elliot wrote in the *Sunday Telegraph*: "More firmly . . . than before in his work, he shuns the Irish malaise, the fever of imagery that can blur meaning. He speaks straight out." The disparate characters are held together by this consistent preoccupation. Caroline Moorehead, writing in the *Spectator*, noted that "Desmond Hogan's *Children of Lir* is a collection of short stories: it could be fragments of a single work, instances in the life of a single hero, the one constant 'I,' wound round a single theme."

In 1982 a short story by Hogan was included in a collection of new short stories published by Penguin, *Firebird 1*, which is intended to be an annual publication presenting both "leading authors" and "new voices" (Hogan being included in the first category). His story "Thoughts" demonstrates clearly the consistency with which his fiction continues to develop certain themes: the meeting of strangers, escape from a confined society, metamorphosis, and the effects of violence. Eugene recalls his childhood in rural Ireland and his meeting with an older and more experienced girl, Gráinne Dempsey, who has just returned from Paris. Gráinne's memories explore the changes in her own identity caused by her life in Paris and her inability to remake herself in the image of her formed by her lover in Paris. Gráinne provides Eugene with images of an ideal and of escape from the limitations of Irish culture, much as the Irish boy does for the woman in "The Last Time," one of the stories in *Diamonds at the Bottom of the Sea*. But in "Thoughts," Gráinne's idealism is linked to the tradition of Irish pacifism: "She came from a place not far from where Daniel O Connell, the Liberator, was born. O Connell was Ireland's leading pacifist." At the same time, "Thoughts" shows a new interest in the form of the story itself; the title links the story with the ideal that Gráinne transmits to the boy, Eugene, and which is imaged by Auguste Rodin's sculpture "La Pensée." Eugene keeps the memory of Grainne's idealism in this image: "Sometimes he doubted but what one could not easily dispense with was an image, an aspiration, Rodin's 'La Pensée'—'The Thought'—self-confrontation, the tentative approach to a work of art which for one moment objectifies our life, arrests its flow, creating something. . . ." The meeting with an ideal imaged in the sculpture becomes a parallel for the meeting offered by the short story.

Hogan continues to live in London and to support himself by writing. He is now working on a third novel, as well as a film script based on "The Sojourner" (a story from *Children of Lir*), which is to be broadcast on Channel 4, the new British independent television channel. He does not intend to return permanently to Ireland; he prefers to visit Connemara and West Galway rather than East Galway, the area he comes from, which he describes as the "claustrophobic centre of Ireland." Hogan has several times insisted that the main literary influences on his writing have not been Irish: "I was never influenced by Joyce. I never liked him particularly." And a major theme of his stories is the liberating influence of foreign culture; often characters find a new identity in their meetings with the world outside Ireland through books, films, or those who have traveled. But like Gráinne in his most recent story—the girl who "never forgot the underside of her nation in Paris; the Kerry storytellers, the Kerry farmers, the widows staring from cottages towards the Atlantic and ultimately towards Boston"—Hogan continues to write of Irish characters and to speak with the voices of Irish storytellers. If he rejects both the grey conformity of contemporary Ireland and the enshrined tradition of literary Ireland, the voice of his stories claims a place in a wider Irish tradition, a tradition that rejects violence; embraces myth, folk tale, and lyricism; and finds its truest identity in its meeting with other cultures.

Plays:

A Short Walk to the Sea, Dublin, Abbey Theatre, October 1975;

Sanctified Distances, Dublin, Abbey Theatre, December 1976;

The Ikon-Maker, adapted from Hogan's novel, London, Gate Theatre, January 1981.

Radio Script:

Jimmy, BBC Radio 3, 1978.

Other:

"Thoughts" in *Firebird 1: Writing Today*, edited by T. J. Binding (Harmondsworth, U. K.: Penguin, 1982), pp. 131-140.

David Holbrook
(9 January 1923-   )

John Fletcher
University of East Anglia

SELECTED BOOKS: *Imaginings* (London: Putnam's, 1960);

English for Maturity (Cambridge: Cambridge University Press, 1961);

Lights in the Sky Country: Mary Easter and Stories of East Anglia (London: Putnam's, 1962);

Llareggub Revisited: Dylan Thomas and the State of Modern Poetry (London: Bowes & Bowes, 1962); abridged as *Dylan Thomas and Poetic Dissociation* (Carbondale: Southern Illinois University Press, 1964);

Against the Cruel Frost (London: Putnam's, 1963);

English for the Rejected (Cambridge: Cambridge University Press, 1964);

The Quest for Love (London: Methuen, 1964; University, Ala.: University of Alabama Press, 1965);

The Secret Places (London: Methuen, 1964; University, Ala.: University of Alabama Press, 1965);

Flesh Wounds (London: Methuen, 1966);

The Quarry: An Opera for Young Players, libretto by Holbrook, music by John Joubert (Sevenoaks, Kent: Novello, 1967);

The Exploring World (Cambridge: Cambridge University Press, 1967);

Object Relations (London: Methuen, 1967);

Old World, New World (London: Rapp & Whiting, 1969);

Human Hope and the Death Instinct (Oxford & New York: Pergamon Press, 1971);

Dylan Thomas: The Code of Night (London: Athlone Press, 1972);

The Masks of Hate: The Problem of False Solutions in the Culture of an Acquisitive Society (Oxford: Pergamon Press, 1972);

The Pseudo-Revolution: A Critical Study of Extremist 'Liberation' in Sex (London: Tom Stacey, 1972);

Sex and Dehumanisation in Art, Thought and Life in Our Time (London: Pitman, 1972);

Changing Attitudes to the Nature of Man: A Working Bibliography (Hatfield, Herfordshire: Hertis, 1973);

English in Australia Now (Cambridge: Cambridge University Press, 1973);

Gustav Mahler and the Courage to Be (London: Vision Press, 1975);

Sylvia Plath: Poetry and Existence (London: Athlone Press, 1976; Atlantic Highlands, N.J.: Humanities Press, 1976);

Education, Nihilism and Survival (London: Darton, Longman & Todd, 1977);

Lost Bearings in English Poetry (London: Vision Press, 1977; New York: Barnes & Noble, 1977);

Chance of a Lifetime (London: Anvil Press Poetry, 1978);

Moments in Italy (Richmond, Surrey: Keepsake Press, 1978);

A Play of Passion (London: W. H. Allen, 1978);

English for Meaning (Slough, Buckinghamshire: National Foundation for Educational Research, 1980).

David Holbrook is a prolific author, mainly of nonfiction. He is probably best known as an educational theorist and particularly as the author of *English for the Rejected* (1964), which broke new ground through a special concern for the less academically

able child. He has also made some impact as a poet, with *Imaginings* (1960) and five other volumes of verse. It is probably fair to say that without this reputation established in other areas his success as a novelist would have been slight; nevertheless he has, especially in *Flesh Wounds* (1966), demonstrated that he can write competent fiction.

David Kenneth Holbrook was born in 1923 to Kenneth Redvers and Elsie Grimmer Holbrook. He was brought up in the provincial city of Norwich, the principal urban center of the region of East Anglia, where he attended the boys' grammar school as a scholarship pupil. He was still at school when the war broke out, and the air raids on Norwich provided material for his later fiction. In 1941 he won a form of bursary, known as an "open exhibition," to Downing College, Cambridge, where he became a pupil of the critic and teacher F. R. Leavis. After a year at Cambridge, Holbrook joined the Royal Armoured Corps as an officer. His tank troop was landed in Normandy on D day, and on "D plus 14" he was wounded quite seriously. He recovered in time to serve in the Ardennes and on the Rhine crossing. When the war in Europe ended, he returned to Cambridge to complete his studies; he took an honors degree in English in 1947 and an M.A. in 1952.

Like many other bright young graduates, Holbrook worked in London as assistant editor of a "little magazine" for a few years, but he also did some part-time teaching. On 23 April 1949 he married Margot Davies-Jones; there are four children of the marriage: Susan Magdalen, Kate Cressida, Jonathan Benedict, and Thomas Simeon David. In 1951 Holbrook broke with London literary circles "to serve a more real community," as he was later to put it; he became first a schoolteacher and then a tutor in adult education. This period, spent mostly in East Anglia, provided material not only for his later writings about education but also for his fiction: "Mary Easter" and "A Time to Plant," the first and last stories in the collection *Lights in the Sky Country* (1962), reflect his experience.

A new phase opened for Holbrook in 1961 when he was made a research fellow at King's College, Cambridge. On the termination of this fellowship in 1965 he was awarded a Senior Leverhulme Research Fellowship, and in 1968 he moved to Jesus College, Cambridge, where he was college lecturer in English until 1970. It was during this period spent in Cambridge in academic employment that he produced his finest work. Best known are the pioneering books on education and on the teaching of English. In trying to contribute to reform in

English teaching, Holbrook has aimed always to bear in mind the primary need in all human beings, whether clever or not, to make sense of their lives. He links this inner need with what can be made available from the inheritance of civilization.

For example, his books for less academically gifted children are full of poetry from reputedly "difficult" authors like Blake, Roethke, Ezra Pound, and Emily Dickinson, as well as folksong and children's own arcane lore, because this folk literature is relevant to their own experience. This was a revolutionary notion at the time but has since become widely accepted. Holbrook also encouraged children to write creatively, for he believed that by producing their own work they could come to a better understanding of literature, which might otherwise literally remain a closed book to them. *English for the Rejected* was especially original in pioneering the notion that academically ungifted children can nevertheless express themselves in quite sophisticated ways in their writing if only they are encouraged to do so. This experimental work with slow learners was based on his own experiences as a teacher of such children, experiences reflected in fictional form in *Lights in the Sky Country*.

Since the early 1970s Holbrook has branched out increasingly into other fields. If he has developed what some critics of his position see as paranoia about pornography and its baleful influence on contemporary cultural life, and if his growing involvement in existentialism, psychoanalysis, and what he calls "Daseinsanalysis" has led to a number of books both published and still unpublished about which commentators are divided, his works of a more orthodox kind, such as his study of Sylvia Plath and his book on Mahler, have been praised by critics who do not necessarily share his views on what he calls "the crisis in the humanities."

Briefly, what he means by this phrase is that we shall have no creativity of any significance unless we find truly "creative themes." He believes that there is a profound philosophical problem behind the lack in our time of "genuine creativity," and that this has to do with "what it is possible to believe." This in turn, he considers, raises problems of our concept of knowing. We need to develop, he argues, ways of looking at the world which are not "imprisoned in the limited perspectives of scientific positivism and reductionism." He pins his hopes upon the development of "philosophical anthropology," which he believes marks a breakthrough toward the rediscovery of man's intentional capacities and a view of the world not confined by mechanism.

In his fiction, Holbrook is above all autobiographical. There seem to be both negative and positive reasons for this; negative, in that he finds it difficult to "invent" much in the way of a story (and where he does, as in "Mary Easter" in *Lights in the Sky Country*, the result is often rather feeble); and positive, in that, as his poetry reveals also, he believes passionately in honesty and directness on the part of the writer. As a poet he has not flinched from probing in public his domestic difficulties and other conflicts and tensions in his private life. As a novelist, he draws heavily on his childhood, adolescence, student days, and war experiences: as a general rule, the more direct and uncensored the reporting, the more vivid the writing tends to be. At its best, his fiction about his childhood, especially the stories in *Lights in the Sky Country* entitled "I Can't Understand the Damn Boy" and "How I Became an Atheist," has a vividness which occasionally approaches that of James Joyce in *A Portrait of the Artist as a Young Man*.

First published as early as 1947 in a short story magazine, "I Can't Understand the Damn Boy" tells how a student stumbles upon a fellow pupil who has hanged himself in the "dark corrugated iron shed" which serves as the school's primitive lavatory; unable through terror to relieve himself in the normal way, the child then wets the floor of the classroom. Later at home his mother is angry at having to change his pants, and his father comments, at what appears to be the child's incomprehensible behavior, "I can't understand the damn boy." "How I Became an Atheist" tells of a family row about religion which leads to the collapse and sudden death of an itinerant parson who lodges in the house. The impact of such violent occurrences on a largely uncomprehending child is, as with Joyce, vividly portrayed.

These stories are, however, miniatures; in his novel *Flesh Wounds*, written at Cambridge during the 1960s, Holbrook attacks a full-sized canvas and shows a considerable advance in fictional technique. Although this first novel was not published until 1966, Holbrook had clearly been working up to it for some time. It is a competent, vivid, but fairly conventional war novel. Its hero is named Paul Grimmer (compare other Holbrook characters, such as John White of "Somewhere to Lay Your Head" and John Grimmer of "A Time to Plant"; not surprisingly, Holbrook's mother's maiden name was Grimmer, and several other people appear under their real names or thinly concealed ones, for example, Leavis as Beavis). Paul is beginning his studies at Cambridge and having his first love affair. He has to leave Lucy, however, when he joins the army; perhaps inevitably, the relationship ends once he has been trained to be an efficient killing machine. The scene changes to Normandy, where the D-day landings are vividly described; Holbrook is particularly good on the confusion of battle and the appalling waste of war. Paul is wounded and sent back to England but later returns to Europe and in newly liberated Brussels meets and sleeps with a kindly young woman whose husband is also at war. The novel ends with Paul's return, as a freshly demobilized soldier, older and a great deal wiser, to a Cambridge he had left as a raw recruit.

Reviewing the book, fellow-novelist Thomas Hinde praised *Flesh Wounds* for its "openness and sincerity," and a journalist on the local Norwich newspaper agreed that the book "glowed with warmth and living detail."

A Play of Passion (1978) takes us back to Paul's schooldays and especially his friendship with the director of the Norwich Maddermarket Theatre, an actual amateur theater still active today, whose world-renowned director at the time of the novel, Nugent Monck, Holbrook has said "it would be absurd to try to disguise." The agonies of adolescent sexuality in the early 1940s in a provincial British city are well described, as is the boy's first serious quarrel with his parents. The novel is strong on atmosphere, setting, and characterization, and its authenticity as a record of a vanished age is undeniable. Holbrook makes no secret that he has barely altered the way things were in his youth. The novel is a sort of Bildungsroman in that it leaves Paul, newly bereaved by the death of his father-surrogate, Monck, on the brink of manhood as he prepares to see his humble world transformed by the cosmopolitan splendors of Cambridge, which he has just entered as a freshman.

Pursuing this vein, Holbrook has been writing a series of novels on Paul Grimmer, his *alter ego*. As yet unpublished are "The Gold in Father's Heart," in which Paul is a small boy of about eight; "The Inevitable Price," which takes up the story where *Flesh Wounds* leaves off, roughly 1947 to 1954; and "Nothing Larger Than Life," which is set in the early 1960s and deals generally with the "relation with woman" and specifically with the effects of Mrs. Grimmer's death on Paul's marriage. Other novels in preparation or seeking a publisher are "Worlds Apart," a love story about a progressive young woman teacher in Australia (where Holbrook spent five months in 1970); "Jennifer," which centers on a young couple, a baby's cot death, and a final moral resolution; "Duffy's Diggings," about the adventures of a small boy (not Paul Grimmer

29.

He was in the turret now, and his tank was leading the troop. The road ahead was clear of enemy. But one never knows. As he rounded the bend Paul saw what seemed to be a cinema commissionaire on a motor cycle : this was his first reaction to the *with a side-car* sharp grey uniform. Then, as he knew it was a German he began automatically, with a chill in his stomach, give a fire order.

Gunner traverse right . . .

But then over the intercom came the voice of his codriver

'He's looking dead, sir.'

The man was stiff, and dead since the first hour. His cycling coat was stitched with the same dark holes from thigh to shoulder. In the goggles and helmet the contorted dead white face was hideous, the eyes squinny in the goggles. In the falling gloom he seemed a statue to mortality : Paul felt his heart beating lowly. But he grinned at some infantry who grinned at him from a stable : they had seen his reaction, and had seen the turret move.

The whole regiment pulled into a wood between Cazelle and Cambes. There were fields rather like English fields in Suffolk, tall elms and an orchard towards the outskirts of the village itself. Patrols were out, and they kept

Page from the manuscript for Flesh Wounds

this time); and finally, the story of a virologist who loses faith in scientific positivism and suffers from hallucinations and marital difficulties. Thus, even when Holbrook's fiction is not openly based on his own life, much of his own experience goes into it nevertheless, and opinions expressed in his other, discursive writings evidently inform it. Although fiction is not as central in his work as poetry, he says, he finds it useful for its fullness and range and as an antidote to what he sees as the "false solutions" proposed by Kingsley Amis and other British writers of whom he strongly disapproves. There is more than a hint, in David Holbrook, of the voice crying in the wilderness, a quality he shares with his teacher Leavis and, more distantly, D. H. Lawrence, whose prose style he imitates in his early fiction.

It is clear that David Holbrook would passionately repudiate the aesthetic theory which underlies, say, the writing of Iris Murdoch. She is quoted as having said once that if the hero or heroine of one's novel is really oneself bearing a fictitious name, one should tear up the manuscript and begin again. Indeed, perhaps not surprisingly, the difficulty with Holbrook's conception of the novel form is that he is, as a consequence, rather weak on plot. His books read like a personal chronicle and rely heavily on detail, some of it admittedly interesting and even vivid, to compensate in some measure for the naivete of the "and then. . .and then. . ." sort of approach. Holbrook seems to work best in the short story centered on one absorbing episode or incident and dependent on one sharply-etched character, as in "Youth's a Stuff Will (Probably) Not Endure," which features Paul Grimmer awaiting the draft in 1942 and working as a temporary truck driver on demolition work, clearing bomb damage in Norwich. The situation is unusual and therefore interesting, and Paul's working-class workmates are vividly brought to life. But all too often in Holbrook's fiction reality is not sufficiently distanced and the imagination is allowed no play. Paradoxically, the reader feels an implausibility in situations which almost certainly occurred in real life.

Ultimately, perhaps, Holbrook is not, at bottom, really interested in fiction at all; but, rather, in illustrating in thinly-veiled autobiography the theories about life, spontaneity, wholeness, and so on, which he pursues in his more recent polemical writing. In these increasingly controversial books of the 1970s (when he held no academic position but worked as a free-lance writer), he seems to be losing touch with his audience, even betraying a lack of sureness as to what his real audience is, and so has been in danger of becoming reductive, simplistic, and even strident. The path to more than one kind of hell can be paved with the noblest of intentions. One hopes that the author of *Flesh Wounds* is not going to become increasingly unpublished as a novelist after his promising debut in the craft of fiction. In 1981 he was appointed to F. R. Leavis's old position as Fellow and Director of English Studies at Downing College, Cambridge, and what this will mean to Holbrook's future as a writer will be extremely interesting to watch.

Other:

Children's Games, edited by Holbrook (Bedford, England: Gordon Fraser, 1957);

Iron, Honey, Gold, edited by Holbrook (Cambridge: Cambridge University Press, 1961);

People and Diamonds, edited by Holbrook (Cambridge: Cambridge University Press, 1962);

Thieves and Angels, edited by Holbrook (Cambridge: Cambridge University Press, 1962);

Visions of Life, edited by Holbrook (Cambridge: Cambridge University Press, 1964);

Charles Dickens, *Oliver Twist*, edited by Holbrook (Cambridge: Cambridge University Press, 1965);

I've Got to Use Words, edited by Holbrook (Cambridge: Cambridge University Press, 1966);

Children's Writing, edited by Holbrook (Cambridge: Cambridge University Press, 1967);

T. F. Powys, *Mr Weston's Good Wine*, introduction by Holbrook (London: Heinemann, 1967);

The Cambridge Hymnal, edited by Holbrook and Elizabeth Poston (Cambridge: Cambridge University Press, 1968);

Plucking the Rushes, edited by Holbrook (London: Heinemann, 1968);

The Case Against Pornography, edited by Holbrook (London: Tom Stacey, 1972; New York: Library Press, 1973);

The Honey of Man, edited by Holbrook and Christine McKenzie (Melbourne: Nelson, 1973);

"Youth's a Stuff Will (Probably) Not Endure" in *New Stories 1*, edited by Margaret Drabble and Charles Osborne (London: The Arts Council of Great Britain, 1976), pp. 146-157.

Reference:

Gordon Morrell Pradl, "Toward a Moral Approach to English: A Study of the Writings of F. R. Leavis and David Holbrook," D.Ed. dissertation, Harvard University, 1971.

David Hughes
(27 July 1930-　)

Elizabeth Holly Snyder
and
Jay L. Halio
University of Delaware

SELECTED BOOKS: *A Feeling in the Air* (London: Deutsch, 1957); republished as *Man Off Beat* (New York: Regnal, 1957);

J. B. Priestley: An Informal Study of His Work (London: Hart-Davis, 1958; Freeport, N.Y.: Books for Libraries Press, 1970);

Sealed with a Loving Kiss (London: Hart-Davis, 1959);

The Horsehair Sofa (London: Hart-Davis, 1961);

The Road to Stockholm and Lapland (London: Eyre & Spottiswoode, 1964);

The Major (London: Blond, 1964; New York: Coward-McCann, 1965);

The Cat's Tale, text by Hughes and Mai Zetterling, illustrations by Pat Marriott (London: Cape, 1965);

The Seven Ages of England (Stockholm: Swedish Radio, 1966);

The Man Who Invented Tomorrow (London: Constable, 1968);

The Rosewater Revolution: Notes on a change of attitude (London: Constable, 1971);

Memories of Dying (London: Constable, 1976);

A Genoese Fancy (London: Constable, 1979).

David Hughes is, and seems always to have been, something of a maverick. Never a popular novelist, he appears more interested in satisfying needs that are important to him rather than those calculated to win him either critical or commercial success. Not that he has failed in the former: several of his books, both novels and nonfiction, have been very well received. But he goes his own way, preoccupied with the deleterious effects of two world wars and the threat of a still more disastrous third, and even more deeply concerned with establishing and preserving some kind of personal integrity as an individual and as a writer. In trying to find his own "voice," or stance, he has often taken chances, sometimes with little outward success, as in one or two of his earliest novels. But he appears to have learned from his failures and remains uncomplacent in his successes, all of which make him a writer worth reading and worth watching.

David John Hughes was born on 27 July 1930 in Alton, Hampshire. Seven years later, he moved with his family to Wimbledon in suburban London, where they stayed until the outbreak of World War II forced them to retire again to Hampshire. After the war, they returned to Wimbledon, and David attended a minor English public school, King's College School, until 1949, when he began his national service as a pilot officer in the Royal Air Force. Eighteen months later, at his father's urging, he entered Oxford and read English language and literature, taking his degree in 1953. Of his Oxford years, he has said that he read extensively, "ne-

David Hughes

glecting the syllabus with deliberate folly" in favor of books which interested him more. Rather than spend his time taking copious notes at lectures, he would wander into the garden of Trinity College on a summer afternoon, "too close for safety to the panic of examinations," and read Hemingway's *Fiesta* (*The Sun Also Rises*, as Americans know it). He read Arnold Bennett extensively in his second year but also much J. B. Priestley, who was a still earlier and pervasive influence. Among the other "unfashionable" writers who have influenced him one way or another, or in whom he has read deeply, are D. H. Lawrence, H. G. Wells, Virginia Woolf, Charles Dickens, and Marcel Proust.

After leaving Oxford, where he edited the magazine *Isis*, Hughes worked for two years as an assistant editor for *London Magazine*, which was just beginning publication, and then for a book publisher. At twenty-six, he gave up full-time jobs in preference for free-lance writing, except for a brief period when he worked for *Town* magazine. At twenty-eight, he married the Swedish actress and film director Mai Zetterling. By this time, Hughes had already begun publishing novels and nonfiction. With his wife, he also made a number of documentary films for the BBC on such diverse topics as Iceland, Sweden, and the gypsies of southern France. From 1964 to 1968 they collaborated on full-length films in Scandinavia, Hughes creating the scripts and his wife directing the productions. Fiction writing continued along with a travel book, *The Road to Stockholm and Lapland* (1964), written for the BP Touring Service, and a social history, *The Seven Ages of England* (1966), written for Swedish Radio. Later Hughes and his wife moved to the south of France for four years and tried living off the land, but in 1974 they returned to London, where Hughes has lived ever since (except for a year and a half when he taught at the University of Iowa Writers Workshop). His marriage to Mai Zetterling broke up in 1976, and he has since remarried. He and his second wife, Elizabeth, have one child.

Although they introduce themes that continue to interest him, Hughes's first two novels were not the most auspicious beginnings to his career as a writer, and his third, *The Horsehair Sofa* (1961), was a disaster. Yet Hughes gained something from writing these books, which have long since gone out of print and are difficult to find (Hughes himself abandoned his only copies when he left France). The first one, *A Feeling in the Air* (1957), is more a novella, or long short story, than a full-length novel and is told in a conventional third-person narration. William Gunner, a successful advertising executive,

has suffered a breakdown as the result of overwork, too much drink and tobacco, and remorse over his second wife's death (he is divorced from his first wife). On doctor's orders, after a period of hospitalization, Gunner goes to Wender, a small town in Wales, for an enforced holiday. Hardly a popular resort, the town is all but deserted after September, but there Gunner meets Venetia Stallybridge, who runs the local hotel, and two minor clerics from the village church. In the brief period he spends among them, several events occur that compel Gunner to reassess his life; however, though the book ends with his precipitous flight from Wender and the affair he has begun with Mrs. Stallybridge, it is unclear how or if he will use the new freedom he believes he has gained.

The bitterness and anticlerical attitudes that color *A Feeling in the Air* are intensified in Hughes's second novel, ironically entitled *Sealed with a Loving Kiss* (1959). But the characters here show scarcely any advance over the poorly developed ones of his earlier book, and their motivations are even more obscure. Hughes's prose style, however, gathers strength and sureness and anticipates some of his later successes. Rex Benbrook, formerly a medical doctor and now working for the *Journal of Christian Thought*, finds no assuagement to his deepening malaise either in the church or in his affair with Barbara Hemming, a simple, affectionate young woman he has met in London. His cruel treatment of Barbie is matched only by the insolence and rudeness he shows to his associates at Dorterfield Grange, where his journal is overseen and published by a pompous and pietistic churchman named Bray-Porter. Tormented by the evil and hypocrisy he finds almost everywhere, Benbrook is apparently driven by still deeper forces. On Christmas Day, in the cottage he has borrowed outside Oxford, he tells Barbie that he hates the church "for the dead hand it reverently lays on the good life." But what that "good life" is Benbrook has been unable to discover, as he sends Barbie away for good and remains in the desolate countryside entirely and willfully alone. Although critics found Hughes's picture of the seedy clerical society of Dorterfield Grange "utterly convincing" and his brief tale told "with great delicacy in a beautifully modulated prose," they were not otherwise impressed.

Meanwhile, Hughes's first book of nonfiction, *J. B. Priestly: An Informal Study of His Work* (1958), earned well-deserved praise. Dedicated to his father, Fielden Hughes, who had encouraged David's ambitions as a writer, this critical study is indeed informal but nonetheless perceptive and illuminating. Priestley had long interested Hughes, who first came to know him through his wartime broadcasts in 1940, when his voice rivaled Churchill's in helping British morale during the Battle of Britain. Throughout this commentary—a not inconsiderable undertaking, given Priestley's huge output even then—a good deal of Hughes himself shines through, as he recounts various experiences associated with his reading of Priestley's work over a long span of years. Probably helped by his work as a journalist, Hughes's critical stance, like his prose style, is self-assured without ever appearing arrogant or, worse, supercilious. The book is obviously written by someone who has long admired Priestley's fiction, plays, and essays but retains an independence of judgment and an essentially balanced view. It is regrettable that Hughes has not produced more works of this kind.

His third novel, *The Horsehair Sofa*, shows Hughes unpredictably attempting bedroom farce with very little originality; although some scenes do succeed in being funny, the final effect is one of not quite overwhelming tedium. Told in the first person by a young man of unbelievable naivete and ineptitude, Marcus Gore, the novel swings through a number of farfetched episodes beginning with Gore's wedding and proceeding through his bumbling attempts to find with his not unwilling wife the expected conjugal bliss. In the process, he falls prey to jealousy (of a virile Italian and his wife, the servants hired by his wife's mother), to an outrageous quack specializing in sexual problems, to a private detective simultaneously hired by his wife and himself, and in general to his own social timidity and ridiculous fantasy life. His wife, Priscilla, is unfortunately barely realized as a character, although her potential for improving the comedy seems considerable.

Not until his fourth novel, *The Major* (1964), does Hughes's real talent for fiction come into its own. Written in only a week, it is a crisp, totally coherent and unified satire against the aggression and violence usually associated with (but by no means limited to) the military. Critics, who acclaimed the work, noted its "nice balance between horror and farce," the "vitality" of the writing, and the confidence Hughes displayed in this "odd, disturbing book." The satire focuses mainly upon an army major named Kane, who returns from peacetime service in Germany to the tranquil English countryside around Salisbury, where he is based and has a home. Not expecting an early reassignment, the Major had let his house on a long

lease to an elderly couple who plan to spend their last years there. But the Major is determined to get them out, so that he and his small family can live there, and in this personal campaign he very effectively, if brutally, reaches his goal. He is much less successful in reaching the professional goal assigned to him by his commanding officer, General Girdlestone—getting the inhabitants of a tiny village out of their homes and into new prefabricated ones elsewhere so that the army can carry on their maneuvers. The novel demonstrates the barely suppressed violence of the English which they must admit to and come to terms with if their society is not to collapse, as indeed the Major's collapses—and he along with it. At the end, Hughes makes his point explicit through Ulla, the Kanes' Swedish au pair girl whom the Major has raped and threatened to kill: "England is still a country that wants war and misses war," she explains to her father, "and if people don't get it forced on them by other countries, they make their own or find substitutes for it."

In his book on Priestley, Hughes had said: "To be read at all the writer must simplify, compromise, and therefore admit failure in his heart of hearts every time he finishes a book. If your aim is partly that of a poet, to distill the essence of life, then like Virginia Woolf you avoid the direct statement and the conscientious narrative which will shatter your delicate laboratory. If, on the other hand, you are occupied with the somewhat coarser pursuit of discovering the nature of life, you will probably gain in power and certainly in readership if you make your statements as blunt as possible." In *The Major* Hughes has undoubtedly gained in power while sacrificing something of the delicately modulated prose of his first two novels, although ironically he does not appear to have gained proportionately in readership. *The Road to Stockholm and Lapland*, published the same year, also shows him attaining full command of his abilities. As evidence of his increasing confidence and strength, he takes the reader on several journeys at once, not only through the low countries and West Germany into Scandinavia, but also through social, literary, and architectural history on a personal tour Hughes takes with his wife Mai. An excellent travel book, it accomplishes exactly what such a book should do: it makes readers feel that they have been to all of the places described, and it makes them want to go there, too.

Drawing on his experiences of making films for BBC television, as well as on his voracious reading as a young man, Hughes's next novel, *The Man Who Invented Tomorrow* (1968), is a thoroughly sustained combination of comedy, satire, and farce rivaling anything like it in contemporary fiction. Hughes's powers were now at their peak, and critics generally applauded his success in developing both characters and theme. The story concerns the making of a television film to celebrate the centenary of the birth of H. G. Wells. Directed by a fading, arrogant, philandering "personality" named Raymond Armstrong, the film is eventually a failure. But the experience of watching Armstrong assemble writers, cameramen, actors, secretaries—a whole production crew—and then take them on various locations to shoot the film is, for the reader, as full of insights into today's television culture as it is hilarious. For the novel is not without its serious aspects, though these are never solemnly presented: the comedy prevails. But like all good comedy, it is not pointless. Using often quite unlikely characters as vehicles to make his case (and thereby enhancing the comic effect), Hughes attacks the "commercialism, knavery, meretricious values, false standards" that Wells foresaw and that still afflict us. Whatever mistakes in conception or execution Hughes might have made in *The Horsehair Sofa*, he makes none in what is probably his best, or at least his most amusing, novel to date. In the process, he provides an ongoing commentary on the life and works of H. G. Wells, whose image he consistently evokes in the dual perspective of his time and ours; indeed, in this novel, Hughes becomes more and more interested in the handling of multiple time frames, an aspect of his writing that he continues to develop in subsequent books.

By the end of the 1960s, Hughes was apparently undergoing some deepening personal crisis that was also linked to his perception of a worsening world situation, certainly a worsening situation in Western Europe and specifically England. He records aspects of this inner turmoil in a strange, difficult book, *The Rosewater Revolution: Notes on a change of attitude* (1971). Neither fact nor fiction, fantasy nor memory, it is a combination of all of these, for to Hughes "each seemed valid only when working with the others." In his introduction he says that the book "is about a late twentieth century man, who happens to be a writer, trying to arouse his own well-kept feelings on the state of his country, his world, himself, and to arouse those feelings even at the risk of inner violence, before he gives up the struggle and chooses comfort. It is an essay in self-destruction, with a view to creating a better man." The narrative, such as it is, revolves around three visits to the Herefordshire village of Monnington-upon-Wye at different seasons of the

year. Part 1 is heavily weighted down with copious "notes" printed in smaller type on pages facing the narrative; part 2 contains, instead of notes, interchapters (also in reduced typeface); but part 3 eschews both and is more or less straight narrative. Throughout, Hughes is concerned with the recurrent themes of time, war (including the English civil war of the seventeenth century, fought partly in Herefordshire), and the "killing" question of religion. Engaged in his own internal civil war "to become anyone other than himself," Hughes invents an antiself named Hyde (with appropriate references to R. L. Stevenson's character) and creates fictional counterparts to four dead friends. By coming to terms with his dead friends, he hopes to come to terms as well with "the dead millions of the world wars, who haunt us all." Although in the end he does not appear to have reached these several goals—he lacked "enough love," among other things, and "the patience to be a real revolutionary, a true creator"—nevertheless the experience was meaningful and showed Hughes, for example, that though he had not found the way to regard the sacrifice of the millions of war dead as intensely valuable to the world, such a way did exist and he would look for it properly "later, in another work." This is a promise Hughes kept when he wrote *Memories of Dying* (1976). Having fought out his own civil war ("the first of them at least"), and having buried "the enemy, the man I might have become" (Hyde), Hughes ends the book in relative peace.

By this time, with his wife Mai, Hughes was living in the south of France, attempting to live off the land, possibly one outcome of his "internal civil war." His next book, *Memories of Dying*, was not published until after his return to England. It is a novel of expiation that *The Rosewater Revolution* anticipates both in form (it glides almost imperceptively between first- and third-person narration) and subject matter (it concerns the guilt caused by two savage world wars and their brutal aftermath). On a holiday trip to Nice, Richard Flaxman, the narrator, becomes convinced that another, older man named Hunter has begun invading his consciousness. Hunter is guilty of some terrible crime and victimizes Flaxman with his burden of guilt for five harrowing days, during which Flaxman somehow relives the other's experiences and finally frees himself of guilt. The crimes Hunter believes he has committed include killing his superior officer during the trench warfare of World War I and then returning to England and marrying the officer's widow. This crime is compounded when he feels he has also precipitated the death of Virginia, his new

Dust jacket for Hughes's 1979 novel, in which he recreates the world of his adolescence during the late 1940s in Wimbledon

wife, in an air raid after their only son is born. After a miserable childhood, the boy also dies—of drugs and alcohol during his first year at Oxford—and again Hunter feels responsible.

Flaxman actually had known Hunter, who was his history master at school years before in the town where Flaxman grew up but which he has not revisited until this strange obsession brings him back—just in time for old Hunter's funeral. The entire experience is one that forces the narrator to "get to the bottom of my century." Although what he sees there is far from pretty, Hunter's interment at last releases Flaxman from the dead hand of the past. Free now to return to his wife and children with love, he is hopeful, too, of yet making with them "something of the mess," of together seeing "the childish beauty abounding an inch beneath the squalor and the pain," of saying "goodbye at last to my habit of killing, as slowly cruelly as I knew how, all the good in me that hung over, unused, from childhood, from before the wars started." Thus the book ends—a superb, brief novel that masterfully

interweaves various time frames and narrators and demonstrates Hughes's consummate control of his medium and his themes. It also reveals a good deal about the creative process, for Flaxman is surely a surrogate for the novelist seized with a fictional idea and motif that will not let him go. The critics loved it. As J. Mellors in the *Listener* said, Hughes's technique allows the novel "to cast its own spell on the reader and haunt him with its many themes and questions."

A Genoese Fancy (1979), Hughes's most recently published novel, was actually written while he was still in France and is dedicated "For Father at 80." The dedication is appropriate, for the novel invokes and recreates the world of Hughes's adolescence during the late 1940s in Wimbledon. At eighteen, Lionel Smith is suddenly orphaned when, on Christmas Day, his parents die in an automobile wreck. He goes to live with his only other relative, Uncle Norman, who feels responsible since the Smiths were on their way to fetch him for Christmas dinner when the accident occurred. Middle-aged, gloomy Norman operates a small grocery store and lives as a confirmed bachelor until Lionel moves in with him for the few months remaining before he begins his national service. Meanwhile, things begin to happen as, however reluctantly, Uncle Norman starts taking an interest in his nephew, gets him to sit for the Oxford entrance examinations, and (under Lionel's bookish influence) develops some ideas about improving future prospects not only for his relative but for others. Norman gets elected to the city council, takes over a friend's bakery, and, after Lionel is inducted, arranges for him to be sent to the RAF's officer training school. Lionel has no wish really to become an officer and is far from certain about going on to Oxford, which has admitted him: his main interest at this stage in his life is falling in love. Hughes deftly plays Lionel's and Norman's adventures off against each other, mixing into his treatment of them generous doses of compassion and tender affection as well as considerable humor.

The world of adolescence is bewildering to both men, not the less so for Norman who comes to it so late. Although again Hughes won praise from reviewers, his novel—one of the warmer and more attractive ones published in recent years—has so far missed a wide readership.

At present, David Hughes is at work on another novel which he calls "Imperial German Dinner Service." Whether or not he eventually finds the popular readership his mature novels deserve, his work should continue to interest anyone seriously concerned with contemporary fiction—British fiction or any other.

Other:

Sound of Protest, Sound of Hope: Protest Songs from America and England, chosen and introduced by Hughes (Stockholm: Sveriges Radio, 1968);
Evergreen, songs selected by Hughes (Stockholm: Swedish Radio, 1977).

Jim Hunter
(24 June 1939-   )

Susan Matthews
St. Anne's College, Oxford

BOOKS: *The Sun in the Morning* (London: Faber & Faber, 1961);
Sally Cray (London: Faber & Faber, 1963);
Earth and Stone (London: Faber & Faber, 1963); republished as *A Place of Stone* (New York: Pantheon, 1964);
The Metaphysical Poets (London: Faber & Faber, 1965);
The Flame (London: Faber & Faber, 1965; New York: Pantheon, 1966);
Gerard Manley Hopkins (London: Faber & Faber, 1966);
Walking in the Painted Sunshine (London: Faber & Faber, 1970);
Kinship; a Novel (London: Faber & Faber, 1973);
Percival and the Presence of God (London: Faber & Faber, 1978);
Tom Stoppard's Plays (London: Faber & Faber, 1982).

Jim Hunter's seventh and most recent novel, *Percival and the Presence of God* (1978), marks an apparent change of direction in his work as a novelist. The earlier novels focus on the pressures of family life, whether between the generations, between husband and wife, or between adolescent friends and lovers. The settings of the first six novels are contemporary, moving from the 1950s in *The Sun in the Morning* (1961) through the 1960s and 1970s and including an interest in changing societies that runs parallel to the domestic concerns of the main narrative. But in *Percival and the Presence of God* Hunter moves beyond the mainly realistic conventions of his earlier work into a mythic world of Arthurian legend. The nonnaturalistic elements present in the earlier novels (highly wrought passages of poetic description, fragmentation of the narrative through shifts in time or perspective, and careful patterns of image and symbol) dominate his most recent novel.

Jim Hunter was born in 1939, in Stafford, the son of David and Gwendolyn Castell-Evans Hunter. His father was a teacher, but as a conscientious objector he worked as a lorry driver during the war, often taking his young son with him. His family were Quakers and he had a Quaker upbringing. After his parents separated, he was sent to a mixed, progressive Quaker boarding school at Ackworth in Yorkshire. The school took pupils from many different backgrounds, including some from disturbed homes, and some of its progressive ideas are echoed in the school attended by Karen in Hunter's 1973 novel, *Kinship*; "Even nowadays people still talk about it as whizzy and advanced," she tells her lover, Howell. "But really we were very, very sheltered.... we were saved a lot of the grubbier inhibitions of the outside world."

As a schoolboy, Hunter had written poetry, but it was while at Cambridge, where he read English from 1957 to 1960, that he had his first short stories published. Three stories, "An Expert at Make-Believe," "Requiescat," and "The Father," appeared in 1960 in the first volume of *Introduction* (a Faber collection of stories by new writers) alongside stories by his contemporaries Alan Coren and Ted Hughes. Two of the stories were incorporated into Hunter's first novel, *The Sun in the Morning*, written, while he was still an undergraduate, in twelve weeks in 1960 and revised later the same year. He had been encouraged in his writing at Cambridge by Donald Davie, and E. M. Forster read and commented on a first draft of the novel. Hunter had been impressed by the trilogy *U. S. A.* by John Dos Passos, and he decided to fragment his account of growing up in the war years and the 1950s by using the contrasted viewpoints of six characters: four boys and two girls. He wanted to exploit what he thought of as his distinctive ability as a young novelist—the knowledge, even if superficial, of a range of social backgrounds. The novel draws on his memories of traveling in his father's lorry and of visits to the homes of friends around Barnsley during his school years at Ackworth. It is only gradually, as the novel moves between the six children, that their stories begin to link up in the setting of the north country mining village of Emthorpe. No single viewpoint predominates. The serious, withdrawn, middle-class Philip, whose memories open the novel, allows Hunter to develop his power of atmospheric description. In the more extroverted Terry, Hunter describes the growth of an adolescent's emotions and sexuality, while Clare allows the author to explore the effect of a Quaker upbringing narrower and less tolerant than his own. In the more external picture of working-class Joe and his younger brother, Danny, Hunter portrays the changing social and sexual morality of the postwar years. Passages which take the reader into the

Jim Hunter

thoughts of the characters are set within an objective narrative, and the fragmented stories are placed against short summaries of changing events in the public world, but the novel never fully conceals its origin in separate short stories. The tendency of Hunter's novels to fragment into separate consciousnesses and broken narrative provides characteristic strengths as well as weaknesses. Reviewing the book, Martin Seymour-Smith praised Hunter's ability to write seriously about "ordinary lives" and saw his "lack of a plot" as evidence that he wrote with "honesty and rare tenderness, not cleverness." *The Sun in the Morning* won the Authors Club award for the best first novel of 1961.

Hunter graduated from Cambridge with first-class honors in 1960 and spent the next year as a postgraduate student at Indiana University studying American literature, getting his first experience of teaching, and exploiting his English accent to work as a radio and television announcer at the university broadcasting station. Indiana also provided him with the setting for his next novel, *Sally Cray* (1963), which was written partly in the United States and partly—after his return to England—in Bristol. Sally is the daughter of an English academic, Robin Cray, who goes with his wife to take up a post at Indiana University. The novel focuses on the impact of her parents' separation on Sally's adolescence at school and university in America, and ends with her return to teach at a school in London.

Perhaps as a reaction to the problems of using six main characters in his previous novel, Hunter here comes closer to adopting a single viewpoint and a straightforward narrative structure than in any of his subsequent novels (other than his seventh, *Percival and the Presence of God*). It may also be because *Sally Cray* is probably Hunter's least successful novel that he avoided using its structure and viewpoint again for so long afterward. It is in the attempt to portray the thoughts of an adolescent girl, Sally, that the novel is at its least convincing. In subsequent novels, Hunter writes best of female characters who are somehow reserved or set apart from the main action: the wife, Freda Stock, in *Earth and Stone* (1963) is distanced by the family's shared but unspoken knowledge of her approaching death from cancer; Linda, the wife of the main character, Douglas Cameron, in *The Flame* (1965), is distanced by her husband's absorption in his mission, while Alison in *Kinship* (1973) is set apart by her depression or madness (she is in fact confined to a hospital during much of the action of the novel). Other women appear as wives or lovers; their role is important in that they influence the main characters, but they do not provide the central consciousness through which the action of the novel is experienced. The settings in *Sally Cray* are often powerfully described, especially in Sally's trip west across the United States and in the final section when she returns to England and sees the drabness of Surrey and London with eyes tuned to the brightness of America. As in *The Sun in the Morning*, Hunter seizes on an opportunity to move beyond the private experience of an individual to a viewpoint which spans, impressionistically, a town or a country.

After qualifying as a teacher at Bristol University, gaining a certificate of education with distinction in 1962, Hunter took up a teaching post at Bradford Grammar School. During the very cold winter of 1962-1963, his first term there, he wrote his third novel, published in England in 1963 as *Earth and Stone*, but in the United States the following year under the title Hunter had originally chosen, *A Place of Stone*. The change of title for the British edition was required by the publishers, Faber and Faber, who had just brought out another book with Hunter's original title. The American title comes from William Butler Yeats's poem "To a Friend Whose Work Has Come to Nothing." Bill Stock is a painter who, failing to fulfill the promise of his early talent, has settled into a life of accepted mediocrity. His wife, Freda ("Of the whole family, except for her son. . . the most intelligent, the best educated, the widest read"), has refused to use her talent for music, has come to accept the mutual separateness of her marriage, and has transferred her hopes to her son, Christopher. Into this situation of settled failure, the knowledge of Freda's illness and impending death brings a new tension. In this novel, Hunter writes (with a growing conviction) from within the imagined consciousness of several of his characters and moves easily from impersonal narration to internal monologue, from character to character, and, above all, from person to place. As the narrative structure and viewpoint become more complex, Hunter places more emphasis on the symbolic organization of the novel, relating character to setting: Bill's character is related to the landscape of moor and rock, and Freda's to the cultivated interior of her home. Although this technique is effective in establishing the contrasting characters within the family, it seems labored when Hunter tries to incorporate the landscape symbols into the narrative climaxes of the novel, when Freda's death is glimpsed by her husband, Bill, as a distant detail of the rocky landscape he is struggling to depict in his painting.

Still in Bradford, Hunter wrote *The Flame*, a book which, like his first novel, spans England and sketches in behind the central characters figures glimpsed in a range of settings. Jane Hodge, reviewing *The Sun in the Morning* in 1961, wrote: "It is not often, after finishing a first novel, that one finds oneself still pursuing its characters down their imagined futures, but the young people of . . . *The Sun in the Morning* linger in the mind." In *The Flame*, Philip, Terry, Danny, and Kathy reappear, though briefly. After two novels limited to the private world of the family, Hunter again adopts a wider perspective, setting the individual consciousness against a changing society. But *The Flame*, unlike *The Sun in the Morning*, is focused on a single theme: Hunter traces the rise of a fictional nationalist movement, "New Vigour," in which the moral idealism of its leader, Douglas Cameron, is used by others to exploit racist feeling. Writing two years before Enoch Powell's speech predicting the growth of racial tension in Britain, Hunter examines the way in which a conservative backlash could develop in response to the growing liberalism of the early 1960s and could then foster racial tension.

The book's two central characters are brothers, contrasted in character and outlook. Douglas Cameron is the charismatic leader, the visionary driven by a strong moral sense, who moves on from work in youth clubs to the creation of a national movement, whose emblem is the flame. Martin, the younger brother, is the tolerant out-

sider; he is expelled from school for a minor offense, visits America, and returns with his "coloured" wife, Jordan. Hunter uses "coloured"
throughout and is generally rather coy despite liberal intentions: "he never exactly thought of her as
being coloured, it was simply a nice Cleopatra colour really. . . ." Hunter uses Martin's viewpoint, as
he earlier used Sally Cray's, to present an outsider's
view of Britain, and a wide range of voices tell the
full story. Excerpts from the press, television,
Douglas's autobiography ("The Capacity for Greatness"), and the thoughts of Douglas's followers alternate with an impersonal narration. Included also
is a voice that speaks for the shared experience of
the nation to explain, for instance, the power of
Douglas's image: "If . . . we projected something of
ourselves into that image, still it was what we
wouldn't ourselves own; we drew back from it at
last, and thrust it out."

The brothers provide a clash not only of
temperament but also of moral outlook, dramatizing, at times too schematically, a recurrent debate in
Hunter's fiction. In Douglas, moral determination,
the ability to fit experience into a coherent pattern,
dominates; in Martin, tolerance and openness prevail. Douglas attacks the "revisionist" Christian, including the Quakers, whose "position today is one
of such 'tolerance,' in matters of belief and moral
thinking, that it is indistinguishable from license."
Hunter suggests that moral condemnation derives
from fear: in Douglas's followers there is "a very
genuine hatred of sin, coming from the horror of
vulnerability." Yet Hunter's portrayal of Douglas
Cameron does not lack sympathy; Douglas, who
shares Hunter's love of mountains (and reflects, "A
friend once jokingly suggested to me that my devotion to mountains was what he called my lust for
power. . . ."), is distantly but effectively drawn. In
the picture of the tolerant, pragmatic Martin,
Hunter is sometimes more schematic. Martin finally
rejects Douglas's philosophy:

> Redemption; sin. . . . He shook his
> head away from the words, grimacing. They
> were so implausible, so inaccurate. They gave
> no help. But the image of Douglas would be
> better if it admitted dependence, and vul-
> nerability. Vulnerable he was. . . .
>
> Martin, who did not believe in good
> and evil, walked almost in a frenzy of moral
> revulsion across the living-room floor. . . .
>
> to exorcise the sense of evil, or malign
> fate, or something else that he didn't believe
> in, which shivered through him and would

not go. It had happened to him once or twice
before, an almost nausea of horror; and always at the evil of a supposed good.

Bill Stock in *Earth and Stone*, concealing from his
wife his knowledge of her cancer, and Douglas
Cameron in *The Flame*, driving his wife Linda to the
point of breakdown, are both convincing portraits
of "the evil of a supposed good." But Hunter's attempt to portray the evil of the unscrupulous politician, Russell Blenkiron, who wrests from Douglas
Cameron the leadership of "New Vigour," is less
successful.

During his years in Bradford, Hunter also
wrote two short critical books, *The Metaphysical Poets*
(1965), and *Gerard Manley Hopkins* (1966). Aimed
mainly at school students, their presentations are
lucid and uncontroversial. Nevertheless, the choice
of authors is appropriate. In his work on Hopkins,
Hunter presents a writer who sees pattern and
meaning in the natural world, while in his discussion of the metaphysical poets he stresses the opposite theme, the perception that the universe does
not conform to the pattern of traditional beliefs.

Hunter's novels are linked by their studies of
how the individual reacts to the more rigid beliefs of
the previous generation or attempts to form and
impose his own pattern. In his first novel, *The Sun in
the Morning*, the theme is implicit in the study of
adolescents growing up in a changing society. But in
later novels, the figure of authority is often found to
be flawed or vulnerable. *Sally Cray* presents not only
a picture of Sally's adjustment to her father's tolerant and flawed beliefs, but more briefly and effectively glimpses Robin Cray's reaction to the
schematic beliefs of his own father, a Baptist minister: "His father, it became quite clear to him, oversimplified things; whatever law or influence gov-
erned the vivid world, it was something much huger
and vaguer and subtler than the neat little
marionette showman of Arnold Cray's sermons."
Bill Stock, the painter in *Earth and Stone*, is finally
and painfully brought by the death of his wife to
accept the instability of his rigid world. The distant,
unrecognized figure of his wife disrupts his painting of rocks: "He wasn't painting the cliff-edge, but
the intrusion of the one figure, of humanity, altered
the whole prospect and marred it; he sat back
against the hot encrusted stone and waited for the
person to pass on." At the end of the novel, he
welcomes the presence of his daughter in his landscape: "the human person, such a one as Sheila,
there took over the whole scene and gave it a pulse."

In *The Metaphysical Poets*, Hunter describes writers responding to the destruction of a rigid system of belief: "the writers hover between belief and disbelief; often they use the protective device of irony, to avoid committing themselves. But above all they are excited—and frightened—by man as individual, the free-ranging figure who might not be bound at all—who could be quite sure?—by the gods or God, or by morality."

In 1966, Hunter returned to Bristol to take up the post of senior English master at Bristol Grammar School. In his next novel, *Walking in the Painted Sunshine* (1970), the wide perspective of *The Flame* narrows and Hunter concentrates on a young couple, Rich and Judy, and their relationship to an older friend, Allen. But the characteristic themes reappear as their private world is placed in a wider context. The title is taken from a poem by Louis Simpson that Hunter uses as an epigraph:

> They want me to be poor, to sleep in a room
> with many others—
>
> Not to walk in the painted sunshine
> To a summer house,
> But to live in the tragic world forever.

Allen is a theater producer, working in youth theater; Rich and Judy have met while rehearsing a play with him. The novel reflects Hunter's growing interest in drama, developed by working on school productions, and his friendship with a young teacher and theater producer he had known in Bradford.

The novel tells of the young couple's visit to Allen's cottage in Scotland, but the trip is not the escape into a private world that Rich and Judy expect. Memories of the past are intensified as they think of a friend, Peter, who also worked in Allen's production and who committed suicide; nor can Rich forget his mother, who is seriously ill. The Scottish idyll is broken by the arrival of a tramp at the cottage, and Hunter frames the account by scenes of the drive back from Scotland which open and close the novel.

The scenes in Scotland, which contain some of Hunter's most highly wrought descriptive writing, take on the quality of dream or drama within this frame. Allen, in Scotland, seems to Rich and Judy to offer a world which is all-inclusive. Drama, he tells his young protegees, aims "to act out—no, that's loading it too much—but to *act*, in profound and intense fantasy, all we are not and might, at the ultimate, be." Allen, in Peter's diary, is characterized as a shaper of experience: "You cannot imagine him growing old. Whereas people like me will live ninety years knowing all the time the thing he never believes, that there is no shape to things." If, as Benedict Nightingale suggests in a review of *Walking in the Painted Sunshine*, Hunter's sensitivity "comes irritatingly close to affectation in some of the description," it is also true that this novel shows a confidence and accomplishment greater than in any of the previous novels. And the "affectation" of the imagery and description is appropriate to the character of the theater director, whom Rich and Judy leave at the end of the novel.

Hunter stayed at Bristol Grammar School for nine years. During this time his work as a teacher became increasingly important to him, as he worked to improve the teaching of English literature and to devise new syllabi for the instruction of A-level (that is, advanced) pupils. His second novel conceived in Bristol, *Kinship; a Novel*, contains a number of references to his private life there. Not only is the novel set in Bristol, but Nick, the highly articulate son of the central character, Howell Mount, is a composite portrait of a Bristol Grammar School boy. The flat in which Karen, Howell's lover, lives is drawn from Hunter's own Bristol flat. *Kinship*, like the earlier *Earth and Stone*, explores the stresses in a family—between Howell and his disturbed wife, Alison, and between Howell and his adolescent son, Nick. Howell tries to hold the family together and to preserve his sense of order and clarity. Secretly visiting Karen, he rejects a sense of guilt: "In the very knot of illogic, uncontrol, treachery: order and structure were brilliant in the air. . . . No, he wanted to say to his wife's psyche, quietly haunting him: no, there can't be evil. For if this disloyalty is not evil then nothing can be; and this is goodness." Karen is more convincing in her relationship to Howell than as an independent character: her role, like that of Bill Stock's daughter or Douglas Cameron's wife, is to force the central character to admit his vulnerability. Hunter links Karen with flute music; Howell listens to her playing: "The sound made him tremble; it freshened and touched him. It was all vulnerable music. . . ." At the end of the novel, it is the wife, Alison, "in all her absence of intensity," who provides the continuing strength for the family. The tone of the ending, with its dogged optimism and its acceptance that there is no pattern or order, recalls that of *Walking in the Painted Sunshine*. There, Rich rejected Allen's certainty of meaning for the openness of movement: "Motion, to Rich now, makes certain of being." Here, Alison has finally to support Howell, the firm upholder of value. She tells her son: "He's a man who sees goodness as a possibility, where I see. . . a confusion of motives and compulsions. He sees patterns, where I would like to see and believe in them, but see really only drifts of air and time."

Kinship opens with a set piece, a family Sunday lunch which is disrupted by Alison's bleakly pessimistic outburst. "At the Sunday dinner, Alison began talking. Roast beef before her untouched, small crisp saucers of Yorkshire pudding half full of gravy; softly they lost their heat." This opening, written in Bristol, exceeds in intensity the rest of the novel, which was completed in Oxford, where Hunter spent a term at Merton College on a schoolmaster fellowship. But if there is a loss of intensity, the novel does become more fluent. There is more dialogue than in previous novels, and the characters are more articulate. Hunter attributes both qualities to the greater mechanical ease he found in using a typewriter for the first draft of this novel.

Dust jacket for Hunter's 1978 book, the first of six historical novellas planned on the theme of heroism

From Bristol, Hunter moved in 1975 to Weston-super-Mare, a west country town (in the new county of Avon, previously Somerset) where he had done his practice teaching in the early 1960s. There he became deputy headmaster at Broadoaks School, a large, noisy comprehensive, which gave him his first experience teaching students of varied ability levels. His seventh novel, written in Weston, marks an important change in his career as a novelist. In late 1973, Hunter had formed an ambitious plan to write six novellas linked by the theme of heroism, all with historical settings. *Percival and the Presence of God* is the only one completed (although Hunter planned another about Hitler's youth movements, and he started work on a third dealing with terrorism in a fictional east European state). But it was the medieval setting of the Arthurian legend that allowed him to write perhaps his most successful novel.

In all of the stories, Hunter intended to set a twentieth-century consciousness into a historical setting, deliberately introducing anachronisms into the text. Alison, Howell's disturbed wife in *Kinship*, in her sense of distance from her husband's optimistic humanism, tells her family:

> We're no longer . . . theologically gifted. We lack the medieval training—they were always finding out the enemy in their midst. Even at home, the arras rustled; in a smile, they saw the hollowness of death. Nowadays, bless our outmoded souls, we rationalize it all away. All gone, all the fear and all the caution.

In *Percival and the Presence of God* the hero finds himself in a similar position. It is the first of Hunter's novels to use a first-person narrative (although the earliest draft was written in the third person), and this viewpoint allows Hunter to show Percival's constant struggle to align his knowledge of the knightly code, taught him by his tutor Mansel, with the irrational, strange reality he encounters. His modern consciousness confronts him at every turn with the gap between legend and reality. He knows that the story he tells will be formed by his listeners into the satisfying pattern of legend: "My story goes round to meet me now, I've started a legend indeed, though it holds no giants."

The physical reality undermines the pattern of the code, not least in the fine description of a fight with which the novel opens: "The teeth at the right of his mouth were stove in, from some injury long ago, molars skewed inwards, the lines of the gums contorted." Percival is forced to question his own role: "My voice sounded thin and impossibly young, in the wide air, after the days within the house." The contrast between the consciousness of the narrator and the world described allows Hunter to create a strange and disorienting world, one which contains the inexplicable as well as the harshly physical. Percival takes part in a strange ritual at the castle of Henged in which he witnesses the sudden aging of his host. The novel, which Hunter conceived almost as a gloss on T. S. Eliot's poem *The Waste Land*, ends by affirming the value of Percival's code and of his journey in search of Arthur. Lying injured, he is rescued by a mad girl:

> The crazy girl taught me my destiny. More and more, it seems a parallel; after my dryness and doubt, I believe all might yet be a pattern of God's. . . .
>
> In the possibility of meaninglessness, codes may be more important than ever. . . .

As Rich, at the end of *Walking in the Painted Sunshine*, sets off on a journey in the knowledge of his mother's illness, so here Percival journeys on, haunted by the suffering of his host, Henged: "Even now, when I think of that face in its ceremony of suffering, shrivelling and collapsing with pain, witnessed by the helpless company, I think of reducing the *time* he must suffer."

Percival and the Presence of God is Hunter's shortest novel, and the concentration of the writing shows clearly the extensive polishing, rewriting, and revising that the text underwent. Attempting to characterize Hunter's style, Robert Nye, reviewing the book in the *Guardian*, suggested that "it reads . . . as though Browning had tried his hand at an idyll, if not of the King, then of the King's men. . . ." Valentine Cunningham said in the *New Statesman* that "Percival, in relating what is now his old story, has learnt from William Golding. . . ." The Arthurian world that Hunter chose carries with it the echoes of so many other writers (of Malory, Tennyson, and T. H. White, for example) that an innocently unliterary treatment would hardly be possible. The influences are felt by the reader but no single influence dominates.

Hunter has moved confidently out of the realistic tradition that confined all his other novels. When his first novel was published in 1961, it was for his sensitivity, openness, and lack of "cleverness" that he was praised: all qualities appropriate to the tradition of realism. Martin Seymour-Smith stresses

Hunter's apparent naturalness, commenting on the loose structure of *The Sun in the Morning* that "Every novelist has struggled with the artificiality involved in plot-making." Subsequent novels made it clear that Hunter's strengths were not only those of realism. The realism of *Earth and Stone* masks its careful use of symbol and setting, while the pseudodocumentary style of much of *The Flame* conceals its insistent and sometimes schematic moral concern. In *Walking in the Painted Sunshine* structure and style become even more important: the affectation of the poetic description comments on the values of its characters. In *Kinship* it is striking that the most powerful and convincing writing is not the dialogue or drama, but the elaborate set piece of the opening, in which the familiar scene of a family dinner becomes strange and threatening. Hunter's closeness to literature as a teacher seems finally to be acknowledged in the new direction that his writing takes in *Percival and the Presence of God*. The limitations of the setting he uses reveal the seriousness of his concern as a novelist with the patterning power of narrative and with the force of contrasting kinds of language. At the same time, the artificiality of the form heightens, by contrast, the innocence and freshness of the narrator, Percival, and releases in the writing a greater imaginative force than in any of the previous novels.

In 1978, Hunter left Weston to become headmaster of Weymouth Grammar School, and in 1981 he moved to the headmastership of a Quaker school in Reading. Since becoming a headmaster he has had less time for writing. However, a critical book on Tom Stoppard was published in 1982. Hunter, who has never married, intends to continue writing novels, perhaps retiring early from teaching, at sixty, to concentrate on writing fiction.

Other:

"An Expert at Make-Believe," in *Introduction* (London: Faber & Faber, 1960), pp. 145-159;

"Requiescat," in *Introduction* (London: Faber & Faber, 1960), pp. 160-170;

"The Father," in *Introduction* (London: Faber & Faber, 1960), pp. 171-179;

Modern Short Stories, edited by Hunter (London: Faber & Faber, 1964);

The Modern Novel in English Studied in Extracts, edited by Hunter (London: Faber & Faber, 1966);

Modern Poets, volumes 1-4, edited by Hunter (London: Faber & Faber, 1968-1969);

The Human Animal, Short Stories for Schools, edited by Hunter (London: Faber & Faber, 1973).

Dan Jacobson
(7 March 1929-   )

Anne Fisher
University of Delaware

BOOKS: *The Trap* (London: Weidenfeld & Nicolson, 1955; New York: Harcourt, Brace, 1955);

A Dance in the Sun (London: Weidenfeld & Nicolson, 1956; New York: Harcourt, Brace, 1956);

The Price of Diamonds (London: Weidenfeld & Nicolson, 1957; New York: Knopf, 1957);

A Long Way from London (London: Weidenfeld & Nicolson, 1958);

The Zulu and the Zeide (Boston: Little, Brown, 1959);

No Further West: California Visited (London: Weidenfeld & Nicolson, 1959; New York: Macmillan, 1961);

The Evidence of Love (London: Weidenfeld & Nicolson, 1960; Boston: Little, Brown, 1960);

Time of Arrival and Other Essays (London: Weidenfeld & Nicolson, 1963; New York: Macmillan, 1963);

Beggar My Neighbor (London: Weidenfeld & Nicolson, 1964);

The Beginners (London: Weidenfeld & Nicolson, 1966; New York: Macmillan, 1966);

Through the Wilderness (New York: Macmillan, 1968);

The Rape of Tamar (London: Weidenfeld & Nicolson, 1970; New York: Macmillan, 1970);

The Wonder Worker (London: Weidenfeld & Nicolson, 1973; Boston: Little, Brown, 1973);

Inklings: Selected Stories (London: Weidenfeld & Nicolson, 1973);

The Confessions of Joseph Baisz (London: Secker & Warburg; New York: Penguin, 1977);

The Story of the Stories: The Chosen People and its God (New York: Harper & Row, 1982).

Born in South Africa in 1929, Dan Jacobson writes strikingly about his homeland. A pioneer in South African fiction, he has won praise for his work on this and other subjects from critics and a certain amount of popularity with the public in both Britain and America. His fiction includes nine novels, one a Literary Guild selection, and six volumes of short stories. He has received the Somerset Maugham Award for fiction, the John Llewelyn Rhys Memorial Prize, and the *Jewish Chronicle / H. H. Wingate* award. He has also twice been a creative writing fellow at American universities. With his winning realistic style he portrays not only natural settings but also intriguing characters, social tensions, and human relationships with equal clarity and insight.

Jacobson is the youngest son of Jewish immigrants, Hyman Michael and Liebe Melamed Jacobson, to Kimberly, a small South African town where he grew up. After graduating from high school at the age of sixteen, he studied English for three years at the University of Witwatersrand, Johannesburg, and graduated with a bachelor's degree at the head of his class in 1948. After graduation he worked on a kibbutz in Israel for two years before he made his first trip to England and took a job in London teaching English. In 1951 he returned to South Africa where he held a public relations job and then worked as a journalist on the *Press Digest* in Johannesburg. He was twenty-two years old.

Since childhood Jacobson had wanted to be a writer, and he had made several attempts, all unsuccessful. He made admittedly awkward attempts at poetry and short stories at the university, and in London he wrote a novel, which went unpublished. Undaunted, at the age of twenty-three he made two important decisions: he wanted to write seriously; he would ultimately settle in London to do so. First he went back to his hometown where he worked in his father's business with his two older brothers for two years. Although Kimberly was hot and dry, a rather ugly mining town, it suited Jacobson. There he found the setting and the leisure he needed to begin his creative work. During this period in South Africa, he wrote a draft of his first novel; revised stories, which began to be accepted by magazines; and acquired an agent.

In 1954 he made his permanent move to England after marrying Margaret Pye, a student of mathematics he had met on his previous visit to London. She was originally from Rhodesia, and they were married in Capetown just before leaving for England. They now have two sons.

The year after his marriage Jacobson's novel *The Trap* (1955) was published. Like four later novels and most of his short stories it is set in South Africa. *The Trap* draws on his boyhood experiences at the two farms his father owned and his firsthand familiarity with relations between the white ruling class and black serving class. The themes of the novel are corruption, violence, and betrayal, particularly those kinds that are peculiar to the South African social situation.

Van Schoor, owner of a ranch, prides himself on his good relations with his black workers, or Kaffirs, as they are called. He believes he is on particularly good terms with Willem, a servant whom he trusts completely. When Willem informs him that Setole, another worker, has been making homosexual advances to him and his son, Van Schoor dismisses Setole at once, despite Setole's ominous warnings that something bad is happening on the farm. Willem then goes secretly to the home of Machlachlan, a dishonest white butcher, to discuss the theft of Van Schoor's sheep. Machlachlan is corruption personified. He not only steals sheep, but when he becomes afraid that he may be suspected of the act, he goes to the police and informs

on Willem. Being black, Willem has no power to refute Machlachlan's word. When Van Schoor discovers Willem's disloyalty, he is so upset that he beats the man savagely. This is the first time he has ever beaten a servant, and the book ends with the suggestion that he will continue to use violence, even toward his wife, in the future.

The ranch can be seen as all of South Africa; the situation between Van Schoor and his servant epitomizes the country's racial problem. The worst part about the situation, as described in the novel, is that everyone involved is hurt by what is happening. The "trap" encompasses all the characters. The same kind of symbolism is used in Jacobson's next novel.

Like *The Trap*, Jacobson's second book, *A Dance in the Sun* (1956), is short and has a single-episode plot. Two college students, the narrator and his friend Frank, are hitchhiking to Capetown when they are waylaid at Mirredal, a tiny village along the way similar to Jacobson's hometown of Kimberly. The boys find lodgings in the house of Fletcher, an eccentric, opinionated, middle-aged man, and his wife. During their night's stay, they become involved with the strange goings-on of the place.

First the boys meet Joseph, an ex-servant of Mr. Fletcher's. As the story unfolds, the boys discover that Louw, Mrs. Fletcher's brother, has gotten a child by Joseph's sister. Since this act is considered unthinkably bad between a white and a Kaffir, the sister and the child have been disposed of and Louw kicked out of town by Mr. Fletcher. Joseph wants to know what has happened to his sister, but Fletcher treats him badly—as he treats all blacks—and will not tell him. When Louw returns home on the same night the boys are staying at the Fletchers, he angrily destroys everything he can lay his hands on in the house in return for the treatment he has received. Meanwhile Joseph has told the boys his story, and they, as liberals, are on his side. While hiding out in the boys' room during his brother-in-law's rampage, Fletcher discovers that the boys are willing to serve as witnesses in Joseph's behalf; he breaks down. As the book closes, Joseph has gained power over Fletcher.

The house in this story, like the ranch in *The Trap*, represents South Africa. The house is divided within itself as well as against the blacks. Louw, ironically, is the most moral character because he can accept the blacks as people. However, his frustration with the situation leads him to take action against his own race. The ending, with Joseph in power, hints at what will happen in South Africa if the whites do not show more tolerance.

The Trap and *A Dance in the Sun*, later combined under one cover, were well received and drew attention to Jacobson as a promising writer. His style in these books, as in the rest of his works, is clear and perceptive. As in many contemporary novels, the writing is realistic. Jacobson says that reading D. H. Lawrence's works was one of the things that encouraged him to write in such a direct style.

The same year that *A Dance in the Sun* was published Jacobson accepted an invitation to Stanford University in California as a fellow in creative writing, where he joined Yvor Winters, the poet and critic, and the English poet Thom Gunn on the faculty. After a year he returned to England. The year at Stanford provided Jacobson with time to complete his third novel, *The Price of Diamonds* (1957), which, like his first two novels, is short and is set in South Africa.

The theme of *The Price of Diamonds*, a moralistic, comic novel, is corruption. Gottlieb and Fink, two Jewish businessmen in the diamond mining town of Lyndhurst, are fast friends. One day Fink, the dominating personality of the two, goes on an errand. While alone in the office Gottlieb accidently receives a packet of illicitly obtained diamonds. This gives Gottlieb the idea of pulling off a deal with the illicit diamond buyers of the town to show his partner that he is a real man of action. He does not succeed but instead loses the friendship of his partner and gets himself into trouble with the police. The police agent, however, falls in love with Gottlieb's secretary and consequently lets Gottlieb off the hook. Meanwhile Fink is struck down by some hoodlums in the street for taking the side of a Kaffir, and he lands in the hospital. Gottlieb recovers his moral balance, goes to the hospital, and is reunited with his friend. The story ends with Gottlieb throwing the bag of diamonds down an unused pit.

The diamonds in the book seem almost evil in themselves since every man who gets his hands on them is corrupted. As Gottlieb discovers, the "price of diamonds" is much too high. This book was not as well received as Jacobson's first two novels. One weakness is that the characters seem to come right from stock Jewish humor and are not very well developed.

A general lack of development in his works was something Jacobson sought to change at this point. Indeed his first few books could almost be

called expanded short stories with their allegorical characters and concentration on one incident. With his next book he began to develop a greater fullness and complexity.

The Evidence of Love (1960) is a longer, more powerful tale about a black-white love affair. The novel portrays relations between the races in South Africa with great psychological depth. The protagonist, Kenneth Makeer, is a Cape colored boy. Although Kenneth longs for education, wealth, and other privileges, his position as a colored person in South Africa makes his ambitions seem impossible to achieve. But Kenneth's skin is light enough for him to pass as white; therefore, when Miss Bentwisch, a rich, eccentric old lady, takes a fancy to him, she sends him to England to study as a white man. She expects Kenneth later to use his position to serve his people. However, after Kenneth begins to study in London and Miss Bentwisch dies, his newfound sense of freedom causes him to lose his sense of direction. Passing himself off as a white man, he courts Isabel, Miss Bentwisch's former white protegee who is also studying in London at the time. Kenneth falls in love with the girl; however, even after Isabel learns his true identity as a Cape colored man, the couple get married.

The ending of this novel does not quite follow from the rest of the story, as one critic noted. The last chapter presents the couple two years later on their way back to South Africa where they know they will meet resistance to their marriage. They bravely do this as evidence to all of South Africa of their love for one another. They are promptly put in prison for six months.

The Evidence of Love seems to be a transitional work between Jacobson's earlier, simpler books and his final, ambitious novel about South Africa, *The Beginners* (1966). All the themes of his earlier works are present to some degree in this long novel, published six years after *The Evidence of Love*. Starting with the original immigrants to South Africa and ending with a child born in London to the grandson of these immigrants, Jacobson traces the lives of the members of a Jewish family. Although the story centers on this family and on the theme of Jewishness, it also encompasses more universal themes. The main theme of the book is the idea of human consciousness, which sets humankind above other forms of life. Jacobson shows, by tracing the individual lives of the members of the family, that the most important ideal to follow in life is one's own human individuality. The story follows the lives of many different characters. However the principal figure is Joel Glickman.

Joel, a young soldier returned home to South Africa in 1945, feels confused about life and is undecided about what to do with his own. He gains some understanding from his college professor, who quotes Pascal to the effect that man is superior in the universe because he is conscious of it and of himself. This idea is of infinite comfort to Joel, who had hitherto been struggling with worries about the worthlessness of life.

When Joel falls in love with a girl involved in the Zionist movement, he becomes involved in the movement also and is sent to Israel to work on a kibbutz. However his girl friend, who was to accompany him, marries someone else. Joel leaves the settlement after a period of time because he does not want to make Zionism his life's work. He does not want his Jewishness to be confined to what is traditionally Jewish. He returns to the university and then goes to England, where he marries Pamela, his father's ex-secretary. Although Joel is never really satisfied with himself, when he takes his mind off himself he is fairly happy.

The personality of Joel's brother, David, stands in contrast to Joel's. David's inner life is much more stable. He is a religious loner. Though he does not completely accept the orthodox Jewish religion as his grandmother did, he does have a firm belief in God. Joe's father also presents a contrasting way of life. He is a successful businessman and also a firm supporter of the Zionist movement, although he does not go to Israel until he visits Joel there. Yet when all his children have grown up, he and his wife settle there. At the end of the story each of the characters is still, in a sense, beginning. The book ends on a happy note with Joel in England anticipating the birth of his second child.

The Beginners is Jacobson's most autobiographical novel. His work on a kibbutz in Israel gave him the firsthand knowledge he uses to write about Joel's experiences. Like Joel, he decided not to give his life to Zionism; like Joel, his father owned a butter factory. Joel's University of Witwatersrand is Jacobson's also.

Financially *The Beginners*, a Literary Guild selection, was Jacobson's most successful book. It was also well received by critics. *The Beginners* has been called "one of the finest South African novels yet produced."

After *The Beginners* Jacobson moved away from South African subjects. He had written much about South Africa partly because he had felt pressure to write something about his homeland and partly because he had felt the need to expose social problems of the country. After *The Beginners*, however, Jacobson felt that he had done his duty and that he needed fresh material for his work. He therefore went off in an entirely new direction to write his most highly praised novel, *The Rape of Tamar* (1970).

Although he took no interest in the Bible as a child, Jacobson developed a strong interest in the Old Testament as he grew older. The idea for *The Rape of Tamar* came when Jacobson was reading the Second Book of Samuel. The novel's plot is actually taken directly from this story of King David's spoiled and only daughter, raped by her half-brother Amnon whom Absalom, another of David's sons, consequently murders.

The novel is narrated by Yonadab, a malignant schemer who takes part in the action as he tells about it. Yonadab calls himself a ghost from the past, and he moves easily between the time of King David and the year 1970. He encourages Amnon to rape his half-sister; then, when Absalom has him beaten for being Amnon's friend, Yonadab becomes Absalom's spy on Amnon and helps arrange for Amnon's death. His narrative—cynical, realistic, and entertaining—makes the reader sympathize with his crimes, to a certain degree. This sympathy or escape into the role of a villainous character, Jacobson believes, is even more pleasurable for the reader than if the protagonist were good. He says that, because people fantasize more about doing bad things, an evil character offers more chance for catharsis.

The basic theme of the book is the struggle for power in human situations. The conflict between David and his sons for political power and Yonadab's yearning for power (and hence his betrayal of people) both illustrate this theme. The book is a witty social satire as well as an entertaining fantasy. The presentation of King David and the high government officials, all with their petty self-concerns and weaknesses, constitutes a satire on modern day politics. A tour de force, the novel is Jacobson's best work so far.

The Wonder Worker (1973) is another fine example of Jacobson's fiction. Like *The Rape of Tamar*, this novel is totally different from his previous work. The story, set in London, is about a boy named Timothy who believes he has supernatural powers. He believes, for example, that he can turn himself into solid objects to escape from the real world. As he grows up, his psychotic delusions become worse and worse until he finally is led to theft and murder in order to obey the calling of some power that he imagines controls him.

to *mop* the tears that brimmed under her
eyelids and ran down her cheeks.

*in the shabby, familiar room. Even as she answered
his question he was* ~~looking~~ *staring about it, at every ugly,
hired item they had lived with, and thought of as their own.*

"Because I love you." She had raised her head and was

looking ~~looking~~ at him with a small, forlorn, defenceless, *pale* ~~pretty~~ face.

Only the cheek on which she had been resting her hand showed

the faint *er* colour, ~~i████████████~~ "Because I want to

have a baby too. I want to have your baby. Please don't leave

me, Michael." *Her voice shook for the first time on that sentence.*
"I love you." *But she went on to say again, quietly,
Then she closed her eyes, too,*
~~my stillness was gone: her words had set in motion things in~~
~~his The pressure was upon him again; it was within him; in~~
himself which he could not name — ~~tears,~~ heat, regrets, tenderness
~~his hands; his chest, which could not contain its strength and weak~~
~~es, fears,~~ which flowed out of him so fast he felt himself

~~in dissolution, falling, a flux, a current, which flowed steadily,~~
                         nor did she; *until they heard*
~~only to her.~~ He did not move; ~~██████████████████~~
*a strange, cracked whimpering ████████████. Jill ██████
and ran █████ and came to his chest, kneeling beside it. They were shy to*
~~████████████~~ *touch one* the quietness of the house seemed to him
*another. Suddenly they both laughed, nervously and excitedly. Then
their hands met.*
uncanny. ~~But~~ One ironic point of his consciousness ~~█████████~~
shone with a bright fixed light, signalling to him
the flux ~~and told him~~ that if he was to leave her, he would have

to do it now, tonight. He could stay there no longer. Their

arrangement was at an end.

~~██████████~~

So
~~He~~ stayed. But four years *were* to pass - years of long separat-
ions and anguished meetings, of many ~~████~~ *letters,* ~~████~~ *and tears -*
and ~~████ ██████████~~, before Michael Lewin, ~~an~~/lecturer, ~~in~~
university
~~modern history~~ and Jill Stanlake, spinster, were finally married

in the Hampstead Registry Office.

"I love you, too." The words were wrenched
out of his chest, ~~████████~~ leaving a hollow
that was filled instantly with a hot flux of
emotions he could not name — regrets,
fears, anxieties, tendernesses, exultations,
the light was gone.

Final page of the first draft for "Led Astray," collected in Through the Wilderness and Other Stories *(1968)*

Timothy is not the only main character. Another level of reality is represented by the narrative structure in which the story is related by a man (under psychiatric treatment) writing about Timothy. As the novel progresses these two planes of reality become intertwined, so that by the end the author and Timothy, who have had much in common throughout the story, seem to be the same person. Both are lonely characters whose inability to form meaningful relationships with others leads them to lose touch completely with reality.

The relationship of reality and fantasy is the subject of the novel. It is hard to tell what "really" happens and what does not since so much of the action occurs within the minds of the characters. Often interpreted as a discussion of the process of writing fiction itself, *The Wonder Worker* elaborates on the relationship between reality and literary illusion.

From the time Jacobson had moved to England in 1954 until shortly after *The Wonder Worker* was published, he had been living from his writing, not only novels but also numerous short stories and free-lance literary journalism. His books sold fairly well, and one of his short stories, "The Zulu and the Zeide," was adapted into a play. He taught twice more in the United States, once in 1965 as a visiting professor at Syracuse University and once in 1971 as a visiting fellow at Buffalo College of the State University of New York. Otherwise, he devoted his time fully to writing until 1975 when he took a job teaching English at University College, London, where he still works. He does not feel that this job has hindered his writing, although he no longer writes short stories, which some critics feel are his best work—he has had six collections of his stories published.

In 1977 he completed his eighth novel, *The Confessions of Joseph Baisz*, which he had worked on for four years. As in *The Rape of Tamar*, the narrator of this novel is malevolent, and betrayal is the central theme. The book is set in the imaginary totalitarian state of Sarmeda, ruled by a dictator, the Heerser; a political party, the Phalanx; and a dreaded police force, the Compresecor. The corruption and violence of this state are mirrored in the actions of Joseph, the main character. Joseph begins his adulthood as a soldier and then rises to the position of bodyguard for Serle, a government official whom, on one occasion, he trips down a flight of steps so that he can be alone with Serle's wife. Later Joseph also turns on the wife, Gita, accusing her of being responsible for his actions. Joseph then works for the Compresecor and gets the job of kidnapping two children. After their father commits suicide in grief over the kidnapping, Joseph marries the children's mother.

Joseph has a talent for treachery, and paradoxically he comes to love the people he betrays, feeling a strange, protective power over them. After this job with the Compresecor, Joseph works in a prison. He has great success at his job, until one day at an assembly he discovers his sister, Beata, calling out to him from the ranks of the women prisoners. Rather than be disgraced in the presence of the Heerser, Joseph denies knowledge of her. This is the act that finally undoes him. Previously the people he had betrayed and then loved had been people to whom he was originally indifferent. Beata, however, had been a sustaining and loving force in his life, so that when he betrays her, he starts to hate her. This feeling sets off a chain of reactions in his attitude. He now hates all his victims, including himself. The story ends with his suicide.

Jacobson admits that betrayal is a subject that concerns him greatly. There is evidence of this preoccupation in many of his works, including *The Rape of Tamar*, *The Trap*, and especially *The Confessions of Joseph Baisz*, for which Jacobson received the *Jewish Chronicle* / H. H. Wingate award.

Such themes as betrayal, racial problems, religion, human consciousness, and power are the major subjects of Dan Jacobson's fiction. From the social morality and naturalism of his early South African novels, to the depth of characterization in *The Beginners*, to the originality and wit of his masterful later works, his writing is gripping and realistic, sensitive and warm. Jacobson is disappointed that his books have not sold better, although he has been well treated by critics and reviewers.

He has recently completed a new novel, *The Story of the Stories: The Chosen People and its God* (1982), that involves both the Old and New Testaments. Jacobson once said that his goal as a writer was to give others the same special kind of pleasure that he had always had in reading good books. It is safe to say that he has achieved that goal.

Radio Script:
The Caves of Adullan, BBC, 1972.

Other:
Penguin Modern Stories (Harmondsworth, U. K.: Penguin, 1970).

Interviews:
Ian Hamilton, "Dan Jacobson," *New Review* (October 1977): 25-29;

Ronald Hayman, "Dan Jacobson in Interview," *Books and Bookmen* (February 1980): 45-46.

Bibliography:
Myra Yudelman, *Dan Jacobson: A Bibliography* (Johannesburg: Univesity of Witwatersrand, 1967).

References:
Pearl K. Bell, "The Gift of Metamorphosis," *New Leader* (April 1974): 17-18;

Midge Decter, "Novelist of South Africa," in her *The Liberated Woman and Other Essays* (New York: Coward-McCann, 1971);

Michael Wade, "Apollo, Dionysius, and Other Performers in Dan Jacobson's South African Circus," in *World Literature in English*, 13 (April 1974): 39-82;

Renee Winegarten, "The Novels of Dan Jacobson," *Midstream* (May 1966):25-29.

Robin Jenkins
(11 September 1912-   )

Glenda Norquay
University of Edinburgh

BOOKS: *So Gaily Sings the Lark* (Glasgow: MacLellan, 1951);

Happy for the Child (London: Lehmann, 1953);

The Thistle and the Grail (London: MacDonald, 1954);

The Cone-Gatherers (London: MacDonald, 1955);

Guests of War (London: MacDonald, 1956);

The Missionaries (London: MacDonald, 1957);

The Changeling (London: MacDonald, 1958);

Love is a Fervent Fire (London: MacDonald, 1959);

Some Kind of Grace (London: MacDonald, 1960);

Dust on the Paw (London: MacDonald, 1961; New York: Putnam's, 1961);

The Tiger of Gold (London: MacDonald, 1962);

A Love of Innocence (London: Cape, 1963);

The Sardana Dancers (London: Cape, 1964);

A Very Scotch Affair (London: Gollancz, 1968);

The Holy Tree (London: Gollancz, 1969);

The Expatriates (London: Gollancz, 1971);

A Toast to the Lord (London: Gollancz, 1972);

A Far Cry from Bowmore and Other Stories (London: Gollancz, 1973);

A Figure of Fun (London: Gollancz, 1974);

A Would-Be Saint (London: Gollancz, 1978);

Fergus Lamont (Edinburgh: Canongate, 1979).

Robin Jenkins once wrote, "The serious novelist in Scotland today is very much on his own." Certainly, Jenkins's role within the Scottish context is an idiosyncratic one. Despite his involvement with the realism fashionable in the 1950s, the time at which he began his writing career, he also displays an inclination to the Scots tradition of tales of fantasy and adventure. Except in his use of dialogue, he makes little concession to the writing in Scots favored by the Scottish literary renaissance movement; nor does he use the techniques of modernism. He has been described as the most important single figure in the Scottish novel since World War II—he is certainly one of the most prolific—yet he remains relatively obscure. Despite the serious critical attention and praise that have been given to his work, he virtually refuses to comment upon it. The man has much of the enigmatic quality of his novels. Yet, although he may be ambiguous about his own attitude, he makes his main concerns quite clear. Love, faith, and innocence are the recurring themes in his novels, always leading to a questioning of the existence, or possibility of existence, of a pure type of goodness in man and society. He never affirms or denies but in his novels explores in narrative terms the existence of any kind of absolute truth.

Born in the west of Scotland in 1912, John Robin Jenkins was educated there, gaining an honors degree in English at the University of Glasgow in 1936. Although he describes his time at the university as a discouragement to him as a writer, breeding in him a skepticism of academia, he went on to become a teacher, spending much of his career at Dunoon Grammar School. However, he also taught abroad at Ghazi School in Kabul, Afghanistan, 1957-1959; in the British Institute in Barcelona, Spain, 1959-1961; and at Gaya College in Sabah, Malaysia, 1963-1965. While he is now retired and

Robin Jenkins

shelves of public libraries than in university collections.

His first novel, *So Gaily Sings the Lark*, was published in 1951. It is firmly placed within one of the major traditions of Scottish writing that deals with escape from the city into the countryside in order to reassess values and to find a more satisfactory way of life. Jenkins, however, develops his novel so that the country is shown to contain the same kinds of threats to human values as the city, because the same destructive human passions are present. In many ways the novel is unsatisfactory, but the use of certain vivid incidents to create a significance beyond themselves shows the beginnings of Jenkins's basic method.

It was with his second novel, *Happy for the Child* (1953), given prominence through a *"Daily Sketch* Book Find" award, that he achieved real recognition. The novel is about the experiences of a scholarship boy from a poor home sent to the local grammar school and describes the strain caused by split allegiance to two very different social situations and sets of attitudes. Jenkins here seems not only to have found a setting suited to his purposes—the slums of a small west-of-Scotland town, used again and again in his later works—but to have discovered the ideal subject for a study of innocence and corruptibility—the child. The novel also contains another aspect of Jenkins's work that is developed in later novels: the fantastic or grotesque personality. Here it emerges in the character of Gourlay, the ruffian acquaintance of the educated hero, John. In contrast to John, the typical Scottish "lad o' pairts," making good through struggle and sacrifice, Gourlay belongs to a darker, more primitive society. His world—of little grace, of cynicism, and of failed ambition—has made its inhabitants into bizarre caricatures of normal social types. Unlike the overly sensitive hero, Gourlay fights his way through a world he cannot understand. Yet it is a world which impinges on that of John's, both practically and emotionally. Gourlay adds little to the novel in the way of perception, yet his vivid personality acts as a reminder of the more threatening face of humanity, always present but usually pushed out of man's consciousness. By the end of the novel Gourlay has, appropriately, been pushed into a minor role, but in later works Jenkins returns to similar characters who are forced into fantastic roles through the barbarism of their circumstances, connecting the reader to a world which could seem too sordid, even too dangerous to acknowledge, if portrayed realistically.

living on a farm outside Dunoon, he spent some time in 1980-1981 on a writing fellowship at York University in Canada. Although his personal experiences bear close relation to the settings of his novels, he is reluctant to divulge biographical details, believing that a writer's private life should remain so, whereas his work is for the public. Any approach to Jenkins's novels must therefore be critical rather than biographical, although Jenkins's attitude is equivocal, holding that critics have received his novels too seriously, failing to appreciate their inherent irony. Certainly his status as a writer remains a paradox: although writers on Scottish fiction admire him, he has never achieved international academic recognition, perhaps because of the apparent lack of technical innovation in his work, and his novels are more likely to be found on the

Jenkins uses this mixture of the real and fantastic to express the dichotomy inherent in his own view of the world. He displays a severe and demanding view of man's morality. Above all he appears to abhor spiritual lassitude, a sign perhaps of Scotland's Calvinist inheritance. And yet existing alongside his desire for an absolutist morality is the claim of his own atheism and an awareness of the difficulties presented by a contingent reality. His novels therefore mix seemingly absolute characters, either good or evil, with ambiguous action and a shifting narrative perspective. In the role of narrator he moves from description of one character to another, revealing only certain aspects of their personalities and showing how these personae are capable of mutation through circumstances. Characters, reader, and even narrator all achieve on different levels an awareness of the uncertainty of their own natures, of the mystery of personality. The novels thus become subtle mockeries of man's assumption of self-knowledge and of fiction's use of realism.

This technique can be seen in his third novel, *The Thistle and the Grail* (1954), concerned with linking Scotland's two main objects of fanaticism, religion and football. Although one character, Andrew Rutherford, a local football-club chairman, could be described as central in that he is a focus of Jenkins's moral doubts and ambivalences, he is never allowed to occupy the stage for too long. The novel is a saga of a small football club's attempts to win the cup for the first time in years; the whole town is involved and details are given about the individual characters connected with the team and their personal problems. Everyone expresses an opinion of the situation, one attitude canceling another. Not only does this process of shifting narration teach the reader to assess the validity of what is said, but it also leads to the disturbing phenomenon of a novel apparently without a moral center. Jenkins has described his purpose as being "to tell the truth about the human situation," and in this particular world the human situation seems completely bleak. Only one man, Tinto Brown, an old, dirty reprobate, shows any flame of finer humanity, and it is largely concealed by his repellent exterior. Yet, through this grim depiction of the human situation, Jenkins appears to desire to create a vision of goodness in such a way that it can be accommodated within the framework of realism which he has established.

This aim is most noticeable in *The Cone-Gathers* (1955), winner of the Frederick Niven Award and widely recognized as one of Jenkins's finest works. Goodness in this novel is shown in the form of two brothers, one of them mentally underdeveloped and physically malformed, the other his aggressively protective guardian. Their job is to climb the highest trees to gather pine cones in the isolated world of an aristocratic estate. The hunchback, a symbol of that purity not usually found in man, becomes the object of malevolence for Duror, the Iago-like figure of the local gamekeeper, who sees in the innocent's deformity a physical reflection of the evil he knows to be within himself. His increasing hatred for the hunchback leads to conflict between the two forces, a hunting of good by evil which causes the other characters in the novel to reassess their own values and judgments. Jenkins's treatment of the owners of the aristocratic estate may be slightly unconvincing, but the novel, set within their closed, microcosmic world, is written with a force and a simplicity that gives its events a universal power. The strength of the novel is in the images it creates, the most striking being that of the brothers perched in their tree gathering cones: a symbol both of their natural goodness isolated from the world beneath and of their vulnerability to that world, ultimately to the gun of the gamekeeper.

In *Guests of War* (1956) Jenkins returns to social realism in a tale of the evacuation of a Glasgow town to the country during the war, but with *The Missionaries* (1957) and *The Changeling* (1958) he again uses images of the fantastic and bizarre. In *The Missionaries* a group of officials and police is sent to a small west coast island, recently bought by a millionaire, to evict a band of religious fanatics who believe that the island possesses some special powers and have refused all offers of rehousing elsewhere. This belief does seem to have some claim to truth, for once the official "missionaries" reach the island their skepticism is shaken by a series of strange incidents that affect the moral stance of each individual. Yet simultaneously, the anachronistic, even fraudulent, nature of the religious group is revealed. The novel lacks the focus of *The Cone-Gatherers*; the attempt to trace the personal quest of each character is unsuccessful within the scope provided. Nevertheless, the incidents themselves have a resonance and significance similar to those of a Robert Louis Stevenson romance.

The Changeling would appear at first to be one of Jenkins's more realistic novels. A well-meaning Glasgow schoolteacher takes his poorest, slyest, and most intelligent pupil on holiday with his family, again on an island. Yet once there the teacher is made to question the motives behind his action, the schoolboy is made to discover where his own allegiances lie, and good intentions in general are thrown into relief against the noncompromising reality of existence. The schoolboy's past life in Glasgow is constantly present in the surrealistic figure of a fellow urchin who dogs his footsteps, his brightly striped cap always and inescapably bobbing behind the hero. By the end of the novel this more grotesque side of his life has taken over, and the book finishes on a note of melodrama. Yet this melodrama is necessary to show the effects of the repressive "normality" which the teacher has tried to impose; the novel ends with a resurgence of the world which both parties were trying to exclude.

In a statement about his role as a writer, Jenkins hinted at the theory behind his literary technique. He said that Scotland should admit to its smallness and that failure to do so "has robbed us of a rich native concentration without giving us in return a confident, spacious outlook." In choosing to explore this narrowness in his fiction, he has to find means of rendering a limited reality in such a way that it does not seem trivial or dull. By introducing elements of the fantastic, he is not so much extending the boundaries of this narrowness as he is breaking them down altogether, thereby emphasizing their limitations. There is a danger in this—that of moving into the realms of melodrama without any other significance. Indeed, this is a problem which beset his subsequent novel, *Love is a Fervent Fire* (1959).

Jenkins's next novel, *Some Kind of Grace* (1960), however, heralds a significant change in his work. This is his first novel to move outside a Scottish context, something which he had admitted in 1955 he was reluctant to do, and to many his first novels remain the most popular and most accessible. But his own experiences in the Far East and his observation of Scots abroad clearly created for him an interesting dialectic between a ruling class in fear of the realities of a foreign environment and the still subservient peoples of a developing nation beginning to experiment with the power they hold through their more primitive but more passionate experiences. His concerns and themes are still the same, the world of the downtrodden native replacing that of the child. These people provide the tension between innocence and corruptible savagery in which Jenkins is so obviously interested. *Some Kind of Grace* is about a couple who disappear while on a religious expedition among the hill tribes of an eastern country similar to Afghanistan. They have gone not only with missionary purposes but also with a wish to find some isolated, innocent place in which goodness can flourish. As the novel points out, that kind of isolated innocence needs to contain a certain cruelty to protect it from the outside world.

Having gained confidence in this kind of setting, Jenkins goes on to integrate primitive and civilized societies in his next novel, *Dust on the Paw* (1961), perhaps one of his best, and certainly one of his most ambitious, works. Through a wide spectrum of characters, each with a subtle and complex personality, he explores the inhibitions and limitations of the conquering races in "Kalimatan." He does this by concentrating on their relationships with the native people who are about to gain their independence. The contrast between personal ethics and personal practices, between public idealism and public pragmatism, is the main feature of the novel. This structure allows Jenkins to create a series of situations in which barriers are either set up or broken down. Through divisions of class, color, and religion, he reaches out to the deeper divisions both between human beings and within the individual psyche, and through these contrasts returns to his ultimate concern—the division of good and evil. This kind of world and these themes occur with great frequency over the next ten years of his writing career. He often returns to the same characters, creating new situations in which variations on the familiar themes can be explored and introducing the reader to a new set of moral dilemmas. In 1962 he published *The Tiger of Gold*, in 1964 *The Sardana Dancers*, and in 1969 *The Holy Tree*, regarded as one of his finest novels, along with *Dust on the Paw*, both more memorable than the majority of his novels set abroad. *The Expatriates* was published in 1971, in 1973 a book of short stories, *A Far Cry from Bowmore*, with subtle and savage pieces which fully exploit the conciseness and the use of implication common to the short-story form, and in 1974 *A Figure of Fun*.

During this period Jenkins also wrote three specifically Scottish novels. *A Love of Innocence* (1963) again features children and an island setting. It is one of the best examples of Jenkins's technique of shifting from one character to another. The story concerns two young boys, orphaned when their father murders their mother. They are sent to a children's home and subsequently to a small island for adoption. The story, however, begins first with the world of the matron of the orphanage; then it moves to the life of her friend, who is responsible for finding suitable foster parents; and only after this are the children allowed to occupy the center of the stage. But not for long: the novel moves on to the affairs of the other people on the island and ends with another islander about to adopt another child. The interesting aspect of this device is the way in which characters, once discarded, fade from the plot and become enigmas to the reader. There is a closeness to life and to the "human situation" in this; very rarely does reality follow through to a neat conclusion. Yet it is disconcerting to find such a representation in fiction. One rather looks to fiction to tidy up the complexities of reality or at least indicate the potential for doing so. Only by the vacuums that he creates does Jenkins point to any assertion of potentiality or value. It is left to the reader to discern the forces which produce these gaps, which push man into reticence, and to derive from this condition some kind of moral direction.

A move toward capitalizing on this kind of emptiness can be seen in *A Very Scotch Affair* (1968). By pointing to lacunae, Jenkins is not only making a statement about what is needed to supplement these spaces but is also commenting on the circumstances that produce them. Having established this approach, he then goes on to experiment with different means of representing these situations. This experimentation takes him in two directions: either he can focus on one individual, making his the main consciousness in the narrative; or he can create individuals who gradually retreat from the center of the novel and cannot therefore be explained or controlled by the narrator. *A Very Scotch Affair* and *A Toast to the Lord* (1972) can be seen as prototypes of these two different methods, leading, respectively, to the later novels *A Would-be Saint* (1978) and *Fergus Lamont* (1979).

Jenkins has described how friends reprove him for writing about "such unpleasant people," although he tends to glory in what he describes as "taking the lid off the dustbin." Indeed, Mungo, hero of *A Very Scotch Affair*, and Agnes, in *A Toast to the Lord*, are two of the most unpleasant people one could hope to find in literature. Mungo is a vacillating dreamer, philanderer, and egotist, and Agnes is presented as a sexually repressed, scheming, religious fanatic. Yet closely related to their unpleasantness is a paradoxical sense of value and worth. For example, in deciding to leave his dying wife and adolescent family to go to Italy with his wealthy mistress, Mungo is betraying basic moral obligations. But in fulfilling his lifelong ambitions, he is casting off the restrictions that have been imposed by his Calvinistic society and by the material restrictions of his environment. Although his departure may have been responsible for the death of his wife, he is actually making an affirmation of his

life, in the sense of enriching his experience and remaining true to his own nature. He may not fully succeed, but the value is in the attempt. The value is also implied by the way in which the reader is gradually drawn into an understanding of the world of Mungo's morals and reasoning.

In *A Toast to the Lord* this process is completely reversed. At the beginning of the novel, the narrator is extremely close to the consciousness of Agnes. But as she becomes more a force of manipulation in the plot, in a very melodramatic and evil way, she moves out of the center of the novel. It is as if her "goodness" or "evil," which is left unclear, is beyond normal narrative comprehension. At first this is shown in the discrepancies between Agnes's interpretation of events and the accounts of others, but by the end of the novel in her fanaticism she has moved completely away from any kind of norm which could be used to judge "truth." Thus, the final serenity she achieves can be seen as a supreme callousness beyond the comprehension of the reader, or it can be seen as genuine "joy in the Lord" which the mass of humanity cannot share because it lacks her single-minded devotion.

This idea of the retreating character, whom the reader is finally unable to judge, is developed in *A Would-be Saint*, Jenkins's most enigmatic novel. Gavin Hamilton, the would-be saint, retreats physically from a world which finds his kind of virtue unacceptable. His retreat into a lonely existence as a forestry worker is paralleled by the escape of the character from the omniscience of the narrator. Gavin's final actions are, therefore, left unexplained, and the reader is pushed into the role of an uninformed spectator. By this technique Jenkins raises serious questions about the power of the novel to deal with goodness in fictional terms and to give it a comprehensible basis in reality. The failure of the narrator is not a failure on Jenkins's part, but it is an indication of certain areas of experience which cannot be catalogued in this literary form.

Jenkins's most recent novel is *Fergus Lamont*, which also seems to mock its own form and to parody the conventions of Scottish literature, and for this reason provoked mixed reactions from the critics. Yet it can be seen as Jenkins's most complete achievement in that he finds a means of combining a retreating character with a great deal of introspection. He does this through the device of making the hero, Fergus, a writer himself, aware of the lack of truth in the format which he uses and, like Jenkins, trying to escape from this by creating fantasy. The novel is written in a first-person retrospective manner, but with interspersed comments from the writer of "the present." This apporoach allows the reader to accompany the character in his retreat from the form; because the reader is permitted to share in Fergus's mocking of his own characters and actions, the moral division into good and evil becomes more blurred. Paradoxically, distrust of the narrative leads to a greater trust in the character. As in most of Jenkins's novels, the distastefulness of life forces man through strange means to an affirmation of hope.

At present Jenkins has just completed a historical novel, a new field for him. As yet unpublished, it is about the Great Disruption of the Scottish churches in 1843. Yet it seems fairly certain that his themes and concerns will remain the same. He is also working on a novel about a more familiar subject—a young boy who declares war upon the world; a theme which he imagines will provoke even more dislike among critics because of its unflinching approach to the darker side of man's nature. But both novels accord with the intentions Jenkins has expressed regarding his depiction of the Scottish character: "We have been a long time in acquiring our peculiarities; in spite of ourselves they are profound, vigorous and important: and it is the duty of the Scottish novelist to portray them." This statement can be extended to Jenkins's treatment of human nature as a whole. The peculiarities he deals with belong to man in general, and although he may often appear to wish to shock his reader in the manner he presents them, the effect intended is a forced recognition of self. It is through this idiosyncratic assertion of the universal that Jenkins's work succeeds in becoming "profound, vigorous and important."

References:

Paul Binding, "Ambivalent Patriot. The Fiction of Robin Jenkins," *New Edinburgh Review*, 53 (Spring 1981): 20-22;

Moira Burgess, "Robin Jenkins, A Novelist of Scotland," *Literary Review*, 22 (Winter 1970): 409-412;

David Craig, "A National Literature?" *Studies in Scottish Literature*, 1, no. 3 (1963-1964): 151-169;

Douglas Gifford, "Scottish Fiction Since 1945," in *Scottish Writers and Writing*, edited by Norman Wilson (Edinburgh: Ramsay Head Press, 1977), pp. 11-28;

Gifford, "Scottish Fiction 1978," *Studies in Scottish Literature*, 15 (1980): 241-243;

Gifford, "Scottish Fiction 1979," *Studies in Scottish Literature*, 16 (1981): 197-199;

F. R. Hart, "Novelists of Survival" in his *The Scottish Novel* (London: Murray, 1978), pp. 272-286;

Allan Massie, "Interview with Robin Jenkins," *Weekend Scotsman*, 26 January 1980, p. 1;

Edwin Morgan, "The Novels of Robin Jenkins," *Listener*, 12 July 1973, pp. 58-59;

Alastair Reid, "The Limits of Charity," *Scotland's Magazine* (October 1958): 43-44;

Alastair R. Thompson, "Faith and Love: An Examination of Some Themes in The Novels of Robin Jenkins," *New Saltire*, 3 (Spring 1962): 62-63.

B. S. Johnson

(5 February 1933-13 November 1973)

Morton P. Levitt
Temple University

SELECTED BOOKS: *Travelling People* (London: Constable, 1963);

Albert Angelo (London: Constable, 1964);

Poems (London: Constable, 1964; New York: Chilmark, 1964);

Statement Against Corpses, by Johnson and Zulfikar Ghose (London: Constable, 1964);

Street Children, text by Johnson and photographs by Julia Trevelyan Oman (London: Hodder & Stoughton, 1964);

Trawl (London: Secker & Warburg, 1966);

The Unfortunates (London: Panther, 1969);

House Mother Normal: A Geriatric Comedy (London: Trigram, 1971, limited edition; London: Collins, 1971);

Poems Two (London: Trigram, 1972);

B. S. Johnson

Christie Malry's Own Double-Entry (London: Collins, 1973; New York: Viking, 1973);
Aren't You Rather Young to be Writing Your Memoirs? (London: Hutchinson, 1973);
See the Old Lady Decently (London: Hutchinson, 1975; New York: Viking, 1975).

B. S. Johnson's suicide in 1973 seems in many ways the fulfillment of his life as a novelist: there are few writers for whom life and art are so inextricably bound. This is not to suggest that one should look to Johnson's novels for the facts of his life or for the causes of his death. But he spoke so insistently of his novels as "truth," made such frequent use of incidents and characters from his life in his novels, and died so soon after completing the most intimate and compelling of them—an account of the life of his mother, occasioned by her recent death—that it is impossible to consider separately his art and his life. Above all other subjects, Johnson wrote of the painful yet life-giving process of integrating novels and life. Reading his books, observing his life, one discerns not merely a rare individual—restless and disturbed, imaginative, challenging—but also the single most forceful exponent in this post-

modernist age of the most characteristic technique of the age, self-reflexive art: his books tell both of his life as a novelist and of the state of the novel in England today.

Critic Bernard Bergonzi said of Johnson in *The Situation of the Novel* (1970) that he has "propagated. . . the idea that fiction is lying, and in other respects undesirable," that "for an English writer Johnson is remarkably conscious and theoretical in his ideas about what he wants to do," that his "considerable talents seem to me unnecessarily limited by his doctrinaire attitudes." Such mixed readings are typical of English critical judgments of Johnson, yet even mixed they are distortions; they underestimate his accomplishment and misrepresent his theoretical views. It is not so much the belief that fiction is lying which Johnson sets forth, as the obverse insistence that for him the novel must be truth. "The two terms *novel* and *fiction* are not, incidentally, synonymous," he writes in *Aren't You Rather Young to be Writing Your Memoirs?* (1973), "as many seem to suppose in the way they use them interchangeably. The publisher of *Trawl* wished to classify it as autobiography, not as a novel. It is a novel, I insisted and could prove; what it is not is fiction. The novel is a form in the same sense that the sonnet is a form; within that form, one may write truth or fiction. I choose to write truth in the form of a novel." Many of his principal novelistic truths are derived from his own life.

Born in London, in Queen Charlotte's Hospital Annex, on Goldhawk Road (near the Stamford Brook station of the District Line train); raised in Hammersmith, West London; and educated at King's College, London (graduating in 1959, with honors in English), Bryan Stanley William Johnson lived most of his life in London. As novelist, poet, dramatist, editor, filmmaker, and writer of plays and documentaries for BBC radio and television—a true modern man of letters—he was naturally based in London, and London was often his subject. (He even coedited a book with Margaret Drabble, *London Consequences*, whose purpose was to raise funds for the Greater London Arts Association.) The occasional excursions beyond the city, as when he served as first Gregynog Arts Fellow at the University of Wales, in Aberystwyth, in 1970, serve merely to confirm his essential status as Londoner. In such novels as *Albert Angelo* (1974), *Christie Malry's Own Double-Entry* (1973), and *See the Old Lady Decently* (1975), is some sense of the middle-class and lower-middle-class neighborhoods in which Johnson lived for most of his life, with his parents, on his own, after his marriage and the births of his two children.

Thus he describes Claremont Square in Finsbury, across from which he writes *Christie Malry's Own Double-Entry*, and visits Chester Square in Belgravia, where his mother once worked as a servant, wonders how it looked in 1922, and describes its modern appearance—the mature trees in the garden and the sign warning off trespassers, the dull, stuccoed houses with their "fortress-doors," sure signs of urban change in the midst of apparent stability. Johnson's work is never naturalistic and never simply autobiographical, but from it the reader may also learn something of the social history of London in this past half-century.

In 1964, Johnson married Virginia Ann Kimpton, who appears as Virginia in *Albert Angelo* and as Ginnie in *Trawl* (1966) and *The Unfortunates* (1969). "I think of her, Ginnie, in connection with home,. . .[with] the concept of my home. . . . Which means here, in that home, making that home: with me." Their daughter appears beside him in his room in *See the Old Lady Decently*, as he attempts to write of his mother's life.

> Suddenly she leaves the room, not saying
> *Night Night*, and the loss is   noticeable. I
> call her, she does not return, the loss is

Women in Johnson's novels are associated not only with stability and continuity but also with betrayal: virtually all of his male protagonists have been and/or feel that they will be betrayed by women. Their inability to verbalize their loss may make it appear still more intense. This is a matter of novelistic technique, however—designed to evoke the reader's involvement in deciphering and sharing the emotion—and not necessarily one of private experience. What these novels depict intimately and unmistakably is Johnson's concern for his craft: it is the artistic process as it grows out of the life—and not the autobiography itself—which is revealed in these novels.

The protagonist of *Travelling People* (1963), Johnson's first novel, is named Henry Henry, and he is an essentially fictional character. Although the novel won the Gregory Award for 1963, Johnson writes, "Since *Travelling People* is part truth and part fiction, it now embarrasses me . . . and I will not allow it to be reprinted; though I am still pleased that its devices work. And I learnt a certain amount through it. . . ." He learned, among other things, that his art requires the immediacy of his life as an artist. Henry Henry is not Bryan Johnson. He is given no real background, and his seriocomic experiences at the Welsh resort at which he endeavors

to withdraw from life—but where he is drawn consistently into life, into involvement with others—are not those of his creator. (Although Henry Henry, too, reads *Ulysses* there.) But the wound which he bears and which he so cherishes, a wound engendered by life and delivered by a woman, would seem to be the same that is borne and cherished by Johnson. Still, the novelist demonstrates throughout the fictitiousness of this account; through the shifting styles and points of view of *Travelling People* (a different point of view for each chapter, ranging from apparent omniscience and the use of the central intelligence to first-person narration by the protagonist, his journal and letters to internal monologue and its more specific variant, stream of consciousness; even to a film scenario and typographical tricks learned from Laurence Sterne and from James Joyce), all that remain constant are the separateness and the intimacy of Henry Henry and B. S. Johnson. Thus, "Soon, Kim went to sleep, and Henry went into the back of his mind, a private world where he could live untouched and where no one else could ever penetrate: always excepting myself, of course."

This is not the sort of Trollopian omniscience which is reborn in Drabble, nor even a simple parody of those new English Victorians whom Johnson has dubbed "literary flatearthers." At issue here is the act of writing itself, as it is reflected onto the novel whose composition is both its subject and its theme, the novel which we are reading and in which, as we read, we see Johnson at work on its creation. Such self-reflexive creation calls renewed attention to the novelist and to his craft (at a time when other English novelists are preternaturally modest about the potential of their art). It is a means of adapting modernist technique to a postmodernist world which, in England at least, would deny artistic self-consciousness. It is a means of both distancing and effecting immediacy between the novelist and the world of his novel, an obvious heightening of the romantic obsession with poetic creation but in a more human context which lessens the romantic artist's godlike proclivities. The immediate source of self-reflexiveness in postmodernist fiction is Jorge Luis Borges; its modernist analogue is the dramaturgy of Bertolt Brecht, which similarly calls attention to itself to remind the viewer that this is merely art and not life, and which thereby, paradoxically, heightens awareness of the significance of the art. Self-reflexiveness as a contemporary form may also be found in films, in opera and the theatre, even in comic strips.

Johnson's contribution to the process of literary reflexiveness is to make himself a character-novelist in his novels—not merely a fictional character based on himself as novelist, as in the stories of John Barth, or even one called at times by his name, as in Borges—not a persona at all, but the actual character of the artist living and working at his art. Because the life of the character in the novel emerges from the novelist's own life, life and art in Johnson's novels are indissolubly linked; Johnson would have the reader believe that this union, in fact, is life and not simply some literary exercise. His suicide, soon after he had completed his intimate, imaginative account of his mother's death, suggests, perhaps, that he should be believed, that even in life he would not fully separate art and life.

This self-reflexive narrative process is advanced, albeit gradually, in Johnson's second novel, *Albert Angelo*, which appeared in 1964. Its narrator is an architect who supports himself by working as a substitute teacher of slum children. The theater which he attempts to design, unsuccessfully, in his spare time is an obvious metaphor of the novelist's art: "Of course, I would really like to be designing a Gothic cathedral, all crockets and finials and flying buttresses, but I must be of my time, ahead of my time, rather, using the materials of my time, . . . in accord with, of, my age, my time, my generation, my life." But this is a fiction, and Albert's creator abhors fictions ("telling stories is telling lies and I want to tell the truth about me. . . "). So Johnson intrudes, drops the fictional pretense, the metaphors about art, and speaks directly in what seems his own voice: explaining the changes which he has made in his (autobiographical) sources, explaining the narrative and typographical techniques (for example, holes in certain pages for seeing into the future; "To dismiss such techniques as gimmicks . . . is crassly to miss the point"), explaining his goals ("another of my aims is didactic: the novel must be a vehicle for conveying truth, and to this end every device and technique of the printer's art should be at the command of the writer . . . as to make my point about death and poetry"). It is in *Albert Angelo*, says Johnson, that "I really discovered what I should be doing." *Albert Angelo* ends with the narrator's death at the hands of his students, his creations in a metaphoric, fictional sense. This tension between creator and creations and a similar resolution of the reflexive conflict—"my point about death and poetry"—may be found elsewhere in Johnson as well.

The unnamed narrator of *Trawl*, for example, is a writer who embarks on a fishing trawler in order to achieve some distance from his past and to make possible a new start in his life (will all "be right with her, with Ginnie, . . . it must be right with her") and in his art. The seasickness from which he suffers throughout the voyage makes writing difficult but facilitates the processes of memory and renewal, of regurgitating a troublesome past and cleansing the spirit. *Trawl*, writes Johnson, "is all interior monologue, a representation of the inside of my mind but at one stage removed; the closest one can come in writing." The metaphors of *Trawl*—the sea voyage, the seasickness, the act of trawling ("Why do I trawl the delicate mesh of my mind over the snagged and broken floor of my past")—are fairly conventional, but they work well within Johnson's personal frame. Seasickness, then, becomes identified with "betrayal," that most common term. "I was seasick yet again," the narrator says on the voyage home, "just as I was the first few hours out. It was as though I had gained no immunity, as it were, from the earlier sickness." And so, devoid of immunity as he is, he remains needful yet suspicious of women, although he recognizes that his demands on them, as on himself, may well be unreasonable: "I have been through some rough old emotional times, it becomes clear, yes. So have the women, to be fair. Always I was trying to make them conform to some concept I had of what a relationship could be . . . a dangerous concept, I see, . . . but I certainly believed it to be true . . . and still believe it, still search for it." But with Ginnie, who may be that figure awaiting him on the pier, he concludes, it will be all right after all. "So: towards this vision of a future not more than five years off: Ginnie as wife, a child, a son, perhaps . . . freedom to work as I have to work, a home: in the far hope of that happiness, I give life one more chance: towards the chance of that future I shall voyage honestly and hopefully." *Trawl*, which won a Somerset Maugham Award for 1967, is the most optimistic of all Johnson's novels, yet even here there is potential ambiguity. Even here he accepts responsibility, as artist and man, for what he has made of himself and recognizes that neither part of his vision, artistic nor human, may be quite true: "I create my own world in the image of that which was, in the past: from a defective memory, from recollections which must be partial: this is not necessarily truth, may even be completely misleading, at best is only a nearness, a representation. . . ." But such an approach to truth, at this point of his career, is the closest he can effect in a novel. For this reason perhaps, he backs away somewhat in the novels which follow from his own life.

The Unfortunates names its narrator B. S.

Johnson, but it is not his life which is at issue here, and London is merely the place to which he returns at the end of his encounter with the past. The action of the novel is set in Nottingham; the protagonist is Tony, Ph.D. in English and a friend and supporter, now two years dead; B. S. Johnson is the reporter who travels to Nottingham for the day to cover a soccer match. "Sub inspires City triumph, from B. S. Johnson, City. . . . 1 United. . . . O," reads the headline of his story in the *Observer*. The headline attests to Johnson's lifelong enthusiasm for soccer and to the unusual structure of this book; it is reproduced on the inside cover of the box in which *The Unfortunates* is packaged. The twenty-seven sections which make up the narrative, from unbound single leaves to twelve-page sections, one titled "First" and one "Last," are designed to be read in random order. "If readers prefer not to accept the random order in which they receive the novel, then they may re-arrange the sections into any other random order before reading." The result of such random shufflings is a highly subjective, disjointed time scheme, a sense of simultaneity which shifts along with the shifting sections. The narrative moves back and forth, more or less at random, conflating past visits to the city with this one, telescoping scenes of Tony's struggle with cancer, his death and burial, the birth of his son, the discovery of his illness. The randomness of the reading—whichever randomness it is—is akin to that of memory, as Johnson the narrator recalls the friend who encouraged him to write his first novel. He fears, however, that he "sentimentalizes" Tony's death, as with Tony he had "overdramatized" his former girl friend Wendy's betrayal. Recalling Tony's life connects him inevitably to his own. "The moment at which *The Unfortunates* occurred was on the main railway station at Nottingham . . . when I came up the stairs from the platform into the entrance hall, it hit me: I knew this city, I knew it very well. It was the city in which [had lived] a very great friend of mine, one who had helped me with my work when no one else was interested. . . . The dead past and the living present interacted and transposed themselves in my mind. I realised that afternoon that I had to write a novel about this man, Tony, and his tragic and pointless death and its effect on me and the other people who knew him and whom he had left behind." Now, in the novel, standing on the railway platform that will lead back to London and to Ginnie, his wife, he identifies once again with his dead friend. "My death would be far easier than his in front of this train, not suicide, just death, this instrument of death, as it were, I do not want to die,

no, but this uncommon way of dying presents itself to me now as a preferable one to his, . . to remind me I may not go as he did, that there are some better, because quicker, ways, the thought occurs, should relieve, even please.   And passes." Even in so unconventional a form, presumably at some distance from his own life, Johnson retains the power to involve and to move us.

House Mother Normal: A Geriatric Comedy (1971) and *Christie Malry's Own Double-Entry* are more conventional novels, conventional at least in the sense that, although they make use of images and insights derived from the novelist's life, they do so in a frame which acknowledges that they are fictions and make no claim to be truth. They are wonderfully comic and predictably imaginative. "The ideas for both . . . came to me whilst writing *Travelling People* (indeed, I discussed them with Tony) but the subsequent three personal novels interposed themselves, demanded to be written first." *House Mother Normal*, which is subtitled *A Geriatric Comedy*, is set in a nursing home and consists of the memories and

Dust jacket for the American edition of Johnson's 1973 novel about a man who attempts to balance the evil in society with a series of terrorist acts

reactions of eight elderly patients, each section twenty-one pages in length, one of them (for a senile patient) almost entirely blank. The narrative concludes with the comments of their house mother, ostensibly normal, who addresses the reader directly and who admits, on the twenty-second page of her narrative ("outside the convention"), that "I too am the puppet or concoction of a writer (you always knew there was a writer behind it all? Ah, there's no fooling you readers!)." The work is clever enough but decidedly minor; only its theme of memory and experience projecting into the present, of death and poetry, achieves for it some of the immediacy which is associated with its creator.

Christie Malry's Own Double-Entry makes similar reflexive gestures but is still more removed from involvement. Its title character, having mastered double-entry bookkeeping, decides to balance society's evils with his own (a series of terrorist acts). Yet he is but an entry in a larger balancing act, the puppet of his ostentatiously omniscient creator, who consciously avoids social and psychological realism, who denies the independent lives of his creations, who questions the appropriateness in our time of the novel form, and who finally eliminates his character with a sudden case of cancer and appears himself at Christie's deathbed. "And the nurses then suggested that I leave, not knowing who I was, that he could not die without me." In *Christie Malry's Own Double-Entry*, distant from emotion as it may be, Johnson kills off not merely his hero but those conventions of the novel, neo-Victorian and postmodernist, which activate most of his contemporaries in England. Having disposed of the corpus, as it were, this lesser work—fiction, not truth—prepares him and his reader for his final and most successful novel, also occasioned by a deathbed scene.

In 1971, Johnson's mother, Emily, died of cancer, and her son set out to celebrate her life and that of the mother country which had helped to form her. *See the Old Lady Decently* was planned as the first volume of "The Matrix Trilogy"; the succeeding volumes, "Buried Although" and "Amongst Those Left Are You," were never written. Something of their intent and significance, however, is apparent in the running title of the projected trilogy: "see the old lady decently buried although amongst those left are you." Johnson would not be left long among the survivors; this book serves as memorial for both mother and son. With its epigraph from *Tristram Shandy*, its sources in family documents and memories and recent tape-recorded interviews, its analogues in history and

myth, *See the Old Lady Decently* is Johnson's most ambitious work. Yet its elaborate apparatus is never a bar to feeling. Typographical tricks are everywhere: documents are reproduced, photographs described, letters and poems numbered consecutively. Titles are used as in a Brechtian performance: his mother's age is measured against that of the century (for example, "20 (12)" for 1920, when Emily was twelve and her father's coffin was returned from France); sections marked GB, for Great Britain, are narrated as by a tourist guide, and those marked BB, for Broader Britain, the empire, consist of passages from texts detailing the influence of the home country upon the colonies; quotes from Erich Neumann's *The Great Mother: An Analysis of the Archetype* are marked N and provide a still broader, universal perspective. In the midst of the decay which afflicts nation and empire—and his mother's body as well—the archetype provides the possibility of fertility and renewal. The novel ends not with Emily's death, which inspired it, but with Bryan's birth ("from Em, Me"), as in *Tristram Shandy*, a further sign of potential continuity. Yet he is an Rh-negative child, destined to be an only child: again ambiguity and also, perhaps, a foreshadowing of his life and his death. The intimacy between novel and life is again self-evident. Even the clearly fictional passages (marked V for Virrels, the Belgian-born cook under whom Emily had worked as a young girl, an experience which Johnson reconstructs on his own), even those scenes of imagined kitchen life in the past may be marked by present immediacy. It is while he is writing V3, "all my pencils in preparation, girding up my 3H Venus, my 2H Staedtlers, my Faber Castell THE WINNER HB," that his daughter intrudes into his study and book. These are old pencils of his, "the stumps so short they have become anonymous and can only be deployed by using a crayon holder I bought secondhand in the covered market at Newtown, Montgomeryshire, less than a year ago, thus prolonging my writing life—how superstitious I am about with what and on what I write—by an indefinite period, probably years. For I shall never buy a new pencil again." He would not need to.

When he killed himself "in a moment of despair" at the age of forty, Johnson was mourned as "one of the most naturally gifted writers of his generation. He was also one of the very small number to commit himself whole-heartedly to the experimental presentation of fiction." These two statements, in the parlance of contemporary English novel criticism, are intended to be contradictory. "He was a combative but immensely likable man," the *Times* obituary continues. "To meet him was to feel, as did most of his English admirers, that his natural gifts and his chosen method of using them were in perpetual conflict. . . ." Johnson might have predicted such a response. He had argued that he was not an experimental writer ("Certainly I make experiments, but the unsuccessful ones are quietly hidden away . . ."), that he was not doctrinaire or even very radical in his theoretical views ("Most of what I have said has been said before. . . . What I do not understand is why British writers have not accepted it and acted upon it"). His belief, quite simply, was that contemporary novelists are obliged to consider the modernist example, and particularly that of James Joyce, in constructing their works. Such a belief, in postmodernist, neo-Victorian England, as simple as it sounds, is very nearly literary heresy. It accounts for both Johnson's ambiguous reputation in England and his appeal to those who admire Joyce and the modernists.

In *Aren't You Rather Young to be Writing Your Memoirs?*, Johnson insists that he refuses to allow his reader to "impose his own imagination on my words. . . . I want him to see my (vision), not something conjured out of his own imagination." Yet he clearly demands the reader's involvement—in working through an unconventional and daring text, in sharing not just the intellectual challenge and humor but also the felt emotion. In *See the Old Lady Decently*, completed just a few weeks before his death, a narrative made distant by its elaborate technique yet intimate because of involvement with the technique, one feels not just Bryan Johnson's loss of his mother but his own loss as well. This final effort of his, one of the triumphs of self-reflexive technique in the postmodernist novel, demonstrates clearly the difficult distinction between what is life and what art, and also the price that one may need to pay for following such a vision of truth in the novel.

Plays:
One Sodding Thing After Another, London, Royal Court Theatre, 1967;
Whose Dog Are You?, London, Quipu Basement Theatre, 1971;
You're Human Like the Rest of Them, London, Basement Theatre, 1971;
B. S. Johnson versus God, London, Basement Theatre, 1971—includes *Whose Dog Are You?* and *You're Human Like the Rest of Them*.

Screenplays:
You're Human Like the Rest of Them, British Film Institute, 1967;
Up Yours Too, Guillaume Apollinaire, British Film Institute, 1968;
Paradigm, Elisabeth Films, 1969.

Television Scripts:
The Evacuees, BBC, 1968;
The Unfortunates, BBC, 1969;
Charlie Whildon Talking, Singing, and Playing, BBC, 1969;
Architecture of Bath, BBC 2, 1970;
The Smithsons on Housing, BBC 2, 1970;
On Reflection: Sam Johnson, London Weekend Television, 1971;
On Reflection: Alexander Herzen, London Weekend Television, 1971;
Not Counting the Savages, BBC-TV, 1972;
Hafod a Henref, Harlech Television, 1972.

Radio Script:
Entry, BBC Third Programme, 1965.

Other:
The Evacuees, edited by Johnson (London: Gollancz, 1968);
London Consequences, edited by Johnson and Margaret Drabble (London: Greater London Arts Association, 1972);
All Bull: The National Servicemen, edited by Johnson (London: Allison & Busby, 1973).

References:
Michael Bakewell, Introduction to *See the Old Lady Decently* (London: Hutchinson, 1975);
Tony Curtis, "The Poetry of B. S. Johnson," *Anglo-Welsh Review*, 26 (1976):130-142;
Morton P. Levitt, "The Novels of B. S. Johnson: Against the War against Joyce," *Modern Fiction Studies*, 27 (1981-1982): 571-586;
Philip Pacey, "I on Behalf of Us: B. S. Johnson, 1933-1973," *Stand*, 15 (1974): 19-26;
Pacey, "B. S. Johnson and Wales," *Anglo-Welsh Review*, 28 (1978): 73-80;
Patrick Parrinder, "Pilgrim's Progress: The Novels of B. S. Johnson," *Critical Quarterly*, 19 (1977): 45-59;
Robert S. Ryf, "B. S. Johnson and the Frontiers of Fiction," *Critique*, 19 (1977): 58-74.

Jennifer Johnston
(12 January 1930-   )

Fleda Brown Jackson
University of Arkansas

BOOKS: *The Captains and the Kings* (London: Hamilton, 1972);

The Gates (London: Hamilton, 1973);

How Many Miles to Babylon? (London: Hamilton, 1974; Garden City: Doubleday, 1974);

Shadows on Our Skin (London: Hamilton, 1977; Garden City: Doubleday, 1978);

The Old Jest (London: Hamilton, 1979; Garden City: Doubleday, 1980);

The Christmas Tree (London: Hamilton, 1981; New York: Morrow, 1982).

Jennifer Johnston is the author of six slim, critically acclaimed novels. She has won several awards: among other prizes, *The Captains and the Kings* (1972) won the *Yorkshire Post* Fiction Award for the Best First Book and *The Old Jest* (1979) was

Jennifer Johnston

named the Whitbread Book of the Year for 1979; *Shadows on Our Skin* (1977) was shortlisted for the Booker Prize.

Johnston is nominally Protestant, but chiefly Irish. She lives about a mile from the Londonderry border, next to the River Foyle, in a house like those around which she centers most of her novels—a Georgian Big House, once held by a wealthy Anglo-Irish landowner. The house is necessarily large: she has nine children, four from her first marriage and five stepchildren. Her second husband, David Gilliland, is a solicitor in Londonderry. She finds children an "enormous pleasure.... a sort of *investment*, rather like my books. They become more interesting as they develop, and there are all sorts of wonderful surprises later on." Her novels are all about children on the verge of adulthood.

Her novels are also, either directly or indirectly, about Ireland and its troubles. From her study, she can hear Provo bombs exploding in Londonderry and army helicopters overhead. Ireland is her inspiration: "I like the damp fields, the men in dark suits. Since the Troubles have started, I've been miserable out of the country," she says. British soldiers on the streets of Ireland make her uncomfortable. She, like many others, feels that "they shouldn't be there." After nearly twenty years of rearing children, she began shaping her view of Ireland into fiction and rose in only three years to literary prominence. A *Times Literary Supplement* reviewer said of her in 1974, "her special talent is to distill and refine the whole tragi-comic experience of Ireland and offer us in remarkably spare, accurate little novels, a handful of people and scenes and smells that convey more about her country than whole volumes of analysis and documentation."

She is especially interested in the differences in class and religion which have sparked the violence. The Anglo-Irish theme is strong in her work, especially in its effect on human relationships: "What fascinates me are seemingly inexplicable relationships. What draws people together? What holds them?" She shares few of the attitudes of the decaying Anglo-Irish gentry, but the sorts of people she describes have been continually in and out of her life.

Jennifer Prudence Johnston was born in Dublin on 12 January 1930, the older of two children of illustrious parents. Her father is Denis Johnston, one of Ireland's best contemporary playwrights, author of such plays as *The Sythe and the Sunset* and *The Old Lady Says No*. Her mother is Shelagh Richards, an actress, director, and producer. Jennifer was born part albino, a problem which has necessitated her wearing heavy smoked glasses, and which contributed to her shyness as a child. However, when she was six, she sometimes acted small parts in pantomimes she wrote herself.

She claims that she has not had an interesting life. Her parents separated before the war and she saw little of her father after that. She lived with her mother and her brother, Michael. She grew up virtually without religion, because her family has been "mixed for generations," she says. But when Jennifer was thirteen, she discovered that she had never been christened, and "for the two weeks between learning about the news and the baptism ceremony, I had a fortnight's torture, for fear I would die and go to Limbo."

She was educated at Park House School. In a short piece she wrote for the *Irish Times* in 1972, she claims to have become "almost incapable of working" because of her "fourteen years or thereabouts" at "a delightful school [Park House] where the only thing of any use I learnt was that it was terribly easy and apparently quite acceptable to slip adequately through life without working." One of the results of such training, she emphasizes in the same article, is that she knows "no grammar." She refers to herself as "The Queen of Commas," a writer who liberally and randomly sprinkles commas because she lacks knowledge of the subtleties of other forms of punctuation. At Park House she wrote plays for student production. She remembers writing a play in which she intended to give her brother the central part of a heroic rabbit, and she was crushed when the role was given to someone else.

Johnston attended Trinity College, Dublin, where she was a classmate of J. P. Donleavy's. (She attended one of the rambunctious "Ginger Man" parties during which furniture was broken to pieces.) She failed exams, left Trinity College, and immediately married Ian Smyth, who later became a lawyer for the National Film Finance Corporation. They moved to Paris, then London. She had four children in fairly rapid successsion: Patrick, Sarah, Lucy, and Malachy. During this time, she did not write, but always felt that she should be acting, that she was destined for the stage. So, in 1960, she got a very small part as a Salvation Army girl in Bertolt Brecht's *Saint Joan of the Stockyards* at the Dublin Festival. She did not enjoy the role and turned from acting to writing brief "little things." When she was thirty-five her husband bought her a typewriter, and she pounded out a play she later judged "very bad." She dates the collapse of her first marriage from the beginning of her serious writing. A literary agent told her that, although the play was "perfectly frightful," she did have writing talent and that she should write a novel. She went back to work and produced *The Gates* (1973), which was rejected with the kind comment that it was "charming, but too short." Her next effort, *The Captains and the Kings*, was accepted by Hamish Hamilton, even though it was shorter than the first novel. It was published in 1972. In one year it won three awards. Hamish Hamilton decided to reconsider *The Gates* and published it in 1973.

Johnston prefers not to discuss the influences on her work. She loves Russian novelists, especially Tolstoy. She has read and admired *The Real Charlotte* by Somerville and Ross, and she loves Aiden Higgins's books, especially *Langrishe Go Down*, and also McGahern's novels and Brian Moore's. She says that she reads Proust "for a penance because I ought to like him."

Although somewhat unnerving in its shifts in point of view, *The Gates* is a remarkably understated and firm novel. It is the story of Minnie McMahon, the orphan of a Communist journalist and his colleen wife, who was not good enough to be brought to his Italianate family home in Donegal. Sixteen-year-old Minnie has been at school in England, living with her Aunt Katherine and Uncle Bertie, who strongly encourage her to stay and marry some wealthy "chinless" Englishman. She prefers to return to the decaying ruins of the Big House at Donegal and to the Major, her uncle Proinnseas. There, Minnie discovers a chest full of her father's books: Dostoevski, Tolstoy, Gorki, Joyce, Lawrence, Yeats, and the like. She reads them "to fill in the gaps of her education," and, after a conversation with herself via her "ghost," she decides to become a writer. She sporadically maps out her own novel. One is to understand that her perceptions are those of a writer.

Her uncle, although pleased that she wants to stay in Donegal, is withdrawn and noncommittal, unable to give her advice about her future. His estate reduced to the enormous, cold, mostly unused house and one family of employees, he now mysteriously whiles away his time in the boot room.

One night, when he cannot make it up the stairs, Minnie helps him and discovers his secret. In the boot room are fourteen bottles of Johnnie Walker, one hidden in each boot. She pours them all out.

Ivy, the Major's housekeeper, has known his secret, but she has chosen to remain and look after the old man. She cooks, complains, and functions as the nurturing center whose sharp but prejudiced views balance and correct Minnie's romanticism. Ivy's wrath is uncontainable when Minnie begins hanging around with Kevin, the only lad of her age in the area. Kevin is one of the eight dirty children of the Major's only employee, Kelly, a drunken tenant farmer. Ivy sees the sexual dangers of the friendship which could lead Minnie to an untenable alliance. Minnie sees them too; she argues with her ghost, even admitting that Kevin stinks, that his hair probably has nits. Yet when she sees his desperation to leave Ireland and try for a better life in England, Minnie plots to keep him at home. She plans great amelioration—not just for him, but for the decayed estate, her uncle, and herself. She will somehow get money to start a vegetable garden which will become a profitable business. The opportunity presents itself. Mr. Maguire comes from America with his wife, seeking his ancestral roots. They wish to buy the huge eighteenth-century gates of the estate. The Major indignantly refuses to sell. Minnie and Kevin decide to steal the gates and sell them anyway for the £100 needed to begin their garden. They do so, and Kevin leaves to deliver the gates to the Maguires. Days later, Minnie receives a letter: Kevin, desperate for a new life, has taken the money and gone to England. The incident draws forth the first real communication between Minnie and her uncle: "No doubt you thought you could turn your precious Ireland into a paradise with a hundred pounds." The Major touches Minnie's hand. "We all want the world to be perfect, and there are moments, luckily brief, in some of our lives when we feel we have to do something about its imperfection. It's, ah, it's inadvisable."

Jennifer Johnston's Ireland is a graveyard of derelicts, those who could not or did not leave to find a better life. Minnie's view of it is worth trusting, since she is a joint product of Ireland and England. Minnie's emotional attachment to Ireland and her naivete blunt the edge of Johnston's otherwise brutal glimpses of wasted lives. The stinking turf-fires, unwashed bodies, and violence attract Minnie; here at least is life—and possibility.

Each chapter of the novel begins with an excerpt from Minnie's diary and then quickly moves to an omniscient narrator, providing a conversation between the returning young woman and her world. There is also the ghost, with which Minnie argues her positions, often comically. This dialectic, which she sometimes conducts while also talking with other people, can be confusing to the reader. Time also occasionally shifts within Minnie's imagination, creating still another juxtaposition in point of view: Minnie confronts the possible.

Minnie's efforts to repair the present lead her to confront her past. Her father's books are the intellectual tools, and Big Jim Breslin, the "shrivelled and almost weightless" hotel proprietor is the emotional tool. He, like her uncle, remembers the finer days, but he, unlike the Major, has warm memories of Minnie's father. Through Breslin, Minnie is able to see the unselfish side of her father's political decisions. Breslin fleshes out the past for her as the future withers away within his body. There is no release from the diseased torment of his life, and he, like Kevin, wants to leave Ireland, only he expects to leave it by dying. He wonders why anyone would choose to stay.

This is Johnston's central issue here: why, indeed, would anyone choose to stay? She offers no answer except in Minnie's compulsion to do just that. Perhaps the answer is not in a panoramic politic or nostalgic Irishry. Johnston concentrates on the small, deft touches that constitute character, and, presumably for Minnie, it is these touches, pleasant or unpleasant, that hold her: Kevin's hair shining with oil, smelling of turf-fires; Uncle Proinnseas's sentences, always left hanging; his Labrador bitch's rotten teeth and fetid breath; Mr. Kelly's leering, vicious sexuality; Ivy's aromatic, floury potatoes, mutton chops, and sprouts.

Reviews of Johnston's first novel expressed dismay in her handling of the Maguires, accusing her of depicting outdated, stereotyped Americans. Even before the novel was acknowledged as her first rather than her second, reviewers found unmistakable "first novel" trappings such as set-piece descriptions and repetitions of trite metaphors. Critics, however, unstintingly praised her adeptness of characterization. Most expressed the hope that the author would learn to flesh out her spare works, adding causality and complexity without losing the economy of language which lends them vitality. All saw her as a potentially masterful writer.

The Captains and the Kings, Johnston's first published novel, won an award from The Author's Club in 1975 as well as the *Yorkshire Post* Fiction Award for the Best First Book and the Robert Pitman Literary Prize. Like *The Gates*, it is a story of decay, personified by another sensitively drawn and isolated old man, Charles Prendergast. Mr. Prendergast, like Uncle Proinnseas, has shut door after door of his Big House and confined himself to one small area, just as he has shut himself off from life and commitment. Haunted by memories of his cold, beautiful mother's constant disapproval, he has never attached himself, not to his wife, Clare, who died even more a stranger to him than she had been when they married, and not to his daughter, Sara, who was farmed out to her grandparents as soon as she was born. Prendergast is left with his piano, his whisky, and his ghosts. He is attended by memories of his mother's scornful schoolgirl laugh as she impeccably poured tea from a silver pot into her opaque cup each afternoon at four. He converses with his dead brother, Alexander, killed in World War I, who had attracted all his mother's love and attention. Prendergast's only live companion is his dead wife's drunken gardener, Sean, who loathes him and who remains faithful to Clare's memory by tending her flowers.

Prendergast forms a reluctant friendship with a persistent local boy, Diarmid, who skips school to visit him and play with boxes of toy soldiers, residuals of Prendergast's childhood. The two devise an elaborate war game on the nursery floor. When Diarmid's parents decide to send him off to work, he runs away from home straight to the Big House. He and Prendergast establish themselves for a seige. But they are found out, and Diarmid is coerced by his brutish Irish-Catholic parents into signing a confession attesting that the old man abused him sexually. Prendergast, while waiting to be arrested, plays Chopin's Nocturnes better than ever before. Just as the guards come to arrest him, he falls dead.

The action is wedged entirely between the setting out and the arrival of the two guards. Prendergast's death is perhaps too convenient a denouement for a tale of Irish decay, but in his final confession of love for the boy, there is a kind of redemption that renders the death itself and the consternation of the guards immaterial. Diarmid has been Prendergast's one last attempt, however reluctant, to connect. Just as the boy has chopped away at the overgrown pond weeds to clear a spot for swimming, he has carved a small inroad into Prendergast's alienation.

In Irish folklore, Diarmid kills the guardian of the "Quick" tree to acquire the magic berries which have the power of restoring to the age of thirty anyone who eats them. The betrayal of Prendergast by Johnston's Diarmid destroys the old man. Diarmid acquires Prendergast's prized war medals,

which may help provide money for his future, but his future in a world of much hatred and many missed opportunities is as uncertain as Prendergast's brief redemption.

Unlike *The Gates*, this novel is full of chances and missed chances. As Diarmid and Prendergast drift off to drunken sleep before the parents and priest burst in to seize them, Prendergast advises: "the great thing is to protect yourself. Keep yourself out of the way of the slings and arrows of outrageous fortune." When Prendergast does take an emotional chance, outraged townspeople hurl accusations which destroy him, but Johnston draws the unmistakable conclusion that it is indeed nobler to suffer the slings and arrows than to protect oneself by avoiding chances.

As in *The Gates*, there is no wresting blame from any quarter. Prendergast's wasted life is clearly his fault, as is the Major's in Johnston's earlier novel. Sean is as responsible for his bitter lies as is Kevin Kelly for his absconding with the £100. Rather than assigning culpability or explaining the entire affair in terms of fate, Johnston offers the reader only the sadness of unfulfilled potential. A *London Magazine* reviewer commented, "The sadness comes from the sense that, after all, happiness on this earth is not very far off, even for the old and sick, and presumably the poor; and the terrible thing is how hard it is to receive it, not how hard it is to give it up."

Critics have complained that Johnston skips around in the chronology of her narrative; they have suggested that this is an intoxication with freedom to which playwrights are particularly prone when they begin novel writing. But the clutter of memories and present anxieties, of lapses and sudden insights, forms an accurate view of an old man's final effort to find meaning in his detached life.

In Johnston's third novel, *How Many Miles to Babylon?* (1974), the setting departs from total concentration on the isolated Big House. The action is split between an Anglo-Irish estate and Flanders of 1915 during the Great War. Her first two novels contain fleeting accounts of life in the trenches, but here Johnston depicts actual life there—the smelly socks, sugared rum tea, and the cold, wet sleeplessness. The story is told as the memoir of Alexander Moore, under sentence of death for shooting his childhood friend, Jerry Crowe, to save him from an ignominious deserter's death by firing squad. The theme is male innocence, which is allowed only a small step toward maturity before it is cut off by death.

Alexander is an only child, early forced into

loneliness by the barrier of class. He is ordered to give up Jerry, a local stableboy and his only friend, because of "the responsibilities and limitations of the class into which you are born," as his father tells him. So he is restricted to the tensions of the Big House, where his ineffectual father and vicious, beautiful mother conduct silent warfare. (Johnston has said about this situation that, although she does not write about her family or from personal experience, since she was working on this novel at the time of her divorce, the "terrible tension of unconfronted hostilities" felt by a sensitive child no doubt echoed her own.)

Alexander's mother urges him to enlist in the British army, partly to pry him from the influence of his gentle, tipsy father, with whom he is at last beginning to form a relationship, and partly to fulfill her romantic notions of war, heroism, and manhood. When he refuses, claiming that his father needs looking after, she informs him for the first time that her husband is not his father. Consequently, after a drunken night with Jerry, both he and his friend enlist. Alexander is made an officer; Jerry, a private. But the two manage to stay together, as the narrowed eyes of Major Glendinning watch the unequal friendship. When Jerry returns after deserting for several days to try to find his wounded father, the Major sentences him to be executed in the field and assigns Alexander the task of executioner. But instead, Alexander visits his friend in the guardroom, encourges him to sing a ballad from their homeland, and, during the brief happy moment, shoots him.

As in *The Captains and the Kings*, the entire action of the story takes place in a moment of recollection framed by a present which is only a brief wait before death. *How Many Miles to Babylon?* is told in first person by a narrator who, like Prendergast, lacks the ability to make connections. As with Prendergast, the chances of Alexander's life have been thwarted by his cowardice. He has allowed himself to be wrenched from his father, from Jerry, and from his pacifistic beliefs by his mother's cruel strength. When Alexander finally does make a decisive move, the action simultaneously destroys him and saves him.

The two Irelands Johnston first explored in *The Gates* are evident here as well: that of the Anglo-Irish and of the Irish peasant and rebel. *How Many Miles to Babylon?* offers flashbacks of the Big House before its fall, but rumblings of the 1916 Easter Rebellion can be heard in Jerry's predictions: "The Germans are going to fix all those eejits in Europe, the British are going to fix the Germans,

and we . . . are going to fix the British."

Johnston has been accused of offering the reader a pastiche of prewar Ireland too strongly reminiscent of Yeats and Siegfried Sassoon, replete with swans on the lake and foxes in the field. Alexander even quotes Yeats throughout his narrative. The hero's struggle to free himself from the oppressive memories of an overpowering mother is similar to that of Rupert Brooke, and naturally the sensitive emotions of the young man in the trenches recall Wilfred Owen and Robert Graves, as well as Brooke and Sassoon. Furthermore, some have suggested that Johnston's war is not an authentic war, but a mere evocation of stench, chilblains, and screams of the wounded. But, as reviewers have pointed out, a writer who reminisces clearly and poignantly and one who suggests the feeling of war without reference to the maneuvers and gunshots of war will naturally bring to mind those who have preceded her.

The novel was reviewed more widely than her previous two, always favorably. Her talent in portraying war scenes, with which she has no experience, has been compared with Stephen Crane's. However, some reviewers continued to complain of the strain her extreme compression puts on the narrative, as details are sometimes made to carry more symbolic weight than they can bear. But all agreed that her strength lies in her economy and boldness and that *How Many Miles to Babylon?* evidences these qualities at her best.

Shadows on Our Skin, moves entirely away from the setting of Johnston's previous novels. The story takes place in present-day Londonderry. Joe Logan, a twelve-year-old Catholic schoolboy, lives at home with his tight-lipped, respectable mother, who must work outside the home to support Joe and his father, her drunken Irish-civil-war-hero husband. Joe is a dreamer and budding poet who stays in trouble at school for his inattentiveness. He meets Kathleen Doherty, a chain-smoking young schoolteacher from Wicklow whose interest in him wins his adoration. She invites him to tea and encourages his poetry. She takes him up Grianan and shows him an Ireland of the past, of mountains and clouds "grey and white and sun-shot as if the sea were boiling up into the sky." Johnston here creates a tension which one feels will eventually well up in Joe Logan's poetry: the wide expanse (from which Joe and Kathleen are driven by a fierce rainstorm) which stands for the unattainable past contrasts with the constricted present where life is ugly and fearful.

Joe's brother Brendan returns from England

to commiserate with their father in memories of his Free State hero days and to seek out glory of his own by joining the Provo (the provisional wing of the Irish Republican Army). When the British army smashes the front window late one night, Joe must hide his brother's gun before it is discovered. In his first frighteningly decisive act, he stuffs it in his knapsack under his books, carries it away and drops it in the river. But his allegiance to his brother comes to an abrupt end when he learns that Brendan has fallen in love with Kathleen and has hopes of eventually marrying her. In a jealous rage, Joe blurts out her secret: she is engaged to a British soldier and will be returning to him at the end of the school term. Brendan and his Provo friends retaliate by beating her up, cutting off her hair, and sending her away. The novel was later made into a television film.

Joe organizes his world with words. They provide a safe structure with which to combat the confusion outside: "To write words down on a page, pattern them not even write them down, hear the song of them in your head, hear nothing else for a few minutes, that was safe too." But Kathleen tells him a poem must be more than pleasing sounds and pretty pictures. It must have "substance." "How can words have substance? That was something you could hold in your hand." He crosses out his insubstantial poem. Immediately thereafter, he finds Brendan's gun, no "toy," something he can hold in his hand. He shoves it into his schoolbag; once again, "substance" has intruded in his life and must be dealt with. At another time, Joe says aloud the word "substance" as he touches his hated father's "soft, mouldering skin." Finally, when Joe realizes that through his jealous temper he has destroyed all that mattered in his world, he knows that there is "no safety," and in this realization he is ready, one assumes, to provide substance for his word pictures, to accept the reality of pain, ugliness, and chaos, and shape this reality into new meaning.

This novel, like Johnston's others, is primarily concerned with a sensitive adolescent child's struggle to interpret old age and its hopelessness as well as the entire adult world and its cruelty. Like her other novels, this one ends with a betrayal. But, as in *The Gates*, one is led to believe that the betrayal will bring new understanding and growth to a vigorous, creative mind capable of readjusting.

Critics praised Johnston's ability to portray what have by now become stock scenes of Irish troubles and create from them an everydayness which remains believable. Some have suggested that Kathleen's motives are not clearly understood and that her relationship with Joe and Brendan strays beyond the bounds of realism. But Johnston does avoid sentimentality, especially through her unrelenting verbal economy.

Johnston's fifth novel, *The Old Jest*, is set in Ireland of the 1920s. The title is from Turgenev: "Death is an old jest, but it comes to everyone." However, the novel, like her others, is focused on life, that of an adolescent at the juncture of adulthood faced with momentous decisions. The heroine is eighteen-year-old Nancy Gulliver, whose travels are emotional rather than physical. Johnston uses the diary technique once again, and once again the diary entries are only short interior introductions to a predominately third-person narrative. Other characters follow the same configurations as Johnston's previous ones: Nancy's grandfather, a retired general who fought in the Boer War, has faded off into senility, another of the author's portraits of pathetic old age. The servant Birdie is a version of Ivy in *The Gates*. Angus Barry, Nancy's newfound friend, is very like Minnie's dead revolutionary father and shares political beliefs with

Dust jacket for the American edition of Johnston's 1981 novel, an unsentimental portrait of a woman's dying

Brendan in Johnston's fourth novel.

The Old Jest follows the pattern of her previous works: innocence-betrayal-growth, but Nancy Gulliver is Johnston's strongest character emotionally and her most insightful one so far. Like Minnie in *The Gates*, Nancy is an orphan. Her mother died in childbirth, and her father was a revolutionary and a wanderer who disappeared "irrevocably." Nancy still searches every stranger's face for a sign of the father she has never seen.

In Nancy's first diary entry, the sun is shining, but her peaceful, secure childhood, as well as her exterior life as the pampered daughter of the Big House family, is about to end. Nancy thinks she loves Harry, a bland stockbroker who is courting Maeve Casey. Nancy's jealousy prompts her to foolish behavior. However, what Nancy really loves is security, which she feels slipping away from her as she becomes more aware of pain in the world. But she finally cannot respect Harry's choice of a solid job, a charming mate, and an unruffled maturity. Other choices present themselves: her Aunt Mary has chosen to hide from reality until the last moment, when lack of money forces her to sell the family estate to Maeve's father for a housing development. Mary drinks and imagines life is still made up of cucumber sandwiches and tea in porcelain cups. The senile old general meanwhile sings his hymns, a refrain throughout the novel which constantly forces the reader as well as the characters themselves to acknowledge the presence of death which shapes the perspective and meaning to life. "Change and decay all around I see," he sings.

In her secret hut on the beach, Nancy discovers a man, obviously educated, but an outcast or fugitive. He is about the age her father would have been, and she imagines that perhaps he is her father, returned from romantic adventures. He is not her father, but he is indeed involved in dangerous busines. Nancy allows him to stay in the hut and to read her books. He, in return, introduces her to another adult world, one in which ideals cause pain. He is a republican, an Irish revolutionary who has chosen his outcast life not from any personal need—he was born a gentleman—but for idealistic reasons. He has a gun, which Nancy despises, but she comes to understand its necessity. From him she learns that pain is part of change and that some changes are necessary and good. Nancy delivers a message for him to a young man in Dublin and thereby unwittingly becomes the accomplice to the killing of twelve British soldiers. When she returns from her mission, soldiers swarm the neighborhood looking for a man who is easily recognizable as her friend in the picture they show her. She runs to warn him, but she is too late. As he steps from the hut, they gun him down.

Nancy's grandfather's hymn the next morning is appropriate—as always—to the novel's theme: "I fear no foe with thee at hand to bless." Nancy is now less afraid of change and death and is ready to make choices, to structure her life into its own pattern. "Next week we must positively start to get organized," Aunt Mary claims.

Reviewers often mentioned the lack of period detail in the novel: the focus remains on the people rather than on the setting. Johnston frequently strains horror through innocent bystanders, with the focus on the bystanders rather than on the horror. This quality is especially noticeable in this novel, and British reviewers of the work have praised it. Some have said that Johnston is at her most intelligent and most moving in this fifth novel. However, to the *New Yorker* reviewer "the disparate alliance on the beach remains an implausible vision."

In this novel, Johnston states most explicitly the central struggle which occupies all her fiction: safety versus change. The perpetual hymn-singing of the old man is a cry for an unchanging world, death representing the farthest extreme of that wish. Nancy declares, "I like to be safe." But her Aunt Mary tells her, "You must move, re-energize. Don't just drift as I have always done. Your grandfather's dead and I am dying. Not. . . that I have ever lived. I've been happy, calm and useless most of the time. The great thing to remember is that there's nothing to be afraid of."

In a 1980 review of *The Irish Journals of Elizabeth Smith*, Johnston said of Smith: "She could never have been a novelist, although her observations are crisp and vivid, because she can never avoid moral comment." In her own fiction, Johnston's characters typically try to escape having to make choices, and if Johnston can be said to be guilty of voicing her own moral comment, it would be simply that one must choose, that a failure to choose is a failure to live.

Interviews:

Elgy Gillespie, "Jennifer Johnston," *Irish Times*, 3 March 1973;

Jeremy Bugler, "Writer With a War Outside," *Observer Magazine* (26 October 1975): 10;

Clare Boylan, "Jennifer Johnston: slim volumes, big talent," *Cosmopolitan* (November 1980): 93.

Gabriel Josipovici

(8 October 1940-   )

Linda Canon and Jay L. Halio
University of Delaware

BOOKS: *The Inventory* (London: M. Joseph, 1968);

Words (London: Gollancz, 1971);

The World and the Book: A Study of Modern Fiction (London: Macmillan, 1971; Stanford: Stanford University Press, 1971);

Mobius the Stripper: Stories and Short Plays (London: Gollancz, 1974);

The Present (London: Gollancz, 1975);

Migrations (Hassocks, U.K.: Harvester Press, 1977);

Four Stories (London: Menard Press, 1977);

The Lessons of Modernism and Other Essays (London: Macmillan, 1977; Totowa, N.J.: Rowman & Littlefield, 1977);

The Echo Chamber (Brighton: Harvester Press, 1980);

Vergil Dying (Windsor: Span Press, 1981);

The Air We Breathe (Brighton: Harvester Press, 1981);

Writing and the Body (Brighton: Harvester Press, 1982).

Novelist and literary theorist, playwright and university lecturer, short-story writer and critic: Gabriel Josipovici is all of these. His erudition is surpassed only by his sensitivity to language and artistic form, making him one of the leading experimentalists writing fiction in Britain today. Modernist and postmodernist writers such as Franz Kafka, Marcel Proust, T. S. Eliot, Alain Robbe-Grillet, and Claude Simon have deeply influenced him, but his work also reveals his fondness for Igor Stravinsky, Pablo Picasso, and Georges Braque, among those in other fields of art, as well as Roland Barthes, Ludwig Wittgenstein, Maurice Blanchot, and other philosophers and thinkers of this century. As his critical essays show, his knowledge extends well beyond this century, for he has written interesting and informed essays about Dante, Chaucer, Rabelais, and Hawthorne.

Gabriel David Josipovici was born on 8 October 1940, in Nice, France. His father, Jean, was of Rumanian-Jewish descent, and his mother, Sacha Rabinovitch, was the daughter of a Russian-Jewish doctor who had settled in Cairo around 1905 and married into a well-estabished Jewish family. His parents, who had been studying in France when he was born, separated when he was three years old. After the war his mother decided to move out of France back to Egypt (where her family still lived) so that Gabriel would avoid the rigid French school system. They settled in Maadi, Egypt, and Gabriel attended the English schools, such as Victoria College in Cairo (1950-1956). At fifteen Gabriel went to England to finish school at Cheltenham College, which he attended 1956-1957. After that, as he was too young to enter Oxford, he spent a year exploring London, visiting museums, attending concerts and theatrical performances, and in general experiencing the culture which Maadi could not provide. In 1958 he entered St. Edmund Hall, Oxford, on state scholarship to read English literature. He was graduated in 1961 with a first-class honors degree, and by 1963 he was married and teaching

English at the University of Sussex in Brighton. Today he still lectures there in a variety of courses.

Though they do not require it, Josipovici's five published novels as well as his short stories and plays gain in clarity and significance when approached through some understanding of his literary theory. His ideas are found in a number of critical essays, many of them collected in *The Lessons of Modernism and Other Essays* (1977), and particularly in *The World and the Book: A Study of Modern Fiction* (1971) where he explains his ideas on modernism and its development. For Josipovici, modernism was primarily "a calling into question of the norms and values not just of the nineteenth century, but of Western art and culture since the Renaissance. What all the moderns have in common," he goes on to argue, " . . . is an insistence on the fact that what previous generations had taken for *the world* was only *the world as seen through the spectacles of habit*." It is the achievement of modernists such as Picasso, Stravinsky, and Eliot that they reexamined the foundations not only of the medium in which they were working but of the entire Western tradition that lay behind it. In the process they created new works of art and compelled others to drop the "spectacles of habit" and look at art and its traditions afresh.

Josipovici's own achievements, like those of many contemporaries, continue the process, demanding that we approach their work with fewer preconceptions and expectations. For Josipovici, just as modern art is antirepresentational, the modern novel is "to some extent anti-novel," and "the best way of coming to grips with it is to understand the premises of the traditional novel." These premises are a product of the seventeenth century and more generally of the Renaissance which helped give rise to "realist" fiction and the basis in verisimilitude on which it depends. But there were alternative premises, as Cervantes, Rabelais, Swift, and Sterne, among earlier writers who stand outside of that tradition, show. As the modernists realized, the norms of the Renaissance do not necessarily correspond with the structure of reality, despite having "strong roots" in human psychology. The modernists did not argue that traditional norms were wrong; they maintained that other ways of looking at reality were also valid. "Habit and laziness, not faulty vision" were what the modernists were trying to fight, and in his criticism and fiction Josipovici also requires that we forego habitual attitudes and take a more strenuous approach to literature, reading books as they ask to be read, not as we are used to reading them. Some of Josipovici's critics,

unfortunately, have failed to cooperate in reading his work in that way, and thus they fall to complaining and carping that nothing much happens in his novels, or he really has little to say in his stories. "It is our view of what a book *ought* to be, of what a novel *ought* to do," Josipovici says, "which comes between us and the understanding of much modern fiction"—including his own fiction, he might have added.

In the concluding chapter of *The World and the Book*, Josipovici expands on this conflict between writer and reader. "By insisting that his book is a book and not the world," he says, "the author recognizes that *reading* is itself an activity, and he makes of it, in fact, the subject-matter of his work." Using examples from Jorge Luis Borges, Samuel Beckett, William Golding, and others, and developing the analogy of viewing reality through spectacles or frames, Josipovici argues that both the artist and the reader must recognize that removing the frames does not help us to see the world as it really is; the reality that must be seen is "the fact that we are condemned to see through frames," and this is what brings with it "a kind of freedom, for it stops us from falling into the trap of thinking that meaning inheres in words, objects or events." But since it is a normal human tendency to think in this way, the remedy must be repeated over and over again. Although each of Josipovici's novels differs from the others, they all make this essential point.

The Inventory (1968), Josipovici's first novel, is superficially about Joe Hyman, a lawyer, who is sent by his firm to take an inventory of the belongings of an old man who has just died. In the flat he meets two of the man's relatives, Susan and Gillian, cousins, and Gillian's unruly children, who spend time with Joe as he makes out his lists, parts of which precede and thus punctuate various sections of the novel, which is told mainly through dialogue. The structure and style are spiraling and sparse. Except for the inventory lists, little exposition is offered; instead, Josipovici juxtaposes motifs and time schemes and uses repetitions, Stravinsky-like, to gain a kind of "cubist" effect. Joe takes a long time to complete his task, for he believes he has fallen in love with querulous Susan, whose relationship to old David Hirsh and his son, Sam, he tries to get her to explain in a series of repetitive, increasingly anguished monologues. Was she in love with Sam? Susan's answer to her own question gives an indication of the texture of the novel as well as Josipovici's intense interest in language and its relation to reality: "I don't know. People cheat all the time. They say I love him or he loves me or I hate him, but things aren't like that, there isn't anything solid like love or hate, there are only stirrings, bits and pieces of emotion, nothing you can put down clearly and label, nothing you can talk about, saying I love or he loves or they love, just indeterminate feelings, emotions, as soon as you say: This is what happened, or That is what happened, as soon as you do that it's false, you've added something, taken something away. . . . You start out saying something and you end up by saying something else, words pile up, one on top of the other, and you try to pull them back, to make them mean what you want, but they go on rising higher and higher until you don't recognize them any more or the things they are saying. . . . How can I explain anything when as soon as I begin it turns into something else, something I never meant to say, but something that I now see could be true, is true, at least as true as any of the things I was going to say and didn't. . . . Nearly every day for a month, or two, or six, I saw two people. At the end of that time something happened. Why? Was there a reason? Now they are both dead and all that's left is this furniture, their belongings, their *havings*. And what does this tell us about their *beings*? Nothing. Precisely nothing. So what do you want me to tell you? What? What?"

As a first novel, *The Inventory* aroused interest among critics and readers, many of whom failed adequately to appreciate his second one, *Words* (1971). Although the anonymous reviewer in the *Times Literary Supplement* recognized Josipovici's real talent and part of the basic point of his novel, he betrayed a bias in favor of more realistic fiction, or the traditional novel, which *Words* is not, however much it borrows the recognizable conventions of dialogue and social intrigue. Like *The Inventory*, *Words* unfolds mainly through dialogue but without any long monologues and with a slightly more generous use of exposition. Jo, Louis's former lover, writes to Louis and his wife, Helen, and asks to visit them in their home near Southampton, where she will board the *Queen Elizabeth II* en route to meet her husband in San Francisco. Already visiting are Louis's brother and his wife, Peter and Tina, whose marriage seems shaky. Reluctantly, Louis agrees to the visit, whose purpose never seems entirely clear: was it just for old time's sake? for Jo to see if she could seduce Louis again and get him to run off with her? or to introduce her strange and silent child, Gillian, to them? or to meet Louis's wife? Through the endless and seemingly pointless chatter which occupies most of the dialogue, Josipovici epitomizes the strains upon modern marriage and life generally—its emptiness, ennui,

shallow human relationships, ego trips, and so on. But above all he shows the power—and the powerlessness—of which words are capable.

During these years, Josipovici was also engaged in writing literary criticism, stories, and plays. His play, *Evidence of Intimacy*, won the *Sunday Times* NUS (National Union of Students) Festival award in 1970. His first major volume of criticism, *The World and the Book*, was published both in England and the United States the following year, with most reviewers finding it an extraordinary and valuable piece of work. Typical are comments by R. W. Uphaus, who, recognizing Josipovici's considerable "learning and judgment," said: "At its best Josipovici's book is truly creative, for, like all good art, it transforms the reader's consciousness in such a way that we will never quite be able to return to our customary ways of reading literature." David Lodge, himself a literary critic and novelist, wrote a full length essay for *Critical Quarterly* on the book and ended with a discussion of the first two novels as they relate to Josipovici's critical theory. Although he disagrees with several of Josipovici's points and indeed his basic argument concerning the traditional novel, he acknowledges the strength of the book and its overall significance. He sums up its major thesis: "Like Eliot . . . Josipovici is an exponent of the idea of a Second Fall. . . . For Josipovici, too, the Second Fall, though long in preparation, occurred precisely round about the seventeenth century, and the dire consequence for literature was not a dissociation of sensibility, but realism. It is from literary realism . . . that modern fiction had freed us, restoring to us— not the unified and divinely meaningful universe of medieval Christianity, for that is lost forever, even to Christians—but something equivalently valuable and liberating for modern man: an understanding of the laws of existence, of the nature of human consciousness and human perception." But Lodge goes on to argue that "subtle and perceptive" as Josipovici's defense of modern fiction is, it is "damaged rather than reinforced by his prejudice against what he calls 'the traditional novel'—a prejudice which leads him not only to travesty the latter, but to deny its continuity with the former." Whether Josipovici's view of the traditional novel is prejudiced or not, as Lodge believes, his book stimulated much serious discussion of the issues he raised and continued to raise in subsequent critical work.

In 1974 Gollancz brought out a collection of Josipovici's stories and short plays under the title of one of its longer stories, *Mobius the Stripper*, which won the Somerset Maugham Award for fiction— later taken away because of Josipovici's foreign birth. As in his literary criticism and novels, these stories and plays show Josipovici's abiding interest in perception, primarily, and with the ways of establishing or ascertaining personal identity. Like a Talmudist or Thomist, Josipovici puts his characters through interrogatories, most directly and obviously in "The Reconstruction," a story entirely in dialogue that begins and ends with "Don't stop. Go on. Don't stop." The story simply called "This" (Josipovici has a predilection for short titles—"Colourings," "Refuse," "One" are some others) is likewise entirely composed of a dialogue between two characters, one questioning the other, who is trying to explain fully the significance of what he has seen on a walk down the sea front. Although it is merely the sight of a man and a child looking out of a window, the experience seems fraught with meaning; for example: "And remember that the plane not only divides, but brings together. . . . The plane allows me to relate to the world and the nearest thing to a window is perhaps language, which also separates in order to bring together." Like so much else in Josipovici's fiction, however, statements like this lead to further questions, and questions to still more questions, as the story ends.

The title story, subtitled "a Topological Exercise," shows Josipovici experimenting in other ways as well. Dividing his pages in half, he uses the upper half for a fairly straightforward account of a rather grotesque character called Mobius, a male stripper who speaks broken English and is very serious about his work. The lower half presents the related account of a writer and his large-footed girl friend, Jenny, who eggs him on to leave his typewriter—the serious-minded pursuit of *his* work—to gather experience, including the experience of seeing Mobius in action. The title, theme, and structure of the story thus derive from the concept of a Mobius strip, a single-surfaced geometrical figure that consists of a rectangle twisted 180° adjoined end to end. Similarly, in the play *Dreams of Mrs. Fraser*, which was first performed at the Theatre Upstairs, Royal Court, London, in August 1972, the stage is divided into two roughly equal areas, each having its own set and alternately lit or in total darkness as the thirty very brief scenes require. Performed entirely by two characters (a tape recording is also used), the action shifts between the sets (the actors changing costume rapidly, as necessary), fusing its two related parts.

Josipovici's success thus led John Mellors to describe him in the *Listener*, early in the following year, as "a born writer not afraid of the dark" and to comment on his tendency to ask questions "about

identity, truth, memory, death, and the relationships between mind and body and the writer and words." Recognizing several of Josipovici's literary forebears, he concluded that "his poetry is that of a late twentieth century Lewis Carroll whose Alice must wait for Godot when she wants intensely to get to Sidcup."

Like Josipovici's previous novels, *The Present* (1975) is told mainly in dialogue, although an omniscient narrator inserts bits of description here and there, always in the present tense. The three main characters are Reg, his wife, Minna, and their lodger Alex, a schoolteacher. The two men enjoy playing chess, Minna keeps house, and Alex goes to choir practice once or twice a week: a very ordinary existence—or so it seems. Then Alex commits suicide apparently by jumping from his window; Minna has a nervous breakdown and is hospitalized, where she is visited by Reg and Alex; scenes appear where Minna is married to Alex and has two children, both girls, whom they take on a picnic; and the novel ends with the three adults back in the small flat where Minna describes her long walk back from Greenwich, as she has done earlier in the novel. How much, then, has actually happened, and how much is Minna's fantasy? The puzzles in the book are evidently designed to force the readers actively to think: What is reality? What is happening? They cannot remain passive and allow the narrative to flow through them. Comparing *The Present* to the "texts" of Robbe-Grillet, critic Peter Ackroyd accurately remarked that "Josipovici creates more powerful effects because he lingers upon the human surface of the world. . . . The narrative is constantly interesting because the language has a lightness to it and it can float free of its themes. Old-fashioned 'characters', when they are created within this elliptical range, can come into their own instead of becoming the transparent integers of 'thought' and 'feeling'."

Despite the generally favorable, though not quite enthusiastic, critical reception of his fiction, Gollancz turned down Josipovici's next novel, *Migrations* (1977), which shows a still stronger influence of Robbe-Grillet, and his second collection of short fiction, *Four Stories* (1977), was published by the Menard Press with financial assistance from the Arts Council of Great Britain. In the same year, also, his second book of criticism, *The Lessons of Modernism and Other Essays*, was published by Macmillan. Although the essays collected in this volume were written over a six-year period beginning in 1970, usually for a specific occasion, Josipovici believed that they were closely related to each other in

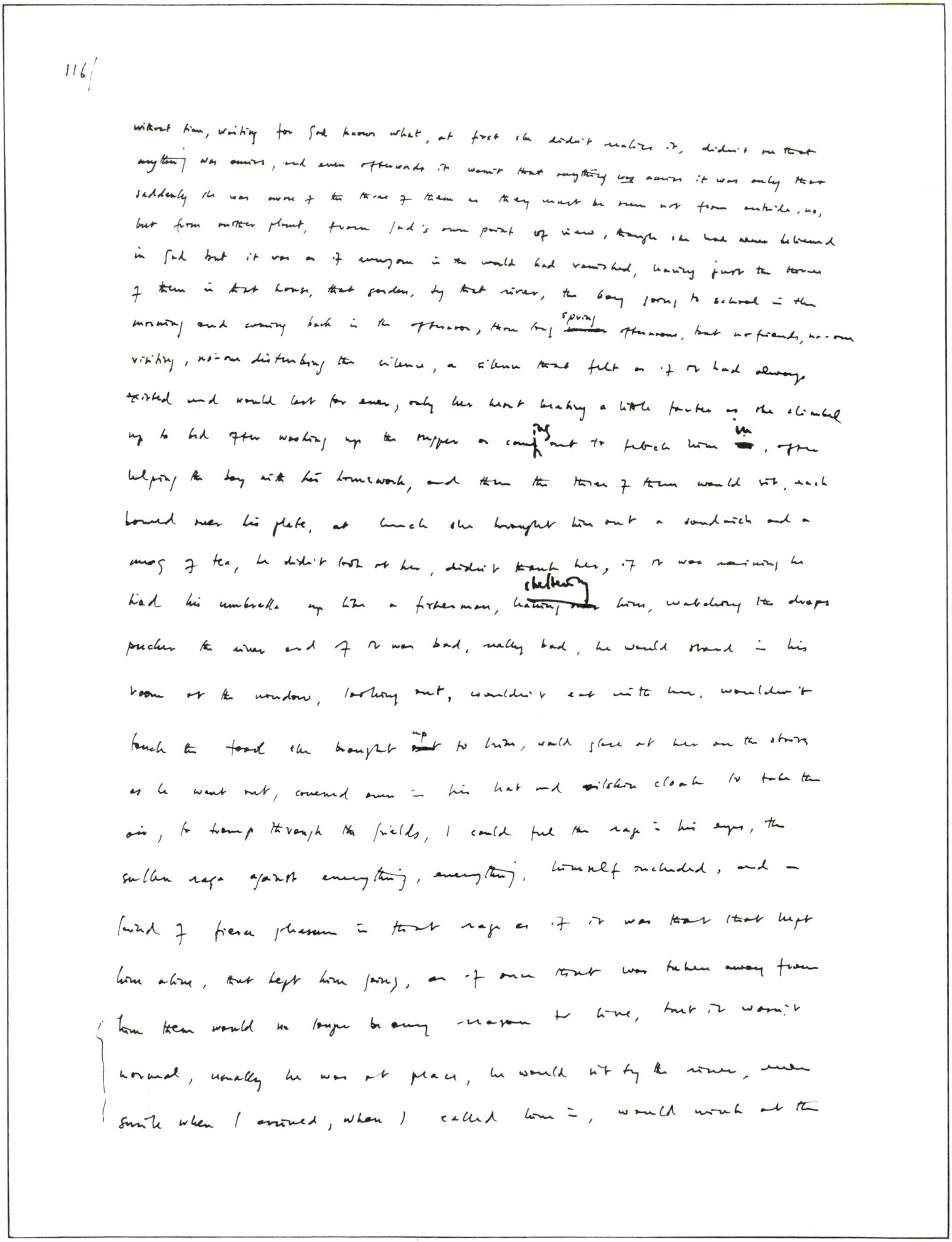

116/

without him, waiting for God knows what, at first she didn't realize it, didn't see that anything was amiss, and even afterwards it wasn't that anything was amiss it was only that suddenly she was aware of the three of them as they must be seen not from outside, no, but from another planet, from God's own point of view, though she had never believed in God but it was as if everyone in the world had vanished, leaving just the three of them in that house, that garden, by that river, the boy going to school in the morning and coming back in the afternoon, those long spring afternoons, but no friends, no-one visiting, no-one disturbing the silence, a silence that felt as if it had always existed and would last for ever, only her heart beating a little faster as she climbed up to bed after washing up the supper or coming out to fetch him in, after helping the boy with his homework, and then the three of them would sit, each bowed over his plate, at lunch she brought him out a sandwich and a mug of tea, he didn't look at her, didn't thank her, if it was raining he had his umbrella up like a fisherman, sheltering him, watching the drops pucker the river and if it was bad, really bad, he would stand in his room at the window, looking out, wouldn't eat with her, wouldn't touch the food she brought up to him, would glare at her on the stairs as he went out, covered over in his hat and oilskin cloak to take the air, to tramp through the fields, I could feel the rage in his eyes, the sullen rage against everything, everything, himself included, and a kind of fierce pleasure in that rage as if it was that that kept him alive, that kept him going, as if once that was taken away from him there would no longer be any reason to live, but it wasn't normal, usually he was at peace, he would sit by the river, even smile when I arrived, when I called him in, would wave at the

Page from the manuscript for The Air We Breathe

their concern not only to understand "the general problem of the possibility of culture in the modern world" but also to explore "the question of the limits of artistic expression," especially as these issues are raised in works like Thomas Mann's *Doktor Faustus*. Recognizing the conflict in modern critical theory between advocacy of the "impersonal" self and the terrifying destructiveness in shedding the self, he continues in his preface: "Art, the making of an artefact, becomes the means whereby the artist frees himself from the shackles of the self without disintegrating into chaos. In this view the artist is no longer either thinker or prophet . . . ; rather, he is a gymnast, developing his potential with each new exercise successfully mastered." The essays cover a wide range of authors and ideas related to these central concerns, and the title essay includes some acute observations on the teaching of literature. (It was first delivered to a meeting of the National Association of Teachers of English at York, 27 March 1972.) In another essay, called "Linearity and Fragmentation," Josipovici makes a comment that has a direct bearing on what he has been trying to achieve in his own writing:

> The principles of fragmentation and discontinuity, of repetition and spiralling, which we found underlying the works of Kafka, Eliot, Stevens, Proust, Robbe-Grillet, Virginia Woolf, and Beckett, do not reveal anything so banal as the final disintegration of the Western Imagination. What they perhaps reveal is a disintegration of a notion of Truth, and of the power of the intellect alone to discover that truth and embody it in works of art, which men had to take for granted in the centuries following the Renaissance. The fragmented or spiralling work denies us the comfort of finding a centre, a single meaning, a speakable truth, either in works of art or the world. In its stead it gives us back a sense of the potential of each moment, each word, each gesture and each event, and acknowledges the centrality of the process of creation and expression in all our lives.

This "spiralling" is perhaps nowhere more evident in Josipovici's novels than in *Migrations*, which depends (like the nouveau roman in France, to which it is indebted) upon a series of repetitions, however slightly varied, of events that give the novel its basic structure. The main character is a man, apparently in considerable agony of body and soul,

who is trying to understand his predicament. Unlike the previous novels, *Migrations* contains a good quantity of description as well as dialogue in the narration, which begins with the man in a bare room lying on a bed from which he arises from time to time to look out the window at the shops and cafes in the High Street, or to vomit violently in the sink. He imagines himself (or recalls) walking down the street waiting for a pub to open and then ordering beer, falling down on the pavement near a lamppost, lying in a hospital. In each repetition, some details are added, as in the various scenes in bed or with a woman, one of whom tries to get him to stay calm and not speak, while another (a prostitute) expresses willingness to hear him talk if he wishes (he doesn't), and still a third sits on a sofa and, like a character in "The Reconstruction," urges him to go on speaking. Emblematic of the structure and theme of this novel is the man's description of trying to sweep out the corners of his being or, reminded of a doctor who once cleansed his sinuses, to scrape out every part of his body. A recurrent motif is the image of Lazarus emerging from the grave, his shroud constantly unwinding until what is revealed is nothing but a little pile of dust. "And that is how it is and how it will be, when all can be spoken and we come back at last to our homeland," the man explains to the woman. "We live in that grave, in those clothes, in the pressure between nothing and everything, we live by perpetual movement from place to place but we want oh so much want to escape to say it all to come home at last to the right place our rightful place our rightful space. As if that was possible." If death is "the end of all migrations," the flux that characterizes existence, then identity must be sought elsewhere. At last the man sees that "We are in the interstices. In the intervals. We are that which moves between the spaces. Which conjures up the spaces. . . . Yes. That is what we are."

The Echo Chamber (1980), Josipovici's fifth novel, returns to the style of *Words* but with a significant difference: like a mystery thriller (the genre it parodies), it builds up suspense concerning an event and reaches its climax and epiphany only on the last page. Peter, a young man, is welcomed into the home of his Aunt Marion, who has fetched him from a hospital where he has been since having a kind of breakdown. Her house in the Cotswolds shelters a large number of others, including her daughters and their children, several men, a childless couple who share the house with her, and Miss Lear, a poet who was nurse to Peter's mother. Yvonne, one of Marion's daughters, spends much time talking with Peter, urging him to look behind the veil, or cloud, that obscures his memory of what caused his illness. Gradually he finds he can, although at one point he becomes so restless and upset that he avoids Yvonne and wishes to leave. Finally, as they are on one of their many walks, the veil lifts completely. What Peter sees, however, is not only the memory of an event but the premonition of a disaster about to happen before his very eyes.

The social milieu Josipovici creates in *The Echo Chamber* is excellent, and one is tempted to suggest that he has begun to make some concessions to traditional fiction. But these may be more apparent then real: Josipovici's interests, first and last, are in exploring human consciousness. In this sense, the novel, like his others, is a study in phenomenology, but as an artist studies it. The epigraph is from Wallace Stevens and clearly suggests the title: "When the mind is like a hall in which thought is like a voice speaking, the voice is always that of someone else."

In 1979 Josipovici wrote a ninety-minute monologue for Paul Scofield that was performed on BBC Radio's Third Programme. It was called *Vergil Dying* and was later published by Span in 1981. In the winter of 1981 he gave the Lord Northcliffe Lectures at University College, London, under the title *Writing and the Body*, which were published in 1982.

Gabriel Josipovici plans to continue teaching six months a year and to devote the other half of his time to writing. His most recent novel, *The Air We Breathe*, was published in late 1981.

Other:

The Portable Saul Bellow, edited by Josipovici (New York: Viking, 1974);

The Modern English Novel: the reader, the writer, and the work, edited by Josipovici (London: Open Books; New York: Barnes & Noble, 1976).

Reference:

David Lodge, "Onions and Apricots; or, Was the Rise of the Novel a Fall from Grace? Serious Reflections on Gabriel Josipovici's *The World and the Book*," *Critical Quarterly*, 14 (Summer, 1972): 171-185.

Maurice Leitch
(5 July 1933-   )

Gordon Henderson

BOOKS: *Liberty Lad* (London: MacGibbon & Kee, 1965: New York: Pantheon, 1967);

Poor Lazarus (London: MacGibbon & Kee, 1969);

Stamping Ground (London: Secker & Warburg, 1975).

The subject of Maurice Leitch's three brooding and pessimistic novels is Northern Ireland. It is not the Northern Ireland of hunger strikes, political demonstrations, guerilla ambushes, and stone-throwing confrontations between Catholics and Protestants that one might expect. Although he does not entirely ignore secular violence, Leitch focuses instead on the spiritual toll the country's split personality has taken on its inhabitants. His Ulster is a place of little beauty, no nobility, no hope. His characters tend to be grotesques, too twisted and weakened to save even themselves. All want to leave, but few ever do.

Leitch was born to Protestant parents in Muckamore, County Antrim, and was educated at area schools and in Belfast. He taught in a primary school in the town of Antrim for six years and contributed free-lance articles and scripts to the local newspapers and BBC radio. In 1962 he began working full-time for the BBC in Belfast and continued there as a features producer until 1970, when he moved to London.

Like many first novels, *Liberty Lad* (1965) is a novel of initiation. In telling of a young teacher's last year of freedom before he must come to terms with the squalid truths of Northern Ireland, Leitch draws on his experiences of growing up in a small industrial village and of teaching students whose

apathy and lack of opportunity rarely let them rise much above it. Frank Glass, the twenty-four-year-old schoolmaster, lives with his parents in a shabby row of redbrick homes built a hundred years earlier to house the workers of the local linen mill. The mill in Kildargen is slowly shutting down and with it the hopes of Glass's parents. His education alienates him from their working-class world, and his Protestant upbringing cuts him off from the Catholics of the village. "Anything I found out about them," he says, "has been secondhand, because living in a community like this, one where the proportions are seventy-five for us, twenty-five for *them* (an inflammable mixture) division starts early—separate housing estates, then separate schools, separate jobs, separate dances, separate pubs." He looks down on Catholics as "a people with a past and no interest in the present, because they have been frogmarched back to that past so often that they have long ago given up any claims to right now." But

he also envies them for "their calm inner knowledge of what they are, who they are and where they came from."

Feeling no such sense of identity, Glass isolates himself behind a conviction that he is better than those he sees around him and is somehow different. He lectures his parents on the folly of their stoic resignation and—romantically rationalizing his constant sarcasm as "the old deadly derision, the curse which we are all born with in this cold cynical northern province"—looks with mocking disdain on the petty rivalries of his fellow teachers and the affected manners of the Protestant gentry. Glass's drinking companion and partner in derision is Terry Butler, whose homosexuality and the need to conceal it make him also feel he is a displaced person. Both soon find, however, that an air of disdain offers little real protection against the realities of life in Antrim. When a scandal threatens to expose Terry's homosexuality, he has no choice but to emigrate. Glass's own fantasies of sexual passion are frustrated when a married secretary at the school, who leads him along by arranging secret meetings, repeatedly refuses to go to bed with him out of fear of being exposed and censured. He is also thwarted in his bid to become principal of the school when he finds that he is expected to pay with homosexual favors for the support of a local politician. By the end of the novel, Glass has been sobered by failure, compromise, and the death of his father. At the funeral in the closing scene, he weeps not for his father but "for the loss of something else, me, as I had been once, three, four years . . . a year ago." Whatever sense of superiority he may retain over Antrim and its spiritually stunted inhabitants, his future stretches ahead, there and among them.

The novel's chief strengths are its physical descriptions of the decaying town and its often humorous accounts of Glass's experiences in the classroom and among his fellow teachers. Leitch is less successful in integrating homosexuality into the novel as a metaphor for social and cultural sterility or in engaging the reader's sympathy for what is happening to Glass: the adolescent arrogance that masks his sensitivity makes him an unattractive protagonist, as does the self-pity with which he finally begins to meet responsibility. The novel, however, was generally well received, with most reviewers praising it for its honesty and exuberance.

If Glass is merely unattractive, the central character of Leitch's second novel, *Poor Lazarus* (1969), is positively grotesque. But he is also much more powerfully drawn. A Protestant shopkeeper in the predominately Catholic village of Ballyboe, a few miles north of the border separating Northern Ireland from the South, Albert Yarr is coarse, sadistic, and misogynistic, a man of cruel humor who humiliates his aging father in front of customers by setting fire to his newspaper and then dowsing him with water, and who thinks it a "a great gas" to roll up his car window on the necks of female hitchhikers and drag them stumbling behind him. Also a man of brutish sexual appetites, he becomes so tormented by his increasing impotence that he first browbeats and finally physically abuses his pregnant wife, Ruby.

As the novel begins, Yarr is teetering at the edge of madness, kept just short of the brink by drugs and periodic electroshock treatments. At the root of his problems is the isolation he feels among the villagers at a time when IRA border attacks have made it unwise for them to patronize his shop. His position is analogous to that of a black shopkeeper living among whites in the American South during a Ku Klux Klan flare-up: "He lived his life in an anthill, a tolerated guest, ignored, as they moved about skirting him carefully, day to day, but one false move and they could turn on him, picking his bones white any afternoon they chose." Complicating his frustrations is the social and intellectual superiority he feels over his neighbors, who meet his pretensions with maddening indifference: "All those faces, not showing enmity, just nothingness. It couldn't be described, just borne." While Glass's sense of superiority finds an outlet in derision, Yarr's is kept bottled inside, souring first into disgust, then into hatred, and finally into paranoia. He remains buried within himself until someone comes along to lift him, like Lazarus, out of his isolation. The agent of this resurrection is Edward P. Quigley, a Canadian television producer who comes to Ballyboe to film a documentary on the old country and enlists Yarr as his unofficial guide.

But Quigley is also facing a crisis. After a series of unsuccessful assignments, he must make good on this one or lose his job. His boss wants slick journalism; Quigley sees himself as an artist but does not realize that his vision is too limited to create art. He comes to Ballyboe expecting an Irish Shangri-la but, even with Yarr as his guide, cannot reconcile his cliched expectations and the corruption he sees oozing below the shamrocks. Like Yarr, he is accustomed to using people callously. In their symbiotic relationship, Quigley strokes Yarr's ego to learn about Ireland. Yarr in turn uses Quigley, but he expects much more from him: he thinks his association with this important outsider will give him stature in the village, that his insider's knowledge of Irish life will win Quigley's friendship, and that this man's acceptance of him as an equal will at last raise him out of his chronic depression. All of Yarr's expectations, however, are frustrated. The cruel jokes he engineers to amuse Quigley only widen the gap between him and the villagers; their wary indifference heightens his conviction that they are conspiring against him; and his role as a pimp for Quigley fans his rage at his own impotence. The final crushing of his expectations comes when he reads the journalist's diary and learns that Quigley is not only a Catholic but also considers Yarr a twisted oddball. This betrayal pushes Yarr over the brink of madness and into destruction.

Poor Lazarus is an ugly book but an engrossing one. The plot is firmly controlled as it moves forward in scenes alternating between the points of view of the superficial Quigley and the tormented Yarr and builds to a climactic cock fight that lays bare the underlying cruelty, sadism, and insensitivity of rural Ulster. Leitch's handling of physical and emotional landscape is reminiscent of Faulkner's in the Snopes novels, and his characterization of Yarr is masterful. Albert Yarr is a monster of banal desires, made pathetic by his desire for dignity and tragic by his attempts to control his madness. The irony of the novel's conclusion calls to mind Yeats's vision in "The Second Coming." While Quigley tries to convince himself that with the birth of Yarr's child everything will become bright and good, the reader is more likely to think of Yeats's rough beast slouching toward birth in a world where things fall apart and "the worst are full of passionate intensity."

Poor Lazarus was a best-selling novel and a critical success. It was awarded the *Guardian* fiction prize for 1969. The *Times Literary Supplement* praised Leitch for "making a distinct contribution" to the "modern literature of man on the edge of the abyss," and the *Observer* applauded the novel for conveying forcefully "the bigotry and sullen hatreds of Northern Irish life . . . its coarse indolence, stupidity and stunted sexuality."

After the publication of *Poor Lazarus*, Leitch moved from Belfast to London in 1970 to work as a scriptwriter and radio drama producer at the BBC's central offices. He is now head of BBC Radio's drama features. The subject matter of his novels, however, has remained the Northern Ireland of his boyhood. In *Stamping Ground* (1975), he moves from the 1960s of his first two novels back to the 1950s. He also shifts his setting to an isolated valley deep in the hills of Antrim, where he is able to deal with more elemental conflicts than he had in the

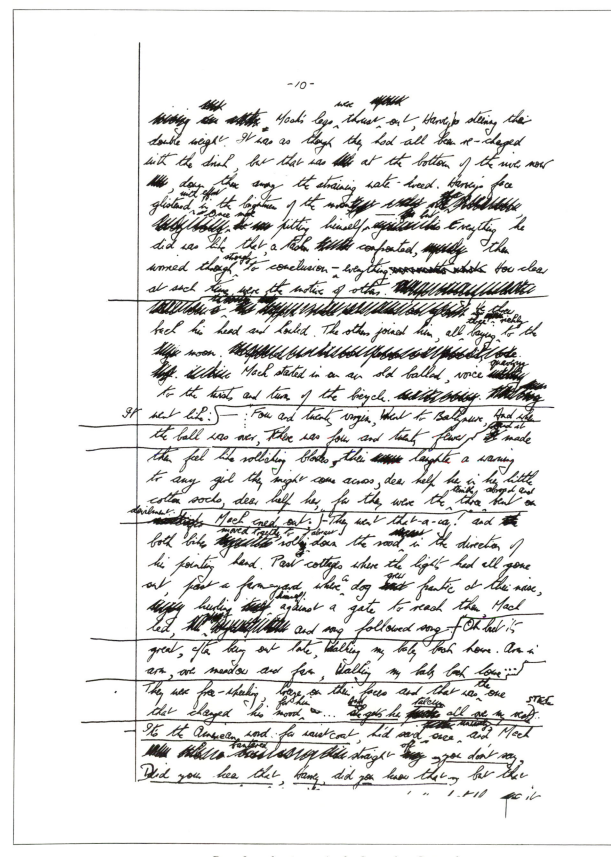

Page from the manuscript for Stamping Ground

earlier books. The valley itself becomes an antagonist, with the pumping beat of the dam at its heart acting as a chorus to the events. Frank Glass again appears as one of his characters, this time as a college student working on a farm during summer vacation. Working with him are two friends: Harvey, a muscular, slow-witted Clydesdale of a boy, and Mack, a moody and sometimes violent practical joker. The dull, simple work of the farm requires only plodding physical exertion, and Frank notices that even at meals they are like "farm animals, recouping lost energies, holding in and on, cunning, watchful." The only thing to engage their imaginations is an occasional film at the village movie-house. The boys all wear their hair cut close "in the current American film-star mode" and imagine themselves as "private-eyes, jazzmen, champion boxers, submarine captains, gamblers and gigolos." Their heroes are Broderick Crawford, Lloyd Nolan, Richard Widmark, Cornel Wilde, Lex Barker.

The novel's plot has the unity, dramatic inevitability, and mythic overtones of a Greek play, and the recurrent references to movie stars provide an ironic commentary on the imaginative and emotional poverty of characters whose mythology in a more heroic age would have been peopled by gods from Olympus. The novel's two other central characters are Hetty, a young servant girl who is just beginning to feel the stirrings of her sexuality, and Barbour Brown, a retired schoolmaster, whose eccentricities include playing peeping Tom under the guise of bird-watching, and dressing up in an Edwardian costume for midnight strolls through the countryside. His fantasies are drawn from old lithographs rather than from Hollywood films.

The action of the novel takes place over a single day and night, beginning in the afternoon with a puppyish tussle in a hayfield between Hetty and the three boys and ending just before dawn the next morning when they rape her as Brown looks on surreptitiously. In the intervening hours, the boys get drunk at a mountain tavern, attend a rustic dance, and race one another on bicycles through the night; Hetty is given some quaintly Victorian instructions on sex by an elderly spinster, attends the same dance, gets tipsy on her employer's wine, and dances naked through the house; and Brown pursues his voyeuristic ramblings. The forces that draw the five characters together for the final act of violence are stronger and more primitive than any of them are equipped to handle: nature's energy breaking out in harvest, the heat of the night, the steady pounding of the pumping station, the full moon, and, most important, a sexuality so suppres-

sed that it almost has to explode.

The rape itself takes on the aura of a pagan ritual, suggesting nature being ravished and impregnated with new life. Its aftermath, however, makes clear that nearly the opposite is true. Leitch's Antrim has drained his characters of any vital energy. All four are curiously untouched by what has happened. Even after an act of genuine passion, neither Hetty nor the boys can view it in terms of anything but another Hollywood scenario. Glass sees Hetty as "just like someone in the movies," and Hetty, borrowing a line from the film *Casablanca*, raises her wine glass and toasts herself with, "Here's looking at you." She knows that the boys' fumbling efforts have not left her pregnant, that "nothing could possibly come out of that daft performance." Only Brown is affected deeply. In a fantasy he jumbles Hetty's rape together with another that happened in the valley hundreds of years before and imagines that he was the agent of both. Despite his fantasies, it is evident that the sterile old bachelor is incapable of impregnating anything. As the novel ends, Leitch suggests that nothing of value will come of the ritual. Hetty will use her sex as a means of manipulating men; Harvey will continue on as a dumb "farm animal"; the brooding Mack—who proves impotent during the rape—may well become another Yarr; and Glass seems destined to be another barren and sexually confused old bachelor like Brown.

Apart from the power of its narrative, what is most impressive about the novel is the richness and variety of its characterization. With her mixture of innocence and sexuality, Hetty is Leitch's only truly attractive character to date, and Barbour Brown is one of his most fascinating, a man who meticulously records in five large notebooks the comings and goings of the valley's inhabitants and who can, while convinced that his efforts are directed toward a scholarly history, admit in a rare moment of self-knowledge that "he was an old goat who liked nothing better than to watch young girls as they bared their bums in the middle of a wood or behind a hedge." Leitch peoples his landscape with other grotesques and eccentrics: Minnie Maitland, a ladylike alcoholic spinster who presides over a crumbling mansion packed with Victorian antiques and the unfulfilled dreams of her girlhood; the "bicycle-mad McKibbin family," practicing constantly for races they have no chance of winning; Frank Cooley, a cracked, childlike war veteran, and his tormenter Henry Gault, a cruel, cunning farmer who, "in his relationships with other people, resembled nothing so much as someone turning over stones to see what lay beneath and never once betraying a response to what might be found there"; and a character called *Exchange & Mart* because of his mania for ordering bargain items from that publication and transforming his cottage into "a warehouse for Admiralty compasses and binoculars, army surplus water-bottles, haversacks, jack-knives, mess tins, stoves and clothing from every theatre of war—his own uniform . . . a German battle-dress, an Australian bush-hat and R.A.F. flying boots, winter and summer."

After *Poor Lazarus* was published, Leitch said he wanted to get away from writing such obviously regional fiction. *Stamping Ground* proves that, so far at least, Northern Ireland has not lost its fascination for him. It is just as well. His fellow Ulsterman, novelist, and short-story writer, Patrick Boyle, considers *Stamping Ground* his best work to date, calling it "a brilliant success" and "a book that gives fresh insight into the behavioral pattern of the unfortunate people of Northern Ireland." The *Times Literary Supplement* said that, while more uneven than *Liberty Lad* or *Poor Lazarus*, "it is in its way more of an achievement" and that Leitch is "staking out his own corner in modern Irish fiction." The small corner of Ulster that Leitch has staked out is beginning to take on the mythic proportions of William Faulkner's Yoknopatawpha County. As John Wilson Foster has pointed out in a recent study of Ulster fiction, his Antrim is a microcosm for the entire region. Unlike Faulkner's county, however, it is a region that lacks a sense of either faded glory or future hope, and recent history suggests that its problems may be more intractable than those of Faulkner's South. Leitch's pessimism about his native land comes across strongly in his novels. Even the occasional flashes of humor only emphasize the pervading darkness. His readers can only hope that, despite his announced intentions, he continues to plumb its depths and add more memorable characters to its odd populaton.

Reference:

John Wilson Foster, *Forces and Themes in Ulster Fiction* (Totowa, N.J.: Rowan & Littlefield, 1974), pp. 268-274.

Penelope Lively

(17 March 1933–   )

Jane Langton

BOOKS: *Astercote* (London: Heinemann, 1970; New York: Dutton, 1971);

The Whispering Knights (London: Heinemann, 1971; New York: Dutton, 1976);

The Wild Hunt of Hagworthy (London: Heinemann, 1971); republished as *The Wild Hunt of the Ghost Hounds* (New York: Dutton, 1972);

The Driftway (London: Heinemann, 1972; New York: Dutton, 1973);

The Ghost of Thomas Kempe (London: Heinemann, 1973; New York: Dutton, 1973);

The House in Norham Gardens (London: Heinemann, 1974; New York: Dutton, 1974);

Boy Without a Name (London: Heinemann, 1975);

Going Back (London: Heinemann, 1975; New York: Dutton, 1975);

A Stitch in Time (London: Heinemann, 1976; New York: Dutton, 1976);

The Stained Glass Window (London: Abelard-Schuman, 1976);

Fanny's Sister (London: Heinemann, 1976);

The Presence of the Past (London: Collins, 1976);

The Road to Lichfield (London: Heinemann, 1977);

The Voyage of QV66 (London: Heinemann, 1978; New York: Dutton, 1979);

Nothing Missing but the Samovar (London: Heinemann, 1978);

Fanny and the Monsters (London: Heinemann, 1979);

Treasures of Time (London: Heinemann, 1979; Garden City: Doubleday, 1980);

Fanny and the Battle of Potter's Piece (London: Heinemann, 1980);

Judgement Day (London: Heinemann, 1980; Garden City: Doubleday, 1981);

The Revenge of Samuel Stokes (London: Heinemann; 1981; New York: Dutton, 1981);

Next to Nature, Art (London: Heinemann, 1982).

Penelope Lively has been a prolific writer since the appearance of her first book in 1970. Some of her books for children have already been called classics, and her more recent novels for adults have also been highly acclaimed. Britain's highest award for children's literature, the Carnegie Medal, was given to Lively for *The Ghost Of Thomas Kempe* (1973) in 1974, and her second adult novel, *Treasures of Time* (1979), was the winner of Great Britain's first National Book Award for fiction in 1980.

Her theme is often the lasting mystery of the flow of time. Again and again her books show her concern with the continuity of the past into the present, and the subtle relation between collective memory (history) and personal memory. She has always been interested in the jumbled layers of history in the English landscape, where "sixteenth century cottages sprout television aerials and a medieval barn bears graffitti celebrating distant football teams." How differing perceptions of time and memory affect human relations is a central problem, and the abrasions that occur when brash modernity rubs elbows with an older, less fashionable culture. In *Judgement Day* (1980), Lively examines the oldest of dilemmas, the undeserved stroke of fate, the presence of evil, once again in a setting where the past heaves uneasily below a thin skim of today. A novelist of manners as well as of ideas, she builds her highly structured narratives in swiftly moving scenes, and brings them to bright, vivid life in the precise gestures and speech of contemporary men, women, and children.

Penelope Lively was born in Cairo, Egypt, to Vera Greer and Roger Low. Her father was a manager in the National Bank of Egypt. She had no formal schooling, but there were other kinds of education: "I am eight, I think. Or nine. . . . I am in Africa—in Egypt—standing in a desert. There is a war on, off-stage. . . . I am looking at a shallow depression in the sand. Within the depression, curled like a foetus, is the delicate structure of a skeleton. . . . A person. A once-person. This person, I am told, lived here thousands of years ago. Thousands. We have come to this spot in the desert to be shown this person by someone called an archaeologist . . . while above us in a hard blue sky the R. A. F. planes chug toward Tripoli. . . ."

At twelve she was sent to England to attend "that particularly barbaric institution, the English boarding school, where I spent five wretched years and learned little except endurance." She had always liked reading and was quite ready to learn, but "the school aimed at turning out competent hockey and lacrosse players and did not encourage other activities." When *The Oxford Book of English Verse* was found in her locker, she was scolded. She would be taught poetry, complained the headmistress, and therefore there was no need to read it on her own.

But in England she was again made aware of the continuity of the past in the physical landscape. "I am thirteen. . . . I stand in Cheapside, in the heart of the City of London. . . . All around there is a sea of rubble. . . . The bombs have stripped the landscape down to its origins: the medieval street plan, the exposed bastions of the Roman wall. Time is lying there in front of me. . . . I am excited, I am lifted out of the prison of my own head and glimpse something larger."

It is not surprising that she undertook the study of modern history at St. Anne's College, Oxford, where her enthusiasms were no longer frowned upon. After taking her B. A. degree in 1954 she worked as a research assistant in Oxford. At St. Antony's College she met Jack Lively, a research fellow, and married him 27 June 1957. The Livelys have two children, Josephine, born in 1958, and Adam, born in 1961. They live in London and Oxfordshire. Jack Lively, a professor of politics at the University of Warwick, is the author of books on political theory, among them *Democracy*.

A fascination with English history is the foundation for most of Lively's books for children. She has described them as "deeply rooted in the English landscape and . . . , in different ways, concerned with the permanence of place and the strong feeling of continuity that haunts the English countryside and expresses itself so variously—physically in the very structure of fields, roads, woods and buildings; and imaginatively in the folklore and mythology."

In her first book, *Astercote* (1970), the historical continuity is awesome. The people of Astercote fear a return of the Black Death that destroyed their village 600 years before. The glittering eye of the television camera, probing their picturesque despair, fails to see into the heart of the matter, the disappearance of the ancient chalice on which, they are convinced, their health depends. Two children help to bring about its return, and all is well.

Myth and history are mingled again in *The Whispering Knights* (1971), when Morgan le Fay turns up in a Rolls Royce, and in *The Wild Hunt of Hagworthy* (1971) when the revival of an ancient dance with masks and antlers arouses equally ancient evil spirits. In *The Driftway* (1972), runaway children encounter travelers from earlier times on the venerable old road from Banbury to Northampton.

Best-known of these stories in which the past leans hard upon the present is *The Ghost of Thomas Kempe*. Lively intended it to be "a light-hearted book about the trials of a ten-year-old boy plagued by the presence of a poltergeist of a seventeenth-century magician." But at the same time she was trying to suggest to the child reader "something of the palimpsest quality of both people and places, those layerings of memory of which both are composed. And, also, the interlocking of people with place and time—that you and I are, inescapably, set against this or that backcloth, that our lives run for their

short span against the greater continuity of history. Even if you are eight, or nine, or thirteen, and as ignorant as sin, you can grasp that astonishing idea, and be enlarged by it."

Here is James, the young hero of the story, himself undergoing enlargement: "The light ebbed from the church. Shadows began to pack the roof and crowd around the pillars and dark oak pews. The knight and his lady lay on their tomb with worn faces and stiff stone drapery. He was a crusading knight, armoured from head to pointed feet . . . he must have known strange, hot, faraway places, and then come back to die in Ledsham, among elms and willows beside the Evenlode. . . . The church was very dark and quiet now, but not empty, because no place that has been used for so long by so many people can ever be empty. Like all old buildings, it was full of their thoughts and feelings, and these thoughts and feelings seemed to crowd in upon James. . . . "

With two later books for young people, *The House in Norham Gardens* (1974) and *Going Back* (1975), Lively turns away from the fantasies for younger children in the direction of the adult novels to come. In the first of these, fourteen-year-old Clare needs no magic to make her aware of the thoughts and feelings that crowd in upon her from the house in Norham Gardens. For her the house is already thick with the youthful memories of her two old aunts. But in the attic she finds something from a time and place further away: a carving stolen from the primitive people of New Guinea by her anthropologist great-grandfather. For a time Clare is haunted by it, but at last she breaks the hold upon her of the past and reaches into the future by planting a beech sapling as a gift for one of the aged aunts. At the end of the book she looks ahead into her own future, wondering what she will be like: "Someone quite different. She tried to project herself forwards in time to meet her, this unknown woman with her name and face, and failed. She walked away, the woman, a stranger, familiar and yet unreachable. The only thing you could know about her for certain was that all this would be part of her: this room, this conversation, the aunts."

Going Back is a stretch in the other direction. It is told in the first person by a grown woman who returns to explore the house in which she spent her childhood, to relive it in memory. In writing the book, Lively was using her own memories of her grandmother's house and garden in West Somerset. "Not only was the landscape a real one, real and vivid to me, but in describing it I was using that very function of memory that I was trying to suggest in the book—the fragmented, dreamy, preserved quality of selective recollection." Much of the book's charm lies in these lucid remembered fragments:

> We are at the orchid place in the quarry, Edward and I, and a rabbit's head lies among the purple-spotted orchids, where the bees unconcernedly feed, a dreadful, shameful thing, and we turn tail and run. . . .

> In the pond, the goldfish slide under the lily-pads. . . . We lie on our faces, our bodies cold against the flagstones, and stare down at them, so close that our breath dents the water. . . .

In *The Road to Lichfield* (1977), Lively's first novel for adults, "the palimpsest quality" of people and places becomes more complex, the truth about the past more shifty and paradoxical. The life of Anne Linton, wife, mother, and teacher of history, has two poles. One is the village of Cuxing, where she lives with her children and her husband, who is conventional and a little dull. The other is Lichfield, 100 miles away. There her father is dying slowly in a nursing home. Again and again she visits him, and there in Lichfield she falls in love with a married man. As she goes through her father's papers she discovers, to her amazement, that her adultery is mirrored in his own long extramarital affair. Her memories of family life are turned upside-down. Back and forth along the road she drives, bewildered, guilty, enraptured. As everything in her life swings and changes, her father dies, her love is choked off, and only the road remains permanent. The book resounds with thrumming reverberations from the past, with time-shufflings back and forth. For example, when the trendy hostess at a party is unable to explain the original use of the old agricultural tool she has hung on her wall for decoration, elderly Miss Standish speaks up:

> "That's a dibble," said Miss Standish suddenly, "for planting seeds . . . I know because of course I remember it as a child . . . " her voice trailed away.
> "Yes," said Sandra. "Fascinating. Now had we better get on, I wonder?"

Fourteen short stories are collected in Lively's next book for adults, *Nothing Missing but the Samovar* (1978). She has described her dependence on something she calls "the digestion of memory" in writing them. "A number of these have derived from experiences of my own twenty years or more ago; at the time the experiences seemed quite without significance. Years later, I have been able to see them in another light, and use them as the vehicle for a story that illuminates something that was in no way apparent to me at the time."

Here the edgy shifts and changes often lie in the gap between generations. In the story called "Party" an old woman and her grandson are the only innocents in the house. They spend the entire night happily making model airplanes while the middle generation, drunk and lecherous, indulges in an orgy.

In another story, "Interpreting the Past," reverence for antiquity is mangled by the emotional starvations of the dowdy archeologist who is excavating an ancient priory on the thousandth anniversary of its consecration. The ancient bones of a baby are scattered on the floor as Maggie Spink repudiates her lost love: " 'You go nuts that way, mulling things over. Take my word for it. Wipe the slate clean—wham!' She swept her arm across the table in a decisive gesture; sherds and other bits and pieces went flying; she was quite drunk now . . . 'Wham! Bam! Finish!' "

In Lively's second full-length novel for adults, *Treasures of Time*, the smooth contours of the historic past are again rumpled by the seething present. A television documentary is proposed in tribute to the archeological discoveries of the late Hugh Paxton, even though it is clear to the reader that he may have been a little hasty in rushing his findings into print. As the camera crew transforms his perhaps not altogether accurate conclusions into a less than truthful but artistically tidy film, there is a tortured dance on the sidelines by Paxton's mean-spirited widow, Laura; his unhappy daughter, Kate; and Kate's carefree lover, Tom. The quiet center around which the storm gathers is Laura's modest sister, Nellie.

Nellie had loved Paxton and had shared his lifelong passion for archeology, but Laura had married him. As beautiful as she was shallow, Laura had awakened in him another kind of passion. The survivor of their unhappy marriage, Laura is still beautiful, respectable, brutal, and vile. Her sister Nellie has had a stroke and must use a wheelchair. But only Nellie accepts her fate without complaint, while all the others struggle for what they desire. When lightning strikes the lintel of Paxton's neolithic barrow during the filming, its collapse is the prelude to other disasters. Nellie dies. Laura is shattered, even though she had tyrannized her sister for years. Kate, glum and pitiable, loses her

22

flower garden beyond. ~~Orxix~~ *Very like people* ~~admittedly there is the chance~~ ~~that one supposes quite wrong.~~ These two, her and Mrs P. - living on here like this - photo albums, cupboardsfull of Hugh Paxton's stuff, Mrs P. - <u>Laura</u> - bored to tears. Why not go out and find a job? But of course ladies like th t don't. ~~Wrong generations~~ The odd morning in the Oxfam shop; a bit of ~~righteous~~ *organised* indignation about threats to the environment - those would be the only options open. Aunt Nellie, of course, seems to be a different kettle of fish, from what one hears.

And he set off now across the lawn, ~~driven by~~ propelled by guilt and a heave of curiosity, to see if help mightn't be acceptable with this ~~~~ pruning or whatever it was she was up to.

And Nellie, intent on a battle with the suckers of a Madame Butterfly in which most advantages were held by the rose, and in her ~~~~ thoughts not present at all, but busy with the reconstruction of this same spot on an afternoon some thirty odd years ago, turned at the sound of movement and saw a man ~~~~ standing in the dark frame of the yew.

~~Hugh~~ And there surges th t i*exquisite tide* ~~irresistible feeling~~ of pleasure, ~~that with~~ *of excitement,* ~~ludicrously x~~ *of fear* ~~ludicrously recalls the childish thrill of presents, Christmas and~~ ~~birthday - perhaps not after all so ridiculous, maybe he since it is always the same,~~ ~~basits remains sources whatever its sources.~~

And I say quickly, to cover my feelings because I am very unsure, as yet, what his might be, "It's a lovely garden, Hugh - or at least it will be when you can get it going again, of course it's all in a dreadful mess now".

It has been /~~Blighted~~ by the war, as we all are. . . Five years older, gathering ourselves together, starting out again. Hugh does not look five years older; his hair is as thick and black as ever and he has the remains of a Far Eastern tan still: he is recently back from India.

I ~~had~~ have not seen him since 1939, that Hampshire dig. Though *one has* ~~thought~~ - oh yes, thought a great deal, through long *dreary* ~~dull~~ hours ~~of~~ at the Ministry, or firewatching, or sorting ~~~~ evacuees.

And the actuality is up to the expectation, and beyond, and here, now, am I with him on a visit to this house that he is almost certainly going to buy. And this afternoon we shall go up to West Kennet to take some measurements he needs and then back to London, hours of time with him, hours and hours, and ~~then~~ beyond that there stretches ahead the whole amazing unbelievable prospect of the Lillington dig. I shall see him, on and off, all summer.

Beyond the garden, the landscape blazes; it reflects my feelings; it glows and

Page from the revised typescript for Treasures of Time

fiance. Only Tom gets off lightly, exiting in partnership with Tony, whose juggernaut film lumbers forward in spite of everything.

Can the past, the reader is meant to wonder, ever be rightly understood? There are several revelations of Paxton's character as he is remembered by Nellie, by Laura, by Kate, and each view is different. History itself reaching back beyond living memory, is further unreliable, a fact regretted by Tom, as he conducts his own research into the life of a certain seventeenth-century antiquarian: "I probably know more about Stukeley than anybody else in the world. . . . I know the broad course of his life from the day he was born till the day he died. . . . The real breathing cock-and-balls prick-me-and-I-bleed Stukeley is just about as inaccessible as Neanderthal man." *Treasures of Time* was the winner of England's National Book Award for fiction in 1980.

In *Judgement Day* a village church is the center of events, as in the novels of Barbara Pym, whose work Lively admires. But here the miscellaneous blows of fate are more scarifying than the small betrayals that disappoint the women of Barbara Pym's parish halls and vicarages. When accidents happen, are they meaningless random events or acts of God? The central figures who must work out this old puzzle are George Radwell, the vacuous vicar, empty alike of conviction and the gift of human interaction, and Clare Paling, very much his intellectual superior. They meet for the first time before a fourteenth-century wall-painting of Doomsday, the pride of the church. The action thereafter takes place in the apocalyptic glow of the painting. The modest preparations for a church pageant are quietly amusing in the manner of Barbara Pym, until the quiet life of the village is shattered by violence. In an idyllic river landscape the disaster is foreshadowed. Clare looks up to see an RAF display team overhead: "It was astonishing. She was filled with wild exhilaration. The shock of it. The beauty of those shapes fleeing across the dark sky, the brilliance of the colour; the sudden intrusion, the sense of something quite merciless and irresistible blasting its way across the tranquil countryside. There was a hot metallic smell in the air. . . ." Later, one of the airplanes crashes into a crowd, and at the end of the book a neglected child falls under the wheels of a lorry. Clare confronts the vicar:

"Don't you find it pretty difficult to live with?"

"It?"

"Blind fate. The blindness of fate. Or whatever."

"I suppose," he began cautiously, "one has always hoped somehow to come to terms. . . ."

"Come to terms is what one never does. . . ."

Lively's next novel, *Next to Nature, Art*, owes its title to Walter Savage Landor: "Nature I loved; and next to Nature, Art." Here, art is the subject of the study courses offered to a gullible public at the Framleigh Creative Study Centre, but nature gets the upper hand. Framleigh was once itself a work of art, a house and park designed by William Kent in the eighteenth century: "Twenty-five acres in which the disordered was cunningly turned into a contrivance, in which the physical world was made an artistic product, in which nature became art." By the second half of the twentieth century, art has given way once more to nature. Framleigh Hall has fallen into decay. Greenery grows out of the gutters; weeds engulf the grounds; everything has gone to seed. Seedy too are the artists within the house, as nature in the form of the usual drives and passions overwhelms their feeble creative powers. In describing the talents of these delectably repellent people, Lively has dipped her pen in vitriol. The dimness of their gifts is typified by the piece of statuary that replaces a vanished Apollo on a plinth at the apex of the woodland ride—sculptor Paula's *Instrospective Woman*: "an abstract sculpture of welded bicycle frames and silver-sprayed nylon fruit netting."

A little band of victimized innocents has signed up for the week of study. Soon they too become entangled in the luxuriant growth of the psychological shrubbery: "Tessa, stumbling with Bob through the darkened park, steps in a cow-pat and is too chagrined to mention the matter." At first they are reverent, feeling that their artist-teachers are special in some way and are above the grubby requirements of real life: "in real life, you feel everything's a muddle, everyone's out for what they can get, it's me all the way. Here, they've got a sort of perspective, know what I mean? There's things beyond just people that are important. Right?"

But before long they discover that everything is in a muddle here as well. At Framleigh, too, "it's me all the way." Doubts seize them, especially when they discover that the swimming pool is derelict and the kitchen help departed. At week's end the disgruntled students go home, the heir to Framleigh has hornswoggled a pair of wealthy businessmen into investing ("Run as a tax loss . . . Purely a prestige venture . . ."), and, once again, "Framleigh sheds a few more flakes of stucco and settles to another day."

Penelope Lively has been called "one of the best living English children's writers," and, as a novelist for adults, "almost excessively gifted," with "a rare wit and independence of mind." In discussing her own writing she calls it "a peculiar mixture of honesty and deception. Honesty of intention; deception of manner. I have got to try to tell you a story—a tissue of lies—in which I have come to believe with such intensity that you are going to believe it too. . . . I still think that the novel should tell a story. . . . I don't necessarily want to see things nicely rounded off and all the ends tied up. But what I do want is a sense of progression, that one thing stems from another even when the things may be not events but the author's gradual unfolding of characters and their motivations. I want a novel to gather force. . . ."

Asked about the difference between writing for children and writing for adults, she explains, "All writing is the expression of experience. . . . Those of us who are writing for children . . . have a special problem; we are writing for people whose own experience is limited. . . . We cannot make a basic asssumption about the reader's sense of the passage of time and his or her own place in a chronological scheme. When I write a novel for adults I am addressing my contemporaries in a special sense—those who live in the same country of the imagination. Children live in another country, and although it is one we have all passed through, to pass beyond it is to have lost, irretrievably I believe, its language and its beliefs. We have lost the sense of a continuous present, and moved into an awareness of what has been and what is yet to be and our own situation in relation to time."

Memory is the key, she insists. "The one thing we all share is the capacity to remember; the novelist tries to convey the significance and the power of that capacity in fictional terms, to make universal stories out of the particular story that we each carry in our own head. At its grandest, this theme is the most compelling in all literature."

David Lodge
(28 January 1935-   )

Dennis Jackson
University of Delaware

BOOKS: *About Catholic Authors* (London: St. Paul Press, 1957);

The Picturegoers (London: MacGibbon & Kee, 1960);

Ginger, You're Barmy (London: MacGibbon & Kee, 1962; Garden City: Doubleday, 1965);

The British Museum Is Falling Down (London: MacGibbon & Kee, 1965; New York: Holt Rinehart, 1967);

Language of Fiction: Essays in Criticism and Verbal Analysis of the English Novel (London: Routledge & Kegan Paul; New York: Columbia University Press, 1966);

Graham Greene, Columbia Essays on Modern Writers Series, no. 17 (New York & London: Columbia University Press, 1966);

Out of the Shelter (London: Macmillan, 1970);

The Novelist at the Crossroads and Other Essays on Fiction and Criticism (London: Routledge & Kegan Paul, 1971; Ithaca: Cornell University Press, 1971);

Evelyn Waugh, Columbia Essays on Modern Writers Series, no. 58 (New York & London: Columbia University Press, 1971);

Changing Places: A Tale of Two Campuses (London: Secker & Warburg, 1975; New York: Penguin, 1979);

The Modes of Modern Writing: Metaphor, Metonymy, and the Typology of Modern Literature (Ithaca: Cornell University Press, 1977; London: Arnold, 1977);

How Far Can You Go? (London: Secker & Warburg, 1980); republished as *Souls and Bodies* (New York: Morrow, 1982);

Working with Structuralism: Essays and Reviews on Nineteenth- and Twentieth-Century Literature (London & Boston: Routledge & Paul, 1981).

David Lodge is the author of some of the most clever, ambitious, and funny fiction written in England during the past quarter century. His fifth novel, *Changing Places: A Tale of Two Campuses* (1975), won the Hawthornden Prize and the *Yorkshire Post* Fiction Prize for 1975, and his sixth novel, *How Far Can You Go?* (1980), was selected as the Whitbread "Book of the Year" for 1980. He has combined the writing of fiction with a keen interest in its theory, and, in addition to his novels, he has written six books of literary criticism and numerous articles for academic journals. His writings on literary theory, especially *Language of Fiction* (1966) and *The Modes of Modern Writing* (1977), have made him one of the foremost critical speculators on the novel form. While carrying on this prolific writing career, he has been a professor of English literature at the University of Birmingham.

Lodge's novels have all been focused largely on his own experiences and on the environments he has known best—lower-middle-class Catholic family life in a South London suburb; a childhood spent in wartime England and an adolescence in austerity-ridden postwar London; life as a graduate student and as a literature professor; married life; and life inside the Catholic church after World War II. For his characters and for his settings he seldom ventures from academia or the Catholic church. In most of his novels his protagonists are literature students or college professors, and a majority of them are also enlightened Catholics. The author himself is "a believing Catholic of a very liberal kind theologically," and most of his novels have at least some Catholic statement set in them. Taken as a whole, his fiction forms an interesting chronicle of the vast changes which took place in the Catholic church and in the attitudes of the Catholic community in the years following the war. One crucial area of such change involved the attitudes of individual Catholics toward official church teachings regarding sex and birth control, and one of the recurrent themes in Lodge's stories is the struggle of his Catholic characters to reconcile their spiritual and sensual desires.

He is undoubtedly at his best as a writer of comic fiction, one very much in the British comic tradition of Evelyn Waugh and Kingsley Amis. Unlike many of his contemporaries, Lodge has retained his faith in traditional realism as a vehicle for his fiction, and his stories never veer off into fantastic or apocalyptic visions of life such as those found in so many other postwar novels. His rhetoric is usually unobtrusive and his style is crisp and conversational. As an academic critic and teacher of

literature with a particular interest in prose fiction, he has inevitably been self-conscious about matters of narrative technique, and his fiction, like his criticism, shows a deep sensitivity toward language. Further, his novels have often reflected his interest in critical theories; this is especially true of *The British Museum is Falling Down* (1965), *Changing Places*, and *How Far Can You Go?*, where his theoretical interest in the problematic relation of art to reality is built into the fiction itself.

Lodge was born in South London on 28 January 1935, the only child of a lower-middle-class couple. His father, William Frederick Lodge, worked as a saxophonist and clarinetist in dance bands. His mother, Rosalie Marie Murphy Lodge, came from an Irish-Belgian background and was a Roman Catholic. During World War II, he was in London during much of the Blitzkrieg, but he and his mother spent over two-thirds of the war years living in the country in Surrey or Cornwall (he later fictionalized that period of his life in his fourth novel, *Out of the Shelter*, 1970). At age ten, as soon as the war ended, he was enrolled at St. Joseph's Academy, a Catholic grammar school in Blackheath, London, and it was there that he first became vitally interested in Catholicism, as it was taught by the Delasalles, the order of religious teaching brothers who ran the school.

After graduation from St. Joseph's in 1952, Lodge went to University College, London, where he took a B.A. in English (with honors) three years later. After his first year of college, when he was eighteen, he attempted his first novel, "The Devil, The World and The Flesh." A publisher to whom he submitted it responded encouragingly but advised against publication. He took the advice. As in several of his later novels, "The Devil, The World and The Flesh" focused on Catholic characters living in a seedy suburban section of London, and on certain religious interests (several episodes were later incorporated into *The Picturegoers*, 1960, his first published novel).

During his undergraduate days at University College, Lodge met Mary Frances Jacob, another English student. She was the third eldest of seven children in a large Catholic family whom Lodge often visited at their home fifteen miles from London. (He later used them as a rough model for the warm and happy Mallory family in *The Picturegoers*.) Four years after finishing his B.A. degree, he married Mary Jacob.

In 1955 he entered national service, working during most of his two-year stint as a clerk at Bovington Camp in Dorset (a training camp for members of the Royal Armoured Corps). He bitterly resented military life, and several years later, as an "act of revenge," he wrote *Ginger, You're Barmy* (1962), his second published novel, recounting, in near-documentary fashion, the brutality and tedium of existence in an army camp.

During his final year in the army, in the spring of 1957, he began work on *The Picturegoers*. A novel about Catholics living in the dingy suburb of Brickley, its action occurs mainly in three locales there—a decaying cinema (the Palladium), a Catholic church, and a large Catholic household on Maple Street. The story relates the changes in the lives of more than a dozen characters over a year's time, but the focus is on the gradual return to the faith of one lapsed Catholic, a young English literature student named Mark Underwood.

Mark's conversion is effected rather ironically through the influence of Clare Mallory, one of the seven children of a family with whom he lodges while he finishes college. Mark longs to possess her "flawless torso," and Clare, a former novice in a convent, longs to help him rediscover the Catholic faith. Gradually, she falls in love and her own piety becomes less intense; but when she at last offers herself in passionate embrace, he rejects her and soon after announces his own plans to enter the priesthood. The ironic "see-saw" of their attitudes provides much of the story's dramatic tension, as the two young people struggle toward self-awareness. (Like Mark and Clare, several of the more engaging minor figures in *The Picturegoers* are also caught in a conflict between their spiritual and carnal desires.)

Lodge defines nearly every character in the novel in terms of his or her responses to the cinema. For a pathetic teddy boy named Harry, for instance, the cinema is fuel for romantic fantasies of one day making the "big time," of having money, cars, and big-bosomed "tarts" such as he views on the Palladium screen. For Mark Underwood, by nature contemplative and analytical, the cinema provides much food for deep thought. He decides that "picture-going" has become a "substitute for religion" and frequently draws parallels between "Mother Cinema" and the Catholic church. In an ironic way, such musings over the cinema draw him back toward the church.

Lodge has attempted to orient the whole book around his characters' trips to the cinema. Early in the novel, he describes the habitues of the Palladium one by one as they enter on a Saturday night; he describes their individual responses to the current film, often pausing to offer exposition—through flashbacks—on their lives; and, finally, he describes how the characters go home thinking about the movie in relation to their own dreams in life. But the Palladium ceases to be such an important structural "peg" in the second half of the book, and the plot becomes rather disconnected.

There are other problems. Some scenes appear extraneous; the reader is asked to hold on to too many characters (over a dozen), a few of them only tenuously related to the plot; and there is not enough dramatic interplay between some of the characters and others in the story. But for a first novel, *The Picturegoers* is eminently lively and readable, and most reviewers in 1960 acknowledged this, even while noting the book's flaws. Many of the novel's passages clearly show Lodge's promising future as a comic novelist and as a prose stylist. His alternation of diction, tone, and rhythm as he shifts from his description of the inner thoughts of one character to those of another seems particularly impressive. Such alternation of styles—which he had learned by reading James Joyce's novels, and which he was to employ again in later novels—enables him to delineate sharply the inner lives of a broad range of contrasting characters.

Certain mannerisms in *The Picturegoers* evidence the influence of Graham Greene on Lodge's style. Lodge had read with special interest the works of Greene and Evelyn Waugh and other Catholic writers, and, when, after his military service ended, he returned to University College, London, to take an M.A. degree, he did his thesis on "Catholic Fiction Since the Oxford Movement: Its Literary Form and Religious Content."

After finishing his M.A. work, he married Mary Jacob on 16 May 1959. Unable to find a university post, he took a temporary job with the British Council's Overseas Students Center in London, where he taught English and literature to foreign students and organized various cultural activities. In 1960, while he and Mary were living in Battersea, their first child, Julia, was born, and, in that same year, MacGibbon and Kee published *The Picturegoers*.

Lodge began immediately to write another novel, *Ginger, You're Barmy*, drawing significantly upon his experiences in the British army. The story's first-person narrator, Jonathan Browne, records the difficulties he encounters after he is wrenched out of his sheltered existence as an English student at a London university and is thrust into a crass, dehumanizing military world where his assets—intelligence, critical judgment, and culture—become liabilities. The book interestingly describes all the universals of soldiering, especially of basic training, with its "quality of realism, of nightmarish unreason," but the novel is kept from becoming just another stale army tale by the narrator's detached and often ironical observations and his keen attention to detail.

As Lodge later acknowledged, *Ginger, You're Barmy* is very closely patterned after Graham Greene's *The Quiet American*. Like Greene in his novel, Lodge alternates narrative based on two time schemes: Browne recalls episodes from his months in basic training in Catterick Camp in the Midlands, and in alternate sections he narrates events from his final week in the national service, when he is a clerk in the Royal Armoured Corps at Badmore Camp in Dorset. *Ginger, You're Barmy* also resembles *The Quiet American* in its themes, characterizations, and plot. Both stories treat the theme of treachery and betrayal (the Judas complex). Jon Browne, like Greene's narrator, Fowler, is an intellectual, cynical, detached man, not at all willing to become *involved* in life. Like Fowler also, Browne steals his best friend's woman and ultimately betrays him. His friend is Mike Brady, another conscript, who like Greene's "quiet American" Pyle is a Christian and an idealist willing to fight for what he thinks is right or just in life. In contrast to the self-centered and unfeeling Browne, Brady is a passionate man, a man of conscience and compassion. When a shy, frail, bumbling boy named Percy is bullied by other soldiers, Brady nobly defends him. When Percy accidentally kills himself, Brady works to make sure that the dead boy—who is, like himself, a Roman Catholic—is not "stigmatized as a suicide" and hence denied Christian burial, and he later retaliates against a corporal whose harsh reprimands had helped cause Percy's death. Near the story's end, Brady becomes involved in yet another cause as he helps the Irish Republican Army raid a British armory at Badmore. He is captured through information provided by Browne and is consequently sent to prison. The novel focuses on the changing nature of Browne's relationship with Brady and on a "small advance" which Browne claims he has made as a person—by story's end, he has, like Greene's Fowler, finally become "engagé" and has found a new generosity of spirit (a change of heart which some critics found less than convincing).

Not long after he began writing *Ginger, You're Barmy* in 1960, Lodge accepted a one-year job teaching English literature at one of the redbrick Midlands schools, the University of Birmingham. A year later he was rehired as an assistant lecturer and then began a steady rise through the academic ranks, culminating in his promotion in 1976 to the rank of Professor of Modern English Literature.

During his first four years at the university, he worked on material which was to form his first academic critical book, *Language of Fiction: Essays in Critical and Verbal Analysis of the English Novel*. After its publication in 1966, it became one of the most widely read of contemporary books on the novel. In it Lodge argues that the novelist's language (image patterns, "key-words," and other features of the "verbal texture" of novels) deserves the same kind of close critical attention customarily given to poetry. He first offers a long argument toward a poetics of fiction and then puts his poetics into practice in seven essays dealing with the use of language in the works of seven English novelists.

Over the next fifteen years Lodge established a reputation as one of the ablest critics and theorists of the novel at work in England. During that time he produced dozens of journal articles and five more books of criticism: *Graham Greene* (1966), a short biographical/critical monograph in the Columbia Essays on Modern Writers series; *Evelyn Waugh* (1971), another Columbia monograph; *The Novelist at the Crossroads and Other Essays on Fiction and Criticism*, which collected fourteen of his essays, many of them reaffirming what he had said in *Language of Fiction* regarding the "primacy of language in literary matters"; *The Modes of Modern Writing: Metaphor, Metonymy, and the Typology of Modern Literature*, where he argues the need for "a comprehensive typology of literary discourse" and proposes that such a typology might be based upon Roman Jakobson's theory of the metaphoric and metonymic poles of language; and *Working with Structuralism: Essays and Reviews on Nineteenth and Twentieth-Century Literature* (1981), another collection of his critical articles.

During the 1960s and 1970s Lodge also edited and wrote introductions for Jane Austen's *Emma* (1971), George Eliot's *Scenes of Clerical Life* (1973), and Thomas Hardy's *The Woodlanders* (1974), and he edited *Jane Austen: "Emma": A Casebook* (1968) and *Twentieth Century Literary Criticism: A Reader* (1972). The idea for the latter text he had gotten while teaching courses on literary criticism at Birmingham. He had in the 1960s often collaborated in teaching such courses with his friend and colleague, the novelist and critic Malcolm Bradbury.

With Bradbury also he had collaborated in 1963 in writing a satirical revue titled *Between these Four Walls*. With a third writer, a talented English student named James Duckett, they accepted a commission by a Birmingham repertory theater to write a series of short humorous sketches and comic topical songs. The revue ran for a month.

That experience and his continued association with Bradbury, among other things, inspired Lodge to try his hand at a comic novel, and, in late spring 1964, just after he had completed *Language of Fiction*, he began writing *The British Museum Is Falling Down*. He had for several years been considering a novel about a postgraduate English student whose life keeps taking on the quality of the novels that he is studying in the British Museum, and, when he got an idea for a comic novel about the dilemma of Catholics over birth control, he soon found a way of linking the two stories. The church's teaching on contraception was a topical issue. A pontifical commission was studying problems associated with the family, population, and birth control, and the Catholic world was buzzing with the possibility that the church's teaching on contraception, which had

formerly been thought of as absolutely unchangeable, might, indeed, change. Lodge and his wife were themselves experiencing in 1964 some of the strains that the church's teaching imposed on married people (their second child, Stephen, had been born in 1962), and the author hoped that with his new novel he might in some way affect the winds of change which were already blowing in the Roman Catholic church.

The novel's hero, Adam Appleby, and his wife, Barbara, have already lost three rounds of "Vatican Roulette" using the rhythm method, and, as *The British Museum Is Falling Down* starts, they are fearful, despite a house full of ovulation charts, calendars, and thermometers, that a fourth child may be on the way. Amidst this "surging sea of fertility," Appleby is struggling to finish his Ph.D. thesis (on modern British novels) and is suffering great anxiety over his need to find a job soon. *The British Museum Is Falling Down* tells the story of one day of pandemonium in his life. It is a day he had planned to spend doing quiet research inside the British Museum, but, during the roughly eighteen-hour span of the novel, he fails to open a single book; he tracks back and forth for telephone calls home to see if his wife has started her menstrual period; he discusses contraceptives at a Catholic meeting; he raises a false fire alarm which throws the British Museum into a panic; he gets drunk and disgraces himself at a gathering of academics; he negotiates with a stately Catholic matron who wants to sell him some literary relics and with her not-so-stately daughter who agrees to *give* him valuable manuscripts if he will take her virginity; he watches as his scooter explodes and sends the treasured manuscripts up in flames; he at last lands a job as a book buyer for a fat American who has come to England hoping to buy the British Museum in order to relocate it to the Colorado Rockies; and he returns triumphantly home to make love to his wife, who, immediately thereafter, starts her period.

These events of one zany day are all structured very much according to the scheme of James Joyce's *Ulysses* (1922), and the imprint of that book is everywhere seen (usually for comic effect) through *The British Museum Is Falling Down*. Like Leopold Bloom, Adam—because of the domestic and academic pressures he is facing—becomes increasingly disoriented as his day progresses, and his perceptions of life around him become increasingly phantasmagoric. Like Bloom also, Lodge's hero keeps his mind constantly fixed throughout the day on his home and his wife; he suffers because of his religion; and he has fantasies of grandeur (which, like Bloom's, are always followed by some sort of comic diminution). Among the numerous other explicit *Ulysses* parallels, the most obvious is the "Epilogue," a ten-page parody or pastiche of Molly Bloom's unpunctuated monologue, wherein Barbara Appleby rehearses, in a flowing stream-of-consciousness style, her love life with Adam. She records her husband's triumphant return to the house in Battersea, and, as does Molly's in *Ulysses*, her monologue forms an optimistic and life-affirming end for the story.

Of all writers, Joyce had the greatest influence on Lodge's fiction. The kind of realism seen in Joyce's treatment of Catholic lower- and middle-class life in *Dubliners* (1914) and *A Portrait of the Artist as a Young Man* (1916) is reflected in Lodge's early novels, and Joyce's stylistic variations in *Ulysses* had an even stronger influence on Lodge's later books, especially *The British Museum Is Falling Down* and *Changing Places*. In *The British Museum Is Falling Down* Lodge changes the style and technique from one section to another, and, very much in Joycean fashion also, he frequently shifts the language of the story into pastiches or parodies of various other novelists, among them Conrad, Hemingway, Woolf, Kingsley Amis, Greene, Baron Corvo, Henry James, and C. P. Snow. Through such a parody technique Lodge subtly weaves into his novel's fabric his hero's own professional interest in literary language and modes. (Lodge's own critical interest in the "language of fiction" had led him to examine various authors' styles very closely, and that research made it easier for him to create the parodies when he came to writing *The British Museum Is Falling Down*. As he later observed, *Language of Fiction* and the novel had "a kind of jokey relation to each other.") The parodies also help demonstrate the novel's subsidiary theme that "life imitates art," and they are expressive projections of Adam's own neurotic notion that the events of his life are following the shape of certain scenes from novels he has read.

The British Museum Is Falling Down is unceasingly and vigorously funny; there are frequent flashes of Lodge's natural wit and endless literary jokes, but, more often than not, the humor is of a broad, farcical sort. Yet throughout the book serious undertones give emphasis and point to the author's general levity. His comic and satiric treatment of the current Catholic indecision over family planning is not a frontal attack on the church itself but rather a good-natured tickling meant to evoke laughter and a serious new consideration of the effect of the Catholic ban on artificial contraception

on couples such as the Applebys. Lodge's satire extends also to the academic world, and he takes more than a few pokes at the petty jealousies, pretentiousness, and absentmindedness exhibited by professors in Adam's English department. Much of the comedy, tone, and atmosphere of *The British Museum Is Falling Down* is reminiscent of Amis's *Lucky Jim* (Lodge had noted in *Language of Fiction* a "strange community of feeling" he shared with Amis), but that earlier novel has a more savage satiric edge. Lodge's treatment of academe is gentler, more the lighthearted raillery and ridicule of a member of the family than a heavy-handed attack of a bitter defector such as Amis's hero.

The British Museum Is Falling Down received more favorable commentary from more reviewers than Lodge's two previous novels had, and it represented a real development in his career as a writer of fiction. Despite the frequent parodies, Lodge gave evidence in *The British Museum Is Falling Down* that he was finding his own "voice," his own fictional style, and he mined a high comic vein in the novel that was later to be acknowledged as one of the most notable features of his fiction.

Lodge took the first chapter of *The British Museum Is Falling Down* with him in August 1964 when he went to the United States on a Harkness Commonwealth Fellowship. He went first to Brown University in Rhode Island to study American literature, and during his six months there he found time to complete the novel by early 1965. Soon after, he and Mary and their two children launched a slow journey by automobile across the southern United States, arriving in San Francisco for a three-month stay in the summer of 1965. After that "fairly euphoric year" in America, he returned home to Birmingham and began another collaboration on a satirical revue with Malcolm Bradbury and James Duckett (this time they were joined by a playwright named David Turner). *Slap in the Middle* was produced in a Birmingham repertory theater that fall (1965).

In 1966, Lodge began writing another novel, *Out of the Shelter* (1970), which focuses on two crucial periods in the early life of its protagonist, Timothy Young—his childhood in wartime London and his 1951 holiday trip to Germany (when he is sixteen). The story includes frequent humorous episodes which recall *The British Museum Is Falling Down*, but *Out of the Shelter* is a comparatively sober treatment of several themes, the most prominent being the sexual maturation of the rather priggish young English Catholic boy.

As in *The Picturegoers*, Lodge's main characters

in *Out of the Shelter* are members of a working-class Catholic family in South London. In an opening chapter more than a little like the beginning of Joyce's *A Portrait of the Artist as a Young Man*, Lodge describes the developing consciousness of young Timothy (in a third-person narrative style which simulates child's syntax and diction) and relates the profound effects of the war on the Young family. Following the war, the shy, intellectual youth prospers as a student at St. Michael's Catholic grammar school in London, and his life is "safe, orderly" for a time. The novel's first section is titled "The Shelter"—referring not only to an Anderson air-raid shelter, where Timothy had felt "warm and safe" during the Blitzkrieg, but also by extension to the "shelter" of his home, parents, school, and the Catholic church. In section two, titled "Coming Out," sixteen-year-old Timothy fearfully prepares to embark for the "exotic" land of Germany, where he will spend the summer with his twenty-seven-year-old sister, Kate, who works as a secretary for the American occupation army. (Lodge had made a similar journey to Germany in 1951, to visit his mother's sister.) This holiday, as Timothy himself later observes, is a "turning-point" in his life, and over two-thirds of the novel relates his experiences on the Continent, his slow emergence from and his life out of "the shelter" of his former existence in London.

His "Coming Out" involves his adaptation to several kinds of changes in his life—geographical, cultural, social, and sexual. He ventures into "the Germany of his imagination," into the land of the recent enemy, but, ironically, during his stay there, he experiences culture shock less from the German natives than from "the American way of life" he encounters. Coming from austerity-ridden postwar England, the naive youngster is thrust headlong into an "environment of excess" among Kate's hedonistic American friends in Heidelberg (most of them civilians working for the American occupation army) and joins them in their endless rounds of sunbathing, drinking, dancing, gambling, and dashing around to various fancy resorts in the Bavarian Alps. Gradually he enters into their "spirit of excess" and begins to realize the limitations of English life as he had known it in a Catholic household of the 1940s, a life of dreariness and repression where one had lived always "in anticipation and recollection, never by impulse." However, he never fully accepts the "abundantly pleasurable," insouciant, and free life which he and Kate identify as "the American way"; he only goes, as he says, "sort of half-way." But his journey to Germany does re-sult in a significant testing and readjustment of his values.

Out of the Shelter focuses largely on the way its young hero advances "half-way" toward sexual maturity. The book lacks intensity; it has no sharply drawn conflict or dramatic tension, and, for most of the story, the only real suspense has to do with this question of how and when Timothy will learn about sex. As in *The Picturegoers* and *The British Museum Is Falling Down*, Lodge frequently relates the sexual interests of *Out of the Shelter* with certain religious interests. Timothy constantly relates his developing sexual knowledge to the teachings of the Catholic church. His own religion seems a strange mixture of fear and superstition. He believes that sex is a "mortal sin," that "if you died with it on your soul you went to Hell," and after he and a half-nude sixteen-year-old named Gloria have touched each other's genitals, he immediately thinks to himself, "I must get to confession before I leave for home tomorrow. Trains could crash, ships could sink."

He never quite gets "out of the shelter" of the Catholic church, and neither does his sister, Kate. While in Germany Timothy fears that Kate has become a "lapsed" Catholic, and he worries over her soul. But in an epilogue (an awkward and contrived effort to tie up some of the plot's loose ends), when he visits his sister in America fourteen years later, she tells him, "I've gone back to the Church. . . . As you get older, I think you feel the need for something." In a significant way, Lodge was to return to that theme—of man's "need for something" (which the church has to offer)—in his sixth novel, *How Far Can You Go?*

Out of the Shelter was finished in 1968 and was published two years later by Macmillan. Lodge completed the book just before he moved his family (then numbering five, son Christopher having been born in 1966) to America, where for two academic quarters he was a Visiting Associate Professor of English at the University of California at Berkeley.

The spring of 1969 was a turbulent time in America; among other troubles, the country was at war in Vietnam, and its university campuses were in turmoil caused by the student revolution. For a time during Lodge's first quarter at Berkeley, normal university activities were virtually shut down by a Third World Students' Strike, and during his second quarter there, the campus was disrupted by a bloody controversy over the "People's Park," where a group of young radicals had seized a plot of university land, and the National Guard eventually was dispatched to the campus. Not by nature an activist, Lodge generally remained on the sidelines during

I.

High, high above the North Pole, *[manuscript text with numerous handwritten corrections and deletions]* two professors of English literature approached each other at a combined velocity of 1100 miles per hour. *[struck-through text]* They were protected from the thin cold air by the pressurized cabin of a Boeing 707, & from the risk of collision by the prudent arrangement of the international air-lanes. *[struck-through text]* The two men were known to each other by name *[illegible]* since they were in the process of exchanging jobs for the year; & in an age of more leisurely transportation the *[struck-through]* intersection of their routes might have been marked by some *[correction]* human gesture — *[struck-through text]* but they *[correction: wave]* to each other for the duration of 2 *[correction]* lives, for example, each may *[correction: simultaneously]* focus a telescope, by chance, on the other, with his own hand; or, more plausibly, a little mime of *[correction: mutual appraisal]* *[struck-through text]* played out *[struck-through]* two *[struck-through]* compartments halted side by side at the same station, the first *[struck-through]* *[correction: more self-conscious]* gently relieved to feel himself, at last, only moving off, only to discover that it is the other man's train that is moving first, a common illusion, but one full of symbolic possibilities in this case.... However, it was not to be. *[struck-through text]* *[struck-through text]* Since the two men were in airplanes, & one was bound & the other frightened of looking out of the window, since, in any case, the

First page of the manuscript for Changing Places

all this activity, but once, in late spring, he did join a vigil of protest by the Berkeley English faculty against the presence of armed police and troops on campus. He had been witness to a much milder form of the student revolution (which had had its beginnings in Paris in May 1968) before coming to Berkeley. At Birmingham the previous autumn, students demanding a stronger voice in the government of the university had occupied an administration building. But such disturbances in England had been much less bloody and less explosive and a great deal less political than the Berkeley protests, which involved the whole community and not just academic interests.

Lodge was intrigued by the very dissimilar ways the revolution of the young was happening on the two continents, and his fifth novel, *Changing Places*, which he began writing in 1971, grew out of his desire to explore that cultural contrast. The public revolution pictured in the novel serves as background to a more important "duplex chronicle" of the private lives of two literature professors, one from a California university and the other from a redbrick British school, who exchange jobs (and ultimately cars, houses, children, and wives) for six months. Each of Lodge's heroes gets caught up in some fashion in the student rebellion. Philip Swallow, who goes to the United States as a visiting professor at the State University of Euphoria, stands in a vigil of protest and unknowingly aids a group of radicals involved in the "People's Garden" protest (the "People's Park" episode at Berkeley is recounted in the novel virtually as it had happened). He views firsthand the fierce and bloody conflict between the "University-Industrial-Military Complex" and the "Alternative Society of Love and Peace" on the American campus. His counterpart, an American scholar named Morris Zapp, goes to the Midlands to the University of Rummidge, where he eventually becomes the chief mediator who brings a confrontation between British students and the administration to a peaceful resolution.

But the primary focus of the book is on the personal lives of the two academics who, approaching middle age, find new identities as a result of their moves to new environs. (*Changing Places* is, like *The British Museum Is Falling Down*, a comic "campus novel," with the same sort of zany characters and events depicted in the earlier novel.) Each of the two college professors depicted in *Changing Places* is, at the time of the transatlantic swap, forty years old; each has, for various reasons, a failing marriage and a career which has gone stale. Philip Swallow is a dull, routinized, weak-kneed man. He has published very little scholarly writing and has small chance for promotion at Rummidge. But his "pilgrimage" to the American West results in a "liberation" of sorts for him and ends some of his self-doubts. He finds himself (mostly by accident) a hero of Euphoria campus politics and a radical philosopher. In California Swallow gradually loses his inhibitions: he commits adultery for the first time (with Zapp's college-age daughter) and later moves in with Zapp's liberated wife, Désirée, thus becoming a "new man." Similarly, the submissive Hilary Swallow is attracted to Morris Zapp's take-charge tactics, and Zapp too becomes a "new man" as a result of the strange marital exchange that occurs in the story. In many ways, Zapp is the antithesis of Swallow. He is rakish, vain, sarcastic, and brilliant, and he is "*the* Jane Austen man," author of five books. But like his British counterpart, he has reached a point of mid-life crisis: he has written very little for the past several years; he has found it hard to hold the attention of students increasingly hostile to traditional academic values; he does not want the divorce Désirée is seeking; and he has experienced some recent sexual failures. But, with Hilary in the Swallow household and with the low-key British academics at Rummidge, he no longer feels threatened and begins to project a future for himself in the dark gray Midlands.

What that future will be, exactly, the reader never learns. When the two couples reunite in a Manhattan hotel (as the two parallel plots finally merge), Hilary wonders aloud: "Where is this all going to end?" No one—not even the author himself—ever gets an answer to the question. The four characters sit in the hotel room searching for an ending, like "scriptwriters discussing how to wind up a play." Lodge floats a series of possible endings to his story, but before the reader learns which option the characters choose, the story abruptly concludes. Philip is addressing "the question of endings" when, with a film-script notation that "the camera stops, freezing him in mid-gesture," *Changing Places* simply *ends*. With this conclusion Lodge is poking a little fun at postmodernist fiction by parodying the strangely ambivalent endings which many recent writers have given to their stories. The final pages of *Changing Places* are, in a fashion, a comic version of such endings as that John Fowles gives his 1969 novel *The French Lieutenant's Woman*, where the novelist invites his readers to choose between alternative endings to his story.

(Lodge discusses Fowles's book and other such endings of "postmodernist" fiction in *The Modes of Modern Writing*.)

Lodge is also, in the ending of this novel, taking a playful poke at some theorists of modern fiction, among them Robert Scholes, the author of the 1967 study *The Fabulators*. Scholes had there argued that the cinema has superseded the mimetic possibilities of literature, that the camera has rendered literary realism redundant. Consequently, Scholes has decided, the novel is "dying," and contemporary narrative writers are turning to "fabulations," to nonrealistic literary modes. But Lodge had disagreed, and in his 1969 essay "The Novelist at the Crossroads," he had countered that such "obsequies" over the novel are "premature," and he had affirmed his "faith in the future of realistic fiction." He is further challenging Scholes's ideas in *Changing Places* (and once again his fiction stands in a sort of "jokey relation" to his own critical writings). On the novel's penultimate page, Lodge has Swallow subscribe to those arguments of Scholes and other theorists who believe that methods of conventional realistic imitation are all no longer adequate to portray "illusory" contemporary life. In the Manhattan hotel, Philip views a television picture of a protest march of young California radicals, and he declares: "There *is* a generation gap. . . . Our generation—we subscribe to the old liberal doctrine of the inviolate self. It's the great tradition of realistic fiction, it's what novels are all about. The private life in the foreground, history a distant rumble of gunfire, somewhere offstage. . . . Well, the novel is dying, and us with it. . . . It's an unnatural medium for their [young people's] experiences. Those kids . . . are living a film, not a novel." Lodge presents the whole last chapter of *Changing Places* in the form of a film script. But that represents no capitulation on his part to Scholes's (and Swallow's) theory that the cinema has superiority over realistic fiction when it comes to representing modern "reality"; to the contrary, it is merely a rhetorical strategy. Lodge invokes the visual medium (television as well as film) merely in order to reinforce a verbal communication—a novel, obviously, and one which sensitively enough registers the many discords of contemporary experience, and does so without stretching too far beyond the parameters of a realistic vision of life.

Changing Places, even more than *The British Museum Is Falling Down*, expresses Lodge's interests in the nature of fictional form. The novel's style becomes a major source of its comedy, as the manipulating author tries out a number of different techniques. Three chapters are told from a third-person "privileged narrative altitude (higher than that of any jet)," but three other chapters shift narrative gears—one is presented in epistolary style; another is a Joycean gathering of newspaper items, press releases, underground press publications, handbills, and classified ads; and the final chapter is cast as a film script. The novelist thus often renegotiates his narrative position. *Changing Places* is, in frequently comic ways, a reflexive novel. Lodge's characters themselves often consider the aesthetic problems he is facing in writing his fiction. Morris Zapp, for instance, reads a book titled *Let's Write a Novel*, one passage of which declares: "There are three types of stories, the story that ends happily, the story that ends unhappily, and the story that . . . doesn't really end at all." The last one, it is declared, is "the worst kind." This and other references to *Let's Write a Novel* serve as a comic commentary on Lodge's own story that has no ending at all. The difficulty of the novel writer's task ultimately becomes, in the closing chapter of *Changing Places*, Lodge's subject, and readers are there made to participate in the aesthetic and philosophical decisions that the novelist must make at the end of his story. In its final chapter, at least, *Changing Places* becomes an example of what Lodge in "The Novelist at the Crossroads" calls the "problematic novel," the "novel-about-itself."

Lodge finished *Changing Places* in summer 1973. As soon as Secker and Warburg published the novel in February 1975, it elicited favorable responses from almost all reviewers. The book won both the *Yorkshire Post* Fiction Prize and the Hawthornden Prize for 1975. In 1976 Lodge was invited to become a Fellow of the Royal Society of Literature. Increasingly through the 1970s he was sought after as a lecturer at universities and at literary conferences across Europe. In 1977 he served as Henfield Writing Fellow at the University of East Anglia during the summer months.

He began writing his sixth novel, *How Far Can You Go?*, in summer 1976, and it was finished by autumn 1978. In a fashion Lodge was circling back over thematic grounds covered in his earlier novels. As in *The Picturegoers*, *The British Museum Is Falling Down*, and *Out of the Shelter*, the focus in *How Far Can You Go?* is on the sexual and religious concerns of English Catholic characters. In *Changing Places* he had treated the political, social, and sexual revolutions taking place in the 1960s; in *How Far Can You Go?* he narrows that focus and treats the effect of those and similar revolutions on English Catholics of his generation. The book presents a panoramic view of the vast changes effected inside the church during the era spanning the 1950s up to Pope John Paul II's installation in the late 1970s. Especially in the years following the Second Vatican Council, traditional attitudes of Catholics toward authority, sex, worship, pastoral practice, and other religions changed radically; the traditional Catholic metaphysic faded; and the church came no longer to represent a sort of monolithic, unified, uniform view of life as once it had done.

To chronicle such changes, Lodge in *How Far Can You Go?* traces the fortunes of a group of ten enlightened Catholics over a quarter century of their adult lives (the group includes, among others, a priest, a nun, a physician, a Cambridge historian, and an English professor). He uses an early morning mass in the gloomy church of Our Lady and St. Jude in London to introduce his ten principal characters (at a time when most of them are University of London students), and to outline the Catholic "world-picture" which these young people had been taught to believe in, the complex "synthesis of theology and cosmology and casuistry" which "situated individual souls on a kind of spiritual Snakes and Ladders board," in the "game" of salvation. Lodge significantly sets this mass on St. Valentine's Day. At a party later, one of the students recites the woeful tale of St. Valentine as another mimes an "extravagant display of passion" on a sofa nearby. The irony comes in the fact that Lodge's young Catholics know such a great deal more about the figure of St. Valentine in his aspect as a Christian martyr than they do about his being the patron saint of lovers. A later chapter, "How they lost their virginities," gives a case-by-case rundown of how the repressed young Catholics all fare in their first sexual encounters, either in motels or in marriage beds. Most fare poorly. Lodge's point, one he repeats for emphasis throughout the novel, is that the Catholic youths have generally been ill-prepared for sex, for the acceptance of lovemaking as something pleasurable.

Most of Lodge's Catholic couples spend the 1960s producing "babies, babies" in spite of "strenuous efforts not to," and Lodge launches a vigorous discussion of a subject he had covered before, extensively, in *The British Museum Is Falling Down*—the problems of conscience which married Catholics face because of the church's teaching on birth control. *The British Museum Is Falling Down*, written at a time when Lodge and other Catholics were hopeful that a pontifical commission was about to change the church's ban on contraception, was lighthearted in its treatment of "Vatican

Roulette"; but, in *How Far Can You Go?*, written after Pope Paul VI's 1968 *Humanae Vitae* had produced "no change" regarding church attitudes, the author speaks bitterly, with righteous indignation, about the church's failure to *change* its stance on birth control. Lodge blames the rhythm method for having caused great ills in Catholic marriages—among them, frigidity in wives so fearful of pregnancy and hideous gynecological complications caused by excessive childbearing. Moreover, he suggests that the breakdown of marriages among the Catholic couples in his story is due significantly to the church's past reticence and repression concerning sexual love.

Changing Places had dramatized the growing permissiveness in Western secular society in the 1960s; *How Far Can You Go?* traces the challenge which this new permissiveness gave specifically to the Roman Catholic ethos, then and later. In lively fashion, Lodge first shows the struggles of his characters to overcome their inbred fear that contraception would be a grave sin in the "spiritual game of Snakes and Ladders"; he depicts their subsequent pursuit of erotic fulfillment through "postural variations" during coitus, blue movies, sex "games" and the like; and he finally focuses on the way they all weather the sexual upheavals of middle age (some commit adultery, others are tempted by group sex). With a few exceptions, the characters seem, by the story's end, to have made a fairly satisfactory compromise between their sensual and spiritual longings.

The novel stresses the far-reaching effects which the crisis over birth control had in the church. Most significantly, the debate over contraception caused Catholics to begin reexamining and redefining their views on other fundamental issues, and some of the results of this process are made evident in the novel's final chapter, in the description of a "Paschal Festival" sponsored by a liberal Catholic group. Lodge presents this festival in the rather contrived form of a transcript (supposedly written by one of his characters, a literature professor named Michael) based on a videotape of a television documentary called "Easter with the New Catholics." This transcript reads "like a coda to everything that had happened" to Lodge's Catholic characters "in matters of belief," and it is, in effect, a recapitulation of the novel's primary themes. The Easter weekend festival is a "showcase for the pluralist, progressive, postconciliar Church," and the participants represent well the wide range of special interests (for instance, the "Charismatic Renewal" and the "new theology" of sexual love as something "self-liberating . . . life-giving and joyous") which engaged Catholics in the years following the Second Vatican Council. Through the Paschal Festival transcript, Lodge dramatizes numerous issues affecting the church over the two previous decades—the fading of the Catholic metaphysic; the growing ecumenism; the democratization of the church; certain liturgical experiments; and other similar matters.

Hovering over the festival and over the whole novel is the question of "how far can you go?" It has numerous applications. It applies particularly to the problems of Catholics in regard to sex—to youngsters who during religious instruction ask, "Please, Father, how far can you go with a girl?" and to older Catholics who must decide "how far" to go in the pursuit of erotic fulfillment and "how far" to go in challenging the church's teaching on sex. In a broader sense, the question applies to the important issue of changes taking place inside the church—for example, to the matter of "how far" progressive theologians could go in demythologizing the Bible, or to the problem of "how far" the official church could go in condoning the "new theology of sex" in the 1970s.

To all these questions Lodge responds, "well, you can go pretty far, but . . . ," and it is that *but* which often makes the novel engaging. The author finds the recent changes in the church on the whole "agreeably stimulating," but he also finds them "slightly unnerving" and expresses throughout *How Far Can You Go?* his anxiety that, in their new attitudes toward sex, the church, and the matter of faith itself, modern Catholics may be going a bit *too far.*

Several times in the novel an ingenious analogy is drawn between religious belief and the imagination involved in the reading or writing of fiction. When describing how disturbed his Catholic protagonists become over the "ebbing away" of the "old dogmas and certainties," Lodge observes: "We all like to believe, do we not, if only in stories. People who find religious belief absurd are often upset if a novelist breaks the illusion of reality he has created." And he extends this faith/fiction analogy: "In matters of belief (as of literary convention) it is a nice question how far you can go" in the process of discarding old beliefs and old practices "without throwing out something vital."

That "nice question" is never definitively answered in *How Far Can You Go?*, nor is that of "how far" a novelist can go in destroying the "illusion of reality" in fiction; but Lodge proposes at least a partial answer to the latter query in the way

he writes his novel. First, he carefully creates the "illusion of reality" in the story, by rendering his characters' personalities and actions with such specific, evocative, and interesting details as to make them real to readers, and by interleaving his fiction with a rather bald journalistic rehearsal of key historical events of the 1960s and 1970s (thereby lending the story a certain atmosphere of authenticity). And yet, the author is forever shattering this "illusion of reality" which he has labored to create. He stops, for example, to lecture readers on the novel as it develops, and pauses to help them interpret the symbolic codes involved in the names and physical appearances of his characters (the fiction is thus both itself and an academic commentary on itself). Further, his readers become involved in the very process of his art, for example, when the author writes into the novel his own indecision concerning the selection of a name for a character or when he halts the story to discuss the problematic nature of his art. He admits openly that his protagonists are only "fictional characters, they cannot bleed or weep," but asserts that "they stand here for all the real people" who lived during the era of crumbling faith and growing sexual permissiveness he is chronicling. (His ten major figures are indeed "types," and the whole book is in effect a fictionalized essay, with the individual characters' stories serving as symbolizations or parables exemplifying and animating the novel's ongoing discussions of faith.) But despite his repeated baring of the devices of his art, Lodge manages—especially through his ever-present wit and playful irony—to maintain a strong hold on the reader's attention throughout.

Reviewers greeted the novel very favorably after Secker and Warburg published it in England in April 1980, and it soon won the Whitbread Literary Award for "Book of the Year" in 1980. (It was published in the United States in 1982 as *Souls and Bodies.*) Both *Changing Places* and *How Far Can You Go?* marked significant advances in Lodge's development as an artist. In neither were there the overplayed scenes, the wasted scenes, the crude epilogues, or the shaky (and often imitative) narrative structures which had occasionally marred his fiction of the 1960s. By the time Lodge came to the writing of these two later novels, he had developed his own strong, original, self-confident, narrative voice, one capable of great modulation, and he had gained a firmer control of his material. By 1980 he had established his reputation as a very good minor novelist—and that should not be taken as dismissive, for, as Lodge himself observed in one of his essays, "to be a *good* minor novelist is no dishonorable ambition and no mean achievement."

Plays:

Between These Four Walls (revue), by Lodge, Malcolm Bradbury, and James Duckett, Birmingham, 1963;

Slap in the Middle (revue), by Lodge, Bradbury, Duckett, and David Turner, Birmingham, 1965.

Other:

Jane Austen: "Emma": A Casebook, edited by Lodge (London: Macmillan, 1968);

Jane Austen, *Emma*, edited by Lodge (London & New York: Oxford University Press, 1971);

Twentieth Century Literary Criticism: A Reader, edited by Lodge (London: Longman, 1972);

George Eliot, *Scenes of Clerical Life*, edited by Lodge (Harmondsworth & Baltimore: Penguin, 1973);

Thomas Hardy, *The Woodlanders*, edited by Lodge

(London: Macmillan, 1974);

"Thomas Hardy" and "Graham Greene," by Lodge and Ian Gregor, in *The English Novel*, edited by Cedric Watts (London: Sussex Press, 1976), pp. 95-110, 152-171;

"Thomas Hardy as a Cinematic Novelist," in *Thomas Hardy after Fifty Years*, edited by Lance St. John Butler (Totowa, N.J.: Rowman & Littlefield, 1977), pp. 78-89.

Periodical Publication:

"The Man Who Wouldn't Get Up," *Weekend Telegraph*, 6 May 1966.

References:

Bernard Bergonzi, "A Conspicuous Absentee: The Decline and Fall of the Catholic Novel," *Encounter*, 55 (August-September 1980): 44-56;

Bergonzi, "David Lodge Interviewed," *Month*, 229 (February 1970): 108-116;

Park Honan, "David Lodge and the Cinematic Novel in England," *Novel: A Forum on Fiction*, 5 (Winter 1972): 167-173.

Colin MacInnes
(20 August 1914-22 April 1976)

Harriet Blodgett
University of California, Davis

BOOKS: *To the Victors the Spoils* (London: MacGibbon & Kee, 1950);

June in Her Spring (London: MacGibbon & Kee, 1952);

City of Spades (London: MacGibbon & Kee, 1957; New York: Macmillan, 1958);

Absolute Beginners (London: MacGibbon & Kee, 1959; New York: Macmillan, 1960);

Mr. Love and Justice (London: MacGibbon & Kee, 1960; New York: Dutton, 1961);

England, Half English (London: MacGibbon & Kee, 1961; New York: Random House, 1962);

All Day Saturday (London: MacGibbon & Kee, 1966);

Sweet Saturday Night (London: MacGibbon & Kee, 1967);

Visions of London—includes *City of Spades, Absolute Beginners, Mr. Love and Justice* (London: Mac-

Gibbon & Kee, 1969); republished as *The London Novels* (New York: Farrar, Straus & Giroux, 1969);

Westward to Laughter (London: MacGibbon & Kee, 1969; New York: Farrar, Straus & Giroux, 1970);

Three Years to Play (London: MacGibbon & Kee, 1970; New York: Farrar, Straus & Giroux, 1970);

Loving Them Both: A Study of Bisexuality and Bisexuals (London: Martin Brian & O'Keeffe, 1973);

Out of the Garden (London: Hart-Davis, MacGibbon, 1974);

'*No Novel Reader*' (London: Martin Brian & O'Keeffe, 1975).

Colin MacInnes established his reputation as a new voice in fiction during the late 1950s and early

Colin MacInnes

1960s by introducing fresh subject matter for the serious novel. His London novels investigated the contemporary worlds of immigrant blacks; teenagers who have achieved affluence; prostitutes, pimps, and police. He went on to depict the slave-holding society of the eighteenth century, the Elizabethan underworld and theater, and socio-political decline in present-day England. By profession a journalist as well as a novelist, he fused a command of fact with an imaginative apprehension of reality and a strong moral commitment to humanistic values. His distinctive books are not documentaries but original and unsentimental re-creations of various subworlds in English culture which skillfully imitate the speech patterns of their inhabitants.

MacInnes was born in South Kensington, London, into an upper-middle-class literary and artistic family. His mother, Angela, class-conscious as her son would never be, was the daughter of the classical scholar J. W. Mackail, professor of poetry at Oxford, and the maternal granddaughter of the Pre-Raphaelite painter Sir Edward Burne-Jones;

Rudyard Kipling was a first cousin, twice removed. As Angela Thirkell, MacInnes's mother would become a popular and prolific writer of light fiction during the 1930s and 1940s and, as such, a burden to her son, who did not wish his work to be identified with hers because he felt it gave a "sterile, life-denying" picture of England. Disliking his mother and her values (the feeling was mutual), he admitted publicly that some of his themes were chosen "precisely because they were ones that would disgust her." His father, James Campbell MacInnes, of whose achievements he was prouder, was an accomplished concert baritone—though unfortunately also a heavy drinker (as his son too would later be). MacInnes himself loved music, especially jazz, and wrote *Sweet Saturday Night* (1967), a historical account, out of his fascination with the English music-hall tradition. In 1917, when MacInnes was three years old, Angela divorced her tempestuous and adulterous husband on grounds of cruelty. She, her two sons (Graham, the elder, would become a memoirist), and an infant daughter (who soon died of pneumonia) were by then living in her parents' London house. MacInnes remembered with gratitude how the family custom of daily reading aloud in the evening, begun in his grandparents' cultured household and later continued in his mother's own home, introduced him to the nineteenth-century novel. After Angela's remarriage to an Australian soldier, Capt. George L. A. Thirkell, a metallurgical engineer, the Thirkells immigrated to Australia in 1920, first to Hobart in Tasmania, then to a suburb of Melbourne, where George made a modest living as general manager of an automobile parts firm. MacInnes attended Scotch College in Melbourne, a Presbyterian academy, and enjoyed vacation trips to the prosperous sheep ranches which would later provide him with settings for his two Australian novels. In 1930, a few weeks after his mother had left her second husband (and the Australian environment she detested), he followed her and his younger stepbrother, Lance, to England, back to his grandparents' home again. Though he was devoted to art he intended to spend just one year in England then return to study law in Australia. After constant friction with a grandmother attempting to make him less of an Australian boor, he was sent off to Switzerland instead.

A family friend described MacInnes as unusually beautiful at sixteen, even angelic in looks—but not in temperament. At seventeen he found employment with a British firm based in Brussels, where he remained until he was twenty-one. He spoke French (which he had first mastered by living with a family at Sceaux-Robinson near Paris) almost exclusively and acquainted himself with French literature during these years, which he later deemed a "major influence" on his writing. During this time Graham effected a reconciliation with the father the boys had not seen since early childhood, and MacInnes reverted to his own surname in place of Thirkell, as an expression of loyalty. He also finally acknowledged his own temperamental affinities and returned to England in 1936 to live in London's bohemia and paint. His interest in art would later be reflected in introductions written for catalogues of exhibitions by Australian artist Sidney Nolan and sculptor Tim Scott. The war aborted his new career, and he served in the British army from 1939 to 1945, one year in the infantry and five as a sergeant in the Intelligence Corps, the inspiration for his first novel.

MacInnes began to write seriously in 1945, his first "instructor," as he termed it, being radio. Returning to London after demobilization (to remain there for most of the rest of his life, never marrying) he wrote some 1500 radio scripts for the BBC in the next few years. By 1948 he had completed his first novel, *To the Victors the Spoils*, but could not find a publisher until two years later. Largely autobiographical in the way of many first novels, *To The Victors the Spoils* is a slow-moving, first-person account of Sergeant "Mac" in British Intelligence during the closing days of the war. Mac passively (and tediously) travels with his unit from Holland to Belgium to Germany, unhappily observing his comrades amass spoils, until finally he takes the initiative and, in the book's most vivid scenes, empties a German prison. The book closes with pointed observations—on the danger of police power and the prison mentality required to maintain it; on the shared culpability for the injustices of the war; and on responsibility for others. All these themes recur in MacInnes's later novels. Likewise the moral earnestness, the painstaking, mundane detail, the avoidance of sensationalism, and the heavy reliance on dialogue anticipate the later novels. But MacInnes would afterwards learn to individualize his characters' speech and natures better and to add tension and variety to his plots. Despite its shortcomings *To the Victors the Spoils* was designated Book Find of the Month by the *Daily Sketch* and was recommended by the Book Society.

MacInnes's second novel, *June in Her Spring* (1952), set in Australia, fared less well. As he ruefully observed in 1961, "This short sad lyric about adolescent girl and boyhood in 'The Bush,' the best thing I've yet written, was commercially, and by the meagre notice it aroused, a total failure." His feeling for this well-paced and touching depiction of star-crossed youth doubtless owed something to its autobiographical resonance. His orphaned young hero's father has had a concert career ruined by alcoholism and marriage, like James Campbell MacInnes; was a military hero in World War I, like George Thirkell; and has bisexual proclivities, like MacInnes himself. The book's theme of youth menaced by the faults of its elders had a certain personal immediacy, too. Wisely MacInnes again underplayed the sensational aspects of his plot. In the raptures of first love, sixteen-year-old June abruptly learns about the hereditary mental instability which destroyed her brother's moral capacity, and has now driven her father to suicide, and breaks off her relationship with seventeen-year-old Ben. And yet love has its bittersweet triumph. Through love of June, this confused victim of a domineering and homosexual guardian (once his father's male lover and now his) finds himself and achieves his independence.

With this second novel MacInnes found what were to be his most frequent themes (loss of innocence and growth into manhood) and character (the late teenage male); what is more, he offered his most lifelike rendering of adolescence, with its volatile moods. Assailed by self-doubt, however, he waited four years before attempting another novel, concentrating instead on nonfiction. In the 1950s he started his highly successful career as a journalist which was to continue until his death and include publication in an impressive list of periodicals: *Cahiers des Saisons*, *Encounter*, *Guardian*, *New Left Review*, *New Society*, *New Statesman*, *Observer*, *Partisan Review*, *Saltire Review*, *Spectator*, the London and the New York *Times*, and *Twentieth Century*.

He was living in racially mixed Stepney when, while least certain of his novelistic abilities, ironically enough he found his best fictional direction—social consciousness—and published the books which established his reputation as a novelist: the London novels *City of Spades* (1957), *Absolute Beginners* (1959), and *Mr. Love and Justice* (1960). (These were republished in 1969 in an omnibus edition: in England as *Visions of London*, in America as *The London Novels*.) Autonomous novels linked by a 1950s setting, they recreate worlds hidden within a more often fictionalized London, with great sympathy for social underlings. A keen observer of social change, MacInnes wanted his books to picture the immediate reality of postwar England to counter the English proclivity for ignoring social flux, as if that would cause all those bizarre new groupings to disappear. He evidently also wanted to expose social wrongs such as racial discrimination and police corruption. Many of the same topics are the subjects of his nonfictional contemporaneous essays and articles later collected in *England, Half English* (1961). He also expressed his personal fascination with London in the interpretive text for photographer Erwin Fieger's *London, City of Any Dream* (1962). In his novels his feeling for the here and now of London life released his creative powers; he was able to translate his intimate knowledge of a locale and mores into fiction which develops timeless themes from topical concerns. In *England, Half English* he characterizes his London novels aptly as "poetic evocations of a human situation, with undertones of social criticism of it; wildly romantic in mood and . . . rigorously analytic . . . by implication."

By far the best novel of the three is *City of Spades* because of its firmly controlled indignation over social injustice and its compelling characterization of a young Nigerian. The book owes much to MacInnes's recent personal acquaintance with black emigres, particularly a young man named Hawton, who resided with him sporadically and became the model for the novel's raffish and ebullient black hero, eighteen-year-old Johnny Fortune from Lagos. So taken was MacInnes with Hawton that, after Hawton died of pneumonia in England, MacInnes visited his family in Nigeria and arranged for their adoption of a child Hawton had fathered. The point of view in the novel alternates between Johnny and a twenty-six-year-old white hero, bumbling but well-intentioned Montgomery Pew, newly appointed to the Colonial Department and probably partly a projection of MacInnes himself. A year among Johnny and his friends radically transforms Pew: he loses his respectable standing, his job, and his illusions about English fairness. Yet, once a timorous and inhibited soul, Pew also learns to live more confidently and joyously by consorting with people who do not "deposit our days in a savings bank, like you do. Our notion is that the life is given us to be enjoyed." Johnny meanwhile has lost his own social innocence as the victim of English coldness and active legal injustice in the form of prejudgments, beatings, and perjury. He peddles drugs, is accused of pimping, goes to jail, and finally returns to Lagos, but his spirit is unbroken. Two Englishwomen have paid heavily, though without any bitterness, for loving him: Theodora, who loses her BBC job and her reputation over an ungrateful

Johnny; and young Muriel, who bears his child but is abandoned by him.

While it is a plea for brotherhood, *City of Spades* nonetheless acknowledges the practical realities of the cultural clash between peoples so different as the Africans (and West Indians, who also figure in the narrative) and the English. Theodora's regretful awareness is also MacInnes's, that "we can never really understand each other because we see the whole world utterly differently. In a crisis each race will act according to its nature, each one quite separately, and each one be right, and hurt the other." *City of Spades* was favorably reviewed, and MacInnes began to be recognized as a distinctively new voice in fiction. Although there were some who accused him of being merely a documentary novelist, a sociologist in the house of fiction, like many other reviewers the London *Times Literary Supplement* writer demurred: "The honesty with which Mr. MacInnes states the social problems of London's Coloured population must not be allowed to obscure the fact that he has written not a sociological treatise but a first-rate novel."

The central topic of *Absolute Beginners* is the teenage social phenomenon of the 1950s, especially focusing on independent youth of the less respectable sort. This novel is developed as a coming-of-age tale whose climactic incident is the 1958 Notting Hill race riots. The fast-talking, unnamed narrator, who supports himself by free-lance (preferably pornographic) photography, lives in a colorful slum where he revels in the camaraderie of outcasts like homosexuals and coloureds and in the freedom of being accepted as a man because he can look after himself and pay his own way. On his nineteenth birthday, the riots begin; the shock of their viciousness and, worse, of Englishmen's passive acceptance of it, is the ordeal by disillusionment which initiates him into actual moral and social manhood. Hitherto he and his teenage friends have pugnaciously defended themselves against adult responsibilities, seeing themselves as "absolute beginners" in a brave new social world of their own, with its own mystique and sense of power. But now he exchanges his separate status as dropout for commitment to the brotherhood of man and the obligations of decent Englishmen. MacInnes lets his narrator instruct the reader in the dress, mores, preoccupations, and preferences of teenage culture and, as the sole point of view, saturate the reader in its locutions. Like that of *City of Spades* and all his mature fiction, the breezy dialect is designed, MacInnes explained, to be "true . . . to the minds and spirits of the characters. . . . I tried in each case to re-invent, from reality, a more 'real'—and therefore timeless—language." Fortunately MacInnes does not take the teenage "thing" as seriously as his narrator tries to do, directing his own irony against the youthful delusion that life offers special dispensations to adolescents. The conception of the book is good and its energetic idiom convincing, but the prevailing comic vitality of its teenage life clashes noticeably with the serious tone of the splendidly described riots at the end. Though there were some objections to a clinical quality and to a narrator too mature for his years, reviewers were largely fascinated by the world MacInnes had exposed to them and impressed by his vigorous verbal impersonation.

Mr. Love and Justice focuses its social concerns on police honor and the plight of ponces (pimps). Attacking social respectability, which is translated into laws that are "the licensed keeper of our own bad conscience," the novel defines the ponce as a societal scapegoat. Discriminatory laws make him liable to prosecution on the word of the prostitute whose own trade (so long as she does not solicit publicly) is not illegal, and he is the prey of a vice squad sanctimoniously performing its social mission with an undisguised contempt for truth. MacInnes insists that it is dangerous to delegate too much power to police; the force of individual morality based on love assures more justice than any corruptible public force. In this quasi-allegorical novel, only the two twenty-six-year-old main characters, subjects of alternating chapters told by a narrator, have names: Frankie Love, a merchant seaman turned ponce for lack of a berth, and Edward Justice, a policeman become probationer on the vice squad. Their names identify their social functions, not their convictions or existential values, since Mr. Love, for whom love is only sex, believes in the reality of an absolute, transcendent justice, while Mr. Justice believes in the reality of perfect love. The antagonists gradually merge into Mr. Love and Justice by revealing their capacity for living by both principles. More harshly tested by events than Love, Justice has practiced extortion, perjury, and deception and ponced off his girl's fidelity, if not her body, to advance his career. But he discovers that his deepest loyalties are to the moral force of love, not the corrupt social force of the police. He resigns from his job to save his soul and his love. A rough diamond, polished rather than drastically altered by his experiences, Love meanwhile confirms a deep sense of honor, even under the provocations of English injustice.

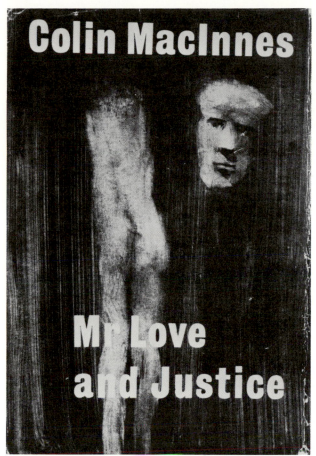

Dust jacket for MacInnes's 1960 novel about law, love, and crime in contemporary London

Cleverly constructed and successful in depicting its main characters, the novel is weakened by excessive set speeches and incredibly villainous minor characters. Reviewers questioned a manipulated plot and over-schematization, and again accused MacInnes of too much interest in sociology; but they praised the authenticity of the milieu depicted by a "modern Hogarth" (as the *New York Times* reviewer put it). Anthony Burgess lauded the entire trilogy in *The Novel Now* (1967) for not exploiting the sensational or lapsing into propaganda; even if MacInnes lacked a "sharp ear" for the actual language of his subjects' worlds and substituted made-up dialects, his work was "psychologically accurate, very enlightening, and full of a real (and quite unsentimental) compassion."

By this time, it was MacInnes's habit to correlate his nonfiction and fiction, using the same material for both. A frequent traveler, he had visited

Poland and East Africa, as well as Nigeria, during the 1950s. Now, after six months of memory-renewing travels in his second homeland, he wrote the interpretive text for the Time-Life picture book *Australia and New Zealand* (1964) and then published his second Australian novel, *All Day Saturday* (1966). A short, nostalgic, modern pastoral, which pairs off (and re-pairs) three couples, *All Day Saturday* pays tribute to honest, unselfish young love, healthy in its physicality and vital in its promise of growth; again, as in *June in Her Spring*, youth is menaced by age. On a single midsummer day in the 1920s, when the locals have convened for the regular all-day Saturday ritual of food, drink, and sport at the prosperous sheep farm of the Baileys, events are enlivened by the intrusion of a tough-minded, belligerent city boy, Norman Culley, who captures the fancy of the middle-aged chatelaine of Cootamundra, Helen Bailey. In a society where, for a brief (and to MacInnes, admirable) moment in history, "the cult of happiness is paramount: hedonistic, mindless, intent upon the glorious physical instant," this fastidious, neurotic misfit, who seeks the perfect spiritual love, has long been estranged from her more realistic, though equally selfish, husband. However, her delusive passion for Norman brings husband and wife together again, after a fashion. Norman more agreeably pursues and wins Helen's young hired companion Maureen, as healthy and uncomplicated in appetites as he, though a far more decent person. Contact with Helen and Maureen has (incredibly enough) changed his cynical sense of love as sex and transformed his selfish devotion to male pride into something like love for a woman. The pairing of Norman and Maureen contrasts with the loveless misalliance of rich and reputedly impotent old Julius and materialistic young Nancy, Helen's second companion. Unfortunately Australian love failed MacInnes here more disastrously than in *June in Her Spring*. Despite some tellingly ironic analyses of local habits, *All Day Saturday* is sentimental in its assumptions and clumsy in its language, as disappointed reviewers were quick to point out.

MacInnes turned to more promising material with his 1969 novel, *Westward to Laughter*, a formal satire on Robert Louis Stevenson's *Treasure Island* and similar blood-and-thunder novels which ignore the realities of Caribbean life. It is (in MacInnes's own words) "a critique of an eighteenth-century slave society in terms of the apprehensions of our times," its narrator a "sort of Candide." Falling from innocence into experience, sixteen-year-old Alexander Nairn, a Scottish Presbyterian recently or-phaned by the Jacobite Rebellion of 1745, leaves his garden eastward in Eden to voyage westward to an absurd world of evil. Sentenced to be hanged at nineteen on the ironically named Joie, Isle of St. Laughter, he writes the episodic first-person memoir which is the matter of the book, ostensibly preserved by the island's pious but hypocritical minister. Shipped off to the British West Indies as passenger on a slaver by his loveless uncle, Alexander jumps ship at Laughter only to be forced into slavery by British "justice," which he flees by joining a pirate crew and a black slaves' revolt. The revolt anticipates modern revolts even as the chattel slavery foreshadows modern forms of slavery. Bitter experience teaches Alexander not only the degradation but the spiritual cost of slavery, since "the free too must lose their freedom; which is any choice whatever of compassion, or, indeed, of human feeling, even most minimal, towards another." Alexander's learning, however, encompasses more than the meaning of slavery. Having been frequently a witness to atrocities and the recipient of abuse and betrayals, rejected by his uncle, and traduced by the planter's daughter he had rescued from a kidnapping (when he really hungers to believe in love), Alexander goes to his death refusing the solace of prayer and only half-joking about preferring witchcraft to Christianity. He has a very modern sense that existence is a moral chaos in which the wicked prosper and the rest are perpetually and pointlessly punished.

To MacInnes meaninglessness is the cost of man's inhumanity to man. This book is a successful novel: well-paced, engrossing, and intelligent; fluent in its prose and skillful in its characterization of Alexander. Reviewers lavishly admired its fresh and "extraordinary" imitation of the verbal style of the eighteenth-century novel. But they were more inclined to find the book an entertaining adventure story than a forceful satire or profound interpretation of history, though they praised the thematic thickening of the genre MacInnes had achieved and his effective assimilation of fact to fiction. There was no longer any assumption that MacInnes was a mere documentarian.

Late in 1969 MacInnes moved from London to Folkestone, Kent, because London, with its foul air and din, frantic modernization, and high prices, had begun to seem unlivable to him. His next, and longest, novel, the thematically ambitious *Three Years to Play* (1970), reflects the move in the fate of its Elizabethan hero: fourteen-year-old Aubrey returns to Epping Forest to settle down after three picaresque and illuminating years seeking his fortune in London. Since MacInnes characteristically keeps an eye on the social scene, the reader learns what Elizabethan underworld life was like when Aubrey falls in among hardworking pickpockets, whores, and panders, controlled in businesslike modern fashion by rival gangleaders. Aubrey, however, also becomes more dangerously involved, at least peripherally, in popish plots which cost him a bit of jail and torture. At sixteen he marries a reformed whore with respectable aspirations, whom he struggles to support, and has a son, whom he names Will after the most impressive man he has met, Shakespeare. Will provides Aubrey's—and the reader's—entry into the daily working world of the theater. And not just the working world. As MacInnes would soon explain in *Loving Them Both: A Study of Bisexuality and Bisexuals* (1973), he admired the prepuritanical Shakespearean age for its acceptance of bisexuality as natural; he therefore also included as a theme in his novel "the sexual patterns of the boy actors who played women's roles"—not to mention the Shakespeare of the sonnets. (The Dark Lady ingeniously enters the novel as a popish Frenchwoman, Marie-Claire, would-be destroyer of the too-revealing poems; she commits suicide by drowning when Will Shakespeare rejects her for flitting between himself and Southampton.)

Aubrey's days of excitement and glory are as brief as youth, as idylls in Arden, and as the stage life of a boy actor, who has "but three years to play." Yet art is long: MacInnes also develops his own version of a familiar Shakespearean theme. Shakespeare sees in the tale Aubrey tells him of evanescent adventures with his London friends the germ of *As You Like It*. Adapting the names and even the sexes of the "real-life" characters, he writes the play as he likes, then arranges for Aubrey (who will play Audrey) and friends to perform its roles. The reader of the novel is consequently obliged to speculate on the relationship of the artist to his creations and of his creations to reality. Aubrey suspects that the play is "far less about my life than his," and Shakespeare confirms it: "all that was ever writ" comes from what a writer reads, hears, and mostly "learns from his own heart," that little we know which is still "a little more than we may know the lives of others." As he did in the story of the genesis of the play, no doubt MacInnes intended to comment on his own art. A cleverly conceived novel with an appealing hero, but too long and slow-moving in its development, *Three Years to Play* received mixed reviews, which ranked it from tedious to competent to lively; from a successful recreation of Elizabethan times and language to poor ap-

proximations of both. Some reviewers questioned an expense of intelligence in a waste of ingenuity.

Out of the Garden, published in 1974, was MacInnes's last novel. In 1975 he would publish '*No Novel Reader*,' a book-length essay on the development of the novel as a genre, with a pertinent prognosis for its successful future because " 'nonfiction,' in its various forms, will never entirely satisfy the instincts of those who prefer a more directly imaginative version of reality." Besides this, "the absurdity of making so sharp a distinction between recorded fact and fiction, will become increasingly apparent." Not surprisingly '*No Novel Reader*' also declares MacInnes's affection for the general reader, who is unencumbered by academic snobbishness and aesthetic preconceptions. In 1976 MacInnes died in London of stomach cancer almost two years after what he assumed was successful surgery to remove a growth. Unaware that he would die so soon and habitually industrious, he was studying Japanese and Gaelic and was still writing articles for periodicals.

For his last novel, *Out of the Garden*, MacInnes returned to a contemporary English setting to develop his most characteristic theme and intention: a loss of innocence which obliges the reader also to see circumambient reality more clearly. The central concern is sociopolitical, with Britain's handling of the crisis in Northern Ireland a particular issue. As the reviewer for the *New Statesman* summed it up, the book is a "treatise on the role of the military in our post-colonial period, using the analytical techniques of Marxism to draw reverse political conclusions." The threat to Britain, in its own declining power, is expressed with Swiftian neatness by the military philosopher who envisions "the last battles of a decaying imperialism . . . fought at its very point of origin": that is, England is the ideal last colony for modern Britain to take over in a military action, since shooting Irishmen has been wonderful training for the home terrain. Couched largely in dialogue, set speeches, epistles, up-to-date catch phrases, and plentiful obscenities, *Out of the Garden* is an ironic allegory, liberally indebted to Genesis for structural effects. The setting for this Eden, however, is a fake Victorian ruin, Otranto Towers and its park—"the Ruin," or England in a state of decline whose roots lie in the eighteenth century, when she began smarting over the loss of her colonies. Rattler (a nefariously decadent aristocrat and former commanding officer who is Mephistophelian in his cynical insights and in his fondness for his chief victim) and his cohort, Lady Aspen—respectively tempters to power and sex and jointly to bitter wisdom—entice a decent working-class family to the garden of original sin. Ostensibly they and the family will soon be opening a horror house, later modified into a pleasure garden at a stately home, for middle-class outings; either way, the ruin will answer the contemporary public appetite for new sensations. Let the lower classes beware of where their presumable betters lead them: the garden is actually a cover for gunrunning to Belfast and, worse, a center for a counterrevolutionary plot led by Rattler to take over Britain and then the world. The family consists of ex-Sergeant Adams, still gullibly loyal to his former officer but increasingly unhappy with his role as civilian supporter; his skeptical wife, Evie, eager to expand her horizons; and their potentially juvenile-delinquent sons, Kik and Mas, who have nicknamed themselves after the Kikuyu and Masai tribes, respectively tillers of the soil and herdsmen in Kenya, where their father and Rattler fought. Kik eventually kills Mas. Finally Evie's father, Mr. Angell, a hard-line Marxist, comes to remove the Adamses to a new life of simpler, more sensible labor. In lieu of a flaming sword he shines the headlights of his battered car full on the estate.

In *Out of the Garden* MacInnes exposes television, public relations experts, military historians and philosophers, property developers and financiers (these last embodied in a character much like Rattler), sexual callousness and kinks, motor-vehicle mania, contempt for foreigners, and the cliches of feminism, Marxism, and nihilism. He also expresses his faith in the good sense of common people as the salvation of society. Reviewers accurately found the book sometimes perplexing but lively and intellectually stimulating; what is more, they found it only too just in its apprehensions about military influence over English life. However, it was also too obviously allegorical and tendentious. Curiously (possibly because ironies so overlap ironies in the book), for the *Times Literary Supplement* reviewer, *Out of the Garden* instead gave the impression of "not really wanting to be taken seriously."

But, though he regularly used comic effects, MacInnes always wanted to be taken seriously. Throughout his career, his fiction was more in danger of overly earnest teaching and telling than of any other fictional failing. He had a regrettable urge to guide the general reader to truth by explaining what the reader might better have discovered unaided and to lecture where he could better have dramatized—or already had. Yet MacInnes also knew how to concoct a tale and phrase the speech issuing from an individual mouth

in a specific setting. Once he had discovered his flair for social consciousness, he wrote fictions which are largely, and sometimes wholly, acts of skillful imaginative apprehension of an impressively varied array of lives, illuminating areas most other serious novelists have ignored; and he did this in novels which are not repetitions of each other. Increasingly, his books were well received by popular audiences, and, consequently, his earlier novels were republished. Critical attention came primarily in the form of a growing number of reviews and occasional inclusion in assessments of current fictional trends. While noting lapses in his fictional technique and denying him profundity, critics praised MacInnes for his verbal versatility and his sincere concern for the condition of England and her lesser folk.

Other:

Sidney Nolan, *Catalogue of an Exhibition of Paintings from 1947 to 1957*, introduction by MacInnes (London: Whitechapel Gallery, 1957); republished as *Sidney Nolan: 11-35*, by Kenneth Clark, MacInnes, and Bryan Robertson (London: Thames & Hudson, 1961);

Erwin Fieger, *London, City of Any Dream: Photographed in Colour*, text by MacInnes (London: Thames & Hudson, 1962);

Ada Leverson, *The Little Ottleys*, foreword by MacInnes (London: MacGibbon & Kee, 1962);

Editors of *Life* and MacInnes, *Australia and New Zealand* (New York: Time, 1964);

Tim Scott, *Sculpture 1961-67*, introduction by MacInnes (London: Whitechapel Gallery, 1967).

Periodical Publications:

"46 Faustroll Court," *Twentieth Century*, 169 (March 1961): 227-237;

"The Writings of Brendan Behan," *London Magazine*, n.s., 2 (August 1962): 53-61;

"Mum's the Word," *New Statesman*, 65 (7 June 1963): 866, 868;

"Dark Angel: The Writings of James Baldwin," *Encounter*, 21 (August 1963): 22-33;

"A Disconcerting Gift," *New Statesman*, 66 (27 September 1963): 402-406;

"A Pre-Raphaelite Memory," *Spectator*, 211 (11 October 1963): 453, 455;

"Michael and the Cloak of Colour," *Encounter*, 25 (December 1965): 8-15;

"Through a Glass Darkly," *New Statesman*, 74 (18

August 1967): 197;

"Exiles Delight," *Encounter*, 36 (April 1971): 34-48;

"A Tardy Revival," *Spectator*, 226 (17 April 1971): 26-27;

"Calypso Lament," *New Society*, 20 (6 April 1972): 4;

"Cancer Ward," *New Society*, 36 (29 April 1976): 232-234.

References:

Harriet Blodgett, "City of Other Worlds: The London Novels of Colin MacInnes," *Critique*, 8.1 (1976): 105-118;

Anthony Burgess, *The Novel Now: A Guide to Contemporary Fiction* (New York: Norton, 1967): 146-147;

Nat Hentoff, introduction to *The London Novels of Colin MacInnes* (New York: Farrar, Straus & Giroux, 1969): vii-xii;

Joseph J. Johnson, "Colin MacInnes's *Three Years to Play*," *Literary Annual* (White Plains, N.Y.: Salem Press, 1972): 322-325;

David Lodge, "The Contemporary Novel and All That Jazz," *London Magazine*, n.s., 2 (August 1962): 73-80;

Graham MacInnes, *Finding a Father* (London: Hamilton, 1967), pp. 95-97, 113-119;

MacInnes, *Humping My Bluey* (London: Hamilton, 1966), pp. 176-179;

MacInnes, *The Road to Gundagai* (London: Hamilton, 1965), chapters 1, 3, 5, 8, 9, 14, 15;

Bryan Robertson, "Perfect Pitch," *Spectator*, 236 (1 May 1976): 13;

Margot Strickland, *Angela Thirkell* (London: Duckworth, 1977), pp. 38, 58-61, 71, 72, 91, 108, 120, 164-165;

G. G. Urwin, ed., *A Taste for Living: Young People in the Modern Novel* (London: Faber & Faber, 1967): 65-68;

Paul West, *The Modern Novel* (London: Hutchinson, 1963), pp. 136-137.

Elizabeth Mavor

(17 December 1927-   )

Teresa Valbuena and Jay L. Halio

BOOKS: *Summer in the Greenhouse* (London: New Authors, 1959; New York: Morrow, 1960);

The Temple of Flora (London: Hutchinson, 1961);

The Virgin Mistress: A Study in Survival: The Life of the Duchess of Kingston (London: Chatto & Windus, 1964; Garden City: Doubleday, 1964);

The Redoubt (London: Hutchinson, 1967);

The Ladies of Llangollen: A Study in Romantic Friendship (London: M. Joseph, 1971);

A Green Equinox (London: M. Joseph, 1973).

Hardly a prolific writer, Elizabeth Mavor's four novels and two biographies, written over the last two decades, nevertheless represent a significant contribution to contemporary English letters. Her novels demonstrate a variety of fictional techniques as well as an ability to blend the world of nature and myth with the ordinary lives of men and women. She is particularly adept at presenting the dual nature of sex (that is, male/female attitudes and feelings in the same person), especially as experienced by women. Her accomplishments re-ceived one kind of recognition when her fourth novel was short-listed for the Booker Prize in 1973.

Descended from William Congreve and a niece of the contemporary writer James Bridie, Elizabeth Mavor was born on 17 December 1927 in Glasgow, where her father was a director in the firm of Mavor and Coulson. She was brought up in an old-fashioned way, with nannies and governesses, and her recollections of childhood are those of peace and tranquillity. She early fell in love with the natural world, and writing, painting, and drawing became lifetime pursuits. She wrote her first story at five and a half. Sent to St. Leonard's, a girls' boarding school, she was taught to play games such as lacrosse, cricket, field hockey, and tennis. The curriculum—quite good, she recalls—was devoted to the classics but also included French, English, art, and mathematics. By seventeen Mavor was writing poetry for her school magazine and wrote short stories at home.

In 1947 she entered St. Anne's College, Oxford, where she took her degree, a third in modern history, in 1950, having decided to read history because she had always loved the past, which continues to hold her interest. Apparently she was more involved in editing the *Cherwell*, a popular Oxford magazine, than in preparing for her examinations. She was the first woman to edit the *Cherwell*, and she also wrote for *Isis*, another Oxford magazine. During her undergraduate years she met several people who were later to become well known, notably critic, writer, and director Kenneth Tynan; novelist John Fowles; and politician Shirley Williams. Iris Murdoch, then an Oxford don, tutored Mavor in Marxist philosophy, but they never discussed writing fiction. Generally Mavor's years at Oxford were happy and carefree ones.

After taking her degree Mavor worked for *Argosy*, a Fleet Street magazine—a job she did not like because, as a woman, she was expected to know shorthand and typing. While her salary as a writer for *Argosy* was miniscule, her parents assisted her financially during those early years, and she led a comfortable existence. She traveled to places such as Italy and Greece, wrote, and enjoyed what London had to offer. On 10 January 1953, she married cartoonist Haro Hodson, whom she had met in Glasgow just before leaving for Oxford. They now live in Oxfordshire and have two sons, Peregrine and Tobias, both of whose names have literary associations.

In 1957 Hutchinson of London founded a subsidiary publishing company, New Authors Limited, to publish first books under a profit-sharing scheme. Although the company took no options on authors' second books, it was hoped that they would want to publish subsequently with the parent firm. New Authors Limited was described as "an attempt to reconcile the frustrations of the new writer who has something of importance to say . . . with the harsh economic climate of publishing as it is today." Directed by Michael Dempsey, it thus became a kind of "fiction nursery," which published the works of writers such as Beryl Bainbridge, J. G. Farrell, Julian Mitchell, and Maureen Duffy. By 1959, when Mavor's first novel was selected for publication, New Authors had already published nine others, including Keith Walker's *Running on the Spot* (1959) and Stanley Middleton's *A Short Answer* (1958).

The readers' reports on *Summer in the Greenhouse* divided three to one, and excerpts from some of them are included in the preliminary pages of the published volume. One report noted Mavor's "bright, poetic thread through chapter after chapter," and another attributed to Mavor "a wider range and a somewhat tougher streak than many of

Elizabeth Mavor

the woman writers who do this rather complicated, atmospheric sort of writing. . . ." The third remarked that, while she had "more sensitivity and talent than many published writers," she was yet another example of someone "who can set down the words beautifully but who has nothing to say." The report went on to complain that this was a general fault in English novels as opposed to American—"the obvious lack of an inspired theme, or driving compulsion, which makes it tremendously good, *despite* its style or its language." The consensus was that, despite its faults (and there are some), Mavor's novel "combines sensitivity of phrase with real imaginative understanding," a view that many reviewers later shared.

Mavor had gotten the idea for her novel about a child's quest and its outcome from a friend, and *Summer in the Greenhouse* (1959) is partly an evocation of childhood and partly a search for a combination of beauty and understanding. In the summer of 1939 nine-year-old Imogen Prescott, an orphan living with her wealthy, widowed grandfather, discovers an old love letter written to him by someone now called Mrs. Peachy, who owns a beautiful painting by Fra Angelico. Imogen decides to run away to Mrs. Peachy's house to see the painting, and en route meets James Faithfull, a poetic young man just out of Rugby, who is also bent on visiting Mrs. Peachy. They travel together the few miles to her home, where they spend several weeks with her as "passionate audience to her play, the play of her life reenacted," until Mrs. Peachy's ne'er-do-well son, Robin, interrupts their idyll. An embittered man in his thirties, he resents his mother's way of life, which he feels is so far from being capable of opening other people's eyes to what is lovely that it can only introduce them to a world of illusion. Yet it is, in fact, the illusion that his mother offers him at the end (that Edward Prescott is his natural father, not the ineffectual Peachy, now dead) which helps restore Robin, on the eve of World War II, to a sense of his own manhood and a renewed will to live.

Central to the novel is the paradox of innocence and experience, though it is not as adequately developed as the related theme of illusion and reality. Mrs. Peachy detains Imogen most of the summer by holding out the promise of showing her the Fra Angelico painting, supposedly at a restorer's

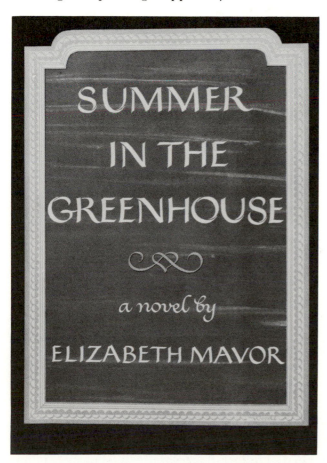

Dust jacket for the American edition of Mavor's first novel, which examines the paradox of innocence and experience

but actually hidden away in a cupboard; by keeping his granddaughter with her, she hopes to get her old beau to visit her again. However, when Robin rather cruelly reveals the hoax to Imogen (ironically just after she thinks she has finally lost her innocence), nothing is made of the incident. At the end of the novel, during an air raid alarm, Imogen discovers the painting at last, but its magical attraction for her no longer exists: "what she had once seen in it now eluded her. . . . It had been quite simply nothing more than a beautiful picture."

Critics responded favorably to the book, which was compared to similar work by established novelists. The reviewer in the *Times Literary Supplement*, for example, compared the novel to the fiction of Elizabeth Bowen and Elizabeth Taylor, adding that Mavor "can evoke with the best those languid summer days which seem essential to this feminine, civilized kind of novel. . . ." At the same time the reviewer noticed several weaknesses in technique, such as occasional obscurity in equating and merging illusion and reality, the use of "veiled symbols" and coincidences, and other artifices "unnecessary to an author whose own feeling for reality is the strongest and most promising aspect of her talent. . . ."

Few, if any, of these weaknesses are apparent in Mavor's second novel, *The Temple of Flora*, which Hutchinson brought out in 1961. To her strong sense of reality was now fused an equally strong sense of the sexual and mythical dimensions of experience. The setting is Thrussel, a rural English village with a decayed church and pagan rites practiced by children in its graveyard. To this town—a "microcosm," as Toby Corbett, one of the main characters, says, "of charming, scabby Europe in decline"—comes Dinah Gage after a disappointing love affair with another woman. Meeting Toby's wife, Sasha, she is encouraged to help in a campaign to revitalize the church, and together they enlist the services of the old priest, Benedict Purefoy.

Sasha's marriage is moribund, and being childless, she devotes most of her time to good works. For a while the trio are successful in their campaign, but their success is more apparent than real. Other forces are at work: the villagers' lust for novelty (as opposed to any deep-seated desire for order), their essentially pagan devotion to the life of the flesh, and a resentment against outlanders, especially those from higher classes who try to control them. Already suspect as an outsider, Dinah compounds matters by spontaneously seducing a young man of the village, Char Smith, one hot summer afternoon, after both have been overcome by stirrings neither fully comprehends. Later, in the company of four "mates," he attacks an old man believed to be hoarding some treasure; but he is let off lightly by the magistrates when Dinah confesses her involvement with him earlier in the day, which apparently had roused in Char emotions he could not handle fully. She then feels she must leave, but Purefoy persuades her otherwise. The awakening she has experienced—that she is not a "biological oddity," as she had thought—becomes a turning point in her life, and a subsequent affair with Toby confirms her heterosexuality and her sense of herself as a caring, sensitive person. For Toby their affair also marks a decided change, even though Dinah finally leaves Thrussel: "Back in the year before that strange and beautiful summer had begun, he had been a different man. A content man, an enclosed whole man, and now he was open, had had windows dashed into his being by the power of love, and he could not see wholly any more. Now he felt things, whereas then he thought them." For Sasha, who has learned of the affair, things are no longer the same either: "I feel that my life is going to move again," she tells Purefoy. Perhaps she will have a child; she is not sure what direction her life will take, but it will be different from the sterile thing it was.

Fertility, plenitude, and ripeness all figure in the novel, which reaches a climax in the great harvest festival planned by Sasha, Dinah, Purefoy, and others trying to revive the church. Their celebration is not so much spoiled as transformed by the raging bull that charges down the center aisle during the service. The symbolism is clear but not forced. Amos Pike, the rural Mephistopheles, is behind the incident, which includes Toby's surreptitious declaration of love to Dinah while shielding her from the bull, and ends with Purefoy's being dragged from the church by the animal he has tried to calm. Although Dinah eventually must, under Purefoy's guidance, give up her claims to Toby and leave the village, she does not renounce her love. Dinah's discovery of love in *The Temple of Flora* is her major achievement, as it is for the other principal characters as well.

Although Mavor's second novel did not receive as much attention as her first, it was generally well reviewed. As one critic said, "In her second novel Miss Mavor walks a fine tightrope between originality and eccentricity.... The resultant tragi-comedy includes some memorable set pieces that never strain our credulity in spite of their extravagance." The same critic also noted her "great gift" for creating atmosphere and sprightly dialogue, but said that she needed to develop her characters with greater subtlety.

During the time her first two novels were being published, Mavor was also at work on a biography of Elizabeth Chudleigh, the Duchess of Kingston. In her preface she says she had become interested in the subject seven years earlier after reading the letters of Horace Walpole, suggested to her by her husband. Struck by Walpole's frequent mention of "a lively demi-rep called Elizabeth Chudleigh," she found her curiosity aroused and sought to learn more about this famous eighteenth-century belle. Her "consuming interest" led Mavor on a quest to discover the duchess's letters, a search eventually completed when she received a microfilm of some thirty-four letters to the Electoress of Saxony for the years 1765-1775. By this time, although she had a wealth of information, Mavor felt she needed to visit those places in England where important events had happened involving her subject: Ashton in Devon, where Elizabeth was born, and the farm at Hall; Chelsea Hospital, where her father was lieutenant governor and where she lived until she was six; Lainston House, Hampshire, where her ill-omened marriage took place. Mavor ultimately saw all of them.

What finally emerged in 1964 was *The Virgin Mistress: A Study in Survival: The Life of the Duchess of Kingston*, a lively biography of one of the most colorful and scandalous women in the eighteenth century, who rose from relative poverty to a position of power and social eminence in English and international society. To attain her goals Elizabeth Chudleigh manipulated the people around her, and on one notorious occasion attended the Venetian ambassador's ball almost naked to attract the attention of prominent males, including the King. Elizabeth believed that money brought freedom as well as position and was persuaded to think of marriage as "an investment in growth shares." Her first marriage was performed secretly, and later, after she married a second time, she was tried for bigamy.

Comparing Mavor's work to several other biographies published during the same period, the London *Times* reviewer considered it the best and liked the "adult and easy" writing it displayed. But the reviewer in the *Times Literary Supplement* was more severe. While acknowledging Mavor's discovery of a great deal of new material, he lamented that this treasure had fallen into "inexpert hands" and listed a number of inaccuracies in Mavor's handling of the period. Her second attempt at biography seven years later received more uniform praise.

In her third novel, *The Redoubt* (1967), Mavor consolidates the strengths of her previous fiction and experiments with new styles and techniques. The depiction of childhood in the early chapters recalls *Summer in the Greenhouse*, and the marvelous descriptions of a storm that causes a seawall to give way are rivaled only by the descriptions of nature in *The Temple of Flora*. The narration shifts between first and third person, as the situation appears to demand. Although the transitions between these points of view are not always clear, they provide a greater flexibility and variation of viewpoint for the novelist, and Mavor later uses this technique in her fourth novel. Flashbacks are used effectively to compare and contrast the lives of the principal characters at the time of the main events, 1953, with significant earlier periods.

Mavor's novel is concerned with love, betrayal, and regeneration, as well as with the natural world, as it contrasts two unsuccessful marriages between younger people with an older couple's happy one. Having known Faber as a child, Eve does not meet him again until years later during her marriage to Archie, whom she has come to see as essentially a destroyer and poisoner, her "death-man husband." Faber, meanwhile, has been married to Cecie, who has borne his children but is otherwise cool, if not frigid, in their relationship. Sensing that Faber, who has done much to reclaim land and turn it into gardens and productive fields, is a creative man, Eve is again drawn to him. They carry on an affair in Lil's inn, Dirty Nancy, and, after Eve has become pregnant with Faber's child, she leaves her husband. Lil has known Eve since she was a child and does not really approve of the illicit affair going on under her roof; her own marriage to Mike was blissful and blessed, and now that he is dead she will probably never marry again, although another of her lodgers, a lepidopterist named Carl Christianson, is drawn to her.

The storm, which is the central episode, causes great destruction in the village, taking the lives of many, including Faber. Miraculously, although badly flooded, Dirty Nancy's is not totally destroyed, and during the height of the storm Lil and Carl help deliver Eve's child under extremely dangerous and difficult circumstances. At one point, to help revive her contractions, Lil climbs into bed with Eve to keep her warm, and later as a kind of sacrificial gesture she throws her wedding ring into the flood and persuades Carl to cast his detailed notes on butterflies and moths into the water as well.

During her labor, Eve hallucinates a great deal and, coming out of her trance, mutters "something about . . . being remade from destruction . . . remade from death," a statement that expresses a major theme of the novel. After the storm the various characters begin rebuilding their lives, some of which, like Carl's and Eve's, have altered permanently. Carl settles down with Lil in a more or less permanent arrangement, though not as her lover. Leaner than before, he is also gentler, less rigid, and more accessible. Eve is wiser and less flighty, knowing she must remake her life alone with Faber's child. Although many critics recognized the power of much of the novel, some found the ending too didactic or the setup too artificial.

Friendship between women, a leitmotiv in all her previous work, became the major focus of Mavor's next two books. *The Ladies of Llangollen: A Study in Romantic Friendship* (1971) is the biography of Sarah Ponsonby and Eleanor Butler, two celebrated eighteenth-century women of well-connected Irish families, who overcame the strenuous resistance of their relatives and spent the rest of their long lives together in a small Welsh village. Their determination was to establish an "ideal" life, and, as their reputation grew, their home at Plas Newydd eventually became a famous stopping place for visitors of every rank, including royalty. What attracted Mavor to write about the ladies, when she had not been contemplating another biography, was the subject matter of Eleanor Butler's paintings. She was curious to know why such scenes as *Gray's Charge at Waterloo* interested a woman painter. When by accident she discovered a book about her in a secondhand bookstore and found Butler's character rather differently described from what she had expected, her interest in Eleanor Butler and her relationship with Sarah Ponsonby grew. She proceeded to gather as much information as possible, traveling to Kilkenny and Tipperary in Ireland as well as to Wales. On one occasion, while she and her husband were copying some letters in one of the great houses they visited, several pugs came dashing into the room barking hysterically. The owner apologized, "I'm so sorry, you know, but they've never seen anybody read a book before!"

Secret or quiet lives—and public ones that reveal a secret or inner self—have always interested Mavor, and she did careful research not only into the lives of the ladies and their familes, but also into the "romantic friendships" of the late eighteenth century, when Sarah and Eleanor began living together. She found that the relationship between the two women was not unique and provided a general description: "symptoms of romantic friendship were 'retirement,' good works, cottages, gardening, impecuniosity, the intellectual pursuits of reading aloud and the study of languages, enthusiasm for the Gothick, journals, migraines, sensibility and often, but not always, the single state." The women's sexual relationship is never made clear and probably cannot be on the evidence available. Mavor speculates inconclusively that their private journals may contain some kind of code, whose key lies in Eleanor's migraines and Sarah's special devotions to her during these periods.

The Ladies of Llangollen received more attention from the reviewers than her previous two novels combined. Her scholarly work as well as her fluent style were especially commended. Typical is Jonathan Keats's comment in the *New Statesman*: "Shunning both cosiness and sensationalism, Miss Mavor uses her own extensive knowledge of the period . . . to emphasize the attraction of the Ladies' wholly eighteenth century triumph for their nineteenth century admirers. . . . She is a sympathetic and consistent biographer, working on a grid of meticulous reference to a great deal of fresh material. . . ." *Choice*, the *Economist*, *Times Literary Supplement*, and other journals and papers also carried favorable reviews of the biography.

Mavor's most recent novel, *A Green Equinox* (1973), like *The Redoubt*, uses a variety of narrative techniques, but its outstanding stylistic quality lies in its passages of lyrical beauty and, in keeping with its subject (the chief male character is an expert on rococo art), its rococolike effects (for example, "Her eyes were wide open. There were morsels of liquid moonlight between their parian lids"). The book is also much concerned with relationships between women, although it opens with an affair between a woman and a married man who is very anxious that his mistress should not meet, let alone have much to do with, his wife. But Hugh Shafto fails to prevent Hero from meeting Belle, an energetic woman like Sasha Corbett in *The Temple of Flora*, and the central episodes concern Hero's unexpected attraction to Belle. This attraction culminates in a sexual embrace while they are both lying in a hospital after an automobile wreck. Hero later thinks that the effect of the typhoid fever she was incubating at that time may have made her especially susceptible to Belle. Whatever the case, when Belle learns of Hero's affair with Hugh, she runs away, taking one of her children with her. Meanwhile Hero recuperates at

Marly, the estate of Hugh's mother, and her relationship with the elder Mrs. Shafto ripens into a love which, if not explicitly sexual, is as close and even deeper than the friendship she had begun with Belle. Mrs. Shafto's death by suicide, when she finds she has a fatal illness, leaves Hero no one to depend on. Like Eve in *The Redoubt*, she now faces having to make her way on her own, but with greater wisdom and strength acquired from recent experiences.

Critical response was favorable, and *A Green Equinox* was short-listed for Britain's most prestigious literary award, the Booker Prize, which is given to the best novel published in English in a given year by a British subject or a citizen of the British Commonwealth, the Republic of Ireland, or the Republic of South Africa. In 1973 the other novels short-listed included Beryl Bainbridge's *The Dressmaker*, J. G. Farrell's *The Siege of Krishnapur*, and Iris Murdoch's *The Black Prince*, which won the award.

At present Mavor is working on "The Cults of Sensibility in the Eighteenth Century," "a love book of history," as she calls it. A draft is already finished and being revised. After that, she plans to write a historical novel about a woman pirate, and she would eventually like to write a nonfiction book about her relationship with her sons, which has been rather stormy, funny, and sad. Mavor is very interested in relationships between parents and children, especially as a mother watches her children grow and develop their own personalities. While she is critical of younger people's attitudes toward their elders, Mavor does not intend her book to be in any sense condemnatory: she is mainly concerned to show the tragedy inherent in the generation gap as it has been fostered by today's social climate.

Among the many writers who have influenced Mavor or whose work she has enjoyed are D. H. Lawrence, Thomas Hardy, Virginia Woolf, and Muriel Spark. She is especially fond of William Golding's *The Inheritors* (1955) and Thomas Mann's *The Magic Mountain* (1927). She is critical of Iris Murdoch's fiction, finding it somewhat overrated. She regards *A Severed Head*, for example, as witty enough but says the characters tend to stereotypes and are manipulated too much by the author. Of her own work, she says she is fascinated by the processes that change a character and his or her outlook, especially as it is affected by a particularly shattering incident. This fascination also explains, in part, her interest in history. As she points out, we know more about the Battle of Waterloo than

Napoleon did, since he only saw it from one vantage point. She expects to continue experimenting with various techniques in her novels and believes that she will never finally settle on any single technique but continue exploring the possibilities available.

She is pleased that the present ambience allows writers greater freedom in their choice and treatment of subject matter, such as sex, than earlier writers enjoyed, and her own work shows an increasing tendency to exploit this freedom.

Ian McEwan
(21 June 1948-   )

John Fletcher
University of East Anglia

BOOKS: *First Love, Last Rites* (London: Cape, 1975; New York: Random House, 1975);

In Between the Sheets (London: Cape, 1978; New York: Simon & Schuster, 1978);

The Cement Garden (London: Cape, 1978; New York: Simon & Schuster, 1978);

The Imitation Game: Three Plays for Television (London: Cape, 1981)

The Comfort of Strangers (London: Cape, 1981; New York: Simon & Schuster, 1981).

Ian McEwan is very much a product of the new British universities, those popularly known as "plate-glass universities" to distinguish them from the older "red-brick universities" at which writers such as Kinglsey Amis or Philip Larkin have taught or still work. Built during the 1960s, they set out to revolutionize curricula and the general structure of academic life in Great Britain. To a significant extent they succeeded, and their graduates are beginning to make a distinctive impact on the cultural life of the United Kingdom. McEwan has perhaps established a greater reputation than any of their other graduates, but the dramatist Snoo Wilson, the novelist Clive Sinclair, and the television drama producer Jonathan Powell, all alumni of the University of East Anglia, which admitted its first students only in 1963, are already well known in their respective fields.

The University of East Anglia, based at Norwich, is particularly important in British literary history of the last two decades because of the presence on the teaching faculty there of two major novelists of the preceding generation, Angus Wilson and Malcolm Bradbury; indeed Bradbury was McEwan's instructor in the master's course in crea-

tive writing that McEwan successfully completed in 1972 with the submission of a dissertation consisting of stories subsequently included in his first book, *First Love, Last Rites* (1975). Since McEwan began writing seriously only in 1970, shortly before enrolling at the University of East Anglia, there can be no doubt that his early writing was significantly affected by his courses there. Equally, those who taught him are not likely to forget the impact he made on them. The way he looked intently and almost accusingly at one through his wire-rimmed glasses was especially characteristic, giving the impression of toughness, sharpness, and great intellectual rigor. These qualities shine through his writings and help account for their typically quiet uncompromising air; their tone is courteous, but not deferential, and they are studiously economical with words.

Ian Russell McEwan was born to David and Rose Moore McEwan in the military garrison town of Aldershot (his father was in the army), and he grew up in such outposts of the empire as Singapore and Libya. He went to a state-run boarding school in England, a common occurrence with children of military personnel serving overseas, and from there to the University of Sussex in Brighton, perhaps the best-known of the "new" universities, where he took an honors degree in English in 1970. During and after his M.A. year at East Anglia, he plunged briefly into the then flourishing post-1968 counterculture. He even made the required pilgrimage to Afghanistan in the days before the Russian invasion made that country less than hospitable to western hippies, but he soon grew bored with their irrationality and anti-intellectualism. In 1974 he settled in London and now lives in Clapham.

Ian McEwan

In one of his term papers at East Anglia, Mc-Ewan noted that Thomas Mann's character Tonio Kröger recognizes in the ordinary the most vital source for art. The more perceptive of McEwan's critics have seen that behind the morbid, even repellent imagery and the sense of impending evil that characterize his writing, there lies a transfiguration of the ordinary which creates a remarkable impact. Fellow-novelist Paul Ableman, for example, felt that McEwan's "spare, rather grey prose" succeeds in engendering the sensory experience he describes. It is certainly true that what remains in the reader's consciousness after finishing a McEwan story is an impression of great vividness, of the blinding clarity of everyday situations and occurrences—especially when the extraordinary intervenes to undermine them. At the same time McEwan's minutely accurate observations are capa-

ble of bringing the extraordinary back to an appallingly familiar reality. At moments like these McEwan reminds one of Kafka, of whom McEwan, noting Kafka's "aesthetic motivation in ordinary conduct," commented in the same term paper that "creative art encourages schizophrenia."

Schizophrenia, indeed, if only of a formal kind, characterizes much of McEwan's own writing. In a review of *First Love, Last Rites*, critic Jonathan Raban noted that this writing is "constitutionally incapable of being appalled," and indeed the contrast between the extreme precision and even beauty of the prose texture on the one hand, and the repellent, often frankly revolting nature of the subject matter on the other, is what strikes the reader most forcibly. It is, of course, easiest to recount the stories' shocking details: in the title story, for instance, the "last rites" of a pregnant rat, savagely destroyed by the narrator, are carried out by his girl friend in the room in which they have lived out their "first love":

> I stood over the rat and prodded it gently with the poker. It rolled on its side, and from the mighty gash which ran its belly's length there obtruded and slid partially free from the lower abdomen a translucent purple bag, and inside five pale crouching shapes, their knees drawn up around their chins. As the bag touched the floor I saw a movement, the leg of one unborn rat quivered as if in hope, but the mother was hopelessly dead and there was no more for it.
>
> Sissel knelt by the rat, Adrian and I stood behind her like guards, it was as if she had some special right, kneeling there with her long red skirt spilling round her. She parted the gash in the mother rat with her forefinger and thumb, pushed the bag back inside and closed the blood-spiked fur over it. She remained kneeling a little while and we still stood behind her. Then she cleared some dishes from the sink to wash her hands.

Such writing would be merely sensational if it were not, like Kafka's, so pointed, so accurate, so incapable indeed of being appalled. In contemporary writing one has to turn to French literature to encounter a similar contrast between the elegance of the language and the disturbing quality of the material; in writing in English McEwan is wholly unique. No one else combines in quite the same way exactness of notation with a comedy so black that many readers may fail to see the funny side at all. Nevertheless, they will be wrong: McEwan is, like Beckett, whom he also resembles in some respects, a comic writer.

Some of McEwan's humor, like that in the following sentence from "Homemade," the first story in *First Love, Last Rites*, is perhaps no more subtle than the jokes of the entertainer Tom Lehrer: "We walked across Finsbury Park where once Raymond, in his earlier, delinquent days had fed glass splinters to the pigeons, where together, in innocent bliss worthy of the 'Prelude', we had roasted alive Sheila Harcourt's budgerigar while she swooned on the grass nearby, where as young boys we had crept behind bushes to hurl rocks at the couples fucking in the arbour." But if this passage is similar to some of Lehrer's songs, like "Poisoning Pigeons in the Park," the macabre twist in the second story, "Solid Geometry," is more refined out-

landish. During one of their frequent violent disputes, the narrator's girl friend or wife smashes a glass jar, which contains a nineteen-century criminal's penis preserved in formaldehyde, and the narrator is left to clear up the mess. Characteristic of McEwan's style is the revolting detail ("my stomach heaved as the foreskin began to come away in my fingers"), but there is a hint of tenderness in what immediately follows: "Finally, with my eyes closed, . . . wrapping him carefully in the newspaper, I carried him into the garden and buried him under the geranium." A few pages later his girl friend apologizes, and he forgives her because "It was only a prick in pickle."

A more wicked form of humor characterizes the brief story "Cocker at the Theatre," which cleverly satirizes the current vogue for nakedness on the stage. An *Oh! Calcutta* type of show is in rehearsal somewhere in London's West End, and the (fully clothed and rather icy) choreographer has arranged the performers in a V-formation and set them all rocking backwards and forwards in time to the rhythms of the simulated sexual act. Unfortunately for her composure, and to the scandalized horror of the effeminate producer, one couple at the end of the V starts making love in earnest. The choreographer stomps out and the stage hands bring a bucket of water to separate the pair (like copulating dogs, of course, though McEwan refrains from underlining the point). They are, however, allowed to finish; the girl runs off to the dressing room and the man, whose name is Jack Cocker, reacts to the producer's sarcastic pronouncement that "you and the little man stuck on the end of you can crawl off this stage, and take shagging Nellie with you. I hope you find a gutter big enough for two," with the surprisingly dignified reply, "I'm sure we will, Mr. Cleaver, thank you." It is characteristic of McEwan's writing that the grotesque situation with its crude farce has been transcended by humanity in much the same way as reality has broken in to this artificial theater setting and emphasized the absurdity of what the actors are doing. It is the naked actors standing uncomfortably about with "no pockets to put their hands in" who are truly pathetic, not Cocker.

Like McEwan's best stories, "Cocker at the Theatre" concentrates on a single idea that it coolly and economically develops; the end is as satisfying as the opening is startling; and under the absurdity and repulsiveness of the subject matter lies a seriousness of intent which makes McEwan's writing, despite the horror and obscenity of the content, the very opposite of pornographic. Not all his stories are as effective and original as this one, of course. "Homemade" is a somewhat lurid treatment of brother-sister incest, which later became the theme of *The Cement Garden*; a not altogether convincing drowning, brought on by a laughing fit, ends "Last Day of Summer"; "Butterflies" is a rather conventional self-portrait of a pervert and child slayer; and "Conversation with a Cupboard Man" owes a little too much to Dostoyevsky's *Notes from Underground*, the hero of which McEwan described as a sick Hamlet stricken with inertia. Nevertheless, when one recalls that stories in this collection were submitted for a master's degree in creative writing, one cannot but marvel at the extraordinary precocity and individuality McEwan displays alongside the more common faults of the student writer: knowingness, literary allusiveness, and a sometimes tiresome desire to shock. The 1976 Somerset Maugham Award for *First Love, Last Rites* was well deserved.

McEwan's next short-story collection, *In Between the Sheets* (1978), is shorter than *First Love, Last Rites*, which was also brief. "Pornography," the opening story, is a black comedy about a man who infects two girl friends with venereal disease and is punished by them for this action and for two-timing them by the surgical removal of his penis. "We'll leave you a pretty little stump to remember us by," one of the girls tells him before he is anesthetized. Castration, like incest, is an obsession in McEwan's stories.

"Reflections of a Kept Ape" is about a failed woman novelist and her literate and articulate pet ape, who tells the reader that the physical phase of their relationship lasted a mere eight days, "the happiest eight days of my life," because "she complained that the friction of our bodies brought her out in a rash, and that my 'alien seed' (alien corn, I quipped fruitlessly at the time) was aggravating her thrush." "Two Fragments: March 199-" is set in a decaying London of the future; the first fragment introduces incest (father-daughter this time) and the second describes the narrator's visit to a former mistress followed by a mysterious encounter with a Chinese family who, evidently motivated by sheer hospitality, offer the narrator a particularly disgusting meal. "Dead As They Come" is a grotesque first-person account of an affair between a man and a life-size female dummy.

The title story, "In Between the Sheets," is an altogether more mature and accomplished piece of work. The sexual pathology involved is more "normal" and so more convincingly portrayed. The story opens in the startling fashion characteristic of

McEwan: "That night Stephen Cooke had a wet dream, the first in many years. Afterwards he lay awake on his back, hands behind his head, while its last images receded in the darkness and his cum, strangely located across the small of his back, turned cold. He lay still till the light was bluish-grey, and then he took a bath. He lay there a long time too, staring sleepily at his bright body under water." He falls asleep and has a dream that proves oddly prophetic. The dream concerns a cafe, a prepubescent waitress, and a coffee machine; he is buying coffee for his former wife, and the girl takes the cup and holds it to the machine. "But now *he* was the machine, now *he* filled the cup." Soon after this dream his fourteen-year-old daughter comes to stay with him for a few days, accompanied by a girl friend of the same age. Stephen is awakened in the night by a disagreeable set of noises, which he identifies as "the sound of his wife in, or approaching, orgasm." He tracks the noises to the girls' bedroom; but when his daughter emerges befuddled with sleep, she appears innocent. He soothes the girl and she is soon asleep once more. As he gazes at her, he sees "in the pallor of her upturned throat . . . from one bright morning in his childhood a field of dazzling white snow which he, a small boy of eight, had not dared scar with footprints."

The power of this story lies in its unemphatic suggestiveness and muted effects. Stephen gets an erection earlier as a result of contact with the two girls, but he is "horrified" as well as elated by it. Nothing unusual occurs, but Stephen is led by his strange dream and by his conflicting emotions over his wife, his daughter, and his daughter's friend to engage in some salutary self-criticism. His wife detests him and has already replaced him with a more vigorous lover, as if to punish him "for all the wasted hours between the sheets." This short story is clear and yet inexplicit, disturbing and yet without the occasionally excessive perversity that mars some of McEwan's other pieces. The realism, as usual, is heightened and intensified, but not so far as to infringe plausibility.

The collection also contains a somewhat unsatisfying experimental prose poem called "To and Fro" and ends with "Psychopolis," a funny, satirical story about an Englishman visiting Los Angeles. The comedy, sharp as it is, adds little to stories, by Evelyn Waugh and many other English writers, which cast a visiting Britisher as an "innocent abroad," a sort of grotesque inversion of the standard Jamesian motif of the naive American "ambassador" in corrupt old Europe. All the usual British clichés about Americans lovingly nurturing their neuroses are there, albeit wittily revived, but the story is memorable for a passage that describes rather well McEwan's own effects as a writer. The narrator is telling his Californian girl friend about a nightclub act he has witnessed. He is not sure whether the act is so clever as to be unfunny, or whether the man just came in off the street in his vomit-stained jeans and took over the microphone. "I've seen acts like that," Mary replies. "The idea, when it works, is to make your laughter stick in your throat. What was funny suddenly gets nasty." Comedy turning nasty is the essence of these stories, as reviewers were quick to note. Hermione Lee was impressed by "their peculiar images of pain and loss," which seem, she said, "to grow in depth" after the first shock has worn off, but she regretted at the same time "an air of mere games-playing" about what she termed "these neo-Gothic pieces." Nigel Williams, on the other hand, had few doubts; for him they were "witty, beautifully written, and original without being monstrous."

Comedy turning nasty could be said to be the essence, too, of *The Cement Garden* (1978), McEwan's first novel. It is a grotesque parody of that sentimental cliche "happy families" in which children play "mummies and daddies" in real (sexual) earnest. The son is masturbating and has his first orgasm at the precise moment his father, mixing cement in the garden, dies of a heart attack. Not long after, the mother dies too, and the children, left to their own devices, decide to bury her in cement in the cellar. Near the end of the novel, in an upstairs bedroom the youthful head of the household is deflowering his elder sister with kid brother dozing in his cot next to them. While the sister's boyfriend frees the entombed corpse, the police arrive. The novel ends in a particularly banal fashion: "It was the sound of two or three cars pulling up outside, the slam of doors and the hurried footsteps of several people coming up our front path that woke Tom. Through a chink in the curtain a revolving blue light made a spinning pattern on the wall. Tom sat and stared at it, blinking." The observation here is not only minutely accurate of the way a police vehicle's flashing light invades a darkened room, it also sets the extraordinary events of the novel in a familiar, realistic context. The novel would be rather silly if its tone were not so obsessive and sustained and if the sharpness of detail and observation were not so intense. *The Cement Garden* is not as satisfying as McEwan's best short stories, perhaps because it is inevitably less economical, almost like an over-extended short story. McEwan has told a friend that he approached the longer form of the novel with considerable misgivings and even trepidation.

The problems are not merely formal, however. It is difficult to see how McEwan can develop much further this line in grotesque horror and black comedy, with a strong admixture of eroticism and perversion, which, with Martin Amis, he has almost made his trademark. Such obsessive writing seems to work best in the intenser mode of the short story; *The Cement Garden* is more impressive in its parts than as a coherent whole. The narrative line is not especially compelling; there are too few twists and surprises to hold the reader's attention for its 120 pages. Vignettes, like the mother's burial in cement, are better than the whole, and the ending, though startling, is in context perfunctory, as if the novel had to end simply because it had to end. The heightened realism of the long-deferred act of incest, though in itself vivid and even convincing, matches less than convincingly with the more mundane realism of the preceding description of the family's existence, and is indeed less credible set against the earlier accounts of strained relations between brother and sister. Nevertheless, the novel remains memorable for its disturbingly authentic depiction of adolescence. Helen Harris felt that "the tension occasionally flags," perhaps because "the emotional deadness of the characters makes them impenetrable, . . . specimens, bodies rather than complete people," but she felt that, even so, the book reflects a "convincing" world. As for John Mellors, he noted that McEwan's characters "come from that country of bad dreams where we live out our fantasies of sex and death," and that McEwan's speciality is to "treat those fantasies as matters of fact." Hermione Lee remarked that "the language hovers, with a perfected chill clarity, on the edge of panic."

In addition to fiction McEwan has written plays for television, and these, like his prose writings, have caused quite a stir. In 1979 *Solid Geometry* was banned at a fairly advanced stage of production by the management of the BBC, on the grounds, they said, of its "grotesque and bizarre sexual elements." McEwan has said that in this play he attempted to "kick over the traces" of television's "powerful, cohesive conventions of naturalism." "Naturalism," he went on to explain, "is the common language of television, not the language we speak, but one we are accustomed to listen to. Simply by association it has become the language of the

State, of an illusory consensus. . . . I thought that formal experiment could therefore really matter, that by calling into question the rules of the common language the viewer could be disoriented and tempted to regard the world afresh." In *Jack Flea's Birthday Celebration*, broadcast by the BBC on 10 April 1976, McEwan's object was similar, to take "a television cliché—a kind of family reunion—and to transform it by degrees and by logical extension to a point where fantasy had become reality." The result is much like the haunting sense of disorientation evoked in several of the stories in *First Love, Last Rites*, to which McEwan feels this play is essentially connected, by date of composition as much as by theme and motif. The review in the BBC journal, *Listener*, spoke of the play as creating "tension well beyond breaking point."

The Imitation Game, broadcast by the BBC on 24 April 1980, is, in contrast, not formally experimental at all. It deals with a subject which greatly interested McEwan: Alan Turing, the brilliant young mathematician brought to Bletchley Park from Cambridge during World War II to work on Ultra, the project to decipher the German "Enigma" codes, and the women who did the repetitive jobs at the listening posts without knowing they were involved in a project to decipher the codes. This superb play was published with the two others in *The Imitation Game* (1981).

Apart from fiction and television drama, McEwan has written a certain amount of literary journalism for such newspapers as the *Times Literary Supplement*, *The Guardian*, and *The Sunday Telegraph*. Because he sees such journalism as peripheral to the serious work of creative writing, he does not do it for a living. McEwan was no doubt fortunate in that his first collection of stories was an immediate popular and critical success, and each successive book has enhanced his standing in the literary life of the country.

McEwan's latest novel is entitled *The Comfort of Strangers* (1981). As their holiday in Venice begins to unfold, Colin and Mary are locked tightly in their own intimacy. Each evening they sit out on the balcony watching the rituals of the canal. They groom themselves carefully, using expensive colognes, before their dinnertime stroll; they choose their clothes meticulously as though somewhere among the thousands they are soon to join, there waits someone who cares deeply how they appear. They have no idea that this is really so, or to what sinister consequences it will lead. Only McEwan could have portrayed the strange, dark entanglement that ensues or its shocking, even horrendous conclusion. Although Angela Huth felt that McEwan's ghost story "has you in its stranglehold from first page to last," one hopes that he is not cultivating a contemporary form of the Gothic to the point of self-indulgence. If he is, he will turn out to be a mere nine-days'-wonder in the British literary scene. If he is not—if, in other words, he can develop and deepen an already formidable talent—then he is likely to become one of the greatest British writers of his generation. For that he needs to progress beyond the macabre and an obsession with self-abuse and incest into wider and more disturbing—because less sensational—realms of human psychology. That near-perfect story, "In Between the Sheets," perhaps points the way.

Interviews:

Ian Hamilton, "Points of Departure," *New Review*, 5 (Autumn 1978): 9-21;

Christopher Ricks, "Adolescence and After," *Listener* (12 April 1979): 526-527.

John McGahern
(1934-   )

Patricia Boyle Haberstroh
La Salle College

BOOKS: *The Barracks* (London: Faber & Faber, 1963; New York: Macmillan, 1964);

The Dark (London: Faber & Faber, 1965; New York: Knopf, 1966);

Nightlines (London: Faber & Faber, 1970; Boston: Little, Brown, 1971);

The Leavetaking (London: Faber & Faber, 1974; Boston: Little, Brown, 1975);

Getting Through (London: Faber & Faber, 1978; New York: Harper & Row, 1980);

The Pornographer (London: Faber & Faber, 1979; New York: Harper & Row, 1980).

John McGahern's fiction continually tempts critics to compare him with other novelists. An Irishman, he has undergone the inevitable comparison with Joyce, which few Irish novelists escape. One critic claims, however, that he writes in the tradition of English romanticism, echoing Keats and Blake; others see him as "post-Beckett," in both tone and style. McGahern has also been compared to Hemingway, Mauriac, and Chekhov and has been called a "Hibernian Camus." The incredibly broad range and diversity of these comparisons, certainly a tribute to McGahern's talent and a testament to his significance as a contemporary novelist, often obscure the essential individuality of his personal vision and style. McGahern's position as not only one of Ireland's most important novelists but also as one of the best contemporary writers of English prose derives ultimately from the originality and uniqueness of his fiction.

Born in Dublin in 1934 to John (a police officer) and Susan McManus McGahern, the novelist was raised in County Roscommon in the west of Ireland. He was educated at Presentation College, Carrick-on-Shannon, and St. Patrick's Training College, Drumcondra, before moving on to University College, Dublin. At the completion of his studies, McGahern left Dublin to work as a laborer in London. He returned to St. John the Baptist Boys National School in Clontarf where he taught for seven years until after the publication of his first novel, *The Barracks*, in 1963. This novel earned McGahern two of Ireland's most prestigious literary awards; he was the first prose writer to receive the

A. E. Memorial Award and was also granted the Arts Council Macauley Fellowship in 1964. Most reviewers praised *The Barracks*, noting a "talent who bears watching."

Set in a small town in the west of Ireland, *The Barracks* describes the death from cancer of Elizabeth Reegan, alienated second wife of a police sergeant. Longing for security and drawn back to her childhood home from a nursing career in London, Elizabeth had married and settled into the routine of police barracks life. Soon, however, she feels "shackled" to Reegan, with whom she shares no intimacy, and to stepchildren whom she desperately tries to mother. Her husband, dreaming of

John McGahern

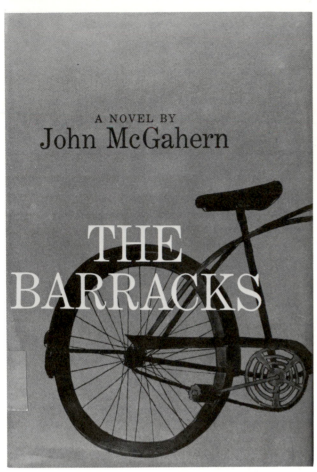

*Dust jacket for the American edition of McGahern's first novel,
which won two prestigious Irish literary awards*

glory from his days as a soldier in the Irish uprising, struggles with his own frustration, as he is continually harassed about rules and authority by a police superintendent.

The discovery of cancer, which forces Elizabeth to come to terms with her life and the possibility of death, brings back memories of London and of her doomed love affair with a young doctor. Echoes of this lover's final words to her—"What is all this living and dying about anyway?"—haunt Elizabeth as the reality of her death becomes clear. Her duties to her family vie with her increasing self-absorption in the fact of her coming death. Elizabeth moves through her days, powerless and helpless, but motivated by need: "her life with these others, their need and her own need, all their fear, drew her back into the activity of the day where they huddled in their frail and human love, together." Elizabeth dies while her husband cuts turf on the bog in a frenzied effort to earn enough money to quit the police force and buy his own farm. In the

final scene, the novel comes full circle as the young son asks his father: "And is it time to light the lamp yet, Daddy?"—the same question he had asked Elizabeth at the beginning of the novel. The cycle of life continues—tragic, shattered, and futile. The final irony of the book is that the expense of Elizabeth's funeral will use up Reegan's escape money.

The Barracks established the theme and tone of McGahern's later fiction. The juxtaposition of life and death, the need to find a way of getting through the mysterious cycle from birth to death, and the acceptance of life as a series of small deaths leading to the final mystery recur. The death that overshadows every life pervades McGahern's fiction. Many of his characters come to realize, as Elizabeth does, that "no one can find anybody to suffer their last end for them."

Elizabeth's alienation and loneliness also foreshadow later McGahern characters. As individuals move "inland" in search of self, they, like Elizabeth, grow increasingly removed from their external environment. Characters vacillate between despair and accommodation; they never quite know why things happen, but they often come to believe what Elizabeth discovers: "And if the reality is this: we have no life but this one—she could only reflect and smile, it must have been the same before her birth and she doubted if she could have ever desired to be born." Ironically, such an awareness brings Elizabeth the only peace she knows. Rejecting religion, she stares at the priest who visits, aware that she has nothing to say to him and that he can give her no comfort. Elizabeth meditates on the significance of faith as she watches the religious devotions that go on around her: "She could only smile and Crucifixion and Resurrection ended in this smiling. As a child she'd been given to believe that the sun danced in the sky Easter Sunday morning, and she'd wept the day she saw that it simply shone or was hidden by cloud as on other mornings. The monstrous faiths of childhood got all broken down to the horrible wonder of this smiling."

Elizabeth's questions become even more significant within the social framework of her life. The realistic details of the small town community and the domestic scenes in the Reegan home embody a social tragedy as pronounced as Elizabeth's personal one. Roger Garfitt sees McGahern's fiction as typical of recent Irish novels which center on "a single articulate person, questioning existence among others who are less bothered, or too busy to care." Barracks life draws together a collection of troubled Irish folk: Elizabeth's neighbor, Mrs.

Casey, desperately lonely and afraid to stay by herself at night; the tipsy guard Mullins, who disgraces the police at Christmas Mass; and the other police officers who pass the time arguing whether Jesus Christ was six feet tall, while lamenting the fact that the appearance of Our Lady at Knock (Ireland's foremost miracle) had never been recognized by the powers in the Vatican. "Nothing short of a miracle would change any of their lives," Elizabeth says, but McGahern's fiction does not allow for miracles. *The Barracks* is a social novel in the sense that McGahern can, as Julian Jebb notes, "create a small world indelibly." The idiosyncracies and tragedies of that world form a backdrop against which Elizabeth's fate is played out.

One of the few reviewers who thinks *The Barracks* is not successful suggests that Elizabeth, while credible herself, becomes incongruous within the setting. The total effect, Anne O'Neill Barna argues, is a "kind of literary gerrymandering—a real person is lifted out of context and attached to a region not her own, and the book seems unreal." Nevertheless, Barna agrees with other critics and suggests that as a first novel *The Barracks* is "full of promise."

After the publication of *The Barracks*, McGahern took a year's leave of absence from school-teaching and went to London to write. His next novel, *The Dark* (1965), was banned by the Irish Censorship Board. This action profoundly affected McGahern's life and created a controversy reminiscent of other notorious battles between Irish writers and the censors in their government and church.

The story of a confused adolescent Irish boy, *The Dark* has been compared with Joyce's *A Portrait of the Artist as a Young Man* because of its confessional overtones. McGahern uses the father-son conflict on which the novel centers to illustrate the gulf between the rigid strictures of a stated personal and community moral ideal and the agonies created when individuals cannot live up to that ideal. The novel is a study in contrasts and ambivalences. The boy, motivated by a deathbed promise to his mother, tries to decide whether to join the priesthood, while he suffers through a natural sexual awakening with its incumbent temptation toward young girls and masturbation.

His father, Mahoney, and a cousin, Father Gerald—the two major forces in the boy's life—have their own personal conflicts, though neither, as Father Gerald honestly confesses to the boy, would ever admit this publicly. In the opening scene, Mahoney berates his son for using an obscene word, yet, in a bed they share at night, Mahoney's sexual

stroking of his son serves as a perverse substitute for his dead wife's love. The terrified boy, who neither participates in nor rebels against the nightly ritual, lashes out at his father in a series of violent, though sometimes silent, domestic showdowns. As the novel develops, son and father reach out toward one another but are continually hampered from communication by personalities and circumstances. Young Mahoney strives for the "impossible reconciliation." Eventually, however, he comes to see his life much as Elizabeth Reegan had seen hers in *The Barracks*: "Lives were lived through in this rathole of security, warding off blows, dealing blows, one desperate cling to stay alive in the rathole; terror of change; neither much risk or generosity or praise, even madness as banal and harmless as anything else there."

Rejecting the priesthood, the boy studies relentlessly to achieve first place in the school-leaving exam and earns a university scholarship. After he arrives in Galway, however, his dreams of a university education shatter when he discovers that his scholarship is inadequate to cover the expenses of a medical degree. Offered a job on the Electricity Supply Board, young Mahoney accepts. Reunited with his father before he leaves the university, he listens quietly to his father's delusions and rationalization and sadly succumbs to a meaningless reconciliation: "You don't hold any of that against me," his father says, "I don't hold anything against you." The father bestows his final blessing on a free, but indifferent, son.

Though chronological, *The Dark* depends primarily on an episodic structure with focus on the individual scene. Despite the confessional tone of the novel, McGahern does not maintain the boy's first-person voice throughout, but shifts from first to second and third person in what Paul Devine describes as an attempt to force the reader to form judgments and conclusions about the events and characters. The gradual elimination of the first-person narrator, with the final chapter in third person, Devine compares to the narrative technique of Joyce and Beckett. The lack of details, such as specific descriptions of the house and farm, the boy's first name, or the exact number of children in the family, reinforces the sense of detachment and objectivity. Counterbalancing this, however, the elaborate descriptions of the boy's sexual fantasies and of some of his personal reactions to people and events suggest the dichotomy between his outer and inner lives. Likewise, the symbolic suggestiveness of the novel's title reverberates through all the suffering and tragedy the novel reveals.

Despite good reviews, *The Dark* created more problems for McGahern than he might have anticipated. Published in England, the novel caused a stir in Ireland involving the Catholic clergy, some of whom had direct control over McGahern's teaching position. The circumstances of the controversy were presented by Owen Sheehy Skeffington in the spring 1966 issue of *Censorship*. In October 1965, McGahern returned from England, only to be told by the school manager, the Very Reverend Patrick J. Carton, that, because of the uproar over the book, he had lost his job. Although Carton admitted he had not read the book, he was adamant about McGahern's leaving. McGahern's marriage to Finnish theatrical director Annikki Laaski, a non-Catholic, which had taken place in a registry office during his leave, complicated the situation. Skeffington suggests that the decision to fire McGahern reached beyond the parish school and directly to the office of the archbishop of Dublin. A Catholic schoolteacher married outside his church, publishing a novel that not only touches on sensitive sexual issues but also portrays a priest who honestly admits to loneliness and doubt, would not be tolerated by the ecclesiastical authorities.

McGahern's publisher appealed to the Irish Censorship Board, but the appeal was rejected by a small majority. McGahern sought help from the Irish National Teachers' Organization which, unsuccessful against the power of the Irish clergy, eventually dropped him from membership. An attempt to raise the issue in the Irish Senate failed when the chairman ruled it inadmissable. Fellow novelist Anthony West, reacting in 1966 to the censorship and its consequences, angrily charged: "Ireland tends to limit this freedom of artistic selection and statement, bending over the artist's shoulder like an old spinsterish schoolteacher and suggesting deletions of what she considers unmentionables." McGahern continued to write and soon began a career as a visiting lecturer in universities in England and the United States. Taking advantage of British Arts Council fellowships, he also traveled and lived in various parts of Europe.

A volume of short stories, *Nightlines* (1970), extends the central symbol of *The Dark* to suggest both an ignorance from which some characters emerge and the darkness of death for which much of life's suffering inevitably prepares us. The settings of these stories include London and Spain as well as Ireland, and some of the characters, like the policeman-father and the guard Mullins, reappear in other McGahern fiction. The first story, "Wheels," with its symbolic title, deals with the re-

curring theme of life as a disappointing cycle in which fathers become children to their sons, and past experiences appear as "all the vivid sections of the wheel we watched so slowly turn, impatient for the rich whole that never came but that all the preparations promised." Woven throughout these stories, this theme reappears at the end in "The Recruiting Officer," where a Christian-Brother turned-lay-teacher sees a version of an earlier self in the brother who comes to recruit boys for his community. The narrator recognizes his own "paralysis of the will" and in the final scene anticipates an evening of drinking at the Bridge Bar, where "several infusions of whiskey . . . will keep this breath alive until the morning's dislocation." Between the narrators of these opening and closing stories, McGahern creates a series of frustrated people seeking escape through imaginary illnesses, drunkenness, and even comic books.

In "Korea" one is reminded of the father-son conflict in *The Dark* when the narrator realizes that his father secretly maneuvers to send him to America in order to get the $250 a month the United States government pays volunteers who serve in Korea. As his father's plan becomes obvious, the young man's eyes are opened: "In the darkness of the lavatory between the boxes of crawling worms before we set the night line for the eels I knew my youth had ended." Like other characters in these stories, this young man moves from the darkness of ignorance into the daylight of insight which ironically suggests a new kind of darkness, the evil nature of his father's motivation. Although the stories in *Nightlines* are not consistently successful, at their best, as the *Times Literary Supplement* critic wrote in 1970, "they deepen and extend one's admiration for this admirable writer." The collection is, as the *Irish Times* pointed out, "formidable."

The issues raised by the censorship of *The Dark* provided material for two novels, *The Leavetaking* (1974) and *The Pornographer* (1979). The first of these, published while McGahern was teaching at the universities of Durham and Newcastle, fictionalizes the events leading up to his dismissal by relating the thoughts of Patrick Moran, a teacher about to lose his job in a Catholic school because he marries outside the church. The fictional life of Moran parallels McGahern's, and the novel echoes characters and scenes from *The Barracks*, including the policeman-father and the death of the mother. The narrator, preparing for an anticipated notice of dismissal, reminisces about his leave of absence during which he found work as a barman in London and married an American woman. Returning to Ireland, he had tried to hide the marriage to save his job, but his landlady innocently exposes the marriage, and the expected consequences quickly develop. Rather than resign, Moran forces the school manager to fire him after the priest's rebuke: "Isn't there thousands of Irish Catholic girls crying out for a husband? Why couldn't you go and marry one of them?" The novel ends with the man and woman clinging to one another in the face of "the turbid ebb and flow of human misery." The narrator, accepting the inevitable, books passage on a boat to London and claims that his leaving is neither a return nor a departure "but a continuing." Love renewed daily is the most he can hope for: "for the boat of our sleep to reach its morning, and see that morning lengthen to an evening of calm weather that comes through night and sleep again to morning after morning until we meet the first death."

Although based on McGahern's own experiences, *The Leavetaking*, as Jonathan Raban suggests, "rehearses a private past which is also a public history." Like other McGahern characters, the protagonist is alienated from his community, a man separated from the attitudes and values of his colleagues and his country. Teaching in a concrete complex "half-arsed modern as the rest of the country," he laments the situation in Ireland: "The church controls the whole setup there. Either you toe their line or you get out." Like Stephen Dedalus, Patrick Moran chooses leave-taking, for only by moving away can he continue to live and grow.

The narrative technique of *The Leavetaking* illustrates one of its basic themes and McGahern's compensation for the misery that life often involves. "All things in actual life, no matter how dreaded," Moran tells himself, "are paltry compared with what the imagination can make of them. . . ." The past, as it rolls through his mind, provides a storehouse of images which allow him to live in two different worlds, that of the schoolroom and that of "memory becoming imagination." Images culled from memory can give relief from the dreariness of the present. Likewise, Moran recognizes, the events of this present day create images for the future.

Implicit in *The Leavetaking* is the relationship between life and art, between the novelist's experiences and the fictional recreation of them. In one of the few published comments McGahern has made on his work, he describes a process where "image after image flows involuntarily now, and still we are not at peace, rejecting, altering, shaping, straining towards the one image that will never come, the lost image that gave our lives expression, the image that

would completely express it again in this bewilderment between our beginning and end. . . ." Such a process operates not only for the novelist who uses thoses images to create a fiction out of personal memories but also for Moran as he sorts through his life.

The two major symbols in the novel, shadow and sea, develop these ideas and show how memory serves to reveal the cyclical nature of life. The shadows of Moran's mother's life, and of her death, fall upon and shape his life in much the same way as the shadows of the flying gulls, introduced at the beginning of the novel, fall on the schoolyard where Moran watches his pupils on his final day of teaching. Moran's mother's death becomes the first in a series of endings, including a failed love affair and the loss of his job, which foreshadow his own death. Like the tide, Moran's life continually flows out of and turns back to his mother's life in the cycle between birth and death. Having betrayed a deathbed promise to devote his life to the priesthood, Patrick now realizes that he has compromised by choosing his mother's profession, teaching, as his own: "My mother's dream for my life, the way that life happened down to the schoolroom of this day, my memory of it and the memory of her dream, and so the tide is full, and turns out to her life." As he prepares to marry in the registry office, in the absence of the Catholic altar and priest, Moran emphasizes the cyclical: "If I believed anything, and it was without conviction, it was that once upon a time we had crawled out of the sea and were making a circular journey back towards the original darkness."

Rejecting his religion, with its promise of eternal salvation, Moran substitutes the day by day renewal of life through love, the "only communion left to us now." The novel then becomes an assertion of the human courage to continue in the face of bewilderment, despite the possibility of failure.

One may speculate that McGahern has dramatized his own personal solution to life's dilemma. He once said that art had become his alternative to religion, "an attempt to create a world in which we can live." He suggests, however, the limitations of his choice: "Religion, in return for the imitation of the formal pattern, promises us the eternal kingdom. The Muse, under whose whim we reign, in return for a lifetime of availability, may grant us the absurd crown of style."

While this statement indicates that for McGahern art cannot offer the compensation that religion does, the success of *The Leavetaking* suggests that his muse has been generous. Critics have noted a few weaknesses in the novel, especially in the second part where McGahern moves away from Irish life to describe London, Moran's American lover, Isobel, and her eccentric father. The novel continued, however, to build McGahern's reputation, with comments like Julian Jebb's in the *Times Literary Supplement*: "*The Leavetaking* represents an achievement of a very high order and substantiates the belief that its author is among the half dozen practising writers of English prose most worthy of attention."

Getting Through, a collection of short stories published in 1978, continues to develop the theme of surviving, as various characters work out ways to get through life, most adjusting to deal with the loss of dreams. The idea of death again predominates. The priest in "The Wine Breath" moves toward an understanding of death as he discovers that "being a man he had no choice, he was doomed to die; and being dead he'd miss nothing, being nothing." In these stories, McGahern's plots again revolve around different kinds of deaths. James Sharkey, after the sudden death of his friend Tom Lennon, looks back on the emptiness of his own life, and allows his mind to race wildly over all kinds of future possibilities: for example, he will find someone to love and will race Lennon's dog in the Rockingham Stakes. But Sharkey stops short, recognizing his "desire for all sorts of such impossible things." Like Sharkey, the narrator of "Doorways," feeling "free" after an unsuccessful love affair, soon discovers that his freedom is illusory: "There were all sorts of wonderful impossibilities in sight. And the real difficulty was that the day was fast falling into its own night."

The symbolic darkness of *Nightlines* and *The Dark* pervades these stories as well, as characters seek respite from their frustrated and gloomy lives. But their escapes succeed only temporarily; the enlightened, like the two lovers in "Along the Edges," discover the greatest challenge: "Well, anyhow we have to face the day." Facing the day together is better than facing it alone. Barnaby and Bartleby, two tramps who inhabit the doorways of Abbey Street, represent most of these characters, and the unnamed narrator's response to seeing them sums up not only some of his own problems but also the major theme of the collection: "Often I want to ask them why have they picked on this way to get through life, but outside the certainty of not being answered I soon see it as an idle question and turn away." Life for McGahern's characters involves a series of expectations which, more often than not, never materialize, and any method for getting

through serves as a buttress against the impending darkness of disappointment and ultimately of death.

The Pornographer, published in 1979, reflects the influence of McGahern's university teaching. He returned to Colgate University in 1978 as O'Connor Professor of Literature, having lectured there in 1969 and 1972. Basic aesthetic questions which the literature teacher continually confronts emerge as themes in *The Pornographer*, a novel that Tom Paulin calls "an exercise in deliberate self parody which plays two improbable fictions against each other."

The plot develops around the adventures of a failed-poet-turned-pornographer who spends his time writing, visiting a dying aunt, and engaging in a sexual liaison with a thirty-eight-year-old woman whom he impregnates. Warned by his publisher Maloney that pornography must be like a story, "like a life, but with none of life's unseemly infirmities," the pornographer soon finds his life and work intersecting. Using the events in his life as the basis for his stories, he enlivens his fiction with sexual feats and erotica absent from his own experiences. Soon the adventures of his two "sexual athletes," Colonel Grimshaw and Mavis Carmichael, become a commentary on their author's own life, which moves along with little direction or purpose.

By the end of the novel, the pornographer recognizes what has been wrong: "By not attending, by thinking any one thing was as worth doing as any other, by sleeping with anybody who'd agree, I had been the cause of as much pain and confusion and evil as if I had actively set out to do it. I had not attended properly. I had found the energy to choose too painful. . . . I had turned back, let the light of imagination almost out." McGahern is suggesting that pornography has this same flaw, that the people and emotions the pornographer ignores do matter, whether in life or in art. Imaginative art, like meaningful life, involves selection and choices which the pornographer refuses to make until the end, when he tells the astonished Maloney that he intends to settle in his childhood home with the woman he loves.

In this novel, as John Thompson notes, "author and narrator are obsessed with the conjunction of birth and death." Confused, the pornographer watches his aunt fight relentlessly against her impending death while he simultaneously rejects his unborn child and its mother, the perenially optimistic Josephine, who naively reassures him that everything will turn out right in the end. The narrator begins to realize, however, that his sexual encounters with Josephine represent momentary escapes from facing the reality of death. Musing over the moments of passion during which their parents had conceived both Josephine and himself, the narrator sees the cycle repeated: "It was as if we were, then, those four other people, now gone out of time, who had snatched the two of us into time. For a moment again we possessed their power and their glory anew, pushing out of mind all graveclothes." For McGahern, sexual union provides the potential to transcend the temptation to despair, as Patrick Moran affirms at the end of *The Leavetaking*. In *The Pornographer*, however, McGahern insists on the need to choose one's experiences carefully. To avoid pain, confusion, and evil, one has to differentiate between meaningful experience and the impersonal exploits which inform the pornographer's life and fiction.

Recapitulating some of the themes of the earlier fiction, *The Pornographer* moves toward a qualified and guarded optimism. While emphasis still falls on the bewildering mystery of life and on the sense that "All, all were travelling. Nobody would arrive," the protagonist exercises more control, recognizing not necessarily answers so much as needs: "What I wanted to say was that I had a fierce need to pray, for myself, Maloney, my uncle, the girl, the whole shoot. The prayers could not be answered, but prayers that cannot be answered need to be the more completely said, being their own beginning as well as end." The decision the narrator makes at the end of this novel represents one step beyond those the protagonists take in *Getting Through*.

While a few critics rate *The Pornographer* as McGahern's best novel, most reviewers find it fascinating but flawed. One problem involves the character of Josephine, who sometimes seems too simple and naive to justify the narrator's wrath. Novelist John Updike claims, "we end up liking Josephine more than the hero does . . . the author has created the character the narrator fails to love." Another problem evolves from the narrator's almost instant redemption; the reader is as unprepared for it as the surprised Maloney. This reversal caused one critic to suggest that at the end it is not clear just what has happened, and that the narrator's chief virtue, his honesty, is not quite sufficient to elicit sympathy. Or, as Tom Paulin notes, "the pornographer's moment of moral awareness sounds very hollow." Despite this criticism, most reviewers comment favorably on the novel's

strengths: a comic element new to McGahern's fiction complements an elegant prose within a carefully balanced structure of juxtaposed scenes.

To many observers, John McGahern has earned a reputation as Ireland's most important contemporary novelist. His fiction, often based on autobiographical experiences, displays both a lyric intensity and a bare, detached objectivity in presenting a hero's personal odyssey through the complexities and ambiguities of modern life. In a unique way, McGahern juxtaposes the barrenness of a Beckett landscape with the minute details and idiosyncracies of day-to-day Irish lives, creating what Jonathan Raban has called "an anatomy of the emotional pathology of Ireland."

Significantly, McGahern has not permanently left Ireland despite the problems he has encountered there. Having traveled throughout Europe and taught in England and at Colgate University, he lives with his second wife, Madeline Green, in Leitrim, where he continues to write. "I suppose deep down," Patrick Moran says in *The Leavetaking*, everybody loves his own country no matter how bleeding awful it is." Probably this reflects McGahern's own view. An Irish sensibility informs McGahern's fiction, and the public and fictional history he creates from his personal life testifies to the degree to which art and life often intertwine. Roger Garfitt describes McGahern's life and work well when he sees in his novels "a movement not toward a resolution of the dilemma, for that's hardly possible on McGahern's terms, but towards a reconciliation with the facts."

References:

Bruce Cook, "Irish Censorship: The Case of John McGahern," *Catholic World*, 206 (January 1968): 176-179;

John Cronin, "The Dark is Not Light Enough: The Fiction of John McGahern," *Studies*, 58 (Winter 1969): 427-432;

Paul Devine, "Style and Structure in John McGahern's *The Dark*," *Critique* 21, no. 1 (1979): 49-57;

Roger Garfitt, "Constants in Contemporary Irish Fiction," *Two Decades of Irish Writing*, edited by Douglas Dunn (London: Carcanet Press, 1975), pp. 207-241;

F. C. Molloy, "The Novels of John McGahern," *Critique*, 19, no. 1 (1977): 5-27;

Owen Sheehy Skeffington, "The McGahern Affair," *Censorship*, 2 (Spring 1966): 27-30.

William McIlvanney

(25 November 1936-   )

Cairns Craig
University of Edinburgh

BOOKS: *Remedy is None* (London: Eyre & Spottiswoode, 1966);

A Gift from Nessus (London: Eyre & Spottiswoode,
1968);

The Longships in Harbour (London: Eyre & Spottiswoode, 1970);

Docherty (London: George Allen & Unwin, 1975);

Laidlaw (London: Hodder & Stoughton, 1977; New
York: Pantheon, 1977).

After the publication of *Docherty* in 1975, William McIlvanney was hailed as the most important
novelist of his generation in Scotland. *Docherty* was
recognized not only as a fine novel (a review in the
Scotsman suggested it was the best Scottish novel
since MacDougall Hay's *Gillespie* of 1914) but also as
a novel particularly relevant to the state of Scottish
culture in the mid-1970s.

McIlvanney, born 25 November 1936, is the

William McIlvanney

son of William Angus (a miner) and Helen
Montgomery McIlvanney. He grew up in Kilmar-
nock, Ayrshire, in West Central Scotland, an area
notorious as an industrial wasteland that had never
recovered from the depression of the 1930s and
that had witnessed the continual decline over forty
years of the industries—mining, shipbuilding,
engineering—on which its late nineteenth-century
prosperity had been built. The area's ethos is
working-class, founded in community traditions
made necessary by the harshness of the environment, but the region was given a new political significance by the rise of a powerful Nationalist
movement in Scotland during the 1970s.

To understand the importance of McIlvanney's achievement and the problems he faced as
a novelist, one must understand the position of
Scots as a language—or dialect—in contemporary
Britain. As a literary language Scots has a long history and reached its widest audience, of course, in
the work of Burns; but in contemporary Scotland it
is the language of the working class, and English is
the language of the middle class. Writing about
contemporary Scotland, the novelist has necessarily
to adopt English as the narrative language—as
Scottish novelists since Sir Walter Scott have always
done—but the life McIlvanney attempts to portray
has as its essential focus the working-class experience, which remains, as middle-class life does not,
distinctively Scottish. The novelist thus enters into
an inevitable conflict with his characters and their
language: while the destiny of Scotland could be
seen as integral with that of England, the author's
English could be offered, as Scott and Robert Louis
Stevenson offer it, as the necessary voice of progress; but in the climate of national revival which
characterized Scottish politics in the 1970s, the English voice of the narrator would only be an implicit
betrayal of the community he sought to describe.

McIlvanney's autobiographical essay, "Growing Up in the West," makes clear that in his own
experience there was a radical division between his
working-class childhood and its values and the experience of being prepared for middle-class life
through the educational system, which, in Scotland,

has always been "English" in language and values: "Much is made of the bright student forging ahead into a new life, while his alienated relatives plod the old ways, bemused and often hurt. Indeed, I've seen so many examples that I've come to believe in a kind of intellectual *nouveau riche*, those who employ their new-found intellectualism to bolster the self-containment of their own lives and to cut their families off . . . the saddest thing is that the families of such bright ones are frequently masochistically delighted by their 'progress.' More than once I've heard working-class parents talk with pride about a son or daughter who is 'away above us noo.' " The dilemma continued for McIlvanney when he became a school teacher in Irvine in Ayrshire, for he was then directly engaged in training those "bright ones" who would be severed from their family background and their native culture.

It is a dilemma, too, which is dramatized in McIlvanney's first novel, *Remedy is None* (1966), its title taken from a poem by the medieval Scots poet Henryson. In its hero, Charlie Grant, the novel presents the image of the conflict between middle-class, English-speaking university life and the Scots-speaking, working-class life of his home. Charlie is called home from Glasgow University to the small town in Ayrshire where his father, a miner, is dying. For his father, Charlie's departure to the university had been the fulfillment of a deeply held ambition to see his children gain all that he has been denied in life, but for Charlie, the university education is a negation of all the bonds that tie him to his family and his community. The pattern of betrayal of working-class values that he feels in himself he sees repeated in his mother, who has left his father for a man who is wealthy, middle-class, and English-speaking. Charlie's bitterness after his father's death leads to an argument during which he kills his mother's new husband, symbolically destroying the middle-class culture for which Charlie has been co-opted and which then puts him on trial for his crime. Trapped between two cultures and two languages, Charlie is incapable of articulating his dilemmas, forced into silence both in the face of his own family and in his confrontations with the articulate English world of the law. What gives the novel such power is that his situation is rendered in a prose style which is ornately English and yet contains the dialect of the working-class community. Charlie's story mimics the tensions of the author's own prose, as McIlvanney attempts to invalidate an English world that he knows will succeed in the end and at the same time to defend a Scots world that he knows to be powerless to defend

itself. *Remedy is None* attracted considerable attention when it was published, winning the Geoffrey Faber Memorial Prize, but the critical consensus has been that its anger and hatred are only fitfully under control: it is a novel trying to say too much. Francis Hart, for instance, in *The Scottish Novel*, comments that "the figurative psychology of complex and extreme inner states overripens at times, and the authenticity of a simple young rustic's nightmare is occasionally lost in the over-analysis of the university novelist."

McIlvanney's second novel, *A Gift from Nessus* (1968), winner of the Scottish Arts Council Book Award, looks at the issue of class from the other side of the barrier, the side that McIlvanney, by becoming a schoolteacher, had to accept as his own. Its setting is not the working-class districts but the middle-class commuter suburbs of West Central Scotland. Its focal character is Eddie Cameron, a salesman barely keeping up with the demands his wife makes upon him for affluence she expected from their marriage and barely keeping his job because of the demands of his relationship with another woman. The plot, more conventional than any of McIlvanney's others, treats middle-class marital tensions. But the personal problems of the characters are constantly counterpointed against the fragmented landscape of decaying inner-city Glasgow, broken by new motorways and blighted with slums, its mixture of old and new reflected in the lives of the central characters. As Cameron climbs the social ladder, he discovers only the nullity of his wife's values. His mistress is hounded by a family still gripped by the puritanical righteousness of the nineteenth-century Scottish Calvinists, and Cameron's relationship with her therefore exists in a limbo between Scotland's anglicized and empty future and its harsh and repressive past. His mistress's family parodies the religious intolerance and emotional sterility that were the constant focus of the novelist's disgust for the works of Robert Louis Stevenson or George Douglas Brown. Eddie's family is drawn from the literary prototypes of the contemporary English novel, challenging the novelist with the split nature of his own inheritance as an artist. Perhaps for this reason English critics have found it the easiest of McIlvanney's novels to accept. Roger Baker was not untypical when he described it in *Books and Bookmen* as "a marvellous piece of work." Scottish critics, on the other hand, have tended to feel that there is an ornate preciousness about McIlvanney's style, which here, in particular, conceals rather than reveals the essential qualities of his characters. Douglas Gifford, for example, in a

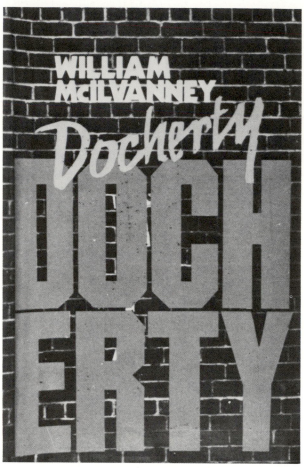

Dust jacket for McIlvanney's 1975 novel, winner of a Whitbread Literary Award

long review of McIlvanney's work in *Calgacus*, takes a stringent look at the stylistic qualities of *A Gift from Nessus* and finds them inadequate. Hart, in *The Scottish Novel*, however, commends the work because "milieu and motive are fixed throughout in modern urban Scotland, and yet the consciousness of being Scottish neither defines the problem nor offers a solution."

Like many Scottish novelists, McIlvanney's answer to this divided tradition was to encapsulate its tensions in a period of Scottish history whose hypothetical future need not be identical with the sterile reality of the present that actually issued from it. *Docherty* (1975), winner of the Whitbread Literary Award, recreates the texture of a working-class community in the years around World War I. The novel is a personal testament to McIlvanney's family and a celebration of Scottish and working-class life, for much of its richness lies in McIlvanney's ear for the dialect of Ayrshire and for the customs of a mining community. The

Docherty family represents stages in a movement toward a consciousness of its real situation in the world. Tam Docherty is, externally, a traditional "hard man" of working-class myth, his physical strength inuring him to the harshness of the labor to which he is committed. A character who might easily have turned into caricature, Tam is one of McIlvanney's finest creations; the author's baroque English prose style is so distant from the terse colloquialisms of Tam's dialect that we see the character both as a man limited by his environment and his inarticulateness and as an intensely compassionate and deeply conscious human being. McIlvanney charts the depths of consciousness to which his characters can give no expression and does so with an awareness of intruding on the essential working-class community language, made up of spoken dialect and, almost more important, of gesture. Tam's hardness is the basis of his humanity, because it allows him to keep intact an inner life that the economic deprivation of his situation would otherwise destroy, but it also prevents his understanding the limitations that the world imposes on him.

Tam's three sons exhibit both the historical pattern of working-class experience and the different responses to their situation that McIlvanney seems to see as inevitable within a Scottish context. Angus, the eldest, adopts the role of "hard man," but in his physical prowess he loses the qualities of compassion and community feeling that make his father the novel's hero. Mick, the second son, experiences the war as an extension of the exploitation of the working classes: he returns wounded, embittered, and politicized but with a harshness that refuses to see humanity except as a force to be moved and opposed. Conn, the youngest, is the inheritor of Tam's conscientious awareness of others but brings to it a greater articulateness, though also a self-consciousness that distances him from the communal life to which his father was central. He is, like his creator, a man struggling to resolve the tensions of living "in twa minds," in two cultures; but *Docherty* succeeds in making that division a fertile conflict, largely because the period setting leaves open possibilities of development which history has, in effect, denied.

With the success of *Docherty* McIlvanney was able to give up teaching and devote himself to writing, though only with the help of a contract to produce a series of detective thrillers based in Glasgow. The first of these, *Laidlaw* (1977), established a character who will make several later appearances since McIlvanney is contracted to produce at least four more thrillers. Laidlaw is a ruminatively philosophical and existentially anguished policeman in a world of decay and violence, and the novel is more than just a potboiler because the conventional format of the detective story allows McIlvanney to experiment with an environment that has proved intractable to the demands of literature.

McIlvanney was writer-in-residence at the University of Aberdeen in 1980 and at the same time began to present a television book program. He also writes a regular column for a recently established Scottish newspaper, the *Sunday Standard*, and is working on a sequel to *Docherty*, which should eventually form the second part of a trilogy. Summing up his place in contemporary Scottish writing, Douglas Gifford has commented of McIlvanney that he, more than any other writer, has "the determination, the epic vision, the willingness to wrestle with the endless difficulties of craft and the honesty to push himself to greater achievement."

Other:

"Growing Up in the West," *Memoirs of a Modern Scotland*, edited by Karl Miller (London: Faber & Faber, 1970).

Stanley Middleton

(1 August 1919-   )

June Sturrock
Simon Fraser University

BOOKS: *A Short Answer* (London: New Authors, 1958);
Harris's Requiem (London: Hutchinson, 1960);
A Serious Woman (London: Hutchinson, 1961);
The Just Exchange (London: Hutchinson, 1962);
Two's Company (London: Hutchinson, 1963);
Him They Compelled (London: Hutchinson, 1964);
Terms of Reference (London: Hutchinson, 1966);
The Golden Evening (London: Hutchinson, 1968);
Wages of Virtue (London: Hutchinson, 1969);
Apple of the Eye (London: Hutchinson, 1970);
Brazen Prison (London: Hutchinson, 1971);
Cold Gradations (London: Hutchinson, 1972);
A Man Made of Smoke (London: Hutchinson, 1973);
Holiday (London: Hutchinson, 1974);
Distractions (London: Hutchinson, 1975);
Still Waters (London: Hutchinson, 1976);
Ends and Means (London: Hutchinson, 1977);
Two Brothers (London: Hutchinson, 1978);
In a Strange Land (London: Hutchinson, 1979);
The Other Side (London: Hutchinson, 1980).

Stanley Middleton is a remarkably prolific novelist. Throughout the 1970s he produced a full-length novel every year. Yet his novels show no marks of mass production, and each offers a clear and fresh insight on his subject—middle-class family relationships in the Midlands of England. Mid-

dleton very deliberately avoids the metropolitan, the modish, the elegant, in favor of a sparse and perceptive realist treatment of provincial life, a sharp and unsentimental view of ordinary people. He has won respect for the careful accuracy of his dialogue and use of detail, his refusal to comfort or to glamorize, and, above all, his concern with human pain and failure.

Middleton was born 1 August 1919, to Thomas and Elizabeth Ann Burdett Middleton, in Nottingham, which is still his home and the background for all his novels. He received a B.A. in 1940 and an M.Ed. in 1952 from University College, Nottingham (which has since become the University of Nottingham). The university awarded him an honorary M.A. in 1975. During and following World War II (1940-1946), he served in the Royal Artillery and in the Army Education Corps. He returned to his studies for a short period; accepted a post teaching English at High Pavement School in Nottingham, where he was educated; and became head of the English Department at Pavement in 1958. He married Margaret Shirley Welch on 22 December 1951; seven years later his first novel was accepted by the New Authors series, which published first novels of promise.

This work, *A Short Answer* (1958), is the least characteristic of Middleton's novels. The later books are strikingly lacking in humor; Middleton's characters occasionally laugh, but the reader rarely shares their mirth. The later novels also ignore almost completely the religious life or religious experience. *A Short Answer*, however, is a jaunty and humorous account of the aftermath of a kind of mystical experience, an apprehension of the presence of "a kind of goodness dominating me and the whole world."

Despite its subject matter, unusual for Middleton, it is very much of its time; like the works of many younger British novelists of the 1950s, it is comic, provincial, irreverent. Sam, the protagonist, decides how religious experience fits into his life and almost commits adultery with his friend Nigel's predatory wife, Megan. *A Short Answer*, which in its discussions about religious experience reflects Middleton's own declared delight in argument, almost entirely avoids the preoccupation with anxiety and death in the later works and ends with Sam safe in his marriage, happy and successful.

Harris's Requiem (1960) is more somber. Middleton is an enthusiastic and well-informed amateur musician. The protagonist of this novel, Thomas Harris, like James Murren of *In a Strange Land* (1979), is a musician; like his author at this period,

he is gradually becoming recognized for his talents. The requiem of the title is composed by Harris after the death of his father; its libretto and the circumstances of its performance and composition reflect the novel's concern with the "defenceless harried by authority"—the power of authority to harrass, manipulate, and waste other people's energies and talents—and with the related theme of death. Grainger Cooke, a powerful magnate, is prepared to treat Harris as a protege until the musician is late for an appointment: the cause of this lapse, which is the death of Harris's father, interests him not at all. Similarly, a school principal lords it over an assistant teacher and nearly destroys the whole fabric of the man's life. Middleton distinguishes sharply between those capable of vital pleasure and those who live through their power over other people. Harris enjoys profoundly his contact with the Bridworth Colliery Silver Prize Band because of the joy and gusto of their music; he resents the wife of one of the musicians for her cold disparagement and ignorance of this joy: "Harris loathed her. She . . . didn't know pleasure. . . . Her sourness sharpened the sweetness. Her stiff upper lips . . . made the world of living people spin." The great achievement of this novel is the way it communicates Harris's delight in his art and the human capacity for delight in general.

This capacity for delight is also seen in Dorothea Seyton of *A Serious Woman* (1961). An ordinary city scene is capable of restoring her peace of mind and sense of values after any emotional storm: "No amount of arguments with her father were going to raise her blood pressure so long as there were still large areas of slate roof for the seeing." This novel is concerned with the relations between Dorothea and the men in her life: her father and the two men who wish to marry her. Dorothea's irritation with her father gradually gives way to an uneasy forgiveness and a quiet love. She marries neither of the two men but through her confrontations with them grows into the "serious woman" of the title. Like many of Middleton's characters, and indeed Middleton himself, she is a teacher; by the end of the novel she has won promotion and also independence. This is Middleton's only use of a female protagonist, and it is largely successful. (It is worth noting that Dorothea treats men as sex objects just as Middleton's male protagonists treat women as sex objects.)

One of *A Serious Woman*'s central themes is elaborated on fully in *Two's Company* (1963), Middleton's fullest exploration of a recurrent theme—a relationship founded entirely on powerful sexual

271

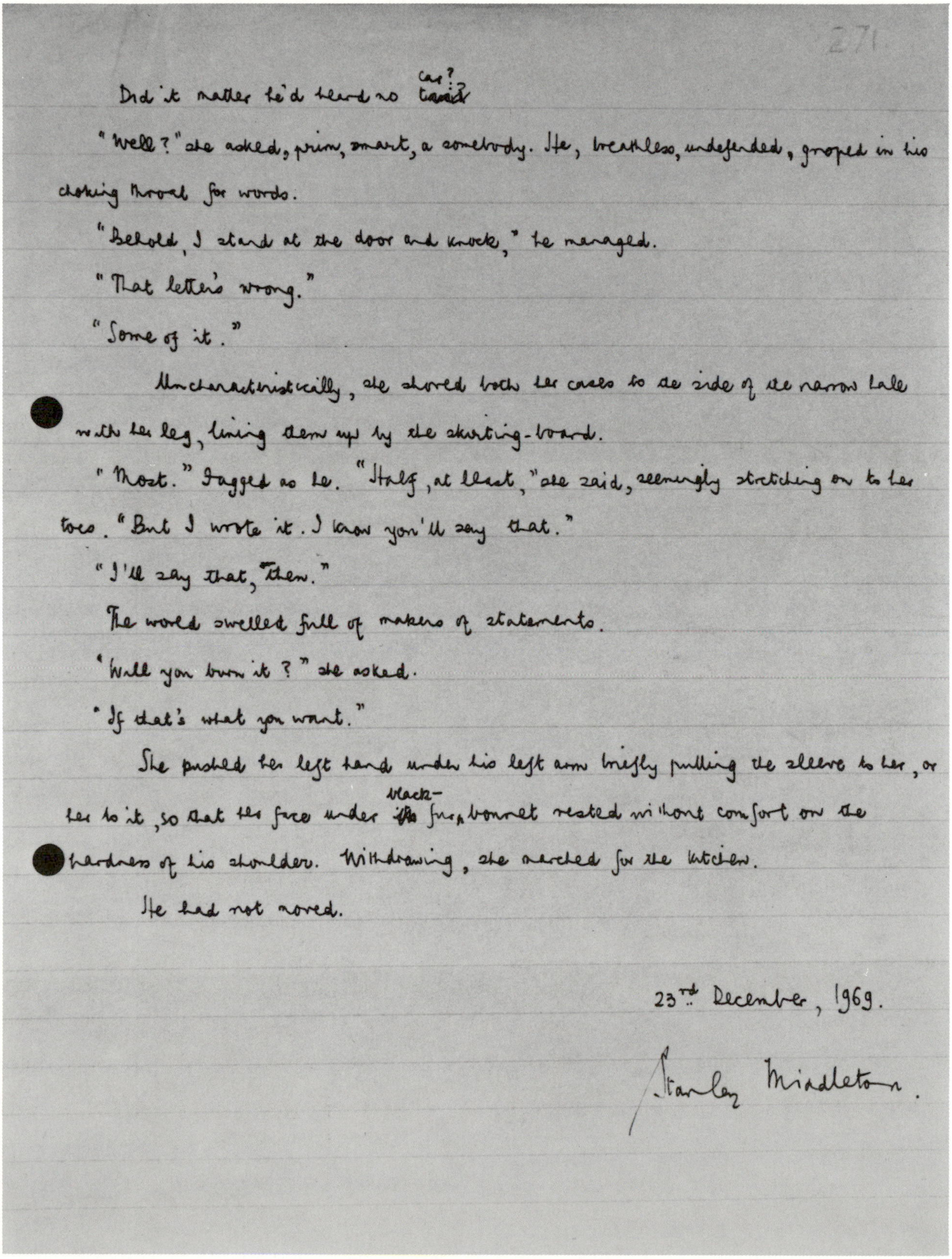

Did it matter he'd heard no ~~taxi~~ car?

"Well?" she asked, prim, smart, a somebody. He, breathless, undefended, groped in his choking throat for words.

"Behold, I stand at the door and knock," he managed.

"That letter's wrong."

"Some of it."

Uncharacteristically, she shoved both her cases to the side of the narrow hall with her leg, lining them up by the skirting-board.

"Most." Dogged as he. "Half, at least," she said, seemingly stretching on to her toes. "But I wrote it. I know you'll say that."

"I'll say that, then."

The world swelled full of makers of statements.

"Will you burn it?" she asked.

"If that's what you want."

She pushed her left hand under his left arm briefly pulling the sleeve to her, or her to it, so that her face under ~~its~~ black-fur bonnet rested without comfort on the hardness of his shoulder. Withdrawing, she marched for the kitchen.

He had not moved.

23rd December, 1969.

Stanley Middleton.

Final page of the manuscript for Brazen Prison

attraction. In his first novel Middleton shows Sam contemplating leaving his wife and children for Megan, whom he knows to be "a silly, perhaps nasty, woman." Dorothea in *A Serious Woman* agrees to marry Malcolm Smith, for whom she has little respect, because of his curly head and broad shoulders. Stead in *Brazen Prison* (1971) remains subject to his destructive and punitive wife, Esther, presumably for her physical attractiveness. In *The Golden Evening* (1968) Jacqueline's incapacity to understand Bernard's reactions to *King Lear* fail to make him aware that she seems to understand almost nothing else about him. Many, perhaps most, of the relationships between men and women in these novels are incomprehensible except as sexual attraction.

Certainly the relationship between Gladys and David in *Two's Company* is at best sterile and at worst destructive, apart from the physical pleasure they give each other. David, who has lost his place at the university and earns his living as a clerk, is a talented guitarist; lively and fastidious, he has inherited the petty snobbery of his prosperous suburban parents. Gladys is a semiliterate and slovenly factory girl, light-fingered and not scrupulously faithful. They meet in a dance hall where David notices that his companion Trevor "could not understand what his friend saw in the girl. He did not understand himself." They make love, and she moves in with him; his parents object, then take Gladys in to try to "improve" her. David and Gladys quarrel, marry, and quarrel again, and eventually move to a new house and a better job in Wales—a new beginning.

Meanwhile a subplot shows the relationship between Trevor and Glady's married friend, Elaine: when Elaine returns to her husband, Trevor follows her, attacks the husband, and in his fury throws the husband's grandmother across the room when she interferes. She dies and Trevor is imprisoned for manslaughter. This subplot, with its totally credible violence and disaster, moves with the same thrust as the main plot. Trevor is bound to Elaine in the same way that David is bound to Gladys; in both cases the sexual bond is essentially destructive.

One of Middleton's most powerful and uncomfortable novels, *Two's Company*, is closely observed, almost entirely convincing. David's confusions and compulsions and the complex class-play of his world are drawn with accuracy and sympathy. Middleton is at his best in his account of David's relationship with his mother, a tangle of love, anger, and self-deception that is fully imagined. It is in David's relationship with Gladys, the core of the novel, that some weakness is evident. The hopeless

relationship is credible, but Middleton never quite communicates the power of physical obsession because although his characters have, very explicitly, penises or breasts, they have no physical individuality, whereas it is characteristic of sexual obsession that it is directed toward an individual. Furthermore, the relationship between David and Gladys seems thin partly because the novel fails to indicate the possibility of any other kind of relationship between the sexes. It is rare in Middleton's novels to find a man and a woman enjoying each other both physically and otherwise. Sexual love is treated as a bond between otherwise incompatible elements. The novels immediately following, *Him They Compelled* (1964) and *Terms of Reference* (1966), are similarly concerned with sexual upheavals and show the same clear sight and refusal to romanticize. The painful accuracy of Middleton's observation had by this time received general critical recognition, more perhaps than pleased the novelist himself. He was to warn a reporter for the *Times* that he would "be after you with a jack knife" if he were "put down as a social realist."

The Golden Evening has a more elegiac tone. A novel of considerable poignance and subtlety, it shows the Allsop family at a time of crisis: Mrs. Allsop is dying, and her children, Bernard and Mary, are both in love. We are shown the counterpoint within the family of the stress of love and the stress of death. The joy of the schoolgirl Mary, with her first boyfriend "blind-happy, lovestruck," is juxtaposed upon the arrangements that follow her mother's death. Middleton also contrasts the end of the parents' relationship through death with the beginning of Bernard's marriage and Mary's courtship. Bernard, watching his father after the funeral, thinks of the family and of how all relationships move toward the inevitable parting. He is, he considers, "a bit of a nobody about to be allied, like his father, to a woman stronger, livelier, wilder than himself. And the join would break. For him. For them all. He grew sorry for himself."

Middleton's great achievement in this novel is his portrayal of this family's values without either diminishing or inflating them. The characters' insistence on "decency," so typical of their class, is shown as a mark of vitality, of humanity. Mrs. Allsop's lapse from her "absolute standard of decorum" in her carelessness about eating and the niceties of middle-class good manners is a clear indication that she is half-dead—it is a corruption. The struggle of Bernard and Mary between the propriety they have been taught and their aroused sexuality is not made to seem as mere repression but as the conflict of two strong powers. In this novel Middleton has used his literary strengths and avoided the display of his limitations.

Wages of Virtue (1969) has a different perspective and a different technique from its predecessors, which cover a comparatively limited time span (for example, early summer to autumn in the case of *The Golden Evening*). This novel, however, follows the development of Daniel Cleaver from childhood to coming of age. *Wages of Virtue* is similar to D. H. Lawrence's *Sons and Lovers*, for here we see the young boy and his loving, ambitious mother; his early school-leaving; his first loves. But while in *Sons and Lovers* the nature of Paul Morel's childhood accounts largely for the nature of his adult life, the early scenes of Dan give the sense that the child is the adult in miniature. Dan sturdily and articulately defying the injustice of his schoolteachers is very much the same person as Dan giving his statement, "not verbose, but fully expressed," at the tribunal dealing with his fate as a conscientious objector during World War II. In both cases Middleton's concern is to reveal how humdrum the realities of such stands are, compared with the principles involved: "What he had imagined as a stand against society, a step towards sanity, had whittled itself away to this, a colloquy with three magistrates or whatever they were in a dusty room." Yet, as the book progresses, Dan's basic lack of any real conviction becomes more apparent—he is not totally convinced of the justice of his case. The man of conviction, Dan's half-crazed friend, Iowerth, ends up gassing himself. This, like many of the other violent events of Middleton's novels (and they have their share of suicides and murders), happens just off-stage. The violence and the conviction are, in fact, just out of focus—and the reader quickly becomes lost, indifferent, in this world of half-lights and half measures.

Yet this novel has power, especially in its early pages: the relationship between the son and his parents and the parents' own relationship are created with great skill and subtlety. The mother, Alice Cleaver, with her obstinacy and strength, is created with generosity and perception, and the father, with his waxing and waning career as an amateur singer, has his inarticulate vitality.

By this time Middleton was producing a novel a year. *Apple of the Eye* (1970) was followed by *Brazen Prison* (1971), which is concerned with a novelist, his creativity, and his marriage. As he had already done in *Harris's Requiem* and as he was later to do in *Two Brothers* (1978), Middleton here creates a work of art within a work of art—in this case a novel within a novel. Encouraged and financially supported by his rich wife, Esther, Stead returns to his native Nottinghamshire to write a novel and while there meets the family of his early love, Iris. Both his wife and Iris are hostile to his art: Iris complains that "no book I've read's been anything like life," and Stead himself accepts the poverty of any art in the face of life: "see how small, how pinched, how thin these masterpieces [by Tolstoy and Dostoevski] are compared with what's digging you in the ribs and treading on your toes."

The novel is concerned with non-communication: with the failure of literature to communicate and the failure of people to communicate. The three marriages portrayed (Stead's, Iris's, and Esther's cousin's) are all extremely unstable. Stead's marriage to Esther is profoundly unrewarding despite their shared sexual pleasure; Stead apparently never notices that Esther is a remarkably destructive, greedy, and manipulative woman. The role of the novel within the novel, which is concerned with an Englishwoman's venture into India, is to underline these failures of communication: "India represented his art with its intractable obstacles, its lack of reward." This novel has a certain dry force, but Middleton's style and manner work against his theme—the theme of non-communication is subversive to his kind of sober realism.

Cold Gradations (1972) deals not only with relationships within marriage but also relationships among the generations. Its protagonist is the seventy-two-year-old widower James Mansfield, a retired schoolmaster whose closest ties are with his brilliant son, David, a wealthy businessman; David's wife, Eleanor; and their children, especially the eldest girl, Sarah. Another family of three generations also appears, the Hapgoods, James Mansfield's friends; one of Clara and Alfred Hapgood's three sons is a hopeless drifter, and he and his slatternly wife have a mentally retarded son whom they dump on the grandparents, just as Sarah, another neglected child, becomes to a large extent her grandfather's responsibility. Clara Hapgood is driven to a suicide attempt by the strain of caring for the boy but is half-crazed by his death; James Mansfield is overcome with grief at the realization that he may outlive his son. None of the relationships within the novel is satisfactory; all bring pain. Nevertheless, the characters cling to these relationships as the essence of their lives. James Mansfield sees Clara Hapgood's devotion to her retarded grandson as pathetic, pointless, and almost obscene; yet it clearly parallels his feelings for his own son.

This concern with the power of faulty human

relationships continues in *Holiday* (1974), cowinner of the Booker Prize with Nadine Gordimer's *The Conservationist*. In comparison to the intervening novel (*A Man Made of Smoke*, 1973), which lacks Middleton's characteristic clarity, *Holiday* is very clean lined. Indeed, its reticence and economy seem overplayed, and although it no doubt deserves its prize, it is not the best of Middleton's work. The holiday of the title is Edwin Fisher's week in the seaside resort where he spent his summer vacations as a child; it is also the break in his life formed by his separation from his wife, Meg, to whom he returns at the end with some relief, just as his father had returned, dumping the suitcases in the hall, with the formula remark, "I'm glad to be home." "*Holiday* is glum and admirable," wrote Jonathan Raban in *Encounter*, thus summarizing the general critical view of Middleton's work at this point in his career, when he was known for what the *Times* called "his punctilious skill as a miniaturist" and the *Times Literary Supplement* labeled "his real and increasing distinction as a chronicler of English life, and of social and personal change in our time."

Distractions (1975) is a more complex work. Like *Holiday* its title is chosen with a grim deliberation. The ordeals of human life lead to the distraction (madness or irrational behavior) of many of the characters; other characters seek or give distraction (diversion) from such distraction (madness). The novel begins with the funeral of Anna Fielding, who has killed herself. Anna's son is living with a neurotic married woman, who is clearly nearing a breakdown. Anna's husband's mistress, Hilda, has fled from a miserable and violent marriage, and her husband is half-crazed by her desertion. Hilda's friend, Elizabeth Mancroft, feels she has nothing to live for and is driven by her loneliness into making sexual advances toward Hilda, while Elizabeth's husband, William, recovering from an operation for lung cancer, falls childishly in love with his young nurse. Another kind of distraction is that which Hilda provides for a small circle of people through her beauty and tact. One character comments, "I expect Brahms was like the rest of us. Uncertain what he managed. Blind. Struggling. On the edge," and from this condition Hilda's gifts provide a kind of respite.

Middleton writes of a world in which tranquillity and happiness are perpetually threatened by the powerful drag toward chaos and destruction. This theme is expanded in *Still Waters* (1976), whose strongest image is the bond of love and enjoyment between Catherine and John Lindsay, even though the novel begins with Catherine's briefly walking out on John because of her unconfessed love for a schoolboy, Douglas Bourne. Like *Distractions*, *Still Waters* is concerned with breakdown; Catherine quickly recovers from her infatuation, but Douglas Bourne's father collapses more seriously so that his family feels uneasily that "he isn't the same person." This work is richer than many of Middleton's novels, for it shows life not only as a whimsical torturer but also as a bestower of gifts. Like Dorothea in *A Serious Woman*, John Lindsay has a moment of "dull sublunary happiness" that briefly transforms his vision; and he is given further joy through the energy of Catherine and the art of his daughter, Frances, a gifted actress.

As *Still Waters* used Middleton's familiarity with the educational system and amateur music (for John Lindsay, the principal of a college of further education, had a lively interest in music-making), so *Ends and Means* (1977) uses his experience as a successful novelist, and, again, as a musician. Eric Chamberlain is a writer of serious suspense stories, and his friend Eli Dunne is a professional musician. Chamberlain's adulteries are coldhearted diversions that cause his wife, Elsa, silent unhappiness; Dunne's adultery drives his wife, Beth, to suicide. Chamberlain's son, John, attempts suicide because of the temporary breakdown of his relationship with his girl friend. The novel is thus largely concerned with the emotional compulsions that lead to a kind of blackmail and manipulation (hence the title); its characters are driven to attempt suicide or kill themselves by their need for love or their inability to bear the pain of consciousness. The more phlegmatic characters, such as Chamberlain and his daughter, Pamela, contemplate with horror and amazement the suffering of other people. An undercurrent in the story is the relationship of the artist to the work of art: John argues fiercely about Ibsen, claiming that his art—and all great art—springs from a sense of failure, while Chamberlain ponders his own work from both the literary and the financial point of view. By this point in his career Middleton was acknowledged to have made "that 'blackish inhospitable' territory, somewhere north of Nottingham," his own. Tom Paulin, writing in the *New Review*, shares the general critical view, one of respect though not enthusiasm: "no one is better than Middleton at investing a condition of average drabness with the qualities of an exact damnation."

Middleton's next two novels also involve the artist and the roots of art. *Two Brothers* (1978) is one of Middleton's strongest works because both brothers, Francis Weldon, the poet, and Jack Weldon, the businessman, have more vitality and individuality than most of Middleton's characters. Jack's gusto is the kind most commonly recognized as signaling vitality—he enjoys food and women, he is strong-willed and courageous—but Francis, although drab and less attractive than his brother, is genuinely convincing as a poet; and when he dies suddenly, the reader suffers a real sense of loss, especially as his death is in sharp juxtaposition to a flashback concerning his love. For, like Middleton's other works, this novel displays the intricacies of sexual relationships. Kathleen, the woman Francis loves and Jack marries, is one of the most sympathetic of Middleton's women. Seeing in Francis's posthumous (and largely autobiographical) papers how parts of their lives are framed, shifted into significance by art, seems to help Kathleen understand her husband and place the same value on the papers that Francis had given them by the sharp focus of his words.

James Murren, the musician of *In a Strange Land* (1979), also comes to see how art asserts life and prevents total, final destruction. The "strange land" of the title, is for various characters, the Midlands or England itself, but it is also Egypt, the land of bondage, sterility, and joylessness from which art can provide a means of deliverance. For James Murren, the Midland town where he spends a couple of years early in his career is a strange land, a place where he never belongs, as Jessica, whom he loves, tells him. In Jessica he finds some consolation, but she recognizes, as he does not, that she is incapable of entering his world. Equally isolated are the Wisniewskis, a Polish couple whom Jessica and Murren befriend. Since the Nazi invasion of Poland, they have lived in England as "strangers in a strange land." They die in England, too, knowing there is no returning home for them; but while Wisniewski is dying, he finds in Murren's talent and Jessica's beauty a lasting pleasure. This is a fine and subtle novel; but when, at one point, Middleton quotes part of Spenser's "Most Glorious Lord of Life" (which Murren sets to music), the beauty, joy, and assurance of the sonnet make Middleton's world seem dingy and bloodless.

Middleton's talents still are not generally acknowledged. *In A Strange Land* was dismissed in *English Studies* (1980) as "slight but readable." A more widely accepted view was expressed by George Parfitt in the *Times Literary Supplement*: "reading him one has the sense of encountering solid achievement, of truths confidently held, beyond anything in Sillitoe, reminiscent of the best of Arnold Bennett, but more than imitation." Middleton has achieved a well-deserved critical respect for his economy and his remarkable accuracy; yet he has never had the general success of some of his less careful and perhaps less gifted fellow novelists. His extreme honesty, his refusal to glamorize, his determinedly provincial content are unlikely to endear him to many in the currently fashionable English literary circles. And indeed perhaps his honesty *is* a limitation. His viewpoint seems so entirely skeptical that—although he records with disconcerting perspicuity and accuracy lapses in conviction, enthusiasm, or love—he does not convey with the same power those other moments when a conviction or a love is wholehearted and transforming. Thus his vision is restricted and distorted, and his world lacks highlight and relief. Intensity is never in focus: in *Ends and Means*, for example, we see through the eyes of one of the coldest characters in the novel. The severity of Middleton's economy is also artistically ambivalent. It can be startlingly effective: in *Still Waters* the novelist never explicitly states that Catherine's infatuation has died; we are made to realize this through action and dialogue. Elsewhere, however, the reader lacks an important dimension because Middleton fails to communicate fully some important quality. In *Distractions* and *Ends and Means* the nature of the relationship between the central couple cannot be fully imagined by the reader because it is never fully communicated by the writer. However, Middleton seems to be moving away from the extreme austerity of some of his novels in the early 1970s to a more satisfying complexity.

Julian Mitchell
(1 May 1935-   )

Simon Edwards
Roehampton Institute

BOOKS: *Imaginary Toys* (London: Hutchinson New Authors, 1961);

A Disturbing Influence (London: Hutchinson, 1962);

As Far As You Can Go (London: Constable, 1963);

The White Father (London: Constable, 1964);

A Heritage and Its History, adapted by Mitchell from Ivy Compton-Burnett's novel (London: Evans, 1966);

A Circle of Friends (London: Constable, 1966);

The Undiscovered Country (London: Constable, 1968);

Truth and Fiction (London: Covent Garden Press, 1972);

Jennie, Lady Randolph Churchill, by Mitchell and Peregrine S. Churchill (London: Collins, 1974);

A Family and a Fortune: a play (London & New York: French, 1976);

Half Life (London: Heinemann, 1977);

Henry IV, adapted by Mitchell from Luigi Pirandello's play *Enrico IV* (London: Eyre Methuen, 1979).

Although Julian Mitchell now regards himself as a playwright and dramatist, during the 1960s he proved himself a novelist of very considerable interest. The author of at least two fine novels, *The White Father* (1964) and *The Undiscovered Country* (1968), he acquired a modest cult following on both sides of the Atlantic. This was partly the result of the way in which the later novel, his last to date, an experimental combination of autobiography and fantasy, confronts very explicitly some characteristic contemporary problems of the genre in its claim to be truthful or "realistic." In his one published excursion into literary theory (the text of a lecture entitled *Truth and Fiction*, delivered at the Royal Institute of Philosophy in 1972), Mitchell has written perceptively about these problems. Very much a professional writer, he is skeptical of academic literary criticism, particularly some of its structuralist varieties, yet he has worked frequently enough in academic contexts to be alert to the development and significance of such criticism. He observes that "imagination . . . is a highly critical as well as a highly creative faculty."

Charles Julian Humphrey Mitchell was born, the son of a successful lawyer, in Epping, just outside London, in 1935. A member of a prosperous middle-class family, he attended Winchester School from 1948 to 1953, before two years of national service in submarines between 1953 and 1955. He read history at Wadham College, Oxford, and, after gaining a first-class degree in 1958, he entered St. Anthony's College, Oxford, where he began research into the political poetry of the early seventeenth century, leading to his M.A. in 1962. His supervisor was the distinguished American historian Lawrence Stone, whose methods and wide-ranging cultural authority, crossing the traditional academic disciplines, he now believes to have been influential in his own intellectual formation. His experience as a research student has also proved directly useful in his more recent work of writing historical drama for television.

Julian Mitchell

518

He has best described his time at Oxford and the atmosphere there in the first autobiographical section of *The Undiscovered Country* and, to a lesser extent, in the imaginative transposition of his first novel, *Imaginary Toys*. Between them the two books suggest something of the literary and social climate of the university and his own involvement in it. With William Donaldson (now best known as the author of the *Henry Root Letters*, witty excursions in popular journalism), whom he had met during national service and who was then at Cambridge, Mitchell founded a magazine, *Gemini*, and edited its first two numbers. Among distinguished contributors were the poets Stephen Spender, Sylvia Plath, and Ted Hughes. This led to their joint editorship of an anthology of new writing from Oxford and Cambridge, *Light Blue, Dark Blue* (1960). Close friends of his at the time were the poet John Fuller, another editor of the anthology, and political novelist and commentator David Caute.

In 1959 Mitchell received a Harkness Fellowship to travel and study in the United States where many of the manuscripts necessary to his literary research were to be found. In fact, his two years in New York, Washington, Austin, and Los Angeles provided him less with information about seventeenth-century political poetry than with materials for his third novel, *As Far As You Can Go* (1963). He also completed his first two novels in the States, *Imaginary Toys* (1961) and *A Disturbing Influence* (1962). The insistent Englishness of their subject matter may be a product of exile, but reviewers tended to find in them the kind of representative voice they were seeking to follow on from the generation of writers dubbed "angry young men." Such a claim now seems inappropriate, and indeed rather than having one "voice," both novels are composed from multiple voices, suggesting an exposure to early-modernist and non-English influences. They read more like fictional exercises than like narratives arising from any deep engagement with the characters and worlds they present. Just this problem of engagement, or the lack of it, seems central to Mitchell's work, and when adequately foregrounded as a theme, as in the later novels, it contributes decisively to his achievements.

Imaginary Toys interweaves the interior monologues, written reflections, and letters of four characters all about to leave Oxford. The most fully presented are Charles Hammond, something of a socialite, although intelligent, anxious, and well-meaning; and Nicholas Sharpe, homosexual, politically aware, and more deeply intellectual. Less interesting is the working-class Jack Evans, given to writing torrid unpunctuated letters of frustrated sexual passion to his girl friend Elaine Cole, who indulges in some rather unconvincing religious meditations. Class and politics enter the thoughts of all four personae, but their real concern seems to be with personal and sexual morality. Like later Mitchell heroes, Charles is puzzled by his lack of any deep feelings; Nicholas, by the difficulties of forming a stable homosexual relationship. The latter describes his ambition as "a responsible hedonism," and the phrase neatly suggests the liberationist culture of the early 1960s that makes up the ambience of the novel. There is a good deal of guilt residually felt by the characters, but little of it is adequately located or explored, with the figures trapped in their solipsistic accounts, and with nothing to counter their undergraduate naivete, other than the general undercutting of the multiple-perspective device. Nevertheless, the book has its interest as period reportage and is evidence of the pervasive influence of certain American writers, especially J. D. Salinger, on English fiction of the time. In that respect it compares favorably with Andrew Sinclair's contemporary *My Friend Judas* (1959), which describes a similar milieu.

A Disturbing Influence extends further the use of multiple perspective, initially giving a greater impression of being stitched together from isolated fragments. One chapter had already appeared as a short story in an anthology, *Introduction* (1960), but the writing is in general more disciplined than in his first novel. The first part attempts to recreate an English country town, Cartersfield, at the time of campaign for nuclear disarmament activism and teddy boys, through a series of recollections by, respectively, a vicar; a secondary schoolteacher named Drysdale (who is one of Mitchell's characteristic, emotionally detached figures); a middle-class adolescent, Edward Gilchrist; and a working-class adolescent. Each low-key narrative style masks more profound, but hardly voiced, intimations of sexuality and death, the "disturbing influences" of the title. The four central figures are joined by additional narrators in the second half, which gives an even more ambiguous account of the vicar's nephew, David Mander, and the impact of his worldliness and sexual precocity on the town during his short stay there, supposedly for convalescence. Mander "lives for the precise moment and its possibilities," and these "possibilities" include the seduction of Edward's sister, Jane, and some kind of homosexual initiation of a group of the town's young men, including Edward. A mysterious fire on the property of a retired brigadier leads to the general's death from an apoplectic stroke and Mander's leaving town with other unspecified changes in his wake. The cumulative effect of both halves of the novel is perhaps intended to resemble that of Joyce's *Dubliners* (1914), equally concerned with an irredeemable provinciality of setting and behavior, equally pervaded by a very subdued apocalyptic note. Relations between characters hardly acquire any dramatic intricacy or force and are largely those between observer and observed. Significantly, everyone seems better able to relate to the amoral and ruthlessly impersonal David Mander than to anyone else. In theme *A Disturbing Influence* belongs to the tradition of the novel of English provincial life, while in technique it is tentatively "modernist," looking back to Henry James and Ford Madox Ford as well as James Joyce.

In 1961 Mitchell returned from the United States to resume his research at St. Anthony's College, Oxford, but preferred to spend the year completing a third novel. *As Far As You Can Go*, reflecting his American experience, incorporates the influence of Henry James quite explicitly but reverses the procedure of *The Ambassadors* (1903), sending its innocent English hero Harold Barlow across the Atlantic for an encounter with a more complex reality. Barlow travels the continent in pursuit of a rich patron's collection of family portraits, which has been dispersed among American owners. He finds himself increasingly attached to and later transformed by the landscape, the people, and the amenities, all of which replace those of an oppressively over-civilized and class-conscious England. He ends up in California laying siege to the most valuable painting, a Nicholas Hilliard miniature, the possession of an eccentric old lady, with whose tantalizingly beautiful granddaughter he also falls in love. The only one of Mitchell's novels to have a central unifying consciousness in the character of Harold Barlow, the work is nevertheless flawed by an inconsistency of presentation, however effective such inconsistency may be in demonstrating differences between English and American settings. Barlow's English life is wry social comedy in the manner of early Kingsley Amis, but in America he develops a complex and earnest moral awareness in the manner of the later Henry James. Mitchell takes great care to have Barlow distinguish between the sources of his disaffection and the fashionable one of anger, but it is not clear that there is a difference. He is only aimlessly critical of English society and his place in it, and his pursuit of personal gratification prevents him from imagining the possibility of social change. If this classic stance of modern liberalism is treated ironically at the outset, it is subsequently justified in an encounter with the more fluid society and values of the United States. American freedom becomes, paradoxically, in itself a kind of commitment.

Mitchell would probably concede that his period in the United States, the first Kennedy years, provided an invigorating climate for this kind of liberalism. Its English face, that of the radical cultural mediator of fundamentally unchanged social structures, is mocked in the figure of a cynical journalist friend of Barlow's, Denis Moreland. As Barlow's mentor he comes to be replaced by the Californian beat Eddie Jackson. First met in an English club, Jackson simply confirms Barlow's anti-American prejudices, but with the beat's reappearance, Barlow is challenged to respond more positively to Jackson's anarchic style of freedom, his combination of aestheticism and hedonism. Jackson is also discovered to be a person riddled by doubt and anxiety, particularly about his own mythicized sexual achievements and his incapacity for love. His morality disturbs and allures Barlow in the same way that Chad's does Strether in *The Ambassadors*, a copy of which remains unread in Barlow's luggage throughout the book. Finally Jackson is castrated by a Los Angeles street gang, and he deliberately kills himself in a stolen car. Paradoxically this action suggests the covert political stance of the novel by pointing to the disfiguring and disfigured sources of wealth and pleasure that both its English and American protagonists seem to assume as a right. Barlow's relation with the girl Diane turns sour; and although he rescues the Hilliard miniature from a fire in which the old lady dies, he leaves California on his own, having apparently learned a modified, or compromised, form of Emersonian self-reliance. More expansive than the early novels, as if in response to the American landscape, *As Far As You Can Go* is also more slackly written. Yet this more relaxed quality of narrative contains far more accomplished sequences of both comedy and high seriousness that look forward to the next novel, in which both dramatic structure and the existence of character as more than a cleverly imitated voice are paramount.

Abandoning his research in 1962, Mitchell set up in London as a free-lance writer. He left the exhausting and unrewarding task of novel reviewing for the London *Sunday Times* and other periodicals to spend the winter in Morocco. Bleak months in a rented room in the small town of El Jadida, near Casablanca, and recurrent illness did not prevent him from producing what is arguably his best novel,

Dust jacket for Mitchell's 1964 novel, winner of the
John Llewelyn Rhys Memorial Prize

The White Father (1964). It builds on his earlier achievement by introducing characters from each of his preceding novels, in particular Edward Gilchrist, of *A Disturbing Influence*, who is now one of two central figures. The other is Hugh Shrieve, who has just returned to England from a long spell in an African colony on the verge of independence. As a district officer in charge of a small primitive tribe, the Ngulu, he is anxious that their interests, indeed the very conditions for their survival, should be protected at the constitutional conference in London. In lobbying a number of influential public figures and institutions in the Ngulu cause, he encounters whole changing areas of British life—political, bureaucratic, and academic, as well as the new forces of big business, the communications and entertainment industries. Feeling estranged from both his family and his old friends, he dislikes oppressively polite and unfeeling behavior, particularly that of his father and his stiff-upper-lipped colleagues in the Colonial Ser-

vice. At the same time he is attracted to the young and their emergent culture, which seems oddly to resemble that of the warm, sexually liberated, feckless, and irresponsible life of the Ngulu. He is joined in his campaign by Edward Gilchrist, just down from Oxford and contemplating a career as a pop singer. Gilchrist's general sense of aimlessness is momentarily countered by his admiration for Shrieve's integrity and purposefulness. In spite of Shrieve's provisional success in winning terms for the protection of the Ngulu, the world explored in the novel, in both London and Africa, appears to be increasingly the product of the more sinister forces of international capitalism, which is shown to be developing, simultaneously and ruthlessly, the new mass culture of postwar Britain and the emergent societies of the third world. Its role is symbolized in the novel by the pervasive presence of the anodyne soft drink *Free*, whose bottles litter the world, and which will clearly compromise the freedom sought by the independent African states. The owner of the British *Free* concession is the megalomaniac Mr. Brachs, who is also shown as controlling both property development in London, whose changed landscape so bewilders Shrieve, and the music business into which Edward is seduced, sacrificing his musical gifts as a jazz pianist for the meretricious world of pop stardom.

By creating two heroes, Shrieve and Gilchrist, Mitchell manages a far more complex and attractive image of the strengths and weaknesses of modern liberalism than he achieved in the simpler portrait of Harold Barlow. With all the easy speed he found in motoring through America, Barlow had managed to skate over the contradictions within liberalism. As a modern "condition-of-England" novel, *The White Father* combines the political range and insight of H. G. Wells's *Tono-Bungay* (1909) with the more finely nuanced study of personal relations and moral dilemmas of E. M. Forster's *Howards End* (1910). If love and responsibility are shown as more deeply compromised, their tenuous triumphs are also more convincing and moving than in Mitchell's earlier novels.

Returning from Morocco to London, he began his first work for the theater, an adaptation of Ivy Compton-Burnett's 1960 novel, *A Heritage and Its History*, which opened at the Oxford Playhouse in 1965 before transferring to London. *The White Father* was awarded the John Llewelyn Rhys Memorial Prize, and Mitchell spent a term as writer-in-residence at Colorado State University in 1965. There he started writing a new novel, *A Circle of Friends* (1966). Almost fastidious in its style, this is another Anglo-American novel. It is both more deliberately comic and even more explicitly indebted to Ford's *The Good Soldier* (1915) than any of his earlier work. It is told by a group of cultured middle-class New Yorkers, a social "circle of friends" presided over by a shadowy and possibly malevolent master of ceremonies, Howard Auchinloss, and including a gauche young Englishman, Martin Bannister. We meet them first in New York, then in the English country home of Henrietta, wife of avant-garde stage director Freddie Grigson. During an amateur production of Henry Fielding's farce *Tom Thumb* directed by Grigson's son, Lawrence, Freddie returns from the States and begins divorce proceedings against his wife, citing Martin Bannister as corespondent. Ultimately Martin reflects that although technically he is innocent of the act of adultery, there is another kind of moral truth, perhaps embodied in the law that judges him, by which he is indeed guilty. There is also a sense in which his guilt is produced by the aesthetic necessity of the novel's form, and although himself a character in that novel, he is able to say of his experience that "it was like seeing my first Cubist painting." The novel's technique might precisely be described as "cubist," giving, as it does, the different partially informed accounts of each of its characters, major and minor alike. In this novel Mitchell moves closer to that radical questioning of the relations between the fictive and the real that informs his next and, to date, last major work. Nevertheless, for all the fineness of its construction, it seems rather slight—its characters have difficulty less with their feelings than in having any feeling at all—here again, perhaps, resembling the characters of Mitchell's model, *The Good Soldier*.

In 1966 Mitchell won the Somerset Maugham Award for *The White Father*. After completing an adaptation for the stage of a second Compton-Burnett novel, *A Family and a Fortune*, he was able once again to escape from the exigencies of novel reviewing and of serving as a member of the Arts Council Literature Panel. He began his most ambitious novel, *The Undiscovered Country* (1968), just before leaving for the Greek island of Patmos.

In a remarkably bold gesture Mitchell wrote the first part as undisguised autobiography. He refers to himself and to many of his friends and contemporaries by name as he describes periods of his life spent at school, in the submarines, at Oxford, in London, and in the United States. Throughout this orthodox and literal narrative Mitchell is pursued and haunted by an alter ego, Charles Humphrey (whose name is extrapolated from the novelist's

own). Humphrey questions, challenges, and abuses many of the assumptions by which the novelist constructs, in both senses, his life. Clearly Humphrey also acts out elements repressed in what is shown as a somewhat guarded personal development, fulfilling different kinds of fantasies. The device is not wholly new and may be traced to James Hogg's *Confessions of a Justified Sinner* as well as to Edgar Allan Poe's "William Wilson." In the second part, however, after the death of Humphrey, Mitchell undertakes to edit, again in a device suggesting Poe as much as Vladimir Nabokov's *Pale Fire* (1962), a fragmentary novel of Humphrey's, *The New Satyricon*. This may be "the undiscovered country" of the title, but what we read of it (and there may well be more that Mitchell has, as it were, suppressed) operates at many levels: as commentary on contemporary society and culture; as extravagant bisexual fantasy; as literary parody and pastiche (although the distinction between the categories no longer holds); and as an account of the human condition in quasi-mythic terms, this last the most oddly adapted to Humphrey's almost Augustan sensibility. The two halves of the novel confront each other starkly; there is no consoling or mediating voice and none of the moral resolution attempted in *As Far As You Can Go*, where the relationship between Harold Barlow and Eddie Jackson offers some less searching parallels. Mitchell writes: "I am a character in one of my own books. Yet I feel I am really a character in one of his (Humphrey's). He never wrote it, and I don't know what to do or say." At another point Humphrey accuses Mitchell: "Your heroes are dim, wet little men who don't care about anything, and feel sorry for themselves because they can't."

Such remarks suggest in some curious way that *The Undiscovered Country* is to serve as an epitaph on Mitchell's own fiction and on what he has come to regard as its failures. It is not in any sense an exercise in fashionable literary politics of the "novel is dead" kind; it is an awkward, disturbing, and impressive work in its own right. Published shortly after John Fowles's *The Magus* (1966), *The Undiscovered Country* shares many aspects of theme and structure with that notably successful and popular novel. Both novels reflect interestingly the journey travelled by English fiction during the 1960s, even if Mitchell himself has felt no call to return to the "undiscovered country" to which it has led.

Now living largely in South Wales, he remains busy as a writer for television and the theater. He has a number of original plays to his credit, including *Half Life* (1977) for the stage and *A Question of Degree* and *Rust* for television. Among many adaptations for the latter medium, he has also written episodes for the historical reconstruction *Elizabeth R* as well as a seven-part dramatization of the life of Jennie Churchill, based on her correspondence. Adaptations of Paul Scott's *Leaving* (1980) and Ford's *The Good Soldier* (1981) have been acclaimed as some of the finest recent writing for television.

Given the title of Julian Mitchell's last novel, *The Undiscovered Country*, there is a nice and probably quite intentional irony in the title of his most recent play, *Another Country* (1981). Here he seems to have literally discovered himself as a dramatist, and rightly the play has enjoyed an extremely long run in the West End in a brilliantly stylish production. It triumphantly demonstrates Mitchell's mastery of a new literary territory, the drama, for articulating the tensions between public and private experience—a theme for which he had, by the end of the 1960s, found the novel form no longer adequate. The play is set in an English public school in the 1930s (although he draws on his own memories of Winchester in the early 1950s) and traces the various social, sexual, and personal pressures that may have led to the creation not only of that famous generation of upper-class socialist intellectuals (Stephen Spender, C. Day Lewis, Christopher Isherwood, John Cornford and W. H. Auden) but also of the equally notorious figure Guy Burgess, a central figure in the network of Russian agents who infiltrated the British Intelligence Service prior to and during the Second World War. Burgess's defection to the Soviet Union in the early 1960s was only one of a series of security scandals involving various homosexual figures in public life, the repercussions of which continue into the 1980s and which also continue to invite those characteristic displays of hypocrisy and prurience by the popular press and the British establishment.

Cornford and Burgess, indeed, provide the models for the two central characters, Tommy Judd and Guy Bennett. With superb economy of effect, trenchant wit, and a brilliant ear for the acerbities of adolescent conversation, the play explores how the apprenticeship to survival in the brutal subculture of the English public school is also an apprenticeship to treachery. It manages to extend a watchful sympathy to even the most stupid and bullying inhabitants of this perverse parentless universe; while in the character of Tommy Judd, Mitchell creates a striking image of moral integrity and honesty that can be achieved and sustained only by a rigorous combination of steely self-discipline and passionate political idealism. Guy Bennett's idealism, on the other hand, can take the form only of passionate homosexual love, which the brutal system cannot permit, even while it appears to encourage homosexuality as the only kind of emotional expression available in this exclusively male world.

Although Mitchell believes he may return to writing fiction and indeed speaks of a project for an ambitious historical novel set in this same period of the 1930s, the encouragement of his recent success on the stage may postpone that return. He feels that he has shed his earlier preoccupation with the novel as an aesthetically enclosed form, which he thinks served to limit his achievement as a novelist. Of the novels *The White Father*, in particular, suggests that this assessment is not wholly true, and certainly Mitchell's continuing vitality as a writer, so recently confirmed, promises also that he may well yet produce rich and interesting fiction.

Reference:

David Lodge, *The Novelist at the Crossroads* (London: Routledge, 1971), pp. 24-32.

Michael Moorcock
(18 December 1939-   )

Colin Greenland
North East London Polytechnic

SELECTED BOOKS: *Caribbean Crisis*, by Moorcock and James Cawthorn as Desmond Reid (London: Sexton Blake Library, 1962);

The Stealer of Souls and Other Stories (London: Spearman, 1963; New York: Lancer, 1967);

The Barbarians of Mars, as Edward P. Bradbury (London: Compact, 1965); republished as *The Masters of the Pit*, as Moorcock (New York: Lancer, 1970);

Blades of Mars, as Edward P. Bradbury (London: Compact, 1965); republished as *The Lord of the Spiders*, as Moorcock (New York: Lancer, 1970);

Warriors of Mars, as Edward P. Bradbury (London: Compact, 1965); republished as *The City of the Beast*, as Moorcock (New York: Lancer, 1970);

Stormbringer (London: Jenkins, 1965; New York: Lancer, 1967);

The Sundered Worlds (London: Compact; 1965; New York: Paperback Library, 1966); republished as *The Blood Red Game* (London: Sphere, 1970);

The Fireclown (London: Compact, 1965; New York: Paperback Library, 1967); republished as *The Winds of Limbo* (New York: Paperback Library, 1969);

The Twilight Man (London: Compact, 1966; New York: Berkley, 1970); republished as *The Shores of Death* (London: Sphere, 1970);

Somewhere in the Night, as Bill Barclay (London: Compact, 1966); revised as *The Chinese Agent*, as Moorcock (New York: Macmillan, 1970);

The Deep Fix, as James Colvin (London: Compact, 1966);

Printer's Devil, as Bill Barclay (London: Compact, 1966);

The Wrecks of Time (New York: Ace, 1967); republished as *The Rituals of Infinity* (London: Arrow, 1971);

The Jewel in the Skull (New York: Lancer, 1967; London: Mayflower, 1969);

Sorcerer's Amulet (New York: Lancer, 1968); republished as *The Mad God's Amulet* (London: Mayflower, 1969);

The Final Programme (New York: Avon, 1968; London: Allison & Busby, 1969);

Sword of the Dawn (New York: Lancer, 1968; London: Mayflower, 1969);

Behold the Man (London: Allison & Busby, 1969; New York: Avon, 1970);

The Secret of the Runestaff (New York: Lancer, 1969); republished as *The Runestaff* (London: Mayflower, 1969);

The Ice Schooner (New York: Berkley, 1969; London: Sphere, 1969);

The Black Corridor by Moorcock and Hilary Bailey (London: Mayflower, 1969; New York: Ace, 1969);

The Time Dweller (London: Hart-Davis, 1969);

The Eternal Champion (London: Mayflower, 1970; New York: Dell, 1970);

Phoenix in Obsidian (London: Mayflower, 1970); re-

Michael Moorcock

published as *The Silver Warriors* (New York: Dell, 1973);

The Singing Citadel (London: Mayflower, 1970);

A Cure for Cancer (London: Allison & Busby, 1971; New York: Holt, Rinehart & Winston, 1971);

The Knight of the Swords (London: Mayflower, 1971; New York: Berkley, 1971);

The Sleeping Sorceress (London: New English Library, 1971; New York: Lancer, 1972); republished as *The Vanishing Tower* (New York: DAW, 1977);

The Warlord of the Air (London: New English Library, 1971; New York: Ace, 1971);

The Queen of the Swords (London: Mayflower, 1971; New York: Berkley, 1971);

The King of the Swords (New York: Berkley, 1971; St. Albans: Mayflower, 1972);

Breakfast in the Ruins (London: New English Library, 1972; New York: Random House, 1974);

The English Assassin (London: Allison & Busby, 1972; New York: Harper & Row, 1974);

Elric of Melniboné (London: Hutchinson, 1972); republished as *The Dreaming City* (New York: Lancer, 1972);

An Alien Heat (London: MacGibbon & Kee, 1972; New York: Harper & Row, 1973);

Elric: The Return to Melniboné (Brighton: Unicorn Bookshop, 1973);

The Jade Man's Eyes (Brighton-Seattle: Unicorn Bookshop, 1973);

Count Brass (London: Mayflower, 1973; New York: Dell, 1976);

The Bull and the Spear (London: Allison & Busby, 1973; New York: Berkley, 1974);

The Champion of Garathorm (London: Mayflower, 1973; New York: Dell, 1976);

The Oak and the Ram (London: Allison & Busby, 1973; New York: Berkley, 1974);

The Land Leviathan (London: Quartet, 1974; Garden City: Doubleday, 1974);

The Sword and the Stallion (London: Allison & Busby, 1974; New York; Berkley, 1974);

The Hollow Lands (New York: Harper & Row, 1974; St. Albans: Hart-Davis, MacGibbon, 1975);

The Quest for Tanelorn (Frogmore: Mayflower, 1975; New York: Dell, 1976);

The Distant Suns, by Moorcock, Cawthorn, and James, as Philip James (Carmarthen, Dyfed: Unicorn, 1975);

The Lives and Times of Jerry Cornelius (London: Allison & Busby, 1976; New York: Harper & Row, 1976);

The Adventures of Una Persson and Catherine Cornelius in the Twentieth Century (London: Quartet, 1976; New York: Harper & Row, 1976);

Legends from the End of Time (New York: Harper & Row, 1976; London: W. H. Allen, 1976);

The Sailor on the Seas of Fate (London: Quartet, 1976; New York: DAW, 1976);

The End of All Songs (New York: Harper & Row, 1976; St. Albans: Hart-Davis, MacGibbon, 1976);

Moorcock's Book of Martyrs (London: Quartet, 1976);

The Transformation of Miss Mavis Ming (London: W. H. Allen, 1977); republished as *A Messiah at the End of Time* (New York: DAW, 1978);

The Condition of Muzak (London: Allison & Busby, 1977; Boston: Gregg, 1978);

The Weird of the White Wolf (New York: DAW, 1977);

The Bane of the Black Sword (New York: DAW, 1977);

The Swords Trilogy (New York: Berkley, 1977);

The Cornelius Chronicles (New York: Avon, 1977);

Sojan (Manchester: Savoy, 1977);

Epic Pooh (London: British Fantasy Society, 1978);

Gloriana, or the Unfulfill'd Queen (London: Allison & Busby, 1978; New York: Avon, 1979);

The Golden Barge (Manchester: Savoy, 1979; New York: DAW, 1980);

The Great Rock and Roll Swindle (London: Virgin, 1980);

My Experiences in The Third World War (Manchester: Savoy, 1980).

Michael Moorcock has established himself at the imaginative forefront of popular writing in the 1960s and 1970s. His editorial work and his own fiction together represent a titanic effort, often against great resistance from the establishments of magazine and book publishing, to reunite the highest literary values with the forms and vitality of popular culture. The immense goodwill and philanthropy displayed even in his most doom-laden visions spring from a living knowledge of a span of popular arts that reaches from Charles Dickens to William Burroughs, from the eighteenth-century commedia dell'arte to the rock band Hawkwind. In the 1960s Moorcock planned and carried out what was almost a one-man revolution in the genre of science fiction and, more important, transformed it in its relation to the larger scheme of mundane fiction. Modest of all his achievements, ferocious in his loves, his artistic desires, and his commitments, he seems to be on the brink of even greater work.

Michael John Moorcock was born on 18 December 1939 in Mitcham, Surrey, the only child of Arthur Moorcock, a draftsman, and June Taylor Moorcock. Like that of his friend and colleague

J. G. Ballard, Moorcock's imaginative fiction has been strongly conditioned by the wartime landscapes of his childhood. Where the young Ballard wandered in occupied Shanghai among drained swimming pools and empty hotels, deserted but undamaged, Moorcock's equally vivid memories are of broken streets and ruined factories, bombers and fighters overhead, and fires in the night. He has remarked that in the contrast between bomb site and bomb shelter he found a powerful affirmation of security. His childhood was spent among ruins of various kinds: after his father deserted them in 1945, Moorcock and his mother pursued an itinerant existence through Mitcham, Norbury, Streatham—the great British semi-detached suburbia.

Moorcock's formal education was a disaster. He failed his eleven-plus examination and went rapidly through a total of ten schools, some of which expelled him. Finally, his mother, observing his hobby of producing homemade magazines, sent him to Pitman's College for a clerical education. Moorcock learned to type and equipped himself for a career in journalism, escaping in 1956, at the age of seventeen, from his second job as office boy to his first professional editorial post, on *Tarzan Adventures*, a magazine for fans of Edgar Rice Burroughs. Moorcock widened its scope with his own fiction, modeled on Burroughs's sword-and-sorcery fantasies, and increased its circulation. He had long been a voracious reader who observed none of the recognized divisions between juvenile and adult fiction. Effectively self-educated, he developed broad tastes and unorthodox literary principles that have sustained his determinedly unconventional career. Having resigned from *Tarzan Adventures* in 1958 after the first of many quarrels with publishers, he went to Paris, where he encountered the last survivors of the bohemian era, and returned to Britain to set up an import business for Olympia Press, smuggling the works of Henry Miller, banned in England at that time.

In September 1958 Moorcock started work for Sexton Blake Library and Amalgamated Press (later Fleetway Publications), continuing his involvement with "the folk-hero business" by editing and writing thrillers and comic strips about Tarzan, Kit Carson, Robin Hood, Jet Ace Logan, the Three Musketeers, and others. At the same time he wrote his first "non-generic" novels, "Duel Among the Wine-Green Suns," "The Quest of Jephraim Tallow" (eventually published in 1979 as *The Golden Barge*), and "The Eternal Champion," and had his first "adult story," a collaboration with Barrington Bayley called "Peace on Earth," published in *New Worlds* (December 1959). During his two years in the Fleetway fiction factory, Moorcock made important friendships with writers Harry Harrison and Jack Trevor Story and illustrator James Cawthorn. He also became involved with the anarchist movement, corresponding with Woody Guthrie and Pete Seeger and working for the National Union of Journalists (while still too young for full membership). His refusal to contribute to comic strips which exploited xenophobic hatred of Germany and Russia provoked a celebrated row with the management: to terminate it, and his employment, Moorcock threw a typewriter through a fifth-floor window. In February 1961 he was back in Europe, climbing mountains in Scandinavia, where he was first introduced to the fiction of Jorge Luis Borges and Italo Calvino. When his money ran out, he hitchhiked to the British Consulate in Paris, fainting from hunger, and was sent home.

At this time British science fiction was almost entirely controlled by E. J. Carnell, literary agent and editor of the three British science-fiction magazines, *New Worlds*, *Science Fantasy*, and *Science Fiction Adventures*. At Carnell's prompting, Moorcock returned to the heroic fantasy of his earliest writings and began the saga of Elric, Prince of Melribonë, with "The Dreaming City," published in *Science Fantasy* for June 1961. Elric was the first distinctive hero Moorcock had created. His stories set the first important strands in the huge interlocking web of Moorcock's fiction and won him his first fan followers. Concerned not merely to follow the conventions of the sword-and-sorcery genre, he created "a hero as different as possible from the usual run." Where Robert E. Howard's Conan and Lin Carter's Thongor are heavily muscled thugs, Elric is a frail albino, dependent for vitality on his vampiric broadsword Stormbringer; he is a philosopher and magician restlessly preoccupied with an elusive balance between the cosmic principles of law and chaos. Moorcock's addition of an introverted sensitivity to a genre whose original popularity lay in the escapism of blithe brutality was surprising but successful. Elric's problems of identity and meaning, purpose and desire, battled out in a crude and violent universe ruled by ambiguous powers indifferent to his values, are essentially problems of adolescent frustration. The stories of this fey warrior appealed to the melancholy romanticism of adolescents in the 1960s and provided a flexible symbolism through which Moorcock could convert his personal experience into popular art. The earliest books of Elric—*The Stealer of Souls and Other Stories* (1963) and *Stormbringer* (1965)—are vigorous but uneven; later stories and revisions of stories, published in *The Sailor on the Seas of Fate* (1976) and *The Bane of the Black Sword* (1977), rationalize the sequence and smooth some of the prose.

In 1962 Moorcock made an attempt to settle down, with a job writing publicity for the Liberal party, and married Hilary Bailey at the end of September. During that same year his first metaphysical science fiction, "The Sundered Worlds" and "The Blood Red Game," appeared in Carnell's *Science Fiction Adventures*. In 1963 with J. G. Ballard he assembled a dummy issue of their ideal magazine, comprising "a cross-fertilisation of popular sf, science and the work of the literary and artistic avant garde," but no publisher would take it up. Fired from the Liberal party job after another disagreement which persuaded him to return to his anarchist commitment, Moorcock struggled to resume a free-lance career in a dwindling market, with his first child, Sophie, to provide for.

In 1964 Carnell left the remaining British science-fiction magazines, *New Worlds* and *Science Fantasy*, when they were sold to a new publisher, Roberts and Vinter. Without telling him, he recommended Moorcock as his successor. Preferring not to be constrained by the generic limitations of a title like *Science Fantasy*, Moorcock chose the editorship of *New Worlds*, where he embarked at once on a campaign to transform science fiction. He gave prominence to Ballard, whose earlier work Carnell had promoted, as an example of a writer who had discarded the plot formulae of science fiction and was reorganizing its imagery into a symbolic panoply all his own. Ballard in turn wrote in praise of William Burroughs, hardly known in Britain then, and called upon science-fiction writers and readers to abandon outer space for inner space. Controversy began immediately. For all its apparent concern for change and the future, science fiction had (and still has) a powerful conservative element. In hindsight, Moorcock's first issues of *New Worlds* seem oddly divided between the extravagant assertions of their editorial matter and commonplace science fiction from established writers like Arthur Sellings, Donald Malcolm, and E. C. Tubb: Moorcock knew he had to retain the existing audience while he cultivated a new one. The only editorial policy of his "popular literary renaissance" was an insistence on originality and intelligence; unfortunately, the resulting diversity and eccentricity of what he offered as "the new sf" were taken to be stylistic requirements. Much frivolity ensued, for which Moorcock was blamed by the hardcore

logicians of science fiction. That, and the fact that his *New Worlds* has always been judged in terms of the genre rather than in terms of the larger postmodernist movement in fiction to which it clearly belongs, have served to diffuse much of its potential impact.

The distinctive double character of Moorcock's career can be seen in the fiction he wrote in 1964 (when his second daughter Katy was born) and 1965. Late in 1964, seeking a new fantasy hero to focus myths not from an imaginary feudal past but out of contemporary urban life, he devised the mercurial Jerry Cornelius and wrote his first adventure, *The Final Programme* (1968), in nine days of January 1965. Beginning his career as a physicist-turned-secret agent, garbed and supplied in the flashiest style of the mid-1960s, Cornelius rapidly developed into an entirely new kind of fictional character, a dubious hero whose significance is always oblique and rarely stable, equipped to tackle all the challenges of his time yet unable to find a satisfactory solution to any of them. At the same time Moorcock was writing pseudonymous pulp thrillers for Roberts and Vinter's Compact imprint—*The Barbarians of Mars*, *Blades of Mars*, and *Warriors of Mars*, a Martian trilogy in imitation of Edgar Rice Burroughs—and another sword-and-sorcery tetralogy, the "History of the Runestaff," whose first draft took him twelve days to complete, at fifteen thousand words a day. Though this work was strictly commercial, to support his family and *New Worlds*, it is thematically inextricable from the Cornelius books, insisting on the inadequacy of heroics and the urgency for individual responsibility in a world which seems pitilessly deterministic one moment and utterly chaotic the next. Moorcock has written many inferior books, but never a dishonest one.

"Behold the Man," the story of Karl Glogauer, a modern social casualty who travels back through time to find masochistic self-fulfillment in the role of Christ, was published in *New Worlds* in September 1966. Controversial as all his work, it won Moorcock acclaim from the science-fiction world, in the form of a British Science Fiction Association Award and, the following year, a Nebula from the Science Fiction Writers of America. Moorcock was beginning to receive some praise for his hard work and some response to his radical proposals, even from the science-fiction community. His career, however, has never been smooth, even in its most successful phases. Economic catastrophe (unconnected with the magazine) now struck at the publishers of *New Worlds*, which was threatened with closure but saved at the last minute by a grant from the Arts Council of Great Britain. This subsidy, though insufficient to finance the magazine entirely, enabled Moorcock, with the assistance of Langdon Jones, Thomas M. Disch, and Hilary Bailey, to change it altogether from its pulp origins into an adventurously designed glossy on the lines of his 1963 model for an ideal magazine. Definitions of science fiction came to have less and less relevance to *New Worlds*, which offered Moorcock his long awaited freedom to write and edit without generic constraints; nevertheless, the continual shortage of funds and the boom in fantasy fiction prompted British republications and American first editions of books from earlier, outgrown phases of his career. Moorcock was in the familiar commercial trap of having to exploit achievements he valued very little to support the work he cared about. The hated and misleading comparisons of Moorcock to J. R. R. Tolkien and Edgar Rice Burroughs came thick and fast. Solicited and perpetuated by avid paperback publishers, they drowned out the more adventurous sound of *New Worlds*, which attracted misinformative publicity and was suppressed by its own distributor, banned by British retail monopolies, and circulated in relative obscurity.

In 1967 when Moorcock made his first trip to America he was already at work on what was to become *A Cure for Cancer* (1971), the second Jerry Cornelius book. He visited Avon Books, who had unexpectedly bought *The Final Programme*, and told them of his plan for a tetralogy developing the character and the narrative technique. The following year Avon published *The Final Programme* (with some unauthorized cuts) and contracted for the next three Cornelius titles. Langdon Jones, assistant editor of *New Worlds*, suggested that Moorcock might try short stories about Cornelius. The first to be published, "The Delhi Division," appeared in the magazine in December, though the first to be written, "The Peking Junction," was reserved for Jones's own anthology, *The New SF*, in 1969. "The Delhi Division" features Cornelius as a miserable assassin with a mysterious colonial past; "The Tank Trapeze," next to appear, intercuts the *Guardian*'s account of the Russian invasion of Czechoslovakia with another tale of assassination, set in Burma, at the end of which Cornelius is shot dead. Manuscripts show Moorcock simplifying complexities, suppressing any passages that comment or explain, condensing plot to a bare handful of scenes and phrases. The process reduces puzzling stories to inscrutable fragments—polished, weighty little enigmas that are all the more fascinating for what

has been removed from them. The effect of the final versions of these and later pieces (collected in *The Lives and Times of Jerry Cornelius*, 1976) is that there are coherent but absent stories, to which they still relate but which are not wholly deducible from the remnants. They invite and frustrate our attempts to isolate the moral and motivational dynamics of their plots, remaining opaque but singularly compelling images. The stories of Jerry Cornelius can be taken as Moorcock's characteristically individual approach to problems of perception, attitude, and decision that have led other experimental writers of the later twentieth century to different narrative techniques. Where the nouveau roman can tempt sterility and seems to clear a vacuum around itself, Moorcock's Corneliana enrich themselves with their infinite allusiveness and engage dramatically (though inconclusively) with worldly events and recurrent catastrophes.

Nineteen sixty-nine also saw the publication of *The Black Corridor*, the story, by Moorcock and his wife, of a spaceflight into madness, and of *Behold the Man*, a novel-length expansion of the prizewinning story. This practice of expanding successful short stories is extremely common in science fiction and often provokes cynical comment, sometimes undeserved, since the novel may represent the conclusion of work-in-progress rather than a capitalization on earlier success. Nevertheless, it is too often true that the eventual novel makes no significant advance on the original story and may detract from it. Some have argued this case against *Behold the Man*. The novel uses a fragmentary technique—part observation, part internal monologue—free-ranging in time, which is appropriate to the schizophrenia of the subject. The fragments accumulate, however; they are centripetal to the point of obsession, leaving no corner of Glogauer's condition unexposed, so unlike the fragments of the Cornelius stories, which orbit about a loose, elusive center. In either form *Behold the Man* is more impressive for its power and its sustained permission of conflicting interpretations of Glogauer's life and death than for its style, which now seems overwrought, however aptly so.

While it would be a futile exercise to construct an image of Moorcock from autobiographical elements in his stories of Glogauer and Cornelius, accounts and reminiscences of his life at the end of the 1960s do much to suggest that the instabilities of his characters reflect the personality of their creator. Glogauer, the masochistic messiah, can find satisfaction only in following a script spelled out for him by history and by the will of the crowd; yet his ministry is in the service of the highest spiritual and humanitarian ideals, and the paradox of time travel makes it possible that the role of Christ is his own creation and always was. By contrast, Cornelius, at once over-ambitious and extraordinarily self-indulgent, demonstrates a crippling moral sensitivity alongside a resolute individualism, a determination to make his own way through whatever the world throws at him. He repeatedly refers to his activities as "capers," but they take place in nightmare versions of the later twentieth century and usually end in tears. Moorcock, gigantic and flamboyant with his wild hair and extravagant clothes, was a cavalier public figure in the *New Worlds* years, disrupting proceedings at science-fiction conventions or playing cowboys and Indians in crowded restaurants. At the same time he lived in a condition of perpetual anxiety and desperation, sacrificing his health, wealth, and domestic peace to an embattled literary magazine with a pitiful circulation. He worked as sole owner, publisher, and editor from 1967 to 1969 in a chaos of mislaid copy and unpaid bills; so strong was his commitment that he forced himself to divert his creative energies into series after series of commercial fantasy writing, detesting them but unable to divorce them from his serious work, using them to reinforce his message of the futility of destiny, the impossibility of idealism. In the service of his literary ideals, he wrote romantic books against romanticism; he wrote heroic books against hero worship and was heroized for them. Nor was he able, financially or psychologically, to shake off his cult: literary recognition within a coterie, without popular enjoyment, could be no achievement at all to him. He was strongly suspicious of respectability but was avid for respect; the unruliness and exhibitionism of his public image at the end of the 1960s masked a sense of moral obligation which could be as devious as it was stringent. Having received payment for a book which he disliked from an American publisher whom he decided had been dishonest, he sat one evening feeding ten-pound notes, one after another, into the fire.

In 1969, with the distributors returning vast quantities of copies of *New Worlds* which had never reached the wholesalers, its staff were to be seen selling copies on the street in Portobello. Moorcock handed over editorial and publishing responsibilities to Charles Platt and returned to the typewriter to raise some funds in the way he knew best—writing more sword and sorcery: the books of Corum and some more of the Elric saga. With his inspiration and permission, other *New Worlds* writ-

ers were contributing their own Cornelius stories to the magazine in this period. James Sallis was the first, followed by M. John Harrison, Brian W. Aldiss, and others. These stories were collected in 1971 as an anthology, *The Nature of the Catastrophe*, edited by Moorcock and Jones. It would seem a singular literary phenomenon that an author should share one of his own highly personal creations with his friends and colleagues, but Moorcock had designed Cornelius as a multivalent and flexible character and was not alone in finding him useful or even in identifying with him. Charles Platt has said of the *New Worlds* team, "Cornelius's spirit was an advertisement for ours. So was his inability to take himself seriously." Cornelius became a totem for the whole new kind of fiction that Moorcock was creating and promoting, an ironic identikit of contemporary styles and attitudes assembled and reassembled by many hands. A prospectus for *The Nature of the Catastrophe*, originally to be called "The Jerry Cornelius Annual," cites precedents from ancient and modern heroic literature for the multiple authorship of tales about a single character: from Arthurian legends to the exploits of Sexton Blake. Cornelius is introduced as an ambivalent index to many aspects of contemporary society: "something of a modern Candide," Moorcock suggests, still intently putting to unexpected use the material of his earlier, less respectable career and resolutely refusing to recognize the conventional demarcation between commercial fiction and literary art. The decision to write *The Final Programme* was a deliberate break with the cliches of sword-and-sorcery, but its early chapters contain deliberate reworkings of two Elric stories. Similarly, "The Peking Junction," the first Cornelius short story, cannibalizes the third of the Runestaff series, *The Sword of the Dawn* (1968).

Despite the efforts of Moorcock and Platt, and the excellence of the issues for 1969 and 1970, *New Worlds* was forced to fold. Number 200, dated April 1970, was the last to appear in a standard magazine format. Moorcock compiled an index and published it, together with two stories (one an extended sentimental joke by Thomas M. Disch and the other a reprinted piece of Victorian apocalyptic speculation), as a funereal "Good Taste Issue" for February 1971. *A Cure for Cancer*, the second Jerry Cornelius novel, received book publication in the same month, having been serialized in *New Worlds* two years previously. Its plot is even more obscure than that of *The Final Programme*, to which it provides an alternative as much as a sequel. Inversions of color, sex, value, and relationship abound. In a Europe occupied by American military "advisors" and dividing into bizarre racial and political factions, Cornelius runs a "transmogrification" service which helps people to secure their own personalities in the flux. While he is on a mysterious mission for the organization, his most important piece of equipment is stolen and misused by his arch-enemy. This black box operates as a key to the "multiverse," a system of worlds parallel in space and time used by Moorcock in his earliest science fiction. To stabilize one person's identity the box requires the sacrifice of another to fuel it (just as Elric's demonic sword, Stormbringer, does). Eventually, in a world turned to ice by the waste of energy, Cornelius abandons his campaign and seeks solace in an incestuous love affair with his resurrected sister, Catherine.

The confusions and enormities of *A Cure for Cancer* are deliberate and cruel. Moorcock has written that "although the tone is light, laconic, the issues are serious—political assassination, manipulation of the individual psyche, erosion of personal and political liberty, U. S. attitudes towards Vietnam, and so on. These problems are examined but not really in a satirical sense because the issues are so complex it is impossible to define exactly what has created them, or indeed, how the problems can be solved." Moorcock's description of his style as ironic rather than satirical is apt. The angle of approach is shallow, glancing in and out again. There is no reluctance to examine the atrocious issues—indeed, the arch, knowing tone of the Cornelius books, especially their dialogue, continually suggests that Cornelius understands the problems better than we do. On the other hand, there is no specific denunciation of the atrocities, nor is there any attempt to propose or imply a doctrinaire solution. The contemporary world has come too far, Cornelius signals; the most we can hope to do is find a way of living with our knowledge of the problems without being corrupted by it, and even this hope may be in vain. Cornelius himself, needless to say, once again pitches his ambition to impossible messianic heights and has to compromise for the rest of the novel. Moorcock rescues *A Cure for Cancer* from the weight of such defeatism by the energy and daring of his imagination, and the novel approaches farce more often than tragic despair. It must also be seen in the context of the ludicrous millenarian optimism fashionable at the time. Insisting that idealism not only dies but also kills, Moorcock had a far harder moral vision to express than he is usually given credit for. Part of the reason for this lack of recognition must be the misleading quality of the style, which is not only light and laconic but elliptical to the point of attenuation. In his attempt at a style which would capture the perversity of the late 1960s, he perhaps went too far and presented a commentary largely indistinguishable from its subject. Nor, with fiction which hands over to its reader so much of the traditional authorial responsibility for continuity and interpretation, can the reader be blamed for misreading.

Refusing to abandon *New Worlds*, Moorcock and Platt had made plans to revive it as a paperback, publishing unclassifiable fiction under a broad "sf" banner as they had done in its magazine format. The first volume of the new series appeared in June 1971 as *New Worlds 1: The Science Fiction Quarterly*, a schedule it maintained for four issues, followed by another six at less frequent intervals. Moorcock edited the first six, Charles Platt and Hilary Bailey the remainder, featuring familiar authors such as J. G. Ballard and Harvey Jacobs alongside newcomers such as Robert Meadley and Richard A. Pollack, and taking the opportunity to reprint some material from earlier issues that had suffered from severely restricted distribution.

In September 1971 Moorcock's *The Warlord of the Air* was published. It is a Wellsian scientific romance presented as a narration of extraordinary adventures by one Oswald Bastable of the 53rd Lancers to Moorcock's grandfather in 1903. Bastable tells of being inexplicably catapulted into the future, and the wonders of the world seventy years hence. The curiosity of his account is that the 1973 he has experienced bears scant relation to the real world of the 1970s. The two world wars never happened and the British Empire still rules, sharing international power with France, Italy, Russia, Germany, Japan, and the Greater American Commonwealth. Helium airships, electric monorails, and steam carriages are the means of transport, and the wireless telephone the means of communication, that unite a world designed according to the Victorian dream. Rudyard Kipling died in the Boer War, Mick Jagger is an army lieutenant, and Josef Korzeniowski, Count Rudolfo Guevara, and others including a "Comrade Spender" are conspirators in a socialist revolution led by Gen. O. T. Shaw. A fanatical racist scoutmaster, called Egan in the published book, bore the name Reagan in the original manuscript. The adventures of the naive Bastable represent another reluctant engagement of the Eternal Champion, peremptorily summoned through the multiverse to a parallel world where history has taken a rather different course. The jokes are diverting but also continually draw attention to the fact that Bastable's new world is a version of our own, with a broad commentary implicit in its design. The Opium War, for example, happened in his as in ours and for the same reasons. *The Warlord of the Air* made it clear that Moorcock's revolutionary sympathies did not stop at the limits of literature. Though the political scheme of *The Warlord of the Air* is rather simplistic and eventually obscured by the technical marvels of the great airship battle, it certainly marks an advance from the safely fashionable anti-Americanism demonstrated in *A Cure for Cancer*.

The Warlord of the Air also shows the first evidence of Moorcock's continuing fascination with Victoriana and his preference for the fantasies of that epoch over the subsequent tradition of science fiction, which his previous writing and editing had done so much to subvert. Nevertheless, 1971 saw the publication of the Swords trilogy, the tale of Prince Corum, yet another avatar of the Eternal Champion in the sword-and-sorcery mode and of a further Elric collection, *The Sleeping Sorceress*: commercial work necessary to pay debts incurred by *New Worlds* and support the Moorcock family, increased by the birth of a son, Max. Ironically, Moorcock's public reaffirmed their enthusiasm for the work which inspired him least, and *The Knight of the Swords* received a British Fantasy Award in the following year. The award was the least of Moorcock's successes in 1972, a year in which he had published three major works, each of which demonstrates that arrival at maturity need not mean the surcease of inventiveness. In these three books his imagination is bolder and more startling than ever, articulated in prose which is at once more disciplined, more flexible, more efficient, and more attractive than he had shown any sign of achieving before.

Behold the Man, by using the license of time travel, had identified Karl Glogauer absolutely with Jesus Christ, while leaving no opportunity for a second coming. *Breakfast in the Ruins* (1972) was therefore an unexpected sequel. In *Behold the Man*, by connecting the messianic urge emphatically with certain commonplace neuroses and offering some ambivalent inferences about worship, sacrifice, and personal responsibility, Moorcock made Glogauer's self-preoccupied biography more widely applicable. In *Breakfast in the Ruins*, by resurrecting Glogauer and sending him out through a hundred years of torture past, present, and future, he makes it apparent that no crucifixion is an isolated incident. A question repeatedly asked in *The Black Corridor* and the Jerry Cornelius stories is, "What is the nature of the catastrophe?" *Breakfast in the Ruins* answers it on every page, but the answer is of no use. Glogauer, now a white English Jew aged about

thirty-one, is seduced by an anonymous black man in London. They spend a night together in a hotel playing sadomasochistic games in the course of which Glogauer allows himself to be painted black all over. Though he starts out as a willing but rather petulant victim, he ends the encounter on top, assuming the persona of a cocky blackamoor dandy, while the black man loses his assurance, his size, and eventually his color. In moments between bouts Glogauer is seen time tripping again, becoming different people of different ages in other years and other places—scenes of various inhumanities, such as Capetown in 1892 or Berlin in 1935. Again and again he makes or tries to avoid making impossible moral choices, in innocence or complicity, compromising himself with corruption, destroying or being destroyed. These alternating texts are offset by quotations from sources such as *With the Flag to Pretoria* and *The Path to Vietnam*, and by a series of problems called "What Would You Do?" in which impossible moral choices are offered directly to us. *Breakfast in the Ruins* is a relentless book. Its subject is everything that is intolerable, that is cause for suicidal despair, yet it makes compulsive, invigorating reading.

The English Assassin was Moorcock's second book in 1972 and his third in the Jerry Cornelius sequence. After the heat death of the world at the end of *A Cure for Cancer*, it is the hero himself who has succumbed to entropy in this volume. Fished out of the sea in a strange semianimate condition, Cornelius is carted around a bewildering world tormented by strange wars, French Zouaves aiding Scottish insurgents against the British Empire, Arabs and Cossacks razing Athens in alliance. Disconnected, highly atmospheric scenes relate to alternative histories of the nineteenth and twentieth centuries, focused on the moral and political problems of a cast of vivid, rather pathetic, characters including Jerry's sister, Catherine, their frightful cockney mother, and their ambiguous ally, the Temporal Adventuress Una Persson, all of whom seem to set a great value on the shrieking corpse of the Messiah to the Age of Science. Moorcock makes use of material and techniques first seen in *The Warlord of the Air*, *Breakfast in the Ruins*, and an early Cornelius short story, "The Delhi Division," employing quotations and references, direct and oblique, to reinforce the enigmatic familiarity of the story. Inserts in the text include news clippings about deaths and miraculous cures of children speeches at "The Peace Talks" and, from a fictitious autobiography, extracts on the subject of historical determinism and the complex interdependence of generations. Moorcock dedicates this book, appropriately, to his father and to his son. Its overall effect is of a world in dangerous and possibly terminal national and personal flux, occupied by people at once closely involved with and poignantly impotent among events that they may not understand any better than we can. Though each is sharply realized, their roles flicker and blur as do the boundaries between private and public and between one possibly factual era and another fictitious one. The unyielding cryptology of *A Cure for Cancer* is replaced by a supple oneiric suggestiveness.

The third of Moorcock's publications in 1972 was *An Alien Heat*, the first of a new trilogy, "the Dancers at the End of Time." Set at the end of the universe, it concerns the last few inhabitants of Earth, an assortment of strange characters equipped with power rings which, by directly altering the basic structure of matter, enable them to make or to do anything they can imagine, including the creation, dissolution, and resurrection of any living thing. There is no longer any division between idea and expression, or desire and attainment, nor any death. Moorcock perceived that these conditions would lead to the extinction of art, of morality, and of all but the mildest emotions. The Dancers drift in a vague, courtly way from pastime to pastime amid incomplete landscapes and architecture of their own devising, interrupted only by the arrival of the odd time traveler from another age. These travelers usually behave in a missionary fashion, determined to impose on the juvenile dilettantes the mores of their home societies, and are politely imprisoned in luxurious menageries designed on historical lines. Bereft of any real inventiveness, the Dancers often entertain themselves with recreations from past eras, and this book and the following ones constitute a gentle farce based on their confusions and misrepresentations of history. One of their number, rumored to be the last naturally born human, is called Jherek Carnelian (Moorcock's work abounds in such "translated" names, anagrams, or puns on characters in other works or from real life). Carnelian opts to revive the major historical theme of romantic love and falls for a Victorian time traveler, Mrs. Amelia Underwood, whose notions of morality and social decency are in humorous contrast with his own paradisal innocence and good-natured spontaneity. When the elastic forces of time snatch her back to her own period, Carnelian follows in a reconditioned time machine and barely survives the horrors of Victorian London. *An Alien Heat* shows Moorcock at his most relaxed and generous, writing with an open-

ness and facility quite unlike the hypnotic or disturbing contrivances of his styles in the Cornelius and Glogauer books.

Short stories about other Dancers at the End of Time appeared in *New Worlds*, now edited by Hilary Bailey, who amicably separated from Moorcock in 1973. Moorcock again won a British Fantasy Award (for Best Writer of 1972), and in 1973 Robert Fuest's film version of *The Final Programme* was released (retitled in America *The Last Days of Man on Earth*). Moorcock was involved in the making of the film in the early stages only and was disappointed by the eventual product. Opinions he has given of it since have grown more and more disparaging, based on the justifiable objection that Fuest trivialized the story's satirical commentary in its trendy imagery and removed its sense of irony altogether. Moorcock has been quoted as saying that Jon Finch, though not ideally cast as Jerry Cornelius, had a better concept of the character than the director did. Moorock's publications in 1973 consisted only of more sword-and-sorcery adventures of Dorian Hawkmoon and Corum, though it was also the year in which *A Cure for Cancer* was published in paperback by Penguin, a house of high prestige, with an excellent cover by David Pelham. In the following year *The Land Leviathan*, the second Bastable adventure, was published. More somber than *The Warlord of the Air*, it tells of Bastable's second journey through time, this one only three years forward, to a 1904 in which the mechanical inventions of a Chilean genius called O'Bean have transformed civilization by automating the world's labor and transport to an almost total degree. However, leisure has brought political unrest, the insurgence of nationalism in the colonies, and eventually war between the great powers. With the use of war machines designed by O'Bean, Europe has been razed and America reduced to barbarism. Bastable meets another Una Persson and another Josef Korzeniowski, this one a submarine captain, and works for President Gandhi in the pacifist utopia of Bantustan until caught up in the campaign of Cicero Hood, the "Black Attila," to crush the country where his father had been a slave.

The Hollow Lands (1974), second of the Dancers at the End of Time trilogy, was published in the same year. The first half of the book concerns Carnelian's frustration over his separation from Mrs. Underwood, the disruptive arrival of a band of alien ruffians, and Carnelian's accidental discovery of a robot Nurse, left over from a previous epoch, who has a time machine in her possession. The rest of the book relates his return to the nineteenth century, where he meets Frank Harris, H. G. Wells, and George Bernard Shaw, and succeeds in abducting Mrs. Underwood from her home and husband. *The Hollow Lands* is less substantial than *An Alien Heat*, more arbitrary in its comedy, even turning, with policemen chasing aliens through the Café Royale, to slapstick.

In 1975 Moorcock officially put an end to the saga of the Eternal Champion in *The Quest for Tanelorn*, which unites all the heroes of his sword-and-sorcery fiction in a journey to a city of peace said to survive even the wildest oscillations of the Cosmic Balance. The book has the air of having been written only because the series and the readers demanded it; Moorcock seems as tired of the eternal campaign as the Champion himself and as eager to have done with it.

The Adventures of Una Persson and Catherine Cornelius in the Twentieth Century, published in 1976, has been rather overlooked among Moorcock's fiction, perhaps because it has little of the glamour fans tend to associate with the name Cornelius. Jerry appears only as a minor and rather unattractive character. Catherine and Una Persson are seen relaxing together in Pennsylvania in 1933 before traveling back to 1910 and working their ways separately through the century, or versions of it, rather as Glogauer was condemned to do in *Breakfast in the Ruins*. Una goes through assorted battles and revolutions, Catherine through a series of ever more perverse and violent sexual involvements with male stereotypes. Characters from *The English Assassin* recur, mostly more conscious and reflective than they were in their previous roles; scenes and descriptions are generally steadier and less remote. The book demonstrates Moorcock's growing concern with female viewpoints, after his protracted cataloguing of male heroics and anxieties. *Legends from the End of Time*, a collection of the related short stories from *New Worlds*, was also published that year, and in November *The End of All Songs*, the final volume of the Dancers at the End of Time trilogy, appeared. Jherek and Amelia, stranded in the Lower Devonian period at the end of *The Hollow Lands*, discover a post of the Guild of Temporal Adventurers, where (with the help of Captain Bastable and Una Persson) they negotiate a way forward to the End of Time. Struggling with many incompatibilities and inconveniences, including the arrival of Harold Underwood, Amelia's fundamentalist husband, they finally decide to return to the peace and solitude of the Paleozoic era, giving up the paradise of idleness and the omnipotence of the power rings, thus fulfilling Moorcock's suggestion

that this, "the last story in the annals of the human race. . . , is not dissimilar to that which many believe is the first."

In March 1977 *The Condition of Muzak* was published in England, completing the Jerry Cornelius tetralogy, which was published by Avon Books in one volume in August, under the title *The Cornelius Chronicles*. Moorcock was awarded the *Guardian* Fiction Prize for the whole work; the paper's literary editor, W. L. Webb, commented: "Michael Moorcock, rejecting the demarcation disputes that have reduced the novel to a muddle of warring sub-genres, recovers in these four books a protean vitality and inclusiveness that one might call Dickensian if their consciousness were not so entirely of our own volatile times."

The Condition of Muzak recapitulates the stories so far, drawing extensively on the first three books and reassembling them into one sequence. Against their familiar vistas of power and war, Moorcock sets another, seedier version in which Jerry is a lazy, feckless working-class lad animated only by dreams of rock and roll stardom. All his friends and enemies appear as threadbare showbiz connections or neighbors in Notting Hill Gate. This, it would seem, is the "real" Jerry Cornelius, the most probable one, and the ubiquitous, bisexual, multi-talented heroes are his "fantasies." Moorcock has played enough tricks with multiple universes for us to be sure that any given reality is not absolute, not the last word; although entropy always tends to a maximum, art (and life) constantly aspire toward the condition of Muzak, and the most liberating rock and roll war cry is finally and swiftly diminished to a television jingle. As Moorcock's friend and fellow writer M. John Harrison put it, "Rather than a bitter revelation of reality, a cancellation of the daydream, we have an alternative. Life is offered as a substitute for the fantasy, which was never offered as a substitute for life."

Yet while Moorcock was healing the fragmented novel and winning literary acclaim, the unstoppable wheels of his commercial career kept grinding. In the same month as the publication of *The Condition of Muzak*, March 1977, *The Weird of the White Wolf*, one of the books rationalizing the saga of Elric, appeared in America; and in September *Sojan*, a collection of Moorcock's juvenilia from *Tarzan Adventures*, was published by Savoy Books in England. In February 1978 the British Fantasy Society published as a small booklet a chapter from Moorcock's still unpublished critical study of fantasy literature. Called *Epic Pooh*, this essay attacks the most popular British exponents of "consolatory" fantasy, from A. A. Milne through J. R. R. Tolkien to Richard Adams, for attitudes of moral and political cowardice he finds exemplified in their fiction. Implicitly Moorcock argues for another British tradition which combines fantasy with psychological and social awareness, a tradition from Charles Dickens through Mervyn Peake, at the end of which Moorcock himself appears. In an interview published at the beginning of 1979, he defined his own literary principle: "I'm attempting all the time to find equilibrium between unchecked Romanticism ('Chaos') and stifling Classicism ('Law'). Pinnochio and Jiminy Cricket. Pierrot and Columbine. Ego and superego. Make your own choice. And in form I'm always looking for a combination (that will work) of the epic and the novel—or the romance and the novel. You will notice that I call very few of my books 'novels' because they are not, classically speaking, novels. They are romances. Scene and idea (allegorical concerns) in general take precedence over characters. . . . The same moral arguments are debated again and again from my earliest (THE GOLDEN BARGE) to my latest (GLORIANA)." *The Condition of Muzak* presents, in its alternate probable and improbable histories of Jerry Cornelius, a confrontation between the modes of novel and romance; though they clash at an immediate level, both eventually express the same entropic vision. *Gloriana, or The Unfulfill'd Queen*, published in April 1978, is Moorcock's most successful integration of the two modes in a story, which is itself one of integration, of Gloriana, Empress of Albion and America, and one of her subjects, Captain Quire, a master of intrigue, torture, and death, a secret agent at first for Gloriana's chancellor and then for an Arabian conspiracy to bring Albion into the power of the Grand Caliph. The pageantry and rich corruption of the scenes contain a complex and cunning psychological exploration, just as Gloriana's vast palace holds a second, shadow kingdom in forgotten suites and corridors inside the walls. Intended as Moorcock's grand conclusion to his fantastic romances, it features not only Una Persson but also Jephraim Tallow, hero of one of his earliest romances, *The Golden Barge*, unpublished until 1979 when Savoy produced it in the course of their dedicated exhumation of Moorcock's juvenilia. With his first and last fantasies in paperback at the same time (each with a cover featuring a painting by Gustave Moreau), his career reached a pause. A public consummation had been attained, leaving him free to enter upon a new phase of writing. Indeed, there was a general clearing of decks in his life at this time: his marriage to Hilary

Bailey, effectively over for five years, was officially ended in divorce in April 1978 so that he could marry Jill Riches the following month. Moorcock started work on "Byzantium Endures" the first book of a new sequence, "Between the Wars."

Since then there has been a lacuna. Financial problems, compounded with the rapid collapse of his second marriage, left Moorcock unable to work for long periods. Separated from Jill Riches in September 1980, he spent much of the year in complete retreat in America. One publication of this year was a Cornelian curiosity, *The Great Rock and Roll Swindle*, first produced in newspaper format and described as "a novel inspired by the film by the Sex Pistols," with whose anarchist antics Moorcock felt some sympathy. *Byzantium Endures* was announced for June 1981; Moorcock, though still beset by problems of tax and litigation, is completing a new book, "The Brothel in Rosenstrasse." In the meantime there has been predictably much reprinting of old standards, publication of unpublished fragments such as *My Experiences in The Third World War* (1980), and the announcement of new romances, including one to be titled "The War Hound and the World's Pain," and a third Bastable book, "The Steel Tsar." Though nothing can now obliterate Moorcock's fame and his achieved ideal of literary values in popular fictional forms, his reputation (and so, to some extent, his future status) are in the balance, pending the appearance of "Between the Wars" which he has referred to, only half-jocularly, as "my *War and Peace*." Whatever course the rest of his career will take, it is unlikely ever to be free of the paradoxes, crises, and surprises that have characterized it so far.

Other:

The Nature of the Catastrophe, edited by Moorcock and Langdon Jones (London: Hutchinson, 1971).

Periodical Publications:

"Play With Feeling," *New Worlds Science Fiction*, 43 (April 1963): 2-3, 123-127;

"New Worlds: A Personal History," *Foundation: the Review of Science Fiction*, no. 15 (January 1979): 5-18;

"Wit and Humour in Fantasy," *Foundation: the Review of Science Fiction*, no. 16 (May 1979): 16-22.

Interviews:

Paul Walker, Interview, *Luna Monthly*, no. 59 (November 1975): 1-9;

Ian Covell, Interview, *Science Fiction Review*, 8 (January 1979): 18-25;

Charles Platt, Interview, in *Who Writes Science Fiction?* (Manchester: Savoy, 1980); republished as *Dream Makers* (New York: Berkley, 1980), pp. 233-242.

References:

Michael Ashley, "Behold the Man Called Moor-cock," *Science Fiction Monthly*, 2 (February 1975): 8-11;

Charles Platt, introduction to *The Condition of Muzak* (Boston: Gregg, 1978), pp. v-xii.

Papers:

The Bodleian Library, Oxford, holds a large and varied collection of Moorcock's papers.

Nicholas Mosley

(25 June 1923-   )

Peter Lewis
University of Durham

BOOKS: *Spaces of the Dark* (London: Hart-Davis, 1951);

Life Drawing, by Mosley and John Napper (London & New York: Studio Publications, 1954);

The Rainbearers (London: Weidenfeld & Nicolson, 1955);

Nicholas Mosley

Corruption (Weidenfeld & Nicolson, 1957; Boston: Little, Brown, 1958);

African Switchback (London: Weidenfeld & Nicolson, 1958);

The Life of Raymond Raynes (London: Faith Press, 1961);

Meeting Place (London: Weidenfeld & Nicolson, 1962);

Experience and Religion: A Lay Essay in Theology (London: Hodder & Stoughton, 1965; Philadelphia: United Church Press, 1967);

Accident (London: Hodder & Stoughton, 1965; New York: Coward-McCann, 1966);

Assassins (London: Hodder & Stoughton, 1966; New York: Coward-McCann, 1967);

Impossible Object (London: Hodder & Stoughton, 1968; New York: Coward-McCann, 1969);

Natalie Natalia (London: Hodder & Stoughton, 1971; New York: Coward, McCann & Geoghegan, 1971;

The Assassination of Trotsky (London: M. Joseph, 1972);

Julian Grenfell: His Life and The Times of His Death 1888-1915 (London: Weidenfeld & Nicolson, 1976);

Catastrophe Practice (London: Secker & Warburg, 1979);

Imago Bird (London: Secker & Warburg, 1980);

Serpent (London: Secker & Warburg, 1981).

During the last thirty years, Nicholas Mosley has had eleven works of fiction published and has gradually established himself among discerning readers of contemporary literature as one of the most individualistic and interesting of postwar English novelists. He has followed his own path with artistic integrity, avoiding every kind of fashionable fiction during a period when modishness has been widespread. As a result, he has not achieved great popular success, and, while he is well known and highly regarded in the British literary world, like some other significant postwar novelists, he has yet to win a substantial academic audience. Perhaps the two most important aspects of his career have been his quest for appropriate forms and his ability to begin afresh as a writer. He has never been satisfied to stand still or to repeat himself with minor variations in the way that some of his better-known contemporaries have done. He has preferred to take risks by attempting something new and different with each novel in an endeavor to invent fictional forms capable of dealing adequately with both the complexity of contemporary experience and the perplexing nature of reality.

Nicholas Mosley was born in London, the eldest son of Lady Cynthia Mosley and one of the most famous and controversial figures in modern British politics, the late Sir Oswald Mosley, and he inherited his father's baronetcy in 1980. He had earlier inherited another title, becoming the third Baron Ravensdale on the death of his aunt, Baroness Ravensdale, in 1966. After completing his schooling at Eton College in 1942, Mosley served as an officer in the Rifle Brigade during World War II, and was awarded the Military Cross in 1944. He left the army in 1946 to continue his education at Balliol College, Oxford, but spent only one year there. In 1947, the year of his first marriage, on 14 November to Rosemary Salmond, he decided to devote himself to full-time writing and moved with his artist-wife to rural North Wales in order to work on a novel.

During the next decade Mosley wrote four novels, three of which, *Spaces of the Dark* (1951), *The Rainbearers* (1955), and *Corruption* (1957), were published. His second novel, "A Garden of Trees," has never been published. Although these books differ in various ways, they also have a number of things in common so that it is possible to group them together as the first phase of Mosley's fiction. All three published novels are relatively long and densely written, often in extended paragraphs and elaborate sentences—Henry James and William Faulkner were important stylistic influences on Mosley at this time. All three books are searchingly analytical about the springs of human behavior and

largely adhere to the accepted conventions of realism even though they are just as much metaphysical as social novels. All three are about the postwar world and look back, to a greater or lesser extent, to the war itself. All three contain something of the existentialist *nausée* of the time, dealing with themes such as alienation, betrayal, and moral decadence.

The title *Spaces of the Dark* is a phrase from T. S. Eliot's "Rhapsody on a Windy Night," an appropriate choice by Mosley since his novel does have affinities with the angst and nightmare quality of Eliot's early poetry. Set just after the end of World War II, *Spaces of the Dark* centers on a young army officer, Paul Shaun, who returns to England bearing a terrible secret and burden of guilt which, as in the case of the Ancient Mariner and other haunted romantic heroes, set him apart from ordinary mankind as an outsider. The secret, not revealed until about one third of the way through the narrative, is that he deliberately killed his friend and fellow officer, John Longmore, during a battle when John's failure as a commander was endangering the lives of his men. In England Paul finds it impossible to communicate any longer with his family or to share their bourgeois values, and he is drawn fatalistically to the two young women who were closest to John: his respectable sister, Margaret, and the totally different bohemian, Sarah Thorne. The book concentrates mainly on Paul's relationships with these two women and on the mounting psychological tension within him as he tries to come to terms with all the conflicts engulfing him. The war casts a truly dark shadow over Paul's present. In the novel's denouement Paul is killed in an act of self-sacrifice while successfully saving the injured Margaret's life. *Spaces of the Dark* is an attempt to write nothing less than a full-fledged tragic novel, a most ambitious enterprise for a beginner in his twenties; if the book does not succeed fully it is because the characters are unable to bear the tragic weight expected of them.

The Rainbearers is less doom laden than *Spaces of the Dark*, and the conclusion is without the finality of death, but there are many resemblances. Like Paul in the earlier novel, the central character, Richard, is an inhabitant of the postwar wasteland and is involved with two women, his wife, Elizabeth, and Mary Livingstone, an Anglo-French girl from his past who reenters his life, so that he too is torn between conflicting loyalties. It is through Mary that the traumatic experience of the war colors the novel, since she has spent the war years in France, helped the Resistance, been tortured by the Germans, and seen her mother shot by the French after the liberation as a collaborator. The lack of direction in Richard's life and his unrealized human potential are connected in some way with his very brief but intense relationship with Mary before his marriage. When Richard meets Mary again after five years, they pick up where they left off, become lovers, and spend an idyllic holiday together in Spain. Mary seems to offer Richard the possibility of fulfillment and happiness, but his inner divisions, combined with a destructive urge, lead him to leave Mary just as he has earlier abandoned his wife. In spite of Richard's reconciliation with his wife, the novel ends negatively rather than positively with the emphasis on lost possibilities, failure, and a pervasive existential malaise.

Corruption differs from its two predecessors in being a first-person, not a third-person, narrative and in having a more complex chronological structure. Mosley's first two novels contain occasional flashbacks but are mainly orthodox linear narratives, whereas the expository stages of *Corruption* involve systematic intercutting between the novel's present and several different pasts. By this means the narrator, Robert Croft, builds up a picture of his intermittent relationship with his cousin and one-time lover Kate Lambourne over the years since their prewar childhood. What triggers his reminiscences is their accidental meeting in Venice during the 1950s, when he is visiting the city with his current girl friend. Mosley's principal male character once again finds himself entangled simultaneously with two women. For much of the book, Mosley's main theme is "the corruption and injustice of a dying world," symbolized partly by Venice but above all by Kate and her decadent life-style. Even more than in his earlier books, the characters in *Corruption* function symbolically as well as realistically, as might be expected from the morality-play title. Yet in the later stages, culminating in a riot, during which Kate reveals (somewhat melodramatically) to Robert that he is the father of her son Julius, there is a break in the pervading bleakness as a sense of redemption and new possibilities emerge. This change in tone is accompanied by a modification of style from the intricate and even convoluted prose of much of the book to a somewhat simpler, more direct idiom. This shift may seem inconsistent since it undermines the mood of oppressive and fatalistic gloom established in the earlier part of the novel as well as in some of the symbolism, but it is also a symptom of Mosley's growing maturity as a

novelist in that he is prepared to subvert the tragic pretensions of his own work by providing a much more open-ended conclusion than in his earlier novels.

With *Corruption* Mosley exhausted one creative vein and did not produce another novel for five years. His next book, *African Switchback* (1958), is a travel book based on his experiences in 1957 while driving from Dakar to Lagos with his friend and fellow novelist Hugo Charteris. In 1958 Mosley became deeply involved with the new Anglican monthly magazine *Prism*, launched Easter 1957 as a platform for advanced theological opinion. Mosley was joint editor for nearly two years, and subsequently became a member of the editorial advisory committee at the end of 1960 and poetry editor in April 1962. Of his numerous contributions to *Prism* before it was absorbed into another publication in 1965, the most interesting from a literary viewpoint are "Christian Novels" (October 1961) and his self-revealing review of J. D. Salinger's *Franny and Zooey* (July 1962), in which he commented: "The importance of this story is that it is about free will, and the way in which one person can touch another, profoundly, when that person needs to be touched. Most clever novels nowadays are about determinism, and the way in which no one has a hope of touching anyone ever." This statement has something of the force of a literary credo since it corresponds to a change in Mosley's own fiction away from the determinism evident in his early novels to more open forms.

Mosley's involvement in Christian apologetics at this time led him into other publications. In 1961 his biography of Raymond Raynes (1903-1958) was published; it is about the saintly superior of the Community of the Resurrection (an Anglican order of monks), who had devoted part of his life to working for the black community in South Africa. Mosley, who first met Raynes in 1950 and was strongly influenced by him, also edited *The Faith: Instructions on the Christian Faith* (1961), the talks Raynes gave during a mission in Denver, Colorado, not long before his death. Mosley's most sustained piece of theological writing is the short book he had published in 1965, *Experience and Religion: A Lay Essay in Theology*, very much a product of his years with *Prism*.

When Mosley returned to fiction in 1962 with *Meeting Place*, he produced a book markedly different from his previous novels. The prose is much simpler, the sentences and paragraphs shorter, and the style more cinematic than analytical. There is a much stronger visual quality in the writing and a harder objectivity in presenting the external world that may owe something to the phenomenology underlying the French *nouveau roman*. Furthermore, the narrative method, though basically linear, is elliptical and discontinuous. In his previous books Mosley had tended to be exhaustive, explaining everything and leaving nothing out; now he is highly selective, forcing the reader to make the connections between the intercut sections and to put the pieces together. In *Meeting Place* reality is much more indeterminate than in his previous novels. The central character is Harry Gates, an idealistic and somewhat innocent religious man who works as an unofficial social worker for a charitable organization, devoting his energies to helping misfits and delinquent teenagers while his own marriage is in a state of crisis. The narrative, notably more comic than its largely humorless predecessors, introduces a wide range of characters from the very well-to-do to the down-and-out, from a Fleet Street tycoon to a former inmate of a Nazi concentration camp, most of whom are involved in a complex network of relationships reminiscent of those in Iris Murdoch's novels. The action reaches a climax when circumstances force Harry to confront his own problems instead of everyone else's and to make a positive decision to rescue his own marriage by traveling to the United States to bring back his American wife, who has returned home. Going very much against contemporary fictional fashion, *Meeting Place* ends positively with a sense of renewal, exemplifying Mosley's belief in the possibility of regeneration, growth, and human creativity.

If *Meeting Place* is an important, transitional step in a new direction, Mosley's next novel, *Accident* (1965), represents the first high point in his career, the vindication of *his* innovative techniques at this time. Mosley's interest in philosophy pervades his fiction, but in *Accident*—the word has a technical meaning in philosophy—the narrator, Stephen Jervis, is an Oxford philosophy don devoted to his discipline as "a process of enquiry"; for Stephen, philosophy "does not find specific answers to specific questions, but rather deals with questions to which there are no specific answers." The world, as Mosley presents it, is characterized by uncertainty, and human attempts to understand it are extremely tentative. The actual story, most of which is presented in retrospect following a road accident at the opening of the novel, is fairly simple and concerns two of Stephen's students, William (upper-class English) and Anna (aristocratic Austrian), Stephen's close friend Charlie and his wife, and Stephen's own

family. Anna has affairs with both William and Charlie, and Stephen finds himself accidentally involved in the emotional entanglements and their human and moral repercussions, culminating in his suppression of the fact that Anna caused the car accident in which William is killed.

Highly distinctive of *Accident* is the spare, compressed, and selective way in which this story of love, marriage, and the "split between our public face and our private helplessness" is told. There is an intense nervous edginess in the writing, with its verbal fragments and staccato rhythms. Phrases and even single words stand as sentences, and the unexpected associations and juxtapositions produce a near-surrealist quality at times. Indeed, there is a considerable tension between Stephen's attempt at rational control and the ambiguities, contradictions, and discontinuities of what he is dealing with; he says himself, "We are all in fragments, disjointed." The difficulty of connecting different experiences is embodied in the prose, with its relative lack of connectives, the avoidance of verbal fluency being a way of undermining the principle of causality. This theme of fragmentation helps to explain Mosley's unorthodox and indeed radically questioning approach to characterization. Asked by William why modern novels "can't just be stories of characters and action and society," Charlie, a writer, replies that "We know too much about characters and actions and society. . . . we can now write about people knowing"; subsequently he adds that "People don't behave in the way we think they do." Stephen observes that "people are not characters but things moving occasionally in jumps and mostly in indiscernible slowness." These quotations illustrate the reflexive nature of Mosley's narrative, challenging its own pretensions to authenticity throughout but not in the ostentatiously obtrusive manner of some postmodernist fiction. Mosley also subverts the tragic potential of the story, offsetting William's death by the birth of a baby to Stephen's wife. The end of the novel stresses continuity rather than finality even though a life and several relationships are ended.

Accident is an unsettling novel in that it challenges many everyday assumptions about reality, people, and the motivation of behavior. In his next novel, *Assassins* (1966), Mosley reverts to third-person narration while employing methods similar to those he developed in *Accident* but with less profound consequences, even though the social and political canvas is much wider. At one level, *Assassins* is a political thriller, but it is unlike any other. The story concerns a crucial meeting between a British foreign minister, Sir Simon Mann, and a political leader from eastern Europe, Korin, who has plenty of blood on his hands and is the target of a would-be assassin. At the beginning of the book, Sir Simon's teenage daughter Mary first breaches the elaborate security arrangements and then accidentally disturbs a young man, Peter Ferec, intent on killing Korin. Peter abducts Mary, and her disappearance has considerable repercussions, as an interesting tension develops between private and public worlds, inner realities and political facades. Mary seems to have more in common with Peter than with all the people determined to rescue her, including her unsympathetic father, and Mosley is at his best in exploring the tentative relationship between kidnapper and kidnapped. In an ingenious twist, Peter not only releases Mary but also pretends to have discovered her by chance, thus claiming credit for her safe return to Sir Simon, a ploy in which she acquiesces. This move creates a situation in which Peter can again attempt to assassinate Korin, though he fails and is himself killed. Mosley's radical transformation of the political thriller, with its elliptical cross-cutting leaving much unexplained, becomes a means of subjecting the world of public affairs and politics, especially the selves of people involved in it, to unorthodox and radical scrutiny.

As narrative, *Impossible Object* (1968) is much less straightforward than *Assassins* and is the most difficult, though perhaps not the most ambitious, of Mosley's novels at this stage of his career (mid-1960s to early 1970s). To judge from the contents page, *Impossible Object* seems to be a collection of eight short stories about complex human relationships, especially love and marriage, and at first glance they might appear to be self-contained. However, at the beginning, at the end, and in between the "stories" are short independent sections printed in italic type. Mosley's interludes are puzzling surrealistic pieces of writing very different from the "stories" themselves, but they introduce certain themes and motifs that also turn up in the main narratives. Indeed, patterns of repetition and recurrence soon become clear in the book as a whole, so that the reader is nudged into finding connections between the eight stories and into discovering the continuities of characters from one story to the next, even though Mosley is most careful to prevent these being obvious. In other words, the reader is forced to work hard to decipher Mosley's code and to assemble the various fragments for himself. Most of the "stories" are told in the first person, but the narrator is not the same person throughout. That Mosley is exploring the possibilities of multiple viewpoints in presenting the central relationship of the novel clarifies the significance of the title, an "impossible object" being one of those trick drawings in two dimensions of a supposedly three-dimensional object that cannot possibly exist in three dimensions. Only from one fixed viewpoint can the three-dimensional version be made to appear as in the drawing; from any other angle it will be seen to be quite different. *Impossible Object* is a reflexive novel in that it is about the representation of reality and about the impossibility of fixing such a relativistic concept as reality: "The object is that life is impossible; one cuts out fabrication and creates reality." If *Impossible Object* looks back to the innovative narrative techniques, especially shifting viewpoint, of writers such as Conrad and Faulkner, it is nevertheless a most individual and unmistakable Mosley novel.

Natalie Natalia (1971) marks the culmination of this phase of Mosley's fiction and, for some critics, is his finest achievement. As usual, the story

Dust jacket for Mosley's 1971 novel about a member of Parliament who sees his mistress as the embodiment of Goethe's daemonic principle

itself is much less important than what he does with it, and his distinctive way of relating this narrative of love, adultery, shame, and breakdown serves to defamiliarize the experiences he writes about and to illuminate them in unexpectedly fresh ways. Mosley's originality in using language, stretching its expressive possibilities to encompass the apparently inexpressible, opens the doors of perception. Unlike many prose writers, Mosley is prepared to take considerable risks with language—risks more usual in poetry than in fiction—to convey the truth as he sees it. The long epigraph to the novel, from Goethe's *Dichtung und Wahrheit*, is about his concept of the daemonic principle, which Mosley's narrator, politician and member of Parliament Anthony Greville, sees embodied in his mistress, Natalia, who is married to a philandering politician. Because she is a living contradiction to Greville, he uses the two names of the title for her, Natalie indicating her "ravenous" nature and Natalia her "angelic" side. *Natalie Natalia* is about their affair and Greville's consequent guilt at deceiving his wife; it is also about the life of a politician who is disillusioned with his professional career yet deeply concerned about the fate of a black African leader, Ndoula, who has been interned without trial in Central Africa. The disorder of Greville's private life mirrors the disorder of his public life. Mosley characteristically stresses the inconsistency of people and the enigmatic nature of human experience, distilling his own brand of comedy from the world he describes. Eventually, in a state of mental collapse while on a political visit to Africa, Greville rides a bicycle into an empty swimming pool, after which he undergoes a process of psychological as well as physical recovery. *Natalie Natalia* attempts more than *Impossible Object* without being so experimental technically, and although some reviewers felt the novel to be uneven and not without passages verging on the pretentious, it received a great deal of justly merited acclaim when it appeared—probably more praise than any other of his novels.

Immediately after completing *Natalie Natalia*, Mosley was involved in a near-fatal road accident that left him in hospital for almost a year. A few years later, in 1974, his first marriage was dissolved, and he married Verity Raymond on 17 July. Between 1971 and 1979 he produced no fiction, which suggests that with *Natalie Natalia* he had come to the end of a particular line of development. During these years he wrote two screenplays and two biographical books. Mosley first worked on the screenplay for a French, Italian, and British coproduction, *The Assassination of Trotsky* (1972), directed by Joseph Losey, who had in 1967 made a film of *Accident* using a screenplay by Harold Pinter. As a by-product of this assignment, Mosley wrote a study of Trotsky, which was published in 1972 with the same title as the film. He then wrote a screenplay based on *Impossible Object*, which was filmed in France by the American director John Frankenheimer and released there in 1973. His most important work of this period is his fine biography of the aristocratic poet Julian Grenfell, who was killed in the early stages of World War I. As the subtitle of this book suggests, *Julian Grenfell: His Life and The Times of His Death 1888-1915* (1976), Mosley is interested in Grenfell's social and cultural context and explores the upper-class ethos of prewar Britain, which Grenfell himself disliked intensely, in an attempt to understand the nation's euphoric response to the outbreak of hostilitites in 1914.

In 1979 Mosley produced his first work of fiction for eight years, *Catastrophe Practice*, his most difficult novel to date, which had most British reviewers at a loss for words. With this book, Mosley launched himself on a most ambitious project, intending to follow this book with six interlinked yet self-contained novels, each dealing with one of the six main characters of *Catastrophe Practice*. Two of these novels, *Imago Bird* (1980) and *Serpent* (1981), have been published so far. Unlike its predecessor, *Imago Bird* received a favorable critical reception when it was published. It is obviously premature to comment on this series of novels since future volumes may modify the view of the books already published, but one thing is clear: Mosley has returned to fiction with an extraordinary new burst of creative energy, as he did once before in 1962 with *Meeting Place*. *Catastrophe Practice*, a compilation of three "plays not for acting" (each with a preface and the last followed by a concluding essay) and a novella-length piece of fiction he describes as "a novel," is the most abstract and theoretical of his books. The six principal figures or "actors" reappear in different guises in the various sections of the book, and there is an elaborate arrangement of correspondences and cross-references throughout, producing unity from apparent fragmentation and dislocation. Using the analogy of catastrophe theory, a recent mathematical attempt to explain discontinuities in the natural world not accounted for by orthodox mathematics, Mosley constructs a paradigm of catastrophe *practice* to investigate the various discontinuities of human experience. It should be noted that Mosley's intense interest in this theme precedes the development of the catastrophe theory itself; he is making use of the theory rather than being influenced by it. Drawing on several philosophers, including Sartre, Husserl, and Popper, as well as the theory and practice of Brecht, Mosley tries to establish a tenable philosophical position for optimism and hope, while also struggling toward literary forms suitable for articulating such a world view. *Catastrophe Practice* is really about the need to liberate consciousness, language, and art from the confines of convention, and in his assault on various forms of convention (such as literary models of tragedy and comedy) Mosley emerges as a modern romantic, though a highly intellectual one. For Mosley, much modern literature, with its predilection for disillusionment and despair, possesses a strongly negative bias, inculcating defeatism and pessimism by falsifying reality. Although *Catastrophe Practice* is very different from his earlier fiction in form, it does not mark a complete change of direction; rather, it represents a new approach to the issues that preoccupied him in his fiction of the 1960s.

This new approach to old concerns becomes more obvious in *Imago Bird*, a comparatively straightforward novel narrated by an eighteen-year-old boy, Bert, who while waiting to go up to Cambridge is staying with his uncle, the prime minister. From the first words of the novel—"Ever since I can remember I have thought the grown-up world to be mad"—Bert attempts to make sense of the perplexing, fantastic, and theatrical world of adult reality, and of the relation between exterior and interior reality. But the process is still more involved and self-conscious because he is also trying to understand himself understanding the world and its random discontinuities. This theme is not new in Mosley: in *Accident*, for example, Charlie argues that the modern novel should not be about people but about people *knowing*. Bert encounters a wide range of people from pop musicians to Young Trotskyites, from establishment politicians to media celebrities, and through his innocent yet penetrating X-ray eyes we see most of these people trapped, without realizing it, in linguistic and behavioral cages of their own devising. In different ways, they are all acting out stock parts in a melodramatic fiction called life, parts they have allocated to themselves. Bert's narrative voice is hesitant, uncertain, exploratory; what might be thought routine and ordinary is for him something to be probed and analyzed, often with startling consequences. Like *Catastrophe Practice*, though in a far more accessible way, *Imago Bird* is about the imprisoning restrictions which conventions impose and about the need to

escape from the world of illusion which they can establish if the human potential for creativity and happiness is to be realized. *Imago Bird* is a decidedly positive novel, though without being facile.

Serpent is a complex narrative involving a screenplay about the Jewish revolt against the Romans at Masada, the fortress where many Jews killed themselves in A. D. 73 rather than surrender; events on an airplane taking the screenwriter Jason, his wife, and influential film people to Israel; and a crisis in Israel itself. The film script and the contemporary action interweave so that some of the film's themes (especially the conflict between devotion and reason, and the individual's relations with and responsibilities to society) are echoed in the present. Mosley is already working on the third of the six planned "sequels" to *Catastrophe Practice* and remains wholeheartedly committed to this large-scale endeavor.

Nicholas Mosley is one of the most original British novelists of the postwar period. His stylistic innovations and his use of modernist narrative techniques have not endeared him to members of the reading public looking for an "easy read," but he has acquired a highly respectful and sometimes enthusiastic following from readers genuinely interested in contemporary fiction. The cumulative effect of Mosley's fiction is probably more important than in the case of many writers, possibly because he has attempted during the last twenty years to challenge a contemporary literary orthodoxy that has sunk much of its capital in what has been called "womb, gloom, and doom." Indeed, his stylistic experiments represent a way of writing an alternative fiction—a fiction rooted in his belief in human possibility, freedom, happiness, and optimism—rather than a fundamentally pessimist fiction. His own artistic progress has been from such an orthodoxy, embodied in his novels of the 1950s, to the work of his maturity.

Screenplays:

The Assassination of Trotsky, by Mosley and Masolino d'Amico, Cinettel / Dino de Laurentiis Cinematografica / CIAC / Josef Shastel Productions, 1972;

Impossible Object, Franco-London Films, 1973.

Other:

Raymond Raynes, *The Faith: Instructions on the Christian Faith* edited by Mosley (Leighton Buzzard: Faith Press in conjunction with The Community of the Resurrection, 1961).

Helen Muir
(4 March 1937-   )

Amanda M. Weir

BOOKS: *Don't Call it Love* (London: Duckworth, 1975);

Noughts and Crosses (London: Duckworth, 1976);

The Belles Lettres of Alexandra Bonaparte (London: Hutchinson, 1980);

Many Men and Talking Wives (London: Hutchinson, 1981).

Helen Muir is becoming known as one of England's finest contemporary writers. Her style is somewhat reminiscent of both Evelyn Waugh's and Beryl Bainbridge's (both of whom she greatly admires), but she has a certain directness of dialogue which sets her apart. A voracious reader of any sort of religious philosophy, she lists religion as her "absolute interest" and is concerned about the present moral state of society. However, she transmits these concerns to the reader without making her message too blatant, and her novels are amusing, zany fun with undertones of the tragic. Commenting on the state of fiction in the summer 1978 issue of the *New Review*, she said, "Good writing and good ideas are not enough. Individuality, eccentricity, certainties, are surely what novels are about. . . ." Muir's novels have these characteristics.

Born to Mr. and Mrs. J. G. Muir of West Kirby, Wirral, Cheshire, Jean Helen Muir is the elder of two children. According to Muir, she and her younger brother, John, had a "perfect" childhood, and the family "couldn't be more devoted" to each other. Until the age of twelve, she attended the local grammar school, where she did quite well. Then she was sent to Adcote, a boarding school in Shrewsbury, which was two hours' distance from her home. She was devastated by the separation from her family and remembers her experience there as a disaster. Muir calls her family one of the greatest influences in her life. Because they were so happy, however, she did not want to break away from them and set up her life elsewhere.

Muir's roots are deeply set in Scotland—both her parents come from the Lowlands—and in a family involved in the arts. As a young woman, her mother received the highest marks on the London drama exams, but could not follow her theatrical vocation because of the poor health of her own mother. Muir believes that her writing talents ultimately came from her grandfather, short-story writer John Muir. Her brother, John, has recently written a play, *The Loudest Tears in Town*, which did well in Germany and has a good chance of being produced in London's West End.

At the age of seventeen, Helen left school for good and started as the most junior reporter at *Birkenhead News*, a small newspaper eight miles from her home. She remembers this time in her life with much fondness. For a salary of three pounds a week her job was to go around to social affairs, such as flower shows, church fêtes, and dances, and write short articles about them: "Night after night, I would go to dances where I'd take the names of the committee, and describe the wives' dresses. You had to have thirty dress descriptions, come what may, and I used to get them all wrong."

After working at this newspaper for twenty

Helen Muir

months, she decided to move to London and in 1956 took a job with the *Hampstead & Highgate Express* writing much the same kind of articles as she had written for the Birkenhead paper. She claims she was hopeless at the job. After a year she inherited some money, quit this job, and concentrated exclusively on her writing. By this time she had had her first short story published in *Punch*, but except for the publication of a few light, romantic short stories in *Punch* and *Woman's Own* her career remained relatively stagnant until the early 1970s, when she spent two years writing her first novel, becoming almost a recluse, only leaving the house to walk her dog.

Around 1973 Muir began writing for the London *Sunday Times* as a sports correspondent. She enjoyed the job tremendously, especially the writing of short profiles on such sports personalities as boxer Dave Green, tennis pro Sue Barker, and Britain's top woman archer, Rachel Fenwick. She had finished her first novel, *Don't Call it Love*, but she did not know any publishers in London. One of her friends suggested that she write Colin Haycraft at Duckworth, who without any recommendations accepted the novel.

Don't Call it Love, published in 1975, revolves around the misadventures of a mixed-up love triangle that includes Earl Orty, a cocky Australian actor constantly on his guard against aggressive women and homosexuals, who he feels are out to get him should he let down his defenses. Joanna, the second of the three, lives in the same house as Earl and sets her mind on seducing the vain Aussie. When Joanna's alcoholic husband, Cedric, comes back from Scotland to reclaim his alienated wife, she does not respond to his advances, and the triangle, according to the *Daily Mail* reviewer, becomes "venomous and fraught with comical disasters." The strength of the novel lies in the intensely funny predicaments caused by the egocentric attitudes of the three main characters.

According to its publisher, *Don't Call it Love* sold well for a first novel. The critical acclaim was also considerable. A reviewer for the *Sunday Times* said that Muir "manages to be very funny indeed—not many novelists made me laugh out loud on a steamy morning on a number 19 bus." On the BBC's *The Book Programme* Robert Robinson called the novel "a very deft bit of work, at times deft enough to remind you of Evelyn Waugh," and, he added, "Helen Muir makes people think like I think people think, and that makes me laugh."

Muir herself feels that *Don't Call it Love* has

some originality, although it ended up different from her initial conception of the novel: "It's not at all the huge thing you imagined, and you are disappointed with the final result." She does, however, describe it as a funny book.

After the success of *Don't Call it Love*, Duckworth asked Muir to write another book to be published the following year. *Noughts and Crosses* (1976), very different in tone from her first novel, is also much more tragic. It examines the relationship between Frances, a doctor's daughter from Cheltenham, and Chris, a half-black ex-convict from the East End. They meet at a party and are attracted to each other by the very things which make them so different. Frances's former lover, David, tries to alert her to the potential problems of such an unconventional match, but she takes no heed. As David foresees, the relationship deteriorates to the point where Frances stays with Chris only out of guilt. The novel ends in violence (including Chris's death), for which the reader is prepared, but life still continues for Frances. She survives relatively unharmed, with only her heavy conscience to remind her of what has happened.

Once again, the critical response was good. In the *Times Literary Supplement* Victoria Llewellyn-Smith commended Muir's ability to present "the mixture of the trite and the unique in everyday experiences," praising her "eye for small detail." Nick Totton of the *Spectator* wrote that perhaps the novel's "strongest quality is a kind of open-eyed directness: no tricks are played on the reader's mind or emotions, and there are no camouflaged dramatic ironies" and added that Muir "has a sophisticated understanding of what is essential."

Muir says that *Noughts and Crosses* is the most autobiographical of all her novels because the relationship between Chris and Frances is similar to one in which she was involved. Unlike Frances, however, she realized that marriage between two very different people would end in disaster. Muir adds that Chris is by no means exactly like the man with whom she was involved. Like other writers, Muir may create a character by starting with someone she knows, but then "it departs, and the image would be slightly different"; she believes that as she goes along the characters take over for themselves. While she thought the novel important for its autobiographical element, Muir was not entirely satisfied with *Noughts and Crosses*. She calls it a "slick" book and says she tried to write it too quickly. Her usual method is to work less rapidly. On a good day, she will produce only two pages of manuscript: "I go

Dust jacket for Muir's 1981 novel, a portrait of a woman experiencing a mid-life crisis

very slowly . . . each thing that I do . . . I have to imagine that they are immaculate and never to be touched again before I can go on. Thinking they're never to be touched again, I probably touch them again about 80 times."

An artistic difference with Duckworth led to a change in publishers around 1977. During the writing of her next novel, *The Belles Lettres of Alexandra Bonaparte* (1980), she again stayed close to home. Her time was spent dog-walking, chatting on the phone with friends, enjoying her relationship with a man whom she has been seeing since 1974, and writing.

The Belles Lettres of Alexandra Bonaparte is written as the memoir of the title character, who, through her charm, wit, and a few white lies, gains the position of secretary to Dr. Wyfield Posset and then fantasizes that his colleague, the handsome Dr. Charles Horenstein, has fallen in love with her. Throughout the novel, she gets herself into ridic-

ulous situations as she is deported from Venice, takes part in international backgammon tournaments, and plots to capture the heart of Charles Horenstein.

Martin Seymour-Smith of the *Financial Times* wrote, "There is a thin (and it is more effective for being thin) cry of despair at the heart of the novel, which makes it more than merely enjoyable. Helen Muir is quite as serious as she is deft and skillful." Felicia Lamb, in *Now*, noted that Muir "has learned much from the masters—Wodehouse, Firbank, Evelyn Waugh. Under the surface nasty things are afoot: betrayal, loneliness, permanent disappointment. But the surface is delicious."

Many of Alexandra's adventures are based on events in the life of one of Muir's close friends. While she was writing the novel, Muir read snatches of it to her friend over the phone, and she seemed to enjoy it. Unfortunately, the woman died before the book was published. Muir describes her as someone who had extravagant ideas and was always arranging something, a good person with good intentions who just always happened to get caught in "escalating circumstances."

Muir's most recent novel, *Many Men and Talking Wives*, published in autumn 1981, is in part a comment on factory farming and the export of live animals for slaughter. Muir feels that such mistreatment reflects the general moral state of society: "We can't live in such an immoral state. . . . We can't have animals having a little life in the dark for a few weeks, and a terrifying death. . . . Here [in England] people can't bear to stop and think." The heroine of the novel, Verity Wilson, spends some of her spare time handing out pamphlets condemning these practices.

Verity is a middle-aged artist who becomes disillusioned with herself and her life when her boyfriend of some years, Christopher Shepherd, leaves her. Her feelings of loneliness and inadequacy are overwhelming, and she turns to her closest friend, Rachel Marsden, for solace. On a suggestion from Rachel, Verity is able to land a job working for the Drew Foundation under Dr. Goulding. He is a charmingly schizophrenic character who takes his job as administrator very seriously at one moment, and the next finds it terribly amusing.

Verity is kept busy organizing the activities of the foundation's foreign guests during their studies in London. When the group tours a stately home in the English countryside, one Mrs. Sobaz is accidentally injured, and the event causes some amusing complications for Verity and her employer. To make matters worse, Rachel has romantic designs on one of the married guests, Colonel Kardag.

Muir's latest effort, the portrait of a woman experiencing a mid-life crisis, is sometimes funny, often strikingly painful, and very real. Verity is not able to complete her paintings, and the man she loves has rejected her. This failure, coupled with her fear that she is growing old, causes her to fall into a deep depression over her feelings of inadequacy and uselessness: "There were no people like her in offices. They weren't wanted at her age." Muir's poignant tone slips easily toward the comic, but at the same time remains believable. Dr. Goulding's frantic activities are a stark contrast to the loneliness of Verity's personal life.

Although Muir's previous novels have tended to be closely knit and consistent, the theme of factory farming in *Many Men and Talking Wives* seems to fall short of these parameters. Perhaps the need to express her personal feelings on the subject caused Muir to make them too obvious. While the sentiments appear consistent with Verity's character, they tend to interrupt the smooth flow of the novel.

Although Muir wrote many romantic short stories when she was younger for *Punch*, *Harper's*, *Queen*, *Over 21*, and *Woman's Own*, at present she "can't think of anything to say" for such magazines. One of her goals is to have a piece published in the *New Yorker*. She would also like to collaborate with her brother, John Muir, in writing a play, but plans for this project are still tentative. Among the writers that she most admires are contemporary writers William Trevor, Beryl Bainbridge, Muriel Spark, Saul Bellow, and Flann O'Brien, as well as Evelyn Waugh, Elizabeth Taylor, and Jane Austen.

Iris Murdoch

(15 July 1919-   )

John Fletcher
University of East Anglia

SELECTED BOOKS: *Sartre, Romantic Rationalist* (Cambridge: Bowes & Bowes, 1953; New Haven: Yale University Press, 1953);

Under the Net (London: Chatto & Windus, 1954; New York: Viking, 1954);

The Flight from the Enchanter (London: Chatto & Windus, 1956; New York: Viking, 1956);

The Sandcastle (London: Chatto & Windus, 1957; New York: Viking, 1957);

The Bell (London: Chatto & Windus, 1958; New York: Viking, 1958);

A Severed Head (London: Chatto & Windus, 1961; New York: Viking, 1961);

An Unofficial Rose (London: Chatto & Windus, 1962; New York: Viking, 1962);

The Unicorn (London: Chatto & Windus, 1963; New York: Viking, 1963);

The Italian Girl (London: Chatto & Windus, 1964; New York: Viking, 1964);

A Severed Head [play], by Murdoch and J. B. Priestley (London: Chatto & Windus, 1964);

The Red and the Green (London: Chatto & Windus, 1965; New York: Viking, 1965);

The Time of the Angels (London: Chatto & Windus, 1966; New York: Viking, 1966);

The Italian Girl [play], by Murdoch and James Saun-

Iris Murdoch

546

ders (London & New York: French, 1968);

The Nice and the Good (London: Chatto & Windus, 1968; New York: Viking, 1968);

Bruno's Dream (London: Chatto & Windus, 1969; New York: Viking, 1969);

A Fairly Honourable Defeat (London: Chatto & Windus, 1970; New York: Viking, 1970);

The Sovereignty of Good (London: Routledge & Kegan Paul, 1970; New York: Schocken, 1971);

An Accidental Man (London: Chatto & Windus, 1971; New York: Viking, 1971);

The Black Prince (London: Chatto & Windus, 1973; New York: Viking, 1973);

The Three Arrows and The Servants and the Snow: Plays (London: Chatto & Windus, 1973; New York: Viking, 1974);

The Sacred and Profane Love Machine (London: Chatto & Windus, 1974; New York: Viking, 1974);

A Word Child (London: Chatto & Windus, 1975; New York: Viking, 1975);

Henry and Cato (London: Chatto & Windus, 1976; New York: Viking, 1977);

The Fire and the Sun: Why Plato Banished the Artists (Oxford: Clarendon, 1977);

The Sea, The Sea (London: Chatto & Windus, 1978; New York: Viking, 1978);

A Year of Birds: Poems (Tisbury, Wiltshire: Compton, 1978);

Nuns and Soldiers (London: Chatto & Windus, 1980; New York: Viking, 1981).

One of the dominant figures of postwar British literature, Iris Murdoch continues to divide the critics; for example, one of the professors of English at Cambridge University, Frank Kermode, thinks highly of her work, while another, Christopher Ricks, has reviewed it extremely unfavorably. But she herself has forestalled some of the critics, at least on the crucial issue of the quantity against the quality of her output. Reviewing Sartre's *Being and Nothingness* in 1957, she concluded with these rather prophetic words: "writers of brief and meticulous articles will always look askance at writers of large, unrigorous, emotional volumes; but the latter, for better or worse, have the last word." She had herself by then published two novels (*Under the Net*, 1954, and *The Flight from the Enchanter*, 1956), a monograph, and a handful of philosophical articles. Some twenty-five years and almost as many books later, she too has become, in the eyes of several critics, a writer of large, unrigorous, emotional volumes. Such fecundity, after all, has not often been

seen since the days of Dickens, Thackeray, or Wilkie Collins.

It is easy, then, to wonder if she is not a kind of modern Collins, an entertaining and accomplished novelist but a fearfully uneven one. How is it possible, her detractors ask, to publish a long novel almost every year and not succumb to facile effects and slick repetition? It is certainly not difficult to criticize some of her books and show how they fall below her usual standards. Reviewers on the whole—with a few distinguished exceptions—greet each new novel as enthralling, undoubtedly, and funny, yes, but excessively complicated and ultimately unconvincing. And academic critics have tended to stop short of any serious confrontation with her work.

Perhaps what makes academics uneasy is a feeling that, despite all the notorious symbolism and the heady moral theorizing, Iris Murdoch is basically a lightweight, even frivolous, novelist, a sort of intellectuals' Georgette Heyer. After all, they say, how can anyone be serious who takes such obvious delight in playing elaborate tricks on her readers? Some critics feel that these antics do not square with an obvious fascination with character and plot (in that order) and an abiding preoccupation with love, reconciliation, and redemption. Yet those critics forget that Henry James too had his mystery plots; that Jane Austen enjoyed teasing her readers; or that Dickens often employed improbable characters and plots while being deeply concerned, himself, with love, reconciliation, and redemption. Are the games Thackeray plays with the reader over Becky Sharp all that different from those Iris Murdoch plays with her enchanters, ingenues, or old lechers? In other words, she draws eclectically on the English tradition and at the same time extends it in important ways.

She is at her best, perhaps, where a perfect "machine"—the sort Collins was so good at constructing—coincides with a satisfying moral concern, in the manner of the greatest English novelists from George Eliot to E. M. Forster; and she is accordingly at her weakest in books like *The Time of the Angels* (1966), where the "machine" is so intricately built that it gets out of hand, or *The Sandcastle* (1957), where the moral thrust becomes too obtrusive. Nevertheless, she is an exceptionally clever writer—perhaps the most intelligent novelist the English have produced since George Eliot—and she is liable, if he is not constantly on the alert, to catch the reader coming and going. In *The Sacred and Profane Love Machine* (1974)—the very title should put one on his guard—the tragic plot resolves (or perhaps rather dissolves) into farce. The author's way of getting rid of Harriet at Hanover Airport can be seen as sleight of hand, the deus ex machina of an incompetent novelist unable otherwise to extricate her characters from an impossible position—that is, if one takes the plot as a serious exploration of a middle-class adultery situation rather than as what it is: a machine, reality metamorphosed into fiction, whose laws are different—very different—from those of life.

A more sophisticated objection to Murdoch's work is that it is not experimental enough and so is out of date in the age of Robbe-Grillet and the *nouveau roman*. She is therefore most often mentioned in the same breath as Angus Wilson or Kingsley Amis, novelists who make no bones about using traditional methods. But she has in fact much more in common with Vladimir Nabokov, with whom no one thinks of comparing her. Her books, like his, are craft-built fictional engines; only superficially are they social satire or realistic documentation. Her choice of the writers who have influenced her most bears out this assessment. For whereas Angus Wilson makes it clear that his greatest debts are to Dickens and Zola, Murdoch cites as her mentors Elias Canetti, Samuel Beckett, and Raymond Queneau—hardly writers one would place in the realist tradition. She *may* write novels that at first read like cruel and witty studies of contemporary upper-middle-class London or Oxford society, but on closer inspection they usually turn out to be something different: not allegories exactly, but decidedly symbolic and universal.

Iris Murdoch was born in Dublin, Ireland, on 15 July 1919 but left Ireland while she was still a child. However, she is of Anglo-Irish parentage on both sides; her father, Wills John Hughes Murdoch, was an Irish cavalry officer in World War I and later a British civil servant. Her mother was Irene Alice Richardson Murdoch. Further back, her ancestors were mainly Irish farmers and soldiers. Because she was an only child, she had what she has called imaginary siblings, who, no doubt, inspired her to tell herself stories. She spent her holidays in Ireland as a child but says she finds it hard to write about Ireland, whose current troubles she finds "too terrible," and indeed her only attempt at treating the subject, not an entirely successful one, is her historical novel of the 1916 Dublin Easter Rebellion, *The Red and the Green* (1965). Otherwise she grew up in the London suburbs of Hammersmith and Chiswick; she attended the Froebel Educational Institute in London and went from there, at age thirteen, to Badminton School, a girls' public school of liberal tradition in Bristol. She started writing for the school magazine almost immediately, and her earliest known published piece appeared in that journal in 1933. There were only two scholars in the school—that is, students holding bursaries, or scholarships—but Murdoch was one of them. A former teacher at the school, Leila Eveleigh, recalls: "She was very homesick [at first] or else just bewildered and Miss Baker's [the school principal's] therapy for that was, in her case, work in the garden under the care of the lady head gardener. I used to meet her pricking out seedlings in the greenhouse quietly and painstakingly." She was, Miss Eveleigh also recalls, good scholastically, particularly so in classics and English, a fine hockey player, interested and gifted in painting (she contributed some woodcuts to the magazine), and though not particularly musical prepared to "have a go." She appears to have been particularly close to Miss Baker, with whom she kept in touch for many years afterward, inscribing copies of her books to the woman she always addressed affectionately as "BMB" and presenting her with a "colourful strong poster-like" painting of Lynmouth harbor, where the school was transferred during the war.

Murdoch went up to Somerville College, Oxford, in October 1938 on an exhibition (that is, a junior bursary), the Harriet Needham Exhibition. The school of which she had been Head Girl still heard from her, and indeed her writing continued to appear in its magazine for some time. The following entry, although written in the third person, was contributed by Murdoch herself: "Iris Murdoch is at Somerville. She is taking Classics and loves her work passionately, and generally takes a zestful interest in the life of the University. She too suffers from a shortage of time and finds a day of twenty-four hours quite insufficient for her needs. She takes an active part in the life of the College and represents the First Year on the Junior Common Room Committee. She is a member of the Somerville Debating Society and also of the Dramatic Society, in whose production of 'The Winter's Tale' next term she is to take the part of Polixenes. She is too busy to play any regular games, but this term is learning to ply a very pretty punt pole on the Isis. The Classical Association, the Arts Club, and the B.U.L.N.S. claim other parts of the day, but her main activities are political and literary. She is a very active member of the Labour Club and helps to run the Somerville branch. For four terms she was advertising manager to 'Oxford Forward,' the progressive University weekly, and now continues her connection as a contributor. She has recently joined the staff of the 'Cherwell,' and hopes next term to subedit that paper. Any time which remains is devoted to the Discussion of Life." The last sentence may be recalled later with affectionate irony in *The Flight from the Enchanter* when the heroine, Annette, abruptly determines to leave her finishing school and tells the principal, "I have learnt all that I can here. . . . I shall go out into the School of Life." The principal, perhaps like an older and wiser Murdoch, replies drily, "As for the institution which you call the School of Life, I doubt . . . whether you are yet qualified to benefit from its curriculum."

Whether or not she benefited from the curriculum of the "School of Life," Murdoch did very well at Oxford, where she read classical moderations and "Greats" (ancient history, classics, philosophy) and took a first-class honors degree in 1942. She was also very left-wing, and, in fact, was a member of the Communist party of Great Britain for a time, an action which in the later 1940s denied her a visa to the United States when she was awarded a scholarship there. This political activity has continued to the present day. She was fiercely hostile toward American involvement in Vietnam and is an active writer of letters to the London *Times*. Her attitudes are not, however, dogmatic or even clear-cut; she opposed the Labour government's policy over comprehensive (all-ability) schools, arguing that socialism and selection are quite compatible and deploring the destruction of the old grammar schools, which, she said, enabled bright students from poor homes to make the most of their potential (or, as the proponents of "comprehensivisation" would claim, join the establishment).

On leaving Oxford she worked as a temporary wartime civil servant (assistant principal) in the Treasury for a couple of years; from this period, no doubt, she derived her extensive knowledge of the British civil service; several of her characters work for that elitist and secretive organization. Then in 1944 she joined the United Nations Relief and Rehabilitation Administration—at school she had been an enthusiastic supporter of the former League of Nations—and shortly after the end of the war in Europe was sent first to Belgium and then to Austria, where she worked finally in a camp for displaced persons. (This experience is also recalled in *The Flight from the Enchanter*, where Nina, the refugee dressmaker, has been born to the east of a line arbitrarily drawn by the Allies and so risks deportation and return to a land abandoned to the the Red Army.) During her stay in Belgium, Murdoch met Jean-Paul Sartre, the subject of her first book, *Sartre, Romantic Rationalist* (1953), and in Austria

she met Raymond Queneau, who became a close friend.

Having failed to gain entry to the United States (one can only speculate how different her literary career might have been if, at this very formative stage of her life, she had been exposed to American culture), she spent a year, more or less as a dropout, in London, during which she read much Kant and no doubt developed even further her extensive acquaintance with almost every corner of that capital city, a knowledge which stood her in good stead for the settings of several of her novels; one critic has even spoken of her "London novels" as almost a distinct subgenre. She returned to academic life in 1947, when she held the Sarah Smithson Studentship in philosophy at Newnham College, Cambridge; although until then she had considered archeology as a career, she was now committed to philosophy. On the termination of the scholarship in 1948, she was appointed Tutor in Philosophy and Fellow of St. Anne's College, Oxford, a post she held until she gave up full-time teaching in 1963. She continued, however, as a part-time philosophy teacher at the Royal College of Art in London until 1967. She was elected a member of the Aristotelian Society, a rather exclusive club of academic philosophers, in 1947, but she allowed her association with it to lapse in the early 1960s. By then her career had changed to that of full-time writer, but she continues to practice philosophy on the fringes of academe, having published her latest academic work, *The Fire and the Sun*, as recently as 1977. This book is about Plato, who has come to exercise a deep influence on her; before that she was much preoccupied with Sartre and existentialism, without ever fully espousing what she sees as existentialism's ethics of irresponsibility. At Cambridge she met Wittgenstein, who was a major influence on her development as a writer, even though she did not adopt his logical positivism.

In the years following her graduation from Oxford, she wrote five novels, which she either discarded or failed to find a publisher for. In 1954, however, *Under the Net* appeared and was an immediate success. Since then Murdoch has written nearly twenty other novels, nearly all of them successful with the reading public.

Fiction is not, however, all the creative writing she has done. There are a number of good if largely uncollected poems, many philosophical-literary essays (the best are collected in *The Sovereignty of Good*, 1970), and two original plays, *The Three Arrows* and *The Servants and the Snow*, produced respectively at the Arts Theatre, Cambridge, in October 1972 and at the Greenwich Theatre, London, in September 1970, as well as two adaptations of novels for the stage, *A Severed Head* written in collaboration with J. B. Priestley (1964), and *The Italian Girl*, done with James Saunders (1968). *A Severed Head* also became a motion picture (Columbia, 1971), and *The Servants and the Snow* was adapted as an opera libretto for the composer William Mathias (first performed at the Cardiff New Theatre on 15 September 1980). Of Murdoch's writing for the stage, it is fair to say that she is good at creating atmosphere but—rather like Sartre in his plays—tends to set up debates in dialogue form so that, curiously, her theater is less dramatic than her fiction. She is also not very good at dramatic plots; the resolutions are somewhat contrived and sudden, lacking the forceful internal logic of the novels. Revelations tend to come so fast at the end that they are merely melodramatic, lacking the ironies with which they are associated in the fiction.

Probably the greatest influence on her writing has been that of her husband, John Oliver Bayley, currently Thomas Warton Professor of English Literature at Oxford, whom she married in 1956. (Her first fiance was apparently killed in the war.) Murdoch and John Bayley enjoy an intimate, even symbiotic, intellectual relationship; they are particularly close in their fascination with Shakespeare and with what Bayley has called "the characters of love." The concept of personality—and a proper respect for it—is central to Bayley's humanism, as it is also to Murdoch's. Bayley deeply regrets that the literary personality—that is, characters in the old-fashioned sense—have sunk in esteem. The authors he most fervently admires, Shakespeare and Tolstoy, are those who endow their characters with the greatest freedom to be themselves. This idea is strongly reminiscent of Murdoch's admonition in a well-known essay, "The Sublime and the Beautiful Revisited," published shortly before her husband's book, *The Characters of Love*, that "a novel must be a house for free characters to live in." It is evident that this is one of the most fruitful literary and critical partnerships of our time, and remarkable in any time.

Murdoch's own ideas about literature have unfortunately not been collected, but her most famous essay, "Against Dryness," first published in *Encounter* for January 1961, has been widely reprinted; it argues polemically for a return to rounded characters and stable values in the novel. As in so much of her writing, she reveals an analytical mind in combination with an Irish heart, steely intellect with emotional warmth. An immensely intelligent and learned person, she would obviously have become a professor or the mistress of an Oxbridge college if she had chosen to remain in academic life. But her passionate interest in people and concern for moral issues have impelled her instead to leave the university environment in order to concentrate on the witty, intelligent, and compassionate novels by which she is best known. And since she has not had any children herself, her books, in a sense, as in the last century for George Eliot, are her children.

She is a keen gardener, devoting her afternoons (she writes mostly in the morning) to her garden in the village north of Oxford where she lives; her particular passion is roses, about which she reveals herself ironically knowledgeable in *An Unofficial Rose* (1962). She is reputed to be a jujitsu expert and lists her hobby in *Who's Who* as learning languages, like her hero Hilary Burde in *A Word Child* (1975). She describes herself as an ex-Christian (Badminton School had a strong religious life) with inclinations toward Zen Buddhism, a faith which is featured in both *The Nice and the Good* (1968) and *An Accidental Man* (1971). She has traveled widely around the world, but it is perhaps Japan which has left the deepest mark on her writing, a mark that appears with especial prominence in *A Severed Head* (1961) and *The Three Arrows*. She has served as a member of the Formentor Literature Prize Committee and has delivered lectures in several countries.

One of her most recent lectures has been expanded to monograph length in the book on Plato, *The Fire and the Sun*, about which Peter Conradi comments, "Murdoch permits herself only a pyrrhic victory in her single combat with Plato over the question of the relations between art and truth . . . the depiction of artists in her books is always a suspicious one." This is borne out by the closing sentences of the lecture: "Plato feared the consolations of art . . . [and] we live now amid the collapse of many . . . structures, and as religion and metaphysics in the West withdraw from the embraces of art, we are it might seem being forced to become mystics through the lack of any imagery which could satisfy the mind. Sophistry and magic break down at intervals, but they never go away and there is no end to their collusion with art and to the consolations which, perhaps fortunately for the human race, they can provide; and art, like writing and like Eros, goes on existing for better and for worse."

In spite of its being the first of her published novels, *Under the Net* fully supports that statement

Dust jacket for the American edition of Murdoch's 1974 novel, in which reality is metamorphosed into fiction

and remains for many readers her finest and most characteristic work. It is easy to see why. The tone, not only of this novel but of much else in her large output, is established in the following passage in *Under the Net*: "The movement away from theory and generality is the movement toward truth. All theorizing is flight. We must be ruled by the situation itself and this is unutterably particular. Indeed it is something to which we can never get close enough, however hard we may try as it were to crawl under the net. . . ." *Under the Net*—the image in the title comes from Wittgenstein's *Tractatus*—is an attempted demonstration of that remark in fictional terms; and those terms owe much to Samuel Beckett's *Murphy* (1938) and Raymond Queneau's *Pierrot mon ami* (1943), two novels which hold pride of place on her hero Jake Donaghue's bookshelf. The debt is made even clearer by the dedication of *Under the Net* to Raymond Queneau, and by the following avowal in response to interviewer Harold Hobson's question, "You admire Beckett?": "Enormously. But

why did he stop writing in the best language? I discovered Beckett long ago, at the beginning of the war. I remember being in an Oxford pub and hearing someone recite the passage from *Murphy* which begins: 'Miss Counihan sat on Wylie's knees. . . .' I was immediately enslaved. I got the book and read it. . . . The influence of that book, together with Queneau's *Pierrot*, upon *Under the Net* should be obvious. I imitated these two great models with all my heart." It is worth looking into the matter more closely in order to discover something about the nature of Murdoch's particular kind of comic fiction.

All three novels are comic in a wry way. Pierrot at the end of his complicated tale bursts into laughter; Murphy wills that his mortal remains be flushed down the particularly noisy lavatory of the Abbey Theatre, Dublin, during the performance of a piece, but otherwise "without ceremony or show of grief"; and Jake, unable at the end to explain a law of genetics to Mrs. Tinckham, laughingly calls it "just one of the wonders of the world." As befits comic novels, all three have intricate plots. And, as for their heroes, Murphy, though passive, is relatively central, for all things lead to him, whereas Pierrot is just a spectator in his own story. Jake is something between the two: a baffled onlooker whose actions nonetheless marginally affect the issues. Alone of the three, Jake is a first-person narrator, and a writer, but—lest we fear a roman-fleuve—"I'm not telling you the whole story of my life," he reassures us.

The tone of all three novels is similar: a kind of Chaplinesque sadness is pervasive under the drollery. It is not easy to read unmoved the account of Murphy's actual dissolution (his ashes are scattered about a barroom floor) or Pierrot's unrequited passion for Yvonne or Jake's final break with Madge. What Jake says of himself applies to all three heroes: "my happiness has a sad face."

Finally, in all three books language is a comic protagonist in its own right. Murdoch's verbal self-consciousness is particularly endearing. She plays cleverly with cliches, for example, as in the words italicized here: "I had acquainted Hugo with something which he needed to know, and we had exchanged *not unfriendly* words. We had even had an adventure together in the course of which I had *acquitted myself at least without shame*. In a sense it could be said that the *ice was broken* between us. But it is possible to break the ice without *burying the hatchet*." And this: the hero can see "no living being" in Farringdon Street; "not a cat, not a copper," glosses Murdoch, who is fond, too, of syllepsis: "He held his head well and the bottle by the neck."

All three writers, as one might expect, are given to a particularly appealing form of donnish humor. Beckett expects his reader to grasp this musical metaphor before sweeping on: "The decaying Haydn, invited to give his opinion of cohabitation, replied: 'Parallel thirds.' But the partition of Miss Counihan and Wylie had more concrete grounds." Likewise, Queneau gives just enough clues to enable the cognoscenti to pick up his many classical allusions.

Similarly, Murdoch expects the reader to know his Rimbaud and what is meant by the Cerberi; she even requires her readers to be as fluent in French as she is: "The *flâneurs* were flaning." The language, in all three writers, is often of such wit that it is hard to refrain from bursting into laughter: for example, at Murphy spluttering over his tea in the cafe like "a flushing-box taxed beyond its powers."

It is clear that Murdoch has studied her masters fruitfully: the filiation, as she told Harold Hobson, is indeed obvious. Her "torments of a morbid self-scrutiny" is a very Beckettian phrase, and "some of my friends think that Finn is cracked, but this is not so" is reminscent of her older compatriot's comic pedantry. Jake's "dreamy unlucrative reflexion" which he enjoys "more than anything in the world" is like Pierrot's; Murphy would accept delightedly the epithet "unlucrative," although he would repudiate any suggestion of dreaminess. He would, however, concur with Jake's thought that "the quenching of thirst is so exquisite a pleasure that it is a scandal that no amount of ingenuity can prolong it."

But there is a more serious side to comedy that is never far from the minds of the creators of these characters: "If fantasy and realism are visible and separate aspects in a novel, then the novel is likely to be a failure. In real life the fantastic and the ordinary, the plain and the symbolic, are often indissolubly joined together, and I think the best novels explore and exhibit life without disjoining them." So declared Murdoch to Harold Hobson later in the interview quoted above. *Under the Net* is an illustration of the indissolubility of the fantastic and the ordinary, the plain and the symbolic. Jake seeks to impose his own pattern on life, and life (Murphy's "rather irregular life") resists Jake's pattern: "I would be at pains to put my universe in order and set it ticking, when suddenly it would burst again into a mess of the same poor pieces, and Finn and I would be on the run." He fantastically misconstrues events and characters, mistaking the substance for

the shadow, and thereby loses his best friend and two girls who have a distinct fondness for him. If only he had known, he thinks, he might have behaved differently: "I had had a wrench that dislocated past, present and future." Fiction is perverse, "like life": X loves Y, who is keen on Z, and Z loves W, who is keen on X. In these circumstances— a grotesque parody of Racine's tragedy *Andromaque*—"love requited," as *Murphy* has it, "is a short circuit." The moral is hard to bear: " 'Some situations can't be unravelled,' said Hugo, 'they just have to be dropped. The trouble with you, Jake, is that you want to understand everything sympathetically. It can't be done. One must just blunder on. Truth lies in blundering on.' " The end mocks all "contrived finalities" because Jake has made the mistake of "having conceived things as I pleased and not as they were." Fortunately in comic fiction the world is never quite so serious, and the damage can usually be repaired: "The ground was strewn with legless torsos and halves of men and others cut off at the shoulders, all of whom, however, were lustily engaged in restoring themselves to wholeness by dragging the hidden parts of their anatomy out from under the flat wedges of scenery, which lay now like a big pack of cards." For, after all, we are in a world of make-believe, and not life itself. Queneau adopts a lighthearted attitude to the quirks of fate, which he exaggerates. The ends are then studiously tied up, in spite of the humorous disclaimer that they are not; "he saw," Queneau writes, "the guileless novel he'd taken part in," a novel that "could have had a dramatic plot but didn't." He is mistaken; nevertheless, it is true that when the play is done, "when the bodies have been carried from the stage and the trumpets are silent . . . an empty day dawns which will dawn again and again." So, too, Celia is graciously accorded a thirteenth and final chapter in which to pick up once more the threads of her life after Murphy's demise and take what pleasure she can in "that unction of soft sunless light on her eyes that was all she remembered of Ireland."

"The end is in the beginning and yet you go on," Hamm declares in Samuel Beckett's *Endgame* (1957), meditating ironically on Heraclitus. The essence of the postmodern comic aesthetic (which Murdoch obviously shares) is that it emphasizes this continuity in things. Comedy begins, and ends, in medias res, untidily, like life. And yet not quite like it; for a work of art, whatever its aesthetic, is self-conscious in a way that life is not. "The above passage," intrudes Beckett's narrator after the paragraph which Murdoch heard being read in an Oxford pub, "the above passage is carefully calculated to deprave the cultivated reader." Likewise, Queneau's narrator knowingly winks at the seasoned novel-fancier: "the classic train launched its familiar wail." And Jake feels that nothing is more paralyzing than a sense of historical perspective, especially in literary matters; he had contrived, he says, to stop himself just short of the point at which it would have become clear to him that the present age was not one in which it was possible to write a comic novel.

Thus although all three books appear to preclude seriousness, all three, paradoxically, are serious, for the theme of each novel centers on a clearly defined symbol. In *Murphy* this is Murphy's mind, which pictures itself "as a large hollow sphere, hermetically closed to the universe without," a figure of Murphy's profound, if happy, alienation. The central presence in *Pierrot mon ami* is the mysterious chapel overshadowed by the garish vulgarity of Uni-Park. *Under the Net* is dominated by Jake's friendship with Hugo, obligingly underlined for us by the author as "the central theme of this book." His conversations with Hugo lead to Jake's writing *The Silencer*, the "genuine" work to which he will return after so many years of hack writing; and it is their friendship which lies, disastrously, at the heart of the novel's complex of human relationships. It also points up the "unutterable particularity" of life, the impossibility of wriggling from "under the net," and contributes toward that blend of fantasy and realism that this novel—matching, like the other two, Murdoch's stated ideal—explores without disjoining.

The maturity, elegance, and stylishness of this first published Murdoch novel are impressive—as are its easy familiarity with other contemporary comic masterpieces and the authority and seriousness of its moral concern. All these qualities recur in the later novels in varying degrees. Indeed, one may divide these works into two broad categories: the more numerous category is that of the ironic tragedy; the other is that of the bittersweet comedy, of which *Under the Net* is the first and perhaps the best. And although Murdoch does not write to formula, her novels do have certain abiding themes and techniques. She is preoccupied with love, with art, with the possibility and difficulty of doing good and avoiding evil. Her techniques are heavily reliant on surprise, suspense, and other dramatic devices. She always writes a highly readable novel, with a strong, gripping narrative and (for the most part) vivid and convincing characters. But at the heart of her stories there is always a moral problem, which,

being the least directive of writers, she sets before the reader for his or her judgment. Her fundamental concerns are with the definition of goodness, the nature and language of art, the relation between contingency and design, and the workings of love and sacrifice in human relationships. She is fascinating and possibly unique, too, in being willing to write in an open and to some extent repetitious way, risking elements of reduplication while sustaining a continuous inquiry into the nature of good and the dialectical contrasts between kinds of love and kinds of good, forms of art and modes of life.

It has often been noticed by critics that there are several "nuns" and many "soldiers" in Murdoch's fiction, either literally or metaphorically. Other figures also recur, like the young and rather foolish virgin, the insecure but morally intransigent boy, the weary and disillusioned middle-aged man, the rapacious and no-longer-quite-so-young female, the old man laden with regrets and unrepented sins, and so on; but it would be misleading to suggest a whole typology, even a worked-out scheme. The point is that Murdoch is concerned above all with moral issues and dilemmas, and since these tend to recur in different guises from one novel to the next, it is not unnatural that the characters who wrestle with them tend to bear a family resemblance to each other.

The Flight from the Enchanter is an early—though distinctly major—novel, visibly inspired by Elias Canetti's *Auto da Fe* (1946), and it has a particularly pregnant title. Each character has some person, idea, illusion, or object by which he is possessed, and each tries to break the spell, to flee the enchanter; for both flight and enchantment are recurrent themes in Murdoch's fiction. In this novel, a pert young girl finds out the hard way that life is a serious business, and a well-meaning older woman burns her fingers through meddling in the lives of others. The girl frivolously attempts suicide, and a tragic misunderstanding leads to the successful suicide of another and worthier character. As in *Così fan tutte* by Mozart, we find here a disturbing combination: under the effervescent comedy lies a serious argument about ends and means, expediency and morality.

Expediency and morality are at the heart of *The Sandcastle* as well. Mor, a middle-aged married schoolmaster, falls in love with a young woman painter, but his formidable wife and precocious children lay their plots with such skill that he fails, when the crunch comes, to run off with her. He and his lover are made very unhappy by this failure, but

Murdoch is not writing a sentimental love story, so it is strongly implied by the narrator that Mor does—if not the right thing—then at least the only thing that makes sense in the light of all the circumstances. But the verdict of the narrative is a harsh one, and it is expressed by the old man whose portrait the painter has been painting: " 'Coward and fool!' said Demoyte. 'Nothing was inevitable here. You have made your own future. . . . Do not deceive yourself. You may meet her once more by accident in ten years' time at a party when you are fat and bald and she is married.' " As part of the trick that his wife has played on him, the schoolmaster will stand for Parliament as a Labour candidate. "If you drop this plan," Demoyte warns him, "if you let her [your wife] cheat you out of that too, I'll never receive you in this house again." But he need not worry: it is clear that Mor will stand by the decision which has been forced upon him. And that, in Murdoch's world, is perhaps more important than the pursuit of personal happiness.

Murdoch's ironic comedies, as the term implies, contain much that is funny and even farcical. In *The Bell* (1958), for instance, the arrival of the bishop to christen the new bell is in the finest tradition of English comedy, a scene worthy of P. G. Wodehouse. And yet *The Bell* is a serious, even tragic, novel, with one attempted and one successful suicide and at least one life ruined during the course of the work. But as is so often the case in Murdoch, if some of the characters go under, others—and often the less obviously or immediately admirable— survive. This is particularly true of the easygoing, even sluttish, heroine of *The Bell*, Dora Greenfield, who would be rather unlikable if her husband, Paul, were not even more unpleasant; it is she, however, with whom the narrator begins and ends the story, and it is she who is selected to survive. And almost by virtue of that fact, she becomes progressively more admirable in the reader's eyes. Murdoch clearly takes much pleasure in questioning moral attitudes in this way. The leader of the lay community at Imber Court, Michael Meade, seems at first to be a worthy man, but gradually his weakness and self-indulgence are exposed by the cool and even merciless progression of the narrative, so that in the end nothing is quite as clear-cut as it appears at first to be. Paul Greenfield is perhaps not such a cruel cad, after all; the aspirant nun Catherine is revealed to be harboring violent erotic feeings for Michael Meade; and the wastrel Nick, her brother, is in a real sense ennobled by his suicide.

The questioning of moral attitudes and, as in *The Sandcastle*, standing by decisions rather than blindly pursuing personal happiness are important considerations in *A Severed Head*. Here Honor Klein, the heroine, says to her lover at the end when, after many hazards and misunderstandings, they come together, "This has nothing to do with happiness, nothing whatever." In the novel, a group of characters rearrange their relationships at least once and in some cases twice during the course of the action. Specifically, the hero, Martin Lynch-Gibbon, realizes that he loves neither his wife, Antonia, nor his mistress, Georgie, but instead loves Honor Klein, who happens to be the half-sister of the lover of Martin's own wife. Palmer Anderson, the brother in question, starts the novel as the lover of both Honor, his half-sister, and Antonia Lynch-Gibbon, and he ends it leaving for New York in the company of Martin's ex-mistress, Georgie Hands. Having run away from Palmer, whose attitude toward her changes dramatically once Martin has discovered him and Honor in bed together, Antonia herself goes back briefly to Martin before declaring that her true passion is Alexander, Martin's brother, who has been her occasional lover for many years. But before he leaves for Rome with her, Alexander has had time to become engaged to Georgie Hands and provoke her to attempt suicide. The only character not linked sexually to any other (although it is implied she has her own affairs elsewhere) is Rosemary, the divorcee sister of Martin and Alexander. And the only two characters who have nothing sexually to do with each other are Alexander and Honor Klein. Otherwise, Antonia loves Martin, Palmer, and Alexander; Georgie loves Martin, Alexander, and Palmer; and Honor is loved by Palmer and Martin: all in that order. Honor's attachments are referred to in the passive voice because she is the rather mysterious dynamo who generates the tensions which cause the others to act; she herself takes no initiatives, except perhaps at the very end when, having seen the others off the stage, she calls on Martin with the evident intention of offering herself to him.

This complex plot, inevitably rather crude sounding in summary, is by no means as frivolous as might appear at first sight. In the final pairings each hitherto morally blind partner (Martin, Antonia, and Georgie) is linked up with a lucid one (respectively Honor, Alexander, and Palmer), undoubtedly for his or her good. It is undeniably better for Martin to grow up into full moral adulthood: he has tended in the past to take refuge in filial relationships with women. The shock of Antonia's adulteries, of Georgie's misadventures culminating in her departure in Palmer's company, and above all of his own demonic passion for the "severed head," Honor, hurls him brutally but salutarily from his cozy Eden. (In mythology, the Medusa's head, cut off by Perseus, turned people who looked at it into stone.) As for Antonia, she has to stop enjoying the possession of three men, who flatter different facets of her personality, and settle for one of them. And Georgie, abandoned by one brother after the other, learns the hard way that a woman makes herself a doormat at her peril. Under the surface comedy of this game of musical beds, therefore, lies a closely argued moral statement: that to play with people is to hurt them, that to abase oneself in love is to invite humiliation, and that only upon mutual respect can a mature and adult love be based. Under the dazzling appearance of comic contingency, too, lies the tougher substance of an almost tragic determinism: one can never really escape from the enchanter but only remain under his or her spell.

The enchanter in *An Unofficial Rose* is a young charmer called Lindsay (who, like many of Murdoch's heroines, has an androgynous name). Randall, a rose-grower, leaves his wife for Lindsay, and his father sells a family heirloom in order to supply Randall with the money he needs to finance his affair in style. The father's motive for this extraordinary action lies in the fact that, many years before, he had failed to leave his own wife for an enchanter who has since become a well-known novelist and (not wholly incidentally) the protector and employer of young Lindsay. So Randall gets his heart's desire because his father once suffered a fatal lack of courage in not grasping his. As for poor worthy Ann, Randall's long-suffering wife, she is courted by a soldier who cannot quite bring himself to seduce her, and who leaves her, tortured by the awareness that "he was paying the penalty . . . for being an officer and a gentleman." The rather surprising moral of this novel seems therefore to be that the deserving will not get their just deserts and that the unworthy will have heaped upon them what they have not merited.

The Unicorn (1963) is undoubtedly one of the best of Murdoch's early novels, certainly one of the most closely studied. Written during the first decade of her career as a novelist, it can usefully stand for them all in terms of symbolism, magic and mystery, and the theme of first love. It is a thriller in the Wilkie Collins lineage crossed with a "romantic" novel of the *Jane Eyre* (1847) variety (with a youngish woman arriving at an ancient castle inhabited by an older man). There are even touches of *Wuthering Heights* (1847) and no end of allusions to

"La Dame à la licorne" (the famous tapestry in Paris), to castles perilous, and to courtly love. But all such allusions are handled ironically, and no single theme offers a key. Once again we find that fiction is not life, but a construct of life's elements; and once again we find the author winking at us through the fine weave of her own tapestry as we see in this passing remark: "It had undeniably the qualities of a wonderful story."

The Italian Girl (1964) is not a wonderful story, as most critics agree. It is one of Murdoch's shortest novels and undoubtedly her weakest. Uncle Edmund returns to the family home after a long absence to attend his mother's funeral, and soon he becomes involved in bizarre goings-on which include the impregnation of both his mature sister-in-law and his young niece by the same male charmer, and the frenzied affair between his brother and the charmer's eccentric sister. After events which are more than usually melodramatic, Edmund discovers that, far from being sexually frigid himself, he is in love with the "Italian girl," the housekeeper who is the latest incarnation of a long line of Italian governesses whom his mother hired. There is no attempt on Murdoch's part to underplay the overt Freudianism of the relationship between an immature adult "son" and his surrogate mother.

Although it was not published next, *The Time of the Angels* shares the weaknesses of *The Italian Girl*, notably an excessively melodramatic plot. The new rector of a riverside parish in London insists on receiving no one, not even his own brother, and we soon discover why: having abandoned his mistress (the black housekeeper, Pattie), he is having an affair with his own daughter. The only sympathetic and even believable inhabitant of this chamber of horrors is the janitor, a Russian refugee called Eugene who lives immured in his memories of pre-revolutionary Russia, and he is left to clear out the rectory when its other inhabitants have moved away on the death by suicide of the incestuous rector who has lost his faith in God.

Opinions are divided about Murdoch's only historical novel, *The Red and the Green*. Although like the other novels of the mid-1960s it betrays an uncertainty of direction, it is more impressive than either *The Italian Girl* or *The Time of the Angels*. This is perhaps because Murdoch is self-confessedly ambivalent about Ireland: on the one hand she feels that she is Irish, at least by descent, and on the other she feels a sort of appalled recoil at the "miserable stupid mixed-up country betrayed by history and never able to recover from the consequences," a situation which offends her rational mind. That a great deal of herself went into this sober yet moving account of the 1916 rebellion cannot be doubted: she clearly needed to write this otherwise rather uncharacteristic book in order to exorcise the exasperatingly muddled romanticism which she inherits from her ancestors and which, her critics would say, mars some of her novels. This necessity is revealed not only by the tone of the novel but also by a detail such as the use of Murdoch's own mother's maiden name, Richardson, as the maiden name of the mother of one of the leading characters. Nevertheless, perhaps because the subject of the Easter Rebellion is an emotional one as far as she is concerned, she does not resist the temptation to have some fairly startling sexual goings-on. The *Times Literary Supplement* reviewer was, however, unfair in calling the book an "implausible bedroom farce"; nearer the mark is critic Donna Gerstenberger's comment that Murdoch was performing at less than her best in this novel by "accept[ing] romanticized absolutes about historical events" and "see[ing] value in such judgments." This tendency may account for an uncharacteristic sentimentality; on the other hand, the historical basis of the material gives the novel a sharp tragic structure and allows it to deal with issues largely unclouded by the symbolism which dogs the other novels of this period of her career.

Murdoch returned to full form with *The Nice and the Good* (1968). This story opens literally on a pistol shot (echoes of Stendhal, except that the civil service rather than politics is involved, and this is hardly a concert). Octavian is burping over his Friday lunch, savoring the afterglow of belched burgundy, and looking forward to his regular weekend at his Dorset country house, when he hears a sound that he recognizes from his army days—the report of a discharged revolver. Joseph Radeechy, one of Octavian's subordinates, has shot himself in a nearby office, as his colleague Richard Biranne at once comes to inform Octavian.

An opening as dramatic as this surpasses even Wilkie Collins for surprise. Less like Collins and more like Balzac is what follows—the filling-in about who Octavian is, what sort of household he heads, who Paula (Richard Biranne's divorced wife) is, and so on. But still within the Collins mode is the art with which very little transpires about Radeechy himself for many pages to come. That is the mystery which, like the secret in Collins's masterpiece, *The Woman in White* (1860), is held back and forms the heart of the novel.

Still, like all Murdoch's works, this is more than just a perverse pleasure to read (though it is that, too). It is a morality: a quasi-Shakespearean comedy (particularly reminscent of *A Midsummer-Night's Dream*) with a happy ending, but much concerned with a crucial nuance in human affairs between the "nice" and the "good." The meaning of this fundamental Murdochian distinction is given obliquely in a number of places: it is the apparent good as opposed to the genuine good, or, in love, the self-gratifying contrasted with the impersonal. Few of Murdoch's characters aspire to the "good" and even fewer attain it: most settle for the "nice," often blissfully unaware of the possibility of another mode of being. Nevertheless, people do need to learn to seek the right path to love, indeed the only path to love: the way of unselfishness. In this novel, Ducane stumbles belatedly upon that path as a result of his brush with death when he plunges into the sea-cave to save Pierce from drowning.

In one of Murdoch's bittersweet comedies, *Bruno's Dream* (1969), a rather feckless character gets the nice girl while the upright (and rather uptight) Miles does not, but there is a certain rough justice about it: "We've all paired off really, in the end," one of the characters realizes; "Miles has got his muse, Lisa has got Danby. And I've got Bruno. Who would have thought it would work out like that?" (The answer to that rhetorical question is, of course, easy: the novelist.) The blurb on the dust jacket of *Nuns and Soldiers* (1980), almost certainly inspired by the author herself, fits not only that novel but all the bittersweet comedies in one way or another: "All the characters are forced into some degree of heroism, and at last muddle and lies are cleared away, and sins are forgiven, though not everybody gains his heart's desire." To that, one need only add that those who do gain their heart's desire are not self-evidently the most worthy.

The very title of the next novel, *A Fairly Honourable Defeat* (1970), contains a harsh irony (and one missed, incidentally, by Penguin's blurb-writer): Rupert's defeat is not honorable at all; it is cruel and messy, like life. Unlike *The Nice and the Good*, this novel has an unhappy ending, and, like so many of the others, it is dominated by an enchanter. This particular manipulator, Julius King, exploits the vanity, mendacity, and cowardice of his fellow creatures in a situation where imperfect beings are related to each other by deep if obscure bonds. Julius does not get his comeuppance as the reader expects (and perhaps hopes), no doubt because he is, in a way, God or at least fate.

At the heart of *An Accidental Man* lies a theme inaugurated by Henry James: that of transatlantic

Dust jacket for Murdoch's 1971 novel about a man who survives through destroying others

love with a college student. Still, like *A la recherche du temps perdu* (1913-1927), it tells the story of its own composition; and, like *Ulysses* (1922), it reflects and meditates upon a masterpiece of classic literature, in this case *Hamlet* (whence the "black prince" of the title, nothing to do, as the reader at first mistakenly thinks, with Edward III's son, the character of English history). But the closest affinities it has are perhaps with Nabokov's *Lolita* (1958). Like Humbert Humbert, the narrator of *The Black Prince* is a conceited and literate deviant who transports his immature loved one away from home and family before being cruelly punished for his pains. *The Black Prince* is a self-styled "celebration of love," but it is also an unremitting exposure of that other face of love: hatred. And following Nabokov, Murdoch tells the story of this unhappy, even doomed, love affair in the context of an elaborate reflection about art. She may well be unaware of—certainly unconcerned about—parallels between her book and *Lolita*; in any case establishing influence is of secondary importance. Putting these two major con-

Dust jacket for Murdoch's 1973 novel, which concludes, "Art tells the only truth that ultimately matters"

misunderstanding. Ludwig Leferrier, expatriate American and potential Vietnam draft dodger, resigns his Oxford fellowship and returns to face the music, ignoring the baffled incomprehension of his English fiancee and her upper-middle-class parents. This is also, except for *The Red and the Green*, Murdoch's most political novel to date. Technically, it is one of her most stunning: the extensive use of letters and of unattributed dialogue to advance the narrative is strikingly new; it bears out her consistent claim that she is by no means satisfied to reproduce the forms of the novel as she has inherited them but has a definite interest in experimenting with different styles and devices, each novel making its own technical innovation (more than perhaps might appear).

Similarly, *The Black Prince* (1973) is, like so many great modern works, a portrait of the artist, although in this case a rather parodic one, since the artist-hero in this book is a retired tax inspector in

temporary works side by side chiefly shows that Murdoch is no less a "modern writer" than Nabokov; she is as much concerned as he is with the nature and status of art. At the end of *Lolita*, Humbert invokes what he calls "the refuge of art" and claims it as the only immortality which he and his Lolita may hope to share. The reader may compare with that statement the last words of *The Black Prince*: "Art tells the only truth that ultimately matters. It is the light by which human things can be mended. And after art there is, let me assure you all, nothing." Even allowing for a hint of self-deprecating irony here, the tone is very similar, and the respect for art as the only available salvation just as great; indeed, Murdoch's confidence is perhaps even greater than Nabokov's: it is after all Humbert Humbert who speaks, in *Lolita*, of "the melancholy and very local palliative of articulate art."

Humbert Humbert's melancholy tone is more at home in *A Word Child*, a sad, ironic tale of a brilliant boy from a deprived background who, by winning various scholarships, makes it to a fellowship at Oxford University, only to lose it all through an affair (with a colleague's wife) that has disastrous consequences. We meet Hilary Burde later in life, when he has "buried" himself in an obscure government office in Whitehall, doing a job well below his ability. His dull but peaceful existence is shattered when his old rival in love is appointed to head the section in which he works. Perhaps rather incredibly, history then proceeds to repeat itself, and Hilary is once again the instrument in provoking an accident which makes his chief a widower for a second time. Hilary is thrust even further into social obscurity, but there is a hint at the end that he will, at the last, be redeemed by the selfless and unreciprocated love of his mistress, Thomasina, who seems to be breaking down his bitter cynicism by persuading him to marry her. This curious, melodramatic story once again reveals that all is not so simple as it appears in Murdoch's world. As we have seen, she herself strongly approves of an educational system based on selection by bursaries and other such means; but her novel is a surprisingly telling indictment of what can happen to a person of great gifts (in this case, as the title implies, a talent for languages) who is raised above his or her normal social environment before attaining sufficient moral and emotional maturity to enable him or her to cope with the enormous pressures involved. Thus the novel has a particularly British obsession with class and social background, and as such it may hold less interest than other Murdoch titles for readers outside England.

In *Henry and Cato* (1976), one of Murdoch's ironic tragedies, Cato the austere priest is cut down to size, and his self-indulgent, easygoing, and even feckless friend Henry inherits wealth and landed property and marries the beautiful fresh young girl he really has no moral right to. Or hasn't he? Cato's high-mindedness cannot prevent the violent death of Joe, the "beautiful" boy from a deprived background whom Cato wishes to "save" less out of Christian charity, it soon becomes clear, than out of a homosexual infatuation which the boy cynically encourages. So perhaps Henry, who is ethically much more modest, is not as undeserving of life's bounties as might at first sight appear. This is perhaps the most Dickensian of Murdoch's novels: the broad humor of the characterization is often similar (Lucius is rather like the sponger Skimpole in *Bleak House*, 1851), the low-life urban setting reminds one of *Little Dorrit* (1857), and the way the characters are introduced and the surprises engineered is characteristic of Dickens's manner. But Murdoch, if she is rewriting Dickens in terms of the 1970s, is doing so very much tongue in cheek. And just as Pip ends up, in *Great Expectations* (1861), older, sadder, and much wiser, so Henry and Cato, two very different prodigal sons, return home at last, chastened, punished, and rewarded in varying degrees.

Perhaps Murdoch's most mature exploration of the theme of personal redemption is *The Sea, The Sea* (1978), which won the coveted Booker Prize for Fiction. A massive novel—over five hundred pages long—it is a major achievement, even by this novelist's high standards. Her steady output has been maturing as well as deepening in quality over the years, but this recent book is one of her best. Certainly its only close rival is *The Black Prince*; and, like *The Black Prince*, it is the story of an obsessive love, an infatuation of tragic proportions.

But whereas fifty-eight-year-old Bradley Pearson, the narrator-hero of the earlier novel, was enslaved by a girl barely out of her teens who could almost have been his granddaughter, Charles Arrowby, the most recent teller of his own sad tale, is a retired theater director who meets again the girl he loved as a boy: Hartley, his own Annabel Lee (as Humbert Humbert would put it). Unfortunately for Charles—but then this is the bittersweet world of Murdoch, where every situation is suffused with irony, and not the cloying universe of Georgette Heyer—Hartley has not been pining for *him* all those years; in fact, she is happily married to a former staff sergeant who evidently (evident, that is, to all but Charles) gives her a very satisfying sex life.

The story of how this monumental and indeed dangerous misunderstanding—the classic quid pro quo of all good comedy—is resolved constitutes the basic plot of the novel. But there are other elements, other themes. For example, we are made very conscious that Charles, not surprisingly for a former actor, is a kind of magician, a comic, even rather parodic, Prospero figure: allusions to *The Tempest* abound, as did echoes of *Hamlet* in *The Black Prince*. Charles is a very destructive magician, though, and he has to recognize, at the end, that he has intervened frivolously, even wantonly, in the destinies of Hartley, of her adopted child, Titus, of his friends Peregrine and Rosina, Gilbert and Lizzie: the list of the people whom his monstrous egoism has damaged or destroyed is seemingly endless.

The theme of the dangerous enchanter is familiar from other Murdoch novels. So is the presence of the sea—not only the cruel unchilding sea lamented by one great poet, Hopkins, but *"la mer, la mer, toujours recommencée"* celebrated by another: Paul Valéry's famous line from *The Graveyard by the Sea* gives this novel its title, and it is significant that the sea, such an important feature elsewhere in Murdoch's world, figures prominently here too. It destroys people (young Titus is tragically, senselessly drowned); but it also cleanses, and that indeed is its principal function. Charles returns from his sojourn by the sea a sadder, lonelier, but wiser and better, man; in a psychological as well as physical sense, his long summer vacation has done him good.

The leading themes, though, as before, are fourfold and related: that of self-deception versus self-understanding; of art versus reality; of reconciliation and love versus enmity and hatred; and of the mysterious, even the magical, versus the familiar and the mundane.

The first theme is obvious enough, in that Charles is patently deceiving himself in believing that Hartley wishes to leave her husband after so many years of marriage. One of the finer ironies of this book is the way Charles sees Hartley as a woman locked up in her nightmares, whereas it soon becomes apparent to the reader how deeply enmeshed Charles is in his own. "It's something childish, it isn't part of the real world," Hartley tells him when he reminds her so insistently of their feelings for each other long ago; and of course she is right. The real world is husband Ben, the little house with

roses round the door and a stuffy overheated atmosphere inside, the collie dog, and the cucumber sandwiches for tea: a world Charles, who never married, cannot begin to understand. A significant detail that shows this up in sharp relief is the visit he pays the house at six p.m. one day. "Six o'clock for me meant drinks," he says. "I had imagined it would be a sensible and humane time to call. In fact I had interrupted their evening meal." His reaction speaks volumes not only for the different worlds in which he and Hartley have grown up and lived out their lives but also for his obtuseness, lack of tact, and deficiencies of understanding. His awakening, when it finally comes, is hurtful to his self-esteem: "I had deluded myself throughout by the idea of reviving a secret love which did not exist at all. . . . How much, I see as I look back, I read into it all, reading my own dream text and not looking at the reality." Reality, indeed, is what the reader, not the narrator, has been aware of almost from the beginning. But by a fine paradox, Charles's movement from self-deception to enlightenment is also a movement, for the former actor, from reality to art:

Iris Murdoch

Charles's story, begun as a kind of memoir or journal, becomes a novel (that is, a work of art) of which he is simultaneously the leading character and the creator. "So I am writing my life, after all, as a novel!" he realizes about one-third of the way through; like so many narrator-heroes in modern literature since Prousts's Marcel and including Nabokov's Humbert Humbert, he is working like an alchemist to transmute his life into art under our very eyes.

But the development is not only an aesthetic one: it has, as always with Murdoch, a moral dimension also. What is here referred to as "the relentless causality of sin" is broken, albeit at great human cost. Charles becomes resigned to Hartley's second and final departure from his life (as he himself says, though without at the time sensing the full force of the parallel, he is a "crazed Orpheus" and she a "dazed Eurydice"). Additionally, he makes his peace at the last with those he has misjudged (like his cousin James, who saves his life when he falls into the sea) and with those he has harmed (such as Peregrine and Rosina, whose marriage he had callously broken up several years before). And the child he had lost before he even knew of its existence (Rosina's, which she aborted to spite him) and the "son" he loses so soon after finding him (Titus, whom he had planned to raise on his own) may finally be replaced with the help of Angie, the impetuous virgin who presses him to let her give him an heir.

There is thus, in spite of everything, something magical about all these events. The pilgrimage of human life, Charles perceives at the end, is "demon-ridden," but the demons are not necessarily always hostile. James appears to live in easy familiarity with them, and it is perhaps with their assistance that he saves Charles from drowning; certainly something very odd happens when Charles gives himself up for dead and is, quite miraculously, saved. There is indeed more to heaven and earth than is dreamt of in his philosophy; and in common with her usual practice (as in *The Bell* or *The Unicorn*), Murdoch leaves that particular mystery unexplained.

As is so often the case in Murdoch's world, Charles begins the painful process of self-understanding only after he has been snatched from the jaws of death. Thus ends what Charles himself calls "another story of death and moral smash-up," although it is only fair to point out that he is thinking more of Henry James's *The Wings of the Dove* (1902) than of his own book-in-the-making. But the description, whatever it makes of James's

masterpiece, does not quite fit *The Sea, The Sea*: a death does occur, but there is a hint of the promise of new life being created with and through Angie; and if there is "moral smash-up," it is the essential prelude to moral regeneration. The same is true of *Nuns and Soldiers*, like *The Sea, The Sea* "very much a love story," in which Gertrude and Tim, against all odds—and particularly the rooted conviction of their friends and relations that Tim is not morally or socially worthy of Gertrude—not only fall in love but marry and stay almost wickedly happy together. Such an outcome may seem "awfully bad form" to the other characters in the story but it is one in which Murdoch evidently takes some delight; she likes to show the morally self-righteous getting their comeuppance. In this, as in other ways, she has much in common with her revered master, James: what could be more unsettling than the discomfiture of Isabel Archer in *The Portrait of a Lady* (1881), of the clever girl who is so morally sure of herself and others? But what could be more exhilarating than Isabel's ennobling realization that she has been grossly manipulated and crudely if effectively misled? In Murdoch, as in James, people are on the whole made better by their sufferings, even someone as initially unprepossessing as Tim in *Nuns and Soldiers*.

Thus it is quite clear that Murdoch writes novels not to advance a cause, expound a philosophy, or portray a society; still less to ensure a future for the English novel, although her intricate plots, particular brand of humor, and sophisticated stance toward her reader may well indicate a way forward that younger novelists can exploit. She writes in order to solve fictional problems. "There is a grace of certainty about being in love," she says in *Bruno's Dream*; "there is a grace of certainty in art but it is very rare." Although her subject matter is usually love (especially its more bizarre manifestations), her true concern is with art, and especially with what she calls "the grace of certainty" that is so rare in art. She is right: it *is* very rare. But, fortunately for us, it is occasionally to be encountered in the works of Iris Murdoch, the only Henry James our age deserves or is likely to produce.

Plays:

A Severed Head, by Murdoch and J. B. Priestley, Bristol, Theatre Royal, 7 May 1963;

The Italian Girl, by Murdoch and James Saunders, Bristol, Bristol Old Vic, 29 November 1967;

The Servants and the Snow, London, Greenwich Theatre, 29 September 1970;

The Three Arrows, Cambridge, Arts Theatre, 17 October 1972;

Art and Eros, London, Olivier Theatre, 2 April 1980.

Other:

"Something Special," in *Winter's Tales 3* (London: Macmillan, 1957; New York: St. Martin's, 1957), pp. 175-204.

Periodical Publications:

"Nostalgia for the Particular," *Proceedings of the Aristotelian Society*, 52 (1952): 243-260;

"Vision and Choice in Morality," *Proceedings of the Aristotelian Society*, supplement, 30 (1956): 32-58;

"The Sublime and the Good," *Chicago Review*, 13 (Autumn 1959): 42-55;

"A House of Theory," *Partisan Review*, 26 (Winter 1959): 17-31;

"The Sublime and the Beautiful Revisited," *Yale Review*, 49 (December 1959): 247-271;

"Against Dryness: A Polemical Sketch," *Encounter*, 16 (January 1961): 16-20;

"Art is the Imitation of Nature," *Cahiers du Centre de Recherches sur les Pays du Nord et du Nord-Ouest*, 1 (1978): 59-65.

Interviews:

Bookman, November 1958, p. 26;

Sunday Times, 17 May 1959;

John O'London's, 4 May 1961, p. 498

Contemporary Literature, 18 (1977): 129-140;

Studies in the Literature Imagination, 11 (1978): 115-125;

Listener (27 April 1978): 533-535.

Bibliography:

John Fletcher, *Iris Murdoch: A Descriptive Primary and Annotated Secondary Bibliography* (New York: Garland, forthcoming 1983).

References:

Frank Baldanza, *Iris Murdoch* (New York: Twayne, 1974);

Malcolm Bradbury, "A House Fit for Free Charac-

ters: Iris Murdoch and *Under the Net*," in his *Possibilities: Essays on the State of the Novel* (London & New York: Oxford University Press, 1973), pp. 231-246;

A. S. Byatt, *Degrees of Freedom: The Novels of Iris Murdoch* (London: Chatto & Windus, 1965; New York: Barnes & Noble, 1965);

Colette Charpentier, *Le Thème de la claustration dans The Unicorn d'Iris Murdoch: Etude lexicale et sémantique* (Paris: Didier, 1976);

Donna Gerstenberger, *Iris Murdoch* (Lewisburg: Bucknell University Presses, 1975; London: Associated University Presses, 1975);

Steven G. Kellman, *The Self-Begetting Novel* (London: Macmillan, 1980), pp. 87-93;

Frank Kermode, *Modern Essays* (London: Fontana, 1971), pp. 261-266;

Modern Fiction Studies, special Murdoch issue, 15 (Autumn 1959);

William Van O'Connor, *The New University Wits and the End of Modernism* (Carbondale: Southern Illinois University Press, 1963), pp. 54-74;

Rubin Rabinovitz, "Iris Murdoch," in *Six Contemporary British Novelists*, edited by George Stade (New York: Columbia University Press, 1976), pp. 271-332;

Lorna Sage, "Female Fictions: The Women Novelists," in *The Contemporary English Novel*, edited by Malcolm Bradbury and David Palmer (London: Edward Arnold, 1979), pp. 68-74;

Richard Todd, *Iris Murdoch: The Shakespearean Interest* (New York: Barnes & Noble, 1979; London: Vision Press, 1979);

Peter Wolfe, *The Disciplined Heart: Iris Murdoch and Her Novels* (Columbia: University of Missouri Press, 1966).

Papers:

The manuscript and typescript drafts of most of the novels, together with other papers both published and unpublished, are held at the University of Iowa, Iowa City. The Bodleian Library, Oxford, possesses the manuscript of the Romanes lecture, which was revised and published as *The Fire and the Sun: Why Plato Banished the Artists*.

John Noone
(7 February 1936-   )

Gordon Henderson

BOOKS: *The Man with the Chocolate Egg* (London: Hamilton, 1966; New York: Grove, 1967); *The Night of Accomplishment* (London: Hamilton, 1974).

John Noone's reputation rests primarily on a powerful first novel dealing with terrorist activities in London during the early 1960s. A second, more experimental novel was less successful artistically and less well received. Although both novels won awards in England, Noone's work has gained little critical notice aside from the usual book reviews, which ranged from enthusiastic to puzzled.

Noone was born in 1936 in Darlington, England, and was educated locally. In 1954 he entered the Durham Light Infantry. After leaving the military in 1956 he entered King's College, University of Durham, where he studied English literature. He has since taught English at various universities around the world, including Alexandria University in Egypt (1961-1965), Libya University in Benghazi (1965-1966), and Kyoto University in Japan (1968-1974). He now lives in Brussels.

The plot of *The Man with the Chocolate Egg* (1966), which won the Geoffrey Faber Memorial Prize for fiction, is relatively simple. A young British soldier steals a hand grenade (the chocolate egg), which he attempts to deliver to his terrorist brother in West London. When he does not find his brother at home, he spends the night at the apartment of friends; is persuaded to act as a pallbearer for a neighbor; and returns to camp, where he is arrested, questioned, and beaten. After escaping from the detention barracks, he hitchhikes back to London, finds his brother dead, and boards a bus, where, presumably, he intends to set off the grenade. In the course of his wanderings, the soldier, Matthew Bright, becomes drenched with rain and develops a high fever, which provides Noone with the opportunity to create his most dramatic effects. As the fever ebbs and returns, the narrative alternates between scenes of vivid realism and bizarre surrealism in which Bright encounters what he imagines to be a walking dead man, a sorceress, and various figures out of Hades. Past and present be-

come jumbled, and in one surrealistic sequence Bright finds himself propelled three times through the same course of events, each time with a disturbingly different outcome. Several reviewers compared the novel to films by Bergman, Hitchcock, Fellini, and Antonioni. The comparison is apt, for the book has the tension, suspense, and air of foreboding of a first-rate psychological thriller.

The most impressive quality of *The Man with the Chocolate Egg* is Noone's ability to create and maintain an atmosphere of mystery and impending doom. The imagery is heavy with blood, violent death, and grotesque aberrations: voodoo dolls and bloated effigies of Guy Fawkes, recurrent images of crucifixion, a mysterious albino who keeps reap-

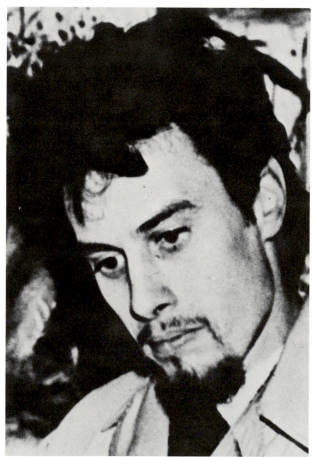

John Noone

562

pearing at the edge of the action, and a dog barking persistently in the distance during several key scenes. The overall effect is that of a nightmare. The *Sunday Times* critic described the novel as "a book which depicts the heavy coldness of horror so accurately it is a relief to be able to close it and look around." Although a few reviewers found the book overly pessimistic and heavy-handed in its symbolism, most praised its intensity, powerfully projected images, well-paced plot, and sharply focused descriptions.

The Night of Accomplishment (1974) is an uneven blend of fiction, autobiography, and mythology. The author/narrator offers this description of it: "The central character of the book is presented as the writer of my first novel, *The Man with the Chocolate Egg*. . . ; the central character of that first book was called Matthew, and the central character of this book is called Luke. In this book, there is another book, which Luke is trying to write. Its title is 'Proteus' and its central character is called Mark. There are therefore three books and three central characters to be considered. . . ." Noone's own first name completes the Biblical quartet of Matthew, Mark, Luke, and John. Luke, who is writing his second novel, is a lecturer in Kyoto, where Noone taught. Sections of the novel-within-a-novel, which is set in Alexandria, are printed throughout the book in a different typeface. Luke's novel is not going well, nor are his personal relationships. He finds his fictional material intractable. "My mind," he says, "is heaped with a jigsaw of ideas, impossible to piece together." His personal life is equally fragmented. A broken heel and displaced vertebrae leave him immobilized, and his marriage is in trouble because of a love affair with a woman who reminds him of his dead sister. Noone writes with intensity and intelligence about the complex interrelationships between an artist's life and his work and about the need to destroy in order to create. He also skillfully brings to life the European academic community in Kyoto. Yet the novel never gains the narrative momentum of *The Man with the Chocolate Egg*. The problem is that Noone too frequently interrupts the plot with lengthy digressions in which he draws parallels between his characters and figures from Greek, Egyptian, Japanese, and Christian mythology. Luke, for example, is variously compared to the unicorn, the lion, the wise centaur Chiron, and the ailing archer Philoctetes; and Noone writes digressive essays on each.

In *The Man with the Chocolate Egg* Noone's allusions to mythology and the tarot underscore the unreality of Matthew's fevered imaginings; in *The*

Dust jacket for the American edition of Noone's first novel, which won the Geoffrey Faber Memorial Prize

Night of Accomplishment the myths are tedious baggage. When the plot keeps its focus on Luke's problems with his wife, his lover, and his writing, the narrative is well paced and interesting; when it gets sidetracked into mythology, it simply is not. The novel won an Arts Council Award but received only passing mention from reviewers, usually in omnibus reviews of several new novels. The *Sunday Times* reviewer called it "an ill-advised stylistic adventure," and the *Observer* critic termed it "an infuriating compilation" by an "amazing egoist . . . conducting his self-analysis in public." Other reviewers were less harsh, but their praise was heavily qualified. Victoria Glendinning in *New Statesman* found the novel "always intense, often fascinating, sometimes maddening" but noted, "if the myths are valid, it surely should be enough for the characters to play their predestined parts without such indecent exposure of their heroic pedigrees." John Mellors in the *Listener* praised Noone as "a learned and talented writer" but complained that "for long stretches the plot suffers almost total eclipse."

When he is writing at his best, as he does in *The Man with the Chocolate Egg*, Noone is a master of narration, description, imagery, and dialogue. Reviewers of that novel were justified in calling him a writer of enormous promise. His second novel, however, only rarely demonstrates his talents. He has published no new fiction since 1974, and with an output of only two novels in fifteen years, his promise remains unfulfilled.

Robert Nye
(15 March 1939-)

Elizabeth Allen

BOOKS: *Juvenilia 1* (Lowestoft, Suffolk: Scorpion Press, 1961);

Juvenilia 2 (Lowestoft, Suffolk: Scorpion Press, 1963);

Taliesin (London: Faber & Faber, 1966; New York: Hill & Wang, 1967);

March Has Horse's Ears (London: Faber & Faber, 1966; New York: Hill & Wang, 1967);

Doubtfire (London: Calder & Boyars, 1967; New York: Hill & Wang, 1968);

Bee Hunter: Adventures of Beowulf (London: Faber & Faber, 1968; New York: Hill & Wang, 1968); republished as *Beowulf, the Bee Hunter* (London: Faber & Faber, 1972);

Darker Ends (London: Calder & Boyars, 1969; New York: Hill & Wang, 1969);

Tales I Told My Mother (London: Calder & Boyars, 1969; New York: Hill & Wang, 1969);

Wishing Gold (London: Macmillan, 1970; New York: Hill & Wang, 1971);

Sawney Bean, by Nye and William Watson (London: Calder & Boyars, 1970);

Poor Pumpkin (London: Macmillan, 1971; New York: Hill & Wang, 1972); republished as *The Mathematical Princess and Other Stories* (New York: Hill & Wang, 1972);

Agnus Dei (Rushden, Northamptonshire: Sceptre Press, 1973);

The Seven Deadly Sins: A Mask, words by Nye and music by James Douglas (Rushden, Northamptonshire: Omphalos Press, 1974);

Two Prayers (Richmond, Surrey: Keepsake Press, 1974);

Five Dreams (Rushden, Northamptonshire: Sceptre Press, 1974);

Cricket: Three Tales (Indianapolis: Bobbs Merrill, 1974); republished as *Once Upon Three Times* (London: Benn, 1978);

Three Plays (London: Calder & Boyars, 1976)— includes *Fugue* [film script], *Sisters*, and *Penthesilea*, adapted by Nye from Heinrich Von Kleist's play;

Falstaff (London: Hamilton, 1976; Boston: Little, Brown, 1976);

Divisions on a Ground (Manchester: Carcanet New Press, 1976);

Merlin (London: Hamilton, 1978; New York: Putnam, 1979);

The Bird of the Golden Land (London: Hamilton, 1980);

Faust (London: Hamilton, 1980; New York: Putnam, 1981);

Harry Pay the Pirate (London: Hamilton, 1981);

The Voyage of the Destiny (London: Hamilton, 1982; New York: Putnam, 1982).

Robert Nye has explored the different modes available to a contemporary writer—poetry, drama, and fiction—yet his work is recognizably of a piece in its approach and concerns. His writing is both traditional and highly individual: traditional in that he works with archetypal themes and myths available to all writers of story and legend both oral and literary, and individual in the forms in which he recreates them.

Nye was born 15 March 1939, in London, into a family of modest background: his father, Oswald Nye, was a clerk, and his mother, Frances Weller Nye, having left school at twelve, never learned to read and write properly. Yet in Nye's account of his childhood and schooling it is possible to see at that point the outlines of the kind of writer he would become. His mother, he says, "was possessed of an innate peasant storytelling ability," and this emphasis on narrative and on traditional materials is an essential element of Nye's novels and stories. His years at Southend High School, a traditional English grammar school, provided him with sound training in the use of language. His wider education, however, he ascribes to the realization at about the age of twelve that he "could get three tickets at the public library for every member of my family and use them all myself since none of the others was much of a reader."

The first medium to which he was devoted and in which he gained his earliest success was poetry; some of his poems were published in the *London Magazine* when he was sixteen. At that age, too, he left school, with no wish to continue his formal education by further study. By this time he was quite sure that writing was to be his occupation and took note of the fact that those three writers whom he then most admired, Shakespeare, Arthur Rimbaud, and Dylan Thomas, "had all done well enough without the benefit of a degree."

Between leaving school in 1955 and commit-ting himself to full-time writing in 1961, he "went through the motions of various non-jobs" as a newspaper reporter, a milkman, a laborer in a market garden, and a ward orderly in a sanatorium. These occupations, however, he saw only as a means to support his writing poetry.

In 1961 he moved with his wife, Judith (whom he had married in 1959), to a remote cottage in North Wales, there to devote himself to writing full time. His first collection of poems, *Juvenilia 1*, was published the same year. That some of the poems were thought by reviewers to be immature in attitude was scarcely surprising since some had been written when he was only thirteen, but the reviews were in general favorable, praising Nye's poetic inventiveness and feeling for language. These early poems hint strongly at Nye's abiding interests, which surface in each literary genre—the word games, the use of myth and legend.

The Welsh cottage had no electricity and relied for its water supply on a spring in the woods; the rent was appropriately low, but even so, the favorable reviews of *Juvenilia 1* did not provide enough income to support Nye, his wife, and their child. Nye says that he was struck by the fact that "here were three of us starving" while the reviewers of his book were receiving fees for their comments. Accordingly, he wrote to the literary editors of those journals where *Juvenilia 1* had been well reviewed, explaining to each his interest in offering himself as a reviewer. This ploy was successful and two of the editors approached began to send him work regularly. Reviewing has continued to subsidize and complement Nye's creative work; in 1967 he became poetry editor for the daily newspaper the *Scotsman*, in 1971 he was named poetry critic for the *Times*, and he regularly reviews fiction for the *Guardian*. As a critic he is well respected (perhaps because as a practicing writer he is less open to jibes often made at those who criticize but cannot themselves create).

A second volume, *Juvenilia 2*, was published in 1963 and won Nye the Eric Gregory Award. Reviews were again good, with the critic for the *Times Literary Supplement* stating, "Here is a proper poet" and referring to Nye's "Gravesian decorum, cool passion and judging concentration." The subject matter of these poems was often more personal—his wife, his son—and the wordplay and the structure were less extravagant.

Literary criticism and poetry did not provide Nye's only outlets at this time. In 1966 his first book for children, *Taliesin*, appeared; in it, as in the poems, may be found the themes which he further developed in the adult novels. Nye has paid tribute to his mother's storytelling abilities and has pointed out that in all his stories "the matter is traditional—it comes from the parish pump, not the well of personal experience." As *Falstaff* (1976), *Merlin* (1978), and *Faust* (1980) were to use the stuff of ballad and legend, so in this children's book Nye takes the story of the ancient Welsh bard and makes of it something at once powerful and humorous. Here Taliesin, defining the nature of true poetry, makes a statement important for an understanding of Nye's stories. A true song, says the bard, is "Not just an old song, not just a new song, but a song both old and new, original and remembered." Nye is keen to emphasize the source of his stories as "Those folk tales which are as it were the dreams of the people coming down to us without the interference of our own identity." Taliesin the bard sings that he "was with my Lord in the Kingdom of Heaven. . . . I am now come here to what is left of Troy. . . ."

In the original "Song of Taliesin" the references are to events in Celtic legend (and thus are impenetrable to most non-Celts); but, as in this version, Taliesin stands for the autonomous power of the song and for the idea of the bard as its vessel. Yet the old songs continue to gain power from the creative spirit working through them, and this is what Nye seeks to do—that is, recreate the myth and, in so doing, breathe new life into it.

During this period in Wales two more sons were born to Nye and his wife, but the marriage ended in divorce. He then married Aileen Campbell, a painter and poet who later studied and qualified as an analytical psychologist at the C. G. Jung Institute in Zurich, Switzerland. Nye had abandoned the cottage in Wales and now settled with his second wife in Edinburgh. They lived there until 1977, when they moved to Ireland, where he is still living.

Meanwhile he had published his second children's book based on the retelling of other Welsh legends (*March Has Horse's Ears*, 1966) and his first novel, *Doubtfire* (1967). Myth and legend are central, although not in the straightforward form found in the children's books. P. J. Kavanagh, the poet and novelist, describes the action of *Doubtfire* as taking place "within the troubled psyche of William Retz (alias Gilles de Retz) enduring a crisis of identity exacerbated by the unattainable nature of Joan Dark (Jeanne d'Arc). It consists of telephone calls into a dead receiver, fantasy playlets, conversations with anti-selfs, descriptions of the nature world . . . descriptions of the creative process, and of

apothegms. . . ." The rhythms and cuts from scene to scene are more akin to cinematic technique than to the traditional form of the novel, and *Doubtfire* lacks the narrative drive and energy of Nye's later novels. Yet even in subject matter the links with Nye's other work, both forward and backward, are there: Joan of Arc was the subject of a poem in *Juvenilia 2*, which was later refined in *Divisions on a Ground* (1976); she and Gilles de Retz also feature in *Falstaff*. The intense concern with language, noted by reviewers of the early poems, continues, with the addition of the lewd jokes which are so characteristic of the novels that follow. Then, too, there is the question of the veracity of Retz's stories, as there is later of Falstaff's history: the nature of fiction is to be considered. Nye has commented: "I do not write short stories as much as tall stories, fibs, lies, whoppers."

His next publication was a return to a work for children, *Bee Hunter: Adventures of Beowulf* (published in the United States as *Beowulf, the Bee Hunter*). Rather than a free translation of the Beowulf legend, this is an interpretation of it. The *Times Educational Supplement* reviewer called it: "A free and beautiful prose adaptation. . . . The story is simplified somewhat and becomes a chilling, bloodthirsty narrative which is redeemed from melodrama by subtle characterisation." As in his novels for adults, Nye makes the people of legend human and accessible.

A collection of short stories, *Tales I Told My Mother*, followed in 1969 and won the James Kennaway Memorial Award. "Rabelaisian" was the adjective most frequently applied to these stories, as appropriate both to their energy and to their content—as in the story of the man who uses the only tool available, his penis, to free himself from a snowdrift. Although each can stand separately, the "nine fictions" of the book build into each other, characters and elements recurring in distorted echoes. As always in Nye, characters from fiction or writers of fiction appear in new guises: Nye says he wrote a whole "lost book" by Emily Brontë in order to quote from it in the story "The Amber Witch."

Another short story, "The Same Old Story," was published in a Penguin Modern Stories collection the following year, and this was followed by two more children's books, *Wishing Gold* (1970) and *Poor Pumpkin* (1971). The former is the tale of the careless king of Ireland and his villainous queen; the latter is a collection of stories based on Eastern and Western folk traditions. "The Witches Who Stole Eyes" and "The Wooden Baby" have strong elements of the grotesque; the modern expression does nothing to emasculate the power of the traditional tales.

The next few years saw Nye in two new roles: as the author of a number of plays and as the editor of several books of poetry. The masque *The Seven Deadly Sins* (published in 1974), commissioned by the Stirling (Scotland) Festival Society, was performed at the 1973 Stirling Festival with masks designed by his wife, Aileen Campbell Nye, and the next year it was performed at the Edinburgh Festival. *Sisters*, which had first been broadcast on radio in 1969, was also performed in Edinburgh (in 1973), as was *Mr. Poe* (in 1974).

Another book of Nye's own poems, *Divisions on a Ground*, was published in 1976. This was the year in which the novel *Falstaff* was also published, and it was with this work, he believes, that he found his own "voice and pitch." Although—with his poetry, his criticism, his plays and fictions—his reputation as a well-rounded man of letters was established, there had until this time been no major achievements and no financial successes: *Falstaff* was published to great critical acclaim in both Britain and the United States.

In reading *Falstaff* one is conscious of Nye's words about his fictions as "tall stories," for Falstaff's memoirs, dictated to a team of scriveners, are in every sense fictions—probably. Falstaff tells the story of his life, but with digressions, like those of Laurence Sterne's *Tristram Shandy*, of stories within stories (of Pope Joan, of King Arthur); meditation on parts of his body; discursions on the nature and name of the Earthly Paradise. Is this Shakespeare's Falstaff? In one sense very much so; he is surrounded by characters whose names at least are from the Shakespearean canon, not only from the historical plays and *The Merry Wives of Windsor*, in which Falstaff appears, but from almost every play Shakespeare ever wrote. Thus he has a cook called Macbeth and a rat Desdemona; loses his virginity with Ophelia; satisfies his aging lust with his niece, Miranda; and claims the sexual conquest of an Imogen, a Perdita, and even a Titania. The encounters with Hal as "the sweet prince," the battle at Gadshill, and the bitter rejection when Hal becomes king contain lines straight from Shakespeare; but Nye, as always in dealing with his source material, has made it his own, so the famous Falstaff meditation on "honour" is both enlivened by a parallel meditation on "onions" and deepened by later reflections on war and battle. For the humor does have serious import. The jokes abound: puns and other verbal felicities (talking of Eden and the Fall, Falstaff declares, "And I am Fall Stuff"); literary "in jokes" (Falstaff affects to despise Gower but falls in love in a church just as Gower recommends in his *Confessio Amantis*); and graphic diagrams of farts. Yet a plea is being made for laughter and for life. "The soul laughs being the root of all forms of vital activity," says Falstaff, and, following Sir Toby Belch, he gives the quintessential put-down to all Puritans: "Because we are suddenly become virtuous shall there be no more cakes and ale?" It is, too, a celebration of what Falstaff perceives as England and English virtues; perhaps what Nye also sees as English, since of his mother and her family he has said, "A farmer's daughter. . . . Of the best blood in England, yeoman stock."

Falstaff has occasional touches of lyricism (as he thinks of "the shifting hedgerows in the fog"), and the only hero he will allow is the native King Arthur, dismissing such foreign contenders as Alexander and Achilles ("a demi-god with weak ankles"). The fun, however, is insistently salacious, a trait some critics found tiresome, although Michael Wood pointed out that "generally it takes on rather an attractive pathos, for we are never allowed to forget that Falstaff is not bragging but lying." Indeed, this relationship between truth, lies, and fiction is at the heart of *Falstaff* as well as Nye's two subsequent novels, *Merlin* and *Faust*.

Again and again Falstaff explores the relationship between truth and dreams: "I was a dreaming boy, only half aware of a difference between the idea inside my head and the world outside." This idea of the dream is interestingly reinforced as Nye's newly crowned Henry V rejects his old drinking companion with the words: "I have long dreamed of such a man as you. But, being awake, I now despise my dream."

Falstaff insists that the nature of the book should be pondered, asking how the reader can be certain of the existence of the characters with whom he [Falstaff] peoples his reminiscences: "I am your author. Agreed. But I am also *their* author." The insistence on questioning the relationship between reality and fiction extends to a questioning of the existence of Falstaff himself. Scrope, one of the scribes of the memoirs, Falstaff's stepson with a Puritan hatred run dry of imagination and of compassion for the old man, declares: "He is a made-up man—he is a lie." Yet in his final confession Falstaff, while admitting to lying, raises the question of whether some of this perhaps unnecessary human activity might not after all have consisted of "true

Robert Nye, photographed by his thirteen-year-old daughter, Rebecca

lies"; because of this query, the final impression is of a man who "exists" in a way denied to the Puritan truthteller Scrope.

The novel won two prestigious prizes, the Hawthornden and the *Guardian* Fiction, and enthusiastic reviews. Kenneth Tynan declared that Nye "writes like Rabelais reborn. The conception is brilliant, the execution full of panache and invention." Other critics favorably compared the book's vitality with that of other contemporary novels: "The rumbustious centrifugal energy displayed throughout makes most contemporary novels seem insipid," one of them said.

In 1981 *Falstaff* was adapted as a radio and stage play, and Nye has expressed particular pleasure that this adaptation recognized and emphasized a point missed by critics when the novel appeared—Falstaff's identification of himself with the Good Thief of St. Luke's gospel. Such echoes of other stories and literary works are an essential part of all Nye's fiction.

Falstaff, then, had bought golden opinions and had shown Nye the area in which he felt his talents lay. His next novel, *Merlin*, is recognizably in the

same mold. As Falstaff tells his own story, albeit via scribes, so Merlin, son of the Devil and a virgin, tells his in similar racy style. As *Falstaff* had used Shakespearean sources, so here the Arthurian legends are a main source: again the addition of this version of the Merlin story to the canon is only accretion and synthesis, not radical change. Like the song of Taliesin which Nye used in his first children's book, the Arthurian materials are themselves ancient, having been worked on and over for centuries. Alan Brien describes the style of *Merlin* as: "A yeasty salty mixture of theological dirty jokes, scabrous scholarly anecdote, sexy pantomime sketches, elaborate scatological images, erudite low comedy and obscene High Criticism." It is obviously far removed from the style and content of Geoffrey of Monmouth or Thomas Malory, but the main pieces of the legend (the faithless Guinevere and the breaking of the Round Table fellowship, Arthur's seduction by Morgan le Fay, Merlin's enchantment by Nimue) are all present.

The *Falstaff* theme of reality and illusion is here too. In the earlier novel there is some entertaining transvestism; in *Merlin* the theme of identity, shape shifting, and illusion is more central. Merlin, who can become any shape, is finally imprisoned in shapes; he who can know the past and the future becomes "a man locked in the present tense." *Falstaff* employs a number of jokes with time, such as Falstaff's women with their Shakespearean names and the rather too early appearance of the potato in Ireland, but these incongruities were incidental. For in the world of Merlin, time has ceased to be linear; events are knitted together by patterns in which significant events are prefigured by earlier ones. So in medieval minds the sacrifice of Isaac prefigures that of Christ, and Adam's grave is at Golgotha, the place of the Crucifixion. Nimue enchants Merlin in order to preserve her virginity, and, calling to mind that his mother too was a virgin, he muses, "Curious, this repeating of things." The Devil is able to quote from a book not yet written—and this causes Merlin to return to a *Falstaff* theme: who is writing this book? He had believed it to be himself, but could it be that the Devil is the author? The idea of free will becomes important: is the world then a book which the Devil writes?

Yet the main impact of the book is through its particular brand of humor. "It is an ingenious and enjoyable entertainment—dirty, funny and intriguing in almost equal measure," wrote Auberon Waugh. There is a good "running gag" about Gawain and some mysterious sexual pleasure known as "the sleeve job"; and a number of excellent incidental jokes are included, such as Lucifer's antifeminism: "Put it down to the closeness of my relation to an all male family of three." The sex, however, which in *Falstaff* holds its place by reason of the old man's lying exploits and an atmosphere of celebration, in *Merlin* seems more intrusive and unpleasant.

Nye's next novel, *Faust*, follows the pattern of history and legend embellished by sex and determinism, jokes and illusion. This time the narrator is Dr. Faust's pupil and follower Christopher Wagner, who tells the story of the last days of Faust's life before his pact with the Devil is due to be redeemed. Once again the nature of truth is in doubt. Wagner, the skeptic, has no real belief in the existence of this pact, yet he finds himself behaving as if Faust were indeed a figure of diabolic powers. Still he sticks doggedly to his task of telling the story: "Let's stick to facts. Believe me the facts about Faust are stranger by far than fiction." Of his master he insists: "I haven't invented him. He's beyond my imaginative range." At first Wagner has no doubts about his own free will in accomplishing his task: "People who believe [in damnation and salvation]

Dust jacket for Nye's 1980 novel. The cover painting is by Salvador Dali.

say 'it is written. . . .' Meaning there's some great book in which we're all characters. Meaning there's some over-all fate which determines our lives. Well, there is no such fate. No Great Book. And 'it' isn't written. I'm writing it." Then, over one hundred pages into the novel, he remembers that Faust has told him that he would in fact write this book. So, although Wagner does not raise the issue explicitly, where or what is free will? Finally Wagner has to realize that he and Faust are bound together in a way that he has not dreamed possible, and he performs "what I was born to do."

This narrator, then, shares Merlin's concern about freedom and, like Merlin, finds himself trapped. Yet there is a sense in which Wagner's plight seems to be more serious, perhaps simply because of his humanity. In this novel the serious issues provide a more effective counterbalance to the jokes and the sexual contortions. Again the jokes are good, some having literary references to the problems encountered by Marlowe and Goethe whose Fausts searched for new boundaries of knowledge ("Mephistopheles didn't tell me much I

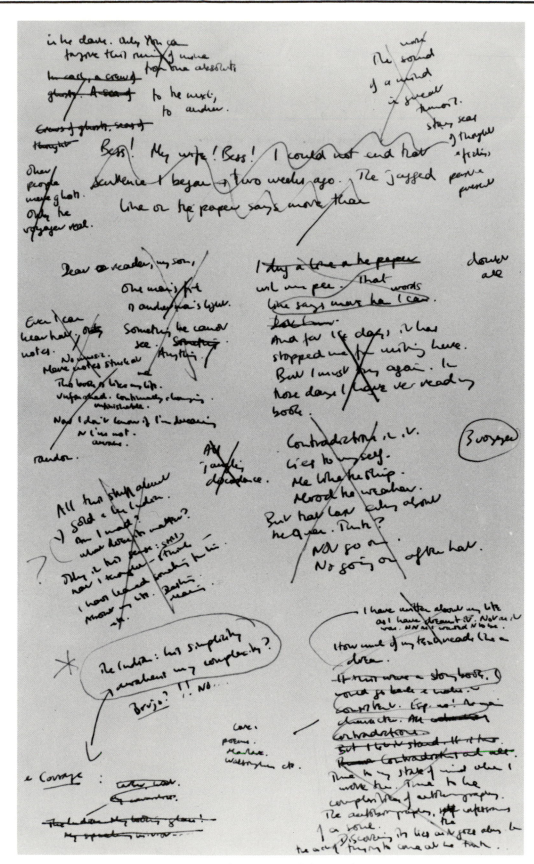

Notes for The Voyage of the Destiny

hadn't worked out for myself"). Others are theological jokes on the study—undertaken by Wagner—of the finer points about angelic movements. Although sex here is with succubi rather than with women, it is less prurient than in *Merlin* and is sometimes inventive in context if not in content, as when Wagner and two girls distract themselves pleasurably during a sermon by Calvin.

A new development for Nye's novels is a greater emphasis in *Faust* on plot. Driven by his own motives or by the pleas of Helen of Troy (who claims to have seen a vision of the Virgin—who looks suspiciously like Helen—promising salvation), Faust, with Wagner and Wagner's girls, travels to Rome. The journey is packed with incident, and although the plot is not the main pleasure that the novel offers, it does provide a tight structure for the disquisitions and the humor, and it adds an extra excitement. The ending, which evokes a concern for Wagner and for his master, and for the fate of both, is genuinely moving in a way new to a novelist the pleasures of whose works tend to be erotic and cerebral rather than emotional.

The three most recent novels, with their mixture of bawdy, learning, and awe, may be alien to the Great Tradition (as defined by F. R. Leavis) but are clearly part of a different English literary tradition, that of the medieval mystery plays and *Everyman*. In a medieval play on the Crucifixion, the soldiers may joke about the problems of fitting Christ's body to the holes in the wood, while in another play Mary's improbable virginity is the subject of ribald humor, without in any way detracting from the intense faith informing the performance and its audience. Laughter was no impiety. Nye agrees that his "mind is essentially mediaeval," and this is a useful point in approaching his writing. In the later novels Nye is concerned to explore the relationships of fiction to fact, of fantasy to truth. While this intense interest in the essential nature of fiction may be found in such central medieval writers as Chaucer and Rabelais, and in modernist authors like James Joyce or Virginia Woolf, it is absent from the novels of the eighteenth- and nineteenth-century realist tradition. The medieval may be seen, as Nye sees it, as more sympathetic to the twentieth-century mind than are the approaches of intervening centuries.

Certainly Nye shows the creative possibilities in their conjunction.

Plays:

Sawney Bean, by Nye and William Watson, Edinburgh, 1969;

Sisters, Edinburgh, 1973;

The Seven Deadly Sins: A Mask, words by Nye and music by James Douglas, Stirling, 1973;

Mr. Poe, Edinburgh, 1974.

Radio Plays:

Sisters, BBC, 1969;

The Devil's Jig, with music by Humphrey Searle, BBC, 1980.

Other:

A Choice of Sir Walter Raleigh's Verse, edited by Nye (London: Faber & Faber, 1972);

William Barnes of Dorset: A Selection of His Poems, edited by Nye (Cheadle, Cheshire: Carcanet Press, 1973);

A Choice of Swinburne's Verse, edited by Nye (London: Faber & Faber, 1973);

"Visakha," in *Scottish Short Stories* (London: Collins, 1973);

"The Lesson," in *Scottish Short Stories* (London: Collins, 1974);

"The Whole Story," in *Factions*, edited by Giles Gordon and Alex Hamilton (London: M. Joseph, 1974);

The Faber Book of Sonnets, edited by Nye (London: Faber & Faber, 1976); republished as *A Book of Sonnets* (New York: Oxford University Press, 1976);

The English Sermon 1750-1850, edited by Nye (Manchester: Carcanet New Press, 1976);

"The Facts of Life," in *Arts Council Stories* (London: Hutchinson, 1978);

"The Second Best Bed," in *Shakespeare Stories* (London: Hamilton, 1982).

Papers:

Collections of Nye's manuscripts are held at the University of Texas at Austin; at Colgate University, Hamilton, New York; and at the National Library of Scotland, Edinburgh.

Edna O'Brien

(15 December 1932-   )

Patricia Boyle Haberstroh
La Salle College

BOOKS: *The Country Girls* (London: Hutchinson, 1960; New York: Knopf, 1960);

The Lonely Girl (London: Cape, 1962; New York: Random House, 1962); republished as *Girl with Green Eyes* (London: Penguin, 1964);

Girls in their Married Bliss (London: Cape, 1964; New York: Simon & Schuster, 1968);

August is a Wicked Month (London: Cape, 1965; New York: Simon & Schuster, 1965);

Casualties of Peace (London: Cape, 1966; New York: Simon & Schuster, 1967);

The Love Object (London: Cape, 1968; New York: Knopf, 1969);

A Pagan Place (London: Weidenfeld & Nicolson, 1970; New York: Knopf, 1970);

Zee & Co.: A Novel (London: Weidenfeld & Nicolson, 1971);

Night (London: Weidenfeld & Nicolson, 1972; New York: Knopf, 1973);

A Pagan Place: A Play (London: Faber & Faber, 1973);

A Scandalous Woman and Other Stories (London: Weidenfeld & Nicolson, 1974; New York: Harcourt Brace Jovanovich, 1974);

Mother Ireland (London: Weidenfeld & Nicolson, 1976; New York: Harcourt Brace Jovanovich, 1976);

Johnny I Hardly Knew You (London: Weidenfeld & Nicolson, 1977); republished as *I Hardly Knew You* (Garden City: Doubleday, 1978);

Arabian Days, text by O'Brien, photographs by Gerard Klijn (London & New York: Quartet Books, 1977);

Seven Novels and Other Short Stories (London: Collins, 1978);

Mrs. Reinhardt and Other Stories (London: Weidenfeld & Nicolson, 1978); republished as *A Rose in the Heart* (Garden City: Doubleday, 1979);

Virginia (London: Hogarth Press, 1981);

The Dazzle (London: Stodder & Houghton, 1981);

Returning (London: Weidenfeld & Nicolson, 1982).

Edna O'Brien

As a contemporary novelist Edna O'Brien is in the unique position of appealing to two audiences: she has attracted the attention of a highbrow literary establishment and of a popular audience that eagerly awaits each new novel. Her short stories appear quite frequently in the *New Yorker*, but she has also been published in *Ladies' Home Journal*, *Redbook*, and *Cosmopolitan*. Among literary critics, opinion on O'Brien's fiction is divided. Reviewed by John Updike, V. S. Naipaul, and Anthony Burgess, among others, her work has drawn judgments ranging from charges that she writes "meretricious trash" or "Gothic malarkey" to comments on her "extraordinary effectiveness and power."

This broad range of audience and opinion arises both from O'Brien's subject matter and from her attitude toward her work. In a 1970 interview with Barbara Bannon, O'Brien stated that she was "very much against literature as such but for the written word with color and life and air in it." Certainly there is color and life in her work. By 1969 five of her novels had been banned in her native Ireland, branded obscene and pornographic.

These novels, and the ones to follow, often brutally and realistically chart a course of affairs where her heroines' emotional and sexual frustrations sometimes lead them into casual sex and liaisons with married men, young priests, and other women. What Stanley Kauffman calls her "lyrics of the loins" created a stir in some quarters, a full-blown scandal in others. How a nice, Irish Catholic convent girl could write so explicitly about sex and so often about despair and disappointment intrigued many critics and readers. The Irish censors, who in banning had promoted many other twentieth-century literary figures, turned their full force against Ireland's latest exile.

The confessional nature of much of O'Brien's prose has likewise led to speculation that little distance separates her work from her life. When asked by Ludovic Kennedy in 1976 how close her stories were to her own life, O'Brien answered: "They're quite close, but they're not as close as they seem. If you write in the first person, which I often do, and if you have a slightly confessional voice—you know, rather than the epistle voice—it looks like that. . . . I think writing, especially semi-autobiographical writing, is the life you might have liked to have had." Talking with Nell Dunn eleven years earlier, O'Brien had also stressed how "close to fantasy writing is" and had suggested that she herself had "pursued pain and humiliation" and emerged to write about it.

Every work Edna O'Brien has written has focused on women, from her first novel, *The Country Girls* (1960), to *Virginia*, a play adapted from the diaries of Virginia Woolf and produced at the Stratford (Ontario) Shakespeare festival in 1980 and in London at the Haymarket Theatre in 1981. Year after year O'Brien has drawn portraits of frustrated women dependent on men, struggling to emerge from the trap that society has set for them and into which they have walked almost willingly, though sometimes unconsciously or indifferently. The prototypical O'Brien fictional family emerges in her novels: irresponsible, drunken father; martyred, submissive mother; cold, detached, cruel husband; lonely, frightened wife; and children about to be sucked into this ongoing cycle. Focusing on the predominant themes of love and sex, O'Brien has explored how these have affected and conditioned the relationships of parents and children, husbands and wives, men and women.

In most of her fiction O'Brien deliberately highlights the sexual drives and attitudes of her heroines. These women, especially Irish women indoctrinated at an early age to the sinfulness of sex,

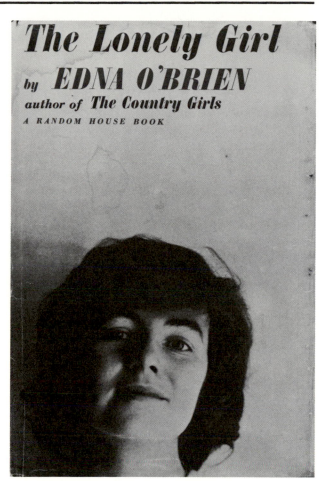

Dust jacket for the American edition of O'Brien's 1962 novel, the second in her autobiographical trilogy

explore numerous responses in their struggles to come to terms with their sexual selves. Taught by mothers to submit to men and warned by their church to remain chaste, they soon find themselves rejected by lovers and humiliated by husbands. Consequently they move through tangled lives, often courting a deliberate wantonness while still searching for Prince Charming, the man with whom they can live happily ever after. That such happiness is impossible echoes through every page of O'Brien's work.

Like sex, love for O'Brien's heroines is a craving. The quest for someone to love is revealed in family interactions: in the child's search for a loving father or father substitute; in the young woman's ambiguous feelings toward a mother whose love she wants but whose legacy she rejects; and in parents, especially mothers, clinging to their children despite inevitable breaches, seeking in them an antidote to the unhappiness of their adult worlds. These women want to be mothers, but they reject the rigid domestic role defined for them; they seek not only lovers and husbands, but love, and are continually disappointed. O'Brien's blend of lyrical realism, most often rendered through a female narrator, defines a sensibility, a tone, an attitude distinctly female.

Edna O'Brien was born 15 December 1932, one of four children of Michael and Lena Cleary O'Brien, in Taumgraney, County Clare, in the rural west of Ireland. In *Mother Ireland* (1976) she describes her years growing up in "a town in a townland that bordered on other townlands of equal indistinctiveness." Her memories include her picture of a "sad irresponsible father" and a sacrificial mother. Not until later, she remarks, did she see them as characters in the drama enacted not only in her home but also in the village, and later in what she calls "the treacherous world" beyond County Clare. In her recollections of Taumgraney she remembers the men as cruel and cross, the women as tender and loving. O'Brien has spoken frequently of the village reading habits: women handing round books of romance, and three popular classics—*Gone with the Wind*, *Rebecca*, and *How Green Was My Valley*—circulated page by page throughout the village, providing escape from a place the novelist describes as "fervid, enclosed and catastrophic." Taumgraney was so enclosed that O'Brien's earliest dreams revolved around romantic fantasies of growing up, marrying the family workman, and settling comfortably into farm life.

Her education, "medieval" by her own accounts, began at the National School in Scariff, which she attended from 1936 to 1941. O'Brien filled her school days with excursions into the glories of the Irish past and her notebooks with "made-up people." At age twelve she continued her schooling at the Convent of Mercy at Loughrea, County Galway, where, trying to live in a self-created state of religious ecstasy, she spent some of her time dreaming up "superb acts of mortification" and the rest committing sins "by the hour." She revealed to Ludovic Kennedy that Jesus Christ, Dracula, and Heathcliff were the loves of her early life. O'Brien tells a prophetic story of being chosen for the coveted role of Our Lady of Fatima in a school play and of falling off the butter boxes she was standing on during the production, much to her own mortification and the nuns' anger. At this point, O'Brien claims, her visions of the Blessed Virgin began to wane, only to be replaced by new fantasies, among them a desire to become a film star.

In 1946 she left County Clare and arrived in Dublin with a suitcase bound with twine and a "head full of fancy." Settling in one of Dublin's poorer districts, she worked in a chemist shop by day and attended pharmaceutical lectures at night. In her first days in Dublin O'Brien discovered a copy of *Introducing James Joyce* and was amazed that for the first time she had found a book that was exactly like her own life. During this time, "I could not decide," O'Brien reminisces, "whether to become a scholar or an adventuress." For a while she tried both, balancing the "nourishment of reading" with the delights of cinemas and pubs. Encouraged by Paedar O'Donnell, O'Brien grew more serious about writing and submitted her first pieces to the *Irish Press* in 1948.

In 1952, defying family and friends, O'Brien eloped with Ernest Gebler, another writer, and soon moved back to the country, to the mountains of County Wicklow. Her two sons, Carlos and Sacha, were born in 1952 and 1954. This marriage seems to have been doomed from the beginning; O'Brien claims she married in response to "a need for and dread of authority" in a "spirit of expiation and submissiveness." The marriage was dissolved in 1964.

O'Brien's move to London in 1959 with her two sons can be seen as another step in her quarrel with an Ireland she felt had warped her with fear and guilt and as a new stage in the continuing odyssey of seeking the person she wanted to be. While she was working as a manuscript reader in London, two publishers offered her a small sum of money to write a novel. *The Country Girls*, published in 1960 and still considered by many to be her best novel, was written in less than three weeks. This novel forms a trilogy with two that followed: *The Lonely Girl* (1962) and *Girls in their Married Bliss* (1964). By 1965 Ireland's country girl found herself the focus of attention in London literary circles.

The trilogy, which begins in a convent school and ends in London, certainly has autobiographical overtones. O'Brien's vivid descriptions in *Mother Ireland* of her life in the convent school, and later in Dublin, leave little doubt that many of the details and incidents in these novels derive from her personal experiences. With the two voices in this trilogy—the brazen, slightly looney Baba, wise (or so she thinks) to the ways of the world and the wiles of men, and the quieter, naive Kate, bullied by circumstances and especially by Baba—O'Brien establishes the two women who continue to appear in her fiction. Embarrassed by her family's poverty, Kate teams up with Baba, daughter of the village veterinarian, in a series of tragicomic adventures in search of sex and a romantic husband. As the trilogy opens, Kate's happiness at winning a scholarship to the convent diminishes after her mother, having left Kate's father and abandoned Kate to Baba's family, drowns in an accident. Alienated from a father whose drunkenness and cruelty have been the source of a good deal of childhood pain and worry, Kate is drawn to both Mr. Gentleman, a rich Dublin solicitor who visits his house in the village each weekend, and to Mr. Brennan, Baba's father, who protects Kate from her father's violence.

Dismissed from school after Baba writes a dirty comment about a nun and a priest on the back of a holy picture, Kate and Baba take off for Dublin, much as O'Brien herself had done, "the country girls brazening the big city." Soon settled in a boardinghouse, they set off on an orgy of smoking, dancing, pubs, and parties in the company of middle-aged men because, as Baba says, "young men have no bloody money." But their adventures come to a halt when Baba contracts tuberculosis. The novel ends with Kate suddenly realizing she has forgotten the anniversary of her mother's death, just as Mr. Gentleman deserts her under the cloud of his wife's nervous breakdown and threats from Kate's father.

The Country Girls sets the tone and theme for the other books in the trilogy. The loss of the mother, the family conflicts and strife, the series of desertions and disappointments in love, and Baba's ridiculing Kate's naivete and poverty but dragging her along with the promise that soon they both will meet wonderful men establish the pattern for the other two novels.

The Lonely Girl, with Kate as narrator, continues to juxtapose the country girls. It opens with Baba (now recovered from illness) crashing a wine-tasting reception, pretending to be a representative from the magazine *Woman's Night*, and Kate standing beside her, mortified in the rubber boots she has to wear because she has stupidly left her shoes on the bus. Kate's introduction to Eugene Gaillard, a documentary filmmaker, quickly pulls her out of the tedious routine of the grocery shop, where she works, into a love affair. Soon, however, Kate discovers that Eugene has a wife and child, and later her father arrives to drag her back to the scorn of her Irish village and a priest who condemns her for walking the path of moral damnation. Kate escapes back to her lover, but the distance between them grows as Eugene begins to ridicule her peasant origins and Kate discovers the gulf between a man "of reason and brain" and a woman desperately desiring to be loved. Eventually Kate returns

to Baba and her former lodgings just as Baba is off to England proclaiming, "Soho, that's where I'll see life." At the end of this novel both country girls are on a boat bound for England, Kate overwhelmed by her disappointment and loss, and Baba carrying pills ("in case we puke") and trying to figure out how to steal some towels. When they settle in England, Baba working in a big hotel, Kate in a delicatessen, Kate looks toward the future: "When I'm able to talk I imagine that I won't be so alone. . . ."

In the last novel of the trilogy, *Girls in their Married Bliss*, O'Brien alternates the voice of Baba with a third-person narrator for the final phase in the lives of the country girls. Speaking of her marriage to Frank, Baba explains: "I knew that I'd end up with him; he being rich and a slob and the sort of man who would buy you seasick tablets before you travelled." She ridicules her ignorant and foolish husband and confesses, without any sense of guilt, "Normally I'm praying he'll fall off a scaffold." Another narrator describes Kate's crumbling marriage, her gradual loss of her child and her husband who chooses another woman to replace her.

Baba and Kate are soon involved with other men, but these adventures lead again to tragedy. Baba meets the drummer Harvey, who boasts that he can make love to twenty-five women a night, and who insists, in one of the most hilarious scenes in the novel, on drumming her into an erotic frenzy. However, Harvey, a typical O'Brien male character, jilts Baba, leaving her pregnant. Meanwhile, on the verge of a breakdown, Kate finally reveals to her psychiatrist that she now sees her mother as a self-appointed martyr and blackmailer. Kate's own role as mother diminishes until, at the end of the novel, Eugene takes her son to Fiji. To a solicitor who asks why she married, Kate replies helplessly: "It seemed to be what I wanted." At the end of the novel, Kate, sterilized to avoid the risk of more children, plans to move back with Baba. Baba, ironically cornered in the end by "niceness, weakness, and dependence," sees Kate as "someone of whom too much had been cut away."

In the country girls trilogy O'Brien has used some of the experiences of her Irish past to construct a fictional world of women destroyed by their dependence on men. Perhaps the most successful character O'Brien has ever created, and certainly the most humorous, Baba seems to have the best chance for survival in this world: she lies her way in and out of situations with the craziest of stories, steals from the refrigerators of men she sleeps with, and asks for very little: "I don't expect parents to fit you out with anything other than a birth certificate, and an occasional pair of new shoes." Of her marriage to Frank, Baba says: "I don't hate him, I don't love him, I put up with him and he puts up with me." But these compromises ultimately defeat Baba; she ends up with a drunken husband, hosting dinner parties for his friends, but still believing that she and Kate can have "each other, chats, their moments of recklessness, the plans that they'd both stopped believing in long ago." And Kate, one of those "serious people," in Baba's eyes so "goddam servile I could have killed her," finds herself trapped by lack of money and power at the moment when "reality caught up with the nightmare."

Of the three novels *The Country Girls* received the most praise. In the *New Statesman* in July 1960, V. S. Naipaul attributed the novel's success to the fact that O'Brien is a natural writer: "The true tragedy lies in the sense of time passing, of waste, decay, waiting, relationships that come to nothing. Yet Miss O'Brien never says so. . . . She simply offers her characters, and they come to us living." Sean McMahon, writing in *Eire-Ireland*, agreed, suggesting that *The Country Girls* established O'Brien as an important Irish writer and *The Lonely Girl* "affirmed this reputation." McMahon criticized *Girls in their Married Bliss*, however, finding it to be "startlingly disappointing" because of its increasingly more strident "note of ironic disillusion."

After the notoriety of *The Country Girls* Edna O'Brien settled in London, continued to write novels and short stories, and began producing screenplays as well. Between 1964 and 1970 three of her novels, *August is a Wicked Month* (1965), *Casualties of Peace* (1966), and *A Pagan Place* (1970), were published, the last winning the Yorkshire Post Book Award for finest fiction of the year. *Girl with Green Eyes* (1964), adapted from her novel *The Lonely Girl*; *Time Lost and Time Remembered* (1966), written with Desmond Davis and based on O'Brien's short story, "A Woman at the Seaside, "; and *Three Into Two Won't Go* (1969), a screenplay O'Brien adapted from Andrea Newman's novel, became popular films. *The Love Object*, a collection of eight stories (five originally published in the *New Yorker*),appeared in 1968 to continue the O'Brien narrative of frustrated and disappointed women.

Missing from the novels written during these years is the humor which enlivens *The Country Girls*. Although Kate's naivete reappears in several other characters, the wisecracking voice of young Baba disappears. The failure of O'Brien's own marriage, as well as her personal experiences rejecting the traditional roles of woman and wife which she had been brought up to believe in, undoubtedly influ-

enced the novels she wrote at this time. Grace Eckley sees *August is a Wicked Month* as a novel which marks a transition between the quests of O'Brien's earlier heroines for fulfillment through marriage and those of her later heroines who realize that this sort of fulfillment is impossible.

August is a Wicked Month, possibly the least successful of O'Brien's novels, focuses on the confusion of a divorced woman trying to redefine her role as mother, rid herself of wifehood, and search for a new definition of herself as a woman. Ellen, a nurse from a rural Irish village, has married, then separated, leaving church and home, and now fends for herself. The novel describes her short vacation to the Mediterranean where, caught between her intense desire for physical pleasure and the residual guilt of her Catholic upbringing, she soon finds herself involved with either masochistic or impotent men. Punctuating the scenes of decadence are her recollections of moments with her young son, which continue to haunt her. However Ellen "had been brought up to believe in punishment," and by the end of the novel she must pay for her sins when her son is killed in a camping accident with his father. In the final scene, much like Kate Brady in *Girls in their Married Bliss*, the heroine waits, neither happy nor unhappy, for the coming of autumn.

August is a Wicked Month reflects O'Brien's growing interest in fictional technique, as symbolism replaces the realistic narrative of *The Country Girls*. In the symbolic structure of this novel the sun becomes "the opponent of dreams," and Ellen's intense pursuit of both sun and sex becomes a purging in the August heat. The obvious and heavy-handed symbolism, however, develops a heroine too vulnerable to be believed, and critics generally responded unfavorably. Ultimately *August is a Wicked Month* suffers from what Lotus Smith called "its self-pitying rancour."

In 1966 O'Brien produced her next novel, *Casualties of Peace*, which centers on the relationship between Willa, a virgin "though tampered with," and Patsy, unhappily married to Tom and about to leave him for another man. Searching for peace after a terrifying marriage to Herod, Willa seeks security with Tom and Patsy; since they came, she feels, "her life had a new order, a solid peace." But in O'Brien's world peace never lasts. Through a bizarre series of circumstances involving Auro, Willa's lover, Tom kills Willa, mistaking her for Patsy. The novel, which begins with Willa's dream of being "slit in multiple pieces" by two strange men, closes with all the casualties of peace scattered about: Willa, dead; Tom, imprisoned; and Patsy, alone. In this novel O'Brien has moved from the decadence of *August is a Wicked Month* to masochistic violence, and the result is disappointing. As some critics have noted, the plot, contrived around a borrowed coat, cannot quite carry the thematic burden O'Brien imposes on it.

By 1970 O'Brien had lived in London for eleven years, but like Joyce before her, she eventually turned to her Irish childhood to recreate in fiction moments from the past. "I believe," she has said, "that memory and the welter of memory, packed into a single lonely and bereft moment, is the strongest ally a person can have. The further I went away from the past, the more clearly I returned inwardly. . . ." *A Pagan Place*, published in 1970, is set in the rural west of Ireland. Talking to David Heycock after the novel was published, O'Brien explained that she wrote *A Pagan Place* because she wanted to get into the "kingdom of children": "I wanted to get the minute to minute essence of what it is when you're very young, when you're both meticulously aware of everything that's going on around you and totally uncritical."

The novel develops from a series of juxtapositions. The village pagan past continually intrudes upon its Catholic present, where the poverty and sterility of daily life are charged with the superstitious lore that permeates the place, and repressed sexuality emerges in sinful and hidden sexual encounters. The minute details of the characters and life of the village show O'Brien at her best. The minor characters, like the nationalistic teacher, Miss Davitt, who goes mad right before the children's eyes, and Hilda, the neighbor who tries to speak to her dead husband even though "she hadn't spoken a civil word" to him when he was alive, are particularly effective. O'Brien's details, like the description of the bedroom wallpaper which had been put on upside down, reveal her talent for suggestive imagery.

In *A Pagan Place* a young girl's family is thrown into a crisis when they discover that Emma, her older sister, is pregnant. The protagonist, shaken by her family's reactions and in the midst of her own sexual awakening, is lured into her first sexual experience by a priest who afterwards quickly rejects her. To atone for her sin she joins an order of nuns dedicated to saving the world. In the final scene, aware that the family's knowledge of her involvement with the priest has severed her from them, the young girl prepares to leave home, hoping her mother will emerge to say goodbye. Disappointed, she hears only her mother's cry, the "howl" that will haunt her for her entire life.

The novel, constructed as a stream of memories, draws on the symbolic and ironic connotations of the word "pagan" to suggest that the Irish villagers, in their guilt, fear, and repression, make sins of the natural pleasures that most attract them and so create a split between what they believe and what they feel. This split ultimately leads to loneliness and cruelty, to mothers who teach their daughters that "love is a form of dope," and to the ironic and wasted sacrifice of the young girl choosing a marriage to God so that she can bring to distant pagans the happiness Christ merited for them.

Discussing her use of the second person, O'Brien explained: "I felt that in every person there are two selves: I suppose they would be called the ego and the alter ego. And then there's almost a kind of negative state where things happen to you and you're not really realizing that they're happening. . . ." The narrator of this novel sounds very much as if she is talking to a younger self, having achieved a mature perspective on the experiences and people of her childhood. Combined with the symbolic implications of setting in *A Pagan Place*, this technique illustrates O'Brien's continuing experiments with form.

The narrative recollection of *A Pagan Place* turns into a Molly Bloom-type interior monologue in O'Brien's next novel, *Night* (1972). Mary Hooligan, adult counterpart of young Baba, settles into a four-poster bed with "satinized headboard" and begins to think about her past. Memories of her mother and her childhood home in the village of Coose; of men, the "cretins, pilgrims and scholars" she has known and loved; of "high teas, serge suits, binding attachments" crowd the slowly moving minutes of the night. Left as caretaker of a vacationing couple's home, Mary appropriates the master bedroom after being haunted in another room by visions of her mother who, like Hamlet's ghost, continues to reappear. The master bedroom is a temporary resting place for Mary's chaotic soul. Claiming she wants to be alone, she still admits to being on the lookout for pals, "pen pals and pub pals." Mary's life spills out as she recollects the many men and women with whom she has seen nights through, some for consolation, some for sexual fulfillment. Saddened by her growing separation from her son, she looks back with horror on her marriage to Dr. Flaggler, not, she admits, a blessed union. As dawn arrives, Mary, though solving nothing, feels refreshed, as one does after a long convalescence. She gladly quits the house and resolves to "live a little" before "the all-embracing darkness descends." Getting through the night, for Mary Hooligan, is a very qualified kind of triumph.

In *Night*, which John Updike called a "brilliant and beautiful book," all past O'Brien heroines merge. A woman, hurt by a disastrous marriage to a cruel man and wise to the tricks of the world, desperately craves the love of her child, of her lost mother, of any man or woman who will have her. But at the same time Mary doubts that love is possible: "You have separateness thrust upon you," she says at the end of the novel. Though Mary Hooligan moves toward what she calls "some other shore," bolstering herself with the fragments of residual hope, her overwhelming loneliness pervades every page.

Although O'Brien did not publish another novel until 1977, in the five-year period between *Night* and *Johnny I Hardly Knew You* (1977) she continued to publish short stories, primarily in the *New Yorker*. Her collection *A Scandalous Woman and Other Stories* appeared in 1974.

In interviews in 1976 and 1977, O'Brien described her dual role as novelist and mother. Divorced at this time for more than twelve years, she was financially independent, with her sons university students at Cambridge and York. While she claimed, in talking to Ludovic Kennedy, that bringing up children by herself had been "glorious" because she had no one to argue with over "clothes and schools," O'Brien acknowledged that living alone often caused one to be extremely removed from people. "I feel," she told Susan Heller Anderson, "that I have been too often used and abused, and angry with myself for allowing it." O'Brien suggested at this time that, although she enjoyed the advantages of London, the city could dry people up. In London people don't tell stories, she claimed, while Ireland is full of stories and curiosity. Despite fifteen years in London, O'Brien still saw herself as a gypsy.

The autobiographical *Mother Ireland*, a blend of myth, history, geography, and personal memories, with photographs by Fergus Bourke, records a pilgrimage back to Ireland. Filled with details of the day-to-day life of the Irish people, *Mother Ireland* reflects O'Brien's ambivalence and pinpoints the ironic juxtapositions she has always seen at the heart of Irish culture. Describing the hill of Tara, the seat of the ancient kings of Ireland, O'Brien notes that Tara is now an "unassuming place." "Six miles away," she writes, "is a holiday camp where girls in plastic hair rollers parade up and down the small toy-like concrete paths, looking for a Mister Right and ironically enough finding

only distraught fathers hauling their children in and out of a Mickey Mouse show." Though nonfiction *Mother Ireland*, with its central metaphor of a woman raped by various enemies, displays the same energy and detail as *The Country Girls*. O'Brien's sharp and disillusioned eye picks up the contrast between the natural beauty of the land and what she calls the "intellectual morass." Readers and critics agree that *Mother Ireland* is not only an exile's autobiographical essay on the land to which she inevitably returns but also one of O'Brien's best pieces.

Johnny I Hardly Knew You, a novel published in 1977, does not enjoy the same reputation. O'Brien creates a first-person narrator who explains, on the day before her trial begins, why she has smothered her son's young friend, with whom she was involved in an affair. As Nora attempts to sort things out, the men in her life—her son, father, husband, lovers—blend into one another to become the male demon who must be slain by the wronged female. Mad Nora wants us to believe that the killing is not a crime, but an aberration caused by men, "the stampeders of our dreams." Obvious Freudian overtones, including Nora's prophetic nightmares and the suggestion that the "terrors that rise up from below . . . will have to be met," carry the narrative along. Like *The Country Girls*, *Johnny I Hardly Knew You* was written in three weeks, but most critics agree that it lacks the originality of the first novel, borders on melodrama, and presents a woman with whom we cannot sympathize. Anatole Broyard, who praises many of O'Brien's other novels, sums up: "I hardly knew him either and I see no reason to regret his demise."

Mrs. Reinhardt and Other Stories, a collection published in 1978, has been enthusiastically received. Benedict Kiely rates these as some of O'Brien's best stories, and Patricia Highsmith, in the *Times Literary Supplement*, nominated the collection as one of the best books to appear in that year. Although the settings vary and the characters come from different classes and backgrounds, these stories like those in her earlier collections highlight frustrated heroines such as Miss Hawkins, the lonely fifty-five-year-old woman who takes up with a twenty-one-year-old transient male, or Hilda, one of "The Small Town Lovers" who ends up as the latest "casualty of peace." But O'Brien's other heroines in *Mrs. Reinhardt* do not as readily succumb; sometimes they show a tendency to resist temptation. In "Ways," for example, Nell, attracted to Jane's husband, retreats out of respect for the rights of her friend. Some of these women discover a qualified kind of peace: Mrs. Reinhardt, jilted by her husband, is reunited with him at the end of the story, "at least for the duration of a windy night." After that? "And by morning who knows? Who knows anything anyhow." In "Clara," O'Brien creates a unique male narrator, but some readers, used to the familiar O'Brien female voice, might echo Victoria Glendinning's judgment: "I never believed in him for a moment."

Mrs. Reinhardt and Other Stories demonstrates a slight shift in the direction of O'Brien's fiction. In his review in the *Times Literary Supplement*, Frank Tuohy notes that "a certain decorousness" seems to have set in which is attributable perhaps to the "chastening influence of the editors of the *New Yorker*." As important as this decorousness, however, could be the peace that a few of the heroines temporarily achieve, especially in relation to men. Edna O'Brien's greatest achievement, her delineation of a female psyche, has also created a limitation: her male characters are often one-dimensional figures who serve as little more than backdrops for her heroines' loneliness, frustration, and disappointment. Hints, as far back as Mary Hooligan in *Night*, suggest that O'Brien wants her women not only to survive, but also to grow, to be independent and even—perhaps—content. A few of the women in *Mrs. Reinhardt* are.

In *Returning* (1982), a collection of stories (several of which had been published in the *New Yorker*), O'Brien again focuses exclusively on the Irish village life dramatized in her earliest fiction. The stories are filtered through an enlightened narrator (all but one is told in the first person) whose memories of her childhood in Ireland reveal the inescapable links to a past she cannot shake. These stories recreate the characters and terrain of the country girls trilogy and recall the narration of memories in *A Pagan Place* and *Night*. The idiosyncracies of village life—the town "dummies" and "maddies," the young girl craving love from an absent mother ("My Mother's Mother") or a favorite nun ("Sister Imelda"), and the frustrated women flirting with the town bachelors or the parish curate—are rendered in that typical O'Brien style which captures the essence of village life in the seemingly insignificant details of daily struggles.

The central theme of returning is carried through all of the stories, not only by narrators reminiscing about childhood experiences, but also by characters like Mabel in "Savages" who went off to Australia and saved for ten years to return to Ireland, only to realize that her coming back has been a mistake. The women who stay are frustrated, sometimes unstable and isolated, but the exiles are often no better off. As the narrator of "The Doll" explains, she has deserted the village for the city, but she now finds herself dangling between two worlds: "I am far from those I am with, and far from those I have left."

Death is a recurring theme in this collection. O'Brien counterpoises Irish burial rituals with the irony of characters who avoid a real confrontation with death because, as the girl in "My Mother's Mother" says, death was "some weird journey you made alone and unbefriended." The narrator of "Ghosts," one of the best stories in the collection, suggests, however, that the dead are preserved in memory. After describing three women from her past life, she finally realizes: "I still can't imagine any of them dead. They live on; they are fixed in that far off region called childhood where nothing ever dies, not even oneself." The interplay between two selves, with the limited perspective of the younger child who often knows something is wrong but does not quite understand what is happening, contrasted with the enlightened perspective of the older narrator, contributes to the success of several of these stories. The ambiguity of these narrators' attitudes toward their memories, some obviously based on O'Brien's own experiences, suggests the relevance of a passage from *Mother Ireland*: "It is true that a country encapsulates our childhood and those lanes, byres, fields, flowers, insects, suns, moons and stars are forever re-occurring and tantalizing me with a possibility of a golden key which would lead beyond birth to the roots of one's lineage. Irish? In truth I would not want to be anything else. It is a state of mind as well as an actual country." As *Returning* demonstrates, that "state of mind" continues to provide material for O'Brien's fiction.

Even Edna O'Brien's strongest supporters admit that she does not always write well, that some of her fiction is "trite" and "second rate." Although she has moved stylistically in twenty years from what Grace Eckley calls the "simple barren naiveté" of *The Country Girls*, through the heightened lyricism of *Night* and *Johnny I Hardly Knew You*, to the sophisticated, realistic narrators of her recent stories, she has always had a unique talent for exposing the minute and telling detail, for capturing the nuances of everyday life. The authenticity of her female voices makes Edna O'Brien a novelist to be reckoned with.

Plays:
A Cheap Bunch of Nice Flowers, London, New Arts Theatre, 20 November 1962;
A Pagan Place, London, Royal Court Theatre, 2

November 1972;

Virginia, Stratford, Ontario, Stratford Shakespeare Festival, July 1980.

Screenplays:

Girl with Green Eyes, adapted from O'Brien's *The Lonely Girl*, Woodfall Production, 1964;

Time Lost and Time Remembered, by O'Brien and Desmond Davis, adapted from O'Brien's short story "A Woman at the Seaside," Rank, 1966;

Three into Two Won't Go, adapted from the novel by Andrea Newman, Universal, 1969;

X Y and Zee, adapted from *Zee & Co.*, Columbia, 1971.

Other:

A Cheap Bunch of Nice Flowers, in *Plays of the Year*, volume 26, edited by J. C. Trewin (New York: Ungar, 1963);

Some Irish Loving: A Selection, edited by O'Brien (London: Weidenfeld & Nicolson, 1979; New York: Harper & Row, 1979).

Periodical Publications:

"Dear Mr. Joyce," *Audience*, 1 (July-August 1971): 75-77;

"Joyce & Nora," *Harper's*, 261 (September 1980): 60-64.

Interviews:

David Heycock, "Edna O'Brien Talks to David Heycock About Her New Novel *A Pagan Place*," *Listener*, 83 (7 May 1970): 616-617;

Joseph McCulloch, "Dialogue with Edna O'Brien," *Under Bow Bells: Dialogues with Joseph McCulloch* (London: Sheldon Press, 1974), pp. 23-29;

Ludovic Kennedy, "Three Loves of Childhood, Irish Thoughts by Edna O'Brien," *Listener*, 95 (3 June 1976): 701-702.

References:

Susan Heller Anderson, "Writing, A Kind of Illness for Edna O'Brien," *New York Times*, 11 October 1977, p. 33;

Barbara Bannon, "Authors and Editors," *Publishers Weekly*, 197 (25 May 1970): 21-22;

Nell Dunn, ed., *Talking to Women* (London: MacGibbon & Kee, 1965), pp. 69-107;

Grace Eckley, *Edna O'Brien* (Lewisburg, Pa.: Bucknell University Press, 1964);

Sean McMahon, "A Sex by Themselves: An Interim Report on the Novels of Edna O'Brien," *Eire-Ireland*, 2 (Spring 1977): 79-87;

Lotus Snow, " 'That Trenchant Childhood Route': Quest in Edna O'Brien's Novels," *Eire-Ireland*, 14 (Spring 1979): 74-83.

Julia O'Faolain
(6 June 1932-   )

Mary Rose Callaghan

BOOKS: *We Might See Sights! and Other Stories* (London: Faber, 1968);

Godded and Codded (London: Faber & Faber, 1970); republished as *Three Lovers* (New York: Coward, McCann & Geoghegan, 1971);

Man in the Cellar (London: Faber & Faber, 1974);

Women in the Wall (London: Faber & Faber, 1975; New York: Viking, 1975);

Melancholy Baby and Other Stories (Dublin: Poolbeg, 1978);

No Country for Young Men (London: Lane, 1980);

The Obedient Wife (London: Lane, 1982).

Julia O'Faolain, novelist and short story writer, is considered one of the most accomplished Irish writers of her generation and one of the few

with a truly international background. While she is at her best in some darkly comic short stories concerned with the position of women, she cannot be categorized merely as a satirist. Her novels range from the burlesque adventures of a young girl in Paris to a brilliant evocation of sixth-century Gaul to the latest, the story of three generations of an Irish political family.

The daughter of writers Sean O'Faolain and Eileen Gould, she was born in London in 1932 and educated in Dublin by the Sacred Heart nuns. After taking a B.A. and an M.A. at University College, Dublin, she continued her education at the Universita di Roma and the Sorbonne, University of Paris. In Italy she met and married Lauro Martines, an American Renaissance historian. They have one

Julia O'Faolain

son and now commute between London and Los Angeles. Julia O'Faolain has worked as a teacher of languages, an interpreter, and a translator.

An Italian government scholarship first enabled her to study in Italy. After her conventional Irish Catholic upbringing, life in Italy was a great change. "Perugia," she says, "was full of landowners' sons. They would have you believe they were like something out of *The Leopard*. Yet, since they were all doing agricultural degrees, they were probably only gamekeepers! Anyway it was a big change from home where men never looked at you." Her first collection of short stories, *We Might See the Sights! and Other Stories* (1968), is divided into Irish stories and Italian stories and reflects her youth in both countries. The biting sardonic tone of the former hits hard at sexual hypocrisies and sexual repressions. Still one shudders to think there are really children like Madge, the heroine of the title story, who believes sex is the crime of the dirty English, and who satisfies her own sexual curiosity and boredom by trying to stimulate and then by beating a retarded child. "First Conjugation" is an excellent study of teenage infatuation in which an introverted adolescent, in love with her female Italian teacher, gets a coldblooded revenge for wounds

inflicted in the classroom. Aunt Adie of "Melancholy Baby" is even more unpleasant. Frantically jealous of her orphan niece's love affair, she is consoled only when the girl contracts a fatal disease. "A Pot of Soothing Herbs" catches bohemian Dublin life in the 1950s. A romantic and reluctant virgin after a night on the town ends up sleeping in a bed with two men, but a bolster divides them and she survives unravished to return to screaming puritanical parents. The delightful captain of "Her Trademark" is a departure into uncharacteristic compassion. A lonely little man, bereft by his mother's death (and probably homosexual), escorts three spinster sisters to Lourdes in search of husbands; he ends up marrying one himself, although the marriage will remain unconsummated. "The Chronic" is a brilliantly funny and recognizable study of another Irish mother-obsessed male, this time a medical student, P. J. Phennessy.

The Italian stories are milder in tone and less concerned with sexual attitudes. Perhaps the best, "That Bastard Berto," shows that the things which intimidated us as children may still continue to do so, and the revengeful hero can finally only offer money to the nun who tormented him as a child. "Dies Irae" points sadly and comically to old age and the way of all flesh, while "Mrs. Rossi" portrays a lonely Italian immigrant woman who is finally hardened by life.

This collection established Julia O'Faolain as an important new voice in Irish fiction. Val Warner found the Italian stories "superior, perhaps because the author finds it easier to distance their material." Roger Garfitt wrote: "Sean O'Faolain and Mary Lavin have both set stories in Italy: Julia O'Faolain has been able to write as it were from inside Italian life." However, the Irish stories have an authenticity to their time and place, Dublin of the 1950s, which makes them classics of a sort—so much so that in 1978 they were republished along with stories from her second collection in *Melancholy Baby and Other Stories*.

O'Faolain's first novel, *Godded and Codded* (1970), is set in Paris. Published in the United States as *Three Lovers*, it is a burlesque account of a young girl's sexual adventures. Indeed, almost the entire action is spent boringly in various beds, and the main character, Sally, is rather shallowly and unconvincingly portrayed. When, for instance, an affair ends in a gruesome abortion, she feels no guilt, a response which does not ring true since Sally is fresh from Catholic Ireland. Her appalling parents are dismissed rather callously by O'Faolain, but they, at least, deserve dismissal for their smugly

Dust jacket for O'Faolain's first novel, a burlesque of a young girl's sexual adventures

religious beliefs. Characters like Sally's pious father undoubtedly still exist, but he is portrayed too broadly to engage the sympathy of the reader. The other characters, with the exception of an old man and an aging mistress, are not particularly memorable. This first novel, which was withdrawn because of a threatened libel suit, has since had mixed criticism. Val Warner found it "déjà vu" and thought the most interesting parts centered on the underground activities of a group of Algerian students in Paris shortly before independence. However J. R. Franks thought Julia O'Faolain would soon be the family member whose name would be used for identification, and Sally Beauman thought she wrote in a style more "pointed than that of her father, and with a cold female eye for the egocentricities of masculine behaviour."

The title story of her next collection, *Man in the Cellar* (1974), is set in Italy. Una, a brutalized wife,

locks her husband in the cellar to get revenge for his beatings but also to demonstrate that she is a person. In this story Julia O'Faolain is at her best and most blackly comic. She inquires into the unequal battle of the sexes and the nature of marriage, leaving us in no doubt as to who the real victim is. "I want Us to Be in Love" is a comic account of an old man's attempt to seduce a young woman. He dies in the attempt, but the unmolested girl now has some sobering realizations about imperfect love. The tender and funny "A Travelled Man" shows an Italian academic in America becoming embroiled in the marital squabbles of his benefactors. In "The Knight" a celibate layman member of an Irish religious society runs down an Englishman who is having an affair with his wife. The story depicts the chauvinism of a smug race and, although described as "gloriously funny" by the publisher, is decidedly sour and gruesome. "It's a Long Way to Tipperary" is another Irish story, full of rain and madness, in which the wife of a displaced Roman Catholic in the British army is converted and goes mad. With the publication of this collection, Julia O'Faolain's reputation was confirmed. John Mellors compared her to Angus Wilson, saying, "Julia O'Faolain has a knack of shattering the reader's complacency, and yet her stories, however ruthless and revealing, are written with wit, elegance and humour."

Her concern for the position of women led her to coedit with her husband, Lauro Martines, *Not in God's Image* (1973), a fascinating documentary history of women from Greek to Victorian times. The book, regarded very highly by feminist and other scholars, has recently been republished by Virago, a London feminist press. Still a committed feminist, O'Faolain says "Women originally invented that shrinking violet thing to attract the protector. Now we've got to protect ourselves instead. Ideally both sexes will end up equally thorny and horny-handed, but meanwhile we have to grow our prickles and thorns. Of course, there's a particularly maddening kind of woman around nowadays who tries to have it both ways. I haven't a daughter as it happens, but if I had, I'd go on fighting the fight through her."

Her interest in the position of women in history led her to write *Women in the Wall* (1975). This novel is a departure from her previous work: it is a brilliant evocation of sixth-century Gaul, reconstructed from original manuscripts. Radegunda, the child bride of Clotair and a spoil of war, is dragged over a dreary Dark Ages Europe until she breaks away from her husband and founds a convent. Agnes, a child of twelve and no mystic like

Radegunda, goes with her and becomes an abbess. Agnes later has a child by Fortunatus, a poet who eventually becomes a priest. The child, Ingunda, walls herself in to atone for her mother's sin, and her voice acts as a chorus throughout the novel. In her visions Radegunda experiences Christ as a lover, while Agnes comes to a kind of mysticism through her love of her child. Radegunda, wanting to establish the kingdom of God on earth, embroils the convent in the chaos of the outside world, but only leaves the way for Chrodechild, a more inhuman member of the religious order, to become abbess. Agnes and even Fortunatus, the fat and greedy cleric, act humanely in trying to save their child, while Radegunda dies and is presumably borne aloft. The novel is not so much a study of mysticism as a study of its failure to help humanity. O'Faolain is saying that we are human and that love can only be expressed in language that humans know. Structurally and thematically her most accomplished book, it has been very highly praised by the critics. Doris Grumbach in the *New Republic* wrote, "Its appearance on lists of the best of fiction this year is inevitable. . . . It absorbs the reader into a time when women were chattels, when 'inherited land followed the spear not the spindle'—into a time when the greatest conqueror was not of the flesh but of the spirit, when the full force of early Christianity made fanatics and saints of its believers."

O'Faolain's next novel, *No Country for Young Men* (1980), is set in modern day Dublin and tells the story of the O'Malley family through three generations, from the Irish civil war of the 1920s to today. The most sympathetic character is a young American who travels there to make a film about the past. He falls in love with a young married woman of the family and is tragically murdered as a result of his curiosity about a past secret. It is through great-aunt Judith, a displaced nun, that this secret is revealed. She is becoming senile but nevertheless is very memorable, if finally a little unbelievable, as a character. Although compelling, this novel is decidedly glum and sour in tone: it is nearly always damp, grey, and raining; characters are constantly described by their rotting teeth. The older members of the family live in a dead past which the very young are eager to embrace. O'Faolain, who has not lived in Ireland for over twenty years, indicates that the past matters enough to affect the present.

O'Faolain now divides her time between Los Angeles, where her husband teaches, and London, where they own a house. But despite her despair about Ireland, she misses it. "L.A. may be liberating

but it's not stimulating; there's no texture to people's minds. What I miss most of all about Ireland is the storytelling. You know how at home in Dublin there's the way people work up stories? There's the Card, the Character—the person who looks terrible ordinary on the outside but someone's aunt will tell you extraordinary stories about him that go on and on and on, you know? That's what I really miss about Dublin, and that, of course, is the preliminary homework that every writer has done for him. My mother Eileen was a prime example of that kind of storyteller—she used to feed Frank O'Connor stories as well as my father."

Strangely, Julia O'Faolain never writes from an American viewpoint: "That's something I'm just not interested in. Also it's a tricky transfer, Europeans writing about Americans, though special people like Paul Theroux can manage it the other way around." However, her latest novel, *The Obedient Wife* (1982), is set in California where Carla, the Italian heroine, has been left with her son by her overbearing husband, Marco. Advised by him to have an affair while he is away, Carla becomes involved with a priest called Leo. While Leo is the product of the new watered-down, trendy Catholicism, Carla represents a highly civilized and secular code. The best scenes in the novel are between these two lovers. The relationship eventually fails, however, not because Carla, who has been brought up on Boccaccio, feels guilty, but because lust as an abstraction holds little attraction for her. An Edna O'Brien heroine would probably have been destroyed by such a passion, but O'Faolain's women look at life more coldly and realistically. This novel has been better received than *No Country for Young Men*. Patricia Craig wrote: "*The Obedient Wife* is an exceptionally polished work; if its ending disappoints feminists, who require gestures of social rebelliousness from their fiction, just as Catholic readers used to require wholesomeness from theirs, it is none the less appropriate, in that it represents an assertion of the values its heroine has lived by."

O'Faolain admits that her father was a great influence on her life and mockingly describes herself as a "Daddy's girl." Her fiction, however, does have its own distinct and important voice. If some of her fiction about Ireland hits too hard in depicting a cruel, grubbing, nasty, and sexually repressed race, her style is always a joy and there is a compassion and mature humor in some of her later work. As Roger Garfitt says: "There is a power of mind behind her work, as well as an irreverently perceptive eye, that catches the intensity of human drives, the essential seriousness of the effort to live, without swallowing any of the trends in self deception. She is an acute observer, who is involved at a level of concern deeper than the substance or sum of her observations."

Other:

Two Memoirs of Florence: The Diaries of Buonaecorso Pitti and Gregorio Dati, edited by Gene Brucker and translated by O'Faolain, as Julia Martines (New York: Harper & Row, 1967);

Piera Chiara, *A Man of Parts*, translated by O'Faolain, as Julia Martines (Boston: Little, Brown, 1968; London: Barrie & Rockliff, 1969);

Not in God's Image, edited by O'Faolain and Lauro Martines (New York: Harper & Row, 1973; London: Temple Smith, 1973).

Periodical Publications:

FICTION:

"No Gentleman Callers in Paris," *Vogue* (1 September 1956): 148;

"Love in the Marble Foot," *New Yorker* (27 April 1957): 99-102;

"Pray for Grace, Poor Little Sinner," *Saturday Evening Post* (25 February 1967): 78-80;

"Political Animal," *Saturday Evening Post*, 241 (7 September 1968): 60-65;

"Lots of Ghastlies," *Mademoiselle*, 68 (April 1969): 245;

"Death Duties," *Kenyon Review* (Spring 1969): 321-335.

NONFICTION:

"A Scandalous Woman and Other Stories," *New York Times Book Review* (22 September 1974);

"Getting Away with Murder," *New York Times Book Review* (20 March 1977): 6;

"Small Town Snobbery in Canada," *New York Times Book Review* (16 September 1979).

Interview:

Elgy Gillespie, "No Country for Young Women," *Irish Times* (23 March 1979).

References:

Sally Beauman, "Fiction: Three Lovers," *New York Times Book Review* (9 May 1971): 38;

Simon Blow, "Cocktail Days," *New Statesman* (6 June 1980): 854, 856;

Patricia Craig, "Playing Fast and Loose," *Times Literary Supplement*, (23 July 1982): 807;

Craig, "Those Dying Generations," *Times Literary Supplement* (13 June 1980): 674;

Doris Grumbach, "Conquerors and Saints," *New Republic* (10 May 1975): 22;

Maurice Harmon, "Generations Apart: 1925-1975," in *The Irish Novel in Our Times*, edited by Patrick Rafroidi and Maurice Harmon (Publications de Lille II, 1976), pp. 61-63;

Alfred Kazin, "Fiction as a Social Gathering," *Saturday Review* (3 July 1971): 19-22;

Hermione Lee, "Most Distressful Country," *Observer* (1 June 1980): 28;

John Mellors, "Animality and Turtledom," *London Magazine* (August-September 1975): 111-114.

James Plunkett

(21 May 1920-   )

Gordon Henderson

BOOKS: *The Eagles and the Trumpets, and Other Stories* (Dublin: Bell Publications, 1954); expanded as *The Trusting and the Maimed, and Other Irish Stories* (New York: Devin-Adair, 1955; London: Hutchinson, 1959);

Big Jim: A Play for Radio (Dublin: Martin O'Donnell, 1955);

Strumpet City (London: Hutchinson, 1969; New York: Delacorte Press, 1969);

The Gems She Wore: A Book of Irish Places (London:

Hutchinson, 1972; New York: Holt, Rinehart & Winston, 1973);

Collected Short Stories (Dublin: Poolbeg Press, 1977);

Farewell Companions (London: Hutchinson, 1977; New York: Coward, McCann & Geoghegan, 1977);

The Risen People (Dublin: Irish Writers' Co-operative, 1978).

James Plunkett's reputation as a novelist was

established almost overnight with the publication in 1969 of *Strumpet City*, a sprawling panorama of Dublin life during the years of labor unrest before World War I. The book was the most popular work of fiction to appear in Ireland in years and soon became an international best-seller with translations into German, Dutch, Spanish, Flemish, Swedish, Russian, and Japanese. Already respected as a playwright and writer of short stories that had been appearing since the early 1940s in Irish periodicals, anthologies, and his own collected editions, Plunkett became recognized with the publication of his first novel as one of Ireland's most important literary figures.

He was born James Plunkett Kelly on the seacoast in Dublin, midway between the respectable suburbs of Sandymount and the pawnshops, public houses, and tenements of Ringsend. His parents were Patrick and Cecilia Cannon Kelly. His boyhood, particularly the time he spent among the dockers, boatmen, carters, and union organizers on the Ringsend waterfront, exerted a strong influence on his writing. He has said that "nothing much happens to a writer after the age of twenty or so that will affect his work; the small store of material which

informs the imagination for the rest of life is made up of the remembered experiences of childhood and youth." His own childhood was, for the most part, a happy one. The Kelly family was working-class, but his father, whom he admired and respected, had a good job as a chauffeur in charge of a fleet of company cars, and the family's homelife was comfortable. As a boy Plunkett found Dublin "a good city to grow up in. The sea was at its feet, its Georgian buildings gave it nobility, its squares and its expanses of water made it a place of openness and light and air."

He found little of this openness, however, at school, where the curriculum reflected the unenlightened social and religious values that permeated Irish life during the 1920s and 1930s. Newly emerged from its fight for independence from Great Britain, the young Irish Free State organized itself around a rigid set of "isms": nationalism, patriotism, isolationism, Gaelicism, and puritanism. "When Revolutionaries attain power," Plunkett wrote, "the last thing they want is any continuation of war's irresponsibility. In their need to create a new respectability and conformity they over-react. All this is understandable but it can be hard to live with." Many of Plunkett's teachers had fought in the war of independence and the civil war that followed. In their teaching they stressed "religious authoritarianism, prudery and a false mode of patriotic expression which sentimentalised history and its symbols out of all truth," he wrote. "Though tender of age and too docile to say so, we were all realists enough to know that this was all bloody nonsense." Religion played a large part in education. At the Christian Brothers School that Plunkett attended in Synge Street, the teachers indoctrinated their students in a Jansenistic brand of Catholicism that "kept our young minds focussed on our essential depravity," he said. "We were experts on Sin: original sin, venial sin, mortal sin, sins of omission and commission, occasions of sin. . . . We were all little anatomists, trained to subject sin and its by-products to endless analysis."

Plunkett found little of this congenial, "especially as the image of Ireland they were giving us bore no relationship to the world most of us were doing our best to grow up in." He left school at seventeen and took a job as a clerk in the gas company, where he remained for seven years. In the meantime he continued to take lessons on the viola and the violin—which he had begun studying at eight—at the Dublin College of Music and the Municipal College of Music, and he played professionally for various musical associations in Dublin.

Soon after leaving school he joined a trade union, "listened with the rest of the Sunday crowd to men who shouted outside the City Hall and Foster Place," and began composing "deplorable little verses" on socialist themes, which he contributed to the satirical magazine *Passing Variety* and other publications. Among the most popular of the street-corner orators he listened to was Jim Larkin, the fiery labor organizer who had unified Dublin's unions during the "Great Lockout" of 1913. Plunkett became increasingly involved in union affairs and in 1946 took a position as branch and staff secretary in the Workers' Union of Ireland, working under Larkin until the labor leader's death in 1947. Larkin became a close friend and would figure in much of Plunkett's later literary work.

When he was still in his early twenties, Plunkett began contributing articles and short stories to such publications as the *Bell*, the *Irish Bookman*, and *Irish Writing*. He took James Plunkett as his pen name, he said, because there were already "so many James Kellys, Seamus O'Kellys, Seamas Kellys and a whole list of them" that using Plunkett was the only way he could make "a distinction between who was what." The *Bell* (and the writers associated with it) strongly influenced his development as a writer. Founded in 1940 by Sean O'Faolain after the outbreak of World War II cut off markets abroad for Irish writers, the *Bell* was Ireland's best and most controversial literary magazine. Its contributors included such prominent writers as Patrick Kavanagh, Flann O'Brien, Lennox Robinson, Peadar O'Donnell, Frank O'Connor, and Elizabeth Bowen. O'Faolain helped Plunkett to come to terms with the religious and political authoritarianism that had troubled him as a teenager. "O'Faolain's polemical writings, such as his book about Daniel O'Connell, *King of the Beggars*, and his editorials in the *Bell*, showed us an Ireland that was not puritanical or obscurantist as had been previously suggested," he said. "One began to see that even the Gaelic League and their publicists were suppressing and distorting the real truth about traditional Irish life, which was rowdy and rejoicing and life-loving."

As an editor O'Faolain helped Plunkett to revise his stories and gave him practical advice on fiction writing. When he sent his early stories to the *Bell*, Plunkett said, O'Faolain "would write back and say not to call a 'meal' a 'repast' and to cut it down and speak plainly and if you didn't have anything to say not to say it." From Frank O'Connor, a frequent contributor to the *Bell*, Plunkett said he learned "something about what it is" to be Irish and how to infuse his stories with "the sense of place and the

sense of identity." The *Bell* published some two dozen of Plunkett's stories and articles between 1942 and 1954, when it ceased publication. Peadar O'Donnell, who succeeded O'Faolain as editor, published Plunkett's first collection of short stories, *The Eagles and the Trumpets* as the *Bell*'s August 1954 edition. It was the only time the magazine devoted an entire issue to the work of a single writer.

The following year the American publishers Devin-Adair brought out *The Trusting and the Maimed, and Other Irish Stories* (1955), an expanded version of the *Bell* edition, containing ten stories. The book, which a recent critic has described as "one of the best volumes to have come out of Ireland," is an impressive collection. At least four of the stories ("The Eagles and the Trumpets," "Mercy," "The Damned," "A Walk Through the Summer") rank among the finest in modern Irish fiction. Several involve young clerks, their lives alternating between the drudgery of the office and the boozy camaraderie of the public house. Some of the best deal with the very young and the very old: the hurt pride of a young boy forced to wear hand-me-down boots to school; a second boy's anguished attempt to reconcile the behavior of his dead father with the Church's stern teachings on sin; a slum girl's desperate efforts to obtain a loaf of bread; the stream-of-consciousness musings of a cracked World War I veteran; and the lonely death of another veteran, still guilt-ridden over having killed a British comrade years before. As in many of O'Faolain's stories of the same period, the pervading view of Irish life is pessimistic, a quality that several American reviewers singled out for special comment. While describing Plunkett as a writer of "considerable talent," the writer in the *New York Herald Tribune Book Review* called his Ireland "too bad to be true," noting that "its men and women are ground down by poverty, indifference and drink; in Dublin there is no romance; in the country towns no tranquility." *The New York Times* reviewer similarly cited its mood of "defeat and resignation" but praised Plunkett for "sincere, honest, reservedly compassionate writing, rising at times in its knowledge to moments of open beauty." Plunkett was the only young writer that Frank O'Connor included in the anthology *Modern Irish Short Stories* he edited in 1957 for Oxford University Press's "World's Classics" series. His is probably the soundest evaluation of Plunkett's early stories and his contribution to the genre: "There is a new firmness and harshness in the work of James Plunkett which is obviously very deeply influenced by that of James Joyce. Though he has still not solved for himself Joyce's problem of reconciling verisimilitude with artistic form, and though he spoils some of his best stories with forced symbolic contrivances, he is obviously a story-teller of high seriousness."

In the same year that *The Trusting and the Maimed* was published, Plunkett became a victim of the sort of ecclesiastical interference in public affairs that O'Faolain had spoken out against so frequently in the *Bell*. At the invitation of the Soviet secretary of the arts, he visited Russia in January 1955 with several other Irish writers and artists. On their return the delegation met with a barrage of criticism in the Catholic press, most notably in the staunchly anti-Communist *Catholic Standard* which demanded Plunkett's removal from the staff of the Workers' Union of Ireland. The press rallied the support of politicians, and soon, Plunkett said, "the county councils were passing all sorts of resolutions condemning us for going to this godless, atheistic country." Despite continued attacks by the clergy, the union stood behind Plunkett and refused to dismiss him.

In the meantime he had begun writing plays for radio. "Dublin Fusilier" was broadcast by Radio Eireann (Irish Radio) in March 1952, followed by "Mercy" (June 1953), "Homecoming" (April 1954), and "Big Jim" (October 1954). The latter play, celebrating Jim Larkin's leadership in the 1913 lockout, is an early forerunner of *Strumpet City* and introduces several characters who reappear in the novel. In August 1955 Radio Eireann invited Plunkett to join its staff as assistant head of drama, a position he held until 1961. His radio play "Farewell, Harper" was broadcast in December 1956. He followed this with an adaptation of his Larkin script for the stage. It was produced as *The Risen People* at the Abbey Theatre in Dublin in September 1958 and subsequently at Unity Theatre in London, where Sean O'Casey contributed an introduction to the program notes, and at the Lyric Theatre in Belfast. The play proved immensely popular and has been revived several times over the past twenty-five years. Its success also led to Plunkett's writing *Strumpet City*. "My publishers [Hutchinson] came over to see *The Risen People* and asked if I would do a novel on James Connelly," he said. "Well, I wasn't particularly interested in that. He was a great man, but I don't warm to him and you need some admiration for that kind of work. I told them I would do a novel on the same period as the play. . . . So I wrote *Strumpet City* about Dublin City and the heroism of the people during the [period that created the] mythology of the Irish working people: 1913. I wanted to put flesh on the

city and to show the city through them." The novel took nearly ten years to complete, with time out from writing after Plunkett joined the infant Telefis Eireann (Irish Television) as one of its first two producers. "When I started writing it in 1960," he said, "we were just starting out in television here. So I had to go off to B.B.C. for training. Even when we began, I didn't have a chance to lift my head for three or four years."

As its title suggests, the subject of *Strumpet City* (1969) is Dublin itself, with the novel's plot and characters contributing to the overall portrait of the city. While he was writing it Plunkett described his novel to a London *Times* reporter as "a picture of Dublin in the seven years, 1907 to 1914. Against the backcloth of social agitation, it is about the attitudes of various strata of society—from Dublin Castle and people of property down to the poor and the outcasts." Any book that takes Dublin as its subject invites inevitable comparison to the works of Joyce and O'Casey. Plunkett has acknowledged the superficial similarities but has noted a difference in scope: "Joyce wrote about the seedy clerk-type part of the city, the slightly respectable. O'Casey wrote about the down-and-outs. But I knew there were other elements too," he said. "There was the clerical crowd and the higher up crowd of company directors. In other words, there were more than just the seedy clerks and the down-and-outs, and more than just the priests and company directors. It was the whole intermingling of them all."

What makes this intermingling possible is Plunkett's use of the 1913 lockout—an event that profoundly affected the whole city—as his backdrop. Starting with a fairly trivial labor-management dispute at one company, events escalate into a general strike and then into a lockout that paralyzes the city for more than eight months. The lockout emerges as an ideological battle between capital and labor, with the municipal government and the Church siding with the Employers' Federation, and English labor and the Irish Citizen Army supporting the strikers. The employers' position is that they would not be justified in paying higher wages because the workers are "damaged material," whose value in the labor market has been reduced by their low energy level and low standard of living. Church and state concur. In the face of this sort of logic, Plunkett said, "Jim Larkin's great task was to create a new social conscience." With Larkin leading the workers, Dublin becomes "a world of picket lines, thundering speeches, convoys that moved under police protection, bitter outbreaks of street fighting that were followed by day after day of apathy and misery." Ultimately the Employers' Federation starves the workers into submission.

Although Plunkett is painstakingly accurate in his handling of historical details, he keeps history, and even Larkin, in the background and focuses on individual Dubliners whose lives are affected in one way or another by the lockout. At the top of the social scale are Mr. Bradshaw, the owner of a decaying row of tenements that eventually collapse, killing several of their occupants; Mrs. Bradshaw, who secretly helps a family made destitute by the strike; and Yearling, a wry, sophisticated, and compassionate company director who takes the side of the strikers. Representing the Catholic Church are Father Giffley, the pastor of a working-class parish who is driven first to alcoholism and finally into madness by the suffering he sees around him; and his young assistant, Father O'Connor, whose personal fastidiousness, social pretensions, and rigid adherence to the Church's Jansenistic teachings make him incapable of understanding or identifying with his parishioners. Father O'Connor serves as Plunkett's bridge between the upper-class world of Kingstown and the tenements of Chandlers Court.

As might be expected, most of the characters belong to the working-class world where the lockout's effects are the most telling: Fitz, a young foreman who loses his job when he refuses to carry out his employer's orders; his wife, Mary, who scrimps to furnish their small flat and then feeds the furnishings piece by piece into the fireplace after the lockout depletes the city's coal supply; Mulhall, a muscular teamster who leads the other workers in skirmishes with strikebreakers before he is jailed and later crippled in an industrial accident; and Hennessy, who is constantly in search of odd jobs to feed his enormous brood and alarmingly fertile wife. At the bottom of the social scale is Rashers Tierney, for whom "God never shut one door but He closed another." Rashers keeps himself alive, for a while at least, by hawking lapel ribbons during the celebration Dublin stages for the visiting King Edward, by serving as a walking billboard for a pawnbroker, and by playing a hurdy-gurdy he accidentally inherits from an Italian street musician. Rashers is the novel's most colorful and most memorable character. Plunkett's description of him is half an indictment of Dublin and half paean to it:

> She had not denied him her unique weapons. Almost from birth she had shaped his mind to regard life as a trivial moment which had slipped by mistake through the sieve of eternity, a scrap of absurdity which would glow for a little while before it was snatched back into eternity again. From her air, in common with numberless others about him, he had drawn the deep and unshakable belief that the Son of God loved him and had suffered on earth for him, and the hope that he would dwell with Jesus Christ and His Blessed Mother in Heaven. His city never offered him anything else. Except her ash-bins.

As the novel ends Father Giffley, another skillfully drawn character, stands on the shore of Dublin Bay and, after a whiskey-soaked internal monologue on God and the devil, decides "to commit something to the sea, a thing he had been fond of doing as a child. He found a pencil and tore a page from his pocket diary and scrawled: *'Time takes all away. This was written by a madman on the shores of a mad island.'* "

For all its descriptions of suffering, *Strumpet City* is a surprisingly optimistic testament to man's essential decency and indomitability. In its tone, its compassionate portrayal of the lower classes, and its use of social upheaval as a backdrop for individual struggles to attain dignity, the novel is reminiscent of *The Grapes of Wrath* (1939). John Steinbeck's famous metaphorical description of a turtle's attempt to cross a busy highway, in fact, is paralleled by a similar scene in *Strumpet City* in which a pigeon dodges a growing cascade of grain as it snatches kernels of wheat from a leaking sack on the Dublin docks. In his handling of the lockout and its hardships, Plunkett avoids both propaganda and sentimentality. As one critic aptly described his approach, "His method is appealingly plain and unsophisticated; his Ireland is given us truthfully and directly in honest, unvarnished storytelling . . . and he himself, though deeply committed, remains completely impersonal."

The novel was a commercial success. Despite its international popularity, however, it received mixed reviews. What troubled critics most is its conventionality of form. Several noted that in its structure and its careful rendering of the surface details of Dublin life, *Strumpet City* resembles a traditional nineteenth-century historical novel. Others complained that many of its characters lack depth or complexity. Even the most grudging of critics, however, conceded Plunkett's skill in recreating Dublin of the period; and the novel received its share of rave reviews. Novelist and short story writer Patrick Boyle, for example, called it "the finest work of fiction to come out of Ireland in nearly fifty years."

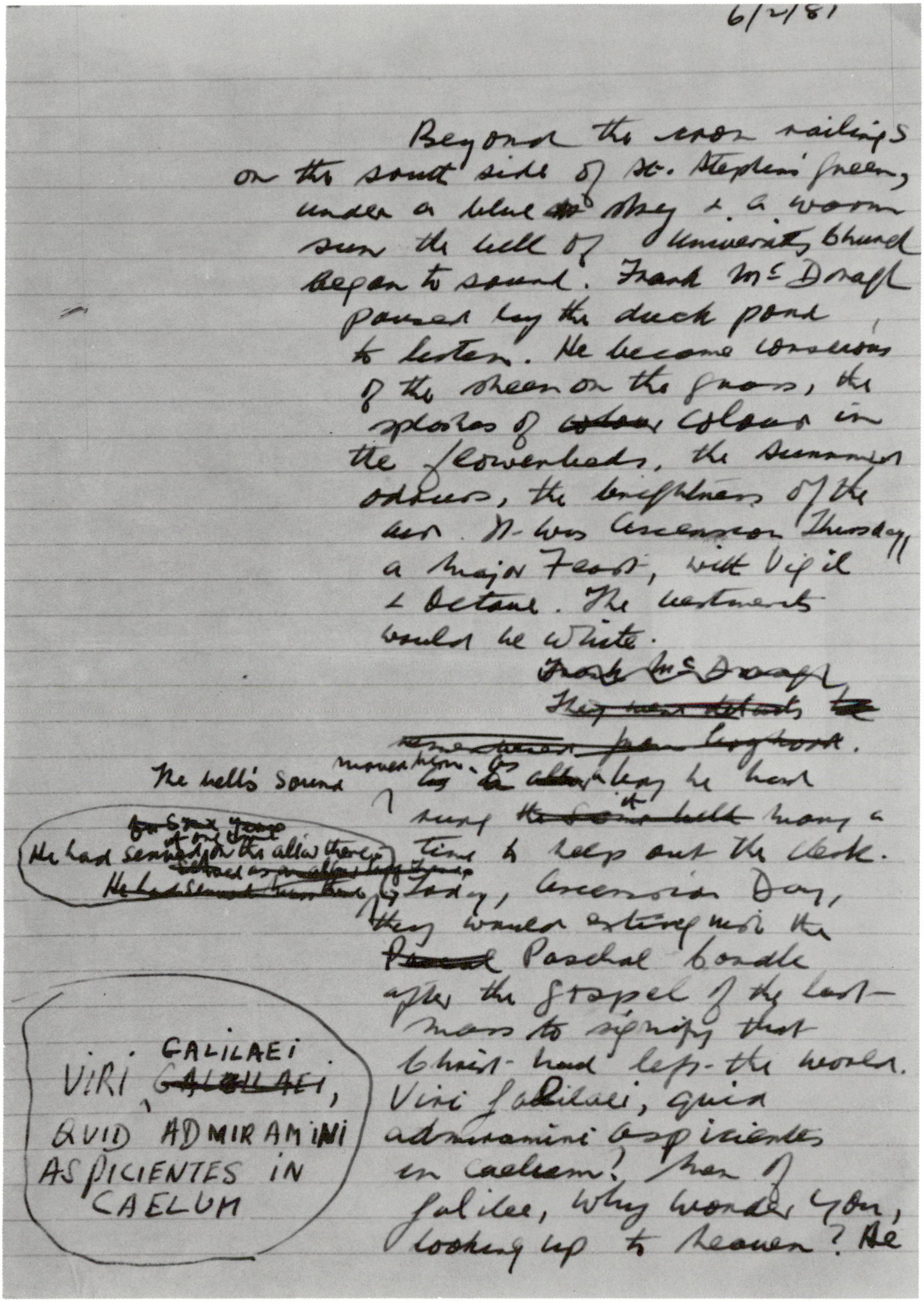

6/2/81

Beyond the iron railings on the south side of St. Stephen's Green, under a blue sky & a warm sun the bell of University Church began to sound. Frank McDonagh paused by the duck pond to listen. He became conscious of the sheen on the grass, the splashes of colour in the flowerbeds, the summer odours, the brightness of the air. It was Ascension Thursday, a Major Feast, with Vigil & Octave. The vestments would be White.

The bell's sound ... he had rung it many a time to help out the clerk. He had served on the altar there. Today, Ascension Day, they would extinguish the Paschal Candle after the Gospel of the last Mass to signify that Christ had left the world. Viri Galilaei, quid admiramini aspicientes in caelum? Men of Galilee, why wonder you, looking up to heaven? He

VIRI GALILAEI, QUID ADMIRAMINI ASPICIENTES IN CAELUM

Page from the manuscript for Plunkett's novel in progress

The *New York Times Book Review* critic said that "James Plunkett knows this world well, and about the Dublin masses he cannot put a comma wrong," adding that the novel's "epiphanies of moments of trust, devotion and loyalty can stand with Joyce's and its unhesitating accuracy of speech with O'Casey's." The book has been published in several editions and was recently adapted by playwright Hugh Leonard as a mini-series for Irish television with a cast that included Peter Ustinov and Peter O'Toole.

Plunkett followed *Strumpet City* with *The Gems She Wore* (1972), an engaging blend of travel, history, and autobiography. He enlivens his descriptions of Dublin, Galway, Sligo, and other Irish places with personal vignettes: the two-week cycling tour of Donegal he took as an eighteen-year-old; the stratagems of three-card-trick men he learned at Galway race meetings; a tour of Irish monasteries with Frank O'Connor, "who collected monasteries and their complicated history the way others collect stamps"; a journey by outboard motorboat with Peadar O'Donnell to the deserted island of Inishkeeragh, the setting of O'Donnell's 1928 novel *Islanders*; and a trip to the Dingle Peninsula with a BBC film crew. His account of this latter incident is typical of the book's style:

> We set out from Castletownbere by helicopter, filmed here and there for some hours and were, from my amateur grasp of navigational matters, firmly in the middle of nowhere when the pilot asked me if there was any place near in which we could get morning coffee. I looked down. There was a great lump of uninhabited mountain below, forbidding cliffs ahead and the rolling sea beyond. The most I knew about our whereabouts was that we were certainly not over the Phoenix Park, but being the only Irishman at hand I had to pretend to be knowledgeable. Seawards the nearest coffee shop would be in New York, so we headed inland.

At a remote public house where the pilot eventually gets his coffee, Plunkett's Dublin accent and a casual reference to local history catch the attention of one of the Irish-speaking patrons:

> "You're not foreign," he said.
> "I am not," I said.
> "Irish."
> "That's so."
> He looked more closely.
> "You have the look of a Dublin man?"
> "Now you have it."

> "A writer maybe?"
> "Correct."
> "James Plunkett?"
>   It was embarrassing. It was also, quite unexpectedly, deeply moving to be recognised in my own country so far away from my own small world.

Plunkett's warmth, humor, intelligence, and obvious affection for the older writers who helped him as a young man raise the book above the usual level of travel literature.

Plunkett's second novel, *Farewell Companions* (1977), also contains autobiographical elements. Like Plunkett, its central character, Tim McDonagh, was born in 1920, grows up on Upper Pembroke Street, and has a father who fought in World War I, worked as a chauffeur, and died when his son is in his teens. Also like Plunkett, Tim works as a clerk and hopes eventually to become a professional musician. Unlike Plunkett (who married Valerie Koblitz in September 1945 and has four children), Tim decides at the end of the novel to enter the priesthood. *Farewell Companions* is a sequel to *Strumpet City*, continuing Plunkett's portrait of Dublin into the mid-1940s. As with most sequels, it suffers by comparison with the novel that preceded it. In the early chapters Plunkett updates the lives of Hennessy, Fitz, and several other characters. As a result, sections of the book have a tacked-on quality. The novel also lacks the background of social unrest that gives *Strumpet City* much of its power and narrative momentum. Much of its action takes place during the 1930s and 1940s, a period when postrevolutionary Ireland settled into such smug complacency, petty political maneuvering, obsessive book banning, and middle-class nest feathering that Sean O'Faolain described the country as "a dreary Eden" and "a grocers' republic." The novel does rise to moments of excitement in flashbacks that recount the terror tactics of the Black and Tans, the opening days of the civil war, and various encounters between the Irish Republican Army and Free State troops.

Most of the novel, however, describes the boyhood, adolescence, and initiation into manhood of Tim and his two friends, Brian Moloney and Des Cunningham. The incidents that fill their lives are unspectacular, but Plunkett brings them skillfully, and often lyrically, to life: Tim's first confession and first communion, boyhood days at summer camp in Donegal, Saturday afternoon football matches, company picnics, and long rambles through the Wicklow Mountains. Aside from an occasional

German bombing raid, World War II barely touches neutral Ireland, but both Brian and Des enlist in the RAF, as much to escape the tedium of Irish life as for patriotic reasons. Among the novel's best scenes are those describing conversations between Brian's father, Cornelius Moloney, a pub keeper and small-time politician, and a character called O'Sheehan, a Celtic scholar who loses his memory in a civil war ambush and periodically lapses into believing he is Oisin, the mythical figure who returned to Ireland after hundreds of years in the Land of the Ever Young and became an old man when he fell from his horse. O'Sheehan's accounts of Ireland's heroic age contrast nicely with the general bleakness of Ireland's present. In both his characterization and his position as a man apparently forgotten by the bureaucracy that is paying him to compile a comprehensive dictionary of the Irish language, he recalls the characters of Flann O'Brien's surrealistically comic novels.

Farewell Companions was a best-seller in Ireland but was only moderately successful in British and American bookstores. Reviewers, however, were generally positive in their appraisals. The reviewer in *Harper's*, while questioning "the wisdom of putting so much talent and effort into such an intolerably dreary period in Irish history," praised Plunkett as "a graceful writer with an impeccable sense of structure and narrative." Nigel Williams in *New Statesman* called the novel "a splendid book, a long, intensely readable evocation of a country graduating from colonial rule to seedy independence."

The Irish Academy of Letters recognized Plunkett's achievements as a writer by electing him to membership in 1970, the year after *Strumpet City* was published. In 1977 his *Collected Short Stories* was published. The volume included six new stories in addition to those he had published in *The Trusting and the Maimed*. Four of these ("The Trout," "The Plain People," "The Boy on the Capstan," and "Ferris Moore and the Earwig") can stand with the best of his early work. His stories have continued to appear in various publications, and he said in a recent interview that he is working on a third novel. His best work to date, however, has been in the short story. Despite the popularity, historical sweep, and richly detailed descriptions of his two novels, they only occasionally match the powerfully focused evocation of Irish life of his best stories. Like O'Connor and O'Faolain, who also wrote novels, his reputation is most secure as a writer of superbly crafted short stories.

Play:
The Risen People, Dublin, Abbey Theatre, September 1958.

Television Scripts:
"The Life & Times of Jimmy O'Dea," Telefis Eireann, December 1964;
"Memory Harbor," Telefis Eireann, 1963;
"Portrait of a Poet," Telefis Eireann, June 1965;
"The Great O'Neill," Telefis Eireann, 1966;
"When Do You Die, Friend?," Telefis Eireann, March 1966;
"Inis Fail (Isle of Destiny)," Telefis Eireann, March 1971;
"The State of the Nation," Telefis Eireann, 1972.

Radio Scripts:
"Dublin Fusilier," Radio Eireann, March 1952;
"Homecoming," Radio Eireann, April 1954;
"Big Jim," Radio Eireann, October, 1954;
"Farewell, Harper," Radio Eireann, December 1956.

Interviews:
Eavan Boland, "Dublin's Advocate," *This Week*, 12 October 1972: 40-42;
Jim Hawkins, "A Visit with Jim Plunkett," *Ais-Eiri*, 3 (Spring 1981): 4-8.

References:
James M. Cahalan, "James Plunkett," in *Dictionary of Irish Literature*, Robert Hogan, editor (Westport, Conn.: Greenwood Press, 1979), pp. 554-560;
Cahalan, "The Making of *Strumpet City*: James Plunkett's Historical Vision," *Eire-Ireland*, 13 (Fall 1978): 81-100;
Godeleine Carpentier, "Dublin and the Drama of Larkinism: James Plunkett's *Strumpet City*," in *The Irish Novel in Our Time*, Patrick Rafroidi and Maurice Harmon, editors (Lille: Universite de Lille, 1976), pp. 209-219.

David Pownall
(19 May 1938-   )

Malcolm Page
Simon Fraser University

BOOKS: *The Raining Tree War* (London: Faber & Faber, 1974);

African Horse (London: Faber & Faber, 1975);

The Dream of Chief Crazy Horse (London: Faber & Faber, 1975);

My Organic Uncle (London: Faber & Faber, 1976);

God Perkins (London: Faber & Faber, 1977);

Another Country (Manchester: Peterloo, 1978);

Music to Murder By (London & Boston: Faber & Faber, 1978);

Light on a Honeycomb (London & Boston: Faber & Faber, 1978);

An Audience Called Edouard (London: Faber & Faber, 1979);

Motocar/Richard III, Part II (London & Boston: Faber & Faber, 1979);

Between Ribble and Lune: Scenes from the North West (London: Gollancz, 1980);

The Bunch from Bananas (London: Gollancz, 1980; New York: Macmillan, 1981);

Beloved Latitudes (London: Gollancz, 1981).

David Pownall's career as a novelist began in 1974. At the same time, he was becoming known as a prolific writer for fringe and provincial theater, as well as for radio, and he remains better known as a dramatist than as a novelist. Three of his novels, *The Raining Tree War* (1974), *African Horse* (1975), and *Beloved Latitudes* (1981), are set in Africa, where he lived for six years in the 1960s. *God Perkins* (1977) concerns a theater company. *Light on a Honeycomb* (1978), less well received than his other books, was puzzling to critics. Pownall's novels are short and quick moving, marked by farce, extravagance, and inventiveness. His true place among contemporary novelists is yet to be defined and secured, with *Beloved Latitudes* the most seriously intended work.

Pownall, the son of a docker, was born in Liverpool in 1938. He went to public school (Lord Wandsworth College, Hampton) on a scholarship for war orphans; he says that in his teens he could not reason his way through to the values of this more advantaged world. At Keele University he took an honors B.A. in English and history and then became a management trainee, later specializing in personnel work, at the Ford plant at Dagenham, Essex, from 1960 to 1963, just after the American takeover of the company. He comments, "I was very depressed about workers and even more about management." He wrote his first (unpublished) novel in this period: "I thought that was marvelous at the time. But later I looked through it and found bits of Conrad, James, Lawrence, you name him he was there. It was like a chorus line of English literature." He was married to Glenys Elsie Jones in 1961, had a son, and was divorced in 1971. Since 1973 he has lived with Mary Ellen Ray, an American actress; they have one son.

In 1963 Pownall took a job as personnel officer at an Anglo-American copper mine in Northern

Rhodesia until 1969, when the country had become independent (as Zambia). He was in charge of a labor force of 12,000 in a town of 65,000. "I went out like any family man in need of a job," he says. "I was no idealist, although I learnt what it was like to feel persecuted. . . . I was certainly sympathetic to Zambian independence, although the actual achievement of it was a nightmare." Africa changed him, Alex Hamilton writes in the *Guardian*, because "it was a confusing experience, shot through with brilliant flashes of illumination. He went to Africa one kind of person and came back another. He came back having shaken loose an exuberant comic talent." While in Africa, Pownall turned to theater after he incurred a serious injury while playing his favorite game, rugby. The copper companies had built some well-equipped theaters as part of an attempt to lure workers to isolated bush towns, and Pownall regretted that the plays performed were European. Soon he was writing short plays about the current situation in Zambia, and after a while he was writing so much that he felt he had to commit himself to writing, "ashamed of the featherbed" of a second occupation. Pownall's years in Africa, writes Hamilton, "changed him from an organisation man to a writer—a disorganisation man. Becoming a writer broke up his marriage: his wife's views of the lunacy of his aims were shared by everyone in that society."

After leaving his job, Pownall began a novel while sailing home to Britain. Paul Vallely in *Radio Times* reports, "Thirty thousand words flowed easily and he was rather pleased when he showed them to a friend and travelling companion. It took the man three days to pluck up the courage to tell Pownall that this was 'the most bloody boring book' he had ever read in his life." Back in England, Pownall worked in the northwest with Century Mobile Theatre, touring from a base at Keswick. In 1971 he settled at Lancaster, in Lancashire, working simultaneously as public relations officer and playwright-in-residence at the newly opened Duke's Playhouse. He also directed plays at Lancaster and had other plays presented in Manchester and at the Traverse Theatre, Edinburgh. Additionally, he wrote radio plays, finding radio "ideal for the quieter scrutiny of home situations, of fathers and sons and mothers in their intricate webs." His first fiction appeared in 1974.

In 1975 he formed a touring company, Paines Plough—named after the pub where the company's original meeting was held—based first in Lancaster and, from 1978, at Warwick University. Pownall's first plays for the company were shaped mainly as showcases for the talents of specific actors; particularly praised were *Music to Murder By* (1976), *Motocar* (1977), and *Richard III, Part II* (1977). Later successes were *An Audience Called Edouard* at the Greenwich Theatre, London, in 1978, and *Livingstone and Sechele* at the Traverse, Edinburgh, in the same year. Pownall's first play for BBC, *Return Fare*, was screened in 1978, and *Follow the River Down* came the next year. Pownall's fiction is thus only one part of a busy life that includes many other types of writing as well as involvement in the organization of two theater companies.

His first novel, *The Raining Tree War*, is set in Zonkendawo, a mythical country in central Africa, in the period immediately before and after independence. Pownall creates a large cast of blacks and whites, all grotesque and somewhat contemptible and mostly randy and drunken. They include Bwana Cat's Eyes, the Chinese agronomist who has failed to promote ping-pong among the Africans; Humphrey Fluellen, the Welsh actor who left Britain because television had put him out of work; Sergeant-Major Loudwater, who marches oddly because of his piles; the biologist Dennis, whose passion is to discover leaf-eating beetles and who is almost shot for desertion when he wanders off seeking more beetles; Desaix L'Ace, who runs an air-charter company with one plane, a 1914 German Focker found on a plantation in Tanganyika; and Tarzan Cool Guy (once called Sixpenny Cassava Root), a wrestler who always has to lose because he is fighting white South Africans in front of white audiences. After independence Tarzan is unemployed because South Africans are not allowed into the country. The story is about enrolling most of these characters, when drunk, into the Territorial Emergency Force, which marches north for an unsuccessful attack on the priestess Maud and the Muntu, suspected of being Chinese-backed separatists. Pownall's plots are not as important as his characters; he creates wild characters, then searches to find something for them to do. The extravagant style is often black farce, with the author showing a perhaps distasteful superiority to all his characters.

The Raining Tree War was highly praised. Godfrey Smith wrote in the *Observer*: "Pownall has done for emergent nationalism in his first novel what Joseph Heller did for war in *Catch-22*: he has rendered it somehow tolerable by making it ridiculous. . . . Nothing as funny has come my way out of Africa since *Black Mischief*." Susan Hill in the *Times* was equally impressed. "The writing is in parts quite brilliant, there are dozens of situations and styles, black humour and light humour, belly-laughs and

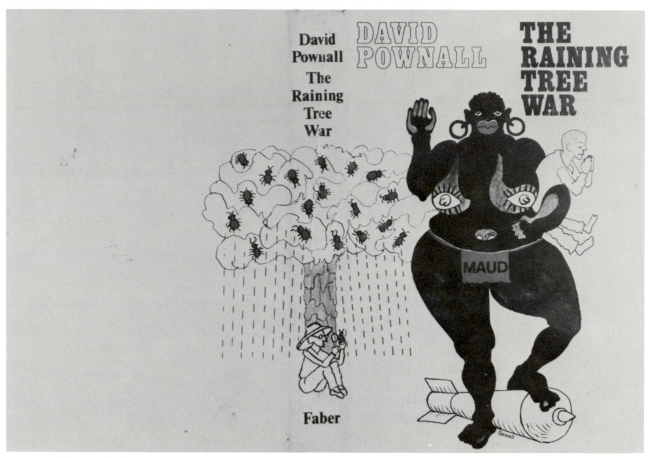

Dust jacket for Pownall's first novel, set in a mythical central African country at the time of its independence

smiles of appreciation at clever subtleties, but Mr. Pownall never loses his way, never makes a false move. . . . This is not a first novel of promise, it is a fully-fledged achievement."

African Horse is also set in Zonkendawo, with some of *The Raining Tree War*'s characters reappearing. The main figure is Hurl Halfcock, who comes from England to work as an industrial relations officer. He hopes that in Africa he can both find his animal-self and prove his Theory of the Three Races of Man: exploiters, exploited, and mystics-and-misfits. The first black he meets, the charcoal-burner Mushikishu, tells Hurl that he is "talking a load of shit about mankind." From then on, as Valentine Cunningham in the *Times Literary Supplement* puts it, "the black loons steadily refuse to be coons, refuse to be considered neatly as either the old exploited or the new exploiters." Hurl is tried for raping Phenomene, mistress of a government chief, though the Bucket-Wheel Excavator Gang, from *The Raining Tree War*, is responsible. This is only one of Hurl's many sexual, political, and al-

coholic adventures: he even has an identity crisis and believes he is a hippopotamus.

Lorna Sage in the *Observer* praises *African Horse* as "a gargantuan farce that can accommodate the real-life spectaculars being acted out there." Peter Ackroyd of the *Spectator* also saw it as a new view of contemporary Africa and "the only novel to bring this puzzling life into the light without pomposity or the slow, grinding tedium of 'serious' novels." In *Stand*, H. B. Mallalieu argued that Pownall makes us "believe that life is like this, larger and more eccentric than we think," adding that the style was "Swiftian in its sharpness." Ackroyd described the prose as marked by "astonishing and sustained inventiveness," with "some moments of subdued lyricism, sharp polemic and blunt description which would do credit to a different kind of novel altogether." Ackroyd claimed that *African Horse* was "close to the spirit of such narrative epics as *Tom Jones* and *Don Quixote*," concluding: "I have a feeling that Mr. Pownall has created a comic landscape which will supersede Blandings Castle, Ambrose

Silk, Lucky Jim and the rest of the old boys."

My Organic Uncle (1976), collecting seventeen short stories, followed. Four of the stories were previously published in *Nova* and four in the *London Magazine*. They range widely in place: Zambia again, but also the Mediterranean, Lancaster, the Liverpool docks, and a Cheshire country house. Several are farces, but Pownall also displays realistic and tragic approaches.

In the title story a dreary old man is trying to sell his organs to some medical institution. "A Place in the Country" pictures a young widow's attempt to avoid regressing to where she was before her marriage by moving from Liverpool to the country. "The Gift" describes how a huge Hereford bull is brought from Britain to serve the small cows of the Mtebe. "The Reluctant Ferryman" is an African superintendent of a cemetery who takes on the unpopular job of hearse driver. In "The Walls of Shimpundu" a black miner tries to understand the racism—the "walled city" of whiteness inside his head—of the dying white foreman, nicknamed Shimpundu. The only answer the miner can find is death itself: "Shimpundu's eyes held nothing but a wide clear plain as broad as Africa itself, and the walls of Shimpundu lay submerged beneath the flood of red, forgiving waters."

The story most admired by John Mellors of the *Listener*, "The Walls of Shimpundu" was "a serious and moving look at colour, class and comradeship." Nick Totten of the *Spectator* found in the book "a cumulative power: the power of a warm intelligence that brings together scraps of disparate experience into a surprisingly coherent fabric." Anthony Delius in the *Times Literary Supplement*, however, found that in the stories "the Africans tend to be, as servants, ministers or chiefs, rather more impressive figures than the whites around them, yet they are all different versions of the same person, all touched with the same childlike insouciance." Pownall's stories, wrote Delius, combine "the humdrum, the exotic, a touch of sickly sweetness with an unconvincing addition of the improbable. They start out with considerable zest and then limp home to something which seems to be excruciatingly contrived."

Pownall not surprisingly turned his wild, extravagant humor loose on an easy target, a theater company, in the novel *God Perkins* (1977). The small and struggling Dramacart theater company has a new play by its resident playwright, Ben McHugh, which causes unprecedented audience walkouts. The novel traces a Theatrefund investigation, turning mostly on McHugh's being insufficiently

working class to merit support and on his efforts to complete another play, *The Blinding Light*, which is to be built around St. Paul's sudden conversion on the road to Damascus. The spare Perkins generator the company has is to be used on stage as a contemporary counterpart to St. Paul's rearing horse, and the company's engineer sees his chance to be on stage, too, astride the Perkins. The usual Pownall farcical complications follow. Somebody's drunken brother is brought back from Canada to compose music for *The Blinding Light*; though he once wrote "The Ontario Power Line Pulsations," he turns out to be only an ex-composer. Some of the company want to perform *A Midsummer-Night's Dream* for a rich man's party on an island because he may become a useful patron, while others reject this idea as elitist.

Lorna Sage in the *Observer* found *God Perkins* "irresistibly funny"; its author has "energy to spare." "Much of the comedy is provided by grossly ingenious slapstick, but it works because the characters have the resilience to carry it off.... McHugh is bound to win out in the end. And so, surely, is David Pownall, given the multi-coloured fun he can extract from a mean, grey world." The anonymous reviewer of the *Sunday Times* found the novel "clever and funny.... Satire on fringe theatre that should be read by all aspiring thespians. David Pownall takes a Puckish delight in ridiculing actors, directors, producers, patrons, playwrights, the Arts Council, and worst of all, ART itself. It will be difficult to watch an 'experimental' play again without recalling the fiascos that attended every Dramacart production." Peter Prince, however, in the *Times Literary Supplement* judged the novel a failure as satire: "When he tries for satire, however, Mr. Pownall is often decidedly shaky. We need to be able to trust a satirist's small, everyday perceptions—otherwise it is difficult to follow him confidently into his large fantasies. I am not sure Mr. Pownall earns that basic confidence." Prince also confesses, "I got lost well before the end." He believes "the theatre world is naturally so full of humour that it seems almost perverse of David Pownall to have written in such a frantically farcical style. So many people are being so busy all the time no single figure ever stands still long enough to establish himself."

Light on a Honeycomb is set in Rougerossbergh, which, like Lancaster, is "standing proud of the land like a burgher's belly in bed . . . clock-crowned with an ever-late municipal timepiece, ponderous with tides, puissant, pyramidal." The main industry is the carpet-plant of Sir Alphonse Bourge. However, a sociologist at the university asks, "What do most people *work* in, either on the giving or the receiving end?" and answers, "Madness in all its subtle forms, and crime. Rougerossbergh's major industry is mental instability." Pointing to the town's three mental hospitals, he asks, "Who is curing whom?" Dr. Zander, a psychiatrist who at the end becomes a patient, is introduced, along with Kevin, an inmate encouraged to "create"; Mrs. Patel, who runs a strange Yoga and Meditation Center; and many more characters. Finally, the Class War Action syndicate, made up of "squatters, pot-heads, junior reporters, sociology students, male nurses and Marxist actors (at rest)," comes out of the honeycomb of the limestone beneath the town to destroy it.

Critics found *Light on a Honeycomb* confusing, and most comment was negative. Francis King wrote in the *Spectator* that he had enjoyed the earlier novels, but this time he was "tedium-stunned." Eric Korn in *Times Literary Supplement* identified the problem as the novel's extravagance: "Where anything can happen, it doesn't matter a lot if it does; there can be no surprise, and no delighted shock, when the reader is already punch-drunk; and the deep rhythm of the action is swamped." John Mellors summed up negative criticism in the *Listener*: "The book suffers from both verbal and conceptual anarchy, mainly because of the author's over-inventiveness. Before one idea can take root it is replaced by another. The result is fantasy run wild."

Beloved Latitudes returns to Africa, to a prison with only two occupants. They are Male Sebusia, former president of an unnamed country, with hints of Kwame Nkrumah and of Idi Amin, and Neville Tyldsley, his white adviser and former minister. They are soon to be executed by Hubert Hiwewe, an intellectual returning from exile in California to be the new dictator. Before their deaths, Sebusia dictates his memoirs to Tyldsley. Two kinds of leadership in contemporary Africa are contrasted through the leaders.

This savage, intelligent comedy was widely praised. "Pownall writes wittily and economically, and achieves considerable feats of ventriloquism with Sebusia and Hiwewe," wrote Anthony Thwaite in the *Observer*. Stuart Evans in the *Times* commended "the consistently sharp but compassionate satire aimed at political, social, familial and individual targets." Peter Ackroyd in the *Sunday Times* concluded: "The humour . . . has intensified. In his previous work, it was tacked on to the narrative as a matter of farce or satire, but here it rises out of the theme itself. In the process, his writing has acquired more strength. . . . Pownall treats fiction as a kind of

brilliant lie, sacred and yet at the same time malevolent."

Only six out of more than twenty plays by Pownall have been published—all written in about ten years. Occasionally he works with conventional stories: the upper-class girl who falls in love with a stable-boy in *Fences* (1976), the discharged mental patient going to live with his brother in *Return Fare* (1978), the old man reliving his life as he follows the river to its mouth in *Follow the River Down* (1979). Pownall studies local history in such Lancaster plays as *Buck Ruxton* (1975), about a murderer in 1935, and *Lile Jimmy Williamson* (1975), about the millionaire owner of the linoleum factory who was also MP for the town for many years. History more distant in space and time provides him with the starting point for *Gaunt* (1973), about John of Gaunt, and *Livingstone and Sechele*—the African chief Sechele was the missionary's first convert.

Usually, however, something quite unexpected breaks through, in fantasy and ritual or in concept. Richard III is brought together with George Orwell through the popularity of a board game, Betrayal, in 1984 in *Richard III, Part II*. Don Juan and Don Quixote appear amid the street fighting of the Spanish civil war in November 1936 in *Seconds at the Fight for Madrid* (1978). In *Barricade* (1979), realism is abandoned as Spanish gypsies try to awaken a young Englishman politically. Similarly, blacks and whites in a Rhodesian mental hospital start to act out symbolic oppression in the second half of *Motocar*. Manet's painting *Le Dejeuner sur l'herbe* provides the starting point for *An Audience Called Edouard*, and soon Karl Marx steps up out of the river. Most difficult of all, in *Music to Murder By* (1978), a California woman musicologist conjures up the ghosts of Gesualdo, an Italian Renaissance composer, and Philip Heseltine, alias Peter Warlock, a scholar and composer who killed himself in 1930, for an illustration of creativity and violence. In a BBC radio play, *Flos*, broadcast 10 October 1982, and in a stage play, *Excessus*, to be produced in March 1983 at the Bush Theatre, London, Pownall is experimenting with themes and materials for a novel in progress. Described by its author as "the life and adventures of a fictional twelfth-century English mason, pilgrim, and heretic," the novel will be called, like the radio play, *Flos*.

Pownall may have suffered by being prolific, neglected just because he cannot be neatly placed and pigeonholed. The plays display greater versatility than the novels, and few of them are bewildering, as *Light on a Honeycomb* is. Though the first two novels set in Africa offer little insight into the continent and its problems, *Beloved Latitudes* engages more seriously with current issues. Pownall's most characteristic tone, that of three novels and most of the short stories, resembles that of Tom Sharpe—wild, inventive farce marked by instant excitements rather than by carefully evolving plots.

Plays:
As We Lie, Zambia, Nkana-Kitwe, 1969;
How to Grow a Guerrilla, Keswick, Century Theatre, 1971;
All the World Should be Taxed, Lancaster, Duke's Playhouse, December 1971;
Gaunt, Lancaster, Duke's Playhouse, March 1973;
Lions and Lambs, Lancaster, Duke's Playhouse, 1973;
Lile Jimmy Williamson, Lancaster, Duke's Playhouse, 30 January 1975;
Crates on Barrels, Fylde Arts (Lancashire tour), 1974;
Buck Ruxton, Lancaster, Duke's Playhouse, November 1975;
Ladybird, Ladybird, Edinburgh, Traverse Theatre, December 1975;
A Tale of Two Town Halls, Lancaster, Duke's Playhouse, November 1976;
Motocar, Edinburgh, Traverse Theatre, February 1977;
Richard III, Part II, Edinburgh, Traverse Theatre, August 1977;
Seconds at the Fight for Madrid, Bristol, Vandyck Theatre (University Drama Department Summer School), 11 July 1978;
An Audience called Edouard, London, Greenwich Theatre, 19 October 1978;
Livingstone and Sechele, Edinburgh, Traverse Theatre, 4 August 1978;
Barricade, Warwick, Warwick University Arts Centre, 24 January 1979;
Later, London, Kings Head, 1980;
Beef, Stratford, Theatre Royal, 9 April 1981;
The Hot Hello, Edinburgh, Traverse Theatre, 29 October 1981.

Radio Scripts:
Free Ferry, BBC, 1972;
Free House, BBC, 1973;
An Old New Year, BBC, 2 January 1974;
Fences, BBC, 31 May 1976;
Under the Wool, BBC, 1976;
Butterfingers, BBC, 21 September 1981;
The Mist People, BBC, 6 December 1981;
Flos, BBC, 10 October 1982.

Television Scripts:
High Tides, ATV, 1975;
Mackerel Sky, ATV, 1976;
Return Fare, BBC-1, 1 November 1978;
Follow the River Down, BBC-2, 1 July 1979;
Room for an Inward Light, BBC, 1980;
The Sack Judies, BBC, 1981.

Other:
Introduction 5 (London: Faber, 1973)—includes four short stories;
Beef, in *Best Radio Plays of 1981* (London: Eyre Methuen, 1982), pp. 63-111.

Interviews:
Merete Bates, "Laying Down the Lino," *Guardian*, 29 January 1975, p. 8;
Alex Hamilton, "Bwana Takes All," *Guardian*, 16 March 1977, p. 8;
Paul Vallely, "The Missionary and the Rainmaker," *Radio Times*, (8-14 December 1979): 22-23.

Christopher Priest
(14 July 1943-   )

John Fletcher
University of East Anglia

BOOKS: *Indoctrinaire* (London: Faber & Faber, 1970; New York: Harper & Row, 1970);

Fugue for a Darkening Island (London: Faber & Faber, 1972); republished as *Darkening Island* (New York: Harper & Row, 1972);

Inverted World (London: Faber & Faber, 1974); republished as *The Inverted World* (New York: Harper & Row, 1974);

The Space Machine: A Scientific Romance (London: Faber & Faber, 1976; New York: Harper & Row, 1976);

Real-Time World (London: New English Library, 1976);

A Dream of Wessex (London: Faber & Faber, 1977); republished as *The Perfect Lover* (New York: Scribners, 1977);

An Infinite Summer (London: Faber & Faber, 1979; New York: Scribners, 1979);

The Affirmation (London: Faber & Faber, 1981; New York: Scribners, 1981).

Christopher Priest is perhaps the most versatile and gifted of the younger British writers who have grown up within—but are, in different ways, extending or transcending—the genre of science fiction. Priest has already established a select but growing reputation in France, the Netherlands, and Australia, as well as at home. A professional writer of fiction, he has never written for the stage and his rare attempts at television or film writing have come to nothing. He is, apparently, the author of novels (other than those listed above) which he had published under a pseudonym; but he will neither confirm their existence nor reveal what his pseudonym is.

Born in Cheadle, a suburb of Manchester, to Walter Mackenzie and Millicent Alice Haslock Priest, he was (he reports) not an only child and did not have an unhappy childhood. He was (he goes on):

educated at Manchester Warehousemen, Clerks' Orphan School (but was neither warehouseman, clerk nor orphan), 1951-59. On leaving school in 1959 he was articled to a London firm of Chartered Accountants,

where he stayed for the next six years. He realised at this point that accountancy was not for him and so left the profession—to sighs of relief all round. His next move was to enter industry, sending in a job application to Faber & Faber—which unfortunately was not successful. His next employment was with a greetings-card manufacturer, then a mail-order publisher—neither of which held any fascination for him. Therefore, by the mutual consent of educators, accountants and industrialists, he became a full-time writer in 1968.

Priest began to write in 1965, selling his first

story ("The Run") in the same year. Although he did not feel himself cut out for accountancy, he admires the professionalism of accountants and seeks to emulate it in his chosen career as an author:

> Professionalism embraces all aspects of the writing activity. It means that one should never write at less than one's best. That one should take an interest in the business side of one's work, and see that both sides of a publisher's contract are abided by. That one acts correctly, and abides by a code of practice. In these matters, and others, I have failed in the past, and will probably do so again, but an awareness of them constitutes a principle that influences every moment of my writing career.

Soon after Priest began to write full time, Charles Monteith of Faber and Faber saw a couple of his stories, "The Interrogator" and "The Maze," and commissioned him to extend them into a novel; they constitute in fact the basis of the first ten chapters of *Indoctrinaire*, which Faber published in 1970, but which, perhaps characteristically, Priest revised in 1979, making it stylistically more polished but somewhat less spontaneous.

Of the craft of writing, Priest has said, "it's a process of the unconscious, even though one consciously employs experience and craft and skill," and he clearly attaches great importance both to the largely unconscious origins of the imagery and to the slow, careful work that goes into making that imagery into a readable and memorable story. That the process is a mysterious, even unknowable, one he never doubts: "it is a process of expression and communication, and it is inexpressible and incommunicable."

Although he does not repudiate his affiliation with science fiction, Priest says that he is a writer first and a science-fiction writer second, that the connection perhaps arises from the fact that "those ideas that appeal to me come out speculative in nature." But a change does seem to have occurred quite early in his career:

> I started realizing that "sf", something that had appealed to me for a relatively short period in adolescence, was actually a decadent and rather unhealthy thing . . . at the same time my interest in speculative or fantastic themes remained. . . . I can trace this change to the writing of *Fugue for a Darkening Island*. I started that book as an sf writer, but by the time I had finished it I was no longer. I wrote virtually nothing for the next three

years, while I tried to understand the change that had taken place. The book that followed, *Inverted World*, is by a paradox the one most people think of as my most "sf-y" book . . . but if I had set out to write it as sf (or as I then conceived of it) I would never have written it at all.

The novels since *Fugue for a Darkening Island* (1972) he sees as "critical essays" which "pass conscious and intended comment on their literary antecedents"—*The Space Machine: A Scientific Romance* (1976), for example, is "a critical essay on the scientific romance, saying, if you like, that we shouldn't take H. G. Wells for granted"—with *The Affirmation* (1981) serving as "a sort of summation of the critical novels."

Priest is thus a very self-conscious novelist almost in the French manner, meditating on his own work and on that of others (he was for a time reviews editor of the science-fiction journal *Foundation*). He has been awarded such literary prizes as the British Science Fiction Association Award for *Inverted World* (1974) and the Ditmar Award for *The Space Machine*. He now lives in Harrow in Middlesex. Apart from novels and short stories, he has published a certain amount of uncollected journalism and a book for children on filmmaking.

"It is a curious paradox," writes J. G. Ballard in the preface to his *Vermilion Sands* (1971), "that almost all science fiction, however far removed in time and space, is really about the present day. . . . Perhaps because of [its] cautionary tone, so much of science fiction's notional futures are zones of unrelieved grimness. Even its heavens are like other people's hells." This is not always true: there is a more optimistic vein in some science fiction, perhaps best represented by one of the classics of the genre, Isaac Asimov's "Foundation Trilogy" (1951-1953), in which, against great odds and in spite of near-disaster, the best of mankind's achievement survives the collapse into decadent barbarism of the First Empire and the galaxy is finally made "safe for ever." Some science fiction, on the other hand, involves puzzles or paradoxes, a kind of black surrealist humor such as marks Priest's first novel, *Indoctrinaire*, and his third, *Inverted World*, both of which are concerned with distortions of time or space. *Indoctrinaire* tells how a circular clearing of stubble in the middle of the Brazilian jungle exists 200 years in the future: in moving out of the trees on to this plain the characters step across two centuries of time. British scientist Elias Wentik is drafted there in mysterious circumstances; when he returns to England he finds it in the middle of a war and his family evacuated from London, he knows not where. In despair he awaits the impending nuclear holocaust, since in spite of everything he decides not to go back (or perhaps forward) to the safety of the future.

Inverted World, though Priest's third novel, had been "simmering" in his mind since 1965 and has more in common with *Indoctrinaire* than it has with his second (and perhaps finest) book, *Fugue for a Darkening Island*. The "inverted world" of the title is Earth City. To its inhabitants it is an oasis of peace, order, and civilized values, built on another planet by an enlightened visionary when earth itself was engulfed in disaster and barbarism (a recurrent theme in science fiction). It is a place where the physical laws governing earth are inverted—"we live," one of the inhabitants declares, "in a large but finite universe, occupied by a number of bodies of infinite size." The picture they have of their world is cast in doubt by the attitude of an intelligent outsider, an English nurse named Elizabeth Khan, to whom the city appears to be "not much more than a large and misshapen office block." Their world view is finally shattered when it becomes clear that it is not the exterior world that is different but their perception of it. Imprisoned in their inherited and unquestioned beliefs, they have for ages been laboriously winching their "city" forward on rails in a continually frustrated attempt to maintain it near the elusive "optimum" where they claim spatial and temporal distortion is at its minimum. It comes almost as much of a shock to the reader to realize that they have been dragging themselves across Spain and Portugal in a post-"Crash" world and, having reached the western seaboard of the European landmass, are about to haul themselves into the endless stretches of the Atlantic. The alternative world view by which they have lived for so long turns out to have been a mere mathematical abstraction based on a hyperbolic curve, and they are saved only in the nick of time from the suicidal consequences of believing in it any longer.

In spite of its rather unsatisfying trick ending, *Inverted World* is not without disturbing features which link it with the satirical utopias of earlier literature. One is the technique of ironic contrast—set up between an imaginary or ideal world and our own—which is the staple of Swiftian or Voltairean satire and is not lost even on the hero himself:

> Perhaps unfairly, I formed an impression that I should not care to live on Earth planet, as most of its existence seemed to be a series of disputes, wars, territorial claims, economic pressures. The concept of civilization was far advanced, and explained to us as the state in which mankind congregated within cities. By definition, we of Earth city were civilized, but there seemed to be no resemblance between our existence and theirs. Civilization on Earth planet was equated with selfishness and greed; those people who lived in a civilized state exploited those who did not. There were shortages of vital commodities on Earth planet, and the people in the civilized nations were able to monopolize those commodities by reason of their greater economic strength. This imbalance appeared to be at the root of the disputes.

It is no coincidence that *Fugue for a Darkening Island* is more "prophetic" (in the Orwellian sense at least) than either of the other two novels and less like classic science fiction. It is described by its publishers variously as "imaginative fiction" and as "a novel of the future." This future, like that of *Nineteen Eighty-Four*, is not especially remote; in fact it is uncomfortably close to home. The "darkening island" is Britain; more particularly, the southeast of England in which the entire action is played out. A nuclear holocaust in Africa has driven millions of blacks to seek refuge elsewhere, and many thousands land illegally in England, provoking racial tension on a scale hitherto unknown. A right-wing government attempts to impose a tough policy of control, opposed by liberal elements (among which the hero Alan Whitman numbers himself). The Africans take up arms to defend themselves; the whites react in kind. Law and order breaks down; atrocity and counteratrocity disfigure communal life. Alan Whitman—the epitome of the ordinary man in the street, a modest college lecturer unhappily married with a young daughter—is not much better at coping with this situation than most of his compatriots; perhaps less so, in that he is a moral and physical coward who has opted out all his life from difficult political, personal, and moral decisions. He is the sort of man who having seduced a girl blames the sexual failure of their subsequent marriage on her and takes up with a string of mistresses with whom he is scarcely less indifferent. His only deep relationship is with his daughter, Sally: he stays with his wife only on her account. His personal slide into barbarism is precipitated by the one occurrence which can provoke in him a "combination of terror and hatred": the discovery of Sally's mutilated body near a brothel set up by the blacks for their troops, one of many female victims who have been murdered for failing to "co-operate."

This novel is thus much more unsettling than *Indoctrinaire* and *Inverted World*. It is also more insistently and disturbingly erotic: the other two, like much science fiction, are perfunctory in their treatment of sex. There is, too, an uneasy tension between liberal attitudes on the one hand and deep-seated anxieties about racial conflict on the other: if *Inverted World* features "tooks," primitive people whom Earth City exploits with good conscience, it does not betray fear of them in the way *Fugue For a Darkening Island* does. The point is that Priest's second novel appears less censored by his own enlightened feelings than the other two; and for that reason it is a more honest, more disturbing, and altogether more satisfying book. It by no means deserves that ugly contemporary epithet "racist"; but it is too clear-sighted to suppress the probability that white people in the situation of a "darkening island" would oppose mass black immigration, that the blacks would resist measures to expel them, and that if nothing were done to defuse the confrontation, the consequences for all parties to the dispute would be ugly and cruel. What Priest is writing about, in a word, is what Ingmar Bergman in one of his greatest films refers to as "the shame" (in fact, the movie may have inspired the book: the imagery of the end is very similar in both cases—the refugee boat, the shapeless bodies in the sea, and so on). The shame is what anyone would experience in a situation of social breakdown for which he would necessarily feel obscurely responsible.

Fugue for a Darkening Island is also the most interesting technically of Priest's novels. It is written from several temporal viewpoints: Alan's boyhood and precocious sexual experiences, his student days and developing relationship with his future wife, his married life and various mistresses, the worsening political situation as the African problem grows in menace, the different stages of the breakdown of normal British life; all these moments in time are visited in turn but in no particular order. As in many nouveaux romans, the reader is expected to find his own bearings from internal indications; none of the individual sections of narrative extends for more than a few pages. The style, too, resembles the impersonal, inexplicit manner familiar in French experimental writing.

But much as it owes to other contemporary fiction, *Fugue for a Darkening Island* is a genuinely original work of art. It is science fiction only in the broadest sense of the term; like the best of the genre, it transcends simple definition. At the same time it is comfortably at home in a long tradition of moral and didactic fiction, playing utopia (in this case the town on the south coast, an unnatural oasis of order and calm in a world of chaos, which offers Whitman shelter for a time) against the horrors of reality. A reality that is not contemporary is not unthinkable either: it is clear that Priest's consciousness, like that of the rest of his generation—he was born in England two years before Hiroshima—is seared by an awareness of the hydrogen bomb, which casts its shadow not only over the "darkening island" but also over the world of *Indoctrinaire*. "It is one thing to imagine an atrocity," Whitman confides, "it is something else again to witness it"; for, as Robert Jay Lifton has pointed out, "we are all survivors of Hiroshima simply by living in a world in which the bomb was dropped." If one of the functions of literature is to remind and warn, Priest's work fulfills it powerfully. Like Artaud in the theater, Priest no doubt sees his task as being to alert us that we are not free, since the heavens may at any time fall about our ears.

Priest surprised his readers with *The Space Machine: A Scientific Romance*. As the subtitle suggests, this is an affectionate return to the imaginative adventures of Victorian fantasists—especially Wells, whom Priest has advised us not to take for granted—but with a sharp and even ironic sense of modern perspective. The year is 1893, and the humdrum life of young commercial traveler Edward Turnbull is enlivened only by his fervent interest in the new pastime of motoring, through which he meets and befriends Amelia Fitzgibbon. She takes him to the laboratory of her guardian, Sir William Reynolds. One of the most eminent scientists in England, Sir William is building a time machine, and from this discovery it is a short step into the future. As the couple emerge into time set ten years later, they discover that a terrible war is devastating England. Indeed that war of 1903 is only the beginning of a series of adventures (including a journey to Mars) which culminates in a violent confrontation with the most ruthless intellect in the universe.

Much classic science fiction—and not only *The Time Machine* and *The War of the Worlds* by H. G. Wells—is lovingly parodied in this curious novel. A more humorous and more cheerful story than *Fugue for a Darkening Island*, it ends on a distinct note of hope: "I took Amelia into my arms. I kissed her passionately, and, with a joyous sense of reawakening hope, we sat down on the bedstead to wait for the first people to arrive." This hopeful ending reflects nineteenth-century science fiction more than that of an older contemporary such as

FIRST DRAFT   THE WATCHED.

Sometimes, Jenessa was slow to leave in the mornings, reluctant to return

to the frustrations of her work, and when she lingered in his house on these

occasions, Ordier had difficulty in concealing~~his~~ his impatience. This

morning was one such, and he lurked outside the door of the shower-cubicle

while she bathed, fingering the smooth ~~plastic~~ leather case of his binoculars.

Ordier was alert to ~~her~~ Jenessa's every movement, each variation in sound giving

him as clear a picture as there would be ~~i~~ if the door were wide open and

the plastic curtain held back: the spattering of droplets against the

curtain as she raised an arm, the barely detectable change in the ~~towel~~

pitch of the hissing water as she bent to wash a leg, the fat drops plopping

soapily on the tiled floor as she stood erect to shampoo her hair. He could

visualize her/body glistening in every detail, and he lusted for her.

He became aware that he was standing too obviously by the door, too

transparently waiting for her, so he put down the binoculars-case and went

into the kitchen and ~~mixx started some~~ boiled some coffee. He waited until it had

percolated, then left it ~~to simmer~~ on the hot-plate. Jenessa had still not finished; Ordier

paused by the door of the cubicle, and knew by the sound of the water that

she was still rinsing her hair. He could ~~see her~~ imagine her with her face

uptilted towards the spray, her long dark hair plastered flatly back above

her ears~~xxxxxplxxxxxfxwaterx~~. She often stood like this for several minutes,

letting the water run into her open mouth, then dribble away, coursing down

her body; twin streams of droplets would fall from her nipples, a tiny rivulet

would snake through her pubic hair, ~~by buttocks and thighs would~~ a thin film would gloss her buttocks and thighs.

Again ~~torn restless with distractions of~~ torn between desire and impatience, Ordier

went to his bureau, unlocked it, and took out his scintilla detector. He

checked the batteries first; demonstrating the instrument to a close friend

a few weeks before, he had discovered to his surprise that his house had

become infested with several of the tiny devices, and since then he had been

checking every ~~few~~ days. The batteries were still sound, but he knew he

would have to replace them again soon.

First page of the draft for "The Watched"

Ballard—or even the earlier work of Priest himself. As Tom Hutchinson commented in his London *Times* review, "the narrative is, at times, not tightly enough organized, but the Wellsian tone is always cunningly caught: a sense of urgency gradually becoming a shrill alarm." Hutchinson was particularly impressed by the characterization, which he found "delightfully realized" and entirely credible. Amelia Fitzgibbon, he says, is a "Mary Kingsley-type of woman who, despite all galactic hazards, manages to keep her virginity intact until the entirely moral moment." Reviewers were also impressed with the skillful way in which Priest introduces Wells himself as a character in a story clearly intended to delight Wells aficionados, succeeding perfectly in that aim.

A Dream of Wessex (1977)—published in the United States under the title *The Perfect Lover*—is not a Victorian vision underpinned (and to some extent undermined) by a late twentieth-century perspective within the writing but an imaginative reconstruction of Wessex (Thomas Hardy's literary creation) in the twenty-second century. A group of scientists "dream" an alternative society into being with the help of a "Ridpath projector"; this society, 150 years in the future, is based upon an extrapolation of contemporary trends and is shaped by the hopes and expectations of those taking part. The entry of a single antipathetic character into this team of dreamers is sufficient to change the corporate vision violently. In the climax of the story the whole question of reality is placed under severe scrutiny, and eventually the hero and heroine emerge unscathed—but in the projected universe of the future, and beyond recall. Of this and other stories David Wingrove has written that Priest's use of the secondary fiction, "the supreme conjuring act in his repertoire," is "almost a statement about the craft of writing itself."

Priest's latest novel, *The Affirmation*, is summarized thus by its publisher: "Peter Sinclair is 29 years old. His father has just died, he has lost his job and his apartment, his mistress has left him. He arranges to stay temporarily in the country cottage of a family friend. There he begins work on an autobiographical manuscript, one with which he intends simply to recount the story of his life, but one which soon develops into an act of imaginative reconstruction, a statement of metaphorical identity. Fascinated, the reader watches as Peter drifts between the increasingly shadowy world of outer reality, and the plausible inner world of memory and imagination. The central characters are living in two worlds simultaneously. Which is the real world, which the hallucination? Which is reality and which is the dream?" Although critic John Naughton found it a "rigmarole," *The Affirmation* shows Priest working toward a major sequence which he has thought of calling "The Dream Archipelago," perhaps in unconscious homage to Solzhenitsyn's haunting *Gulag Archipelago*.

Priest is a remarkably literate and self-conscious writer. He is also an extremely skilled one whose craft as a prose stylist is singled out by commentators for particular praise. It is widely agreed that he stands head and shoulders above the run-of-the-mill science-fiction writer. He is very articulate about the art of science-fiction writing as practiced on different sides of the Atlantic, as his afterword to the collection *Stars of Albion* (1979) shows. He is also an excellent literary critic, as his comments on his older colleague and mentor, J. G. Ballard, and others reveal:

> J. G. Ballard's influence has been of a different order, although he is himself an excellent stylist. Probably no single writer of science fiction, here or anywhere else in the world, has done so much to change our ideas of what sf could be *about*. His attitude to the genre has been disconcertingly Dadaist—the André Breton of sf. Ballard has asked questions to which no answers were possible within the canons of sf, yet answered them himself with his own work. "Inner space" has become a catchphrase, sometimes applied pejoratively, yet it was Ballard who first described the inner landscape, and it was Ballard who first wrote about it, and it is still only Ballard who can take us there and make us understand it.

A novelist as lucid and as skilled as Christopher Priest will doubtless go far. Although his books have attracted favorable reviews and one or two excellent essays, he does not appear to have achieved the major breakthrough into popular success that he deserves. He is at least as good as Ian McEwan, who has achieved much greater notoriety and whose books probably have higher sales. But recognition cannot be far off, and perhaps it will be *The Affirmation*, a story of madness which seems to have cut all of Priest's remaining links with the genre of science fiction—links which have probably resulted in his being unfairly typecast in the past—that will prove to be the occasion of his acceptance as one of the most gifted of the younger generation of British novelists.

Other:

Anticipations, edited by Priest (London: Faber & Faber, 1978; New York: Scribner, 1978);

Stars of Albion, edited by Robert Holdstock and Priest (London: Pan, 1979).

Periodical Publication:

"The Profession of Science Fiction: Overture and Beginners," *Foundation*, 13 (May 1978); re-printed in *Vector*, 93 (May-June 1979): 10-11.

References:

John Fletcher, "Cultural Pessimists: The Tradition of Christopher Priest's Fiction," *International Fiction Review*, 3 (January 1976): 20-24;

David Wingrove, "Legerdemain: The Fiction of Christopher Priest," *Vector*, 93 (May-June 1979): 3-9.

Barbara Pym
(6 June 1913-11 January 1980)

Paul Binding

BOOKS: *Some Tame Gazelle* (London: Cape, 1950);

Excellent Women (London: Cape, 1952; New York: Dutton, 1978);

Jane and Prudence (London: Cape, 1953; New York: Dutton, 1981);

Less Than Angels (London: Cape, 1955; New York: Vanguard, 1957);

A Glass of Blessings (London: Cape, 1959; New York: Dutton, 1980);

No Fond Return of Love (London: Cape, 1961);

Quartet in Autumn (London: Macmillan, 1977; New York: Dutton, 1978);

The Sweet Dove Died (London: Macmillan, 1978; New York: Dutton, 1979);

A Few Green Leaves (London: Macmillan, 1980; New York: Dutton, 1980).

Barbara Pym was born in Oswestry, Shrop-shire, the elder daughter of Frederic Crampton and Irene Thomas Pym. She was educated at a private school in Liverpool and at St. Hilda's College, Oxford, where she studied English literature and took a B.A. with honors in 1934. The Anglican church and higher institutions of learning—including Oxford itself—both found their way into her fiction. During World War II she served with the WRNS in both Britain and in Italy (as did the heroine of *A Glass of Blessings*, 1959). Her working life after the war was spent at the International African Institute in London, where she became assistant editor of their journal, *Africa*. Her first novel, *Some Tame Gazelle*, appeared in 1950.

Between that date and 1961 five other novels

of hers were published. All enjoyed a modest critical success and won her a band of admirers. Certain territories of English life became associated with her—those inhabited by librarians, anthropologists, the clergy, men and women (particularly the latter) on the fringes of learned life. All her novels are distinguished by an amused shrewdness of eye and ear; furthermore, these works combine irony with delicate psychological insights raising them above mere comedies of manners.

After 1961, however, Pym found—to her sur-prise and distress—that the fiction she wrote was not wanted by either publishers or agents. She persevered with writing, moving to a quiet room in London, away from her editing work and her home, in order to practice her craft intently; but still her work was rejected, and her earlier books all went out of print. While never ceasing to work on her fiction, she came to believe that she must write for herself alone; she also began to doubt the merit of her previous work. In 1974 she retired from her job and went to live with her sister, Hilary Walton, in an Oxfordshire village.

In February 1977 the *Times Literary Supplement* invited a number of distinguished literary figures to name their choices of most overrated and under-rated writers of the century. Two of these, the critic and biographer Lord David Cecil and the poet Philip Larkin, nominated Barbara Pym as their choice for most underrated writer; they praised her for her perceptiveness and her wit. The publishing and media worlds made an almost instant volte-face. Her then most recently written novel (*Quartet*

Barbara Pym

church affairs and infinitely respectful of the pious life, she was no fervent born again Christian and preserved a gentle skeptical attitude (even though this stance did not preclude worship). Nor did her wide-ranging knowledge of English poets, from the Elizabethans to the late Victorians, mean that she revered the past above the present; as her novels indicate, she took the liveliest interest in the fashions, mores, mannerisms, and beliefs of the changing world around her and was concerned in exploring what dictated them, what conditioned their ability or failure to survive.

Some Tame Gazelle, Pym's first novel, establishes the concerns and—to a limited degree—the world of her subsequent fiction. It depicts the lives of Belinda and Harriet Bede, two unmarried sisters in their mid-fifties, who live in a quiet village. The novel's theme is indicated by the quotation, from the minor Victorian poet, Bayly, from which its title is taken:

> Some tame gazelle, or some gentle dove,
> Something to love, oh something to love.

" 'Something to love,' that was the point," Belinda reflects at the close of the book; in life, appropriate or responsive recipients for one's capacity for love do not always appear, despite the folklore to the contrary. In the end, Pym indicates, it is surely best to come to terms with this sad fact—with humor and with charity—and to opt for modest outlets. Belinda has been secretly in love with the local archdeacon for many years. A vain man, he chooses most of the time to ignore what he does in fact perceive. Harriet lavishes attentions on young curates to the point of making herself look foolish. Yet the tendernesses these unrequited loves bring out in both sisters are valid and acceptable releases of deeper feelings, and as such they are to be respected.

Some Tame Gazelle is episodic in form, and—upholding humorous acceptance of a confining existence—it tends to move from comic set piece to comic set piece. This forward movement detracts somewhat from the central, sober subject; and the attempt of the last chapter to unite the more serious strands of the novel and to close on a mood appropriate to the governing motto suggests that hereafter Pym will strive for greater tightness of form.

She achieves this tightness in *Excellent Women* (1952). Set in London, the novel focuses on an unmarried woman not dissimilar to Belinda Bede (and to her creator) in class, temperament, and situation—though she is younger. The novel is told in the first person, and its controlled but very indi-

in Autumn, 1977), rejected many times, was immediately bought by Macmillan, the publisher to whom it had been sent shortly before the article's appearance; Jonathan Cape, the publishing house that had let all her early books go out of print, straightaway announced its intentions of reissuing them (an intention which has now been realized). Television programs and newspaper interviews followed in the wake of this distinguished championship of her work, and her three subsequent novels received detailed and sympathetic reviews.

Pym had become accustomed to a quiet life and had grown cynical about the integrity of the literary world, and her renaissance, while it undoubtedly pleased her, did not change either her mode of existence or her wariness of the media and its values. She was a shy, if gregarious, person much more interested in private activity than in public notice. Observant and guarded in her personal contacts with people, she nevertheless suggested an inner life of which she affords brief but telling glimpses in the contemplative moments of her fiction. The English church and the English poetic tradition, she said, were what had meant the most to her during her life. Yet while she was well versed in

Dust jacket for the American edition of Pym's second novel, about the disorganized marriage of a former naval officer and an anthropologist

vidual voice—self-deprecatory, sharp, amused—is responsible for the work's great unity and consequent intensity of impact. Pym is also more at home in an urban setting than she was in the somewhat fossilized and stereotyped village of *Some Tame Gazelle*. Random meetings of imaginative or emotional significance, which provide entrees into unsuspected social worlds, become a most distinctive feature of Pym's fiction; clearly they are more a part of a metropolitan than of a rural pattern of life.

In *Excellent Women* the narrator becomes involved with her emotionally disorganized neighbors, Rocky and Helena Napier, he a handsome former naval officer, she an anthropologist. The narrator's sensitivity, as well as her emotional uncertainty, is revealed in her ability to enter—as sympathetic, shrewd, and accepted visitor—disparate spheres: her old school frozen in custom, her local church, anthropological meetings, even the raffish metier of the Napiers' married existence.

In *Jane and Prudence* (1953) Pym returns, for

the greater part of the book, to the countryside. Ten years before the opening of the novel, Jane Cleveland has taught English literature to Prudence Bold at an Oxford college. They have become friends, though their natures are as different as their subsequent lives are to be. Jane, as the novel begins, is the wife of an unworldly rural vicar; Prudence has opted for a humdrum job at a cultural institute and a life of unsatisfactory love affairs. Though yielding interesting and entertaining scenes, the contrast between the two women and their milieux is perhaps, on the one hand, too overt and, on the other, too lacking in the fruitful metaphoric power of the most successful fictional antitheses. The London episodes are far more deft than the country ones, where there is a tendency for the author to slip into the farcical-pastoral.

Less Than Angels (1955) returns to the world of anthropologists which *Excellent Women* introduced—indeed figures from that novel are referred to in this one, a device that Pym uses repeatedly. *Less Than Angels* is perhaps Pym's subtlest and strongest achievement. It has two pivotal centers: the love of two women for a young anthropologist, Tom Mallow, and the award of a research grant for anthropological studies. While retaining rich and observant comedy, this novel is more somber, more concerned with complexity and ambivalence of feeling than its predecessors. The emotions of the two women are rawer, not only in respect to Tom but also in respect to their own situations. By the end of the novel Tom has died, and—compassionately but alarmingly—Pym reveals how little effect the death of this apparently magnetic man has, even on those who cared for him most ardently.

Pym declared of this book: "It is surely appropriate that the anthropologists, who spend their time studying life and behaviour in various societies, should be studied in their turn." This anthropological approach—noting rituals of suburban or working life, conventions observed, conventions broken—pervades *Less Than Angels* (not only in application to the anthropologists of the novel) and distinguishes all Pym's subsequent fiction as well.

A Glass of Blessings bears resemblance to *Excellent Women* in its first-person narration and its mood of mellow acceptance of frustration as an inevitable part of the human condition. However, it retains the unflinching vision of *Less Than Angels* in its examination of complex feelings and their social manifestations. Wilmet, the central figure, is married to an affluent civil servant who, at this stage of their married life, makes no appeal to her deeper personality. Her feelings go out to an old friend's brother, Piers, who is something of a failure, broody and imaginative, and surely a suitable object for her emotional superfluity. She is puzzled by his diffident response until she discovers that he is homosexual, his partner a simple, earnest young man brought to life by a host of kindly, humorous details. Wilmet accepts not only Piers's orientation but his specific relationship also, assimilating it into the pattern of her own social life. Acceptance is all; it provides enrichment as well as sanity.

No Fond Return of Love (1961) also has as its protagonist a woman romantically obsessed by a man about whose private life she knows little and whose character she has only partially assessed. Her obsession leads to a quest for more extensive information about him and his life, a quest making use of many of the anthropological fieldwork devices of *Less Than Angels*. This is the most densely populated of all Pym's books. Submerged middle-class worlds—touching each other but isolated in interests and in inhibitions—are brought up for merciful but amused scrutiny: a conference of compilers of learned indexes, a private hotel on the Devon coast, a London florist's shop.

Sixteen years of enforced silence followed, as Pym was unable to attract a publisher. The first novel produced at the end of this period, *Quartet in Autumn*, is markedly different from any of the previous six, but perhaps most particularly from its predecessor, *No Fond Return of Love*. After that novel's amplitude and amiability, this one shows an austerity of form and vision. Two women retire from an office where they have carried out unspecified tasks. Work may not have meant much to them, but its absence creates a frightening void. Indeed, each member of the quartet of job associates that gives the book its title inhabits a world informed by loneliness and ennui. This world is attributed to the amorphousness, the cultural rootlessness of contemporary English society, something which, however, has to be accepted. No well-meaning institution, such as the church or a social club, can prevail against it.

This novel's successor, *The Sweet Dove Died* (1978)—actually written before *Quartet in Autumn*—is also spare in style and taut in form. It is, above all else, a study in selfishness and by extension an indictment of a society that not only endorses it but, in fact, encourages it: the English haute bourgeoisie and its peripheries of the 1970s. The novel focuses on the conscious selfishness of Leonora Eyre, well-off, middle-aged, and unmarried, who desires that only the agreeable and tasteful enter her life and who is ruthless in her dealings with more threatening elements; the unconscious selfishness of the youthful object of her infatuation, James, a charming, feckless, self-indulgent bisexual; and the indifference amounting to selfishness of the world through which they move. Chilling though it is in its uncompromising moral vision, the book is not without the compassion and humor which so characterized the earlier novels.

At its best Barbara Pym's fiction combines, in an extraordinarily intricate way, the interior and the exterior. Great attention to detail and an accurate—and anthropological—ear for speech result in each of her various milieux coming to life as organic and convincing entities. But at the same time the inner life is never neglected; for all the diversity of persons and places, every book owes its shape and unifying emotional atmosphere to the sensitively exposed mind and heart of the central figure.

Shapeliness and unity do not distinguish her posthumous novel, *A Few Green Leaves* (1980), written while Pym suffered from terminal cancer. Percipient in its demonstration of how traditional country mores have been partially eroded by infiltrations and intrusions from other, more amorphous worlds, it lacks precisely the empathetic central character that draws the disparate unto itself. For that reason the novel lacks the moral impetus of its predecessors. Nevertheless, in certain episodes—the abandonment of the widower vicar by his romantic-minded sister, for instance—Pym's tart, feeling comedy reveals patterns in outward behavior and inward mood such as her work at its finest has always done.

Ann Quin

(17 March 1936-?August 1973)

Judith Mackrell
Oxford University

BOOKS: *Berg* (London: Calder, 1964; New York: Scribners, 1965);

Three (London: Calder & Boyars, 1966; New York: Scribners, 1966);

Passages (London: Calder & Boyars, 1969; Salem, N.H.: Boyars, 1979);

Tripticks (London: Calder & Boyars, 1972; Salem, N.H.: Boyars, 1979).

Ann Quin was one of the major figures in a group of experimental writers who emerged in Britain during the 1960s. Although, unlike others in this group, she did not concern herself with literary manifestos or even, initially, regard herself as an experimental novelist, her work reveals a growing concern with the technical possibilities of the novel and with the articulation of areas of experience that had largely been ignored by writers of the previous decade. Her early work has, in fact, been most frequently likened to the novels of Natalie Sarraute, both in its techniques and also in its attempt to capture the fleeting and subterranean movements of her characters' minds and feelings. The later novels are perhaps closer to the work of more contemporary writers like Robert Creely and Alan Burns in their development of a more fragmented and apparently random organization of material and a greater variation in style and technique.

She was born in Brighton, Sussex, where she lived alone with her mother, Ann Reid Quin, her father, former opera singer Nicholas Montague, having abandoned them soon after she was born. Although she was not a Catholic, she was educated at the Convent of the Blessed Sacrament in Brighton, which she recalls as alien and claustrophobic: "A ritualistic culture that gave me a conscience. A death wish and a sense of sin. Also a great lust to find out, experience what evil really was." Although she showed little interest in her formal education, she read a great deal and wrote continuously, mostly stories to entertain herself.

She describes herself as living largely in a fantasy world of her own creation, a habit, which when she was seventeen, transferred itself to a passion for the theater. She decided to join a theater company

as an assistant stage manager, but the job lasted only six weeks, and when she subsequently tried to enter the Royal Academy of Dramatic Art, she ran away from the audition, paralyzed with fear. This brief, unhappy experience with the stage convinced her finally that she wanted to be a writer, and she began first to devote herself to writing poetry, "mainly religious and surrealistic."

For the next three years she took a number of secretarial jobs, in both London and Brighton, during which time she also had her first serious love affair and wrote a novel. The book was rejected by several publishers, but she was undeterred and began work immediately on another. However, it was while working on this second novel that she had her first serious breakdown. She had left London to take a summer job in a hotel in Cornwall, but the unpleasant, arduous work left little time for writing. Almost immediately after running away she found herself unable to leave her bed and subject to terrible hallucinations; but after having visited a psychiatrist several times she was able to recover sufficiently to decide that "the loneliness of going over the edge was worse than the absurdity of coping with day to day living." For the rest of her life, however, she suffered from recurrent periods of illness—probably some form of schizophrenia—when her usually extroverted and enthusiastic nature changed dramatically to one of silence and withdrawal; clearly these experiences influenced considerably the extent to which her novels explore areas of madness in her characters' lives.

Back in London she managed to finish the novel, which had developed into "telephone directory length of very weird content, without dialogue." Although it too was rejected, she did receive a letter of encouragement from the publisher; therefore, she began work on another, *Berg*, which after several versions was accepted for publication by John Calder in 1964.

Like all of her novels *Berg* is highly autobiographical in its underlying emotional impulse if not in particular detail. (Here the underlying impulse relates to Quin's absent father, about whom she wove an intense fantasy life.) It tells the story of

Alistair Berg, a frustrated and rather seedy young man, who goes to a seaside resort with the intention of finding and killing his father, Nathaniel (who had deserted Berg and his mother soon after Berg was born). In many ways the logic of the novel's plot parallels Freud's use of the Oedipal myth, though some of Quin's friends and critics suggest that her plot evolved from an instinctive grasp of Berg's (and her own) situation, rather than from a fully deliberated schema.

When Berg sets off to find Nathaniel he leaves behind him his mother, Edith. As his relationship with her is highly dependent and emotional as well as constricting and frustrating, it is clearly responsible for the anxiety and contempt with which he views other women. However, when he arrives at his father's boardinghouse, he transfers this feeling (now explicitly sexual) to Nathaniel's mistress, Judith, whom he seduces as part of his "revenge." Though Berg also plots continually for ways to kill Nathaniel, he never actually succeeds, but instead substitutes three symbolic deaths—two of which are of objects close to his father, the third the actual death of a man whom he chooses to identify as his father. Another farcical, even more complex variation on the theme of the Oedipal triangle derives from an incident in which Berg, trying to avoid discovery in his father's room, dresses up as Judith and is faced with (or fantasizes) the drunken advances of Nathaniel, who is thereby dealt some measure of sexual humiliation. Yet Berg's resolution of his conflict, despite its symbolic enactment, is never really achieved: the novel ends with the sinister return to the boardinghouse of a man closely resembling Nathaniel, and Berg's relationship with Edith is never even confronted, let alone resolved.

Running through the narrative are also clear parallels to *Hamlet* and *Crime and Punishment*. Berg is both an unbalanced and a highly reflective villain, chronically uncertain about his identity and subject to long fits of procrastination, during which he either gets immersed in the contemplation of his situation or else tries to work himself up to the crime. From these periods it emerges that his desire to kill Nathaniel does not derive solely from the conscious need to avenge his desertion and the unconscious need to assert himself against the paternal rival; he also desires to forge an independent and significant self through a supreme act of defiance against society.

Despite the seriousness of the emotions and the issues with which the novel deals, however, the narrative frequently exhibits a strong vein of surreal fantasy and farce. The latter is particularly strong in the account of Berg's symbolic murders (for example, his desperate attempts to dispose of the ventriloquist's dummy, which he seems seriously to imagine is his father's corpse) and of course the ludicrous seduction scene between Berg and his father. The frequently surrealist quality of the prose not only contributes to its black humor but also conveys a sense of the strange world that Berg's consciousness creates for itself. For although during much of the narrative Berg's thoughts and perceptions are conveyed with an exact if rather imagistic realism, a shift in the language or an unusual focus on a detail transforms the everyday world into a suddenly strange and fantastically significant place.

> Crossing the park: a subterranean world surreptitiously risen; here a million star-fish pinned on the forelocks of a hundred unicorns driven by furious witches. A transformation that held itself occasionally in suspense, but for how long would it be like this?

Berg clearly inhabits a world that is frequently distorted by the almost hallucinatory quality of his fantasies and obsessions, yet Quin is able to evoke a sense of his fluctuations between "madness" and sanity simply by means of such stylistic shifts, without imposing any external narrative exposition or judgment. Although most of the novel is told in the third person and Quin as omniscient author unobtrusively (and very elliptically) relates Berg's story, she attempts to create the impression that the shape of the narrative and the movement of the language are dictated by the movements of Berg's own mind. His world and the other characters who inhabit it are always filtered through his perceptions, and the reader has to notice for himself, either through carefully placed details or snatches of dialogue, the objective reality and desperate humor of certain situations. Quin, in fact, is attempting to develop a technique that will appear to render a faithful impression of the continuous and subjective present of Berg's consciousness. Just as actuality and fantasy are abruptly juxtaposed, even merged, so are past and present, and even thought, speech and, action—Quin does not use quotation marks to indicate dialogue or to break the continuity of Berg's speech and the thoughts that precede it. (It was these last qualities in Quin's style which caused many critics to liken the novel to the works of Sarraute and other new novelists; however, Quin had not read these authors, and more plausible influences, which she notes herself, are to be found in

Virginia Woolf and Dostoevski.)

Although Quin does succeed in giving a vivid and immediate quality to many of Berg's experiences, the other characters exist largely as functions of Berg's own drama; Quin does not give them an autonomous and individualized existence, and they frequently emerge not simply as shadowy, but sometimes as highly implausible in their manner of speech and behavior. The revelation and manipulation of Berg's own consciousness also have moments of contrivance and implausibility. The occasions when he lapses into a surreal or highly metaphoric mode of perception are sometimes too consciously "literary"; Berg is by profession a hair restorer with no clear "literary" background, and at these moments he seems simply to function as a rather thin persona for Quin's own images and ideas. In general, however, both the style and the structure of the novel show a considerable degree of technical skill.

Berg received a great deal of attention for a first novel. Although certain reviewers criticized its "thinness of plot" and failed to see its style as anything other than evidence of a willful obscurity, others saw it as a work of considerable depth and originality, important particularly for the way in which it parallels certain qualities of the French new novel in a style and setting that are "unmistakeably English."

The novel's success had important results: first, Quin began to be known among other writers of the literary avant-garde; second, she was awarded two fellowships—the D. H. Lawrence Fellowship from the University of New Mexico in 1964 and the Harkness Fellowship (for the most promising Commonwealth artist under thirty) for the years 1964 to 1967. Both of these enabled her to spend the following years in America. Between completing *Berg* in 1962 and setting off for America in 1965, however, she had, after recovering from glandular tuberculosis, spent much time traveling in Ireland and Greece and had virtually completed her second novel, *Three*.

This novel, published in 1966, is an exploration of the triangular relationship between a married couple, Ruth and Leonard, and a young girl, S, who comes to stay with them. Though convention and habit give them the appearance of a stable and united pair, the couple are in fact bored, frustrated, and self-divided. The girl views them as representatives of a solid, complacent world and wants to expose them to each other, to smash the routine of their marriage; yet she also desires to be recognized and accepted by them. A strong element of sexual

tension exists among all three characters, and the novel traces the fluctuations in their allegiances and their responses to each other.

Three bears certain underlying resemblances to *Berg*. The triangular relationship between the three characters can in part be understood in the light of the same Oedipal pattern; and, as in the case of *Berg*, Quin again places the quest for identity—for a significant self—at the center of the girl's conflict. Unlike *Berg*, however, S has a convincing literary ability and the fragments of her tapes and journals, which make up a considerable part of the narrative, indicate that part of this quest has been channeled into the creation of a literary self—the self that both writes and is written about. But her failure to define herself as she would like through her relationship with Ruth and Leonard finally seems to propel her to suicide. This is a solution which *Berg* too had considered (but rejected), but for S it has an ironically successful effect: after her death Ruth and Leonard become increasingly obsessed by her, by their possible responsibility for her death, and as a result they grow increasingly violent and direct in their questioning of each other and of their marriage.

Much of their time is thus spent in studying S's tapes and journals to discover possible motives for her suicide; through these much is revealed about S's attitudes toward the couple. These extracts also provide background information about S's past and her character, some of which relates quite clearly to Quin's own life. Like Quin's, S's life includes an absent father, a repressive school, and periods of illness and breakdown. Significant too is S's ambiguously sexual role in the triangular relationship, since the idea of triangular relationships is something that fascinated Quin not only in her novels but also in her own life. Tragically, S's drowning prefigures Quin's own death in 1973.

The other important function of these extracts is the opportunity they provide for an extended experimentation with language and prose forms. S's style is actually close to Quin's in its use of highly fragmented, elliptical sentences and in its vivid, economical juxtaposition of precisely caught impressions and the fleeting thoughts and emotions which they evoke. At times this style is extended to an almost free-verse form, in which the movement of the language is not dictated by linear thought but by the poetic association of words and the associative force of ideas, thoughts, and feelings:

. .Hallucinations
falling.

Apples. Half eaten into.
Hooded
Skulls
nod. Hands beckon. Voices call
from mouths
that do not open. Eyes broken
into
shrouded
layers of grey tissue take on forms

At its best this method creates a distilled, almost suspended picture of S's mind; at its worst it falls into a mechanical and rather mannered fragmentation of what is essentially a rather straightforward narrative. There are fragments, too, of Ruth's and Leonard's journals, written in a characteristically more conventional style and, like S's, they reveal important facts about their lives and characters. Thus Ruth's rather irritating frigidity and primness are explained by Leonard's sexual incompetence, and his rather shoddy dilettantism is seen in the light of his yearning for lost emotional and artistic possibilities, qualities that underlie their attraction to S, who is young, sensual, and apparently free of their own feelings of waste and frustration.

As in *Berg*, plot, character, and chronology develop in a very gradual and nonlinear fashion, without the overt exposition and judgments of the author, though the characters here are more consistently plausible and more fully drawn. This result is partly because the diary sections give each his or her own voice and viewpoint, but also because Quin succeeds in giving Ruth and Leonard, in particular, a very characteristic mode of speech and apprehension. Yet although the novel manages to maintain an almost phenomenological faithfulness to the subjective experience of the three characters as individuals, it also succeeds in creating an impression of the combined identity of the three: the moments of shared obsessions and emotions during which they almost become the fluctuating aspects of a single self (an idea which was to become much more explicit in her next novel, *Passages*).

Like *Berg*, *Three* had several appreciative and intelligent reviews—some of which were by other experimental novelists: B. S. Johnson, Robert Nye, and Alan Burns, for example, from whom she received not only friendship and encouragement, but also a growing sense of the directions her writing and her experimentation might take, a sense too of herself as part of a literary avant-garde.

While in America Quin spent much of her time traveling, particularly in California and New Mexico. She also continued to write, producing sev-

eral short stories and her third novel, *Passages* (1969), which reflects her earlier travels in Europe. The introduction to this book describes it as a mirroring of "the multiplicity of the meaning of the very word passage" and goes on to explain something of its theme and structure:

> This theme expresses itself through the wanderings of two people—a woman in search of her displaced/dead brother, and her lover, a masculine reflection of herself, in search of himself. Constantly moving, they live out their disparate, entangled existences, snatching at futile hopes, reluctant to give up, afraid of the outcome.
>
> The novel form, reflecting the schizophrenia of the characters, is split into two sections—a narrative and a diary, annotated with those thoughts that provoked the entries.

The narrative section seems initially to have been written by the woman and the diary by the man, each recording both the external events and impressions of their travels and the thoughts, emotions, and fantasies that underlie their actions (the diary perhaps attempting a greater organization and analysis of its material). Yet whereas in *Three* the individual characters remain distinct, despite the frequent interweaving of consciousnesses, the two characters in *Passages* cease very quickly to be discernible individuals. The "I" form of both sections rapidly begins to alternate with a third person form, suggesting some objectification or depersonalization of self; and sometimes it shifts entirely to the voice of the other character, suggesting not so much a dual perspective as an actual merging of identity into a single mind or single voice. Comments, descriptions, and feelings—which are unconnected in any way with either speaker or with the apparent present of the narrative—appear frequently in the text, and even where they are explicitly connected, it is clear that both characters often participate in each other's ideas and fantasies.

Even more than in the previous novels, past and present, fantasy and reality merge in an almost undifferentiated form, as Quin abandons completely the impersonal authorial narrative. She is exploring not simply the confused and fragmented workings of her characters' minds but showing, too, the ways in which they reflect and are part of each other and how they are bound together in what seems to be a shifting sadomasochistic relationship. Each character, or each voice (for it is finally impossible to decide if there are one or two people involved), dreams of doing violence to the other or to him/herself, either sexually or emotionally; and each fears the power that the other has over him/her. Escape is both desirable and impossible; hence they continue to drift along together.

Quin's extension of her earlier technique is not simply motivated by this more extreme psychological subject matter, however, but by more consciously experimental or formal considerations. As in *Three*, she pushes her elliptical prose style to a point where it becomes close to free verse, and the replacement of linear or causal logic for a more associative method is even more pronounced. In the diary sections the spatial organization of the prose suggests a new range of technical possibilities. Spaces of varying lengths are inserted between the different entries, and the marginalia in the left hand column (mostly ideas and statements that may or may not have an overt relationship with the text of the entry, along with extracts from Jane Harrison's *Prolegomena to a Study of Greek Religion*) are organized in what seems to be a random, but is in fact a highly deliberate, relation to both entries and spaces. Quin thus achieves a threefold relationship between two levels of thought and silence, a relationship that, though frequently lacking any explicit causal logic, develops a series of resonances and suggestions (an idea that was possibly derived from her interest in the music and writings of John Cage). This new interest in other avant-garde techniques is also evident in her use of the "cut-up" method: in certain sections of the diary, fragments of other extracts—of dreams, thoughts, and fantasies—reappear in a new, scrambled form, possibly to create new connections between previously disparate trains of thought.

Passages is a much more ambitious novel than the previous two, for although it deals with similar themes (loss of identity; the relation between reality and obsession or fantasy; the analysis of particular psychic states—either through symbolic action or, as here, through the casting of two individuals in roles which can be seen to represent two aspects of a schizophrenic mind), it does so with a much greater literary originality and with much less reliance on discernible plot and character. In parts of the novel, for example, the shifting of the narrative from first to third person frequently achieves a dramatic sense of alienation, and generally Quin succeeds in her attempt to evoke the obsessively interrelated personality that the two "people" become. As in *Three*, the interweaving of thought, perception, and emotion is carefully worked, and, in particular, the fragmentary impressions of place are very fine;

Quin is able to evoke a whole atmosphere, a whole climate through highly evocative detail: "We drank small cups of black coffee, thick, sweet. And sucked halva. Bread from an oven, in another part of the house. A spiral stairway he went down. She looked in the round mirror. Walls of mirrors. Circles of water, trees, faces edged off by shifting light." She suggests also a sense of the vivid but transitory impressions that are the peculiar privilege of the traveler. Her handling of the poetic resources of language is perhaps at its finest in this novel. Yet despite this more elaborate treatment of form and language, she can also articulate very recognizable elements in the couple's relationship, such as their frequent alterations from pleasure to dullness and despair, or the strange tension of violence which binds them in their shifting power relations.

But in some passages the writing seems, as in *Three*, to become mechanical or abstract. Certain fantasies/episodes (like the whipping scene and the woman's interrogation by the police) bear the mark of cliched sensationalism, and the woman's search for her dead brother is not realized with sufficient psychological force. (This was one of Quin's own obsessions, for in her article "Leaving School" she describes how at age fourteen she met her half brother—who later died—and, like the woman in *Passages*, imagined herself as Antigone. Like the autobiographical elements in *Berg*, it may be that this theme was too personal for her to be able to dramatize it successfully in an external form.) The diary narrative is not always wholly successful either. On occasion the marginalia are not of sufficient intrinsic interest or do not set up any real resonance in their relation to the rest of the text, and their presence thus becomes an irritating distraction. Sometimes, too, the reflections and analysis in the diary descend to the level of rather banal aphorism, and though possibly intended to reveal the speaker's rather stultifying self-absorption, they lack the perspective of a distancing irony.

Many reviewers found *Passages* a difficult and irritating book, though Marion Boyars, Quin's publisher and close associate, feels that the reviews reflected the bad choice of critics rather than the novel's artistic quality. Quin herself regarded it as her most important work but sensed that the communication of her personal experience in fictional form had become much more difficult.

Her last novel, *Tripticks* (1972), is in many ways a more impersonal work, though it derives from her travels around America and from her extreme dislike of New York. Its chameleonlike narrator-hero drives across America, claiming to be pursued by his first ex-wife and her husband, but appearing rather to be in pursuit of them. During his journey, the series of bizarre incidents that occur and fantasies he experiences are juxtaposed with flashbacks from the past, all of which have a dual purpose. On the one hand, they reveal the hero's erotic obsessions and paranoia; on the other hand, they satirize, either through style or theme, some aspect of American culture: its materialism; its uncritical acceptance of fashionable ideas and jargon; its crass notion of psychology; and the loss of individual contact and humanity within a mass-produced ideology. The ensuing collage of styles and perspectives—which are frequently exaggerated or distorted to the point where they become surreal—is thus intended to mirror the cacophony and bizarre quality of American society. The text is also punctuated with illustrations by Carol Annand—illustrations frequently reminiscent of Roy Lichtenstein's pop art—which contain fragmented images from American culture and from the man's sexual fantasies.

In certain passages the parody or satire is witty, accurate, and expressive, as in the section where Quin gives a surreal edge to the regimented, impersonal world of the motel and the fast-food culture in which individuals appear to have even less autonomy than the food they consume: "My cheeseburger spat contemptuously at the matron who flipped it. The meat was quickly silenced by the bun that drank its red juice all the way past the cash register and into the dining room, where I sat inconspicuously in front of a huge picture window. . . ." Particular incidents or flashbacks point cleverly to the nature and background of the hero's sexual paranoia—that he is, for example, unable to find a relationship that functions outside the realm of fantasy, and that he seems to lack the virility and the imagination to fulfill the fantasies that his women have. Yet as a whole, the narrative is too dense a confusion of styles and images to sustain the humor and point of the satire or to provide any coherent insight into the hero's consciousness. Indeed the novel's humor frequently falls into a rather vacuous and heavy-handed "zappiness" and the surreal edge into a gratuitous verbal exercise that does not really communicate a sense of the bizarre and the shocking. The illustrations, too, though witty and pleasing individually, are frequently positioned in a way that does not actually sharpen or develop the point of the narrative, but simply adds to the jumble.

Certainly this confusion has its point, for Quin intends her hero to be a typical representative of a mass-produced society: one who has lost his own identity to the point where all he can utter is the jumble of ideas, words, and images that have been fed into him over the years, and who has no personal viewpoint that can give them coherence or order. Thus at the point where he finally believes that he has been trapped by his ex-wife, he describes his experience in the following terms: "Fear for safety and sanity, helplessness, frustration and a desperate need to break out into a stream of verbal images. . . . I opened my mouth, but no words. Only the words of others I saw, like ads, texts, psalms, from those who had attempted to persuade me into their systems." Yet because the narrative lacks a consistent ironic perspective, this point is neither developed nor analyzed, and the satiric element remains a rather glib and superficial attack on what are essentially very easy targets. There were few sympathetic reviews for the novel, and the *New Statesman* critic went so far as to describe it as a "piece of self gratification" which "promulgates nothing more than the work of an artist at the end of her tether."

Artistically this was not in fact the case, though shortly after finishing *Tripticks*, while traveling in Sweden, Quin did suffer another serious breakdown and had to spend a month in a London hospital, unable to speak. However, she again appeared to recover and began work on her next novel, "The Unmapped Country." From the fragment which is published in *Beyond the Words* (a 1975 collection of experimental writing edited by Giles Gordon), this work appears to be a fairly straightforward treatment of her experiences in hospital, as well as a continuation of her interest in intermingling fragments of narrative, dialogue, and diary entries.

She also decided to extend her formal education, and in 1972 she entered Hillcroft College to prepare for university entrance examinations. Though her teachers seemed to show little appreciation of Quin's highly personalized approach to literature (she was not, in other words, an average student), she was awarded a place at the University of East Anglia for the following year. It was only a month before she was due to enter university, however, that she died—presumably having committed suicide, though the coroner's verdict on her death was an open one. She had always tried to avoid treatment for her mental illness, and her friends and associates generally assume that her death by drowning must have been related to it.

Quin was only thirty-seven when she died. From the evidence of her published work, it seems that she was gaining an increasing mastery and range of both language and form. The control and assurance evident in "The Unmapped Country" suggest that she had probably not yet achieved her potential. What she did write, however, stands as a considerable and highly original contribution to the experimental tradition in English literature.

Other:

"Eyes that Watch Behind the Wind" in *Signature*

Anthology (London: Calder & Boyars, 1975).

Periodical Publications:
"Leaving School," *London Magazine*, July 1966;
"Mother Logue," *Transatlantic Review*, 32 (1969): 101-105.

Papers:
Quin's manuscripts and publishers' correspondence are held in the Lilly Library, University of Indiana, Bloomington, Indiana.

Frederic Raphael
(14 August 1931-   )

John P. Kent
West Chester State College

BOOKS: *Obbligato* (London: Macmillan, 1956);
The Earlsdon Way (London: Cassell, 1958);
The Limits of Love (London: Cassell, 1960; Philadelphia: Lippincott, 1961);
A Wild Surmise (London: Cassell, 1961; Philadelphia: Lippincott, 1962);
The Graduate Wife (London: Cassell, 1962);
The Trouble with England (London: Cassell, 1962);
Lindmann (London: Cassell, 1963; New York: Holt, Rinehart & Winston, 1964);
Darling (New York: New American Library, 1965);
Orchestra and Beginners (London: Cape, 1967; New York: Viking, 1968);
Two for the Road (London: Cape, 1967; New York: Holt, Rinehart & Winston, 1967);
Like Men Betrayed (London: Cape, 1970; New York: Viking, 1971);
Who Were You With Last Night (London: Cape, 1971);
April, June and November (London: Cape, 1972; Indianapolis: Bobbs-Merrill, 1976);
Richard's Things (London: Cape, 1973; Indianapolis: Bobbs-Merrill, 1973);
Somerset Maugham and His World (London: Thames & Hudson, 1975);
California Time (London: Cape, 1975; New York: Holt, Rinehart & Winston, 1976);
The Glittering Prizes (London: Lane, 1976; New York: St. Martins Press, 1977);
Cracks in the Ice: Views and Reviews (London: W. H. Allen, 1979);
Sleeps Six and Other Stories (London: Cape, 1979);
Oxbridge Blues (London: Cape, 1980);
After the War (London: Cape, 1981).

Since 1956 when his first novel appeared, Frederic Raphael has produced fourteen novels, two volumes of short stories, a biography of Somerset Maugham, a volume of book reviews and broadcast talks, a collection of essays on the reading of writers, and translations of works by Catullus and Aeschylus. He has also written numerous film and television scripts, several of which have been published in book form. Such productivity has been accompanied by a continuing high standard of literary art that has made his novels among the most well received of the postwar years. His interests are never shallow, his technical ability has continued at the highest level, and his vision of contemporary society is tempered by wit and a wry self-knowledge. As a psychological outsider, Raphael can look on English society with a delight in its nuances of speech and its subtleties of character that are sometimes too familiar to be remarked upon by the writer more entrenched in that society. Raphael is in many ways a satirist—a propensity not often remarked upon—of contemporary English society, a spy at the heart of the English middle class, who, one feels, could at any moment become a double agent.

Frederic Michael Raphael was born in Chicago, Illinois, on 14 August 1931, the only son of Cedric Michael and Irene Mauser Raphael. His father, an employee of the Shell Oil Company, was British and his mother, American. The family lived in the United States until 1938, when, just before the beginning of World War II in Europe, they moved to Putney, a borough of southwest London, where his father had taken a new job.

After he had spent some time in "a typical middle-class preparatory school," he went to Charterhouse, one of the better known British public schools, where (unlike at his previous school) he was unhappy. However, through the attentions of a sympathetic teacher, Charterhouse provided him with an interest in the classics and later, in 1951, with the means for a major classics scholarship at St. John's College, Cambridge.

The cause of his unhappiness at Charterhouse seems to have been a sporadic antisemitism by fellow students, together with a feeling of isolation because of his anomalous position in society: "I had no sense of belonging to a society. I was a so-called Jew parked among so-called Christians; I was born in America and had my home in England; I had no brothers or sisters and I claimed no friends."

At Cambridge, where he read classics and later moral sciences, he was affected greatly by the philosophy of Wittgenstein as taught by his disciple, John Wisdom; Wittgenstein, who died in Cambridge in 1951, had ceased to teach several years before Raphael's arrival there. Raphael has remarked, with perhaps no hint of hyperbole, that "Wittgenstein swam into one's consciousness rather as that of Jesus must have into that of the early Christians." He left Cambridge with an MA (Honors) in 1954, and in the following year he married Sylvia Betty Glatt; they have two sons and a daughter.

Frederic Raphael has made a name for himself in at least three areas: as a novelist, as a writer of film and television scripts, and last as a book reviewer for the *Sunday Times* and other quality newspapers and magazines. His recently published book of collected reviews, *Cracks in the Ice: Views and Reviews* (1979), consists of reviews mainly from the *Sunday Times* but also from the *Listener* and the *New Statesman* as well as transcriptions of talks on the BBC.

Several of the talks given on the radio are autobiographical; one in particular, "Why I Became a Writer," is useful to a reader of Raphael's novels for the paradigm it gives of his emotional attachment, or lack of attachment, to his Jewish forebears: "Jews who refuse to admit what they are are generally regarded with disfavour. But what are we? And am I one of them? Though I cannot, I suppose, claim to be a racial hybrid, since my grandparents were, as I have said, all Jewish, I have no sense of

Frederic Raphael

religious certainty or racial allegiance." Many of his novels—one might almost suggest that a motif runs through them—try to answer these questions. Later in the same talk he commented further that "the Jewish experience in the 20th century remains obstinately at the heart of my consciousness. Shall I be making a terrible confession if I say that I am not particularly fond of Jews? I feel at ease with certain of them. . . . I dread gatherings of Jews and even that crucial instance, the state of Israel, fills me with contradictory feelings: its policies dismay me, yet its destruction would leave me in a state of incurable guilt and anger." In certain of his works—*The Limits of Love* (1960), *Lindmann* (1963), *Orchestra and Beginners* (1967), *April, June and November* (1972)—he explores, usually through character, the complex fate of being Anglo-Jewish.

Raphael is as well known as a writer of film scripts for the large and small screen as he is as a novelist. Indeed, the list of his credits and awards for that kind of work is long. In his preface to the film script of *Two for the Road* (1967), he defends the serious writer who can accept his part in the production of a film: "The inability or unwillingness to be imaginative in terms of film has become a virtue not so much because film is not an art as because it is an industry. The evidence may still point to the folly of associating with the bitch-Goddess of Hollywood . . . but that is not at all the same thing as saying that the form itself is necessarily contaminated." And indeed, Raphael seems to have been convinced by his own argument. Since 1964, he has written at least eight film scripts, for one of which, *Darling* (1965), he received an Oscar for best original screenplay, together with several awards from British organizations. While most of the scripts he has written for television have not been seen in the United States, one, *The Glittering Prizes* (1976), appeared on public television stations in 1979. It is a series of television plays dealing with the young people who were at Cambridge in the 1950s and with their subsequent careers, amatory as well as economic.

Raphael has several times asserted that a major impetus to write was his reading Somerset Maugham's *Of Human Bondage* (1915). He has said that his anguish at being a "squalid little public-school Jew-bait" forced him to find avenues of escape; and his future seems to have been set with the reading of Maugham's novel: "Philip Carey's club foot was my Jewishness. If Maugham's anguish could be written out and dignified by print, so then could mine. My revenge would never be physical, for the enemy was too powerful and too numerous,

but through books I could enjoy the last laugh. . . . And to be published was to be accepted. . . . Is it very shameful to confess that an element of revenge has never been wholly absent from my work?" If Raphael has not followed Maugham very far in the kind of novel that he writes, he does seem to be fairly consistent in his continuing interest in the situation of the outsider, especially the Jewish outsider, in English society. Raphael's novels do not deal exclusively with this topic, but the theme is never very far away.

Raphael's first novel, *Obbligato* (1956), is interesting because it *is* his first novel, but it contains little of literary value. Although we can already see the writer's ability to characterize through dialogue even slight differences in the social class or intellect of his characters, protagonist Frank Smith's rise to fame through chicanery and a certain ability on the trumpet, allied with some rather obvious satire on the world of "entertainment," gives us no real indication of Raphael's future work. His second novel, *The Earlsdon Way* (1958), deals with suburban complacency, futility, and prejudice—the staples of so many novels about such an easy target—yet what raises it above the ordinary is Raphael's clear-sighted knowledge of the world he portrays, both the physical world in all its details and the psychology of the English bourgeoisie in its terrifying obtuseness. The hardly disguised antisemitism of the middle class, portrayed in its reaction to Mark Epstein, is shown with sureness of touch, especially in the dialogue; Raphael knows exactly *what* is said, and how innuendo and tired jokes, the common coinage of the country-club set, serve to dehumanize the outsider.

Raphael's third novel, *The Limits of Love*, an extended history of several generations of an Anglo-Jewish family living in London, depicts the tensions of a younger generation in revolt against a culture the virtues of which it is not yet completely aware. The Adler family live in Cricklewood, a borough of north London. The parents are Isadore and Hannah; their children are Susan, married to Ben Simons, a Communist; Colin, lately a major in the army; and Julia, a schoolgirl. The time is just after World War II. The moral center of the novel lies in Paul Riesman, the protagonist, who arrives rather late in book 2 and eventually marries the Adler's younger daughter.

Book 1, while introducing the Adler family, is also a brilliant evocation of an Anglo-Jewish milieu that in its children is rapidly losing the cohesiveness and indeed the clannishness that an older generation knew. While much of this new Diaspora can be accounted for by historical forces, British society—with its emphasis on a complex class structure and the virtues of finally acquiring middle-class gentility—contributes a great deal to the self-hatred seen in the protagonist and several of the minor characters. Colin Adler, for example, is petrified by the thought that his neighbors and the fellow members of his golf club will find out that he is Jewish. The Riesmans, the parents of Paul and friends of Colin Adler and his wife, Tessa, comment on the possibility that a new synagogue might be founded in their pleasant suburb:

> "Of course a synagogue is the last thing we want out here. I mean you know what happens: the brethren simply arrive in their coach-loads."
> "Jaguar-loads," Colin said.

Paul Riesman, the lover and, later, husband of Julia Adler, is the most self-reflexive of the younger generation. He aspires to be a writer and succeeds in his trade, but his success does not reconcile him to his fractured state. It is only after his marriage to Julia that he finds the beginnings of a reconciliation in his experience with his new mother-in-law, Hannah Adler. Her solidity, her ability to accept life, is based on her sense of community, the community of Jewishness. A woman of no great intellect but with an immense openness to life, she revisits with Paul the scenes of her earlier days in the East End of London. The effect on him is strong: "He loved her because she loved what was true, because she acknowledged the truth, because she came from this street where Jewish people lived, where people were born Jews and grew up Jews, where they did not doubt or think of escaping what they were."

The novel as a whole is impressive in its realism, in its exploration of Paul's dilemma, and in its articulate presentation of the milieu. Yet Paul's problem comes rather late in the novel, and the parallel situations of Colin and Susan Adler seem rather peripheral. Susan thinks she will find community in the Communist Party, Colin in the anonymity of the English bourgeoisie. Although neither one does achieve his or her goal, each eventually reaches a kind of calm. But it is Paul who carries the moral burden of the novel and carries it extremely well.

A Wild Surmise (1961) is a different kind of novel altogether. The small South American country of San Roque harbors an English oil company, Sarroco, and a United States naval base. It has a dictator with a beautiful daughter and a population which is made up of mostly poverty-stricken Indians, with remnants of aristocratic first families. Into this world comes a young Englishman, Robert Carn, whose intelligent cynicism masks a certain naivete about the world and himself and who impinges upon the life of the town and its inhabitants, both native and foreign, with considerable effect. Most affected are the young personnel-relations man for the oil company, Bruce Fairley, and his wife, Jessica. Robert Carn's odyssey to his putative death among the Indians involves the whole community. Fairley and his wife are made to take a close look at the worth of their lives, especially the human worth of Bruce's job. The oil company is shallowly manipulative, and the local political forces, the nationalists and the communists, are murderous in their political maneuverings. Part of a shipment of oil, which would become a glut on the local market at an inopportune time for Sarocco, is illegally distributed as cooking oil to the Indians by the nationalists, with the result that large numbers of the Indians die. Carn is in part responsible for this action and its results, and his efforts to recruit Bruce Fairley to aid the Indians, as well as his own decision to stay and eat with the Indians in the mountains, is an expiation and a kind of justification for his life.

The construction of the novel suggests a debt to cinematographic techniques, with rapid cutting between scenes for usually significant purposes and with a wholly admirable use of dialogue to produce individuality of character, even in the minor figures. There are faint echoes of Conrad's *Nostromo* (1904) in Raphael's picture of modern colonialists in San Roque; if the oil is not as socially corrosive as the silver of the San Tome mine, it does affect decisively the lives of many people. Further, Raphael reveals only in piecemeal fashion the information we need to judge the major character, who remains a mystery until near the end of the novel.

Raphael's next two novels, *The Graduate Wife* (1962) and *The Trouble with England* (1962) are, compared to *The Limits of Love* and *A Wild Surmise*, rather slim. Yet the writer is never negligible when he is dealing with the emotional and moral lives of married couples. The graduate wife is Joyce Heywood, wife of Nicholas and mother to Lindsey and Julian. The novel details her "graduation" from a rather infantile dependence upon a group of male friends of the family, known as the "gangsters," all of whom have been to private school and some to university with Nicholas. She graduates to becoming a woman who finds she is capable of dwelling in herself, depending neither on the past nor on her persistently unimpressed husband. Joyce is also a graduate of Oxford and the daughter of a judge. Thus she is, like her husband, impeccably middle class. But as for many, Nicholas's and Joyce's university days are the apogees of their lives. At Oxford wit and sparkle exist, profundity is thought to reign but rarely does, and the descent for many into the quotidian round is very difficult. Joyce manages to become her own woman through an encounter in central London with a rather mysterious and arrogant stranger, a Mr. Van Benius, driver of a Rolls-Royce with which she collides in her small car. Angered by his insistence that the fault is hers, she is goaded to reply in strong language, whereupon he loses his temper and attempts to strangle her. He fails, but this curious indication of her significance—"Joyce put her fingers to her throat as if to a new necklace, as if to touch a new gift"—is later strengthened when, after losing the subsequent court case to Van Benius, he suggests that she become his mistress. She rejects his offer, but on his insistence that he give her something, she elects to drive his Rolls-Royce several times around Regents Park. Her ability to arouse strong emotions of both anger and lust in a man of substance such as Van Benius, even though she finds him personally repellent, gives her a new power and maturity. Later at home, recounting only part of the incident to Nicholas, she makes known her desire for another child, for a break with the past, for a different future: "'I refuse to be disappointed any further. You must admit there's something tediously juvenile about the gangsters. One must graduate sometime.' She turned and walked briskly to the front door."

The Trouble with England deals with the interaction of two English couples on the Riviera. Ian and Betsy are rather dull and smug, while Mike and Josie have a certain warmth and moral dynamism. Their relationship is detailed with irony, brilliant dialogue, and an emphasis on the moral contrast between the two. The interest stems more from the details of middle-class England than from the expected moral judgments.

If *The Graduate Wife* is the exploration of one major action in the protagonist's life, *Lindmann*, Raphael's perhaps most significant work up to this time, is a much more comprehensive investigation, an investigation into the nature of guilt and its expiation. Both in technique and in emotional intensity the novel goes beyond anything Raphael had previously attempted. The plot, if it can be called that, conveys very little of the power of the book. A British civil servant during World War II had, on orders of his government, refused to give Palestine

entry visas to some six hundred Jews from occupied Europe who were stranded on the S. S. *Broda* at a Turkish port. The Turks as a result would not allow them ashore, nor would they allow repairs to be done to the dilapidated ship. Instead, they towed the *Broda* outside Turkish territorial waters and set the ship adrift, whereupon it sank with the immediate loss of all but two of the Jewish refugees. The guilt-ridden civil servant has a mental breakdown and takes on the identity of one of the surivors who later died—a man called Lindmann.

For the first fifteen chapters of the book, we do not know that this Lindmann is the civil servant James Shepherd. Yet the false identity begins to break down in the last three chapters. This crumbling of the false identity is brought about by the protagonist's reading of a film script about the *Broda* tragedy, written by Milstein, an ambitious friend. Shepherd/Lindmann's only response to the script when asked, "Well, how *true* do you feel it is?" is to remark, "What I feel about the script is—that I am mistaken. I am mistaken. That is all. If this is the result—I am mistaken. That is all."

Shepherd has taken on the historic Lindmann's identity in an attempt to expiate his guilt, but this action is not presented as either heroic or morally acceptable. After the reading of the powerful film script at a meeting punctuated by the vulgar badinage of a producer named Loomis, Shepherd's comments show his awareness that his insane impersonation of Lindmann, for whatever seemingly moral reasons, is a species of plagiarism, in the same way as the script is the falsification of an event so horrible that its use as a subject for a film denigrates it. As Shepherd realizes in his delirium: "The most subtle and nauseous forms of plagiarism are those which occur in living, when we take others' misfortunes to ourselves and at once dramatize ourselves and diminish them." Even Milstein's tainted affection for Shepherd/Lindmann will result in, ironically, more of the same: a television series on difficult psychiatric cases, including the protagonist's. Milstein remarks to Fine, a psychiatrist and friend of Shepherd/Lindmann's: "I do want to do this series. It could be bloody marvellous, I really mean. It's the only thing to be done for Lindmann, if you know what I mean."

Orchestra and Beginners is a return to the more orderly paths of the English middle classes. In a novel of some five hundred pages, Raphael traces the psychological history of Linda Strauss, nee Tayfield, during the first years of World War II. Her husband, Leonard, is Anglo-Jewish, while Linda is an American. Their milieu is that of the well-to-do upper middle classes, those who went to Claridges for lunch when the cook had trouble with the rationing. They have a son, Mark, who goes to the obligatory preparatory school, where he discovers the pains and few pleasures of English boyhood. The Strausses also have a daughter who remains a determinedly shadowy figure throughout the novel.

The book deals in detail and at length with the strains of a marriage in which a young American wife is trying to find her own way of life with a husband who not only is fixed in and supported by English society but whose consequent self-assurance enfolds and stultifies her. While Leonard is in Switzerland doing something for British Intelligence, Linda tries to develop a satisfactory relationship with her son, who is more interested in conforming to public-school protocol than to the needs of his affectionate mother. She, therefore, turns to a school friend of Mark's, Patrick Conrad, who is desperately in need of maternal love, but whose past and present persecutions by his schoolfellows lead him to an accidental death. When Leonard returns from the war, Linda is more mature—having had space and liberty to develop—and the potential for a balanced relationship between them is at last possible.

The novel's excellence lies in its brilliant reproduction, mainly through dialogue, of an atmosphere of nervous tension that permeates both the society at war and the individual marriage. Again, one is impressed by Raphael's ability to depict the psychological convolutions of intelligent and articulate people and, in this novel especially, the attractive decadence of some aspects of British society at the beginning of a war.

Greece before, during, and after World War II is the setting for Raphael's ninth novel, *Like Men Betrayed* (1970). Artemis Theodoros's life is wasted; on the losing side during the Greek civil war and a man of sensitivity, intelligence, and poetic powers, he suffers violence, exile, and betrayal. The rhythms of Greece, the concrete details of Greek life, are brilliantly evoked, while the corruption endemic to politics raises more familiar echoes.

Who Were You With Last Night (1971) is narrated in a virtual monologue by the protagonist, Charlie Hanson, formerly a sailor in the Merchant Navy and now a salesman for an industrial park. In his demotic English he reveals his ambiguous attitude toward his wife, Lola, and, indeed, to women in general. Hate and love are inextricably mixed in Hanson's mind, and yet the story is told with such Rabelaisian humor and honest self-knowledge that

the reader cannot but acknowledge the truth of his experiences.

The conclusion, however, is rather unconvincing. Charlie Hanson is surprised by an intruder in his employer's office. Hanson himself is there illegally, making love to a rather superior secretary, Jean Haughton; the intruder unfortunately turns out to be a rather unpersuasive symbol of justice:

> "What's important is what I represent, isn't it?"
> "What you represent."
> "Which is justice in a way."
> "Ah!"
> "That's what I represent. I don't have to have a name."

The novel thus turns into a morality play.

April, June and November (1972) is a novel about the bright young people who come down from Oxford or Cambridge, get jobs in BBC television or write books, and talk, talk, talk brilliantly yet exhaustingly. Daniel Meyer is a well-known film director who is not sure where his happiness is to lie. For a time he thinks it might lie with Nancy Lane, a beautiful divorcee, or perhaps with Rachel Davidson, an actress and flower child. But Daniel is a destroyer of relationships and fights with both women. And yet, Meyer's intentions are good—children are what he claims he wants; but he never seems to be able to actualize his good intentions, in part perhaps because of the effete society in which he exists. Daniel Meyer as hero can only exist, it seems, playing soccer, a game that is the only thing his friends take seriously.

The virtues of *April, June and November* are many: the descriptions of a fortieth birthday party and of the Greek landscape are excellent, and the dialogue is well done. Yet there is something self-indulgent about the novel. Dialogues go on too long, jokes are told for the sake of telling jokes rather than to illuminate character, and wit becomes an end in itself.

In happy contrast is *Richard's Things* (1973), in which a complex state of mind is suggested in prose that has been stripped of the boisterousness of Raphael's previous novels. Kate Morris's husband, Richard, dies of a heart attack while away from home on business, and she finds out he has been having an affair with a young French girl, Marie-José Clavand, known as Mijo, who is an employee at his firm of landscape gardeners. In fact, Mijo had accompanied him on the business trip, and it was she who had called the ambulance. Kate moves

the theatre together. It was rotten and they left at the interval. Both of
them agreed that the intellectual pretensions of the stage were evidence of the new
decadence. Maxine was slimmer and seemed younger than Victor had ever known her.
The maternal puffiness of her face had been refined by Oxford food and by the serious regime she had imposed on herself. She was too old, she said, for undergraduate
nonsense and she had worked with a rare diligence. Her chance had come late and
she was determined not to fluff it. Thanks to Pip's generosity, she had lived
very comfortably. She had a large allowance and she was dressed in a leather suit
which Victor found indelectable. Her hair had been done by a man in South Moulton
Street. But what particularly enchanted Victor was her appetite for serious talk.
They went to a restaurant club and talked until they were the last people there.
She had taken a room at the Dorchester, for the night. She proposed that they continue
to analyse the relationship between intellectual style and social content, in the
comfort of her hotel. He was seduced less by the smart new clothes and the quite
maredkly smarter new accent than by her ravenous interest in his opinions. They
went only slightly furtively past the porter, amused to think that no one would
ever credit the loftiness of their motives.

It must have been three or four in the morning before anything personal was
said, and then it was said quite impersonally: "I married the wrong woman, you know.
I thought that Wendy and I would have conversations like this all our lives, but
she never wanted to."

"I should never have said anything if you hadn't," Maxine said, "but of course
I could have told you that the minute I met her, that night at your house when I
was supposed to play the kennel maid."

"I had no idea that you had a mind at that point," Victor said. "I don't mind
confessing it, I was terribly snobbish, and I still am, I daresay, except that
you're not the same person as you were then, are you?"

"Thanks to Pip," she said. "We shouldn't ever forget that."

"The difficulty," he said, "is to know how we ever shall.

"Times have changed," she said. "I don't imagine that he's been exactly the
faithful spouse out there in Los Angeles, do you?"

"They aren't noted for it, I'm told, and I assume environment will do its

Page from the revised typescript for "Oxbridge Blues"

620

from hatred of the girl to a lesbian relationship with her in a desperate attempt to keep in contact with Richard through the person to whom he seemed to reveal a different self. As long as Mijo exists in Kate's life, Richard is not dead. But the relationship does not last; its bases were false from the beginning, and the full momentum of Richard's death inevitably comes.

Kate is entirely believable in her disbelief at Richard's infidelity; she has been married to him for sixteen years and has thought they were happy. She has a teenage son at boarding school, and she is well off in a modest way. Even her rather rapid love for Mijo is believable because it is artfully downplayed. *Richard's Things* has an aesthetic completeness, a sense of form which Raphael had not completely achieved since *Lindmann*.

California Time (1975), Raphael's Hollywood novel, is not, as one reviewer remarked, "an easy read." He has attempted to write the novel in a series of presents, a construction that, with the book's alternating typography, adds to the nightmarish quality of the southern California landscape. The novel is a juxtaposition of images and wordplay, of past and present, which achieve the effects more of an experimental poem than of prose fiction. When Victor England, a well-known English film director, returns to sign a contract in a Hollywood that has seen better days, the hotel in which he is staying is taken over by the Mafia, and the studio with which he is dealing changes bosses in some commercial shenanigans. Victor has an affair with Bella, who mysteriously turns into his daughter, a cripple; there are also many flashbacks. Victor's previous amatory adventures are presented, and finally his deal is concluded. These broken images produce a rather powerful emotional effect, which is only slightly hindered by Raphael's predilection for some rather corny puns.

The Glittering Prizes, his most recent novel, a spin-off from his television series of the same name, is a book about the mutations of ambition among a group of young people. We follow them from Cambridge, where they meet, through their subsequent marriages, divorces, successes, and failures. The "gangsters" of *A Graduate Wife* live again in more detail, perhaps, but essentially the figures in the two works are the same kind of people: witty, literate, ironic Cambridge graduates.

The critical reception of Raphael's novels has been characterized by a continual harping on one theme: his dialogue is brilliant, but his ability to pull his novels together into unified wholes is somewhat lacking. American reviewers have been more re-

ceptive than the English, who are generally more acerbic, and, one suspects, less objective. As early as *The Limits of Love* the theme was sounded: Raphael "loves writing in dialogue and much of his drive, it seems to me, goes to waste through a lack of selectivity," remarked the reviewer for the *Guardian*. The *New Statesman* admitted that "while we have one brilliant scene after another, the scenes do not quite jell together as a final satisfactory narrative." *A Wild Surmise* brought slightly better reviews. Critics praised the "robust, chop-licking prose, and above all . . . the characterization-through-dialogue which gives it compulsion," but again many reviewers insisted that dialogue was his only expertise: "All that really emerges is the dialogue, reproduced with the fidelity of the tape-recorder," Patricia Hodgart remarked rather acidly in the *Spectator*. The personal odyssey of Carn, the central character, was not particularly well received: "a weakness in the story," "less successful . . . is the central character." *Lindmann* had a better reception. Haskell Frankel suggested that "*Lindmann* moves him out of the category of 'writers to watch' and into that rare company of 'writers to follow,' " while the *New Statesman* saw parts of the novel as having "a sustained brilliance that can scarcely be questioned," yet the novel "doesn't sustain itself as a whole." P. N. Furbank wrote, "The central idea of the novel is really a stunning one," but at the same time he found "much dead weight." *Orchestra and Beginners* drew tempered praise from the *New York Times*, which said Raphael's "dialogue is brilliant to the point of excess," while the *Times Literary Supplement* wearily commented that here was "Yet another long, sad novel about cruel little boys in a fee-charging boarding school," while adding that "if the author can edit this self-indulgent novel, concentrating on his main theme, he could make a first-rate film script from it." *Like Men Betrayed* elicited the same response from Neil Millar in the *Christian Science Monitor*: "This is a novel of luxuriant talent desperately in need of pruning," and, again, "When Raphael's characters are talking, his ear for cadence and emphasis is faultless." *Richard's Things* had a better reception. The novel led the *New York Times* book reviewer to claim that "not many novelists have so complete a mastery of their art," while the *Times Literary Supplement* saw only a "clever but barren exercise in technique."

Raphael's work since 1956 has been consistent in its brilliant use of dialogue, in its critical interest in the urban middle classes, and in its dissection of that febrile world where art and commerce intermingle. Perhaps he has not yet completely achieved his early promise; but certainly with *Lindmann* and *Richard's Things* he has written two fully realized works of literary art that will guarantee his place in any history of the modern novel.

Screenplays:
Nothing But the Best, based on Stanley Ellin's short story, Columbia, 1964;
Darling, Embassy, 1965;
Two for the Road, Twentieth Century-Fox, 1967;
Far from the Madding Crowd, based on Thomas Hardy's novel, MGM, 1967.

Other:
Bookmarks, edited and with an introduction by Raphael (London: Cape, 1974);
The Poems of Catullus, translated by Raphael and Kenneth McLeish (London: Cape, 1978);
The Serpent Son: The Oresteia of Aeschylus, translated by Raphael and Kenneth McLeish (Cambridge: Cambridge University Press, 1979);
The List of Books, compiled by Raphael and Kenneth McLeish (New York: Harmony Books, 1980).

Piers Paul Read
(7 March 1941-   )

Philip Flynn
University of Delaware

BOOKS: *Game in Heaven with Tussy Marx* (London: Weidenfield & Nicolson, 1966; New York: McGraw-Hill, 1967);
The Junkers (London: Secker & Warburg, 1968; New York: Knopf, 1969);
Monk Dawson (London: Secker & Warburg, 1969; Philadelphia & New York: Lippincott, 1970);
The Professor's Daughter (London: Alison/Secker & Warburg, 1971; Philadelphia & New York: Lippincott, 1971);
The Upstart (London: Alison/Secker & Warburg, 1973; Philadelphia & New York: Lippincott, 1973);
Alive: The Story of the Andes Survivors (London: Secker & Warburg, 1974; Philadelphia & New York: Lippincott, 1974);
Polonaise (London: Alison/Secker & Warburg, 1976; Philadelphia & New York: Lippincott, 1976);
The Train Robbers (London: Alison/W. H. Allen, 1978; Philadelphia & New York: Lippincott, 1978);
A Married Man (London: Alison/Secker & Warburg, 1979; Philadelphia & New York: Lippincott, 1979);
The Villa Golitsyn (London: Secker & Warburg, 1981; New York: Harper & Row, 1982).

Piers Paul Read was born in Beaconsfield, England, the son of poet, essayist, and art critic Herbert Read and Margaret Ludwig Read. When Read was eight his family moved to the rural north of Yorkshire, the scene of Herbert Read's own childhood, which he so movingly described in *The Innocent Eye* (1947). The elder Read was a humanist, anarchist, and skeptic, a lifelong opponent of the capitalist system whose political concerns would provide a major theme of his son's novels. That influence was balanced, however, by the religious convictions of Read's mother, whom her son has remembered as "an emotional, musical, unpredictable convert to Catholicism." At his mother's insistence Read was sent to Ampleforth College, a private school run by Benedictine monks, that would provide much of the material for the first part of his novel, *Monk Dawson* (1969).

Read left Ampleforth with relief at the age of sixteen. Rather than directly entering a university he spent six months in Paris, where he watched with interest the death throes of the Fourth Republic. After a short visit to Germany and time spent working for a London publisher, he entered St. John's College, Cambridge. He has described his years there as "agreeable but unexciting," the dons elusive, and the undergraduates "on the whole less interesting than the people I used to meet at home." Beginning as a student of history, he switched briefly to moral sciences (philosophy), despaired at the dominant linguistic approach, and returned to the study of history. He had already decided to become a writer, but both his father and the English tutor, Hugh Sykes Davies, warned him against the pernicious effect of reading English literature in an academic setting. Because of that warning he is now an accomplished stylist and, by his own standard, "wretchedly ill-read."

Read's history studies included readings in American history and the history of political thought, both of which would provide material for his analysis of capitalist culture in *The Professor's Daughter* (1971). Because of his father's long interest in politics and his own recent exposure to French

Piers Paul Read

public affairs, he joined a number of undergraduate political clubs. But Read's awareness of and interest in Marxist thought stopped short of total conversion. Although, as he has written, he was at this time "a revolutionary by nature" and although Marxist thought impressed him as "an effective revolutionary ideology," he was never able to master Hegel's writings and "so never had a sufficient grasp of Marx to call myself a Marxist." After taking his B. A. in 1961 and his M. A. in 1962, Read lived for two years in Germany, the first year working for a publisher in Munich and the second as a Ford Foundation Fellow in West Berlin. As Read

later wrote, "Perhaps because my mother had a large measure of German blood, I had always been fascinated by the Germans and had chosen to come to Germany to try and digest their 'undigested past.'" In 1964 he accepted a position as subeditor of the *Times Literary Supplement*, then joined his father on a two-month visit in 1965 to Japan, Thailand, Laos, Cambodia and South Vietnam, returning to England in time for the publication of his first novel, *Game in Heaven with Tussy Marx* (1966).

The book was advertised as an "experimental" novel, although the technique and tone remind a reader of earlier experiments—by Laurence Sterne, perhaps, or Virginia Woolf. In heaven the narrator, a dowager duchess, and Karl Marx's daughter, Tussy, look down upon processions on the mountaintops and highlands of Britain. The processions—described by the narrator as "a revival of the Forty-Five, of the Levellers, the Chartists and the Pilgrimage of Grace too"—are seeking a leader, a hero, one Hereward (historically a leader of the Saxons against William the Conqueror). The "game" involved is the narrator's attempt to construct an admittedly fictional history of Hereward, the revolutionary saint for whom contemporary men and women seek.

Read makes due obeisance to the modern concern with fiction's "truth." That philosophical/technical concern, along with other themes, and the tone of this first novel are important to an understanding of his later work. Read here employs themes that mean much to him: the emptiness of secular society ("he can see the despair of his fellow countrymen who [have] lost hope in their community under any form—empire, nation or welfare state . . ."); the danger of social stagnation ("their instincts are clogged by customs no longer related to the form of their society"); the importance of marital fidelity ("I can see no logic for it but I know that fidelity is a good thing and the measure of a man's calibre"); and the strange connection between Communist and Christian ideals ("as different and intertwined as body and soul, heaven and earth"). But the tone in which these themes are treated is ironic, the tone of a young novelist not wishing to be laughed at as too earnest. Did Read lack the courage of his own concerns? "Why must he hide his feelings like that?" asks the dowager concerning Hereward. "He has to use the idiom of his time," replies the narrator. "Otherwise no one will understand him; he will seem ridiculous. . . . If the times reduce Hereward to speaking the truth in tones of irony, cynicism, and contempt, he will still be speaking the truth." Some years before, another Catholic novelist, Evelyn Waugh, had written of "the simple truth" with "a facetious intonation" (*Put Out More Flags*); when he dropped his facetious mask in *Brideshead Revisited* critics hissed and Waugh was stung. Either Read was determined not to make the same mistake or, a good thing for a Catholic novelist, he was keeping all his options open for his art. In this and later novels, Read adopted the idioms of his time—the idioms of cynicism, nihilism, sociological/biological determinism. Until the writing of *Alive: The Story of the Andes Survivors* (1974) he would play games with his readers: fiction's truth and Read's own truths would be veiled.

In spring 1967 Read visited his fiancée, Emily Boothby, who was teaching school in Uganda; with her and a cousin he then made a circuitous return to England via Kenya, Zanzibar, Ethiopia, Egypt, and Libya, locations that would eventually be used in *The Professor's Daughter*. After visiting Emily's father, who was at that time ambassador to Iceland, Read and his fiancée were married on 28 July 1967 in Strasbourg, France, where the ambassador had been subsequently posted as British envoy to the Council of Europe. Perhaps drawing on this exposure to diplomatic life, certainly drawing on his earlier sojourn in Germany and research into German affairs, Read produced in 1968 his second novel, *The Junkers*. Years later, commenting on his politics at that time, Read wrote, "It seemed to me, as I studied the Nazi era, that the only plausible alternative to National Socialism in the 1930s was Socialism *tout court*. Thus if all other things had been equal I would at that time have called myself a Marxist: I might even have joined the Communist Party, but I was always inhibited from doing this by my Catholic faith which was always stronger than my ideological convictions. Indeed the convictions were the inspiration of the Faith. It seemed to me then that liberty, equality and fraternity could only be justified by the Christian hypothesis that God meant men to be free, equal, and fraternal. I still think this, but no longer believe that Communism or Socialism is the necessary expression of his command."

Read's description of his own state of mind while he was writing *The Junkers* does not prepare a reader for the finished novel. What evolved was not a statement of Christian fraternity or, despite the presence of one Communist saint, a celebration of communism. The novel is a complex horror story, a study of the twentieth century's great symbol of evil, Nazism. It also plays upon the paradigm of comedy, with lovers from different worlds overcoming obstacles to give birth to a brave new world in a closing wedding feast. The nameless first-person narrator ("This is what happened to me in Germany") is a member of Read's own generation, a diplomatic adviser to the British Commander in Berlin. He describes himself as an Englishman who believes in fair play, one who takes pride in shrugging off his father's generation's obsession with the horrors of World War II. He is also a veteran of joyless seductions, a sensualist who has deep contempt for the pleasures of the flesh. An expert on German history and finance, he feels no real sympathy for the people or the country. A rootless modern, an uninvolved expert with no personal feeling for the subject he studies, he is also Read's first portrait of the artist.

This narrator's art is an imaginative reconstruction of the lives of the von Rummelsberg circle—a group of Pomeranian Junkers who had been caught up in the rise of the National Socialist party in the 1930s. The narrator has been ordered to investigate the past of Karl von Rummelsberg, whose emergence as a political leader in postwar Berlin troubles the Allied authorities. But the narrator feels an unusual, personal interest in this investigation: he is attracted to the physically flawless, perhaps virginal, Suzi von Rummelsberg, the ward or daughter or mistress of Klaus's brother, Helmuth von Rummelsberg, a diplomat turned nightclub impresario. The investigation proceeds on two levels, historical and personal, as the narrator attempts to reconstruct the von Rummelsbergs' past and to discover Suzi's true relationship to the von Rummelsberg circle: "This is what we know and what we suppose. I began to lead their lives in my mind with facts and fantasy as I led my own on the ground with arms and legs, mouth and eyes."

The format Read employs on the historical level is that of the intelligence dossier, which includes names, dates, and "what we suppose." The racism, betrayals, and atrocities he gradually discovers (or supposes) in the von Rummelsbergs' history are paralleled, on the personal level, by the prejudice, sadism, and abortions within his own family and sexual affairs. The investigator is himself an agent and victim of deceit. He lies to Suzi and his political superiors; he is deceived by the von Rummelsbergs to forward their own postwar ambitions. Through alternating dossier reconstructions and first-person narrative, the artist/narrator/investigator moves toward a choice between his love for Suzi (the best thing in his life) and his repulsive suspicions concerning Suzi's true father (the worst thing in his imagination). Read's message seems, at first, to be one of tolerance and chastened hope: the

Nazis were no worse than the rest of us; they destroyed Jews but the United States bombed Hiroshima and Dresden; forget the past and move into an enlightened, forgiving, internationalist Europe. But, as in a well-constructed horror story, the last pages surprise us, betray our hopes, confirm our fears. It is not that the Nazis were no worse than the rest of us. The rest of us are as evil as the Nazis—a more damning, fearful, lapsarian indictment. Evil is real and pervasive; the narrator's attempt to rise above the historical past is a refusal to recognize the human past, the human condition in which evil is entangled with men's noblest aspirations—to save Germany through Hitler, to save Europe through communism, to save oneself by staying aloof from politics and cultivating one's own garden. In a scene near the end of the book, having received the blessing of the godlike/ Prospero-like Helmuth von Rummelsberg, the book's nameless hero/Adam/Ferdinand suspects that his Suzi/Eve/Miranda has betrayed him—that their brave new Europe may be flawed by the unexpected presence of Caliban/Suzi's true father/the former Nazi sadist at the wedding feast.

The Junkers won Read both critical attention and two awards, the Geoffrey Faber Memorial and Hawthornden prizes. At the time of the novel's publication in England in 1968, Read's first television play, *Coincidence*, was produced by the BBC. Read himself was completing a two-year visit (1967-1968) to New York and Massachusetts as a Harkness Fellow, gathering material that he would use in *The Professor's Daughter*. What immediately followed *The Junkers*, however, was a novel that explored the psychology of an English saint, a character like Edward von Rummelsberg, the Christian-Communist idealist of *The Junkers*. The novel was *Monk Dawson*, Read's first detailed analysis of Roman Catholic life, a novel that would shortly win the Somerset Maugham Award for fiction. The subject of Catholicism before and after Vatican II is one of which Read writes with personal knowledge. The title figure, Edward Dawson, is a Catholic boy educated in a Benedictine school that caters to children of the upper-middle class. His early humanitarian impulses are tempered by his teachers' belief that we must serve our fellow man for God's sake, not man's. Taught to distrust the pleasures of the flesh, affected by the theater of Catholic liturgy, driven by desires to "help people," Dawson becomes a Benedictine priest and teacher—just as his father's family had provided clergymen, doctors, and civil servants to the East India Company or the British Empire. But Daw-

son's concern with personal saintliness makes him a poor teacher of adolescent boys, while his desire to help others leads him to question a school dedicated to teaching only affluent children. A Catholic educated in the stable 1950s (as was Read), Dawson becomes a casualty of the 1960s, "a small molecule of the phenomenon of religious turmoil that became so evident all over the world."

As the post-Vatican II Catholic church reassesses its relationship to secular concerns, Dawson rushes into local social causes "with the fervour of a frustrated saint." Because his superiors add to his frustrations, he transfers to the secular clergy and becomes a parish priest in London, a guest-preacher and confessor to fashionable Catholics. But Dawson becomes increasingly confused about distinctions between social, psychiatric, and religious concerns. In a series of articles written for a London paper, he assumes the Jansenist position that faith, not good works, is the essence of religion. In his own life and pastoral encounters, however, faith is not enough: he longs to bring comfort to others in ways that his priestly office does not allow. On enforced retreat at a Trappist monastery, a world of silence far removed from the cries of London, he acknowledges that he has "outgrown all the nonsense" learned at school.

Putting things of childhood behind him, Dawson leaves the priesthood and begins a series of secular encounters in his attempt to serve mankind in more effective ways. The most serious encounter is his affair with Jenny Stanten, a wealthy young woman to whom Dawson had at one time given instruction in the faith. Established as Jenny's live-in lover in a fashionable town house, a condition envied by his secular friends, Dawson attempts to construct a new heaven to match his new earth. He becomes a crusading journalist, rejecting religion in Comtean fashion as no longer necessary in a rational age. But human irrationality and the contradictions of his own life-style frustrate his liberal, secular ideals. At a fashionable charity-masquerade ball (secular humanism in its most liturgical and flabby form), Dawson celebrates a make-believe Black Mass (even evil in this setting lacks conviction) and literally chokes on the words. Shortly after, Jenny leaves him for a trendy Marxist to conduct guerrilla theater in Venezuela.

Like many of Read's central figures, Dawson is a man whose lights have failed. Like his suicidal father, Dawson contemplates taking his own life as a philosophic statement. At novel's end, however, he chooses a different kind of statement and escape, joining the same Trappist community in which he had earlier renounced religious life. Visiting him there, Dawson's friends find a man who is at peace, a man now convinced that there is "great confusion in our generation between social and religious morality—between the exigencies of human life and the deference . . . due to God." Dawson's friends—perhaps some of Read's readers—feel anger and confusion. The distinction between what is due to man and what is due to God is explored, in a different revolutionary setting, in Read's next novel, *The Professor's Daughter*.

As an Englishman visiting New York and Massachusetts in 1967-1968, Read was fascinated by the crisis in East Coast liberalism—another light that, for a time, was failing. In *The Professor's Daughter* he created and examined an American scene that was in some ways complementary to his picture of the English Catholic world of *Monk Dawson*. His focus here is generational conflict within the family of Henry Rutledge, an Eastern aristocrat, Kennedy Democrat, and professor of political theory at Harvard. Rutledge, his wife, Lilian, and his friend and political ally, Bill Laughlin, are all part of the generation that, after World War II, determined to make liberal American ideals the standard of world civilization. Kennedy's election is both a public and a private satisfaction to the Rutledge circle, an affirmation of that sense of destiny and virtue that had sustained them since their youth. Kennedy's assassination, in turn, is the beginning of both public and private confusion for Rutledge. Called to Laughlin's Virgin Islands retreat to plan a new political strategy, Rutledge discovers Laughlin's naked ambition and Lilian's naked body under Laughlin. Despite his own past casual infidelities, Rutledge is shaken: "Is it possible, he thought, that I mind this . . . this banality more than the death of the President?"

Personal failings overshadow public virtue as Rutledge and America move into the mid-1960s. His marriage now a guilty compromise, Rutledge finds solace in the company and admiration of Louisa, his sixteen-year-old daughter. But on a trip to Europe and Africa, where Louisa's emerging sexuality is heightened by the attentions of Rutledge's foreign colleagues, the professor has a moment of near-incest with his daughter, an encounter that Louisa does not fully comprehend, but one that fills her father with remorse and self-disgust. At the same time Louisa's social conscience is awakened by the sight of African poverty and by Henry's unsatisfying rationalizations of the Rutledge family wealth. As Henry guiltily withdraws from his peerlike intimacy with her, Louisa is introduced by a school

friend to Marx and Proudhon. Emotionally and politically the generations drift apart.

Matriculating at Berkeley, Louisa quickly enters the counterculture—first living with, marrying, and divorcing a veteran of free speech and antiwar movements, then living with a middle-age beatnik who initiates her into the gymnastics of Kama Sutra. By 1967 she has returned to Boston, a suicidal nymphomaniac who seeks to "have herself besmirched and split and sated by any man she could find." Rutledge, feeling his failures as father and husband, is unable to continue his seminar on political thought with customary objectivity. In private conversation with one of his students, a Jesuit priest who has lost faith in God, Rutledge asks if Louisa is a sinner or a social casualty. The priest answers that Louisa and her peers are victims of corrupt capitalist values, the only cure for which is revolution. But the priest—restating Monk Dawson's final position while rejecting Dawson's application—distinguishes between the saint, who practices virtue through a subjective process of the will, and the hero or social revolutionary, who grasps with his intellect the logical necessity of social revolution. Revolution is what is owed to our fellow men; virtue is what is owed to God, if God exists. The priest, for whom only his fellow men exist, convinces other members of Rutledge's seminar to attempt a symbolic revolutionary act. Their target is Congressman Laughlin, now a strong supporter of the Vietnam war and still the selfish lover of Lilian Rutledge. Henry Rutledge, for whom politics is no longer real, accepts the priest's distinction but, like Monk Dawson, chooses God, sainthood, and virtue. He gives his own life to save that of his wife's lover. After his self-sacrifice, an act that Louisa sees as ultimately foolish, his daughter and her friends commit themselves to the political campaign of Eugene McCarthy—"to give the system one final chance" under the man who, in Read's view, most poignantly confused the roles of saint and hero in the 1960s.

British and American critics praised the intelligence and wit of *The Professor's Daughter*, but they also regretted the novel's resolution, "mucked up . . . in mere melodrama." In Russia, however, Soviet critics were delighted by Read's apparent condemnation of capitalist values, and Read was invited to visit Russia as a guest of the Soviet Writers Union. Before and after that visit Read wrote radio and television plays, *The Family Firm* (produced in 1970) and *The House on Highbury Hill* (produced in 1972), while working on a novel that was possibly not what his hosts had hoped his visit to Russia

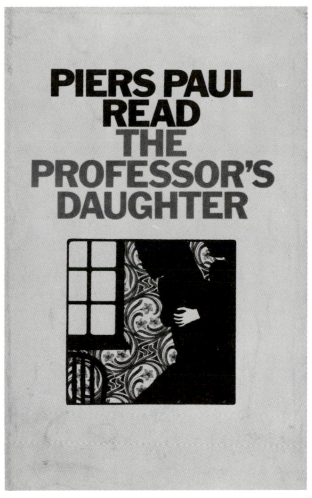

Dust jacket for Read's 1971 examination of American culture

would inspire. *The Upstart* (1973) is an adaptation of two traditional prose forms, the rogue/criminal autobiography and the account of spiritual conversion. Although the principal scene is London of the 1960s, Read's main point of reference is the eighteenth century. His rogue hero, Hilary, is born of a loveless country vicar and a warm but socially ambitious Yorkshire farm girl. Thrown into daily contact with Mark and Harriet Metherall of Lasterby Hall, Hilary swallows whole the Metheralls' aristocratic values and rejects his loutish cousins. But friendship with the Metheralls brings a series of exquisite social defeats and embarrassments: "If I had lived in the eighteenth century the issue which perplexed me could have been more clearly expressed: I should have worried as to whether I was a gentleman. Since now this word was put at the entrance to every public lavatory, the question was more complicated, though in essence it may have remained the same." When Hilary appears at a

dance in the wrong kind of jacket, the question is answered for him by the Metheralls. In rejection and reaction Hilary develops a revolutionary's hatred for the Metheralls' kind. At the same time he rejects his father's cold, sin-obsessed Christianity: "Like a psychologist's rat, I shied automatically at the least intimation of Christian injunction. I grew to loathe such words as meekness, chastity, and humility, and at eighteen was already determined to be assertive, lascivious, and proud." After a few months at Cambridge, where he cultivates poker and repulses the advances of his morals tutor, Hilary escapes to London to join the biologically determined struggle of "ten million, rootless, friendless urban vermin." He is by this time a nihilist, a moral relativist, a thorough cad—a man whose gods (father, Metheralls, Cambridge) have all failed him.

In London Hilary pursues two successful careers, that of burglar preying upon the rich and that of painter preying upon the rich. The parvenus who buy his fraudulent paintings are the very men whose town houses he loots. Joining forces with a band of fences, deviants, and pimps—all alumni of his public school—Hilary recruits for their bordello, drowns a baby born to one of his prostitutes, and accidentally murders an old man. Throughout these horrors only one thing touches him—the pitiful social pretensions of a woman he has robbed and then seduced. Raised in Slough (of Despond?), a lower-middle-class suburb, the woman is, like Hilary, an *"ancien combattant de la guerre de classes."* Her hopeful, hopeless, graceful tea set, mats, and sugar tongs move Hilary to tears.

Nothing else moves him. A success in his two chosen careers, he suffers from ennui, but chance encounters with Mark and Harriet Metherall focus his energies on a course of private revenge. He breaks the aimless Mark at gambling tables and seduces the married, unfulfilled Harriet. For a moment—seeing Harriet's heavy, naked body—he is moved to tears again, but her snobbery steels him against that touch of grace, and he resolves to debauch the youngest Metherall, the schoolgirl Martha, telling the reader, "My pleasure nowadays was in the frustration of nature in one form or another." In that satanic pleasure he is himself frustrated. Martha, though seduceable, is also indestructibly normal and healthy, blessed with wit, compassion, and a social conscience. Mark Metherall, forced into steady employment, finds purpose in his life; Harriet, divorced by her husband, is partly ennobled through her suffering, and Hilary proves to be an agent of redemption for others. At the climax of his long-planned revenge, a trial at which he is charged with seducing a minor, he feels pity for the publicly humiliated Metheralls. Indifferent to the verdict, he bungles his defense and is sentenced to three months in prison.

Before entering prison Hilary takes tentative steps toward his own redemption. He attends the deathbed of his father, the rector of Lasterby, who dies in fear of his own damnation. Hilary is seized with the fear of death "like an infectious fever." Once in prison, sharing his cell with a good thief (Irish, Catholic, and repentant) and a bad one (English, atheistic, and self-righteous), Hilary passes through stages of self-contempt, repentance, and despair, before feeling "the possibility now that there was a father beyond the grave—not the rector of Lasterby but his father too—who was waiting for my embrace, who was ready to accept it and forgive me and take me as a sobbing child into his arms." The conversion is violent, radical, and consciously designed to affront a modern secular reader. But, despite his equally conscious and misleading use of the language of determinism, Read has chosen to work in a literary tradition that recognizes the metaphysical reality of sin, grace, and redemption. Read prepares his reader subtly and explicitly by episodes of grace and sterility throughout this rogue's progress and by quoting, as his epigraph, from Julien Green's *Diary*: "In each one of us there is a sinner and a saint. . . . If the man is a sinner . . . the saint develops as best he can on the imaginative plane (a yearning for holiness). That is why a sinner who is converted never starts from scratch. He has made some progress during his life of sin." Hilary receives the sacrament of confession, marries the pregnant Martha as his penance, and, such are God's mysterious ways, must abandon his plans of monkish solitude to become the master of Lasterby Hall, the paradise once lost. Solaced by "the consolations of nature"—rural solitude, his newfound love for wife and children—he submits at the end of the novel to God's apparent plan: "Soon it will be five o'clock, when I shall go up to the nursery and have tea with Martha and the children. And in time I shall die. Between these two appointments there is nothing of importance." England in the 1960s merges with England in the 1700s; a modern sinner joins Barry Lyndon and Moll Flanders; sin, guilt, and repentance link Augustine, Bunyan, Wesley, and Read.

Before *The Upstart* was published, Edward Burlingame of Lippincott, Read's American publisher, suggested that Read write a nonfiction treatment of a real-life tragedy, the October 1972 crash in a remote part of the Andes of a plane chartered by a Uruguayan rugby team. Despite repeated searches the plane was not discovered; Uruguayan and Chilean officials soon abandoned any hope that survivors of the crash could have survived the mountain snow. But ten weeks later a mountain peasant found two survivors who had left the broken plane in search of help. At the crash site fourteen more of the forty passengers remained alive. They had survived by eating the flesh of those who died.

Writing a history, working with documents and interviews, relieved Read of the problems of point of view and fiction's truth that had confused some of his early novels: "Nothing in this book departs from the truth as it was told to me by those involved." And writing about those involved—pious Catholic Uruguayans brought face-to-face with questions of conventional morality, self-sacrifice, and their God's inscrutable will—allowed Read to discuss religious themes with a freedom that he had not yet permitted himself in fiction. This book's religious piety and sacramental vision could not be dismissed by readers as merely the writer's own. These things had really happened, these emotions really had been felt: "This is the story of what they suffered and how they remained alive." In this book Read had no need to disguise his own voice in the idiom of his time or of the eighteenth century.

Alive tells the story of the Andes survivors in terms of the Christian culture they shared and understood. The book's epigraph is John 15:13, "Greater love hath no man than this, that a man lay down his life for his friends"; the central symbol, for Read as well as the survivors, is the sacrament of Holy Communion. The young men of the amateur rugby team had overcome their horror at eating human flesh by connecting their experience to Christ's first Eucharist. In deciding to eat those already dead, each of the young men offered his own body to his surviving comrades in the event of his own death. They later remembered that at nightly prayers they had felt a mystical unity. By the end of their seventy days in the wilderness, having watched their friends die and having suffered extreme pain and hunger, the sixteen felt purified, ennobled. "In situations such as this," one dying boy wrote in a note to be given to his parents, "even reason cannot understand the infinite and absolute power of God over man. I have never suffered as I do now . . . though I have never believed in him so much."

Read himself probably found something suspect in the culture in which these boys were raised. Their Uruguayan families were affluent conservatives, part of a stagnant middle class that was in some ways similar to those that Read had dissected in his novels. The boys had been educated by the Christian Brothers, muscular Christians whose principal concern was not political or religious sophistication but moral lessons learned by playing rugby. In extremis, however, what might have been shortcomings proved to be their strengths. Without religious piety, their rugby-team ethic, their close family ties, the social cohesiveness, the young men would have despaired and perished. Distanced by his role as reporter or historian, effective in his sparse prose style, Read seems to let their story tell itself.

Read produces books so quickly that it is dangerous to speculate on how the writing of *Alive* may have influenced the novel that followed two years later. Nonetheless, Read almost lays his cards on the table in *Polonaise* (1976). Tracing the fortunes of a family of displaced Polish aristocrats, the novel also tells in detail of the philosophic pilgrimage of artist-skeptic Stefan Kornowski. Kornowski strips himself of theism, Catholic morals, and "Polishness" at the same time that his sister and family lose their virginity and land. Living amid genteel poverty in Warsaw in the 1930s, Stefan and his sister discover communism—for Stefan a purely intellectual exercise, for his sister a vehicle to express her hatred of the capitalist order that has humiliated and dispossessed her. But, although he envies the historical righteousness felt by his comrades in the party, Stefan cannot subjugate his fiction to the purposes of party propaganda. Cynical, detached, a personality similar to that Read exhibits in his own writing style, Stefan analyzes his commitment to Marxism as he had earlier dissected and rejected the Catholic religion of his youth. The passion for social equality, he sees, is an aesthetic rather than an ethical urge. Without God, without belief in Christ's injunction to love our fellow man, without the chance genetic gift of sympathy, there is no ethical imperative to help our fellow man. "Your mind is moulded by twenty centuries of Christian belief," he tells his brother-in-law Bruno, the committed Marxist, "and though you say you are atheists, your whole philosophy is shaped by Christian beliefs and has no justification without them. The Soviet Union is not a new development in the evolution of human history; it is Holy Russia under another name." Meanwhile Stefan's fiction, while free of the restrictions of Marxist ideology, remains a series of aborted pornographic fragments—partly conditioned by his early traumatic exposure to sex, primarily frustrated by his lack of moral vision. As an artist and a man he remains uncommitted, both

Faust and Mephistopheles at once, watching life "with lizard eyes" while still longing for some absolute.

Seeking relief from his creative sterility through action, Stefan joins the Communist forces recruited for the Spanish civil war, only to desert before ever reaching Spain. Seeking ecstasy, the ultimate experience, he plots to murder a young girl in the throes of orgasm, only to be diverted by a practiced whore. Deserting family and country as the Nazis invade Poland, Stefan flees to America in an act of self-willed escape from instinct and inheritance, only to spend the 1940s in creative frustration. By the 1950s, weak in health and spirit, he has drifted to Paris, where his sister has remarried, joined the bourgeoisie, and raised her son by the martyred Bruno. In Paris the artist finds his theme: the innocent love of Bruno's son, Teofil, and an English girl who has been traumatized, like Stefan, by an early sexual experience. Assuming the role of creator-artist-God, Stefan watches the young couple, guiding their development and writing the minutiae of their lives down in his notebook. But their relationship and Stefan's emerging novel are both threatened when the girl's debauched and snobbish parents, unhappy with the match, introduce their daughter to an accomplished seducer. Miserable at seeing the impending loss of innocence, Stefan is forced to examine his own misery—a feeling his philosophy of amoral egoism cannot comprehend or explain. "We escape from God without much difficulty, but it is not so easy to escape from the Good." Why does he care? Nature is amoral; only conscience treasures the good. But if conscience is in conflict with nature, what force beyond nature directs conscience? At work on those questions in the introduction to his novel, Stefan dies from a heart attack; we are led to believe that his longing for the good has led him back to God.

Polonaise seems to come close to being a personal statement. Read maintains his customary cynical, objective tone; Stefan Kornowski may be only one more specimen in Read's collection of modern pilgrims, an example of the creative consciousness that Herbert Read had often analyzed in his essays. But Stefan's dissection of various ideals is so acute and unsparing that it is difficult not to think that his final groping toward moral theism is not of special value in his creator's eyes. And Read's next novel, *A Married Man* (1979), would be even more explicitly moral, even Catholic, in its theme. But between the publication of *Polonaise* and *A Married Man*, in spring 1976 Read was invited by W. H. Allen and Company to meet the paroled executors of what Britons called "the Great Train Robbery," the theft of £ 2,500,000 from the Glasgow-London mail train in 1963. The thieves wished to sell their combined memoirs; the publisher wanted Read—still fresh from the commercial and critical success of *Alive*—to perform a task similar to that which he had done for the Andes survivors. Read was interested, but skeptical about the project's worth: the story of the robbery and subsequent investigation had already been told by individuals on both sides of the law. Read was convinced to accept the job, however, when the thieves and their literary agent revealed a previously unsuspected aspect of the case: the robbery had been financed by Otto Skorzeny, the Waffen SS commando who had engineered the rescue of Mussolini and, perhaps, created ODESSA, a worldwide organization of former members of the SS. Fascinated since the writing of *The Junkers* by the doings of ex-Nazis, convinced by the apparently corroborative evidence provided by one of the thieves' wives, Read began research for *The Train Robbers* (1978).

Like *Alive* this new nonfiction book explored the central theme of all Read's fiction—the psychological reality of moral good and evil. He was clearly fascinated by the ethics of professional thieves, which he presents as at least as admirable as the ethics of ordinary businessmen. He was also impressed by the ubiquity of graft among police officials, legal witnesses, and train dispatchers. But selfish crime, white- or blue-collar, becomes boring, and nothing in this story allowed Read to reach the level of moral vision he had reached in *Alive*. Perhaps more disappointing to the author, the dimension of the story that had drawn Read to this project (the Skorzeny/ODESSA connection) remained for him unfocused and, worse, unconfirmed. Research in Germany and an interview with Simon Wiesenthal, the Nazi hunter, led him to doubt the claim of German involvement. Later, interviewing Ronnie Biggs, the train robber who remained free in Rio de Janeiro, Read was told that the German connection was a fraud, a hoax concocted by the robbers' literary agent to make their memoirs more attractive to a publisher. Read suspected that Biggs himself might be part of the Skorzeny network, trying to throw Read off the scent. Caught in a web of possible deception similar to that in which the narrator of *The Junkers* finds himself, Read confronted the other robbers with his suspicions. Some admitted the deception; some denied it; what was Read, fiction writer, to do with the possibly fictitious tale that W. H. Allen wished to publish as fact? Read wrote: "Even though I was

satisfied now that I was near the truth, I could never be certain and thought it best to leave the story as they had told me and let each reader decide upon its veracity for himself." So the book ends, leaving readers—if not Read—in a position of doubt similar to that of the readers of his admittedly fictitious excursion into the ex-Nazi world of *The Junkers*.

At best *The Train Robbers* is investigative journalism; at worst a well-told tall tale. But a knowledge of things criminal, and the fear he himself had felt in his dealings with men who were capable of violence, has served Read better in *A Married Man*. In its narrative pace, economy of cast, and coherence of plot, this book is Read's best work to date, entertaining in its truthful depiction of the rhetoric of egotism and evasion, disturbing in its revelation of the presence of sin. The married man is John Strickland, a successful barrister and father of two, whose accidental reading of Tolstoy's *Death of Ivan Ilyich* focuses his middle-age suspicions that his life has been misspent. Wed to an attractive Catholic woman but contemptuous of the hypocritical morality of his wife's affluent Catholic acquaintances, Strickland tries to recapture his own youthful vision of the good—socialism. Despite the objections of his Conservative friends he becomes involved in the Labour party at a moment, 1973, when labor strikes are crippling the country. But this possibly idealistic public commitment is matched by his pursuit of what appears another good, the libidinous daughter of the man who he thinks is his best friend. On a personal level Strickland's ethics are ad hoc, situational, unlike the code ethics of his Catholic wife that include "some dubious notions such as sin and redemption." Just as the English law that Strickland serves is based upon precedent rather than abstraction, Strickland's ethics are based upon what other men in his social station think and do: "Thus brawling and shop lifting were punished while buggery and adultery were not, because many if not most of John's friends were either sodomites or adulterers but would never fight in a pub or steal from a chain store." Strickland's father-in-law, the saint figure of this novel, remarks that the arrival of the birth-control pill may be the most significant social event in modern times: marital fidelity, once a matter of practical necessity, is now an abstract commitment. Strickland's social circle, unaccustomed to abstract commitments, fornicate with untroubled consciences. And Strickland, despite his commitment to social-political justice, is a slave to his own wayward lusts.

Against a background of electrical blackouts caused by striking unions and of attacks upon private property committed in the dark (a physical lapse into near-chaos and old night), Strickland pursues his political career, standing as a Labour candidate. He is troubled, however, by occasional fears that his socialist commitment may be as fickle as his lust: "for while science, agriculture, banking or business had objective values on which all men were agreed, politics—like art and love—depended upon subjective judgments of different individuals, each encased in his own egoism." Inexorably Strickland's situational ethics, his enthrallment to what feels right at the moment, draws him into ethical blackout. Angered by his wife's suspicion that his politics are only an extension of his ego, feeling like a modern Prometheus chained by family ties, Strickland becomes deeply involved with a woman who shares his genteel socialism. But the woman—an heiress, hedonist, and sometimes social worker—admires the unhypocritical vitality of the young criminals whose cases she has studied. At her urging Strickland successfully defends a guilty criminal whom Strickland, in haste to go on holiday, had represented carelessly on an earlier charge. In this second defense, prompted by both guilt and lust, Strickland bends the law. Small crimes lead to large: after a disillusioning weekend with his mistress, Strickland returns home to find his wife and her lover murdered. Gradually Strickland realizes that his mistress has hired the young criminal to murder Strickland's wife.

That realization and Strickland's victory in politics are overshadowed in his mind by another discovery, a packet of letters exchanged between his wife and a Catholic priest. The letters trace his wife's spiritual suicide, her despair at Strickland's egoism, her emotional need and vulnerability to the advances of Strickland's best friend. They also contain the priest's sensitive statement of the Catholic position on marital fidelity—a position of absolute moral commitment to which married persons must cling despite the promptings of immediate emotional and physical needs. Strickland discovers that commitment in himself through his reveries upon his married life. Without regret he abandons his political career. Without recrimination he leaves the mistress-murderess whose cold egoism he now sees as only different in degree from his own. Watching his Catholic children praying at Mass he contemplates belief in a God who might help him know himself.

Read's tenth book, *The Villa Golitsyn*, was published in late 1981. He has accomplished much already, winning readers, prizes, and critical atten-

tion, but his stature among modern British novelists is still somewhat uncertain. He has not yet written a best-selling novel, nor has the critical attention that he has received been uniformly friendly or encouraging. His obvious strengths have been recognized—his "calm, graceful prose," his "cool, wry, tough intelligence"—but the explicitly didactic and religious strain that has emerged in his later novels has put some critics on their guard. Several novels have been criticized as lapses into melodrama; others have been damned for dramatizing "that dismal Catholic scenario which insists that God may only be approached by way of man's complete physical and emotional degradation." Like any other novelist, Read is entitled to his own scenario. What appears to some critics to be melodrama might be examples of God's intervening grace to readers who share Read's ontology. But the Catholicism that provides Read's fiction with its moral center could prove to be the artist's liability, narrowing the subjects or circle of readers he can touch. He has dealt with the major *isms* of our time on a personal level, with a sharp eye for domestic detail and a keen ear for the rhetoric of moral confusion. If his own mature religious certainty does not limit his imaginative sympathy with varied human sinners, he soon may join the thin ranks of major modern moral satirists.

References:

Susan Heller Anderson, "Piers Paul Read Asks 'What Do I Write Now?'," *New York Times*, 10 December 1979, C15;

James Brockway, "Going Down Bravely," *Books and Bookmen* (February 1977): 22-23;

David Holden, "Blow-Out," *Spectator* (18 May 1974): 611;

Melvin Maddocks, "Hope Against Hope," *Time* (25 October 1971): 92-94;

John Mellors, "Books," *London Magazine* (December 1973- January 1974): 155;

Mellors, "Stern Stuff," *Listener* (25 November 1976): 688;

Peter Prince, "Humiliations," *New Statesman* (7 September 1973): 321;

"Prodigal's Progress," *Times Literary Supplement* (7 September 1973): 1017;

Michael Rogers, "Books," *Rolling Stone*, 23 May 1974, p. 90;

Nick Totten, "Polarities," *Spectator* (20 November 1976): 22;

Jonathan Yardley, *New York Times Book Review*, 7 November 1971, pp. 38-39.

Bernice Rubens
(26 July 1928-   )

Judith Vincent
College of Ripon & York

NOVELS: *Set on Edge* (London: Eyre & Spottiswoode, 1960);

Madame Sousatzka (London: Eyre & Spottiswoode, 1962);

Mate in Three (London: Eyre & Spottiswoode, 1966);

The Elected Member (London: Eyre & Spottiswoode, 1969); republished as *Chosen People* (New York: Atheneum, 1969);

Sunday Best (London: Eyre & Spottiswoode, 1971; New York: Summit, 1980);

Go Tell the Lemming (London: Cape, 1973);

I Sent a Letter to My Love (London: Allen, 1975; New York: St. Martin's, 1978);

The Ponsonby Post (London: Allen, 1977; New York: St. Martin's, 1978);

A Five Year Sentence (London: Allen, 1978); republished as *Favours* (New York: Summit, 1978);

Spring Sonata (London: Allen, 1979);

Birds of Passage (London: Hamilton, 1981).

Bernice Rubens has written eleven novels, most of which have been well received by the critics. Her fourth, *The Elected Member* (1969), won the Booker Prize, Britain's most important and most coveted literary award. While her first four novels earned her acclaim as a perceptive and witty chronicler of Jewish family life, in her subsequent books she has extended the range of her subject matter, and in each one she seems to have set herself some new stylistic challenge. If there is any single feature that characterizes her work, it is an interest in investigating the narrow dividing line between despair and enjoyment of life and in exploring the lives of those people whose existence is delicately balanced on that line.

Bernice Ruth Rubens was born in 1928 in Cardiff, Wales, one of four children of Eli and Dorothy Cohen Rubens. Her father was born in Russia and had come to Wales as a refugee. Because her family and most of her family's friends were Orthodox Jews, her background is one of rich cultural complexity, combining the inherited traditions of her Jewish emigre family with the firsthand experience of growing up in South Wales during the years of the Depression and World War II. After attending Cardiff High School for Girls, a school noted for its high academic standards, from 1938 to 1944, Rubens went on to read English at University College, University of Wales, graduating with honors in 1947. To the period she spent at the university, Rubens attributes her rather late development as a novelist; she found that the formal academic study of literature overdeveloped her respect for language and for other writers, thus inhibiting her own creative use of language. She says firmly that a degree course in English would be the last thing that she would recommend to any aspiring writer.

On 29 December 1947 Rubens married Rudi Nassauer, a writer, and took a post as an English teacher at Handsworth Grammar School in Birmingham, England. She found little enjoyment in teaching. Soon, however, in an almost accidental way, another career possibility opened up when a friend who was making a documentary film about debutantes, finding himself with an unsatisfactory

Bernice Rubens

script and a nearly exhausted budget, asked her to write a script for him. After writing the script, Rubens became involved in making the film and enjoyed her first taste of the process. She resigned her teaching post and since 1950 has been working in England as a free-lance documentary filmmaker. She has written and directed films—including *One of the Family* (1964), *Call Us By Name* (1968), and *Out of the Mouths* (1970)—for such organizations as the National Society for Mentally Handicapped Children, the Society for the Blind, and the United Nations. Her career as a filmmaker continued without serious interruption as she raised her two daughters: Sharon, born in 1952, and Rebecca, born in 1954.

Rubens did not complete her first novel until 1960—and it was indeed her first novel; there are no abandoned or rejected manuscripts of earlier attempts. *Set on Edge* explores the lives of the members of a Jewish family, the Sperbers, centering on Gladys, the eldest child. Gladys's childhood passes by as she helps her mother care for her four younger brothers and sisters, all of whom succeed in leaving home, contracting along the way some bizarre marriages. Finally only Gladys remains, and as she reaches middle age, her family, becoming aware of her spinsterhood, makes unsubtle and unsuccessful attempts to marry Gladys off. Not until she is sixty is a husband found for her, but he dies during their honeymoon, leaving her with nothing but a bedroom suite. This furniture becomes a subject of dispute between Gladys and her mother when she returns with it to the family home, where she remains with her mother until the old lady dies, leaving Gladys the sole occupier of the house.

The novel examines how the members of this family exploit one another, with Gladys seeming to fall victim to them all. Yet even when the characters' behavior toward one another appears most insensitive, it is never malicious, and the family bond is not broken or even threatened. As individuals they have little in common—their initial impulse is to break away from one another—but they constantly reassemble at the family home even though each of these reunions ends in a quarrel. While there is no obvious pleasure in Sperber family life, Gladys never appears more pitiable than she does at the end of the novel when she is finally alone. There is no longer anything within the family to give her a sense of belonging, and her loneliness inflicts great pain.

That the family is Jewish has no particular significance in itself, but the features of Jewish life as Rubens draws them serve to point up her theme.

Her characters are aware of belonging to a small and enclosed community that is only a small part of a larger, looser, and ill-defined society. As a result family life is claustrophobic but at the same time more secure. The Sperber family circle lies within the wider circle of the Jewish community, beyond which lies a yet wider circle of society, its circumference barely discernible by the Sperber family. These concentric circles hold one another in place and give a feeling of narrowness and constriction to the innermost circle, the family, and the sudden dissolution of this innermost circle on the death of the mother is responsible for Gladys's sense of displacement.

In this first novel one of Rubens's greatest skills is already apparent: though there is nothing inherently comic in the life of this family, the novel is shot through with a dark humor. The writer's humor is rather Chekhovian; she distances the reader from her characters and reveals a comedy in their situation that never for a moment becomes accessible to the characters themselves. The function of Rubens's humor here and in her other novels is to solicit compassion for her characters while always keeping the reader distanced. The book was greeted by critics as a very promising first novel; her eye for detail, in particular, was praised. The *Times Literary Supplement* reviewer called *Set on Edge* "Jewish writing at its best."

In her next three novels, *Madame Sousatzka* (1962), *Mate in Three* (1966), and *The Elected Member*, Rubens continued to draw on her Jewish background for setting and explored broadly similar themes. Madame Sousatzka's situation is in many ways the reverse of Gladys Sperber's. Having fled without her parents from Hitler's Germany and having arrived in England as a refugee at the age of twenty, Sousatzka has never had the opportunity to belong. In Germany she left behind a promising career as a concert pianist, and in England she supports herself by giving piano lessons to untalented pupils. She shares her house with eccentric tenants. "Uncle," an emigre countess who insists on the title "Uncle Countess" but is known as the dirty countess on account of her personal habits, lives in the basement busying herself with crossword puzzles; Cordle, an osteopath, lives upstairs surrounded by charts of the human body and dreams of becoming famous in his profession. When the novel begins, Sousatzka is forty-five years old and has just fallen in love for the first time but has been deserted. She meets a talented eleven-year-old pianist, Marcus Crominski, whom she takes as a pupil. Her generosity in offering to coach Marcus without payment astounds the boy's mother, but Sousatzka hopes that her coaching will make Marcus into a famous pianist and that through his success she will achieve recognition. Yet as the relationship grows between the pupil and teacher, Marcus becomes more important to Sousatzka's emotional needs; she will not share the child with anyone and thus will not allow him to perform in public. Her possessiveness threatens his career, and her teaching method, in which she believes fervently, is deforming the child physically as his shoulders become more and more rounded. She fights Marcus's mother for the boy's affection and Felix Manders, an impresario, for control of the child's career, losing both battles. As Marcus slips away from her, she also loses her house and her tenants. Sousatzka belongs nowhere and is able to form no bonds. At the end of the novel all that remains to her is her unfailing belief in her teaching method, which no one else shares.

Mate in Three probes again the simultaneously protective and destructive drives that exist within personal relationships, this time in the relationship among a wife, her husband, and his mistress. While reviewers remained impressed by Rubens's style, some complained that in her second and third novels she handled her material too schematically.

Rubens's fourth novel, *The Elected Member*, explores these themes more effectively, however, as Norman Zweck, the central figure of the book, breaks under the strain of belonging to his family. At the beginning of the novel, Norman is already unable to cope with this burden, and his chosen route of escape has led him to drug addiction. His family—his father, Rabbi Zweck, and his sister, Bella—see his condition as a matter of shame because Norman, a clever young man and a successful lawyer, has been the pride of the family, a symbol of its success and achievement. His addiction requires them to acknowledge that their family life has not squared with the happy and united image that the now dead Mrs. Zweck has forced upon it, and they want Norman cured as much for their sakes as for his own.

As Norman's addiction increases, Rabbi Zweck and Bella attempt to bully him out of it or to ignore it while the past events in the Zweck family, which have contributed to Norman's present condition, are revealed through the recollections of family members. Mrs. Zweck, reveling in maternal pride, trapped her children in an unnaturally long childhood, forcing Norman and Bella to pretend to be three years younger than they actually were so that Norman would be admired as a child prodigy. Bella, now in her late thirties, still wears white ankle socks and has never married; her recollection of family life reveals an incestuous childhood love between herself and her brother, and her ankle socks seem to hurl a daily accusation at Norman. Another sister, Esther, at Mrs. Zweck's insistence, has not been mentioned in the family since she eloped with a gentile, an action that Mrs. Zweck believed to have destroyed the family. Norman remembers that when she eloped, Esther drove his best friend, David, to suicide. Esther, however, recalls that Norman persuaded her to elope with John by telling her that David was a homosexual. Guilt and blame for events that have befallen this family move from one member to another as the various points of view are presented, and Rubens refuses to apportion blame. Instead, she explores how the Zweck family destroys itself and how Norman comes to be cast in the role of scapegoat.

As in her first novel, the family's Jewishness is used to intensify the theme. Rabbi Zweck's position within the tight-knit Jewish community and the regard his mother has fostered for Norman in this community add to the pressures generated within the family. Rubens handles her material with great skill, weaving back and forth between past and present and revealing her characters from different angles, constantly forcing the reader to reassess them. The awfulness of the situations in which her characters find themselves is relieved throughout by her characteristic humor. Rubens richly deserved the Booker Prize, which she won for this novel in 1970, as well as the recognition the award brought her.

While she was producing these four novels, Rubens continued with her filmmaking. In 1967 she directed a film about children in care for the Granada television company's series *This England*. In 1969 she won the Blue Ribbon Award of the American Documentary Film Festival for *Stress* and was commissioned by the United Nations to make a film about agriculture in the Far East. While working on this project she spent some time in Java, an experience which provided material for a later novel, *The Ponsonby Post* (1977).

One of the surprising features of Rubens's novels, considering how much this author works in the medium of film, is how little the descriptive writing in her fiction appeals to the visual sense. Apart from small details that lodge in the minds of the characters, such as Marcus Crominski's concern about the color of his mother's hats or the irritation caused to her family by Bella Zweck's white ankle socks, Rubens does not concern herself with the physical appearance of her characters. Descriptions

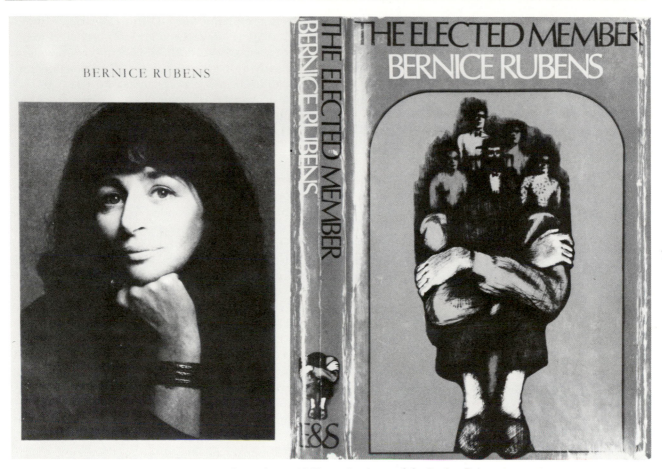

Dust jacket for Rubens's 1969 novel, winner of the Booker Prize

of the settings of the action are used sparingly, too. She does not allow her reader to be distracted from the interplay of characters, and in her early novels, where there is very little plot, the reader is further directed toward character.

In her fifth novel, *Sunday Best* (1971), Rubens attempted something quite new, abandoning her tested and familiar setting of Jewish family life and experimenting with first-person narrative. The novel's narrator is George Verry Smith, a transvestite, who for six days each week is a sober schoolteacher. On Sundays, however, dressed in women's clothes and wearing makeup given to him by his amused wife, he becomes Georgiana. This way of life has become routine until a series of events, including the death of a neighbor, a scandal at school, and the murder of a colleague, upsets George/Georgiana's balance. Georgiana progressively takes over until George is eclipsed, and Georgiana, who renames herself Emily Price, leaves behind wife and school and sets out to live alone. As this transformation takes place, George's childhood

is revealed; his resentment of his father, his love for his mother, and his father's death are clearly connected with the change he is undergoing. He blames himself for his father's accidental death because, he says, he *wished* his father dead. But George's recollection is selective; later in the novel, his mother reveals to his wife that the "accident" that befell his father was engineered by George, a secret she has kept, but not allowed George to forget.

Rubens's use of first-person narrative is particularly effective in the early part of the novel as Georgiana and then Emily take over George. The narrative experiment is only partially successful, however. Later in the novel, after Emily has left home, a third-person narrator has to be introduced to keep George's wife and mother in the story, where they are still required. This sudden recourse to third-person narration causes a disruption and unevenness in the novel. Rubens felt under pressure when trying to follow up her prizewinning novel and had deliberately experimented with new material and a new approach. Critical response to this experimentation was mixed; some critics were disappointed to find the savage humor of her earlier novels lacking in this book, while others considered her portrayal of character more skilled than that in *The Elected Member*.

Rubens was next persuaded by friends to write a television play. She was not particularly happy with *Third Party* (1972), saying that she did not like writing fiction for television and does not intend to attempt any more television drama.

In her next novel she returned to an exploration of the conflicts between wife, husband, and mistress that she had dealt with earlier in *Mate in Three*, though in *Go Tell the Lemming* (1973) the treatment of the subject is quite different. The action moves from London to Italy and back to London. Angela Morrow, a production assistant, and her estranged husband, David, come together briefly on location in Italy to work on the film David is producing. The lives of Angela and David as well as those of the leading lady, Daphne, and her husband follow patterns similar to the film script, in which the wife kills herself after her husband deserts her for another woman. While filming is taking place, Daphne's husband visits her, bringing with him his mistress. Daphne attacks her husband's mistress and then makes an unsuccessful suicide attempt. Angela rehearses in private a suicide attempt, which she has no intention of carrying through in earnest, and subjects herself to a series of promiscuous sexual encounters in which she and her victims suffer humiliation of different kinds. The similarities between these situations and the differences between the reactions of the women to their husbands' infidelities are evident enough, but what conclusion the reader is supposed to draw is less certain.

The most interesting feature of this novel is the portrayal of Angela Morrow, who, like George Verry Smith in *Sunday Best*, has a divided personality. The two Angelas, however, are not as distinctly separate as George and Emily, and one personality does not supplant the other. Rather, both Angelas coexist throughout the book. The one Angela is the character involved in the action of the novel, a public Angela; the second is known only to Angela herself, a private Angela. The first Angela confides to the second her hopes and distresses and calls upon her for advice that is never forthcoming. The second Angela is a woman who could cope with the situations in which the first founders and who mocks the failures and vain hopes of the first. This Angela seems to have been brought into existence to fill the vacant space left in Angela Morrow's life

when her husband moved out to live with his mistress. Angela and David's marriage, like many others portrayed elsewhere in Rubens's novels, is filled with impulses toward mutual destruction, and the second Angela takes David's role of antagonist. The two Angelas batter each other with more terrifying mental violence than in any other relationship in Rubens's novels. The portrayal is all the more frightening because it is unrelieved by Rubens's customary humor. This novel was received cautiously by critics; while the book was evidently meant to shock the reader by its violence, critics complained that it lacked impact because the characters provoked little sympathy.

Rubens's next novel, *I Sent a Letter to My Love* (1975), is a poignant tale, whose themes are much like those of her first novel, *Set on Edge*. *I Sent a Letter to My Love* deals with the members of the Evans family, centering on Amy Evans, a middle-aged spinster who, like Gladys Sperber, has never escaped from home. The family is Welsh, not Jewish, but the small seaside town, from which the family seldom ventures forth, has all the claustrophobic features of the Jewish community in *Set on Edge*. Comparison between the two novels reveals development of Rubens's skills as a novelist. In this book she is thoroughly in control of her material.

Amy Evans's story is unveiled with great compassion. Her mother has love for Amy's crippled brother, Stan, but for Amy she has "Amy-hate"; Amy's father takes little notice of her; and as a child she has learned to hate herself. She has had no lovers, only a single, silent, sexual encounter with a nameless French soldier—silent because they had no common language. Since her parents' deaths, she has devoted her life to caring for Stan, who demands love but is unable to give it. Her only friend is Gwyneth, another lonely spinster of Amy's own age. In a last desperate attempt to find love, Amy places an advertisement in the personal column of a newspaper, using a pseudonym to avoid detection by Stan or Gwyneth. Only Stan replies, and brother and sister write to each other as lovers. Amy finds pleasure in the correspondence and discovers a side to her brother's character that she had not previously suspected, but Stan, unaware of the identity of the woman to whom he addresses his love letters, wants a flesh-and-blood lover, whom he finds in Gwyneth. This final rejection is a fatal blow to his sister; Amy takes to her bed before Stan and Gwyneth's wedding day and never again rises from it.

Rubens's deftness in writing dialogue is well demonstrated in the brief and endlessly repeated conversations between Amy, Stan, and Gwyneth, which convey convincingly, and with great economy, the monotony of their lives. In this novel, the critics agreed, Rubens had regained her delicacy of touch in character delineation and had produced a work of sensitivity and compassion. Rubens has an acute ear for speech and dialect, seeming to capture even the accents of her characters in the dialogue. Perhaps it is these qualities which have made this novel particularly suitable for stage adaptation. *I Sent a Letter to My Love* was produced as a stage play in 1978 at the Long Wharf Theatre in New Haven, Connecticut, with Geraldine Fitzgerald cast in the role of Amy. In the following year it was staged at the Greenwich Theatre, London, with Rosemary Leach playing the leading role, and in 1981 a film version, made in France and starring Simone Signoret, premiered in New York. Rubens did not write the stage script or the screenplay for the film, but at present she is working on the script for a film version of *Madame Sousatzka*.

The Ponsonby Post, published in 1977, is a product of her 1969 visit to Java. The book attacks savagely the attitudes of Europeans working for the United Nations. The Ponsonby Post, named after a practical man who suggested that the various U. N. projects in Java should be coordinated and that there should be some liaison with the Javanese authorities, is held by Hugh Brownlow, who finds the Europeans working in Java bitterly divided among themselves on personal and nationalistic grounds. Their one shared conviction is their determination to keep themselves as remote as possible from the local population. Through Rubens's depiction of Brownlow's friendship with the local police chief and with a ten-year-old shoeshine boy who is also a part-time drug trafficker, the reader is made aware of the chaos in Java, where civil war is imminent, corruption is rife in the city, and poverty is destroying the country. While the police chief struggles to maintain civil order, the Europeans aid him by adding two murders and a complaint about a stolen pair of shoes to his files. With the exception of Brownlow, all the Europeans are grotesque and unsympathetic characters. Though well-intentioned, Brownlow is rendered wholly ineffective in his post by obstruction from European colleagues. An unusual feature in Rubens's work is this novel's complex plot, which includes Brownlow's being taken prisoner by a Javanese guerrilla group. While the author admits happily to a lack of interest in the mechanics of plot, that of *The Ponsonby Post* is handled skillfully. Indeed, the novel was described by one critic as a thriller. Ironically, her well-developed

and entertaining plot may have hidden from some readers the novel's satirical and more serious purpose.

A Five Year Sentence (1978) returns to the theme of loneliness. Accustomed since her childhood in an orphanage to being told from day to day what to do, Miss Hawkins is overwhelmed by the prospect of retirement, of being cast adrift at sixty. She resolves to kill herself, but on the day of her retirement, she is presented with a five-year diary, the first gift she has ever been given. She views the gift as an instruction to go on living and to write in the diary each day. Yet she does not know how to fill its blank pages; she needs instructions before she can act, and she must act to provide material for her diary. Deciding to make the diary issue its own directives, Miss Hawkins writes instructions in the diary each night, reads them the next morning, and acts accordingly. The diary's commands become bolder and bolder; eventually it tells her to find herself a man. With Brian Watts she discovers companionship and sex, but Brian and the diary lead her to destruction. The only action that Miss Hawkins performs impulsively is the murder of the matron of the orphanage where she grew up. There is a nasty twist in the tale; to begin with, the diary seems to open up to her the things Miss Hawkins has missed in life, but before the five-year sentence is completed, everything, including what little she had at the start, has been snatched away from her through the consequences of actions she does not recognize as her own. This carefully constructed novel was short-listed for the Booker Prize in 1978. Some critics, however, felt that this novel indulged too much in pathos.

Spring Sonata (1979) presents familiar Rubens themes in a wholly original, surrealistic manner. Its narrator, Dr. Brown, presents his credentials and convinces the reader of his sanity in a preface. He then reveals the contents of a notebook he has found in the womb of a pregnant woman on whom he has performed an autopsy. The notebook is the diary kept by Buster Rosen, a child who refused to be born and stayed in the womb for nearly four years. Buster's reports of his eavesdropping on the family he should have been born into make the reader sympathetic to his refusal to come out and join them. Within the womb he retains a loving relationship with his mother and she with him; in the Rosen household he hears mostly cries of anguish as the members of the family inflict emotional torture on one another. Appalled by this life, Buster cuts the umbilical cord and releases himself and his mother into oblivion. The novel is a remarkable flight of fancy, but deeply pessimistic. One critical response to this novel was to point out that there is nothing particularly original in the dissection of family life, but what distinguishes Rubens's approach is not so much her unusual perspective as the savage humor she employs.

In *Birds of Passage* (1981), Rubens deals with loneliness on a grander and more ambitious scale than in her earlier treatments of this theme, examining the case histories of six lonely people on a cruise liner. Mrs. Walsh and Mrs. Pickering have promised each other, through the long years of their respective marriages, that they would take this holiday when they were both widows. Mrs. Dove has had the holiday thrust upon her as a prize; she is accompanied by her daughter, who has recently been deserted by her husband. Mr. Bowers has been recently widowered, but his marriage died long before his wife. Wally Peters is unmarried and has always been alone. The novel reveals that, though there is only one term to describe the state, loneliness takes many forms. The enforced togetherness of the cruise serves to highlight the characters' problems and often seems to mock their situations. While each has come aboard ship with different hopes, all seek some kind of escape. As is the habit of cruise liners, though, the ship delivers them literally and figuratively back to the port from which they embarked. Reviewers of this book expressed some concern that the individual case histories were insufficiently differentiated and that Rubens tended to become repetitive.

Rubens has already begun her next novel, which she describes as her most ambitious yet. It will trace the fortunes of a Russian-Jewish family over a period of more than a century. Although she continues to make films, spending two or three months a year on them, writing has become her main interest. Recently she has been working on a film about women and rural development in South America, Cuba, South Africa, West Africa, India, and Pakistan. While her films are always documentaries, there is still some link between them and her novels: her films are often about the underprivileged and the handicapped; in her novels she examines the plight of the emotionally handicapped and underprivileged.

Rubens's themes may be insistent and even limited, but her treatment of them prevents any kind of predictability in her work. Her novels show a progressive development in her skills; as a craftsman, she is dexterous and inventive. For many of her readers, though, the attraction of her novels lies in the compassion she shows toward her wounded and vulnerable characters and the humor with which she is able to suffuse painful and potentially tragic situations.

Paul Scott
(25 March 1920 - 1 March 1978)

Margaret B. Lewis

BOOKS: *I Gerontius* (London: Favil Press, 1941);

Johnnie Sahib (London: Eyre & Spottiswoode, 1952);

The Alien Sky (London: Eyre & Spottiswoode, 1953); republished as *Six Days in Marapore* (Garden City: Doubleday, 1953);

A Male Child (London: Eyre & Spottiswoode, 1956; New York: Dutton, 1957);

The Mark of the Warrior (London: Eyre & Spottiswoode, 1958; New York: Morrow, 1958);

The Chinese Love Pavilion (London: Eyre & Spottiswoode, 1960); republished as *The Love Pavilion* (New York: Morrow, 1960);

The Birds of Paradise (London: Eyre & Spottiswoode, 1962; New York: Morrow, 1962);

The Bender: Pictures from an Exhibition of Middle Class Portraits (London: Secker & Warburg, 1963); republished as *The Bender* (New York: Morrow, 1963);

The Corrida at San Feliu (London: Secker & Warburg, 1964; New York: Morrow, 1964);

The Jewel in the Crown (London: Heinemann, 1966; New York: Morrow, 1966);

The Day of the Scorpion (London: Heinemann, 1968; New York: Morrow, 1968);

The Towers of Silence (London: Heinemann, 1971;
     New York: Morrow, 1972);
A Division of the Spoils (London: Heinemann, 1975;
     New York: Morrow, 1975);
The Raj Quartet (London: Heinemann, 1976; New
     York: Morrow, 1976);
Staying On (London: Heinemann, 1977; New York:
     Morrow, 1977).

When Paul Scott was awarded Britain's premier literary award for fiction, the Booker Prize, in 1977 for his last novel, *Staying On*, it signified belated recognition for a writer who had been producing a distinguished series of novels for twenty-five years, with very little attention from the British literary establishment. His greatest achievement, *The Raj Quartet*, a tetralogy of interconnected novels, which was followed by a short sequel, *Staying On*, was published between 1966 and 1977 and brought him the wide following that has steadily grown since his death in 1978. *The Raj Quartet* provides a unique insight into British and Indian society at the time of Indian independence in 1947, and these powerful, slow-paced novels with their detailed, concrete world pose questions about the nature of the British Empire and of British society that

had not been asked since E. M. Forster's *A Passage to India* in 1924.

Although readers of Scott's novels may feel that the ease and familiarity of his descriptions of the Indian landscape and social scene must suggest a writer who was born in India, they would be mistaken because Paul Scott was born in north London in 1920, the second son of Tom and Frances Scott, both commercial artists. Paul Scott attended Winchmore Hill Collegiate School in London but left at age sixteen to train as an accountant, a safe career in the eyes of his self-employed family. He married the novelist and short story writer Nancy E. Avery in London in 1941. Scott did not visit India until sent there in June 1943 as an officer cadet in World War II. As an air supply officer he traveled widely throughout India, Burma, and Malaya, moving easily in the varied society of civilians and military, of British and Indians. After returning to England from India in 1946 Scott used his early training in accountancy to join a small publishing firm, Falcon and Grey Walls Press, as company secretary. In 1950 he became a director in a firm of literary agents, Pearn, Pollinger and Higham (later David Higham Associates). He had written poetry and drama during and after the war, but now he turned to fiction and produced five novels between 1952 and 1960, when he gave up his work as a literary agent to devote himself to writing the longer and more substantial novels that he had been wanting to attempt for some time. Scott visited India in 1964, financed by his publishers, and there found inspiration for *The Raj Quartet* and *Staying On*. The British Council enabled Scott to make further short visits. In 1976 and 1977 he was a visiting lecturer at the University of Tulsa, Oklahoma. He died of cancer in London in 1978, shortly after receiving the Booker Prize.

It is curious to think that the rich, imaginative world of Paul Scott's fiction should have emerged from the unremarkable house in north London where he lived very quietly with his wife and his two daughters for twenty-seven years. He paced the streets of Golders Green, transforming the roads and buildings into his imaginary Indian cities. *The Raj Quartet* is full of details that are always right, as the distinguished historian Max Beloff confirmed in an article largely concerned with the historical aspects of the novels, where he finds that "Of those writers who have attempted to distil the last years of the Raj in fictional form, the most ambitious and the most successful is undoubtedly Mr. Paul Scott." Scott himself has said, "It's important to get the small things right," and these details give the novels

Paul Scott

their unfailing historical and psychological veracity.

Scott spoke often about his "obsession with the relationship between a man and the work he does," and this emphasis on work is fundamental to a study of his characters in the novels. His characters function through the work they do, and Scott saw this involvement with the rewards of work as an extended metaphor, explaining that "A story about men at work in Anglo India is the metaphor particularized." Scott's emphasis on work is one of the important distinctions between the world of E. M. Forster's *A Passage to India* and the world of *The Raj Quartet*. In a masterly lecture, "India: A Post-Forsterian View," given to the Royal Society of Literature in 1968, Scott admitted to some irritation at being regularly compared to Forster, because, while he felt that Forster spoke superbly for his age, Forster's India was not the same as the India of *The Raj Quartet*, a nation on the verge of partition and independence: "The Anglo-India I took my own passage to was not quite the same as the one Forster knew and brilliantly recorded. The differences were marginal, but they existed." Scott had reservations about Forster's tendency toward caricature in his portrayal of the stuffy British administrative class, where he feels that "a moral judgement is entered against them, without evidence for the accused being admitted." Their absurdity is made more acute by the absence of evidence about the actual work done by the Anglo-Indian hierarchy: "without the aura of occupation they lack what was their chief justification." Scott saw the work of the colonial administration as the expression of their ideology; when the ideology failed, so did their belief in their work. For him the final period of the British Raj in India was the last time when liberal philosophy had practical meaning, and he contrasted the earlier British colonials with the new technocrats of the 1960s, who accept well-paid jobs overseas, but have no philosophy of service.

The idealism that permeates all Scott's writing is evident from his earliest published work. In 1941 his long poem *I Gerontius* was included in the Resurgam Series of poetry pamphlets, published during the darkest days of World War II and dedicated to "rebuild a new world where men are truly free." *I Gerontius*, a religious poem divided into three sections, "The Creation," "The Dream," and "The Cross," is undeniably derivative of Eliot and Yeats in its cadences. A brief introduction by Clive Samson suggests that "It records the thoughts and emotions experienced by the author before entering the Army: war and human suffering are its back-

ground, the desire for religious belief its implication."

After the war, while at the Falcon and Grey Walls Press, Scott had an early success with his stage play *Pillars of Salt*, which was selected as a prizewinner in a Jewish Playwriting Competition organized by the Anglo-Palestinian Club. Although not a Jew, Scott was already making the theme of racial persecution a powerful motif in his work, and in his own brief introduction to the play, which was published in 1948 with three other winners as *Four Jewish Plays*, he refers to the Jewish tragedy as "a knife in the heart." The play is a parable about war and persecution, set in an imaginary mountain state where the forces of totalitarianism are strengthening daily. The threatened Jews remain helpless and unwilling to defend themselves, frozen like Lot's wife, who was changed into a pillar of salt. Eventually positive but violent action comes from two young non-Jewish brothers, who find that their unformed ideas of life have become clear and hard as a result of persecution and betrayal in their own village. *Pillars of Salt* is a young man's play, slightly awkward in its dialogue, but interesting for the energy of the ideas behind it. Although this play has never been performed, adaptations of his novels for radio and television, mainly by Scott himself, have had considerable success and have brought Paul Scott's Indian world to a wide public.

Johnnie Sahib, Scott's first novel, was rejected seventeen times before finally being published in 1952 but was then awarded the Eyre and Spottiswoode Literary Fellowship Prize. The novel employs Scott's experiences as an air supply officer in India to explore the idea of command and the loyalties that can be a powerful force in the close confines of a small army unit. Cap. Johnnie Brown (called Johnnie Sahib by his devoted Indian soldiers) is an unconventional section leader whose charismatic influence over his men causes conflicts between him and his fellow officers at the base and eventually leads to his posting elsewhere. The novel is concerned not so much with the active service of the air supply unit, which was dropping ammunition and supplies for the Burma War, but with the tensions between the officers and men, and the question is prominently posed as to whether the soldiers work for the war or for their leader.

Published a year later was *The Alien Sky*, a slender novel also set in India, which deals with a theme that was to become one of the central issues of Scott's later works, the feeling of almost tragic alienation that comes to a man who has dedicated his life to India and Indians and is now rejected at Independence, his former proteges unwilling to shake his hand. The character of Tom Gower is skillfully drawn and encapsulates the moral dilemma of the colonial who genuinely feels that his work, now discredited, has been worthwhile. The second major character in *The Alien Sky* is an American, Joe MacKendrick, who is traveling in search of his brother's past. The pattern of memories juxtaposed with present experiences that echo the past and the figure of the solitary traveler who seeks to piece together a story became familiar modes of presentation in Scott's later work.

Although *A Male Child* (1956) is set in London, the protagonist Ian Canning has just returned from military service in India, and his friend Alan Hurst has also been in the East and longs to return. The novel evokes the drab, chilly winter of 1946-1947 when England was slowly recovering from the effects of World War II. Again the novel's emphasis is on personal relationships and memories, given added poignancy by the fact that Canning has contracted a mysterious tropical disease that may be bringing him close to death. There are some intensely felt moments in Canning's relationship with Alan Hurst's extraordinary family, but the novel seems to lack the distinctive qualities that Scott's Indian novels possess.

The Mark of the Warrior (1958) returns the reader to the East, to the jungle warfare of Burma in 1942 and to the world of men in action that Scott first depicted in *Johnnie Sahib*. Major Craig is haunted by the death of a young officer, John Ramsay, for whom he felt responsible, and in trying to exorcise the experience from his conscience he reenacts the event, thus causing the death of Ramsay's younger brother. The novel is once more concerned with the qualities involved in leadership, in men working together, and in the crucial need for support from the team. The structure of the novel is too contrived to work entirely successfully, and Major Craig lacks the depth of characterization that his role seems to call for.

Scott gave himself more room to explore character in *The Chinese Love Pavilion* (1960), the last of his novels dealing specifically with British soldiers in Malaya and India during World War II. Here Scott was beginning to develop the sensuous, poetic prose that, linked to a more pronounced symbolic structure, was to suggest the fascination that the East has always held for Western visitors, which in this novel include the fanatic collector of orchids and sometime guerrilla, Brian Saxby, and

the young officer Tom Brent, whose family has served in India for generations. "India was of my bone," says Tom Brent, and Brian Saxby teaches him how to love the country to which they both have become inextricably bound.

The Birds of Paradise (1962) uses Scott's increasingly sophisticated blend of narrative techniques to filter the memories of a solitary traveler to the East, William Conway, who is escaping from a broken marriage and his uneasy role as a successful businessman in London. Conway is haunted by a brief episode during his childhood in India, during which he and his friends Dora and Krishi, an Indian prince, visited an island on a lake in the palace gardens, where brilliantly colored, stuffed birds of paradise hung suspended in a large cage. This central image of the mysterious birds of paradise is carefully woven through the novel, which culminates in a visit to the island by the three friends, now middle-aged. They find that the birds of paradise are still flying in their elaborate cage, but they are beginning to show signs of age and neglect; a poignant comment on both the splendor of the Raj and the vanity of the Indian princes of the Independent States, as well as on the vague, never to be attained aspirations of youth, seen from solitary middle age. The structure of the novel is a delicate layering of memories and flashbacks, allowing the reader to see how Conway's childhood experience in India and his fascination with the wonderful birds of paradise provided him with the most intense and meaningful moments of his life. *The Birds of Paradise* blends a delicate approach with intense emotion and accurate detail, an achievement that Scott surpassed only in *The Raj Quartet*.

The narrow range of *The Bender* (1963) seems to fit uneasily into Scott's series of novels with exotic settings in India or the Far East. A curiously slight work, the novel deals with a middle-aged Londoner, George Spruce, whose life has been shaped and largely destroyed by an unexpected inheritance which has made it unnecessary for him to find a job, yet keeps him on the brink of poverty. It is possible to see in the background of this mildly humorous novel and its satire of fashionable London in the 1960s Scott's preoccupation with the crucial importance of work for the definition of one's role in life and for the recognition by one's fellows of that role. *The Bender* is also about social class, the British caste system, that is so important in *The Raj Quartet*. Unfortunately the strands of the slight plot never seem to allow a more than superficial exploration of the problems behind it, and this novel must remain

Scott's least successful work.

The strangely disjointed structure of Scott's next novel, *The Corrida at San Feliu* (1964), may well have been related to a period in which Scott seems to have been perturbed by the relationship between life and art, between illusion and reality. The reader must gradually piece together a series of apparently unconnected fragments left behind by the imaginary novelist Edward Thornhill, who with his wife, Myra, has been killed in a car crash while returning to his Spanish villa after a bullfight (corrida). The fragments are introduced by a long-standing friend and business associate who has made the decision to publish them. Within this fictional framework Scott gives the reader a filing cabinet of oddments all supposedly written by Thornhill: two short stories, one set in Africa, one in India; two alternative openings to a novel set in India; and a short novel, "The Plaza de Toros." This disjointed montage may be baffling on the first reading, but gradually Scott's technique of stacking up the memories and experiences that figure in the consciousness of the imaginary novelist Thornhill and relating these to the ever-present image of the bullfight as a comment on life ultimately leads to what Patrick Swinden has called "A disturbingly original treatment of some of Scott's familiar themes."

Scott revisited India in 1964 and found the raw material he was to transform into the five novels on the decline of British rule in India, *The Raj Quartet* and *Staying On*. Although each novel can be read independently, rich rewards are gained from reading the novels as a complete entity. Here is evidence of a mastery of the genre that must place Scott among the handful of writers who have made a significant contribution to the novel in this century.

The Jewel in the Crown (1966) opens with an uncompromising statement that "This is the story of a rape," and so it is; a crime whose significance can never be eradicated; a crime which still reverberates in the final pages of the fourth novel, *A Division of the Spoils* (1975). Not only is one white woman raped in *The Jewel in the Crown* but another is attacked. Daphne Manners is raped by a gang of Indian youths while secretly meeting her Indian lover, Hari Kumar, in the Bibighar Gardens. A missionary schoolteacher, Edwina Crane, has her car overturned by an unruly mob, and her Indian assistant teacher is beaten to death in the road. These crimes are skillfully linked to the political turbulence of the "Quit India" riots of 1942, and the response to the civil unrest forms the major part of the novel, with the reactions of civil and military forces, of Indian judges and English memsahibs, of petty criminals and Indian princesses all woven together to give the novel its rich texture and alluring moral complexities. Not only do different characters reveal different views of the same incident but they present them through a variety of literary forms. The reader must evaluate letters, memoirs, formal reports, a journal, a legal deposition, and omniscient flashbacks, all dealing with basically the same events seen from different points of view. As Scott adds layer upon layer of detail to the plot, it becomes clear that making any kind of moral judgment of the events or the people involved in them is going to be impossible, and the reader finds himself participating in the decisions and crises that the novelist has depicted so vividly.

The arrest and conviction of Hari Kumar for Daphne's rape polarizes the tensions between the Indians and the British and introduces the ambiguous figure of Ronald Merrick, District Superintendent of the Indian Police, whose outwardly upright character is steadily undermined throughout the four novels. The British Establishment may have secret doubts about Merrick, but his authority is never questioned. Only the Indians never forget his injustice and never forgive his false conviction of Hari Kumar and his friends, even though they know that it is hopeless to try to combat the power of the Raj.

A powerful motif haunting all the novels is the old nineteenth-century print of Queen Victoria on her throne accepting tribute from her loyal Indian subjects; India is the "Jewel in the Crown" of the Empire, and in exchange for tribute the Raj offers that curious paternalistic quality known as "man-bap" by the Indians—translated to mean "I am your father and your mother." The print of the "Jewel in the Crown" appears in many situations, some ironic, some poignant. The notion of responsibility on the part of the English administration is codified by this painting and further confirms Scott's sympathy for the old-fashioned ideals of Empire.

Scott's portrayal of the corrupt Superintendent of Police, Ronald Merrick, which begins in *The Jewel in the Crown*, is deepened in *The Day of the Scorpion* (1968), which opens with the arrest of Indian politicians at the time of the "Quit India" riots of August 1942. More emphasis is placed on the politicians and the soldiers in this novel, and the effect is to circle round the crime in the Bibighar Gardens and to see it from a different angle, that of Hari Kumar. The perspective is enhanced by a chronological advance of two years when, in a dramatic and revealing episode that forms the centerpiece of the novel, Hari Kumar at last breaks his silence and tells his story to an emissary from the governor who has come to question him in jail. The investigation comes at the request of old Lady Manners, aunt of the attacked girl who has since died in childbirth. Lady Manners arrives at Kandipat Jail heavily veiled, in a purdah car, to listen unseen to the investigation. The darkened car, normally used to carry high-caste Hindu ladies still in purdah, carries an aura of seclusion and mystery and adds drama to Lady Manners's secret visit and to the startling evidence that Kumar provides of Merrick's ill-treatment of prisoners. Lady Manners leaves convinced both of Kumar's innocence and of the sense of disaster looming over the relationship between Indian and British in the final years of colonial rule. "The barrier that separated us was impenetrable," Lady Manners realizes, as, weeping, she gazes at Hari through the thick glass and metal slats in Kandipat Jail. Political tensions continue to increase as the Congress party gains in power, and the credibility of British rule is both undermined by the revelations of Superintendent Merrick's sadistic behavior toward the Indians and strengthened by the eventual reopening of the investigation into Daphne Manners's rape and the release of Kumar. It is strengthened also by the undeniable moral force of the memsahibs (the wives of the Anglo-Indian rulers and bureaucrats) in the hill station of Pankot, in the foothills of the Himalayas, especially in the developing character of Colonel Layton's daughter, Sarah, who is regarded as "unsound" because of her increasingly unorthodox views by the other Anglo-Indian women, but who is one of the few who begins to cross the barriers between the races and to assess rationally the meaning of British involvement in India. Sarah sees in Merrick "our dark side, the arcane side," and, while his heroism as an officer cannot be denied, Sarah recoils from his dismissal of the code of conduct that lies behind the tradition of service in India. Merrick regards the Indian Army officers with their care for the families and wives of the Indian troops ("man-bap" again) as amateurs; he is the new man, the professional, and his cold professionalism ensures that he is distrusted by the British and hated by the Indians he controls.

The Towers of Silence (1971) puts even more emphasis on the women behind the British military and civil lines. Most of the novel is set in Pankot, and as well as the Layton family, it develops the tragic figure of retired missionary schoolteacher Barbie Batchelor, who comes to Pankot as a paying guest and whose lower-middle-class background (her

father was a clerk and her mother a dressmaker) places her outside the circle of the British rulers of India, with their private incomes and private schools. Like Lucy Smalley in *Staying On*, Barbie is snubbed and persecuted by the memsahibs of Pankot, and these characters allow Scott to explore his concern for the English class system as manifested in India ("We have our Brahmins, our workers, our untouchables," he has said). Superintendent Merrick's highly ambivalent role is played out in the background of this novel, but he continues to bring a sense of evil wherever he goes. Merrick, like Barbie Batchelor, is not "one of us" (that is, one of the hereditary British rulers of India), and the uneasiness of his presence keeps alive the memories of the civil disturbance that he quelled so ruthlessly in 1942 and which is so graphically described in *The Jewel in the Crown*.

The final volume of *The Raj Quartet*, *A Division of the Spoils*, deals extensively with the ultimate retreat of the British and the partition of India in 1947. The clash between Hindu and Muslim becomes a matter of systematic mutual slaughter, and juxtaposed to this pattern of increasing violence is extensive political discussion on the part of Indian and British politicians, at one point telescoped into a description of a series of cartoons in a Bombay newspaper. The violence is particularized in the savage murder of Merrick by the young Indian boys he sexually exploits and in the graphically described butchery of Sarah Layton's Muslim friend, Ahmed Kasim, who is one of a large group of Muslims torn from a train and killed before the eyes of the departing British. The depiction of this scene and the bloody aftermath, in which Sarah and her future husband, Guy Perron, try to assist the wounded, is eloquent evidence of Scott's deeply held view that the British were responsible for the deaths of the quarter-million people who were killed after the Indian subcontinent was partitioned into India and Pakistan.

Scott has always been sympathetic to the feelings of the elderly, and the same understanding is revealed in his depiction of Col. Tusker Smalley and his wife, Lucy, in *Staying On* (1977), the coda to *The Raj Quartet*. Set in 1972, the novel gently satirizes the new India of sophisticated, wealthy businessmen and politicians, corrupt property dealers, and fashionable hairdressers, as Scott depicts the now elderly and fragile Tusker and Lucy, who first appeared in *The Day of the Scorpion* as rather dull but useful appendages to the military station in Pankot, still making their home there after the other British have gone home. The profu-

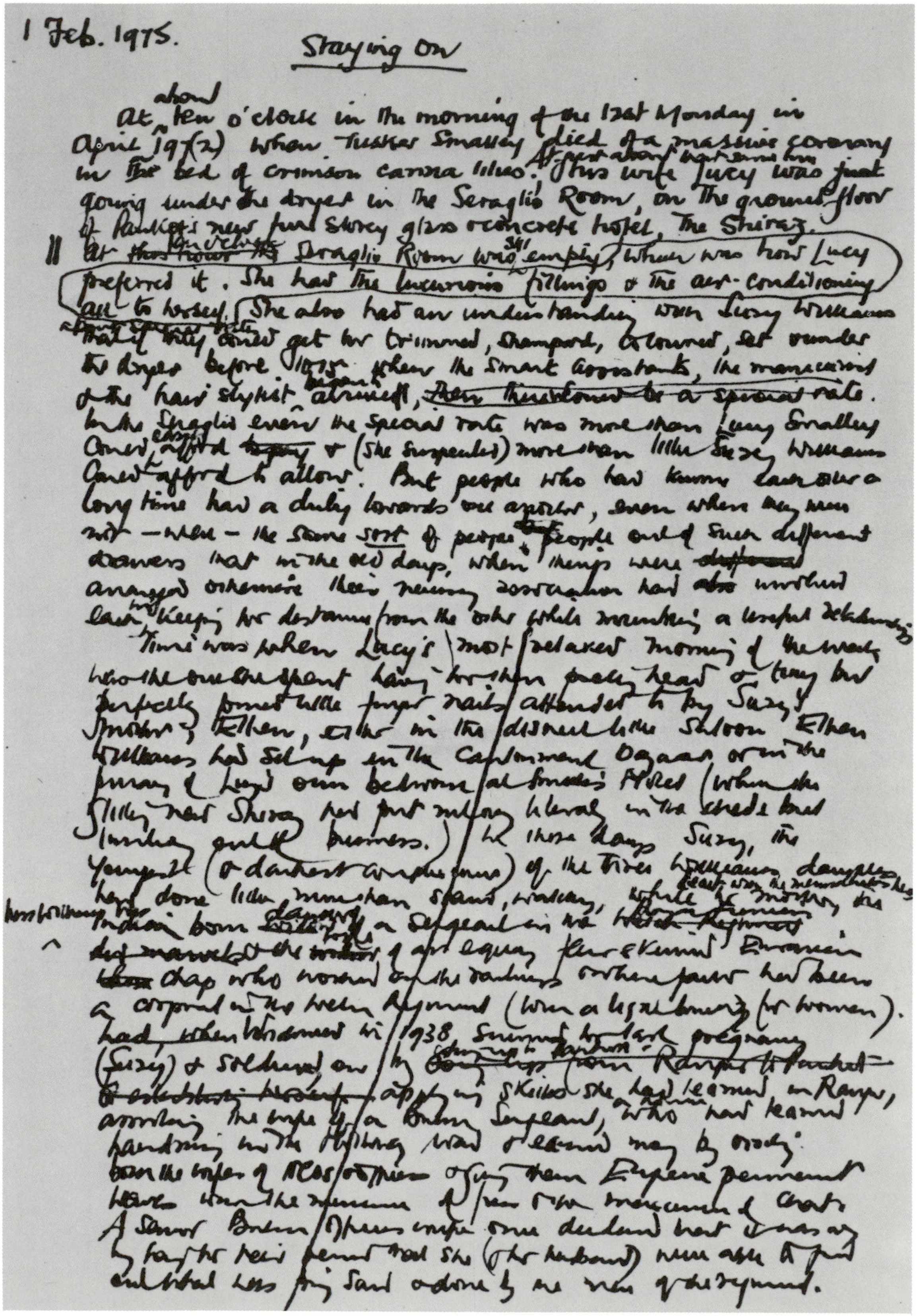
1 Feb. 1975.

Staying On

At about ten o'clock in the morning of the last Monday in April 197(2) when Tusker Smalley died of a massive coronary in the bed of crimson canna lilies, his wife Lucy was just going under the dryer in the Seraglio Room, on the ground floor of Pankot's new four storey glass & concrete hotel, The Shiraz.

First page of manuscript for Scott's last novel

sion of characters found in *The Raj Quartet* has been distilled to these two figures. Tusker's death at the opening of the novel leaves the remainder of the narrative—with most of the emphasis on Lucy's thoughts and her imaginary conversations with a friend of Sarah Layton's whom she is expecting to visit her from England—to work toward his death in the now-familiar patterning of memory juxtaposed to present at which Scott had become so adept. The sensitivity of the relationship between Tusker and Lucy is heightened, not destroyed, by the humorous handling of their essentially uncommunicative marriage, and the portrayal of their Muslim servant Ibrahim is a masterpiece of comedy. *Staying On* may seem to have the quality of a miniature painting after the vast canvas of *The Raj Quartet*, but it has all the unique qualities of a miniature: clarity of definition, minute attention to detail, and total concentration on the subject.

Paul Scott's steady development as a novelist occurred without attention from academics, although the general reading public always appreciated his work. Being elected Fellow of the Royal Society of Literature in 1963 was one of the few marks of recognition he received from the literary world before the publication of *The Raj Quartet* in the nine years between 1966 and 1975, which enhanced his reputation considerably. The award of the Booker Prize in 1977 for *Staying On* led to a huge increase in sales of his books throughout the world. It was not until after Scott's death, however, that scholars began to acknowledge his considerable achievement. Sophisticated narrative techniques and sympathetic historical insight work together in Scott's later fiction to provide a triumphant vindication of the old-fashioned literary virtues of characterization, plot, and narrative detail. His moral questioning goes to the heart of the role of man in society, whether in Anglo-India or a wider world.

Television Plays:
Lines of Communication, BBC, 1952;

The Alien Sky, BBC, 1956.

Radio Plays:
Lines of Communication, BBC, 1951;
The Alien Sky, BBC, 1954;
Sahibs and Memsahibs, BBC, 1958;
The Mark of the Warrior, BBC, 1960.

Other:
Pillars of Salt, in *Four Jewish Plays*, edited by Harold F. Rubinstein (London: Gollancz, 1948);
"India: A Post Forsterian View," in *Essays by Divers Hands* (London: Oxford University Press, 1970).

References:
Max Beloff, "The End of the Raj—Paul Scott's Novels as History," *Encounter* (May 1976): 65-70;
Richard Rhodes James, "In the Steps of Paul Scott," *Listener* (8 March 1979): 359-360;
Caroline Moorehead, "Getting Engrossed in the Death Throes of the Raj," *Times*, 20 October 1975, p. 7;
Arthur Pollard, "Twilight of Empire: Paul Scott's *Raj Quartet*," in *Individual and Community in Commonwealth Literature*, edited by Daniel Massa (Msida: University of Malta Press, 1979), pp. 169-176;
K. Bhaskara Rao, *Paul Scott* (Boston: Twayne, 1980);
Nancy Wilson Ross, "Paul Scott, Unsung Singer of Hindustan," *Saturday Review* (24 June 1972): 58-60;
Patrick Swinden, *Paul Scott: Images of India* (London: Macmillan, 1980);
Francine S. Weinbaum, "Paul Scott's India: *The Raj Quartet*," *Critique: Studies in Modern Fiction*, 20, no. 1 (1979): 100-110.

Papers:
There is a collection of Scott's papers at the Humanities Research Center, University of Texas, Austin.

Tom Sharpe
(30 March 1928-   )

Simon Edwards
Roehampton Institute

NOVELS: *Riotous Assembly* (London: Secker & Warburg, 1971);

Indecent Exposure (London: Secker & Warburg, 1973);

Porterhouse Blue (London: Secker & Warburg, 1974);

Blott on the Landscape (London: Secker & Warburg, 1975);

Wilt (London: Secker & Warburg, 1976);

The Great Pursuit (London: Secker & Warburg, 1977; New York: Harper & Row, 1978);

The Throwback (London: Secker & Warburg, 1978);

The Wilt Alternative (London: Secker & Warburg, 1979; New York: St. Martin's, 1980);

Ancestral Vices (London: Secker & Warburg, 1980).

Tom Sharpe

Tom Sharpe is that comparatively rare phenomenon, a contemporary writer who manages to make a living from his novels alone. With only two of his novels published in the United States, the combined sales of his works in paperback approach two million in Great Britain. After a life spent as a teacher and a photographer in South Africa and England, he began writing fiction at the age of forty-one. His novels of grotesque and savage farce (the dust-jacket blurb for his most recent, *Ancestral Vices*, 1980, describes it, unashamedly, as "insensitive") draw on a range of cultural and intellectual preoccupations that resemble those of earlier comic novelists such as Thomas Love Peacock and Aldous Huxley. However, the methods of their construction are closer to those of English popular novelist Dornford Yates, whose work Sharpe loathes, and P. G. Wodehouse, whose satiric style he respects. To prepare himself for writing, he reads Richmael Crompton's William books for children and uses snuff. With the great Augustan satirists, such as Swift and Pope, Sharpe shares a fascination with popular literature, which he sees as at once necessary and corrupting, and his most effective writing can attain similar effects of ironic counterpoint, moral subversion, and even, at times, a bleak moral grandeur, though it can also decline into the repetitively mechanical.

Reviewers were universally enthusiastic about his earlier work, but recently they have begun to take him to task for a lack of generosity toward his characters and the failure to develop wider perspectives on human behavior, criticisms that may not be justified. Nevertheless, his sixth novel, *The Great Pursuit* (1977), did suggest movement into a new dimension of seriousness without abandonment of the remarkable inventiveness and comic energy that informed his previous work; moreover, *The Great Pursuit* escaped the formula of each of the other novels to the extent of being some fifty pages longer. Characteristically Sharpe claims this length to be merely the result of using a new typewriter with different spacing, and he would still prefer to have pruned it. Three more novels, each with its own strengths, have tended to disappoint that promise of development. One hopes that with a growing confidence in the size of his constituency of readers, he will indeed be prepared to risk further experiment.

Sharpe's childhood and adolescence were remarkable and have left important traces on all his work. He was born to a fifty-eight-year-old Unitarian minister, George Coverdale Sharpe, and his wife, Grace Egerton Sharpe, in Holloway, London, in 1928 and was brought up in Croydon and at boarding schools. He ran away from Bloxham school, in Buckinghamshire, and then attended Lancing College. His father, a former socialist, had become a committed Nazi and systematically educated his son as one. At school, during the war, Sharpe wore a German military belt, an improbably provocative mark of his family's politics. His discovery, in late adolescence, of the reality of the German concentration camps was wholly traumatic. This encounter with the insanities and evils of racism was later compounded by his years in South Africa, where he went to work after two years of national service as a marine (1946-1948) and after earning an M. A. degree in history and social anthropology at Pembroke College, Cambridge. He reached South Africa initially through connections of his family (a remarkable one which had made and lost fortunes in various colonies of the Victorian Empire), and after a few months with a finance corporation he worked for the Department of Non-European Affairs in the black township of Soweto, outside Johannesburg. In 1952 he began teaching white children in Natal and opened his own photographic studio in Pietermaritzburg in 1956. Throughout this period he was attempting to write serious political plays. Of nine plays written, only one was produced, at the fringe Questors Theatre in Ealing, London, in 1961. This production was to prove a turning point in his life. Because of it, he was arrested by the Special Branch of the South African police, imprisoned, and deported.

Arriving in England, without job, money, or qualifications, he taught for a few months at Aylesbury Secondary Modern School before returning to Pembroke College to train formally as a teacher. He began lecturing in history and liberal studies at the Cambridge College of Arts and Technology in 1963, and his eight years there form the basis of his version of the campus novel, *Wilt* (1976). After the publication and succcess of his first two novels, *Riotous Assembly* (1971) and *Indecent Exposure* (1973), he left his job to become a full-time writer and has subsequently produced a novel almost every year. He now lives quietly, with his American wife, Nancy Anne Looper Sharpe, and their three daughters, in Dorset. He writes every morning—single chapters of his novels often require over a dozen drafts—and gardens vigorously within his four-and-a-half acres most afternoons. His 1930s suburban house is on a quiet street that runs between two factories in the small market-town of Bridport. Passing through the house, one comes upon a surprising pastoral vista of lawns, woods, and rose gardens leading down to a deserted railway cutting and sheep-grazed water meadows. Sharpe confesses a preference for reading gardening books rather than literature, as the writers he is most like to enjoy and admire can only disrupt what he sees himself as trying to achieve as a writer.

The first two novels have a number of characters in common and are both set in the South African town of Piemburg, whose "mediocrity was venomous." The town is clearly modeled on Pietermaritzburg where Sharpe had worked. The novels may both be read as satirical improvisations (despite the intricacies of their plots) on a remark made in the first work about a mental hospital, where the inmates perform a lunatic masque, resembling the masques in Jacobean tragedy and reenacting the last hundred years of South African history: "There didn't seem to be any significant difference between life in the mental hospital and life in South Africa as a whole. Black madmen did all the work, while white lunatics lounged about imagining they were God." Contemporary psychiatric practice—particularly through the figure of a monstrous blond woman therapist, Doctor Von Blimenstein—and other aspects of modern medicine, including heart transplant surgery, which was pioneered in South Africa, are incidental targets in both novels. Sharpe's preoccupation with sexual deviation as distorted human energy suggests complex indebtedness to modern psychological theories about the relations between sexuality and political and social power, both at their most distorted in South African institutions. Sharpe's using sexuality in both an exploitative and a symbolic sense is another aspect of the ambiguous relationship his work has with popular literature.

Both novels are more concerned with the tensions between Boer and English legacies within South African society than they are with those between black and white communities, though problems between the Boers and the English are seen as exacerbating, if not determining black-white tensions. Piemburg is an English enclave within Afrikaans territory. *Riotous Assembly* concerns the investigations made by the Boer-dominated police force into offenses against the absurd laws forbidding interracial sexual relations, supposedly committed by the long-established English family the Hazelstones, residents of the local great house, Jacaranda Park. The elderly Miss Hazelstones, daughter of the insane general, Sir Theophilus, has been having an affair, based on a mutual rubber fetishism (a recurrent motif in Sharpe's work), with her black cook. Miss Hazelstones claims responsibility for his murder though it seems more likely that he has been literally buggered to death by her drunken clergyman brother, Jonathan, the Bishop of Barotseland. The characters to emerge most strongly are the equally repulsive, mutually hostile, Boer policemen. These include Kommandant Van Heerden, pitifully obsessed by the sangfroid social style of the English, who, he believes, can do no wrong, and his second-in-command rival Lieutenant Verkramp, a Boer ideologue and compulsive author of secret reports to BOSS (the South African secret police) on almost the whole English community, all of whom he regards as potential Communist subversives.

The dirty work of these superior officers is carried out by Konstabel Els, a brutal thug whose pleasure in killing and torture gives the lie to the hateful racial theories that both Van Heerden and Verkramp believe to be the basis of civilization. Inevitably they both despise Els, whose anarchic violence threatens to compromise them when they lay siege to Jacaranda Park in order to prevent the news of the outrages there from infecting the whole district. Outrage succeeds outrage, however, when Els occupies an impregnable pillbox built by the paranoiac Sir Theophilus and, with his extraordinary armory of lethal weapons, threatens singlehandedly to eliminate the whole invading local police force and army. The total confusion of the battle scene is depicted in a deadpan style, as suggested in this description of the attackers' armored cars that Els has blasted to pieces: "its occupants trickled gently but persistently through a hundred holes drilled in its side." The tendency of the police to regard black Africans merely as objects is thus savagely reversed. The combination of this style with wildly cruel invention creates a black humor which captures beautifully the collective insanity of South African "civilization." There is a further strain of black humor in the tortured religious speculations of the Bishop of Barotseland, particularly when he realizes that the fundamental images of Christianity are those of torture and suffering. The bishop is eventually captured and sentenced to death while Konstable Els is recruited as

an emergency hangman and Kommandant Van Heerden, his heart in poor condition after the chaos he has unleashed, negotiates for a transplant of the bishop's heart, thus hoping to acquire some of the envied English racial characteristics. The overriding tone of the novel prevents the reader from sympathizing with the bishop, despite his realizations, but this strain of latent humanism does suggest a function of Sharpe's imagination that cannot easily be accommodated by his chosen form but reappears in later novels to create a kind of eloquent power.

Indecent Exposure extends the rivalry between Van Heerden and Verkramp, who calls in the predatory Dr. Von Blimenstein to conduct some aversion therapy on the Piemburg police to cure them of their persistent breaches of the law forbidding sexual relations with blacks. Their penises are wired to electric-shock machines while they are shown photographic slides of naked black women. While the local police are thus incapacitated, Verkramp also arranges for a team of twelve agents provocateurs to create enough outrages in Piemburg to justify mass arrests among its English residents. These outrages culminate in the explosions of a herd of ostriches, which, having been persuaded to swallow gelignite, have been released around the town. Verkramp's excesses have been made possible by the absence of Van Heerden, who has been pursuing his anglophilic fantasies on vacation with a group of expatriate English who have formed a Dornford Yates Club and are acting out, at a suburban country house, fantasies of upper-class life. The two plots meet when the police, now recovered from their therapy, believe they have identified the source of sabotage as this group of English and attack their country house, White Ladies. The ubiquitous Konstabel Els, who has been acting as a servant at the house, reappears to give chase to the masquerading colonel, who is dressed in women's clothing. This brutal parody of an English fox hunt exposes the sanctimonious English justification of blood sports (just one element in the ideology on which South African society is based). Ironically, Els seems to have become transformed into a positive representation of the life force, thus anticipating a more sympathetic rendering of the will to survive in the next two novels.

Indecent Exposure includes a whole series of wild reversals, particularly of sexual roles and identities. For example, in a scene that also coincides with the point where reality and literary fantasy meet, the English group at White Ladies act out "Berry Puts Off His Manhood," the climactic chapter of Dornford Yates's *Jonah and Co.* Sharpe's probing of the instinctual life, awkwardly and paradoxically couched in racial terms, is here part of his questioning of the basic nature of reality, which, without being overtly moral, rescues the book where it hovers dangerously on the verge of the mechanical. He tests reality also by introducing an imprisoned Communist, Geisenheimer, thus offering the kind of politically weighted critique of South Africa that Sharpe ultimately eschews. The total effect of the two novels suggest, however, a political radicalism that is challenged in the next novel, *Porterhouse Blue* (1974).

In *Porterhouse Blue* the faculty of a Cambridge college, Porterhouse, attempts to resist the moves toward modernization initiated by a new master, Sir Godber Evans, a retired Labour cabinet minister. Porterhouse serves as a microcosm of contemporary England; through a series of scandals, frequently sexual, the contradictions of progress are given complex comic realization, in spite of the savagery with which both its opponents and proponents are presented. Outstanding in this gallery of villains is the aristocratic Sir Cathcart D'eath, a graduate of Porterhouse who stands for much of the ideological and institutional inertia bedeviling English life; his conservatism finds a "populist" face in the novel's real hero, the college porter, Skullion. The victim of an apoplectic stroke at the end of the novel and immobilized in a wheelchair, Skullion becomes, appropriately enough, the new master of the college after the death of Sir Godber, who, just before his death, has been made to feel the limitations of his crudely Benthamite liberalism. Skullion's opposition to changes at Porterhouse makes him a national celebrity, and although he begins as a servile grotesque, he acquires a self-critical moral intelligence that can incorporate a recognition of the uses to which he has been willingly put by others throughout his time at Porterhouse. Ironically these abuses of Skullion are part of Sir Godber's justification for change, and during his television appearance, when he is interviewed by pundit Cornelius Carrington, "the Jeremiah of the BBC" and a graduate of the college, Skullion becomes more *real*—"as a mirror . . . to a mythical past"—than in his own self-definitions.

The suggestion is that men like Skullion, with their admirable though corruptible resourcefulness, lie at the very center of English history and experience, though they are persistently and culpably disregarded in the power struggles of the ruling class. One of his last perceptions is the bleak observation that "there were no just rewards in life, only

insane inversions of the scheme of things in which he had trusted." This more somber note of illusion and betrayal, together with the oddly archaic imagery of English life that informs the novel, is characteristic of Sharpe's later work. The archaism may be a property of Skullion's sort of conservative "populism," which refuses conventional political analysis and alternatives, a refusal neatly caught by the side of the body paralyzed by Skullion's stroke: "There were no contradictions now between right and wrong, master and servant, only a strange inability to move his left side."

Blott on the Landscape (1975) continues the themes of progress and populism but deals with politicians, bureaucrats, and property development rather than academics. Skullion's role is now assumed by the more marginal though eponymous Blott, the sources of whose violent resistance to change include a library of popular English history, including the work of Sir Arthur Bryant. In fact, Blott is an alien, a German former prisoner of war, who has claimed Italian ancestry and now works as a gardener to Lady Maud Lynchwood. Divisions within the British ruling class are symbolized by the Lynchwoods' marriage. Lady Maud's impotent husband, Sir Giles, plans to divorce her while capitalizing on his £100,000 investment in her Shropshire family home, Handyman Hall. To circumvent a complex reversionary clause that in case of divorce will lose him his share in the property, he arranges, through political and business connections, to have a motorway built through the estate, providing him with handsome financial compensation. The local campaign against the motorway is led, with remarkable deviousness and determination, by Lady Maud, who has her own reasons for wishing to separate from her husband. By means of blackmail and counterblackmail, a fastidious bureaucrat, Dundridge, who is in charge of the motorway scheme, is drawn into the plot. Initially he stands, like Sir Godber in *Porterhouse Blue*, for the facile principles of an impersonal progress. His spiritually enfeebled meliorism is set against the Lynchwoods' two versions of more ruthless "laws of nature." Sir Giles's "dog-eat-dog" justification of naked capitalist enterprise is perversely reflected in his own masochistic sexuality, while an even more stark "law of the jungle," implicitly Social Darwinian, is invoked by Lady Maud, who is allied with the violent, brooding Blott in her battle with the developers. Appropriately, Sir Giles is eaten by lions in the Safari Park that Lady Maud is establishing at Handyman Hall, while Dundridge, humiliated and reviled, adopts some of the tactics of outright force in a spirit of pure vengeance by conducting the motorway construction as a military campaign, "Operation Overland." Blott shares this military spirit and prepares to defend the estate in a prolonged siege, fortifying the gateway from a concealed arms cache. "That was all the bloody world understood. Force," he reflects. His eventual marriage to Lady Maud is evidence of the resilience of the English class system, the capacity of the ruling class for incorporating disparate elements.

Lady Maud's own family is an amalgam of decayed landed interests and ruthless industrialists of the nineteenth century. Her marriage to Sir Giles was clearly an earlier attempt to include a new element of social and political power in the form of property development. As an emblem of fundamental Englishness, Blott is, however, a more troubling figure than Skullion, and Sharpe seems reluctant to make him a fully realized character. He may reflect his creator's South African experience in his notion that "being a prisoner in England was better than being free anywhere else." Yet it is not merely a disillusionment with politics that suggests this similarity. Blott, "not knowing who he was . . . tried out other people's personalities"; he has extraordinary aptitude for mimicry and impersonation that coincides with Sharpe's own avowed methods of creating fiction. As an exploration of what it means to be English, of an ideology whose mentor is Sir Arthur Bryant and which is unbalanced by the radical accounts of, say, George Orwell and E. P. Thompson, the novel is faintly alarming, particularly when the emergence of something like genetic typing as an explanation of character is noted. It is not clear, for example, whether Lady Maud's remark that "evidently the blood of her ancestors ran in her veins" is wholly ironic. Another version of fundamental human decency, the moral stand taken by Mrs. Forthby, the woman Sir Giles pays to flog and humiliate him ("I may be a silly woman and not very nice but I do have my standards"), only partly serves to dissipate this alarm.

Sharpe's next hero, the technical college lecturer in *Wilt*, is a far more self-consciously intellectual version of the "populist" spirit. Henry Wilt is at loggerheads with the trendy rubbish of elegant defeatism spouted by his colleagues at Fenland College and oppressed by the classes of bored industrial apprentices to whom he has to teach literature, as well as by the vulgarity and sexual voracity of his fat wife, Eva; he, therefore, cultivates some of the old-fashioned cynicism and "Little Englandism" that

would seem to have more in common with the postures of the "angry" novelists of the 1950s than with his real contemporaries. The plot involves Wilt's encounter with a fashionably liberated American couple, who are viewed with a savagery recalling that shown toward the police in the South African novels. The wife initiates a reluctant Eva into lesbianism, and, after Eva has left Wilt, he is arrested for her murder. In fact, the corpse discovered is not Eva's but an inflatable life-size plastic doll to which Wilt has become "attached" at a party thrown by the American couple. The antics surrounding his arrest threaten to jeopardize the future of the academically aspiring Fenland College, creating scenes of intellectual pretentiousness and administrative panic that have given the novel something of a reputation among teachers in British higher education during the period of reorganization and expansion in the 1970s. The most compelling part of the novel is the attempt made by the policeman, Inspector Flint, to get Wilt to break down and confess the murder (in a scene pertinent to recent scandals in England about police methods of interrogation).

During his prolonged confinement Wilt develops qualities of resilience which belie his name. In fighting back he appears to accede to a cruder ethic of survival than his previous tenets of defeated liberalism suggested. He acquires a knowledge of the world as perverse, silly, and random—a clear knowledge which liberates him from his doubts about reality and justice. There are echoes of Dostoevski and Kafka here, as Sharpe brings the truisms of an education in modern literature into confrontation with lived, suburban English experience and thus revitalizes the tradition of the absurd. Through this experience Wilt acquires a new sense of rapport with the working-class butchers' apprentices to whom he teaches a course known scathingly in the college as Meat One. With this modified philistinism, which is also a respect for his students' instinctive knowledge of human limits, he determines, at the end of the novel, to teach them much needed practical skills rather than the literature on which our "culture of the word" places too high a value.

Eva too emerges at the end morally purged; she is born again through nearly drowning. This rebirth is partly the result of a crazy encounter, at the end of her adventure in sexual experiment, with a drunken Anglo-Catholic clergyman, St. John Froude, who resembles the Bishop of Barotseland of *Riotous Assembly* and whose extravagant metaphysical speculations are a curious amalgam of the Book of Genesis, William Blake, and F. R. Leavis.

While *Wilt* broaches questions of literary value and cultural significance, *The Great Pursuit* confronts them head-on. Here Sharpe, the lapsed "political" playwright who is now an enormously successful best-selling novelist, treats explicitly the issue of the writer's responsibility. Of all Sharpe's novels *The Great Pursuit* is the most intricate in plot and theme as well as in its complex sympathy toward the characters. Perhaps in part because it has sold less well than his other novels, Sharpe has not extended its methods and implications. The novel deftly employs parallel and parody, the more remarkable in that it threatens to slacken off toward the middle.

The title alludes to F. R. Leavis's *The Great Tradition* (1948) and *The Common Pursuit* (1952), key texts of Leavisite critical orthodoxy, which requires that novels present moral values uplifting to society. This outlook *The Great Pursuit* attacks in the name of a literary culture "where people write without

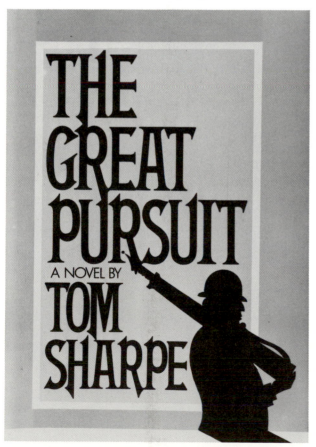

Dust jacket for the American edition of Sharpe's 1977 novel, which espouses writing "without hypocrisy for money"

hypocrisy for money." Yet this new position is indefensible too, and the novel becomes a disturbing indictment of contemporary culture because *The Great Pursuit* also depicts those wider pressures at work in the economics of book production, reflecting the structure of capitalist production as a whole. Sharpe originally agreed to allow a Russian translation of this novel to be published in the Soviet Union, but he withdrew permission after the arrest of Sakharov, and the Russians' refusal to publish Sharpe's letter protesting the arrest.

In *The Great Pursuit*, an aging Leavisite Cambridge don, Dr. Louth, in spite of her lifetime of strictures against popular novels, is the anonymous author of *Pause O Men for the Virgin*, an appalling pulp fiction that articulates years of self-repression. She submits the manuscript of her novel to Frensic, a charming literary agent and eighteenth-century buff, who, recognizing its market potential, sells the paperback rights to Hutchmeyer, a foulmouthed American paperback tycoon. When Hutchmeyer demands that the author should conduct a personal sales campaign in the United States, Frensic persuades Peter Piper to act the part. He is a hitherto unpublished novelist of incapacitating literary integrity for whom Dr. Louth has served as mentor. After beginning his American tour amid wild scenes recalling Dickens's astonished accounts of his popular reception in America in the 1840s, Piper falls into the clutches of Hutchmeyer's wife, Baby, who has had numerous face-lifts. After a fire destroys the Hutchmeyer home, Baby and Piper, both believed dead, run off together to the Deep South, ending up in an isolated and backward community named, significantly, Bibliopolis. Here Baby undergoes her final "face-lift" as a born again Christian. Dickens's novel reflecting his American tour, *Martin Chuzzlewit* (1844), echoes through Sharpe's pages; the swamp-infested Bibliopolis recalls the similar location of the new town of Eden, in which the younger Martin Chuzzlewit is "born again."

Piper, despairing now of his literary aspirations and recognizing, like Wilt, a new order of practical necessity, sets himself up as a writing master. Paradoxically, his School of Logosophy, which defines the world as Logos (The Word), becomes a mirror image of the self-enclosed world of literary production, as conceived by Dr. Louth's most influential work, *The Moral Novel*. While Frensic tracks down the real author of the novel in England, Piper and Baby continue to live off its royalties. After discovering Dr. Louth's authorship, Frensic visits

Piper and Baby in Bibliopolis. There, using her charismatic authority within the community, Baby terrifies Frensic into publishing under his name Piper's dreadful literary novel, *Search For A Lost Childhood*, which the author has spent a lifetime rewriting. Although for years the novel has been considered unpublishable, if not unreadable, when it finally appears as Frensic's work, it meets universal acclaim, a "stigma" that Frensic must bear in an almost Christlike fashion.

Peter Piper is shattered by his knowledge of his mentor's "real" responsibility: "The age of the great novel was over. It remained only to commemorate it in manuscript. And so while Baby preached the need to imitate Christ, Piper too returned to traditional virtues in everything." Reviving the use of quill pens, "the original tools of his craft," which stand "as reminders of that golden age when books were written by hand and to be a copyist was to belong to an honourable profession," Piper begins to rewrite *Great Expectations* (1860-1861): " 'My father's family name being Pirrip, and my Christian name Philip, my infant tongue could make of both names nothing longer or more explicit than Piper. . . .' He stopped. That wasn't right. It should have been Pip. But after a moment's hesitation he dipped his quill again and continued."

This reversion to traditional ways and values is, of course, also part of the "organic community" celebrated by Leavis and his disciples. The whole method of construction in *The Great Pursuit* is the very opposite of the elegant economy of, say, Borges (whose story, "The Library of Babel," is recalled by Bibliopolis), even while it confronts similar questions of origins, attribution, and meaning, not merely in literature but also within the whole system of sign making that is culture. In that respect, the novel is paradoxically a Leavisite text, seeing literary and cultural significance as inextricably linked. What has been called here Sharpe's "populism" may even have Leavisite roots. *The Great Pursuit*'s very expansiveness as a novel ensures that it cannot be read as an idealist critical exercise as the questions it raises are placed in the context of the conditions of literary production as well as of its own production. It then fulfills those Augustan criteria for a wit that is truly *mordant*, that it should bite. Sharpe's finest achievement certainly invites comparison with Waugh (to whose *A Handful of Dust*, 1934, its closing pages also allude), if not with Orwell and Swift.

Sharpe's next novel, *The Throwback* (1978), marks a return to more familiar material and devices. Sharpe says that the extraordinary rhetorical sequences—a vulgarized amalgam of nineteenth-century ideologies from Carlyle, Schopenhauer, Darwin, and Samuel Smiles—delivered by one of its two central characters, Old Flawse, were initially an unconscious echo of Sharpe's father's habits of speech. Given his father's political predilections, the novel may be read as an exorcism, with the elderly man's name suggesting "old flaws." *The Throwback* resembles a literal exorcism as the latter part of the book is haunted by the monstrous old man's thundering voice, but that voice is only a disembodied tape recording played by his lunatic grandson, Lockhart, after his grandfather's death. Both the novel's setting, a vast feudal estate in contemporary Northumberland, and some of its characters owe a debt to an earlier novelist in whom popularity and seriousness meet, Sir Walter Scott, whose biographer was his son-in-law, John Gibson Lockhart. In its use of both sentimentality and the overtly shocking, the novel might derive equally from the bastardized contemporary versions of Scott, such as Catherine Cookson's popular televised series *The Mallens* (also set in Northumberland), and Stella Gibbons's parody of the genre, *Cold Comfort Farm* (1932). Sharpe admits his admiration of both Scott and Gibbons but claims to be writing from "experience." The literary texture of the novel, however, as well as its obliquely personal concerns, suggests precisely what is problematic in the term *experience*. Sharpe admits that the central sequence of the novel is mechanical, his most tedious exercise in perverse ingenuity of plotting. Yet even the word *mechanical* is suggestive in that it literally refers to the devices used by Lockhart to terrify and evict all the tenants of his wife's suburban estate so that he can sell it and restore the floundering fortunes of his ancestral home, Northumberland. Lockhart makes further gains by inserting his name in the typescript of a historical novelist and then suing the man for libel.

Lockhart, illegitimate son of Old Flawse's daughter, has been brought up by his grandfather in total sexual innocence with a morality based on the hodgepodge of his grandfather's reading, which justifies any act of violence. The same morality saturates his unstinting denunciations of the modern world and contemporary progress, a hostility toward the twentieth century echoing that in both *Porterhouse Blue* and *Blott on the Landscape*. A more profound anxiety about origins is suggested by Old Flawse's fear that he may in fact have fathered Lockhart during an act of drunken incest. Lockhart's discovery at the end of the novel that he is not Old Flawse's son is part of the process of exorcism. The novel ends with yet another crazy and violent siege that Sharpe is adept in portraying. Flawse Hall is surrounded by invading tax inspectors, whom Lockhart sees, in another allusion to Scott, as excise men seeking payment of debts accruing from the profits from the sale of Lockhart's wife's London estate. Lockhart fights off the invaders with the aid of amplified tape recordings of military maneuvers, tapes supplied by a remarkably amiable officer from a neighboring army base. Meanwhile, the tape-recorded voice of his grandfather, his dead body pickled and stuffed by a terrified Italian taxidermist, resounds through the house, driving Old Flawse's widow (actually the mother of Lockhart's wife), who may otherwise inherit the estate, to flight and violent death.

One senses that the moral and philosophical dimensions of this novel are only half explored. They are imaginatively represented in the group of retainers and clients of the Flawse estate—a bailiff, a solicitor and a doctor—who, enclosed in the same pocket of time, gather for evenings of "gude crack," as it was known in Scott's day, and of extravagant philosophical speculation. The brilliant comedy of this scene and Sharpe's failure to integrate it into the novel's willfully popular format suggest some of the peculiar shape and blackness of Sharpe's farcical instincts. In comparison, other aspects of the novel are less attractive, especially the depictions of the violent indulgence of Old Flawse's sexual appetites and the contrastingly coy innocence of Lockhart's wife throughout their unconsummated marriage.

The struggle to achieve a broader significance and to confront contemporary political issues in more immediate ways (as the South African novels had done earlier) continues in *The Wilt Alternative* (1979), another siege novel. Henry Wilt, now a head of department at Fenland College, tentatively reconciled to his wife, Eva, and busy with quadruplet daughters, finds his house occupied by international terrorists. When he arrives on the scene, the army is already at loggerheads with the local police force, which includes Wilt's old antagonist, Inspector Flint, who gleefully anticipates the death of both Wilt and his wife. Army personnel persuade Wilt to try to get his children out without alerting the terrorists, but during his attempt Wilt and his family are all taken as hostages. Initially high on chemical stimulants administered by the army, Wilt tries, with final success, to confuse the telephone negotiations between terrorists and authorities so that in the resulting disorder he can rescue his children. This impractical man is once again allowed to improvise his way to practical achievement, serving

further to confirm Sharpe's mistrust of all organized authority and his hostility toward any kind of theoretical knowledge. Thus a left-wing colleague of Wilt's is contaminated by the same odium as the terrorists; all are "doctrinaire shits." The image also suggests a developing scatological vein in Sharpe's humor, an Augustan element hitherto surprisingly rare and reinforced by a running joke about organic waste disposal and the recycling of human feces. (This type of humor reappears in the representation of Victorian plumbing in *Ancestral Vices*.) The terrorists are presented as wealthy jet-setting playboys, while their leader is an extremely beautiful and intelligent German girl, Irmegaard Mueller, who has been a lodger in the Wilts' attic flat. In fact, until she revealed her politics, Henry was fantasizing about becoming a great novelist in the tradition of Proust, Mann, and Gide on the strength of his feelings for this girl. But if Wilt's final revulsion concerning his own sexuality is disturbing, far more so is the apparently endorsed savagery of Eva Wilt's plans to revenge herself on Irmegaard Mueller, plans which are as much a product of her sexual jealousy as of her protective instinct toward her children. Unleashed here is the most violent kind of sexual fantasy, the implications of which Sharpe subtly evades by attributing the actions to Eva, now likened to some kind of primeval feminine principle. The flight from ideology and "all the -isms"—a flight that *The Wilt Alternative* seems to approve—can turn into an anti-intellectualism with a dangerous social and sexual face, which the novel purports to oppose. Sharpe is practiced enough a satirist to recognize this paradox through his presentation of the figure of Wilt. Alternatively, it is not difficult to criticize successful satirical writing in this way, and it will be a measure of Sharpe's true stature as a novelist if he can write his way out of this impasse.

The guarded response of reviewers to *Ancestral Vices* is not surprising. The novel is another excursion into the excesses of the English upper classes, this time represented by the Petrefact family of the Vale of Bushampton. The Petrefacts, like other members of their class portrayed in Sharpe's fiction, are in conflict with the modern world, which in this novel is represented notably by the American Walden Yapp, a professor of demotic historiography at Kloone University, who has been engaged to write a family history.

Yet the reviewers of Sharpe's novels have missed much of his real importance, tending to see each novel as a joyously anarchic squib and calling Sharpe a remarkable intelligence making welcome use of an accessible popular form. In fact, the works taken together create a far more troubled world, brooding on humankind's tenuous reproduction and survival. Thus the novels are apocalyptic, haunted by recurring motifs of sterility, impotence, and both moral and physical perversion.

Hitherto Sharpe has attracted little or no sustained critical attention, although influential reviewer, Auberon Waugh, whom Sharpe acknowledged generously as the sympathetic character Octavian Door in *The Great Pursuit*, has published an interview with Sharpe. The interview disappoints, however, because Sharpe clearly failed to fuel Waugh's "Tory anarchism." He is a far more interesting novelist than this interview would suggest, a novelist with whom criticism of contemporary literature and culture must come to terms if only to explore the relations between the intelligentsia and popular cultural forms. Sharpe's novels, regardless of setting, form a vast and grotesque counterpastoral of contemporary English life as much concerned with myths as realities. He has created a history of England at once both cruel and sentimental, where liberated sexual mores—in which social classes meet in illusory freedoms together with barbarian outsiders disguised in shabby parodies of the conventions—threaten to destroy the contradictory fabric of their inception.

Robert Shaw
(9 August 1927 - 28 August 1978)

Malcolm Page
Simon Fraser University

See also the Shaw entry in *DLB 13, British Dramatists Since World War II*

BOOKS: *The Hiding Place* (London: Chatto & Windus, 1959; Cleveland: World Publishing Company, 1959);

The Sun Doctor (London: Chatto & Windus, 1961; New York: Harcourt, Brace & World, 1961);

The Flag (London: Chatto & Windus, 1965; New York: Harcourt, Brace & World, 1965);

The Man in the Glass Booth [novel] (London: Chatto & Windus, 1967; New York: Harcourt, Brace & World, 1967);

The Man in the Glass Booth [play] (London: Chatto & Windus, 1967; New York: Grove, 1968);

A Card from Morocco (London: Chatto & Windus, 1969; New York: Harcourt, Brace & World, 1969);

Cato Street (London: Chatto & Windus, 1972; New York: Grove, 1972).

Robert Shaw's five novels mix unusual and adventurous plots with solid and serious themes. Though *The Man in the Glass Booth* (1967), which he adapted as a successful play, is his best-known novel, *The Sun Doctor* (1961) is perhaps richer. Asked by interviewer Terry Philpott why he wrote, Shaw said: "First, because I have a childish desire for immor-

Robert Shaw

tality. . . . Secondly, I am a political writer. I feel very radically about some things but only in a certain kind of way, not in a square-on political party way. I would like to influence people to a hard and tough radicalism. That is why I admire Orwell so much. . . . I genuinely love to shock my readership into something. But I am always thinking of how I can get their attention, of how I can shock them out of their smug, middle-class ways. I want to shock them out of their stupor, to shock them into awareness, to make them think. Everybody is shocking them sexually but I am like the Jesuit priest and I want to make the boy *think*!"

Shaw was versatile—a novelist, a playwright, a stage actor, and film star—and made substantial achievements in each area. An interest in sports, cars, and drinking went with his deep historical and philosophical concerns, and his enjoyment of wealth combined with a socialist faith. He once told an interviewer that "It is likely that most people think that there are two Robert Shaws. People who read novels think that there is a novelist called Robert Shaw who has nothing to do with that dreadful actor who they occasionally see on television."

Robert Archibald Shaw was born in 1927 in Westhoughton, near Bolton in Lancashire, the eldest of five children. His father, Thomas Shaw, was a doctor and sportsman. The family moved in 1933 to Stromness in the Orkney Islands and in 1937 to Cornwall. In 1938 Shaw went as a boarder to Truro School, and the next year, when he was twelve, his father committed suicide. Shaw called his mother "the total influence. She is an extremely strong woman, a puritan in the true sense of the word. We were thought of as a family of some social standing, the family to know in the village. While my mother used to tell me not to play with the 'common children,' from her I learnt also real humanity." At school he distinguished himself in rugby, athletics, acting (he played Lady Macbeth in *Macbeth* and Mark Antony in *Julius Caesar*), and in his academic studies, leaving in December 1945 with a scholarship to Cambridge University. First, however, he taught for two terms at a school, Glenbow, at Saltburn, Yorkshire. While there he decided to go not to Cambridge, but to the Royal Academy of Dramatic Art in London. Failing to win a scholarship, he paid the tuition himself.

Shaw played small parts in the summer seasons at the Stratford Festival from 1948 to 1950, reaching the West End in 1951 as Rosencrantz in Alec Guinness's production of *Hamlet*. He joined the Old Vic company in 1951-1952, playing Cassio in *Othello* and Lysander in *A Midsummer-Night's Dream* and going on tour to Europe and South Africa. In 1952 he married an actress, Jennifer Bourke, who is the mother of their four daughters. He was with the Stratford company again in the summer of 1953; then periods of unemployment followed. He was in the cast of Giraudoux's *Tiger at the Gates* in London in 1955 and had his first film part, in *The Dambusters*, the same year. He starred in the first of his three stage plays, *Off the Mainland*, when it was staged at the Arts Theatre, London, in May 1956. Set on a prison island in the Balkans, the play concerned the seduction of the wife of the alcoholic colonel in charge of the prison by his younger brother and ended in two killings.

Shaw's fame as an actor began in the following year with the role of Captain Dan Tempest in a highly successful television series, *The Buccaneers*. His response to this success was characteristic: he withdrew to the country to write his first novel. But from 1957 to the end of his life, stage, television, and film appearances became increasingly frequent. Shaw played four major stage parts in new plays in 1958-1959: Blackmouth in John Arden's *Live Like Pigs* at the Royal Court, London; Lazlo Rajk in Robert Ardrey's *Shadow of Heroes* in the West End; Mitchem in Willis Hall's *The Long and the Short and the Tall* at the Royal Court; and Sewell in Beverley Cross's *One More River* at Liverpool and in the West End. He also appeared in the film *Sea Fury* in 1959.

His first novel, *The Hiding Place*, published in 1959, tells of two British airmen kept prisoner in a cellar in Bonn. Shot down in 1944, they are saved by Frick, who conceals them from pursuers. After a week, he drugs them and puts them in chains. He treats them well, cooking carefully, saving up his limited earnings to buy them slippers, teaching them about German music and writers. He also tells them that the war is still going on though the date is now 1952; they have been captives eight years. One prisoner, Wilson, is finding himself—or perhaps losing himself—writing long descriptions of childhood memories of the Orkney Islands. The other, Connolly, stays angry and resentful, brooding about means of escape and about his wife and young son.

Two-thirds of the book cover one day. Frick makes his first mistake, leaving behind a broom, from which Connolly extracts a nail. At work in a pharmacy, Frick remembers his mistake and waits impatiently for his lunch break to return to the cellar. When he does, there is no time to change into his Nazi uniform, so the Britons see him for the first time in a brown suit. Frick catches Connolly holding the nail and retrieves it. At a regular secret meeting of Nazis that evening, Frick is shocked that his comrades have decided to disband, suffers a heart attack, and is told he must go to a hospital to rest. Puzzling over the problem of caring for his prisoners, he realizes he will now have to release them—which he does, advising them to try to reach Switzerland. By this time we have some sense of Frick as a timid and friendless man whose limited and lonely life is bound up with his love of Hitler and his self-imposed task of caring for the captives. Although Shaw never spells out the precise motives for his behavior, they are clearly implied.

The final section of the book shows Wilson and Connolly slowly discovering the world into which they have been freed. They lie in the sunshine, resting, until they need food and risk a visit to a farm to buy some. They steal a canoe to paddle up the Rhine and learn from travelers and then from an English newspaper some of the truth about the war and the postwar situation. They work at harvesting for a while before going to the British consul, where Connolly learns that his wife is remarried and in Australia. Back in England, they go to look at the house in Regents Park Road where Connolly used to live. After Connolly leaves him, Wilson stays on, staring at the house. As he turns away toward Camden Town, Frick, who was watching nearby, suddenly rushes up behind and offers to work for him and Connolly. Partly because Frick looks too ill to live long, Wilson is on the point of accepting the offer when the novel ends.

Shaw's strange tale is compelling. Though published in both Britain and the United States, *The Hiding Place* received as little attention as most first novels do. V. S. Naipaul remarked harshly in the *New Statesman* that, once the prisoners are released, "nothing happens. All tension disappears, and the novel idles to a tame and disappointing end." The anonymous *Times Literary Supplement* critic also thought the ending had "a bedraggled air of anticlimax," though the basic situation was given "credibility and even absorbing interest." David Boroff was more enthusiastic in the *Saturday Review*, finding it both "a genuine suspense thrill" and "a wise and compassionate look at human beings under stress." Shaw produced and starred in a faithfully adapted television version of the novel, retitled *The Pets*, which was seen in October 1960.

Shaw apparently found time to write his second novel, *The Sun Doctor* (1961), while engaged in two more London stage appearances, as the reporter Watson in Patrick Kirwan's *A Lodging for a Bride* (which opened in April 1960) and as the villain De

Flores in Rowley and Middleton's Jacobean tragedy *The Changeling* (at the Royal Court in February 1961). In 1960 he also covered the Rome Olympics for the *Queen* and chaired the *Bookman*, a television literary program. He appeared in a third film, *The Valiant*, in 1961.

The Sun Doctor won Shaw the Hawthornden Prize in 1962. In the first of the novel's three parts, Benjamin Halliday, aged forty-eight, who has been a doctor in Africa for many years, returns to England to receive a knighthood for his work. Part 2 shifts to the previous year when Halliday, exploring in Africa, is summoned to a remote tribe living in the middle of a marsh. He discovers that the chiefs are sick. Though the tribesmen are, in fact, healthy, the conscientious doctor leaves to gather medical supplies, then returns to live with the tribe for a time. He becomes friendly with a man he calls Friday and is loved by a young tribeswoman, Kamante. He eventually leads most of the tribe back to his hospital at Kotopos, where they remain stubbornly indoors around fires, angering Halliday. When Kamante fails to comprehend his explanation of his work, he impatiently hits her and kills her.

In London again in part 3, after receiving his knighthood, Halliday decides to renounce his work and not go back to Africa. He plans to marry his young housekeeper, has an affair with her, but concludes that he is not capable of sufficient love for marriage. He wanders in Europe, then goes to his father's home in the Orkneys. Here he meets a man who knew his father and comes to a new understanding of the elder Halliday. This prompts a return first to the Kotopos hospital and then to the tribesmen who remained in the marsh, a dwindling number. Close to the end of the novel, Halliday reflects: "The only pattern he was sure of today was a pattern of inconsistencies—that any observation he might make could be equalled by its opposite. That all apparent truths were to be questioned; and once questioned, acted on; and questioned again; and acted on again. Therein lay the thread. . . . He was still a young man. He had the feeling there was much to come." As the book ends, a group of the servants return from Kotopos hospital to the community in the swamp, and Halliday's mission continues.

The Sun Doctor recalls aspects of Graham Green's *A Burnt-out Case* and Saul Bellow's *Henderson, the Rain King*. Halliday questions why he does as he does; what his shortcomings are; what meaning he can put into his life, through service and if possible through love—but this strange fable has no easy interpretatons.

The *Times Literary Supplement* reviewer especially admired the "deceptively simple" style, "requiring the reader's continuous intellectual effort. It startles by the harsh poetry of the scenic descriptions, by unexpected flashes of humour." John Lucas in *Contemporary Novelists* praised the "feeling for place," adding that accounts of "the Angolan swamp and of the natives themselves are probably as good as anything that has been managed in a novel of its sort since *The Power and the Glory*." But Geoffrey Grigson in the *Spectator* was more severe: "It is told so well that a quick read leaves one impressed and surprised, hazarding that an imagination has been at work. . . . My second thought. . . is that Mr. Shaw has written very ably, in the Conrad manner, a backward-looking, second-hand piece of defeatism." Norman Shrapnel of the *Guardian* found the book "a virile and compassionate novel which lifts the spirit," while John Coleman of the *New Statesman* was most enthusiastic: "What is so impressive in *The Sun Doctor* is the certainty of touch and the sheer intensity with which both the choked sudden jungle and Halliday's dealings with its maimed owners are sketched in: here, for once, the confrontation of black and white makes for marvellous metaphors of dignity and courage."

Shaw's New York stage debut came in the fall of 1961, when he played Aston in Harold Pinter's *The Caretaker* for a five-month run. He took the role in the film of the play two years later. (Its U. S. title was *The Guest*.) He was in the movie *Tomorrow at Ten* in 1962 and the next year made another film, *The Luck of Ginger Coffey*, in Montreal. After his divorce, he married his costar, Mary Ure, in 1963. They had two sons and two daughters before her death in 1975.

Nineteen sixty-four was a year of triumphs. His movie reputation was made as a huge, silent blond thug in the second James Bond story, *From Russia with Love*. On television he played Claudius to Christopher Plummer's Hamlet; he acted in his own *The Florentine Tragedy*; and, in the United States, he appeared in the United Nations-sponsored show, *Carol for Another Christmas*. Finally, in the fall he played Mobius in Dürrenmatt's *The Physicists*, directed on Broadway by Peter Brook.

His third novel, *The Flag* (1965), was announced as the first volume of a trilogy entitled "The Cure of Souls," but the other two books were never completed (the second was to deal with the period of the Spanish civil war). Shaw wrote that the work "derives from the life of Conrad Noel, Vicar of Thaxted, who hoisted the flag. He was remarkable—very different from my Vicar, being an Anglo-Catholic, a friend of Chesterton's, an intellectual, and upper class."

The action covers twenty-three days in May 1925. John Calvin, a former miner, stubborn, fervent, devout, has arrived the day before from the northern industrial town of Houghton to become vicar in the Suffolk coastal town of Eastwold (similar to the actual town of Southwold). He is accompanied by his neurotic wife and three children, a teenage boy and girl and the child Betty.

Shaw introduces a sizable gallery of townspeople, among them Lady Cleeve, a young widow who appointed Calvin to the vicarage; her aunt Mrs. Mellors; General Andrews, who unexpectedly supports Calvin because he admires men with backbone; his atheist nephew Robert, who is at Eton; and Richards, a mine-owner and churchwarden, who is the leader of the forces against Calvin. The movements and conversations of many of these characters are presented in a series of very short passages, which intercut the main narrative that concerns Rockingham, an elderly miner and admirer of Calvin's. He leaves Houghton to walk to Eastwold, carrying a big red flag to present to Calvin, and on the way he meets Jean, young and pregnant, who accompanies him. They journey from Sheffield through Lincoln and Boston, where they climb the Stump and first fly the flag at dusk. They go on to Norwich, where several more tramps join the group, and a half-mad "screever" (a sidewalk-artist) attacks and follows them.

Rockingham and his party enter the church just as Calvin begins his first sermon, taking his text from Keir Hardie in *Labour Leader*. Events unfold quickly: Rockingham hoists the flag at the foot of the church tower, beside the Union Jack and the Sinn Fein flag, and Calvin defends this action despite mounting protest. A parish church council sympathetic to Calvin's socialism is elected. While crowds arrive from out of town to tear down the flag, Rockingham takes it to the top of the tower: at the end he falls to his death, taking the screever and one of his enemies, as well as the flag, with him.

Shaw's view of his novel was explained by Norman Shrapnel in the *Guardian*. *The Flag* was not "intended to make any profound statement about the nature of religious faith. [Shaw] is telling a story, founded on actuality and centred on a memorable character. The British are not a religious people to Mr. Shaw's way of thinking, nor have they much spiritual capacity. Though not himself a Christian believer it is a subject that interests him profoundly." But *Time* was impatient with the style of *The Flag*: "What with [Shaw's] ponderous verbosity, irrational shifts of style, difficulties with grammar and punctuation, he makes the reader confident that it didn't really happen." John Coleman in the *Observer* found other faults: "The hopeful, visionary element in Mr. Shaw does result in excesses, notably confessional ones, coups de theatre that come rather wincingly off the page. The general abruptly soliloquises about his sex-life in public, Calvin's son achieves an improbably swift rapport with the general's Etonian grandson [in fact, nephew], and the whole sub-plot of grizzled miner and good-bad girl on the road is wishful rather than felt." But he also saw humor in the novel: "The lofty or ballad side of it is constantly brought down to earth by some very broadsheet humour: a conclave of eloquent tramps in this one, if owing moments to *The Caretaker*, is marvellously comical."

He concluded with a generalization about Shaw's world view: "There is a solitary, devoted to some anguishing cause; there are friends where one doesn't anticipate them and foes in intimate places; people will reveal more of themselves to strangers than to kin. It's an unfashionably extreme view of the human condition, concerned with nobility and moral strain."

Shaw's work from 1965 to 1967 was entirely in films: he appeared as a Nazi tank commander in *The Battle of the Bulge*; then as a handsome, dashing Henry VIII in the movie of Robert Bolt's *A Man for All Seasons*; and in 1967 in the title role in *Custer of the West*, in which Mary Ure also appeared.

Of his experience as an actor, Shaw said in an interview with Terry Philpott: "Films are a business and seldom an art form. It's a director's medium. For obvious reasons there are no good screen writers because anyone with any sense doesn't want to be one. The only films that I have been in that have made money have been the bad ones. . . . There are occasions when you are working with someone like Joe Losey and filming can become art and takes on something special. It is a sort of religious moment when you feel that you are really communicating something. It is probably an illusion but you can also feel it when you write. It has only happend to me rarely with acting. . . .I get bored by any stage play in about four weeks but you also have an audience to respond to you. The great difference is that in the theatre you can dominate the audience, whereas in the cinema you can woo them. . . .There is. . . this child-like side in me that loves acting, and although I curse it at times I think that acting is under-rated."

If *The Man in the Glass Booth* is Shaw's best-known novel, it is probably because of the stage and film versions that carry the same title. The novel is

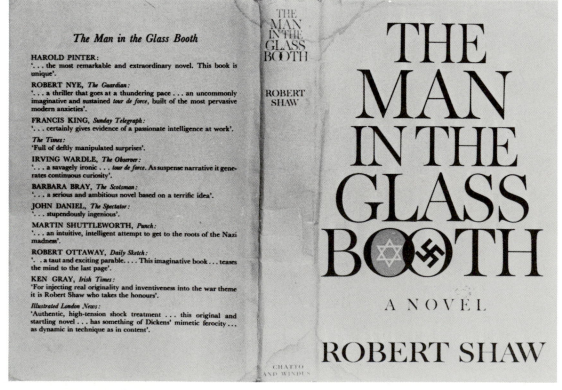

Dust jacket for Shaw's 1967 novel about a Jewish Nazi proud of his role in the Holocaust

about an eccentric New York property tycoon, Arthur Goldman, apparently Jewish, who quotes Hitler and has a secret museum of Nazi relics. Kidnapped and taken to Israel as a war criminal, he is put on trial in a glass dock. (The parallels to Adolph Eichmann, and to Hannah Arendt's *Eichmann in Israel*, are clear.) Goldman welcomes the chance to be the first Nazi to show pride in the extermination of Jews, taking full responsibility for his actions and boasting of his pleasure in his work. So readers wonder, as the *Times Literary Supplement* reviewer said, "Is Goldman what he seems to be—a Jew neurotically obsessed with Hitler's Germany—or is he really a Nazi war criminal disguised as a Jew? Or is he a Jew pretending to be a German pretending to be a Jew?" Even when the fact that he is a Jew emerges, uncertainties are not resolved: "Is he a great Jew, the salt of the earth, a scapegoat for the sins of the world, or is he a vainglorious, insensitive fool, maddened with spiritual pride?"

Daniel Stern took a hostile view of the novel in the *New York Times Book Review*: "The protagonist is both too mad and too directly motivated in his madness, to have the size the author intended. . . . The odor of research clings to it. . . . The irony is without dimension. The surprise is merely stagecraft." Mostly, however, critics wrestled to find ways of describing a novel which moved simultaneously in a low popular style and in a high philosophical one. For Shaw had written both what Robert Nye in the *Guardian* called "a sharp little maverick of a thriller that goes at a thundering pace" and a book that looked directly at the huge and nearly unmentionable facts of the Holocaust without, as the *Times Literary Supplement* reviewer said, seeming "trivial, callous or self-righteous." Melvin Maddocks summed it up in the *Christian Science Monitor* as "a pop-art novel of the absurd that ranges with astonishing vitality from braying comic vulgarities to subtly and scrupulously weighing political guilt and atonement," while Stanley Kauffmann concluded in the *New Republic* that "it is an arrangement of life-size possibilities—in action and psychology—to form a moving allegorical whole. The theme of the book is the pre-eminent moral question of the century: what has happened to evil? . . . Can the concepts of sin and expiation survive?"

Shaw's stage version was seen in London in July 1967 and in New York in September 1968, directed by Harold Pinter with Donald Pleasence as Goldman. Edward Anhalt made drastic changes for the 1975 film version so that Shaw insisted on the removal of his name from the credits. Arthur Hiller

directed, with Maximilian Schell as the man in the glass booth.

Shaw continued his career as an actor after the success of *The Man in the Glass Booth*. On ABC television in 1968 he took the title role in a version of John Osborne's *Luther*, and he played Stanley in the low-budget film *The Birthday Party* by Harold Pinter. In 1969 he was in two film epics: *The Battle of Britain* and *The Royal Hunt of the Sun* (based on Peter Shaffer's play about the Spanish conquest of Peru), in which he played the role of Pizarro.

A Card from Morocco (1969) is Shaw's slightest novel. Set mostly in a bar in Madrid, the book is largely a dialogue between two men, both in their early fifties, whose stories can gradually be pieced together. Lewis, an Englishman, is well-educated, has a private income, has been twice married, and now has an attractive young wife he may not be able to satisfy. Slattery, an American, is unreliable when he talks about himself: he says he was an athlete and is a painter, surviving on the checks from his hated father, once a police chief in Boston. As they get drunk they quarrel and tell each other their secrets. In disjointed episodes, they fiddle with a lavatory to retrieve some hundreds of dollars flushed down it; go skiing, where Lewis breaks his leg and has to go to hospital; and receive a visit from Slattery's father.

Frederick P. W. McDowell in *Contemporary Literature* explained the relationship between the characters: "Slattery is genuine and good-hearted, but his crudity and instability alienate him from his family; Lewis is fastidious, considerate, and socially knowledgeable, but naive about his own nature. The two complement each other, while they possess in common a knowledge that much is missing from their lives with the onset of late middle age. But if they are both wasted individuals ('Once we must have had some promise,' Lewis says), they compensate in vital energy for whatever they may lack in worldly distinction." Robert Nye in the *Guardian* was impressed: "The book's strength lies in the way it compels one's care about a couple of people who remain strangers. We *overhear* their rambling and elliptical conversation. Our sympathies are not solicited, and the author never flatters us or demeans himself by explaining anything except in terms of consequent action. The effect is limited but powerfully cinematic, with the cinema's cold magic of ghosts in colour, larger than life, walking and talking on a wall in a room where the audience sits in darkness, offered a colossal intimacy that denies relationship." But the majority of reviewers were unimpressed and somewhat confused. Ken Stitt in

Tribune, for instance, wrote: "The novel read, there must remain a final doubt as to the purpose of the whole enterprise. Why have we been reading and understanding? Or is the understanding its own purpose?"

Shaw's activities in 1970 included writing the screenplay for *Figures in a Landscape* (from a novel by Barry England) as well as acting in the film and playing the title role in the Broadway musical *Elmer Gantry* by Peter Bellwood (from the novel by Sinclair Lewis). About this time, too, he moved to a big house by a lake close to Tourmakeady, in County Mayo, Ireland. He made two films in 1971, *A Town Called Bastard* and *Labyrinth* (also known as *Reflections of Fear*), and played Deeley in Harold Pinter's drama, *Old Times*, opposite Mary Ure in New York. In November 1971 his third stage play appeared at the Young Vic in London, starring Vanessa Redgrave. *Cato Street* featured the unsuccessful 1820 conspiracy by working-class radicals to kill the whole British Cabinet. Shaw supplied a social context by starting his play with the Peterloo massacre of 1817; he also made the leading plotter female instead of male to give women greater prominence in his drama.

Shaw's last years included a final New York stage appearance as Edgar in Strindberg's *Dance of Death*. He and Mary Ure later starred in the television play, *The Break* (1974), about a civil servant who is a spy. After Mary Ure's death, he married Virginia Jansen in 1976.

Ten film parts, however, occupied most of his time. In 1971 he played Lord Randolph Churchill in *Young Winston*, of which he said: "Hardly anyone knows anything about Randolph so I'll have to be bad not to be able to do something with the part. While he wasn't the equal of his son [Winston Churchill] he was a very remarkable man. It is pleasant to be playing an intelligent man for a change. I have also got my best wardrobe since Henry VIII so that is my vanity satisfied."

The other parts in films included *The Judge and His Hangman*, *The Taking of Pelham 123*, *Diamonds*, *Black Sunday*, *The Swashbucklers*, and *The Deep*. He excelled in 1973 in a modest British film, *The Hireling*, from a story by L. P. Hartley, but was most widely seen as the villain in *The Sting* and as the fanatical shark-hunter Quint in *Jaws*.

Reading of Shaw's crowded life, one might conclude that the novels are merely a by-product of his other activities. This would be unfair: Shaw was serious about trying to become a good novelist. *A Card from Morocco*, a minor novel, was experimental. *The Flag* is a more ambitious work, blending historical and religious themes, though Shaw's historical-political side is best seen in the play *Cato Street*. His other three novels successfully combine the most searching of ideas with the readability of thrillers, and *The Sun Doctor* deserves as high a reputation as *The Man in the Glass Booth* has gained.

Plays:
Off the Mainland, London, Arts Theatre, 30 May 1956;
The Man in the Glass Booth, London, St. Martin's Theatre, 27 July 1967, 142 [performances]; New York, Royale Theatre, 26 September 1968, 269;
Cato Street, London, Young Vic, 15 November 1971, 12.

Screenplay:
Figures in a Landscape, Joseph Losey, Cinecrest, 1970.

Television Scripts:
The Pets, A-R "Play of the Week," October 1960;
The Florentine Tragedy, BBC, 1964.

Interviews:
Norman Shrapnel, "Robert Shaw, Author," *Manchester Guardian*, 21 January 1965, p. 14;
"Pendennis," "Man and Superman," *Observer*, 6 April 1969;
Terry Philpott, "Robert Shaw," *Guardian*, 16 July 1971.

Penelope Shuttle
(12 May 1947 -   )

Kathleen Fullbrook

BOOKS: *An Excusable Vengeance*, published with *Infatuation* by Carol Burns and *The Road* by J. A. Dooley (London: Calder & Boyars, 1967);

Nostalgia Neurosis and Other Poems (Aylesford, U.K.: St. Albert's Press, 1968);

All the Usual Hours of Sleeping (London: Calder & Boyars, 1969);

Branch (Rushden, Northamptonshire, U.K.: Sceptre Press, 1971);

Wailing Monkey Embracing a Tree (London: Calder & Boyars, 1973; Boston: Boyars, 1980);

Midwinter Mandala (New Malden, Surrey, U.K.: Headland Publications, 1973);

The Hermaphrodite Album, by Shuttle and Peter Redgrove (London: Fuller d'Arch Smith, 1973);

Moon Meal (Rushden, Northamptonshire, U.K.: Sceptre Press, 1973);

The Terrors of Dr. Treviles: A Romance, by Shuttle and Redgrove (London: Routledge & Kegan Paul, 1974);

Photographs of Persephone (London: Quarto Press, 1974);

Autumn Piano and Other Poems (Liverpool: Rondo Publications, 1974);

The Songbook of the Snow (Ilkley, U.K.: Janus Press, 1974);

Webs on Fire (London: Gallery Press, 1975);

The Dream (Knotting, Bedfordshire, U.K.: Sceptre Press, 1975);

The Glass Cottage: A Nautical Romance, by Shuttle and Redgrove (London: Routledge & Kegan Paul, 1976);

Four American Sketches (Knotting, Bedfordshire, U.K.: Sceptre Press, 1976);

Rainsplitter in the Zodiac Garden (London: Boyars, 1977; Nantucket, Mass.: Longship Press, 1978);

The Wise Wound: Menstruation and Everywoman, by Shuttle and Redgrove (London: Gollancz, 1978); republished as *The Wise Wound: Eve's Curse and Everywoman* (New York: Marek, 1978);

The Mirror of the Giant: A Ghost Story (London: Boyars, 1980; Boston: Boyars, 1980);

Prognostica (Knotting, Bedfordshire, U.K.: Booth, 1980);

The Orchard Upstairs (Oxford: Oxford University Press, 1980).

Penelope Shuttle's work focuses on the difficulties of human relationships, especially erotic relationships, in the modern age. A poet as well as a novelist, she is an author whose interests spring from the great revolution in personal life-styles in the 1960s and 1970s, especially from the changing status of women. At the same time much of her fiction must be seen in relation to the distinguished twentieth-century tradition of mythopoetic analysis, whose practitioners include Joseph Campbell and Robert Graves. By exploring the subconscious, at times supernatural, forces which drive her characters in their attempts to find satisfaction with

Penelope Shuttle

each other and to understand truly their needs and desires, she directly confronts the dangers and the power of underlying human psychology. The extreme sensitivity of her perceptions is reflected in the highly poetic prose of her novels. Her feminist and poetically symbolic novels have attracted attention from a small but highly literate section of the British reading public.

Penelope Diane Shuttle was born near London in Staines, Middlesex. Her father, Jack Frederick Shuttle, was a salesman and her mother, Joan Shepherdess Lipscombe Shuttle, a housewife. She was educated at Staines Grammar School and Matthew Arnold County Secondary School. Her talent was evident from an early age, and she began having her poetry published when she was fourteen. Shuttle has said that formal education was alien both to her interests and to her gifts. She believes that her work at school was mostly "nonsense," and that her passionate interest in literature precluded academic success. While taking the general certificate of education examination in English, Shuttle wrote for three hours on *Macbeth* rather than responding briefly and meaninglessly to the required battery of questions. Her uncompromising stance kept her from the possibility of entering a university.

The late years of adolescence were difficult for Shuttle. She suffered from agoraphobia, anorexia nervosa, and had a mental breakdown when she was nineteen. During this period of her life she subsidized her writing by working for six months of the year in "dead end" office jobs. Although by 1969 she had had two novels published, she felt that she had no prospects for a life that would afford time to pursue her writing and that she was "fading fast."

Shuttle's two early novels reflect the sense of crisis pervading her life at the same time as they speak directly to the difficulties and pleasures experienced by all human beings attempting to make contact with one another. Her short novel, *An Excusable Vengeance* (1967), published with Carol Burns's *Infatuation* and J. A. Dooley's *The Road* in Number Six of Calder and Boyars's New Writers series, introduces major concerns which run throughout her other novels. The two characters "he" and "she" court each other with great tentativeness and uncertainty. He, in particular, is simultaneously drawn lovingly to the woman and appalled by the force of his physical desires. After the pair's first kiss he is driven by visions of lust which seem to defile his growing love for her. The pair oscillate between approaching and avoiding each other. In a final scene, set by the ocean, he,

struggling confusedly with forces within himself, first reclaims the woman from the sea and then strangles her. In despair and confusion he then buries himself alive in the sand and dies. This early experimental work draws powerfully on images that will become characteristic for the author: a derelict garden; trees infused with mystery; rain that signifies the sad release of powerful emotional reactions; houses that protect as well as entrap individuals; mirrors that both reflect and distort the inner and outer world. The extremely vivid description of the couple's lovemaking is also characteristic. Throughout Shuttle's work is an acute sense of danger as well as pleasure and a highly developed sense that sexual activity is "sacred" and therefore potentially explosive on natural and preternatural planes.

Penelope Shuttle's second novel, *All the Usual Hours of Sleeping* (1969), was compared by a *Times Literary Supplement* reviewer to D. H. Lawrence's *Women in Love* (1920). In *All the Usual Hours of Sleeping* Shuttle's manipulation of words points up the torments of her characters' complex interrelationships. Rachel leaves Tomas because she finds it necessary to travel to discover herself, while Herma, who has previously miscarried Tomas's baby and is herself fighting to retain her inner identity, rejoins Tomas. When Rachel returns with a new lover, Tomas is again drawn to her while attempting to hold together his life with Herma. All three major characters are finally revealed to be siblings. The novel's exploration of the drive of unconscious incest that underlies ordinary lives demonstrates Shuttle's interest in archetypal patterns and her sensitivity to the mystery inherent in sexual attraction.

In 1969 the author was working in Somerset at a secretarial job when she met the poet Peter Redgrove. She moved to Falmouth in Cornwall in 1970 to live and work with Redgrove, who since 1966 has been resident author at the Falmouth School of Art. Their daughter, Zoe, was born in December 1976. Shuttle and Redgrove were married in September 1980, and the relationship has proved a fruitful one for both partners. They have collaborated on a number of novels, books of poetry, and *The Wise Wound* (1978), a psychological and historical study of menstruation. This book, which has been their greatest popular success (it was republished in England as a Penguin paperback in 1980), arose from Shuttle's difficulties with premenstrual tension in 1971. With the assistance of dream analysis and symbol interpretation based on Dr. John Layard's system, Shuttle overcame her distress, and a sense of the sexual and imaginative value of the menstrual period took its place. *The Wise Wound* is a courageous attempt to fit the monthly cycles of women into a poetically stirring and psychologically valid vision of the rhythms of human life. The book has received wide attention in all types of periodicals, ranging from academic journals to women's magazines. The sense of the menstruating woman as a source of power is a common theme in many of Shuttle's novels.

Wailing Monkey Embracing a Tree (1973), Shuttle's third novel, continues the themes that dominated her early work while demonstrating the maturity of her idiosyncratic "bardic" use of language. The topic under consideration is the break-up of a marriage that should never have been made in the first place. Luke and Elinda marry although Elinda is still imaginatively preoccupied throughout the novel with an earlier lover, Matthew, whose baby she has lost in a miscarriage. Matthew, a mysterious figure who appears late in the novel, has deserted Elinda after she has found him in bed with another woman. While he is away, Luke and Elinda try to make a decent marriage though both are "locked within their own private calamities." After Elinda finally reveals to Luke the fact of her entanglement with Matthew, Luke informs her of his own previous marriage. Elinda's dreams, which are a major component of the novel, become violent; the couple quarrel incessantly. Finally Luke leaves. The extremity of Elinda's unhappiness mystically summons Matthew from his travels, and at the end of the novel Elinda has settled with Matthew and her marriage to Luke is ended.

The Terrors of Dr. Treviles (1974), the first published novel that Shuttle wrote in collaboration with Peter Redgrove, portrays a wider ranging group of characters than Shuttle's previous work, but it moves in characteristically surrealistic patterns while dealing closely with the formation and reformation of sexual unions. The book's themes include magic, dreams, sensitive physical states, extrasensory perception, religion, and art. Interlaced with poems, it contains highly mythological images, often borrowed from British and European folklore. The novel has been called a book of "frightening intensity," yet it is one that relates closely, by analogy, to ordinary processes of frustration and desire. The two major characters are Robyn, a brilliant young scientist who is also a witch, and her stepfather, Gregory Treviles, a psychologist who becomes Robyn's lover. The plot traces the release of Treviles from his haunted "terrors" and his movement to freedom, which is finally

signaled by his acceptance of the menage a trois that Robyn has created by the introduction of Dr. Brid Hare, her lesbian lover, into the household. The flow of love between the two women, which is in turn shared by the man, is meant to signal a kind of life-enhancing acceptance of human desire and its fulfillment that had previously escaped Treviles. The book closes with a series of poems called "Robyn's Candle Poems," which echo the mystery of her womanly and "witchy" power in the novel. The authors' purpose in this book has been described as nothing less than a demonstration of "human redemption through imagination and discovery." *The Terrors of Dr. Treviles* is an exceedingly ambitious work, destined to fail on some counts because of its sheer ambition. The prose at times becomes mere musical effect, the situations slightly silly rather than portentous. But for all these cavils the novel is a mature and highly serious work which deserves a wider circulation than it has so far achieved.

Shuttle and Redgrove's collaboration continued in *The Glass Cottage* (1976), a novel in which an English schoolteacher is stabbed by her lover on board the SS *Messenger*. In her wound is found a ticking watch, a bizarre occurrence that gives rise to the major concern of the novel: the effect of the dead woman living on in the psyches of other marginally defined characters who become commenting voices of consciousness on the life and death of the woman. In the study of these reactions time lapses and folds back on itself as do the minds which give a place to the images and hallucinations that keep the woman "alive." The *Times Literary Supplement* reviewer initiated a minor controversy by objecting to "the fact that the murdered woman has more reality and power dead than alive" and commented that the employment of a "sex/murder cunt/wound" analogy in the novel must be taken as "a modern piece of anti-feminism pretending to be myth." Shuttle and Redgrove replied to the reviewer's charges in a highly illuminating statement of their feminist purposes: "Our *The Glass Cottage* is about a murder, which is like the Jesus-Murder in that many people feel guilty about it whether they have actually been involved in it or not. The murder we write about in our novel is The Goddess-Murder, of which any woman deprived by convention or taboo of her natural abilities of menstruation is a victim. We suppose that a religion could be based on a goddess who sheds her blood in sacrifice from which life arises, and our book partly satirizes attitudes which are dismissive of this possibility." In 1976, when this joint letter was published in the *Times Literary Supplement*, the authors were already

②

from work in ~~progress~~ progress; Penelope Shuttle 1 Arwyn Place Falmouth
                                        Cornwall UK

strong as I was before...
          But christ how
          I want to begin! It aches in me, a prodigal distance of
                                                              all my
ital   The idea of beginning is immense. It dazzles   exhibition,

me, hurts my eyes; I flinch, I dare not open my eyes

to the beginning, though the idea of it thuds through
                                                        slips
me, to the core of me, to my sex, those roots of silk.

It dazzles, that vast light.

Each day, the burden of it lies in wait for me.
          moderately
I sleep ~~fairly~~ well, I travel the night in dreams
                                              happy at first
exhaled and inhaled, and in the morning, when I

rise from bed, the burden leaps lightly on to my
                          long
back and all day/grows steadily heavier andheavier.
          Jack mike Lewis
But ~~Bran~~ is kind. He does not demand or command.

He waits, encouragingly. H wants to help me out

of this ~~loneliness this corall of~~ aftershock ~~i'm~~ in which I'm

penned, corralled.

→   Sometimes I think if I could wake before daylight

and watch the day begin, it would be easier. If

I could see how the clear grey morning light makes
                                      + will
the outlines of the fields firm and strong,

with no obscurity, the light recognizing the green

shape of turf and hedge, and responding with its
                                    then
gift of clarity, if I could see that I could follow

the patterns of the hours after dawn; ~~and~~ follow the

way the daylight moves through the house. But I

never wake until it is way past dawn, alarm clocks

fail me, and then it is too late, the time of seizing

my opportunity has gone, and the day is already stale.

Any hope of an unencumbered life, of discerning without

Revised typescript page from a work in progress

at work on *The Wise Wound*, and the vehemence of their self-defense, which continued in a further letter, marks the passion with which they regarded this subject throughout the 1970s.

In Shuttle's fourth solo novel, *Rainsplitter in the Zodiac Garden* (1977), the shifting narrative time scheme of *The Glass Cottage* is repeated with great virtuosity. Faustina, the major character, is trapped by the demands of conventional female behavior. Her husband, Micah, wants her to bear him a son while Faustina wants at least a year of childless freedom. She is greatly distressed by Micah's changing her name, which had been Eve, and is tormented by dreams which she can, at first, neither understand nor escape. Faustina, in marrying Micah, has indeed made a bargain with a devil and is further penned in by various acts of betrayal. Her lover Anna, the only person with whom she feels fully alive, marries Faustina's brother, Stefan, leaves Faustina, and returns later to appropriate Micah. Micah also leaves Faustina at one stage of the novel, and the entire book is shadowed by images of desertion and threatening war. Most of the text of the novel is filtered through the pregnant Faustina's mind. In the end, having given birth to a son, Faustina herself, in what can only be seen as a triumphant assumption of choice and responsibility, takes to the open road in gypsy fashion after she finds Anna and Micah making love. This novel is a powerful study of marriage and motherhood and of the choices and limits that confront women tied to traditional roles while they germinate individual responses to their conditions. *Rainsplitter in the Zodiac Garden* has been published in America as well as England, and a French translation was published in 1981.

In *The Mirror of the Giant* (1980), Shuttle's most recent novel, Theron is haunted by the highly erotic ghost of his former wife, Vellet, who has been dead for five years. The ghost is sexually omnivorous, a devouring figure who leaves Theron with no sexual energy to share with his present wife, Beth. Beth's position is therefore tenuous, and when she comes to understand the presence and persistence of the ghost of Vellet, who had been Theron's ward and who was forced into marriage with him, Beth wars with the ghost for possession of the man. Theron and Beth's mentor and comforter is the giant, a prehistoric figure carved into the chalk uplands of the valley in which the novel is set. A phallic figure and a demigod, the giant reveals to them in his

mirror the way out of their enchanted entrapment. Vellet is found to be haunting Theron with his permission. Because he knew she left their house to meet her lover, Theron did not rescue Vellet from drowning, and now he cannot forgive himself. When Beth's former lesbian lover, Ash, returns to her, the ghost of Vellet learns the meaning of love by watching the two women's tenderness toward each other. The ghost has gained what she needed, a vision of love, and she is free to cease her haunting of Theron. Beth then returns to her husband to help him "bear the loss of his haunting." The "reality" of the ghost remains uncertain throughout the novel, but whether Vellet is a product of Theron's tortured conscience or a true supernatural manifestation, the direction of the book remains the same: love is shown to be a redemptive power, the root of contentment and sanity for human beings. The strangeness of the plot is a fine counterpoint to the simplicity of the book's moral statement.

Shuttle's poetry collection "The Child Stealer" will be published by Oxford University Press in 1983. Her current work in progress is a novel provisionally titled "The Making of a Prisoner."

Penelope Shuttle's novels have been received with consistent critical interest. Although she has been accused of "excessively wrought luxuriance" in her prose, it has often been said that in the course of her novels she "earns" the right to her highly idiosyncratic style. Shuttle is a prolific young author of both prose and poetry. That she is highly engaged with the problems of contemporary sexual manners as well as with the mythopoetic implications of these manners has been clear from the first. Peter Redgrove has remarked that Shuttle sees her work as a "testimony" directed toward the enhancement of life. The statement seems apt and many more interesting books can be expected from this still developing author.

Radio Plays:
The Girl Who Lost Her Glove, BBC Radio 3, 3 March 1975;
The Dauntless Girl, BBC Radio 3, 26 February 1978.

References:
Carol Dix, "The Bloody Cycle of the Moon," *Sunday Times Magazine*, 21 May 1978, p. 79;
Sally Vincent, "Such Stuff as Lives are Made On," *Observer*, 3 December 1978, p. 37.

Alan Sillitoe

(4 March 1928 -   )

Catherine Smith

BOOKS: *Without Beer or Bread* (Dulwich Village, U.K.: Outposts Publications, 1957);

Saturday Night and Sunday Morning (London: W. H. Allen, 1958; New York: Knopf, 1959);

The Loneliness of the Long-Distance Runner (London: W. H. Allen, 1959; New York: Knopf, 1960);

The General (London: W. H. Allen, 1960; New York: Knopf, 1961);

The Rats and Other Poems (London: W. H. Allen, 1960);

Key to the Door (London: W. H. Allen, 1961; New York: Knopf, 1962);

The Ragman's Daughter and Other Stories (London: W. H. Allen, 1963; New York: Knopf, 1964);

Road to Volgograd (London: W. H. Allen, 1964; New York: Knopf, 1964);

A Falling Out of Love and Other Poems (London: W. H. Allen, 1964);

The Death of William Posters (London: W. H. Allen, 1965; New York: Knopf, 1965);

A Tree on Fire (London: Macmillan, 1967; Garden City: Doubleday, 1968);

The City Adventures of Marmalade Jim (London: Macmillan, 1967);

Shaman and Other Poems (London: Turret, 1968);

Love in the Environs of Vorenezh and Other Poems (London: Macmillan, 1968; Garden City: Doubleday, 1969);

Guzman, Go Home, and Other Stories (London: Macmillan, 1968; Garden City: Doubleday, 1969);

All Citizens Are Soldiers, adapted by Sillitoe and Ruth Fainlight from Lope de Vega's play (London: Macmillan, 1969; Chester Springs, Pa.: Dufour, 1969);

A Start in Life (London: W. H. Allen, 1970; New York: Scribners, 1970);

Poems, by Sillitoe, Fainlight, and Ted Hughes (London: Rainbow Press, 1971);

Travels in Nihilon (London: W. H. Allen, 1971; New York: Scribners, 1972);

Raw Material (London: W. H. Allen, 1972; New York: Scribners, 1973);

Men, Women and Children (London & New York: W. H. Allen, 1973; New York: Scribners, 1974);

Barbarians and other poems (London: Turret, 1973);

Storm: new poems (London: W. H. Allen, 1974);

The Flame of Life (London and New York: W. H. Allen, 1974);

Mountains and Caverns (London: W. H. Allen, 1975);

The Widower's Son (London: W. H. Allen, 1976; New York: Harper & Row, 1977);

Big John and the Stars (London: Robson Books, 1977);

Three Plays (London: W. H. Allen, 1978);

The Incredible Fencing Fleas (London: Robson Books, 1978);

Snow on the North Side of Lucifer (London: W. H. Allen, 1979);

The Storyteller (London: W. H. Allen, 1979; New York: Simon & Schuster, 1980);

The Second Chance and Other Stories (New York: Simon & Schuster, 1980; London: Cape, 1981);

Her Victory (London: Granada, 1982; New York: Watts, 1982).

Alan Sillitoe

Alan Sillitoe had no plans for becoming a writer; writing seemed a most unlikely, even "inconceivable" career for a factory worker raised in the industrial town of Nottingham, England. Despite, or perhaps because of, his working-class origins, Sillitoe became a writer whose first two works assured him of a place in English letters. The prize-winning author of poetry, plays, screenplays, short stories, and novels, Sillitoe has capitalized on his background in ways few writers equal. Though actual settings vary, Nottingham is never too far distant in his writing.

Uncertainty born of poverty characterized Sillitoe's earliest years in Nottingham. Born 4 March 1928, to Christopher and Sylvina Burton Sillitoe, Alan Sillitoe watched his father, an unskilled laborer, struggle with unemployment during the financially precarious 1930s. Lack of money sometimes meant government assistance in the form of hot meals for Sillitoe and his four siblings and caused frequent moves over rent disputes for the entire family during Sillitoe's early childhood.

School provided a kind of stability in the constant flux of Sillitoe's volatile home life. By age eight he had become a dedicated student with a wide range of interests, particularly topography, which has remained a lifelong hobby and has figured in several of his novels and stories. Despite two attempts, Sillitoe failed the difficult eleven-plus examination, forcing him to abandon plans for grammar school and higher education. He instead spent the next three years in a local school eagerly reading all sorts of adventure stories by authors ranging from Sir Walter Scott to Sir Arthur Conan Doyle. This reading often supplied needed plots for the stories Sillitoe told to entertain his siblings. In 1942 his formal education ended in typical working-class fashion.

At age fourteen Sillitoe quit school and found a job doing piecework at the Raleigh Bicycle factory. After three months, a dispute over wages led to the end of this job and to the beginning of a new one in a plywood factory. Sillitoe found this work boring, and after eighteen months he became a capstan lathe operator at a small engineering firm where he remained until his military service began in 1946. As Sillitoe points out, his interests were those of any Nottingham youth: visiting local pubs, enjoying women, having money for the first time in his life, and spending it as fast as he made it. Factory work soon dulled what creativity he had begun to develop. Escape from such deadening work and the promise of travel made him a willing volunteer for the RAF. Though he was accepted for pilot's training, the end of war with Japan eliminated the need for more air personnel, and Sillitoe began training as a wireless operator.

Stationed in Malaya for the next two years, Sillitoe had ample time for reading. In addition to the adventure stories he had favored as a child, he read Tressell's *The Ragged Trousered Philanthropists*, which explored working-class existence in Edwardian England. Sillitoe admired Tressell's work because it was one of the few novels that treated working-class characters as people rather than as caricatures. While Tressell's work influenced Sillitoe's writing in a general fashion, his Malayasian duty later shaped specific scenes in his third novel.

After his tour of duty in the RAF, Sillitoe returned to England in 1948 for his discharge. Routine medical tests revealed that he had contracted tuberculosis while abroad. Consequently, he spent the next sixteen months in an air force hospital where the enforced isolation prompted another period of reading. Sillitoe's reading this time, beginning with the Greek and Latin classics in translation, represented a deliberate effort to educate himself. Simultaneously, as he began reading books, he began trying to write them. The next ten years represent what Sillitoe terms an apprenticeship spent writing novels that were pastiches of all the authors who most influenced him, from Dostoevski and Lawrence to Fielding and Conrad. As Sillitoe worked through these influences, he said, he learned to write "clear English." Some of his early stories reappear, though revised and reworked, in later fiction, such as *The General* (1960), his second novel. Shortly before his release from the hospital in December of 1949, Sillitoe wrote his first novel and received his first rejection slip. Not discouraged, he remained firm in his commitment to writing.

Sillitoe spent the following year living in Nottingham and writing short stories and another novel, as yet unpublished. In 1951 he retired to his aunt's cottage in Kent, where he met Ruth Fainlight, an American-born poet living with her husband in nearby Hastings. For six months, with Ruth Fainlight's help and encouragement, Sillitoe concentrated on writing poetry. In January 1952, they left together for France. They remained away from England for six years, living first in France and later in Spain. With his limited RAF pension and National Health allowance as the primary sources of income, Sillitoe still managed to write steadily during this period, even writing on book jackets when paper proved too expensive.

While abroad, he met Robert Graves, and in 1954, following Graves's suggestion that he write about Nottingham, Sillitoe began work on *Saturday Night and Sunday Morning*. Having already written a number of short stories set in Nottingham, he started with these brief works and combined them into a picaresque novel. *Saturday Night and Sunday Morning* was finally completed to his satisfaction in 1957. A year and five rejection slips later, the novel was published in 1958, after Sillitoe and Ruth Fainlight had returned to England. The immediate positive response to the novel astounded everyone, including its writer. Assuring the novel of success, the Authors' Club in London awarded Sillitoe its Silver Quill for most promising first novel of 1958.

Praised for its verisimilitude in depicting working-class life, this picaresque account of Arthur Seaton, a lathe operator in a Nottingham bicycle factory, follows his progress toward marriage. The novel immediately establishes some favorite Sillitoe themes: the social injustice inherent in working-class life, the "jungle" of social classes, the mindlessness and monotony of the only work accessible to the lower classes, and the "us versus them" mentality of workers pitted against establishment, whether in the person of politician, policeman, or foreman. Arthur's affairs with two sisters, both married, result in the pregnancy and subsequent abortion of one and Arthur's defeat by the husband of the other. The end of the novel finds Arthur at once rebelling against society and conforming to some of its expectations by preparing to marry. Sillitoe does not consider the novel autobiographical because Arthur represents a compilation of many personalities, including about ten percent of Sillitoe's own, tempered by memories and imagination. An immediate popular success, *Saturday Night and Sunday Morning* remains a favorite of later critics as well as early reviewers.

With his improved prospects, Sillitoe and Ruth Fainlight moved to London and settled in an inexpensive flat where he completed a collection of short stories, *The Loneliness of the Long-Distance Runner* (1959). Advances from publishers allowed Sillitoe to lease a cottage in Whitwell, Hertfordshire, where he readied his second novel, *The General* (1960), for publication and continued work on *Key to the Door* (1961). Two events especially distinguished 1959 for Sillitoe: his marriage to Ruth Fainlight in November and the publication of *The Loneliness of the Long-Distance Runner*. The critical and commercial success of Sillitoe's second work coupled with that of his first signaled the end of his writing apprenticeship.

In 1960 *The Loneliness of the Long-Distance Runner* won for Sillitoe the Hawthornden Prize,

awarded each year for the best imaginative writing by a writer under forty. This remarkable volume contains some of Sillitoe's finest short stories, in which he writes about survivors and the hardships they confront. Several of the stories focus on youths in Nottingham as Sillitoe explores a child's fascination with suicide in "Saturday Afternoon" or follows the Goose Fair adventures of two boys who steal one last ride in "Noah's Ark." In the final story of the collection, Sillitoe describes childish war games led by a childlike adult, Frankie Buller, later subjected to shock treatment by an indifferent society more interested in control than compassion. All the stories emphasize the sense of futility shrouding every aspect of working-class existence, but the title story offers the harshest indictment of the upper classes. In this story, Smith, an unrepentant youth sentenced to a borstal, or reformatory, for theft, deliberately loses a long distance race and its attendant trophy, which the borstal director wants him to win for the prestige of the borstal. Because self-esteem does not come easily for Smith, he refuses to risk its loss by winning a race for the director, much as a trained horse might. Though the protagonist's deliberate and obvious losing of the race complicates the remainder of his sentence, he regrets neither his action nor its consequences, and concludes that "in-laws" and "out-laws" can never see eye to eye. This story explores the resentment the lower classes feel for any of the innumerable ways government, and, by extension, society, dehumanizes them. With few reservations critics welcomed Sillitoe's second work and eagerly awaited his third, which appeared in 1960.

The General proved a disappointment to critics, who quickly dismissed it. Though some criticized it as a hasty effort written to cash in on the success of Sillitoe's earlier two works, *The General* was actually written over a long period of time. It developed from a story Sillitoe first wrote in 1949 and later revised while living in Majorca in 1953, and during the next seven years it went through several more thorough revisions. A fable about war, art, and the nature of man, *The General* chronicles the actions and reactions of an anonymous protagonist, the General, commander of the somewhat barbaric Gorshek forces, and of Evart, conductor of a symphony orchestra that, on its way to the front lines to entertain troops, is captured by Gorshek forces. While awaiting instructions about the orchestra's fate, the General and Evart debate the relative merits of war and pacifism. When the high command's computers demand the musicians' deaths, the General, at high personal cost, arranges for their escape. His decision, influenced in part by the orchestra's moving performance, introduces freedom of choice into the novel's central debate as the General selects integrity over blind obedience and so assures himself of certain disgrace and punishment. His insistence that the orchestra members carry weapons spells a type of defeat for the pacifist Evart as well. Either ignored or condemned by critics, *The General* was made into a film, which also failed to win an audience.

The Rats and Other Poems, also published in 1960, includes the long title poem and thirty-three short lyrics from *Without Beer or Bread* (1957), a small collection of poems published in a limited paperback edition. For the most part undistinguished, the volume did introduce a favorite Sillitoe theme: individual rebellion against the collected pressures of government and other bureaucracies. Though Sillitoe considers himself first a poet, then a novelist, critics regard his fiction much more highly. Interestingly, however, the passage in *Saturday Night and Sunday Morning* that most critics single out for praise was originally a long poem. Sillitoe spent the rest of 1960 preparing the screenplay for the film version of *Saturday Night and Sunday Morning*. Starring Albert Finney, the film proved both a critical and a commercial success.

After a five-month holiday in Tangier, Sillitoe returned in 1961 to London where he rented a flat and began revising *Key to the Door* while he worked on another screenplay, this time for *The Loneliness of the Long-Distance Runner*. As with Sillitoe's first novel, this story translated well into film. Both critics and public responded with quick enthusiasm to the film, which starred Tom Courtenay and Sir Michael Redgrave. *Key to the Door* was published in October 1961 to a generally tentative critical reaction, which stemmed from reservations about Sillitoe's often overworked style and his heavy-handed attempts to inject his political philosophy into the novel. Most critics recognized the merit of the novel's first two sections, which recount the Nottingham childhood of Brian Seaton, older brother of Sillitoe's first protagonist. In contrast, the account of Brian's military service in Malaya, detailed in the novel's last two parts, provoked harsh criticism for its insufficiently prepared for climax in which Brian refuses to kill one of the Communist rebels fighting the British. Sillitoe fails to convince the reader that Brian is willing to die for a system he is only superficially aware of. The author's naive use of political propaganda coupled with the lack of a definite structure weakens a novel that contains some of his most vivid writing. Uneven, but worth-

while, *Key to the Door* evidences a preoccupation with politics that colors Sillitoe's succeeding works.

Shortly after his son's birth in March 1962 and six months after the publication of *Key to the Door*, Sillitoe uprooted his entire family for a year and traveled to Tangier and later throughout Morocco. Here he began his next novel and wrote some of the short stories included in *The Ragman's Daughter and Other Stories*. Published in 1963, this volume met with generally favorable, if not enthusiastic, reviews. Although most critics praised the stories' technical skill, a substantial number of reviewers regarded as myopic and oversimplified Sillitoe's view that society is comprised solely of oppressed workers and oppressing bureaucracies. Most of the stories urge rebellion against the establishment in any form, and, while many of the protagonists cheat their employers more for enjoyment than from necessity, several characters are reduced to scavaging through trash heaps in order to survive. In this

Dust jacket for the American edition of Sillitoe's 1961 novel, a sequel to Saturday Night and Sunday Morning

volume the emphasis on violent rebellion replaces the thorough character development and psychological analysis of the earlier stories. Though resistance to authority colored much of his writing by 1963, politics became even more dominant in later work. Sillitoe's unhappiness with the British system increased after he had an opportunity to observe Communist life.

After his return to England in 1963, Sillitoe received an invitation from the Soviet Writers' Union to visit the USSR, where he spent a month. Later in the year he traveled for four weeks in Czechoslovakia and catalogued his observations in *Road to Volgograd*, which was published in 1964. An individual, highly personal account of his travels, the work reveals much about Sillitoe's own tastes, such as his interest in geography and military strategy and his love of cartography and topography. Distinctly uncritical of Soviet politics, *Road to Volgograd* offers a new perspective on Sillitoe's dissatisfaction with England in general, not just with the handicaps she imposes on her workers.

David Brett's stage adaptation of *Saturday Night and Sunday Morning* opened and quickly closed in Nottingham in spring 1964. A 1966 London production was equally unsuccessful. In its transition to the stage the picaresque structure of the novel became episodic drama, which was not enhanced by interruptions of pop music. A new volume of poetry, *A Falling Out of Love and Other Poems*, also appeared in 1964. Though the poems in this volume showed much discipline and craft, none provoked an enthusiastic critical response. Late in 1964 Sillitoe resettled his family in Spain and for the next four years divided his time between his homes in Spain and England. Despite commuting, he managed to finish *The Death of William Posters* (1965), the first novel of his Frank Dawley trilogy. In this novel Sillitoe takes his argument against social injustice beyond Nottingham.

The protagonist, Frank Dawley, is both older and more ready to rebel than either of the Seaton brothers. While *Saturday Night and Sunday Morning* ends with Arthur's convincing himself that marriage should be his next step and *Key to the Door* ends with Brian's returning to a marriage interrupted by military service, *The Death of William Posters* begins with Dawley's deserting wife, children, and job in order to find freedom and a sense of identity. Dawley creates an imaginary figure, William Posters—a name suggested by the signs Dawley sees everywhere: "Bill Posters Will Be Prosecuted"—who comes to symbolize the underdog workman

apparently hounded by authorities. Dawley's relationship with his first lover ends when his commitment to causes becomes more important than his commitment to individuals. The protagonist's alliances with an eccentric painter, a new lover, and an American revolutionary lead to his enlistment in the Algerian rebellion against France. As Dawley begins his new life as a revolutionary, his old symbol of the oppressed workman, William Posters, dies. Difficulties in style and weaknesses in the conception of Sillitoe's hero prompted critical reservations. The second novel of the trilogy fared little better.

Appearing in 1967, *A Tree on Fire* continues the story of Frank Dawley's own revolution. In this novel Dawley's lover, Myra, and their son return to England and share a home with Albert Handley, the painter who earlier befriended Dawley. The scene then shifts back to Dawley and the desert fighting, which incorporates the most basic of working-class biases—the "us versus them" dichotomy. After attacking with the rebels, Dawley is sick for ten days, and deciding he would be more useful in England raising money for the insurgents' cause, he returns and joins his lover and child at Handley's home. A successful painter but also a confirmed revolutionary, Handley enlists Dawley in his efforts to establish a utopian community, which becomes the subject of the third novel. While reviewers commended Sillitoe's rendering of battle scenes, they criticized his style in other passages. As his characters receded before his theme of violent rebellion, his art degenerated into propaganda.

Though begun in 1967, the final novel of the trilogy, *The Flame of Life*, was not published until 1974, and the delay proved devastating. In this novel, Dawley, Handley, and various members of their families keep trying to establish a utopian community while disrupting the English society around them. Yet their own bickering continually interrupts and delays their revolutionary plots to correct social injustices. Little action, less direction, and too much purposeless theorizing coupled with such stylistic excesses as overlush prose and self-conscious imagery make this novel Sillitoe's weakest. Critics generally agreed *The Flame of Life* added little to Sillitoe's reputation.

In 1966 after the publication of the first novel in his trilogy and while working on the second one, Sillitoe collaborated with his wife in adapting for the British stage Lope de Vega's play *All Citizens Are Soldiers*. In 1967 a group of young actors staged the play, but it closed after only a few performances. While his play was opening and closing, Sillitoe traveled again to Russia. This time, however, he was openly critical of restraints on Soviet writers. Upon his return in fall 1967, he collected his family, and they all wintered in Majorca in a house loaned by Robert Graves. During this period, Sillitoe finished some short stories as he worked on another play, *This Foreign Field*, and readied for publication another volume of poetry, *Love in the Environs of Vorenezh* (1968). Late in 1968 Sillitoe again journeyed to the Soviet Union, but increasing disenchantment with Soviet treatment of minorities has made further travel in Russia unlikely.

Sillitoe's third collection of short stories, *Guzman, Go Home, and Other Stories*, was published at the end of 1968. About the circumstances and pressures that force people together or apart, these stories concern survivors, as Sillitoe's stories often do. In "Revenge," as marital love turns bitter, the protagonist survives both his wife's blundering murder attempt and the contemptuous indifference of his psychiatrists. "Canals" examines the effect of the past on the present in rendering certain things at once familiar and alien. In the title story Sillitoe returns to the theme of his second novel, the interdependence of art and politics, as Guzman, a German war criminal, tries to justify his life to himself as well as to a young English painter. Sillitoe creates sympathy for Guzman by making fun of him. Though the themes are familiar, the writer treats them with a skill and assurance critics applauded. For one reviewer Sillitoe's technique even invited comparison with that of Dickens.

Sillitoe spent most of 1969 in England writing various short stories and a long, picaresque novel, *A Start in Life* (1970), in which he experimented with such traditional comic forms as satire, irony, farce, and parody as he followed in the tradition of Fielding, an author he had long admired. The protagonist, Michael Cullen, flees his Nottingham background, his pregnant girlfriend, and the dubious circumstances surrounding his dismissal for unethical real-estate dealings. Escaping to London, he has a series of adventures that eventually land him in prison. At the end of the novel, Cullen retires to the country, obstensibly to lead a respectable life. Generally receptive to *A Start in Life*, critics appreciated the writer's humor and his skill in manipulating traditional literary forms.

Sillitoe spent part of 1970 working on a utopian fantasy, and in March 1970 the same company that had staged *All Citizens Are Soldiers* produced *This Foreign Field*, but it too closed after only a few performances. Sillitoe spent most of this year finishing the screenplay for *The Ragman's Daughter*, which premiered in 1972. Starring Victoria Tennant, the film met mixed reviews and received little promotion. Though Sillitoe was pleased with the film, it did not enjoy the success of his first two screenplays.

Sillitoe's refusal to complete a census form resulted in a fine in 1971 after seven months of legal maneuvering. He spent the summer of 1971 traveling on the continent with his family. He also joined with his wife, Ruth Fainlight, and his friend, Ted Hughes, to produce *Poems*, a handsome, signed, limited edition of three hundred copies. Sillitoe's fantasy, *Travels in Nihilon*, appeared in the fall of this year.

Exploring the possibilities of life in a totally nihilistic state, *Travels in Nihilon* met critical reserve and public indifference. The novel follows five travelers to Nihilon where citizens value cheating and violence, scorn honor and loyalty, and deliberately create chaos and disaster. The five travelers join an insurrection against the established government but ultimately realize that the rebels are as corrupt as the government they want to overthrow. The farce and satires of some of the adventures do not compensate for the weak multiple perspectives imposed on the novel by five protagonists. Though *Travels in Nihilon* sparked little enthusiasm, Sillitoe's *Raw Material* aroused great interest when it was published in 1972.

Both novel and memoir, biography and autobiography, *Raw Material* attempts to explain how someone of Sillitoe's background becomes a writer. According to its author, *Raw Material* attempts to trace through the "raw material" of his grandparents' lives the events and circumstances which shaped his decision to become a novelist. In part 1 he alternates sections of philosophical speculation, primarily about the relativity of truth, with accounts of family history, in particular biographical details about his grandfather Burton, so that he can examine the interrelationship of a writer and the raw material of his own life. Much of part 2 concerns World War I as Sillitoe interweaves carefully researched facts, memories of relatives about the war, and his own theories about the misuse of power by government and other bureaucracies. The last chapters include anecdotes about more recent family history between commentaries on writing. The book works best when Sillitoe explores his familial relationships. The indirect, oblique analysis of the fiction-making process in these passages succeeds much more than the direct philosophical speculations of the commentaries. Somewhat uneven, the work offers valuable insights about Sillitoe, who considers it one of his most important works. To his gratification, a slightly revised edition was published in 1978.

Later in 1972, at Stephen Spender's invitation, Sillitoe wrote a paper on D. H. Lawrence, "Lawrence's District," which was later included in *Mountains and Caverns* (1975), a collection of Sillitoe's essays. After the undistinguished release of the film version of *The Ragman's Daughter* in 1972, the writer moved his family back to London, ending three years in the Kent countryside. The following year, 1973, he produced his fourth collection of short stories, *Men, Women and Children*, which was well received, in part because it included "Mimic," one of Sillitoe's most memorable stories.

The stories in this collection may share a Nottingham setting, but they focus on limitations arising from character rather than from environment, and geography has little to do with self-image. Only one of the stories, "Pit Strike," indicts, in the usual Sillitoe manner, a society that encourages repressive, unjust conditions. The other stories focus on individuals and the ways they cope with circumstances, not yield to them. The most important story, one of Sillitoe's finest, is "Mimic," about a man who tries to cope with life by imitating it. His relationships with people exhausted, the protagonist is reduced to the impossible task of mimicking nature. His unsuccessful efforts drive him mad, but in the second half of the story he comes to recognize the dangers of self-delusion inherent in mimicry and rids his mind of its collected phantoms. Well received by critics, the stories in this collection represent a technical sophistication even more pronounced in Sillitoe's latest novels.

Always protesting the repression of minorities, Sillitoe has never hesitated to express his markedly pro-Zionist views, which prompted a 1974 invitation by the Israeli Foreign Office to spend ten days in Israel. He subsequently had published two brief articles in a geographical journal as well as an article in the *New Statesman* that detailed his enthusiasm for Israel. Later in 1974 Sillitoe's love of geography led to a series of lectures at Nebraska State University. One of these lectures, "Maps," is included in *Mountains and Caverns*. During this same year, Sillitoe also reiterated his criticism of Soviet repression. Concern for the repressed also marks the poems in *Storm: new poems* (1974), a volume which includes Sillitoe's verse from *Poems* as well as numerous short lyrics published in two earlier small press editions, *Shaman and Other*

Poems (1968) and *Barbarians and other poems* (1973). As a group, the poems reveal Sillitoe's improved control and increasingly skillful technique.

For the next two years, Sillitoe produced little besides *Mountains and Caverns*, which included an account of his early years as well as essays and speeches written since 1963. He remained active in humanitarian causes, often attending conferences, such as the one sponsored by UNESCO to discuss the cultural aspects of Arab-Israeli relations. In November of 1975 Sillitoe was elected a fellow of the Royal Geographical Society, an especially gratifying honor for him. Early in 1976 at a conference in Brussels, he harshly criticized Soviet treatment of Jews by writing a short play, *The Interview*, which was performed in September 1976.

While revising an early story for children prior to its publication as a book, Sillitoe researched the life of a career army officer for his next novel. This book, *The Widower's Son*, published in the fall of 1976 to general acclaim, examines the life of William Scorton, raised by his widowed father, a retired professional soldier dedicated to molding his son in his own image. Conditioned from an early age to perceive life in military terms, first as a young cadet at gunnery school and later as a colonel in the royal artillery, William never comes to terms with his background. He can resolve neither the immediate conflicts with his father, who secretly considers his son better off as a noncommissioned officer, nor his later conflicts with his wife, a brigadier's daughter who can never quite overcome the differences in their backgrounds. Over his wife's objections, William resigns his commission to discover much about life that the army failed to teach him. William's initiation destroys his marriage. Sillitoe's elaborate extended metaphor of marriage as war details the collapse of William's relationship with his wife. His subsequent mental breakdown culminates in attempted suicide from which he emerges with the beginnings of a self-awareness denied him in his army career and in his relationships with both wife and father. Beginning in midlife a new career as a teacher, William prepares to face life on his own terms, no longer colored by the orders and desires of others. In this novel, Sillitoe does more than catalogue the problems caused by working-class origins; he focuses on the inner agonies of one individual.

In 1977 Sillitoe produced *Big John and the Stars*, a story for children which was well received, and later that year, "Pit Strike" from *Men, Women and Children* was dramatized successfully on BBC television. The 1978 *Three Plays* collected *This*

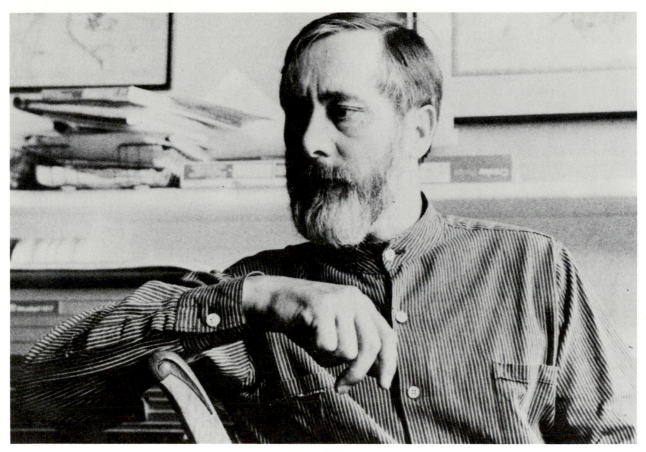

Alan Sillitoe

Foreign Field, retitled *The Slot Machine*; *The Interview*, an expanded and revised version that was performed in March 1978 in London; and *Pit Strike*. During the summer of 1977 Sillitoe and his family spent two months at the invitation of the mayor of Jerusalem at the Mishkenot Sha'anamin, a retreat for celebrated artists. Though Sillitoe recorded his impressions in a daily journal, an account of his experiences has yet to be published. After the publication of *The Incredible Fencing Fleas* (1978), another story for children, Sillitoe released his ninth volume of poetry, *Snow on the North Side of Lucifer* (1979). More important, in fall 1979 Sillitoe produced his tenth, and most ambitious, novel, *The Storyteller*.

The Storyteller chronicles the progress into madness of Ernest Cotgrave, who begins storytelling to escape the violence threatened by the school bully and ends committed to a mental institution following a suicide attempt that renders him mute. Cotgrave retreats into schizophrenia as his life becomes so intertwined with those of his characters that he can no longer distinguish reality from illusion. Peopling his tales with persons and

events from his own life, he is finally so overwhelmed by the multiple personalities that the only response possible to his lover's rejection is attempted suicide. Because he is a mute, Cotgrave's complex oral existence is reduced to "block capitals" on "bits of paper."

Multiple personalities characterize writers for Sillitoe, who pictures the writer as empty before he peoples his mind with his fictional creations. In *The Storyteller* Sillitoe deliberately blurs distinctions between fantasy and reality, as intricate interior monologues become, without warning, perorations before audiences both appreciative and hostile. Though some over-extended metaphors and awkward sentence patterns persist, the word-echoes and refrains, the expert interweaving of inner thoughts and public performances, and the sophisticated treatment of what Sillitoe terms the "same old identity situation" mark *The Storyteller* as one of his finest novels.

Sillitoe again explores the problem of identity in his sixth collection of short stories, *The Second Chance and Other Stories*, published in 1980. Critical reaction was, for the most part favorable, with different reviewers praising different stories. However, "A Scream of Toys," "The Sniper," and the title story were singled out by most. Sillitoe's concern with acting, masks, and mimicry, which dominated *The Storyteller*, figures most clearly in "The Second Chance," a story about a larcenous young man inextricably caught up in his own masquerade of playing the dead son to an elderly couple. Living a lie becomes a leitmotif which echoes throughout the volume.

Sillitoe defies critical attempts to pigeonhole him. Critics labeled him an "angry young man" early in his career, before he had even read much by such writers as Osborne and Braine. Also rejecting the label of working-class novelist, Sillitoe prefers to be thought of as simply a novelist. For him Arthur Seaton is first an individual, then a representative of the working class. In his later novels Sillitoe tempers his concern for social injustice, which dominates the early fiction, with a closer examination of the individual victims of such injustices. As the externalized battles between the working-class and the establishment become the internal conflicts within a single character, Sillitoe continues to draw on his Nottingham origins. His most recent fiction does so with sophistication and skill. For example, Sillitoe incorporates bits and pieces of his own life in his account of Ernest Cotgrave's life in *The Storyteller*, creating an added tension between fantasy and reality. The images of imprisonment, factory, borstal, and conscription in earlier books yield to more subtle metaphors of schizophrenia, suicide, and madness. Not willing to settle for the place *Saturday Night and Sunday Morning* earned him in English letters, Alan Sillitoe continues to explore the writer's limits with volumes of children's literature, poetry, drama, short stories, and increasingly complex novels.

Plays:

All Citizens Are Soldiers, adapted by Sillitoe and Ruth Fainlight from Lope de Vega's play, Stratford-upon-Avon, 20 June 1967;
This Foreign Field, London, Roundhouse, March 1970;
The Interview, St. Martins-in-the-Fields, 16 September 1976; London, Almost Free Theatre, March 1978.

Screenplays:

Saturday Night and Sunday Morning, Continental, 1960;

The Loneliness of the Long-Distance Runner, Continental, 1962;
The Ragman's Daughter, Penelope, 1972.

Television Script:

Pit Strike, BBC television, September 1977.

Other:

Introduction to *Saturday Night and Sunday Morning* (London: Longmans, Green, 1968);
Introduction to *A Sillitoe Selection*, selected and edited by Michael Marland (London: Longmans, Green, 1968).

Periodical Publications:

"Both sides of the Street," *Times Literary Supplement*, 8 July 1960, p. 435;
"Novel or Play?" *Twentieth Century*, 169 (February 1961): 206-211;
"Drilling and Burring," *Spectator* (3 January 1964): 11-12;
"Poor People," *Anarchy*, 38 (April 1964): 124-128;
"The wild horse," *Twentieth Century*, 173 (Winter 1964-1965): 90-92;
"My Israel," *New Statesman*, 20 December 1974, pp. 890-892;
"Writing and Publishing," *London Review of Books*, 14 (April 1982): 8-10.

Interviews:

"Silver Quill for New Novelist: Mr. Alan Sillitoe Looks Forward to Wider Travels," *Times*, 23 April 1959, p. 9;
"Alan Sillitoe," *Times*, 6 February 1964, p. 15;
Igor Hajek, "Morning Coffee with Sillitoe," *Nation*, 27 January 1969, pp. 122-124;
Bolivar Le Franc, "Sillitoe at forty," *Books and Bookmen*, 14 (June 1969): 21-22, 24;
P. H. S., "Very alive," *Times*, 21 July 1969, p. 4;
Brendan Hennessy, "Alan Sillitoe," *Transatlantic Review*, no. 41 (Winter-Spring 1972): 108-113;
Barry Norman, "Alan Sillitoe avoids the complacency trap," *Times*, 26 October 1972, p. 12;
M. Lefranc, "Alan Sillitoe: An Interview," *Etudes Anglaises*, 26 (January-March 1973): 35-48;
Josef-Hermann Sauter, "Interview mit Alan Sillitoe," *Weimarer Beiträge*, 19 (1973): 44-59;
John Halperin, "Interview with Alan Sillitoe," *Modern Fiction Studies*, 25 (Summer 1979): 175-189.

Bibliography:

Robert J. Stanton, *A Bibliography of Modern British*

Novelists (Troy, N. Y.: Whitston, 1978).

References:

Stanley S. Atherton, *Alan Sillitoe: A Critical Assessment* (London: W. H. Allen, 1979);

James Gindin, "Alan Sillitoe's Jungle," *Texas Studies in Literature and Language*, 4 (Spring 1962): 35-48;

John Dennis Hurrell, "Alan Sillitoe and the Serious Novel," *Critique*, 4 (Fall-Winter 1960-1961): 3-16;

Frederick P. W. McDowell, "Self and Society: Alan Sillitoe's *Key to the Door*," *Critique*, 6 (Spring 1963): 116-123;

Anna Ryan Nardella, "The Existential Dilemmas of Alan Sillitoe's Working-Class Heroes," *Studies in the Novel*, 5 (Winter 1973): 469-482;

Marie Peel, "The loneliness of Alan Sillitoe," *Books and Bookmen*, 19 (December 1973): 42-46;

Allen Richard Penner, *Alan Sillitoe* (New York: Twayne, 1972);

Eugene F. Quirk, "Social Class as Audience: Sillitoe's Story and Screenplay," *Literature-Film Quarterly*, 9 (1981): 161-171;

Janet Buck Rollins, "Novel into Film: *The Loneliness of the Long Distance Runner*," *Literature-Film Quarterly*, 9 (1981): 172-188;

D. M. Roskies, "Alan Sillitoe's Anti-Pastoral," *Journal of Narrative Technique*, 10, no. 3 (1980): 170-185;

Roskies, " 'I'd Rather Be Like I Am': Character, Style, and the Language of Class in Sillitoe's Narratives," *Neophilogus*, 65, no. 2 (1981): 308-319;

Michael K. Simmons, "The 'In-Laws' and 'Out-Laws' of Alan Sillitoe," *Ball State University Forum*, 14 (Winter 1973): 76-79;

Hugh B. Staples, "*Saturday Night and Sunday Morning*: Alan Sillitoe and the White Goddess," *Modern Fiction Studies*, 10 (Summer 1964): 171-181;

Ramsay Wood, "Alan Sillitoe: The Image Shedding the Author," *Four Quarters*, 21 (November 1971): 3-10.

Andrew Sinclair

(21 January 1935-   )

Judith Vincent

BOOKS: *The Breaking of Bumbo* (London: Faber & Faber, 1959; New York: Simon & Schuster, 1959);

My Friend Judas (London: Faber & Faber, 1959; New York: Simon & Schuster, 1961);

The Project (London: Faber & Faber, 1960; New York: Simon & Schuster, 1960);

Prohibition: The Era of Excess (Boston: Little, Brown, 1962; London: Faber & Faber, 1962);

The Paradise Bum (New York: Atheneum, 1963); republished as *The Hallelujah Bum* (London: Faber & Faber, 1963);

The Raker (London: Cape, 1964; New York: Atheneum, 1964);

The Available Man: The Life Behind the Masks of Warren Gamaliel Harding (New York: Macmillan, 1965);

The Better Half: The Emancipation of the American Woman (New York: Harper & Row, 1965; London: Cape, 1968);

A Concise History of the United States (London: Thames & Hudson, 1967; New York: Viking, 1967);

Gog (London: Weidenfeld & Nicolson, 1967; New York: Macmillan, 1967);

Adventures in the Skin Trade [play], adapted from Dylan Thomas's short-story collection (London: Dent, 1967; New York: New Directions, 1968);

The Last of the Best: The Aristocracy of Europe in the Twentieth Century (London: Weidenfeld & Nicolson, 1969; New York: Macmillan, 1969);

Che Guevara (London: Collins, 1970; New York: Viking, 1970);

Magog (London: Weidenfeld & Nicolson, 1972; New York: Harper & Row, 1972);

Dylan Thomas: Poet of His People (London: M. Joseph, 1975); republished as *Dylan Thomas, No Man More Magical* (New York: Holt, Rinehart & Winston, 1975);

The Surrey Cat (London: M. Joseph, 1976);

Inkydoo, the Wild Boy (London: Abelard-Schuman, 1976);

The Savage: A History of Misunderstanding (London: Weidenfeld & Nicolson, 1977);

Jack: A Biography of Jack London (New York: Harper & Row, 1977; London: Weidenfeld & Nicolson, 1977);

A Patriot for Hire (London: M. Joseph, 1978);

John Ford (New York: Harper & Row, 1979; London: Allen & Unwin, 1979);

The Facts in the Case of E. A. Poe (New York: Holt, Rinehart & Winston, 1979; London: Weidenfeld & Nicolson, 1979);

Corsair: The Life of J. Pierpont Morgan (Boston: Little, Brown, 1981; London: Weidenfeld & Nicolson, 1981).

Andrew Sinclair's early novels were greeted with enthusiasm by readers and reviewers alike. His first two novels, published when he was in his mid-twenties, met with instant success with the reading public. The critics praised his narrative style and his facility for gentle social satire and predicted that he would take his place among the best-known novelists of his generation. Although

Sinclair has retained his popularity with the general reading public, many critics have felt that his later novels fail to fulfill the promise they saw in his earlier work. Since the publication of his first novel, *The Breaking of Bumbo* (1959), Sinclair's career has developed in many different directions: he has been a university lecturer, a journalist, a translator, and a director of feature films; as well as writing novels, he is the author of biographies and books on social history. His interests as historian and biographer frequently impinge upon his fiction, and some critics have felt that these interests have detracted from, rather than furthered, his development as a novelist.

Andrew Annandale Sinclair was born in Oxford to Stanley and Hilary Nash-Webber Sinclair. His education began at the Dragon School, a preparatory school in Oxford, where he stayed until 1948 when he won a scholarship to Eton College. He found Eton a valuable experience. While there he became aware of the cultural and literary tradition among Eton scholars, particularly among the immediate generation before him, which had included George Orwell. He left Eton at the age of eighteen and did two years service in the army, where he became an ensign in the Coldstream

Andrew Sinclair

Guards, the oldest brigade in the British army. On completion of his national service, he won a scholarship to Trinity College, Cambridge, where he read history, graduating in 1958 with a double first class honors degree.

Sinclair's early life is reflected in his first two novels, though the novels are not autobiographical. In his first novel, *The Breaking of Bumbo*, he drew upon his experience in the army to describe the career of his hero. Benjamin Bailey, known to his friends as Bumbo, survives the rigors of military training and becomes a guardsman. From his secure and privileged base in the Wellington Barracks, Chelsea, he sets out to explore the world of debutantes, to which his position as an officer in the guards admits him, and that of the musicians, models, and wealthy dropouts who live in Chelsea. This existence is disrupted, though, by the suggestion that the guards might be sent to defend British interests at Suez. Uncertain whether his motive is cowardice or a courageous stand for principle, Bumbo attempts unsuccessfully to lead a mutiny.

Sinclair's observation of undergraduate life at Cambridge provided the material for his second novel, *My Friend Judas* (1959), which chronicles the sexual and other adventures of a grammar school boy, Ben Birt, who has won a scholarship to Cambridge. The novel describes the mixture of social classes at the university and the excesses of undergraduate life, amid which the university struggles to maintain its academic traditions.

Sinclair's experience in the Coldstream Guards and at Cambridge did more than provide him with material for the plots of these novels, however. During this period his political views were undergoing changes that influenced the treatment of his material and the tone of his novels. Sinclair describes himself at the time he went up to Cambridge as "an unthinking right-winger," but the political events of the mid-1950s, in particular the Suez crisis and the Hungarian uprising, altered his political outlook. Considering the Conservative government's handling of the Suez affair inappropriate and ineffective, he became a socialist and a supporter of the Labour party. At the time of the Suez crisis, Sinclair was a reservist, but he was not called up for active military service. However, the personal dilemma he would have faced had he been called to fight for a cause in which he did not believe is clearly behind the situation confronting Bumbo. Sinclair's altered political perspective would seem also to have influenced the manner in which he presents the many upper- and upper-middle-class characters in these novels. Presenting a study of a

life-style and attitudes which seem inappropriate in postwar Britain, Sinclair captures very accurately the assumptions and distinctions at work in a class society.

Sinclair's political awareness may also have influenced his next novel, *The Project* (1960), a science-fiction fantasy about a chief scientist who deliberately sends a nuclear weapon (the "project" of the title) off course to Russia. The novel begins with a description of a party on the eve of the launch and continues as the scientist's account of the motives behind his action. At the time the novel was written, nuclear disarmament was an important issue in British politics, and the Labour party was split over whether or not to adopt a policy of unilateral disarmament. Sinclair's personal view about the possibility of nuclear war was pessimistic; as an historian, he observed that the accumulation of armaments eventually led to their use. The novel is a departure from Sinclair's earlier method of social observation and is presented as a kind of fable, but it is less skillfully realized than his earlier novels and lacks their humor.

After graduating from Cambridge, Sinclair followed an academic career. He was a graduate student at Cambridge for one year and then traveled to America in 1959 as a Harkness Fellow of the Commonwealth Fund. While in America in 1960, he married a French writer, Marianne Alexandre. They had one child and were later divorced. Sinclair spent two years in America studying at Harvard and at Columbia University. The fruit of this study was a Ph.D. thesis on prohibition that was accepted by Cambridge in 1963 and became the basis of his first major nonfiction publication, *Prohibition: The Era of Excess* (1962). A requirement of the Harkness Fellowship was that the fellow should spend three months of the academic year traveling in America; Sinclair used this time to cross the United States from coast to coast by car.

When he returned to England in 1961, he became a fellow and Director of historical studies at Churchill College, Cambridge. Despite a rapidly developing academic career, he retained his interest in, and found time for, writing novels. His travels in America provided the foundation for *The Paradise Bum* (1963), in which Ben Birt, the hero of *My Friend Judas*, now a little older and feeling restricted by English society, travels to America, where he meets and marries Anabel. Together they set out to cross from the east to the west coast of America in a car they have won. Neither of them has any money, but they finance their trip through a number of ingenious petty crimes, including theft, blackmail, and fraud. Along with presenting Birt's adventures, Sinclair records an Englishman's response to the American landscape and to American society in the early 1960s.

This novel was soon followed by an attempt to write a story not based on personal experience. Death is the unmistakable theme of *The Raker* (1964), the title of which is drawn from the nickname of its protagonist, John Purefoy. Descended from a Norman family, Purefoy feels out of step with the times and unwilling and unable to adapt to the present. He exists with the consciousness of the death of the past from which he is descended—and of his own forthcoming death—to such an extent that he has no life. Coming into contact with Adam Quince, an obituary writer, Purefoy goes through an antagonistic acquaintanceship with him before the two recognize their affinity. Purefoy eventually poisons himself and bequeaths to Quince the title "The Raker"—a reference to the corpse rakers in London during the great plague of 1665. Throughout the novel Sinclair uses images of the seventeenth-century plague in London to give allegorical significance to the story. In *The Raker* Sinclair experiments for the first time by mixing fiction with history and myth.

Sinclair returned to America in 1963, this time as a fellow of the American Council of Learned Societies. He stayed in the United States for two years, working on a study of the emancipation of American women (*The Better Half*, 1965) and on his first biography, a study of Warren Gamaliel Harding (*The Available Man: The Man Behind the Masks of Warren Gamaliel Harding*, 1965). By the age of thirty he had an established academic career, had produced two works on American social history and a biography, and had written five novels. These five novels established the themes that are recurrent in his work, the most insistent being those of social adjustment within a changing society and of the individual's attempt to face death.

Fiction, history, and myth are mixed more thoroughly in Sinclair's sixth novel, *Gog* (1967), which is by far the most ambitious and most successful of his novels to date. Gog is washed ashore in Scotland, naked and suffering from amnesia, at the end of World War II. There are no clues to his identity apart from the words *Gog* and *Magog* tattooed on the backs of his hands. Hearing that a Labour government has been elected, Gog escapes from a hospital in Edinburgh and sets out to walk to London. On his journey he meets characters of historical, mythical, and fictional significance, such as a tramp called Wayland Merlin Blake Smith, a

Welsh schoolmaster called Evans the Latin, the Marquis de Sade, Sacher-Masoch, and Lady Chastity and her gamekeeper. He also visits such significant places as Stonehenge and Glastonbury, as he is pursued by his family, his wife, Maire, his mother, his grandmother, and his brother, Magnus (Magog). Gog comes to represent the British people, and his brother, Magog, a civil servant, becomes representative of the forces of oppression Gog sets out to destroy. As his journey progresses past and present merge and the boundaries between dream and reality become less distinct. Through Gog's journey Sinclair explores British history and landscape, and he probes at the border between sanity and insanity. He describes *Gog* as "a novel which tries to substitute a view of the past perceived in the present for a conventional analysis of characters or society. It tries to use only the traditional looseness of the saga and the picaresque novel, before the advent of the psychological novel, in order to present at length the complex evidence of the history and myth and memory that produced one Briton in one place at one time." Critical response to the novel was mixed, but those critics who praised it found Sinclair's experiment exciting, and some greeted it as a work of genius. It is a novel of very great imaginative power.

In the year *Gog* was published Sinclair won a Somerset Maugham Award for *The Better Half*. He also gave up his teaching post at London University in order to pursue his writing career and his developing interest in the cinema. In 1967 he became managing director of Lorrimer Publishing, a firm which specializes in the publication of screenplays. His writing career since then has developed in different directions. He has written biographies of Dylan Thomas, Jack London, John Ford, and, most recently, J. Pierpont Morgan; he has written screenplays, including the screenplay of his novel *The Breaking of Bumbo*, and some television plays; he has been a frequent contributor to *Atlantic*, *Harper's*, the *Spectator*, the *New Statesman*, and the *Observer*, and his ability as a linguist has enabled him to translate foreign works into English. In 1969 he became managing director of Timon Films. He has directed several feature films, most notably the film version of Dylan Thomas's *Under Milk Wood*, which starred Elizabeth Taylor, Richard Burton, and Peter O'Toole and was chosen to open the 1971 Venice Film Festival.

Since 1967, however, he has written only four novels. The novels continue his now familiar themes and have well-developed plots, but they are significantly lacking in the inventiveness and power

from Gog

Jolt, bump and sway, looking up at the canvas roof, dark and ribbed as a mackerel evening sky. Drop, jar and shake, a yielding backrest under the back, a smell of incline rank and exotic as rotting grain, its stain yellow as corn-stalks. Lids drowsing, flicking open, drowsing back in the willy-nilly journey, animal out of control. Long, long since, the sprawling laughing lies these dreaming of tall and impossible women on the top of a haycart in the short summer journey, rumble — — rumble from rut to rut down the track to the farm, while the twilight drives the labourers and the small boys home, small boys creeping out from their slums by the docks of Holyhead, small boys winter-white as winter before haying time, brick-red by the autumn before they go back for bad to their coal-black terraces

Page from the manuscript for Gog

of vision present in *Gog. Magog*, a sequel to *Gog* which follows the career of Gog's brother from 1945 to 1970, was published in 1972. In this novel Magog is materially successful; his career takes him from the civil service to the film industry, to the property market, and finally to the world of academia. The description of these stages of his career is entertaining, but ultimately the moral of the novel is trite: Magog discovers that his material success is hollow and that an inevitably changing order must deprive him of power.

In 1972 Sinclair married Miranda Seymour, and the following year saw another departure in his career as he embarked upon film production, writing and producing *Malachi's Cove*, which starred Gregory Peck. His next novel did not appear until 1976. *The Surrey Cat* was inspired by newspaper reports in the early 1970s of sightings of a large black cat roaming the Surrey countryside. The newspaper reports were unconfirmed, and no cat was ever found, but Sinclair used the story as a departure point from which to weave a tale about a small community terrorized by the cat. Some reviewers were quick to point out the similarities between this plot and that of the film *Jaws*, which was popular and successful at the time the novel appeared. However, while the novel is successful as a thriller, Sinclair's other themes lift the novel above this rather banal level. The cat has a certain mythic quality as it stalks its human prey, but the novel seems to develop more in the style of Sinclair's earlier work. Peter Gwynvor, a rather anachronistic lord of the manor and master of the hunt, assumes responsibility for destroying the cat and protecting the village. The village lies in the stockbroker belt, and the characters who live there are mostly upper-middle class. Sinclair provides an incisive study of this class and, in particular, of Gwynvor's dislocation from the time in which he lives. Dying of cancer, Gwynvor is anxious to provide himself with an heir before he dies, so he becomes involved in affairs with two sisters. This subplot provides an opportunity for Sinclair to pursue his death theme as Gwynvor weighs the choice between a slow death by cancer or a death in confrontation with the cat. It is hard to tell whether or not the evocation of D. H. Lawrence in the scene in which Mister Spring, Gwynvor's butler-cum-gamekeeper, makes love to Gwynvor's girl friend, Claudia, as she lies naked in the moonlight upon a pile of dead rabbits, is intended as some kind of literary joke.

This novel was followed by *A Patriot for Hire*, published in 1978 but set in Britain in 1979. It deals with British politics under the pressures of both left-

and right-wing extremism. The patriot, Patrick Abernethy, engaged by a Conservative government to protect a visiting Russian dignitary, Kulushov, becomes involved not only in political intrigue but in personal chaos as he discovers that Kulushov is the husband of his mistress, Alesha, and that Alesha and Kulushov are the parents of Eva, a Russian interpreter with whom he has a brief affair. As the plot unfolds, Abernethy loses hold on the personal and political values with which he has grown up. In an attempt to regain these certainties, he finds himself working with a group of free Poles who are attempting to kill Kulushov in revenge for the murder of Polish soldiers at Katyn during World War II. In a scene reminiscent of earlier Sinclair novels, Abernethy, a man losing touch with the society in which he lives, is warned by his doctor that he does not have long to live.

Sinclair's most recent novel, *The Facts in the Case of E. A. Poe* (1979), attempts to combine fiction and biography. In the novel Sinclair claims he is only the editor and compiler of notes left by Ernest Albert Pons, who believes that he is Edgar Allan Poe reborn in the twentieth century. Without any real desire to be cured of this belief, he consults a psychiatrist, Dupin, whom he has selected because he has the same name as Poe's fictional detective, C. Auguste Dupin. Dupin sends Pons to visit the scenes and places which were important in Poe's life. On this journey Pons is forced to confront his own past and the fact that his family died in Hitler's concentration camps. Sinclair's intention in this novel was to use Pons as a means of bridging time between the present and Poe's own day. The novel is ambitious, but it is only partially successful in its attempt to weld fiction and biography. The necessity of providing the reader with sufficient information about Poe causes the fictional element to be broken up by lengthy passages which are purely biographical, and the fictional character Pons fades from view.

The themes in Sinclair's novels seem to have become obsessive, but he is still experimenting with the forms of his fiction. If not always wholly successful, these experiments are adventurous and interesting. One of the most disappointing features of his novels is his lack of any really convincing or fully developed female characters. Too often his female characters seem to exist only as the fulfillments of the fantasies of his male characters or as objects to be fought over. The character groupings in his novels have tended to become familiar, too; relationships between brothers and between sisters are often used, and his male characters seem to make a habit of having affairs with their mistresses' sisters and daughters. Sinclair has said that his ambition is to make one good film and write one good novel. *Gog* is certainly his best novel to date, and, having one such novel, the reader hopes for another.

Plays:

My Friend Judas, adapted from Sinclair's novel, London, Arts Theatre, 21 October 1959;

Adventures in the Skin Trade, adapted from Dylan Thomas's short-story collection, London, Hampstead Theatre Club, 7 March 1965; Washington, D.C., Washington Theatre Club, 25 February 1970.

Screenplays:

Before Winter Comes, Columbia, 1969;

The Breaking of Bumbo, Associated British Pictures, 1970;

Wasn't This What You Came to See, Timon Films, 1971;

Under Milk Wood, based on Dylan Thomas's play, Timon Films, 1971;

Malachi's Cove, Timon Films, 1973;

Blue Blood, Mallard-Impact, 1973.

Television Script:

The Voyage of the Beagle, CBS Films, 1970.

Translations:

Anthologia Graeca (New York: Macmillan, 1967); republished as *The Greek Anthology* (London: Weidenfeld & Nicolson, 1967);

Bolivian Diary: Ernesto Che Guevara, translated by Sinclair and Carlos P. Hanserv (London: Lorrimer, 1968);

Jean Renoir, *La Grande Illusion*, translated by Sinclair and Marianne Alexandre (London: Lorrimer, 1968);

Masterworks of the French Cinema (London: Lorrimer, 1974).

References:

T. R. Fyvel, *Intellectuals Today* (London: Chatto & Windus, 1968);

Lee T. Lemon, "*Gog* and *Magog*," *Prairie Schooner*, 48 (Spring 1974): 83-84.

Anthony Storey
(10 November 1928-)

Jay L. Halio
University of Delaware

BOOKS: *Jesus Iscariot* (London: Calder & Boyars, 1967);

Graceless Go I (London: Calder & Boyars, 1969);

The Rector (London: Calder & Boyars, 1970);

Platinum Jag (London: Calder & Boyars, 1972);

The Centre Holds (London: Calder & Boyars, 1973);

Platinum Ass (London: W. H. Allen, 1975);

Brothers Keepers (London: Boyars, 1975);

Stanley Baker: Portrait of an Actor (London: W. H. Allen, 1977);

The Saviour (London and Boston: Boyars, 1978).

A former professional rugby player, army officer, schoolteacher, and practicing psychologist who is now a tutor in psychology in the adult education program of the University of Cambridge, Anthony Storey is also—and primarily—a novelist deeply committed to exploring and reviving the latent aspects of the human spirit. So far, his novels have not won either the popular or the professional readership they deserve; Storey refuses to play the fashionable games in which some of his contemporaries indulge, and he remains a very private person, like his brother David, although a very different sort of writer in many respects. While for many years he entertained the idea of writing a novel, he did not do so until relatively recently, but since *Jesus Iscariot* was published in 1967 he has written seven more novels, a biography, and several screenplays.

Born in Wakefield, Yorkshire, on 10 November 1928, Anthony was the second of four sons born to Frank and Lily Cartwright Storey. His father worked in the coal pits, tending the water pumps, and eventually was forced to retire early because of a serious lung condition caused by

Anthony Storey

players, rugby players do not wear heavy padding and helmets, and there is only a five-minute break between forty-minute halves.

In 1949-1950 Storey did his national service as an officer in the British army, serving as a platoon commander in Malaysia, or Malaya as it was then called. While Storey was en route to the Orient, two events occurred that in retrospect appear highly significant. He wrote several pages of fiction that eventually became part of his first novel—the fight between Alistair and Donald in *Jesus Iscariot*—and he bought a copy of Freud's *Outline of Psychoanalysis*, the only book on psychology available on the shelves of the bookstore selling English books in Port Said. By the time Storey returned from Malaya eighteen months later, he knew that book backward and forward, although he does not now regard the book as one of Freud's better ones. During his service in Malaya, which was divided between service along the Thai border and in the Cameron Highlands, Storey and his platoon often escorted convoys to protect them from Communist guerrillas. He tells of having to shoot a guerrilla dead while on patrol once and finding a letter on the body of his victim. It was all in Chinese and, thinking it had some use for intelligence purposes, Storey took it and had it translated. Instead, the letter was one the soldier had written to his wife, beautifully describing the causes for which he was fighting—many of them the very ones Storey himself believed in. Shortly afterward, like Tony Foster in *Graceless Go I* (1969), he was wounded in the ankle and was hospitalized in Singapore.

Returning to Yorkshire in 1950, Storey worked as a schoolmaster in a secondary school in Wakefield. Again, like Tony Foster, his fictional counterpart, he played professional rugby, lived away from home—his relationship with his parents, especially his mother, remained tense—and dated a young woman much like Jean in his second novel. He remained in the Territorial Army (roughly equivalent to the U. S. National Guard) until 1966, rising to the rank of major. In 1953, he decided to go to Leeds University for a degree and began reading English literature there. Disappointed in the way English was taught and studied, he switched to psychology, taking his B.A. in 1956. Since he was not allowed another grant for his return to higher education, Storey supported himself mainly by playing rugby for Bradfield Northern. (The kind of life he led as a rugby player is captured by his brother David's novel, *This Sporting Life*, 1960, which is in many respects a biography of Anthony as a young man.)

working in the mines. The oldest child, Neville, died young. Much of the quality and atmosphere of the family life during Anthony's childhood is vividly and accurately portrayed in his first novel, including his mother's bitter attitude toward her second-born son and the intense rivalry between Anthony and David, the two oldest surviving brothers. At school, a large minority of the pupils were also the sons of coal miners, but many were children of engineers or of unemployed fathers (these were the Depression years). At eight years old, Anthony was already playing rugby, taught to do so on the concrete playgrounds where one quickly learned how to take care of himself. The experience was not unusual for boys in that part of England. Storey attended Queen Elizabeth Grammar School in Wakefield until 1946, when he went to Leeds Teacher Training College. By that time he was also playing professional rugby for teams like Wakefield Trinity, which helped to support him in college although he also had a grant. Storey played professional rugby for many years, until 1960, and still regards the sport as one which involves a considerable amount of intelligence as well as physical prowess and endurance. Unlike American football

On 26 June 1954 Anthony Storey was married to June Bridgewater, a nurse he had met in the hospital when his mother was ill. During the years of their marriage, which ended in 1968, they had three children: Christopher, Jane, and John. After taking his degree at Leeds, Storey worked from 1957 to 1960 for the Home Office in Newton-le-Willows, Lancashire, assessing the psychological needs of delinquent children between the ages of ten and sixteen. It was here that he met the consulting psychiatrist upon whom Roger Wilby in *Graceless Go I* is modeled; the psychiatrist became very interested in training Anthony as his "apprentice," but he really had in mind (as Storey discovered when he examined the papers left in his care following the doctor's death) training him to cure the psychiatrist of his own illness, which eventually led to his suicide. In 1960, Storey and his family moved to Armagh, Northern Ireland, where he worked as a psychologist treating a whole range of learning as well as behavioral problems among children. Finding that the ingrained prejudices of many people, including his son's teacher in school, were having a disturbing effect, he again moved in 1962 back to England, where until 1966 he worked as a psychologist for the Suffolk County Council in essentially the same capacity as he had done in Armagh. When University of Cambridge had difficulty finding an academic to take on the job of teaching in its adult-education program, Storey was hired, and he has been tutor in psychology at Cambridge ever since, taking his M. A. in psychology there in 1969.

It was about this time that Storey turned seriously to writing fiction. He had long felt he had a novel he wanted to write, but the one that actually emerged, *Jesus Iscariot* (1967), was not the one he had been thinking about all those years, although it is closely related to the trilogy he eventually produced and is currently in process of rewriting. Drawing heavily on his personal experiences, the novel is not, however, an autobiography, despite many autobiographical passages. For example, the fight between the two brothers, Alistair and Donald, actually occurred, egged on by their parents, especially their mother, but Anthony never broke David's jaw. If in some psychological sense Anthony and David "lived together" during their early manhood, they never literally shared a flat, as Alistair and Donald do in Leeds while Alistair teaches at the

Anthony Storey (with ball) in his first senior professional rugby match, 1950

university and works toward his Ph.D.; and certainly Anthony never killed a man in a pub. Separating the facts from the fiction is not always easy, but in a sense it may be irrelevant, as Storey uses the facts of experience in his fiction not for their own sake but to work toward some idea of truth. Insofar as he succeeds, the truth that emerges is a more general one than the fact of any personal experience.

The truth that Storey seems to be searching for in *Jesus Iscariot* involves, as the title suggests, the conflicting and contradictory elements in a powerful personality, such as Alistair Shuttleworth's, that leave him feeling at times like Jesus, searching for truth, and at others, like Iscariot, betraying the best part of his nature, the "lyrical and loving" part that attracts Rachel, a young woman from a very middle-class, sheltered environment, to live with him. The novel is also concerned with developing the truth of the relationship between Esau and Jacob, as it is relived in a way by Alistair and Donald. Behind or underlying everything is the sinister and disturbing family life presided over by Jesse, the boys' mother, who has lost her first born, conceived before marriage to Joe, and by Jesse's parents who, she believes, badly let her down at the greatest crisis in her life.

Although the novel did not win any prizes, critical reaction was as good as one might wish for a first book, and generally it was favorable. Reviewers recognized both its strengths and its weaknesses, and a number acknowledged the appearance of an exceptional new writer. The review in the *Times Literary Supplement* is too patronizing and negative but at least glimpses a little of Storey's intention: "Alistair's confusion is such as to suggest that he is seriously unbalanced—a possibility deliberately suppressed by the novelist so that *Jesus Iscariot* can reach after the higher drama of Dostoevskian self-abasement. . . ." Others saw in this first novel something that became much clearer in subsequent ones—the strong affinities between Storey and D. H. Lawrence, another miner's son and visionary novelist.

Graceless Go I, Storey's second novel, followed two years later in 1969. By now his marriage to June Storey had broken up, and he was living apart from his wife and family, to whom he willingly paid alimony and child support. Actually, they lived quite close by, Storey having bought a house not far from his own for them to live in. To help make ends meet, he began taking in lodgers and lived in the sitting room of his six-bedroom house. Again drawing on his personal experiences, his second novel is the one that his friend and mentor in Newton-le-Willows, who had since died, had wanted him to write. The story centers upon Tony Foster's friendship with Roger Wilby, a consulting psychiatrist in Wakefield whom Tony meets while teaching school. It also concerns the affair Tony has with Roger's wife, Dorothy, who has separated from her husband but lives in the same town with their two daughters. Like his real-life counterpart, Roger is clever, perceptive, and sensitive, admired and respected by those who know his professional skill; he is also increasingly addicted to alcohol and drugs and uses his friendship with Tony to help him illegally obtain nembutal and methadrine. Ultimately, he commits suicide after telling both Tony and Dorothy he has planned to do so. By then Tony is attending Leeds University and is married to a nurse, Mary, though he sometimes still sees Dorothy.

Unlike *Jesus Iscariot*, there are few lyrical passages in this novel, whose style is suited to its action: terse, blunt, even brutal. Repeatedly protesting his honesty, Tony frequently lies, especially to his first girl friend, Jean, whom he had not deflowered before going off to Malaya in the army earlier and returned to find a kind of holy whore. In all of his relationships, Tony seems to court agony: his is a tortured, if belated, adolescence, as is Roger's; but Tony survives his. Critical reception of this book was on the whole positive, and reviewers singled out for comment Storey's use of the "Oedipal triangle" as reflected in Roger, Dorothy, and Tony. Among the more appreciative and perceptive reviews was one by novelist Angus Wolfe Murray, who wrote in the London *Times*: "This is a guide into the mind of a disturbed 24-year-old adolescent, not romantic in the style of the '50s, but intelligent and solitary. . . . Figures emerge out of dim landscapes, are introduced and fade quite naturally, no towns, no crowds, no world but the world inside. Even the rugby seems more symbolic than actual. Storey's technique succeeds in suggesting many layers of interpretation, his language fierce and honest. This is writing of the highest quality." It was the sort of reader reaction Storey hoped for but seldom received, especially for his later novels, which increasingly puzzled (when they did not outrage) critics heavily involved in the literary establishment Storey refuses to cater to and in fact vigorously opposes.

Many of Storey's novels have attracted film people, although only *Graceless Go I* has so far actually been filmed. Rex Harrison was initially very interested in it, and Storey recalls the astonishing transformation from nearly abject poverty to relative riches when a check for £1,500 arrived for the rights to his novel. He spent the summer of 1970 in Portofino, Italy, with Rex Harrison and his wife, Rachel Roberts, working on the film script. To Rachel Roberts's relief, Harrison did not finally play the part of Roger Wilby, which was taken by Stanley Baker when the production changed hands (Roberts played Dorothy to Ian McKellan's Tony). Completed with Lynn Hughes's help on the script in 1973, the film version was not very successful, owing largely to the poor job of editing and cutting by two people working independently of each other.

Meanwhile, Storey was at work on his third novel, the first in a projected trilogy, and *The Rector* appeared in 1970. Like all of his novels but one, it was published by Marion Boyars, then part of Calder and Boyars, but since October 1975 a separate firm. It was to her that Storey brought his first novel when the original publisher reneged on the agreement to publish it, and Storey has brought her all his novels since without the intermediary of an agent. Hers is not one of the larger publishing companies in Britain, but she has developed a well-deserved reputation for publishing avant-garde work and is gradually becoming better known both in the United States, where she now has offices in Boston and in Salem, New Hampshire, as well as in Britain. She is not an avid publicist, and Storey's books have not sold well, although outlines and scripts of his books either have been sold or are circulating among film producers.

Storey recounts the occasion when at one point the screen star Rita Hayworth became interested in making a film version of *Graceless Go I* and playing the role of Dorothy; she flew in from America to discuss it with him. She was very businesslike, and after a day's work on the project, Storey took her to King's for dinner at the college high table, where she sat between him and another Cambridge don. She commented upon how beautiful the architecture and portrait paintings were, to which the don replied: "Yes, this is one of the better Tudor fakes." Utterly taken aback by this response, she remarked to herself but in Storey's hearing: "I come all the way from California to have dinner in a Tudor fake!" Her disappointment with Cambridge architecture, however, had nothing to do with her failure finally to make the picture with Storey, who looks back on his meeting with Hayworth with affection, humor, and not a little admiration.

The Rector is the first installment of the novel that Storey had been contemplating for years. It is about Mary, the daughter of novelist Anthony Johnson (another fictional representation, in part, of the author), and the events leading up to and following her announcement that she has "conceived of God." Her conviction, which is unshakable, shatters her fiance, Christopher Arden-Jones, the rector of the local church, who is almost the same age as her father, and it seriously disturbs her mother, Jane. Because he has brought her up to be open, candid, and truthful in all her dealings with people, her father tends to accept what she says, and they become even closer in the course of events. The second half of the novel focuses on Christopher's disintegration, which ends with his confinement in a mental hospital. It is only after her son is born, Mary says, that he will recover and they can be married, but the novel ends before then.

Through Mary, the dominant figure in the novel and throughout the trilogy, which includes *The Centre Holds* (1973) and *The Saviour* (1978), Storey attempts not so much to retell the Jesus myth, transposing it to our own time, as to use her as a vehicle to reawaken the latent human spirit. A key symbol in the church at Ilkley, where she lives and Christopher is rector, is the East Window by William Blake. From the moment of its installation, however, it has never been fully illuminated, and Blake refused to attend a dedication until the ancient oak tree that shaded and obscured the window was cut down. During a storm after Mary's annunciation, the tree cracks down to its roots and falls, revealing the window in all its splendor during certain times after sunrise when the church itself does not shadow it. At this time the picture of the Madonna with the Child on her knee has the sun rising behind it, providing the Virgin especially with a brilliant halo. After the tree falls, the light at last can shine through and on the Virgin, just as after Christopher is rent to his roots by Mary's announcement light shines on and through her.

The Rector was widely reviewed and puzzled many establishment critics, who thus adopted a "wait and see" attitude pending completion of the trilogy. The review in the *Times Literary Supplement* was typical and said, in part: "The notion that Christ's coming would meet with little but scepticism in the modern world is not exactly a new one. Mr. Storey's intention, though, is not to weaken a myth by transplanting it; he uses the fact of Mary's (apparently) pure pregnancy as a point of tension around which complex and sometimes extravagant emotions accrue. Too often, though, the gap between . . . 'normal' reactions and the behaviour forced by crisis widens into an incredible gulf, affecting, among other things, the dialogue, which frequently appears either limply inadequate or incongruous. In many ways, perhaps, *The Rector* is the sum of its miscalculations; but it will be interesting to see where Anthony Storey goes from here." Despite some dissatisfaction with the book's achievement, critical acclaim was such that it was short listed for the Booker Prize that year.

In 1970, also, Storey remarried. His second wife, a French woman named Anne-Marie Guludec, is a schoolteacher whose subject is French. They were married on 22 March about six months before his third novel was published. The following year Storey wrote the film script of D. H. Lawrence's *The Plumed Serpent*, but it has not yet been made into a film. He continued working full time as a tutor at Cambridge in the adult-education program, while trying to devote as much time as possible to his writing. He began to experiment with another, lighter form of fiction and in 1972 produced *Platinum Jag*, a "psycho-thriller" that bears some similarities to mysteries and spy stories such as those featuring James Bond. The main character here and in the sequel, *Platinum Ass* (1975), is a former headmaster, Alistair Cartwright, who is separated from his wife and three children. Drafted into service by "the Department" (presumably a branch of British intelligence), he has many adventures and love affairs, including one with Helene Guludec, a wealthy French woman who bears the same surname as Storey's wife before she was married. Both novels have much to do with attempts to smuggle large amounts of platinum across international borders and accordingly involve underworld characters from "the Organization," who are both well heeled and well armed. Interestingly, the Alistair of these novels bears the same surname as Storey's mother before she was married, and there are other autobiographical allusions,which have nothing to do, however, with the principal events that occur.

In Storey's next novel, *The Centre Holds*, a continuation of the trilogy, the novelist Anthony Johnson explains, "In a sick way, [James] Bond is Jesus." He is Jesus insofar as he, too, searches for salvation, but "in a sick way" because, one supposes, the salvation he seeks has little or nothing to do with the spirit—and a great deal to do with material wealth. This, perhaps, is one connection that may be made between the "platinum" novels and Storey's others. Another connection is between the characters. By this time it is apparent that many of the major figures in Storey's fiction have a family resemblance, not only in their names and per-

sonalities but also in their relation to their author. In a sense, Alistair Shuttleworth, Tony Foster, Anthony Johnson, and Alistair Cartwright all portray different aspects of Storey himself as well as of his personal experiences. The distinction between autobiography and fiction is often a very close one and becomes further complicated when more than one of these personae appear in the same novel, as in *The Centre Holds*. Here, the first-person narrator, Tony Foster (also the narrator of *Graceless Go I*), meets Anthony Johnson and the rest of his family eleven or twelve years after the incidents in *The Rector*. Alistair Shuttleworth, now a television producer and director, also appears toward the end of the novel, which is set some years in the future, suggesting a slight science-fiction slant to the novel (a mistake, Storey now thinks).

If the East Window of the church in Ilkley is a key symbol in *The Rector*, the West Window is the key symbol in *The Centre Holds*. Unlike the "Blake" window, it is not a product of Storey's imagination but an actual thirteenth-century piece of stained glass, a picture of a pregnant woman with a church enclosed within the outlines of her body, its door precisely where the woman's sex is located, and its steeple rising phalluslike between her breasts. In this and in other ways, Storey develops the concept of "God the Mother" and the religious and liberating ideas of sex. As Mary tells Tony, sex is not the "last remaining mystery," as he thinks, but the one twentieth-century man "has to get through to reach the other mysteries." Apparently, she and her fam-

The thirteenth-century stained-glass window that serves as the key symbol for The Centre Holds

ily, which includes her father, Christopher, and her son (simply called "Boy" until he chooses a name—or others choose it for him), all practice freedom from inhibition and taboo, often sleeping in the same bed together. Jane has begun to fade from their lives, which are now lived mostly in a house in France, in the Dordogne, but after making Tony Foster her lover, she brings him to see the family. When Tony brings Boy back to Yorkshire, events begin to crescendo and reach a climax when a riot occurs during a trial involving Alistair and Tony, who have assaulted two policemen they believed were about to strike Mary's son. In the battle, which Mary calls "the massacre of the innocents," many young people, but also many army personnel, are killed or injured. The riot is filmed by Alistair's production crew, and as Mary and Boy walk among the dead and dying, ministering to them, Emma, one of the directors of the film, notices Mary's charisma and the attention it attracts. She thus proclaims the carnage as a "testament to the rebirth of the beautiful life and the Age of the Mother."

In *The Centre Holds*, a title which adapts a line from Yeats's poem "The Second Coming," Storey indicates how his novels are written and how he expects them eventually to be regarded. Tony Foster describes Anthony Johnson as "one of two or three writers who got people reading novels again. Mainly . . . by extending the novel into the common ground between theology, fiction, and anthropology, not to mention psychology." In fact, Storey's novels have aroused more interest among theologians than literary critics, many of whom ignored or were angered by this second book in his trilogy and even attacked him on personal grounds—evidence that something of the book got through or touched a nerve. In a very negative review, which nevertheless recognized Storey's intention "to transform our consciousness while extending the range of the novel," the *Times Literary Supplement* writer betrayed a bias, or entrenched preconception about fiction, and argued that Storey's ideas were "asserted rather than thought out" and that his characters had "little fictive presence." (For readers without such literary "self-consciousness," Storey insists, his characters have a very powerful fictive presence—as indeed they do.) From the response to *The Centre Holds* it is not hard to understand why the final novel in the trilogy, *The Saviour*, went almost totally without comment from reviewers when it appeared.

"My integrity as a writer—such as it is," Anthony Johnson says in *The Centre Holds*, "depends on my not being there in the novel. I put no linking passages, no little descriptions, demonstrating the writer's virtuosity, sensitivity and wisdom, nothing. I wait at my typewriter and when they talk and do things, I get it down. Without comment. I am like a secretary. The servant of the characters." This is a very close description of how Storey conceives of his role as a writer and how he actually composes his novels. He sits in a large easy chair and deliberately empties himself of all thoughts and ideas until the characters appear and begin to talk. He then transcribes events and dialogue on his electric typewriter in his study. The conception of composition is admittedly and unashamedly Platonic (compare the Socratic dialogue *Ion*). In the revisions of his trilogy and in other kinds of writing, however, Storey recognizes the need for a much greater measure of deliberate choices he must make as opposed to being a kind of recording secretary.

In 1974 Storey wrote the screenplay of *Zulu Dawn*, an expensive film which Stanley Baker produced and starred in. Unfortunately, the film lost rather than made money. In his biography of Baker, Storey describes his first meeting with him, high up in his office overlooking the Thames. Several South African businessmen, including a very well-tailored black man serving as their consultant, had come to discuss financing the film. At one point, seeing the shield and assegai hanging on a wall in Baker's office, the Zulu grasped them, let out a cry, and began to dance and sing "a breathy, exciting, fierce pagan song of naked strength and collective power." Urged to continue, he put the weapons down and quietly said he had danced enough. The incident stands out as one of many in the friendship that grew between Baker and Storey and was regrettably cut short by the actor's untimely death a few years later.

When W. H. Allen and Company later commissioned Storey to write the biography of Baker, they also became interested in the second "psycho-thriller" Storey had written, *Platinum Ass*, and published it in 1975. Marion Boyars had seen it and decided against publishing it because she felt it was too much like *Platinum Jag*, which she had already published. Drawing on their greater resources, W. H. Allen produced a more handsome volume than its precursor and generously included excerpts from favorable reviews of Storey's previous novels on the back of the dust jacket. Meanwhile, Boyars published in the same year *Brothers Keepers*, Storey's seventh novel, one that returns to the intense rivalry between the brothers Alistair and Donald, the chief characters of his first novel.

Renamed Cartwright (Lily Storey's maiden name), the brothers are now each successful professionals: Alistair, a psychologist living and teaching in Cambridge and the author of several novels; Donald, a practicing playwright of considerable reputation, who is married to Rachel. Alistair's wife, June, has recently left him, and he is on his own in a house almost denuded of furniture, which she has taken with her and the children. The novel opens as Donald is driving up to visit Alistair, and his irresponsible driving causes a number of rapidly consecutive accidents in which several people die or are injured seriously. But Donald, preoccupied with other possibilities of violence, such as killing his brother, pushes on and does not stop until he is outside Alistair's door. Although Donald's recklessness is a leitmotiv, the novel concentrates on the love-hate relationship between the two brothers and, continuing from *Jesus Iscariot*, their relationship with their parents, about whom Donald's new play, produced in London's West End, is chiefly concerned. The novel also treats Alistair's relationship with one of his former patients, who has escaped from Pentonville Prison and precipitates the final crisis, threatening to murder the man who has tried in the past to help him.

Donald's play, here called simply *Family*, is actually modeled after David Storey's *In Celebration* and is about three brothers who go back to their hometown to help their parents celebrate their fortieth wedding anniversary (in point of fact, *In Celebration* is modeled on the actual event which occurred). In the novel, the parents ask Alistair to arrange for them to see Donald's play, and all four have a meal together afterward. The play, written so close to the literal reality, has a powerful effect upon Jesse, but Joe is better able to take it in stride. After they leave for their return to Yorkshire, another drama unfolds between the two brothers back in the theater, where they reenact some scenes from their past or otherwise reexperience them. In the process, their deepest feelings for each other are revealed.

His shortest novel to date, but in some ways his most moving, *Brothers Keepers* troubled and apparently embarrassed reviewers, who could scarcely avoid the biographical allusions. Neil Hepburn in the *Listener*, for example, complained about the quality of the writing: "wildly unreticent, name-dropping, sententious at times, it is no advertisement for its writer-characters' success." In short, it was too much like listening to the rows of the family next door. The rivalry between Anthony and David Storey is real enough and is as deep as it is longstanding. They rarely see each other, and their relationship is one of rather guarded friend-liness—with emphasis on the qualifier.

During this period, Storey continued writing film scripts, including one of his novel *Platinum Jag*, as well as fiction. In 1977 W. H. Allen published *Stanley Baker: Portrait of an Actor*. If in his fiction Storey himself is very much present in one form or another, in this sensitive, truthful portrayal of an actor he is simply a camera trying to capture in words the essential qualities of the man he had come to know and love. Inevitably, some personal reminiscing appears, but the author consistently refers to himself self-effacingly (if somewhat stiltedly) as "the writer." The camera is always directed at Baker, whom Storey visits at his villa in Spain, where he is recuperating from a serious cancer operation. Baker is dying, as one part of him knows and another part refuses to accept, while he makes plans for his next film or visits with friends along the Costa del Sol. Lady Ellen Baker, to whom the book is dedicated, also frequently appears as the devoted, loving wife trying as hard as she can to remain cheerful and optimistic. Through it all emerges the portrait of a man growing up in "absolute poverty," aided by his teacher and friend Glynn Morse (whom Storey also interviewed along with Baker's sister), getting his chance to act on the stage and in films, and finally being recognized by friends and colleagues, such as Richard Burton, as the fine actor he is. The book concludes with a list, or filmography, of all of Baker's films, including those he produced but did not act in.

The Saviour, the final volume in the trilogy, was published in 1978. Boy is now generally recognized as Jesus, whose name he accepts together with the hostility his presence arouses among many, including Mary's vicious brother, Michael, who finally kills him. By this time Storey had learned to use the attacks upon him and his work for the purposes of his fiction, incorporating similar attitudes and responses among those inspired by his characters, especially Mary and Jesus. Another family is introduced prominently in this part of the trilogy: Martha and her husband, Hector (a policeman), and their emotionally disturbed daughter, Deirdre. Although he still does not say much and the little he utters is usually in question form, Jesus here begins to come into his own at last, sharing and at times overtaking the interest Mary inspires among the other characters and the reader. While some episodes occur in the family home in the Dordogne, where Martha visits and for a while seems transformed, the book begins and ends in England, where Jesus's ministry centers. Near the end, he explains his mission: "I have caused pain and anger.

I have no lesson to teach other than to search for truth within to find the Kingdom of Heaven. Morality comes out of this search. The mystery is plain, simple and wonderful. The mystification is man's making." Hardly traditional Christian teaching, it is identical with Storey's own belief and practice in his novels.

Theologians, who take the most interest in Storey's books, see him as a Trinitarian, doubtless in the same terms that Alistair describes his Trinity in *Brothers Keepers*: "God the mother, God the father and God the child." Again like Alistair, he is searching to regain the wholeness that mankind once enjoyed. Human beings need to recover as adults what they may have had, however briefly, as children—before the "sadisms, masochisms, hysterias, bits of psychoticism" fragmented their lives, leaving them incomplete where once they were whole. Can literature help people to that end? Alistair's mother is clearly skeptical, cuttingly referring to her son's own troubled life. But his plea carries a conviction that underlies all of Storey's serious fiction: "I agree that literature, serious literature, should be liberating, ennobling . . . but not by denying nature . . . by asserting our nature . . . by transcending through acceptance, with eyes open, rather than denial, with eyes closed. . . ."

At present, Anthony Storey lives quietly in a small village a few miles from Bury Saint Edmunds, Beyton, where he has bought two adjacent houses and made them into a single large dwelling for himself and his wife. His parents, now in their eighties, may eventually occupy a part of the house that retains a separate kitchen. Storey now teaches in only two terms at Cambridge, from October to April and thus has the rest of the year to spend entirely on his writing. Apart from reworking the novels that his trilogy on the Second Coming comprises, he has drafted another "platinum" novel and plans to work on various film scripts, television plays, and a new novel. His ambition is to present the characters and substance of his trilogy in a variety of media, for only in that way, he believes, will they have a chance to become a living reality in the popular imagination. But this ambition is not of the utmost importance, and his creative energies are by no means exhausted. Meanwhile, he remains patient, awaiting his true audience.

Of his own work in fiction Storey has said: "My writing—by-pass surgery to the novel—is often though not always compulsively real for readers without literary pretensions. To the extent that this proves to be so, they are good. Each of them, despite the profanities—in all senses of that word—is loving and potentially spiritually-releasing as well as liberating of the imagination." Although establishment critics will demur and seize upon a perceived anti-intellectualism, it is a fair comment, as eventually more readers are bound to recognize.

David Storey
(13 July 1933-   )

Dennis Jackson
University of Delaware

See also the Storey entry in *DLB 13, British Dramatists Since World War II*.

BOOKS: *This Sporting Life* (London: Longmans, Green, 1960; New York: Macmillan, 1960);
Flight into Camden (London: Longmans, Green, 1960; New York: Macmillan, 1961);
Radcliffe (London: Longmans, Green, 1963; New York: Coward-McCann, 1964);
The Restoration of Arnold Middleton (London: Cape, 1967; New York: French, 1968);
In Celebration (London: Cape, 1969; New York: Grove, 1975);
The Contractor (London: Cape, 1970; New York: Random House, 1970);
Home (London: Cape, 1970; New York: Random House, 1971);
The Changing Room (London: Cape, 1972; New York: Random House, 1972);
Pasmore (London: Longman, 1972; New York: Dutton, 1974);
Cromwell (London: Cape, 1973);
The Farm (London: Cape, 1973; London & New York: French, 1974);
Edward, text by Storey, drawings by Donald Parker (London: Allen Lane, 1973);

A Temporary Life (London: Allen Lane, 1973; New York: Dutton, 1974);

Life Class (London: Cape, 1975);

Saville (London: Cape, 1976; New York: Harper & Row, 1976);

Mother's Day (Harmondsworth, U.K.: Penguin, 1978);

Early Days (Harmondsworth, U.K.: Penguin, 1980);

Sisters (Harmondsworth, U.K.: Penguin, 1980);

A Prodigal Child (London: Cape, 1982).

Few contemporary British authors have had as much success writing in two genres as David Storey in fiction and drama. His first novel, *This Sporting Life* (1960), brought him the Macmillan Fiction Award, and his sixth novel, *Saville* (1976), elicited Britain's most prestigious literary award, the Booker Prize for Fiction. He has twice won the *Evening Standard* Drama Award for best play of the year in London, and he is the only playwright ever to have won the New York Drama Critics' Circle Award three times. He has been a prolific writer. During the first two decades of his career, he had seven novels and eleven plays published (over a dozen plays were produced on British stages), and all of his books are still in print, often in popular Penguin and Avon paperback editions.

His novels, usually written in a terse and understated prose, are conventional realistic works in the tradition of the English social novels. All of them treat one or both of these themes: (a) the painful and sometimes insoluble conflict between working-class parents and their educated children; (b) the suffering or psychic disintegration of protagonists (all of them isolated, moody, self-tortured) who cannot balance their inner/spiritual lives with their outer/physical lives, and their attempts to achieve "wholeness," to gain some sort of intellectual or emotional control. All of the novels draw somehow on Storey's experiences, during his youth and early manhood, as a professional rugby player, farm worker, erector of showground tents, artist, and schoolteacher, and all of them graphically chronicle the lives of the "north country" people who live amid the smoke-and-steam-belching factories, mills, and collieries of gray industrial towns in Yorkshire, where he grew up. The major passage in the author's life came when he moved away from these people of the West Riding, and their value system, to join the educated class in London. The effects of his social, geographical, and intellectual uprooting are everywhere dramatized in his writing.

David Malcolm Storey was born in the indus-

David Storey

trial city of Wakefield on 13 July 1933, the third of four sons of Frank Richmond Storey, a Yorkshire coal miner, and Lily Cartwright Storey. In *Saville* and in his 1969 play *In Celebration* the author makes artistic use of the fact that the oldest brother died in childhood, causing his parents much anguish. The second son, Anthony, was himself to become a well-known novelist and screenwriter. The family lived in a housing estate near the Roundwood Colliery where the father worked. David attended Queen Elizabeth Grammar School on a scholarship, and it was there that he first developed an interest in writing and painting. This interest created the first major crisis of his life. As he was to argue in a 1963 BBC broadcast talk giving his views on the genesis of his writing career, the world of the West Riding was "an acutely physical one, a world of machines and labour and commerce, and one in which the artist . . . was not merely an outsider but a hindrance and a nuisance." In fact, in the puritanical working-class community where he lived, *physical* work was considered "good, and mental work . . . evil." Consequently, acting purely from his sense of "guilt" over his love for "interior" things, for painting and writing, he played rugby union and became a forward on his school team. His hard-working father had been fiercely determined that his sons would, through the passport of education, escape going "down pit," and would become middle-class professional men. But the more David learned, and especially the more he pursued his love for art, the more his father came to fear and resent what his talented son was becoming. The young artist became increasingly estranged from his father and laden with guilt that he was not somehow living up to expectations—and the shadow of that guilt is cast long over Storey's novels, reflected everywhere in the relationships of working-class fathers and their educated offspring.

In 1951 Storey enrolled at the local Wakefield School of Art, where he attended classes until 1953. During his second year there, when he was eighteen, he signed a fourteen-year contract with the professional Leeds Rugby League Club, hoping to use the money to help support his family and to lessen his continuing depression over the fact that his father was daily bent over in the pits while he himself sat around painting pictures. Shortly after signing with Leeds, he received a scholarship to the Slade School of Fine Art in London, and for the next three years he studied art during the week and traveled back to the northern counties for each Saturday's rugby matches. At the Slade, he blossomed as an artist: his works won prizes and were included in a number of London exhibitions before he received his diploma in 1956. He has continued to paint and has frequently designed dust jackets for his novels.

It was during this period in the mid-1950s that Storey began writing what was to become his first published novel, *This Sporting Life*, which was substantially completed by the time he left the Slade. His creation of this tale about a brawny but sensitive rugby league hero was (as he acknowledged in his later BBC talk) an "act of despair," an attempt to make sense of his own schizophrenic condition during those unhappy "nightmare" years when in both the worlds of art and athletics he found himself an outsider. His Leeds teammates, all young miners and mill workers, were somewhat wary of the introverted, long-haired youth who spent his week painting pictures in London, and his fellow Slade students, thinking him a moody provincial, similarly kept him at a distance.

The weekly 200-mile train trip across England eventually took on for Storey a metaphorical reality: "those four hours of blackness were a journey across my brain," he later recalled. In his increasing despair, he came to think of Leeds and London as be-

ing representative of the two poles of his own temperament: its *northern*/outer/physical/extroverted/masculine aspects and its *southern*/inner/spiritual/self-absorbed/feminine aspects. And, in an effort to reconcile these warring elements of his own psyche, he began writing *This Sporting Life*, first scribbling rough notes during his London-to-Yorkshire train rides. In creating his rugged protagonist, Arthur Machin, Storey was trying to isolate and come to terms with the "physical" side of his own temperament, which had confused and frightened him throughout his youth. Machin by his own description is a "super ape," a big, powerful battering ram of a man who thrives on tearing other rugby leaguers "into postage stamps." He is estranged from his parents, is at odds with his own working class as well as with the industrialists who own his Primstone team, and has no stable relationships with even his own teammates. He is vain, he constantly strives to dominate others, and he frequently discards acquaintances who have become "withered limbs" of his ambition. And yet, he is by no means simply a truculent, destructive brute. As his perceptive first-person narration of the story reflects, he has a decided capacity for self-analysis and sensitive thought, and on a number of occasions he is shown to have deep and generous feelings for others (feelings which he often tragically cannot articulate). What emerges from this book is a fascinating image of a man struggling courageously—but futilely—to find *wholeness* in his life, to balance the two sharply contradictory sides of his nature.

The novel opens with an account of rugby league action during which Machin has six teeth smashed out (as David's brother, Anthony, actually had experienced as a professional rugby player). Shortly thereafter, while under ether, he drifts back in memory several years to the beginning of his rugby career and to the start of his relationship with his landlady, a dowdy "not-too-young" widow named Valerie Hammond. The first five chapters deftly shuffle the reader back and forth between such flashbacks and several present-tense scenes depicting Machin's attendance at the dentist and at a rowdy Christmas party at the home of the team's owner. Later chapters detail in a straightforward present-tense narrative his developing affair with Mrs. Hammond, his movement through the sleazy world of professional sports, and his response to the depressing environment of the sooty industrial town where he lives.

Machin had first been drawn to rugby league while working as a lathe operator in a factory, when he had perceived the sport as his only chance to escape the oppressive lot of the ordinary working man. Once he has gained the status of a local hero, he can strut through town, the proud gladiator, relishing the fact that "Machin's a name that means something" to the local people. But his exterior successes do not satisfy the lonely and reflective man's longing for roots, for some deeper meaning in his life, and his consequent torment is Storey's central concern in this novel.

On one occasion, when his boss's wife invites him to enjoy a casual affair with her, he refuses, because, as one of his teammates mockingly observes, he "believes in falling in love." As a sports celebrity, he has such "samples" available at every turn, but he remains faithful to the pitiful, washed-out widow with whom he boards on Fairfax Street. It seems incredible that this homely, embittered, withdrawn widow, so fearful of life and so unappeasably a figure of suffering and defeat (she still keeps her husband's boots polished by the hearth) could come to have such a compelling grip on Machin, but he becomes obsessed with playing Pygmalion to her Galatea, with having "the real Mrs. Hammond . . . come popping out." He also finds a rather perverse challenge in the woman's willful indifference to his being a hero and in her refusal to express gratitude for his kindnesses. He buys her a television and a fur coat and takes her family for long Sunday rides in the countryside, but she offers no response. She has her own good reasons for not committing herself to him emotionally. She fears that he wants only to see her give in, to hear her admit her need of him, before abandoning her. His cockiness and "big swash actions" repel her; his brute force often overwhelms her.

And yet despite the perverse and egotistical nature of his initial attraction to the noncommittal widow, and despite his continued "ape-like" behavior around her, Machin gradually comes to feel real love and an earnest need for Mrs. Hammond. In one of the novel's key passages, which offers a revealing window into Machin's deepest feelings, he acknowledges his awareness that he is not "going to be a footballer for ever," and expresses his longing "to have something there for good," a meaningful and permanent connection with Mrs. Hammond. He needs her, he says, "to make me feel whole and wanted." She is willing to give him sexual satisfaction, but he would have her express "some feeling for me" as well. But she never realizes (as does the reader) that Machin could indeed be the answer to her psychic needs and a real source of warmth and security for her and her children. Because of her

temperament and his own inarticulateness, she and Arthur fail, finally, to make the needed affective connection. She eventually throws him out of the Fairfax Street house, and she goes into a decline and dies soon after, with a grief-stricken Machin by her hospital bed.

The final chapter of *This Sporting Life* makes no mention whatever of the love affair. It is the straightforward description of a rugby match. Storey thus meaningfully sandwiches the account of Machin's futile love affair between two slices of brutal rugby action. The narrative returns full circle, but Machin himself can make no return to the prospects he had held years earlier as a rookie rugby star. He is left, finally, with nothing more than his loneliness, the ever-dwindling joys of physical contact on the ice-hard pitch, and his growing fears that with his coming retirement, he will slip back into the obscurity of the life of a factory worker.

In style *This Sporting Life* seems extraordinarily mature and polished as a work of a beginning novelist. The prose—taut, unadorned, directly matter-of-fact—seems particularly well-matched to the narrator's personality, and what pathos exists in the novel (particularly that in the climactic hospital scenes) is effectively filtered through Machin's customary understated manner. The author's realistic descriptions of working-class life and his precise rendering of his Yorkshire characters' dialect are particularly impressive, and so are his graphic portrayals of the industrial landscape of the dreary provincial town, its sky seemingly forever flushed with a hellish crimson-and-orange glare from the local collieries' coke ovens. Here, as in all of his later writings, Storey displays an acute sense of visual imagery—something no doubt engendered during his apprenticeship as a painter—and a sharp eye for the feature and detail of his setting.

Perhaps most impressive of all passages in *This Sporting Life* are the young author's vibrant descriptions of rugby, of the bone-crushing, savage, close-quarters battle. Storey shows that he can write superbly of action. Such violence as that which recurs both on and off the rugby pitch throughout this first novel was to be a feature in virtually all of his later fiction, especially *Radcliffe* (1963) and *A Temporary Life* (1973). The reader of *This Sporting Life* is also given remarkable firsthand sensual impressions of the game—the sounds of the whistles, trumpets, and "animal roars" which greet every success of the home team; the smells of sweat, sewage mud, carbolic, liniment, and leather that permeate every changing room; and the visions of players limbering up freshly before competition and of their slumping wearily into blood-and-mud covered baths afterward (anticipating similar scenes to be dramatized in Storey's 1971 play, *The Changing Room*).

Storey had grown weary of rugby by 1956, and with the encouragement of his new wife, a language teacher named Barbara Rudd Hamilton, he arranged a release from his Leeds city team contract. From 1957 until 1960 he worked as a substitute teacher in the tough schools of London's East End and found it a wretched experience. Dozens of the afflicted young people in his novels and plays are teachers or former teachers, and virtually all of them are made to voice their creator's disillusionment about the profession. The title character in *Saville*, for example, teaches in a Yorkshire secondary school, and says his job is "like being in a prison." A number of Storey's characters who are teachers—such as Howarth in *Flight Into Camden* (1960), Colin in *Pasmore* (1972), and Yvonne Freestone in *A Temporary Life*—are on or beyond the verge of mental breakdowns. Teaching drove Storey into a severe depression, and in 1959, when he began writing his first play, *The Restoration of Arnold Middleton* (then titled "To Die With the Philistines"), his subject was a schoolmaster who cracks up. Storey was at the time discouraged because *This Sporting Life* had been rejected by numerous publishers, and he had begun to doubt that he would ever succeed as a novelist. So he tried his hand at drama, taking off from teaching for a few days during half term to write the play.

Arnold Middleton is a history teacher in his thirties, and he is going mad. It is only very slowly and often through a subtle method of indirection that the playwright makes it apparent why his hero is cracking up. For one thing, he is, like so many of Storey's characters, spiritually impoverished. He longs for a better world of better men, and complains that the "greatest threat to the present century" is the pygmylike condition of modern man's soul. He has himself studied "kingship" and admires adventurers like Robin Hood, but his own life is one of boring school work done amid cringing, mediocre fellow teachers. He suffers also from pressures brought on him by the females in his life, by his jealous and demanding wife, by the unnatural demands brought on him by his sensual mother-in-law, and by the memory of a working-class mother whose expectations he had not met. In a revelatory window to the play's meaning, Middleton stands before a wall and in a rambling verse monologue recalls his mother's admonition, delivered years before: "Please, please my son. / Don't

fail me like your father done." But he *had* somehow failed her, and his guilt over things not done for his mother in his youth contributes to his madness. In the play's original version, Middleton kills himself at the end, but in the 1964 revision produced in 1967 in London, Storey allows his hero hope of a restoration to normality, once he has experienced the "insights that irrationality brings."

Arnold Middleton's madness anticipates the psychic disintegration of dozens of Storey's future characters, in all of his later novels and in a large number of his plays (especially in *Home*, 1970, which is set in a mental institution; *Life Class*, 1974, which describes the collapse of an art instructor named Allott whose mind and marriage are crumbling; and *Mother's Day*, 1978, in which the entire cast are raving lunatics). Storey's literary world is peopled with comic crazies who talk at cross purposes, who collect bottles of their own urine, who go down on all fours and bark like dogs, and, much more frequently, with darkly tragic madmen who withdraw into lonely fantasy worlds. Of these many mad characters, Arnold Middleton is one of a very few who ever manages to retrieve any fragile sort of mental balance.

Shortly after finishing "To Die with the Philistines," Storey got the news that *This Sporting Life*, which eight British publishers had rejected, would be published in the United States by Macmillan and in England by Longmans, Green. The novel was published early in 1960 to considerable acclaim. The young author was immediately hailed by and associated with the "angry young men," and critic Brian Glanville in *London Magazine* called Storey "a gifted, serious and unusual" novelist who "seems potentially a more important writer than either Braine or Amis." With the receipt of the $7,500 bounty that accompanied the Macmillan Fiction Award, which he received for *This Sporting Life*, Storey was able to quit his teaching job in 1960 and began devoting his full time to writing.

In the flush of enthusiasm over the acceptance of *This Sporting Life*, he sat down and wrote another novel, *Flight Into Camden*, in eighteen days. It was published in fall 1960. Like *This Sporting Life*, it traces the course of a doomed romance between two working-class lovers who seem as ill-matched in their own fashion as Machin and Mrs. Hammond in the earlier novel. After dealing in *This Sporting Life* with what he identified as the northern/physical/masculine aspect of his temperament, he turned in *Flight Into Camden* to explore "its southern counterpart—the intuitive, poetic" London world which in his BBC talk he associated with "femininity, with a woman's sensibility and responses." In *Flight Into Camden*, the heroine and first-person narrator, Margaret Thorpe, makes the same "flight" from Yorkshire to London that the author himself had made a few years earlier. Her flight into Camden is made with her lover, an art teacher named Gordon Howarth, who has left behind in the provincial town his wife and two children. *Flight Into Camden* chronicles the struggle of these two lovers to find happiness in their relationship while undergoing severe pressures from their respective families to end their illicit union.

Before going to London Margaret had lived a life of dreary routine divided between her work as a Coal Board secretary (she had attended secretarial college) and her home, where she had been an emotional pawn of her hectoring older brother and her loving but nonetheless oppressive parents. But after her initial joy over the freedom of London, she becomes disenchanted with Howarth, who has drifted aimlessly and unhappily back into teaching, and their union is further undermined by mounting pressures which their families back in the north country bring to bear on them, Howarth's wife begging by correspondence for his return and Margaret's father and brother visiting Camden to seek her return to the family fold.

The parasitic union of the two weak central characters in this novel never commands the reader's attention the way Machin's obsessive passion for Mrs. Hammond does in *This Sporting Life*. Margaret Thorpe's psychic development in the story, her progress away from her family's conventional puritan moral vision and toward a more liberated emotional state where she can fully show her feelings for her lover, is developed by Storey in plausible enough fashion. But the reader of *Flight Into Camden* faces difficulties in trying to determine why Margaret ever develops any such feelings for the indecisive, dishonest, self-pitying, neurotic, cynical, and unrelentingly morose Howarth in the first place. Margaret herself recognizes that he is a moral coward, that he "had only a vast emptiness to turn to." And yet, the reader is meant not to question her compelling passion for this hollow and characterless man, nor to doubt her sincerity when she observes: "I missed Howarth more than I could bear. I was incomplete and lifeless without him." Even less convincingly motivated is the climactic letter which brings an end to their affair. In it Howarth both avows his deep unending passion and tells her he is sending her luggage and plans never to see her again. It is all very confusing, and the reader is left to puzzle over the man's ambiguous reasoning for breaking off the romance and to decipher why Margaret bathes herself in tears upon receipt of this letter from her spineless lover.

Much more interesting is her response to her family, both before and after she takes flight into Camden. As he often does in his writing, Storey sensitively demonstrates in this novel the complexity of familial relationships and captures well the fine shades of emotions among the Thorpes during their tense and dramatic confrontations. Margaret's mother and father—decent, religious, working-class folk, full of good intentions and homely maxims and well-meant aspirations for the success of their children—resemble closely the north-country parents of the central figures in *Pasmore*, *Saville*, *In Celebration*, and the 1973 play *The Farm*. Invariably the fathers of these families have labored for years (usually down pit) to give their children an education, thinking that would mean for them a passage to a better life. But in every case, the dream has disappointing results, for both generations—the children, in moving beyond their working-class origins, seldom find happiness in their new situa-

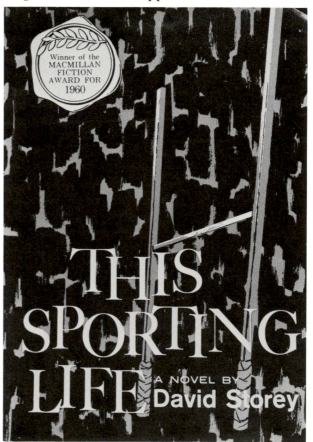

Dust jacket for the American edition of Storey's autobiographical first novel, written as an "act of despair" to reconcile the author's dual careers in art and athletics

tions, and the older generations are often crushed by the discovery that education has led their children to compromise or wholly abandon the social and moral values of the parents. From these roots grow the inevitable—and often insoluble—domestic conflicts that are at the heart of much of Storey's writing. Margaret Thorpe's frustrated father condemns his children's "great educated emptiness" and expresses resentment over their ungrateful attitude toward his sacrifice in the mines. Like most parents in Storey's works, he is an emotional vampire who feeds on whatever love and gratitude he can get from his children. Bound by his narrow, old-fashioned moral code and a faith in family, Mr. Thorpe inevitably disapproves of his daughter's adulterous affair and of Howarth's desertion of his wife and children. The relationship between Margaret and her father—the complete web of love and hatred and gratitude and guilt spun between them—is the most fascinating aspect of *Flight Into Camden*, and their tortured head-on encounters over her "carrying on" with Howarth form the novel's finest scenes. Howarth at one point observes that families can be parasitic and destructive, "like vicious animals, radiant with solicitude, and affection until you touch them," and that they "rear up like crazy beasts." This observation he directs squarely at the Thorpes, whom he justifiably sees as his enemies, and, while it is an exaggerated view, it does contain kernels of truth. The Thorpes do indeed "rear up" when their family circle is disrupted, and—though they mean no malice toward Margaret—they use all means available to them to get her back. She is affected less by her father's rages and occasional outbursts of violence than by the other, subtler means of emotional blackmail—expressions of love, tears, agonized looks, timely illnesses—which both her parents use to coerce her away from Howarth and back to their Yorkshire home.

Through the influence of her older brother, Michael, a university lecturer and an "intellectual gangster," Margaret had developed a contempt for "domesticity and the fatefulness of motherhood," but the novel's final tableau—which depicts her sunbathing on her brother's Yorkshire lawn while her domestic and pregnant sister-in-law beckons her to tea, a visiting clergyman expresses approval of Howarth's return to his wife, and brother Michael drones on in his overbearing way—suggests that Margaret's own destiny will involve just such a domestic somnolence as that which Michael, in contradiction to his own "theories," has settled into with his "little mother." Such a life for

their daughter would certainly please the Thorpes. The question left at the end of *Flight Into Camden* is whether such a life would ever please Margaret.

Flight Into Camden lacks the force and the compelling drama that *This Sporting Life* had contained. The plot of the second novel is slow to develop, and the pace is frequently dull and pedestrian. Storey has no special problems with his use of a woman as his first-person narrator, but his novel does suffer because that woman is mousy, gray, and unremittingly intense and dolorous as she narrates her tale. Margaret simply lacks the diversity of mood and sense of humor that would be likely to engage a reader's interest for very long, and this may in part account for the fact that *Flight Into Camden* was the only one of Storey's first six novels which was out of print two decades after his career began, and the only one which never was reprinted in an Avon paperback edition. Though *Flight Into Camden* created less of a general stir with critics and reviewers than had *This Sporting Life*, it did draw reviewers' praise for the young novelist's potential, and it won for him two notable literary awards, the John Llewelyn Rhys Memorial Prize for 1961 and the Somerset Maugham Award for 1963.

Storey felt that reviewers had generally missed the point about the physical/spiritual dichotomy in his characters' lives in the first two novels, so when he came to writing *Radcliffe* in 1961 and 1962, he was in a "state of irritation" and was determined not to let his audience misread the new story. Toward that end, he steps frequently into that narrative to explain certain matters (something which he rarely does in other novels), and he has his characters talk—endlessly—about the theme of the divided self. He even has one provide what amounts to a gloss for the entire novel: "But just think what if this separate [spirit] were in one man, and the body, the acting part in another? What if these two qualities were typified ideally in two separate men? Then, just imagine . . . the unholy encounter of two such people!" Storey himself imagines just such an encounter through the whole of *Radcliffe*: the central action of the story is the failure, ending in murder, of a tortured, violently passionate homosexual love between two men, one who is made to represent the soul, and the other the body of man. As in the earlier novels, Storey sought in *Radcliffe* to dramatize the powers that stormed in his own being by making one of his protagonists, Victor Tolson, a muscular working-class lad, and the other, Leonard Radcliffe, an intensely self-absorbed artistic intellectual. "Vic was my body, and I was his soul," Radcliffe explains to his father. "It's the division that separates everything in life now." The reader is thus asked to view the relationship between the two men as symbolic of the deep rift that the social and religious traditions of Western society have wrought in man's nature.

Leonard Radcliffe is the effete last of the line in a decayed aristocratic family and lives in a crumbling Yorkshire manor house where his father acts as a caretaker. He first meets Tolson when the lower-class lad rescues him from tormenting schoolmates. Even as a child the brawny, slow-witted Tolson is given to outbursts of sadistic violence, which seem his only means of self-expression, and Leonard often becomes his victim. But Radcliffe comes to depend on Tolson's vigorous physical presence, and, when they are separated for several years, it seems as if he is "physically disintegrating." Only after they are reunited after eight years, when they join a tent contractor's crew, does Leonard once again feel alive, and then his physical dependence on Tolson intensifies when they begin a homosexual love affair among the tents at a work site. Radcliffe mistakenly assumes that their union also implies an emotional commitment, but Tolson soon demonstrates total disregard for his feelings when he has intercourse with a local tart while Leonard lies sobbing in a nearby tent. Tolson thereafter alternately courts and abuses Leonard, wooing him gently on one occasion and on another viciously smashing him with a hammer, and their relationship continues on such a par until Tolson brutally rapes the weaker man, pushing him over the edge of sanity and prompting him to murder. The death scene itself is a gruesome slow-motion nightmare, with Leonard raining a crescendo of bloody hammer blows on Tolson's head, and this Jacobean fifth act is carried further into the realm of horror, as another character (a broken-down stage comedian named Denis Blakely, who had also been one of Tolson's lover-victims) cuts the throats of his children and then commits suicide. Leonard is subsequently incarcerated in a mental home, where he dies of a brain hemorrhage. After these deaths, the novel concludes with the birth of a boy to Leonard's sister Elizabeth, who had herself been raped by Tolson. This child, with its dark and enigmatic "Radcliffe eyes" and the "energetic movement" of Tolson's body, represents a reconciliation of spirit and flesh that had evaded the story's two protagonists during their own lives. But it is difficult to say, exactly, what this strange reconciliation means, and to determine what, if any, metaphysical implications are to be gleaned from this complicated and horrible tale of sexual perversity and violence. For

one thing, Storey's meaning seems too often to become entangled in the swirling poetic symbolism and the melodramatic turbulence of his narrative. There is a general murkiness all through the telling of the tale, a perpetually baffling effort by the narrator to stretch his story into allegory. For instance, the battle between the two homosexual protagonists is to be viewed, as Leonard tells the court, as symbolic of the calamitous body/spirit "split in the whole of Western society." The decaying Radcliffe mansion is further suggested as a symbol of aristocratic old England gone to rack and ruin, a symbol of historic culture and intellectualism as it is threatened by mass society, by the physicality of the workers in the housing estate which threatens to consume it. The faint tom-toms of "significance," the hints that this tale is somehow about the decline of the Western world, sound forever in the edges of Storey's narrative, but the reader is never quite given sufficient coordinates by which he can locate this weighty theme in terms of the actual events of the novel.

In an effort to describe *Radcliffe*, many reviewers mentioned comparable works by Emily Bronte, Dostoevski, and D. H. Lawrence, and Storey's tale does indeed often seem an amalgam of the best and worst elements of those novelists' works. Like *Wuthering Heights* (1847) it chronicles the tumultuous passions of larger-than-life characters, and paints as evocative a portrait of modern Yorkshire as Bronte did with the same terrain in her day. Storey's novel has even more in common with the fictional world of Dostoevski. Radcliffe easily brings to mind Dostoevski's Raskolnikov as he goes feverishly about town fingering the hammer in his raincoat, and his subsequent murder of Tolson is not unlike the ax murder of the old moneylender in *Crime and Punishment* (1866). Dostoevski's hero is evoked again when Leonard confesses and asks the authorities to look on his deed "as if it were the simple illustration of an elaborate theory" (his theory of the "split" in Western man's consciousness). The characters in *Radcliffe* are, like those in many of Dostoevski's books, largely an assemblage of perverse and unpredictable grotesques, and Storey's focus on their bizarre acts of sadism and masochism, of rape, murder, incest, and the like, brings to mind the Russian's own concentration on the base passions of his morally diseased characters. Few streaks of sunshine cross the pages of either writer.

It was inevitable that Storey would be compared to D. H. Lawrence, if for no other reason than the striking correspondence in their lives: each was the son of a north England coal miner; each won grammar school scholarships that helped remove them from their working-class backgrounds; each subsequently suffered through unhappy periods as teachers in London secondary schools; and each took up painting before deciding on a career as a writer. There are important resemblances also in the content of their works and—at least in regard to *Radcliffe*—in their prose styles. Storey's preoccupation with the duality in man's consciousness, with the problem of sexual relationships, with the relations of parents and children, and with the conflict of British social classes are all major thematic concerns throughout Lawrence's writings, too. Also, Storey's tale of an artistic young man's struggle for release from stifling family ties in his seemingly autobiographical novel *Saville* seems remarkably similar to Lawrence's own autobiographical story *Sons and Lovers* (1913). *Radcliffe*, moreso than the other Storey novels, shows Lawrence's influence, especially in its poetic symbolism and its treatment of the sexual obsession of its characters. There are occasional direct echoes of Lawrence, as when Radcliffe complains about Christ's failure to "use his sex" (a complaint Lawrence dramatizes in *The Escaped Cock*). In particular Storey's writing in *Radcliffe* resembles Lawrence's in his use of phallic symbols, in the way he invests ordinary activities (for instance, the riding of a motorbike) with erotic significance, and in his creation of an emotion-filled landscape which so often mirrors his characters' psychic condition.

With its florid romanticism and poetic symbolism and its overheated prose, *Radcliffe* seemed a radical departure from the simplicity and the vigorous realism of *This Sporting Life* and *Flight Into Camden*, and it created a great controversy among critics when it appeared in 1963. One reviewer called it "worthless trash" and another "one of the sweatiest and most ludicrously symbolified novels in years." To the other extreme, Malcolm Bradbury said it was "full of excellencies" and Jeremy Brooks declared that *Radcliffe* "establishes David Storey as the leading novelist of his generation." The consensus among reviewers, however, fell somewhere between these two positions, and John Mellors's observation that *Radcliffe* was a "clumsy, blundering, groping, and yet oddly impressive book" typified the novel's critical reception.

During the early 1960s, after he had quit teaching school, and during the time he was working on *Radcliffe*, Storey supported his family partly by writing nonfiction articles (art reviews, pieces on education, film, socialism) for British periodicals such as *New Statesman*, the *Guardian*, the *Listener*, and *Twentieth Century* and by working on various television and film projects. In 1963 he worked as a director for two BBC television productions, *Portrait of Margaret Evans* and *Death of My Mother*, a documentary on D. H. Lawrence. In the early 1960s he was also asked by film director Lindsay Anderson to convert *This Sporting Life* into a screenplay. The film, produced in 1963, starred Richard Harris and Rachel Roberts, and at the Cannes Film Festival that year it was awarded the International Film Critics' Prize. It has since come to be regarded generally as a classic of modern cinema. Anderson's and Storey's extraordinarily fruitful artistic collaboration on the film was to be extended, eventually, to the British stage, and Anderson directed over half of Storey's plays produced between 1967 and 1980.

After writing the screenplay, Storey was encouraged by Anderson to try his hand again at drama, and he dusted off and extensively revised "To Die With the Philistines," which had elicited only lukewarm responses from theater people to whom he had shown it in 1959. The Royal Court Theatre in Sloane Square, where Anderson was one of the directors of the English Stage Company, agreed in 1964 to produce the play, but it was shelved year after year until a friend of Storey's produced it at the Traverse Theatre Club in Edinburgh in November 1966, under its new title, *The Restoration of Arnold Middleton*. Eight months later, the play appeared at the Royal Court. This nationally subsidized theater, since the mid-1950s a seedbed for some of the best offerings of the British theater, was to produce eight more of Storey's plays in the following decade. After twenty-two performances, the highly praised play was transferred to the Criterion Theatre in the West End, and the *Evening Standard* shortly thereafter named Storey the "Most Promising Playwright" for 1967.

Buoyed by the success of *The Restoration of Arnold Middleton*, Storey began devoting new attention to writing plays, and several of them just "popped out" (as he later put it) in a remarkably short span of several months. By 1970, he had written a half-dozen plays, which were all subsequently produced. Within weeks after the July 1967 Royal Court premiere of *The Restoration of Arnold Middleton*, he had written *The Contractor*, a plotless slice-of-life view of a group of workmen erecting and dismantling a large wedding tent on a lawn. He returned to a novel he had been writing, but remained fascinated by the image of a white metalwork table which he had left setting on an almost bare stage near the end of *The Contractor*, and two or three weeks after he had finished that play, he began another, which he called *Home*, creating four characters who drift casually onstage to sit and talk at that table—only this time he placed it on the grounds of a mental asylum. His characters are inmates there, and *Home* depicts an uneventful afternoon in their bleak lives, when they try futilely to lift their hopeless depressions through communication with others round the table. At almost the same time, in late 1967, Storey spent several mornings laboring on a fourth play, *In Celebration*.

It was to become the second of his plays to be produced. It premiered at the Royal Court in April 1969, with Alan Bates playing one of the lead roles, Andrew Shaw, one of the three sons who have returned to the Yorkshire mining town of their birth "in celebration" of their parents' fortieth wedding anniversary. This play, like *The Restoration of Arnold Middleton*, won immediate favor with London theatergoers. Six months later, *The Contractor* opened at the Royal Court and was even more warmly received. It was transferred the next April to a West End theater, and subsequently elicited for Storey the London Theatre Critics Award for 1970.

In June 1970 *Home* became the third Storey play to open at the Royal Court in a little over a year. Before the end of that year, the play—with the illustrious British actors John Gielgud and Ralph Richardson starring—had been transferred to West End and Broadway theaters, and it won both the 1970 *Evening Standard* Drama Award and the 1971 New York Drama Critics' Circle Award (a prize he was to claim again in 1973 with *The Changing Room* and in 1974 with *The Contractor*). And his success as a playwright was not to wane with the production of his fifth play, *The Changing Room*, in November 1971. This drama, a documentary-style slice of sporting life, recording a Saturday afternoon in the locker room of a rugby league team in northern England, again won recognition as best play of the season in both London and New York.

For almost three years, 1972 through 1974, Storey did a stint as associate artistic director of the Royal Court, and within a nine-month period (August 1973 to April 1974) three more of his plays—*Cromwell*, *The Farm*, and *Life Class*—had their debut at the theater. But none of them received anything like the critical acclaim which *The Contractor*, *Home*, and *The Changing Room* had elicited. *Cromwell*, which focuses on a small group of people who struggle to survive in a war-torn land, had been written in a five-day stretch around New Year's Day 1969, at a time when the fighting in Vietnam and the troubles in Northern Ireland were at a peak, and Storey had

hoped to make with his play some sort of philosophic statement about the war. But he had tried to impose intellectual and spiritual issues on the drama which do not seem to fit the action itself, and, as he later admitted, he had made a "bloody awful job" of *Cromwell*. The critics agreed with that assessment.

Storey's plays produced later in the 1970s found even fewer supporters, even among those who had previously sung his praises. *Night* and *Mother's Day* were staged in 1976. The latter is a wild farce about a middle-class English family, the Johnsons, who spend their days and nights in a remarkable merry-go-round of rape, adultery, incest, group sex, Oedipal longings, parricide, greed, and extortion. It is as if the author has taken the farrago of madness, grotesquerie, murderous hatred, and sexual perversion in *Radcliffe* and given it a wildly exaggerated comic spin. *Mother's Day* received virtually unanimous condemnation when it appeared at the Royal Court in September 1976. Michael Billington, customarily an admirer of Storey's drama, opened his *Guardian* column by declaring, "*Mother's Day* is a stinker . . . a calculated exercise in bad-taste comedy . . . vulgar without being funny." Storey was stung by such disastrous notices, and, when he ran across a group of London theater critics in the bar at the Royal Court the night after his play's debut, he gave them a severe tonguelashing and also began to rain blows upon Billington's head. Such violence notwithstanding, critics gave no warmer a greeting to his next play, *Sisters*, another farce about sexual activities on a British housing estate, when it opened in 1978 at the Royal Exchange Theatre in Manchester. *Early Days*, which the Cottesloe Theatre produced in 1980, was clearly superior to the farces, and was in fact probably the best Storey drama introduced since *The Changing Room* in 1971, but the play itself was largely overshadowed by the critical raves given the magisterial presence of Ralph Richardson in the lead role (Storey had created the play in the early 1970s as a vehicle for the redoubtable British actor). The play is an imaginative character study of a retired politician named Sir Richard Kitchen, who sits in his garden rehearsing the events of his life, the days of his political power, his marriage, and his haunting memory of a childhood trip to the seaside. Michael Billington—either having forgiven Storey for the earlier pummeling in the Royal Court bar or perhaps fearing a reprise of that performance— praised *Early Days*, comparing it to the best qualities of a Wordsworthian lyrical ballad.

Most of Storey's plays rework themes, characters, or situations dealt with in more complex (and usually more somber) fashion in his novels. A good many of them have been direct by-products of the fiction, or vice versa. In 1964, Storey revised *The Restoration of Arnold Middleton* and then turned to material that would be published ultimately as *Pasmore*. The title characters of the two works are obviously cut from the same cloth, both being schoolteachers suffering psychic collapses because of marital dilemmas and unresolved problems related to their upbringing and parents. Of all Storey's plays, *In Celebration* seems the most important in relation to his fiction because it deals directly with important themes common to most of his novels. When Storey got a writer's block while working on *Saville* in 1967, he put it aside in despair, and, using similar material and transposing characters from the novel, he wrote *In Celebration*. *Saville* recounts the childhood experiences of the eldest of three sons of a north-country miner who labors desperately to give his children a better life. *In Celebration* takes virtually the same family and describes an incident many years later, when the three brothers (now in their thirties) return to their old Yorkshire home overnight to observe their parents' fortieth wedding anniversary. All three have become externally successful: Andrew has become a solicitor; Colin, a labor relations expert; Steven, a university teacher. But according to Andrew, he and his brothers are really "wash-outs," men who have lived lives "measured out in motor-cars." Their move into the middle class has meant for them only spiritual impoverishment and alienation from their work and from themselves. And he claims that this psychological and emotional crippling had been set in motion years earlier by their parents' "philistine, parasitic, opportunistic" values and by the "vision of a better life" held perpetually before them by their parents. Steven, the youngest, complains that while their father has found his own work in the mines "significant," the professional work he has educated them for is "nothing . . . at the best a pastime, at the worst a sort of soulless stirring of the pot." *In Celebration* in effect dramatizes the *result* of what the parents are shown doing to their three sons in *Saville*, and Steven Shaw's observation that he and his brothers had suffered "disfigurement" at the "wholly innocent hands" of their parents states the theme not only of the play but of the novel as well.

The Farm similarly focuses on a family reunion which erupts into bitterness and recriminations, this time between a crusty Yorkshire farmer and his four educated children. Like the coal-mining fathers in *Saville* and *Flight Into Camden*, Joe Slattery

is an apostle of the work ethic, and he especially resents the idleness of his son Arthur, a would-be poet who has "never done a day's bloody work." The old farmer disapproves of his son's dabbling at poetry because he believes that "Work's the only bloody thing that's real" (he means *physical* work), and this motif is sounded—without ever being refuted—throughout Storey's writings. The author had grown up in a rigidly puritanical region of the West Riding which had a very simple morality: work is good, indolence is evil, and the influence of that philosophy is everywhere reflected in his literature. Personal relations always break down in his novels and plays, but his characters who do physical work usually find some satisfaction and stability in it: work gives their lives a structure and a dignity which otherwise would be missing, and certain spiritual needs are met in their working for material goods. Such, at least, seems the case for the workers portrayed in *The Contractor*, which is a relatively jovial dramatization of a scene from *Radcliffe* wherein the crew of a tent contractor (named Ewbank in both works) erects a marquee for a wedding. The exchanges of the workmen in the play—mostly lighthearted banter, songs, tale-telling, and good-natured ribbing—differ considerably from the violent, hateful relationships among the laborers in *Radcliffe*. What plot or dramatic tension there is in *The Contractor*—as the crew erect, decorate, and later dismantle the large tent—involves the relationship between Ewbank, who derives obvious joy from working alongside his employees, and his Oxford-educated son Paul, who (like young Slattery) has "never done a day's work in his life." Unlike his father and grandfather, who had worked happily as a rope-maker, Paul cannot "*do* anything at all," and he suffers—like the Thorpe children in *Flight Into Camden*—from his own "educated emptiness." In stark contrast is the blithe young man named Glendenning, who, though he is a stammering half-wit, seems happy and secure while engaged with the other workmen. Storey's point in *The Contractor*—that communal labor can be salvational—is reflected in another form in *The Changing Room*, which like *This Sporting Life* presents a vivid firsthand view of worker-athletes for whom violent rugby forms uneasy recompense for bleak lives otherwise spent in Yorkshire mills, mines, and factories. In the play as in the novel, the suggestion is made that these footballers gain a sort of spiritual renewal as they merge their identities each Saturday into the larger impersonal community of the team.

Another of Storey's plays which has close ties to his fiction is *Life Class*, which includes several important parallels to scenes in *A Temporary Life*. The adult characters of the play are lifted straight from the novel and given new names. For example, Wilcox, the deranged art-college principal in the novel, becomes Foley in *Life Class*, and the play's main characer, Allott, especially in the sarcastic, ironic tone he often uses, resembles Storey's narrator Colin Freestone in the novel. Both are failed artists and failing teachers, and both wind up losing their jobs, Allott because he has orchestrated (or at least tolerated) the mock rape of his life-class model by one of his students. Very much like Arnold Middleton and the title character in *Pasmore*, Allott is a teacher at the end of his tether (especially distraught because his marriage has gone sour), and *Life Class* records the last stages of his crack-up.

Storey's plays have generally fallen into four broad categories: (1) traditional "well-made" plays such as *In Celebration* and *The Farm*, with fairly conventional plots directed toward a crisis; (2) overtly stylistic plays such as *Home* and *Cromwell*, which in their style and—to a lesser degree—content show the influence of Beckett and Pinter; (3) farces such as *Mother's Day* and *Sisters*, undoubtedly among his least successful literary endeavors; and (4) plays such as *The Contractor* and *The Changing Room*, in what Stanley Kauffmann has termed the "New Naturalism" mode. These slice-of-life plays have little or no conventional plot and very little dramatic tension; they simply document in realistic fashion the gatherings of groups of people who share some sort of communal effort and then disperse. Furthermore, the dialogue of such plays is not remarkable—most exchanges between workmen or athletes seem like the small change of time-passing talk. But Storey's documentary vignettes have made extraordinarily good theater, they have drawn the fascination of audiences through their brilliant capturing of the mood or atmosphere of the work site or the locker room, and they have profoundly affected contemporary British drama.

When *Pasmore* was published in 1972, reviewers noted its lean and bony prose, its frequent use of dialogue, and the surgical objectivity of its narration. Some of them were led to conclude that the novel showed the result of a new discipline Storey had learned during the decade since he had written the relatively tumid and sprawling prose of *Radcliffe*. That was not, however, the case. Much of *Pasmore* had been written in 1964, before Storey had even attempted writing his second play. And he had continued to work hard at fiction all through the years he was having such phenomenal success in the theater. Writing novels, he told an interviewer in

1973, had been for him "like working in a coal mine," while creating plays had always seemed a relatively easy task, "a holiday."

Pasmore and Storey's fifth novel, *A Temporary Life*, are both actually transpositions from a larger work of fiction written between 1963 and 1967. Storey had piled up enough money writing film scripts that he could devote those five years to writing a "big work" which he projected as a climax to that "campaign for reintegrating myself" which he had begun with *This Sporting Life*. After dramatizing the incompatibility of body and soul in the confrontation of his two lead characters in *Radcliffe*, the author had intended with his fourth novel to bring about a fusion of the warring elements in man's psyche in the figure of one hero, a powerful property developer named Neville Newman. Storey told an interviewer in 1970 that the theme of what he called his "big novel" involved the "division between those who can make society work for them and those who can't," and Pasmore was one of those "who can't," a foolish foil for the book's other major characters. But in 1967, Storey grew frustrated over his inability to make structural sense of his long work, and he put it aside and began working on plays and on another novel, *Saville*, about an entirely different subject. Subsequently, in order to recoup on his five years of hard work on the "big novel," he sat down and extracted *Pasmore* and *A Temporary Life* from the larger work, extensively reshaping the material as he did so, and the novels were published in 1972 and 1973. In both, the hero of the "big novel," Neville Newman, is glimpsed only barely, as the husband of the mistress of the two books' respective heroes.

As he has so often done throughout his career, Storey in *Pasmore* was reworking situations treated in previous works, looking at them from a wholly different angle. In *Flight Into Camden* he had depicted the marital breakdown and psychic disintegration of a college teacher, viewing it from the perspective of the man's mistress. In *Pasmore*, such a character is viewed more or less from his own perspective, though in third-person narration. *Pasmore* further shares with *Flight Into Camden* an engaging portrayal of the painful conflict between a hard-working coal-miner father and an educated child whose values and private torment he cannot comprehend. But despite such circling back over old emotional territory, Storey offers in *Pasmore* an interesting, imaginatively conceived story with a subtle ironic tone and a sense of humor that makes it superior to the earlier narrative.

Colin Pasmore is almost thirty and is going

mad. A history teacher at a Bloomsbury college, married with three children, and settled in an Islington house that he has lovingly renovated, he suddenly feels a new "fury," a nameless anxiety that "something was wrong" in his life. His work begins to seem "meaningless and absurd," and, though he loves his wife and children, he cannot bear to be near them. To that point, his life has gone exactly according to the pattern set forth by his working-class Yorkshire parents—he has been a "good and certainly faithful son," a "good and faithful husband," and a "good and faithful teacher." And yet, there are missing elements in his life which he cannot identify in terms of his work or family, and he wonders "where had all this faith and goodness got him?" Gradually he drifts from his "decent home" and "respectable marriage" into a sparsely furnished flat and a hollow and bloodless affair with an enigmatic mistress named Helen, a wealthy married woman in her late thirties. Her husband soon puts an end to their union, first by offering Pasmore a bribe, then by threats, and finally by having him brutally beaten up.

Colin treasures the sense of jolly control he feels over his innocent, gullible, and naive wife, Kay, and is disgusted by "her vulnerability . . . her lack of pride . . . that ineffectual look . . . the incapacity to stand alone." That statement becomes hugely ironic by the end of *Pasmore*, as their fortunes seesaw and Kay begins to flourish while her husband dwindles into a weak, whining, and inert lump of neuroses. She is initially shattered by his desertion, but slowly begins taking tentative little steps toward independence, first striking a friendship with a man named Fowler, and subsequently insisting rather harshly that Pasmore visit the children *only* when invited on Sunday mornings. And while her prospects rise, his plunge. Having severed all the connections (family, work) which had given his life shape, he sinks into a morbid depression and becomes virtually "extinct," spending his long lonely days at the flat lying in darkness and staring at his ceiling. He becomes increasingly disoriented, and, on the rare days when he does work at writing his book on evangelical idealists, he scribbles only incomplete sentences. Mostly he sits in slovenly apathy and weeps.

Some reviewers complained that Storey had not properly clarified Pasmore's motivations for withdrawing from his "decent" life into a psychic shell, but they were overlooking the many clues sprinkled through the narrative which suggest that he is another of the numerous Storey characters suffering, as was Steven Shaw in *In Celebration*, from a "disfigurement" at the "wholly innocent hands" of

parents. When Pasmore tells his sister about his problems, she says, "I always felt something would happen. . . . The way my dad sent you out, as his private army." Many other similar passages suggest that Colin's crack-up is a belated reaction to his upbringing. When he travels to his Yorkshire home, he is immediately reminded of his painful ties with his parents, when his father rehearses how he had spent his entire life digging coal so his son could escape the pit and when his mother reminds him that "you owe things to people. . . . You can't go shrugging them off." In an effort to induce his son to return to his "decent" home, Colin's father resorts to all the same forms of emotional blackmail used by the old coal-mining father in *Flight Into Camden*, and, those ploys failing, he finally smashes his son in the face. Colin feels "fear and terror" when the "ghost" of his "father's reaction" pursues him back to his London flat—giving evidence once again that the root of his problems lies in his old Yorkshire home.

Colin cannot achieve the "feeling of wholeness" he seeks until he has learned to deal with this "fear and terror," with the residual guilt over the vague debt he feels he owes, but can never repay, to his parents (and to his class). The resolution of his psychic dilemma comes, finally, in a strange purgation of fire. Alone in his flat, Colin feels his own presence "ignited . . . by flames," and imagines himself falling into a "hole in the ground," a gaping pit of blackness which his feverish brain clearly associates with the mines where his father has so labored on his behalf. Once this brainstorm has passed—once he has completely rebelled from the pattern of "faith and goodness" which his parents had set for him, and once he has made his psychic journey into the "pit" to suffer vicariously with his father—he is able to pick up his life again, and is soon after reconciled both with his parents and with his wife and children.

Does this constitute a happy ending for *Pasmore*? Well, a qualified one, perhaps. Colin is still aware that "somewhere underneath" the Yorkshire landscape his father is still slaving away, and he himself still dreams of the "pit and the blackness." His despair persists even after he has returned to the Islington nest, and his past still exists "all around him, an intensity, like a presentiment of love, of violence," reflecting again his ambivalence toward his parents and the origins of his psychosis. He has obviously not, as the book's jacket claims, experienced "redemption and renewal," exactly. But he has gained some sort of self-knowledge that helps him cope better with the "fear and terror" caused him by his past, and while that may not qualify as a truly happy ending, it is certainly the most upbeat conclusion in all of Storey's six novels.

Storey told an interviewer in 1976 that "it suits me temperamentally to describe things through gritted teeth," and the short, tightly structured *Pasmore* certainly seems to be narrated through clamped jaws, with none of the intrusive attitudinizing which mars *Radcliffe*. Its spare prose is flat and noncommittal and leaves the reader to make what he will of the bare, stripped happenings of the story. Some reviewers thought the prose was too laconic, that it was, as one critic put it, a "deeply evasive and artless novel." On the whole, the critical response to *Pasmore* was lukewarm, at best. And even those who defended it generally overlooked what may be its chief merit—the irony and understated humor involved in Pasmore's domestic adventure. The author's three previous novels had been unremittingly humorless affairs. And Barry Cole, writing in the *New Statesman*, thought *Pasmore* was just more of the same: "Throughout the book there is no sign of wit, humor, or verbal irony. At times it sounds like a case history from a doctor's notebook." But he had misread the book: there is strong comedy in *Pasmore*, though it is very subtly presented and the reader often has to labor to make the comic connections for himself. There is, for example, a certain dark humor in the mafioso-style warnings which Helen's cuckolded husband gives Pasmore, to keep hands off his wife—four dark-suited men suddenly appear at the flat to deliver a coffin, a hearse parks outside, and funereal wreaths soon follow. The narrator never overtly directs the reader's attention to the fact, but there is a highly comic contrast between these methods used by Helen's husband to retrieve his wife and the way Pasmore himself subsequently reacts when he discovers "another man, in public, in possession of his wife." Instead of confronting this other man directly, as Helen's husband had done, Pasmore goes to warn his wife that Fowler is not the sort of person he would have associating with his children, and—in one of the novel's high comic moments—he condemns the other man for being unstable. Pasmore himself never recognizes the keen irony there, nor in the hilariously priggish telegrams he composes (but lacks the nerve to send) to Fowler: "Leave my wife alone homebreaker," he warns. "Adulterer beware"; "Fowler do you believe in the sanctity of marriage." About homebreaking and adultery Pasmore of course knows much, but he sees no connection between his former behavior and his new-found moral stance. There is broad comedy

also in some of the scenes of Colin's darkest moments—as, for example, when he is arrested for loitering outside his own house, or when he later has to be pried loose from his own furniture as he clings to it and begs pitiably to be readmitted to the house and the family he had so stoutly rejected the year before. In one of his telegrams to Fowler, he cries that there is "no justice in the world." There is, however, plenty of comic justice dealt in the fictional world of *Pasmore*, and the reader is meant to enjoy at least some of the agony experienced by the protagonist as the tables are turned on him.

As he transposed it from his "big novel," Storey extensively revised the material that went into *A Temporary Life* (1973). The original story had been set in London and had been narrated by the master builder Neville Newman. In its final form, the story is narrated by an art-college teacher named Colin Freestone, and the action takes place in a Yorkshire town where he is living temporarily in order to be near his institutionalized wife. The story focuses on his engagement with wildly idiosyncratic characters in three very different (and only tenuously connected) worlds: one is the farcical world of the Municipal College of Fine Arts, with its hilariously eccentric majordomo, R. N. Wilcox; another is the tragic world of Colin's lovely but deranged wife, Yvonne, who resides at Westfield Mental Hospital; and the third is the intensely violent and perverse world of the very rich and very powerful property dealer Neville Newman. Increasingly through the novel it becomes clear that the bizarre inhabitants of all three of these arenas of the novel's action are mad, and that the outside world is even more a madhouse than the asylum where Yvonne stays.

Reviewers of *A Temporary Life* generously praised Storey's comic portrait of "Skipper" Wilcox, the more-than-disturbed principal of Colin's art school, who patrols classrooms obsessively seeking out smokers; packs his own lavatory with stolen art objects and bottles filled with his own excreta; lectures against bread, blaming it for the world's "interdenominational strife"; and repeatedly asserts his belief that art is simply a matter of "good digestion." The novel's comic highlight—and one of the most marvelous passages in all of Storey's fiction—comes in the description of Freestone's dinner engagement at Wilcox's cold, dark cottage, when he dines on an unusually frugal meal which includes a toadstool cocktail.

Through Wilcox's world of zaniness Colin sails relatively unscathed, but he does not so easily move through the sea of madness and pathos that surrounds his wife, Yvonne. Her breakdown is analyzed with clinical skill through *A Temporary Life*, and Storey makes her one of the most engaging of all the "afflicted" personalities in his writings. Again like so many of his characters, Yvonne has been psychically wounded by a well-meaning father, who had slaved in the Yorkshire mills so his "ray of sunshine" could go to college and "get out of here." But once out of the working classes, she had become burdened with a horrible guilt over her inability to give back to her own class "some of the things she's had," to repay her father's sacrifice, and she has compensated by taking on all the world's suffering, spending her life in a sacrificial round of service to old people, charities, and the like. In this abstract caring about people, however, she has failed to live up to the expectations of her parents and has failed to make contact with the people close to her, to Colin for instance, who finds more and more that he cannot communicate across the barrier of his wife's madness.

The figure of the mad but compassionate Yvonne overshadows all else in *A Temporary Life*, and her character becomes an especially meaningful counterpoint to the brutal and insensitive Newmans, into whose strange orbit Colin is drawn when he becomes involved with the wife of the rich property developer. In stark contrast to Yvonne and her belief that "it's caring about people you don't *have* to care about that counts," Elizabeth Newman "couldn't give a damn about anything." The flourescent-cool affair she has had with Colin is just another brief stop in her quest for pleasure, as her own daughter acknowledges matter-of-factly: "Mummy has her men." Elizabeth seems well-matched with her manipulative and nihilistic husband, who in a broader and more devastating sense is also on the make and careless of anyone who gets in the way. He and his company are, by his reckoning, "harbingers of progress," constructing modern industrial estates before moving on to "revitalize" other towns. But in Freestone's eyes, Newman is viewed as the arrogant and greedy head of a villainous system which somehow mangles people in its wake. Of Newman and Company Colin observes: "They try and undermine you first by attempting to rouse in you feelings of common decency. . . . Failing that, they clobber you. . . . Failing with that, they compromise you . . . by offering you positions. . . . The one thing you can refuse them is co-operation, until the whole system . . . collapses of its own volition." Just such ploys are indeed tried against Colin, but he holds out against Newman at every juncture. He refuses to abandon Elizabeth even after New-

man's henchmen have clobbered him severely, persisting, as much as anything, out of his own perversity of will, his desire to thwart the powerful businessman. The contest of wills between the two men comes to a bloody climax following a birthday party at Newman's house, where Colin goes berserk and attacks one of his host's aides. (Freestone is a former professional boxer, and he brings to mind Arthur Machin and Vic Tolson in his tendency to express himself through violence.) Colin is eventually beaten unconscious, and when he awakes, Newman—true to Colin's assessment of his methods—offers him a job. Colin refuses co-operation once more, and with supreme defiance sneers, "Do I get your wife as well?"

He will not get Elizabeth at any rate, for she is herself a member in good standing of the corrupt Newman world Colin labels "a regular circus." She deliberately and masochistically provokes her husband to jealousy and violence (he beats her harshly as Colin watches), and Colin finally recognizes that such behavior is part of the Newman family routine, in which not only Elizabeth's adultery but even Newman's retaliation are known quantities. "Wherever we go it gets like this," their daughter acknowledges. Another member of their entourage further observes, "It's always the innocent with them . . . who suffer." There is in the delineation of this Newman world—with its wild weekend parties of the rich and mighty, the exaggerated behavior of their hangers-on, the drinking, the promiscuity, the sudden violence—a strong whiff of *The Great Gatsby*, though Storey's narrator certainly has little in common with the moralizing Nick Carraway who tells F. Scott Fitzgerald's tale.

The Newmans finally move on to seek other affairs and further violence in other towns. Colin is left (thanks to Newman) without a job at the college and winds up sweeping streets for a living. But even that is a gesture of defiance against Newman, who had predicted that he would never "work around here . . . again." Colin is not, finally, a "victor"; rather, he is a *survivor*; he has answered Wilcox's absurdities in kind (for example, by scribbling graffiti on school walls and by unearthing the secrets of the principal's lavatory); he has come to terms with Yvonne's psychic withdrawal, through his own stoicism and his understanding of her plight; and he has met the challenge of the bullying Newman without flinching.

One reviewer of *Pasmore* complained that its author had not made his hero "a man worth feeling for," and the same complaint was voiced in different words about *A Temporary Life*, though the novel generally received warmer reviews than any of Storey's novels since *This Sporting Life*. Freestone, to be sure, is no ideal man, nor even an especially likable one. Like Elizabeth Newman, he seems not to "give a damn about anything at times," and his perpetual cynicism wears thin after a while. But he does have redeeming qualities. He seems to have genuine feelings for his wife, he is attractive in his very cockiness and pugnacity, in his willingness to engage the enemy, and he has something which no other Storey protagonist displays—a sense of humor (a sardonic one, but nonetheless refreshing).

In the same year (1973) that *A Temporary Life* appeared, Storey had another book published, a strange little volume titled *Edward*. It is essentially a book of drawings by Donald Parker, with a slight text supplied by Storey. Some bibliographers categorized *Edward* as juvenile literature, but that it is certainly not—Parker's drawings frequently include images of naked women and are typically irreverent. In one, a dazed nun inspects a lineup of naked bishops. The wonderfully funny drawings are vastly superior to the text, which focuses on the tale of a bishop who finds a mysterious key and cannot discover what it fits. Storey's text is enigmatic and scattered, and it often seems ill-connected to the drawings.

The writer began his sixth novel, *Saville*, in 1967, after he had for the time abandoned his "big novel," and over the next half-dozen or so years he worked on it, as he told Victor Sage, "as a kind of relaxation from writing plays." Much longer than his previous novels (it ranges over 500 pages), *Saville* gives a richly detailed account of the childhood, adolescence, and early manhood of a north England miner's son, who ultimately struggles to escape the strangling bonds of family affection and duty and the oppressive environment of his small pit village, to take flight into London. *Saville* is, as one reviewer noted, "the kind of novel you live in," a curiously old-fashioned naturalistic tale that traces the fortunes of a family of six (the oldest child Andrew dies at age seven, before his three brothers Colin, Steven, and Richard are born) in the village of Saxton in the low hill land of south Yorkshire during the 1940s and 1950s. The book gives a firsthand view of the *family* environment that is so often blamed for having "disfigured" the adults in Storey's earlier novels and plays. The evocative descriptions of the activities and the people of this tiny village in *Saville* give the feeling of firsthand acquaintance, and the book seems fiercely autobiographical in tone. Colin Saville certainly resembles Storey in the way he is born in the early 1930s in a

north-country industrial town, begins a process of social mobility by winning a grammar school scholarship, excels at rugby and expresses an early interest in writing poetry, spends holidays working as a farmhand, and finally flees south to London and to a new freedom of spirit. However, Storey has stoutly denied that the book is autobiographical, and once told an interviewer that "Nearly everything is pure invention" in the novel. Nonetheless, when one considers that the published version of *In Celebration*—written at precisely the same time and about precisely the same characters and themes as *Saville*—is dedicated "To My Mother and Father," one can only conclude that the familial situations in both works have coordinates of some significant sort in the author's own life.

Saville is narrated in Storey's typically minimalist style, in his customarily reticent, noncommittal prose which holds the material at arm's length from the reader. All things are reported dispassionately, with little explanation, and the reader is usually left to assign value to what is being depicted. The third-person narration is generally limited to Colin's consciousness, and the novel's structure basically imitates his memory—the early descriptions of family and village life are mundane and particular, reflecting the narrow perceptions of the growing youngster, and the later portions of the novel become much more abstract and more dialectic, reflecting the impact his education has had on his thinking. Little suspense is created through the first two-thirds of the novel, but Storey commands his reader's constant attention through his creation of many richly idiosyncratic characters and through the finely etched details of his depictions of village life. He masterfully captures the speech, the dialect and syntax and peculiar rhythms of the language of the West Riding people. As always in his writings, his descriptions of physical activities—for example, of Colin's toil with other sweat-and-dust-covered farmworkers cutting corn—form some of the best writing here. Also good are the accounts of Colin's experiences as a student at King Edward's Grammar School and as a teacher at Rawcliffe village; the closely observed encounters between the bullying masters and their raw young charges are as good as any schoolroom dramas in English fiction. Finally, Storey's remarkably graphic painting of the gray old village of Saxton—with its towering colliery headgears, its ash heaps, its smoke-and-steam-filled skies, its stinking sewage ponds—recalls the best of D. H. Lawrence's similar fictional sketches of Midlands mining towns.

More so than any of Storey's other works,

Saville is a powerful social document, illustrating with unblinking objectivity the poverty, the squalor, and the hard lives of the working classes in northern England. "Some men grow out of their environment," says Colin's friend Bletchley. "Whereas others just seem to sink into it." They are the only two Saxton men of their generation not to sink; both rise out of their backgrounds through education. By the material standards of their community, Bletchley becomes more of a success, landing a management job with a manufacturing firm, while Colin becomes only a teacher and a poet. But all the rest of their friends "sink" into the pits or become "factory fodder." The vast inequities in the British social class system are dramatized in *Saville*, especially in the contrast between the harsh, tormented lives of all the working-class lads and that of Colin's friend Stafford, the son of a wealthy mill owner, who glides smoothly and insouciantly through his youth toward an army commission, a stint at Oxford, and a subsequent life of ease.

Nowhere in all of Storey's writings is the dignity of the undignified man better portrayed than in the character of Colin's father, Harry Saville. Despite the dismal social conditions in which he lives, the elder Saville is proud and industrious and determined to keep his own sons out of the pit where a man like himself is "just another piece of muck." He sends Colin forth as an ambassador to live the life he had himself been denied. Together they sit at the kitchen table laboring over the youngster's homework, and when his son wins the grammar school scholarship which will be the key to his deliverance out of the working class, the father bursts with pride. But in his late teens Colin begins questioning his father's values. For example, he rethinks the work ethic his father has instilled in him and weighs the truth of a cynical friend's assertion that the Saville family's philosophy can be boiled down to a matter of "material progress backed by a modicum of religious superstition." Such self-scrutiny feeds his growing bitterness over how he has been misshaped "not through force" but "through love" by his father. He has never, Colin claims to a friend, been allowed to decide for himself what he wants to do, and "in most ways I feel set against what I've been told to become, or felt I ought to become." Once he has become what in his family's eyes is a success and is working as a teacher, he draws his father's envious contempt and suffers when he hears his father mock his "easy" job with long holidays, "no muck, no sweating out your guts." Those words echo Joe Slattery's to his schoolteaching daughters in *The Farm*, and the old

farmer's attitudes are sounded again when Saville derides Colin's "sitting still" and "writing poetry" while others his age are out "doing things" (that is, physical things). Thus Colin suffers, as Storey himself had in early manhood, as he strives to reconcile these two warring worlds of the intuitive and the physical, and as he tries to adjust his own inner aspirations and needs to the expectations of his Yorkshire family and community.

Colin's attempt at self-definition is helped along by his relationship with a middle-aged woman named Elizabeth, who becomes a surrogate mother figure to him and is able to articulate some of the nineteen-year-old boy's psychological problems, which he cannot himself perceive. "You don't really belong to anything," she tells him. "You're not really a teacher. You're not really anything. You don't belong to any class, since you live with one class, respond like another, and feel attachments to none." She is accurate also in claiming that he has remained in Saxton because he is still so "inextricably bound up" with his parents. "I owe them something," he explains. But when he repays that debt in material goods, in household furnishings, he complains loudly to his parents, "It's supposed to be enlightenment I've acquired, not learning how to make a better living."

As his depression deepens, his relationship with his family becomes stormier. He brutalizes his brother Steven, who with his complacent, good-natured personality is the direct antithesis to the ever-earnest and industrious Colin. The older brother envies Steven's insouciant nature and harshly reproaches his parents for giving his brother "chances of freedom I've never had," for not "moulding" Stephen to fit their ambitions as they had him. In his mounting frustration over his brother's lack of determination to "succeed" (after he fails his exams, Steven goes blithely down pit), Colin becomes to him as much an intellectual gangster as ever Michael does to his sister in *Flight Into Camden*.

During that same period of his early twenties, Colin has an even more significant and dramatic relationship with another of his brothers—the one he had never met, Andrew, who had died of pneumonia six months before Colin was born. Colin's parents had looked on Colin as a "bewitching recompense," as a mystical replacement for the dead child, and Colin belatedly resents the fact that he had been burdened by being the repository of two sons' shares of parental hope and ambition. But it is through his own search for this artistic, "unruly," freedom-loving boy that Colin discovers what he himself must be. As a child, Andrew had been "trouble," had repeatedly wandered off from home, spending his short, happy life in constant careless flight. Colin comes to view the child as the symbolic antithesis of his own bound being. Andrew had also been an incipient artist—"He had the nature as well as the gift" to be a painter, his mother reports. The dead boy begins to haunt Colin's dreams and thoughts, and in a strange cemetery scene an image of the "wild, anarchic boy" comes to Colin's mind and he feels an "invisible bond with that figure in the ground," consequently leaving the graveyard with a new "sense of mission, a new containment."

It is still a considerably long time thereafter before he acts on this new "sense of mission" and takes flight into London. But his growing sense of rage and his swelling sense of the possibilities inside himself finally propel him to make the break, and the novel ends as he watches the last trail of "blackish smoke" over Saxton as his train moves south. He thus escapes the bondage of his class and his village, as well as the obsessive love of his family, and bears his emptiness into the larger world. His future is still open, though he seems destined to pursue his dream of being a writer. He certainly seems destined to drag his painful past behind him—until, perhaps, in just such a reunion scene as that dramatized in *In Celebration*, he will be able to exorcise the demons of his past.

When *Saville* was published in 1976, it received what one critic later accurately termed "hysterically enthusiastic reviews" in England. The ultimate accolade paid Storey's sixth novel was the awarding of the £5,000 Booker Prize for Fiction, Britain's most important literary award for fiction.

During the 1960s and 1970s Storey lived with his wife Barbara and their four children in Hampstead in north London. In 1974, he became a fellow at University College, London. After finishing *Saville*, he began work on another similar, but less ambitious, novel, *A Prodigal Child*, which was published in 1982. Like *Saville*, this novel is a straightforward naturalistic tale of a north-country boy's development through adolescence to early manhood and to the threshold of an artistic career. "Concrete and specific," the motto of the art room where Storey's young hero, Bryan Morley, sculpts in this story, also provides a clue to the author's greatest strength here—the rich details which cause the provincial Yorkshire world to spring vividly to life, particularly in the opening chapters which chronicle the growth of Stainforth, a new estate

where "pioneer" tenants are building new homes, carving new gardens, and forming new friendships. Beyond those early chapters, *A Prodigal Child* suffers from occasional prolonged patches of flat dialogue and from the fact that the story is well past its midpoint before its chief dramatic conflicts are clearly established.

The novel concentrates first on the domestic life of Morley's parents, a beer-swilling farm laborer and his sullen, penny-pinching wife, but most of the story focuses on the strange alliance Bryan forms (during the 1930s) with an older woman, Fay Corrigan. She and her wealthy husband take him into their mansion at Crevet and virtually adopt him, paying his way into a posh private school where he can develop his talents as a sculptor. Like the typical Storey protagonist, Bryan feels wholly "cut off" from his parents and his brother and welcomes this "escape" from the lowly life of Stainforth estate. He believes himself a "prince" of "special destiny," and yearns to create something which, without him, "could never have existed." But his development as an artist is of less moment in the novel than his obsessive fixation on Mrs. Corrigan, who is several decades his senior. He feels she is destined to play "princess to his prince," and even as a shy schoolboy his attraction to her is decidedly sexual (he causes a commotion in his school by sculpting her nude figure in clay). Their relationship becomes not only that of surrogate mother and son but also, perversely, that of surrogate husband and wife (the Oedipal drama is played out here just as prominently as it is in Lawrence's *Sons and Lovers*, which Storey's novel strongly resembles). This relationship—Bryan himself calls it "odd, maybe even mad"—is tolerated, even welcomed, by Fay's weak husband, who hopes that it will keep his promiscuous wife at home. It does not, and, during the seven years Bryan is at Crevet and Mrs. Corrigan is waiting for her young charge to grow into manhood (and to become her mate), she engages in frequent affairs with other men. Belatedly she realizes that her alliance with Bryan is a "disease," and becomes despondent over the inevitability of her losing him to her spunky niece Margaret, in whom Bryan sees "a youthful Mrs. Corrigan."

At story's end, a fast-maturing Bryan does indeed seem destined to mate with Margaret, who has all along served as muse to his art, to his desire to become "someone special," and he is enjoying new success as a sculptor (one critic has lauded him as "a prodigal talent"). Like Colin Saville, he plans to pursue his art in London. But unlike Saville and other Storey protagonists who have taken similar flights south, Bryan is reunited with his past before he leaves to meet his future. Admitting to his father that he has "made mistakes," he expresses his desire to return home and to make a "fresh beginning" with his family before going to London. He returns to Stainforth in time for a community-wide party, and, as he watches his neighbors dancing on the estate grounds, he feels it "strange how everything that is full of life has come back here," to the working-class world he had abandoned years before, when he had gone to live at Crevet and to pursue his career as an artist. As he views his parents and their neighbors, he declares, "this is my kingdom, the kingdom of the heart . . . and we are all a part of it." This ending does not really seem justified in terms of Storey's plot, but it is interesting because no other previous Storey protagonist has been able to make such an acceptance of family and of class. Bryan seems to have achieved a wholeness of character, an intellectual and emotional control that has evaded the grasp of virtually every tortured character in Storey's previous novels and plays.

Speaking in 1977 to Mel Gussow, Storey observed that "art is a liberating experience—from yourself." Whatever his next advance in fiction, it seems likely that it will be, as all of his previous novels have been, another step backward in time, as he continues his efforts to "liberate" himself, to exorcise the demons of his own past and to continue that "campaign for reintegrating myself" which he feels he began on those lonely London-to-Leeds-to-London train journeys back in the days of his unhappy youth.

Plays:
The Restoration of Arnold Middleton, Edinburgh, Traverse Theatre Club, 22 November 1966; London, Royal Court Theatre, 4 July 1967;
In Celebration, London, Royal Court Theatre, 22 April 1969; New York, Sutton East Theatre, 1977;
The Contractor, London, Royal Court Theatre, 20 October 1969; New York, Chelsea Manhattan Theatre, 9 October 1973;
Home, London, Royal Court Theatre, 17 June 1970; New York, Morosco Theatre, 17 November 1970;
The Changing Room, London, Royal Court Theatre, 9 November 1971; New York, Morosco Theatre, 6 March 1973;
Cromwell, London, Royal Court Theatre, 15 August 1973;

The Farm, London, Royal Court Theatre, 26 September 1973; New York; Circle Repertory Company, 10 October 1976;
Life Class, London, Royal Court Theatre, 9 April 1974; New York, Manhattan Theatre Club, 14 December 1975;
Night, 1976;
Mother's Day, London, Royal Court Theatre, 22 September 1976;
Sisters, Manchester, Royal Exchange Theatre, 12 September 1978;
Early Days, Brighton, 31 March 1980; London, Cottesloe Theatre (National Theatre), 22 April 1980.

Screenplays:
This Sporting Life, Continental, 1963;
In Celebration, American Film Theatre, 1974.

Television Scripts:
Home, PBS, 1971;
Grace, based on James Joyce's short story, BBC, 1974.

Periodical Publications:
"Commonwealth Art Today," *Guardian*, 3 November 1962, p. 5;
"Journey Through a Tunnel," *Listener*, 70 (1 August 1963): 159-161; republished in *Writers on Themselves* (London: BBC Publications, 1964);
"What Really Matters," *Twentieth Century*, 172 (Autumn 1963): 96-97;
"Marxism as a Form of Nostalgia," *New Society*, 15 July 1965, p. 23.

Interviews:
Special Correspondent, "Speaking of Writing—II: David Storey," *Times* (London), 28 November 1963, p. 15;
Ronald Hayman, "Conversation with David Storey," *Drama* (Winter 1970): 47-53; republished in *Playback* (London: Davis-Poynter, 1973);
Martha Duffy, "An Ethic of Work and Play," *Sports Illustrated*, 38 (5 March 1973): 66-82;
Mel Gussow, "To David Storey, A Play is a 'Holiday,' " *New York Times*, 20 April 1973, p. 14;
Peter Ansorge, "The Theatre of Life: David Storey in Interview with Peter Ansorge," *Plays and Players* (September 1973): 32-36;
Frances Gibb, "Why David Storey Has Got It In For Academics, the Critics, and 'Literary Whizz-Kids,' " *Times Higher Education Supplement*

(London), 2 February 1977, D9;
Gussow, "Talk with David Storey, Playwright and Novelist," *New York Times Book Review*, 28 August 1977, p. 11.

References:
James Gindin, *Postwar British Fiction: New Accents and Attitudes* (Berkeley & Los Angeles: University of California Press, 1962), pp. 96-104;
Frank McGuiness, "The Novels of David Storey,"

London Magazine, 3 (March 1974): 79-83;
John Mellors, "Yorkshire Relish: The Novels of John Braine and David Storey," *London Magazine*, n.s. 16 (October-November 1976): 79-84;
John Russell Taylor, "David Storey," in his *The Second Wave: British Drama for the Seventies* (New York: Hill & Wang, 1971), pp. 141-154;
Taylor, *David Storey, Writers and Their Work*, 239, edited by Ian Scott-Kilvert (London: Longman, 1974).

Emma Tennant
(20 October 1937-   )

Georgia L. Lambert

BOOKS: *The Colour of Rain*, as Catherine Aydy (London: Weidenfeld & Nicolson, 1964);
The Time of the Crack (London: Cape, 1973);
The Last of the Country House Murders (London: Cape, 1974; Nashville: Nelson, 1974);
Hotel de Dream (London: Gollancz, 1976);
The Bad Sister (London: Gollancz, 1978; New York: Coward, McCann & Geoghegan, 1978);
Wild Nights (London: Cape, 1979; New York: Harcourt Brace Jovanovich, 1980);
Alice fell (London: Cape, 1980);
The Search for Treasure Island (New York: Puffin/Penguin, Jr., 1981).

Fantasy, feminism, and political satire are combined in Emma Tennant's novels, which portray humanity's groping, fumbling quest for meaning and purpose today or in the near future. The difficulties of distinguishing between illusion and reality are exemplified by Tennant's often comic, dreamlike narratives and her stunning imagery. Her exploration of the imagination and her depiction of the passing of time show exciting originality, and she is a novelist who is inspiring followers of modern fiction.

Emma Tennant was born in London on 20 October 1937 to Lord Glenconner and his second wife, Elizabeth. A businessman in the City of London, Lord Glenconner retained the title bestowed on Emma's grandfather, while Emma retained the Scottish family name, Tennant. Shortly after Emma's birth, the family moved to Scotland and

remained there until the end of World War II. Her father, who was Special Operations Executive in Cairo and Turkey during the war, and her mother traveled extensively while Emma was a child, and she and her brother, Colin, three-and-a-half years her junior, were "rather isolated," she says. Several of her novels are set in Scotland, where she lived until the age of eight; then the family moved back to London, returning to the family home in Scotland each summer.

In London young Emma attended St. Paul's Girls' School, which was, she recalls, "a very, very good girls' school," but she remembers that she "hated it." She went to Paris at the age of fifteen to study the history of art at the Ecole de Louvre. She did not attend a university because, she says, she "did what was expected of a woman of class" and returned to the Chelsea area of London as a debutante at the age of seventeen for the usual whirl of social activities. In a 1981 review of *Lenare: The Art of Society Photography 1924-1977*, Tennant recalled being presented at court: "In my day (1956) Presentation at Court was on its last legs and knew it. This did not prevent great numbers of girls and their presenters turning up: but the train and the ostrich feathers had gone and the older and younger women were not able to be statuesque or maidenly, or distinguishable from one another as they bobbed before the dais where the Royal Family (or perhaps they were replicas in wax) sat without losing a smile or drumming a finger for hours on end.... My presenter, the wit and author Violet

Wyndham, daughter of Ada Leverson, author of *The Little Otleys* and *Love at Second Sight*, was much amused by all this. It was an odd way to spend a day, in the ox-cart queue up the Mall to the Palace, in a salon where nerves ran to such a pitch anyone would think we were due to audition for Lady Macbeth; and then the flustered curtsey before returning to the jam-packed courtyard and home. Had we lost an innocence, by being shown to the Sovereign in this way? Possibly we had."

In 1957, at the age of nineteen, Emma Tennant married Sebastian Yorke, son of novelist Henry Green. She was much impressed by Green's writing and feels that her first novel, *The Colour of Rain*, written when she was twenty-four, is a reflection of his work. Her first child, Matthew Yorke, was born 24 November 1958. By 1961 Tennant had become an "occasional journalist" for the *New Statesman*. In 1963 she accepted a job with *Queen* as travel correspondent.

The Colour of Rain, published in 1964 under the pseudonym Catherine Aydy, is a conventional third-person narrative that depicts the English upper-middle class way of life and shows the artificiality and shallowness in their lives and marriages. Although one feels little liking for any of the shallow characters and little sympathy for their self-created plights, there is, in afterthought, a feeling of cynical sorrow for the foolishness of humanity. Her publisher considered the novel good enough to submit it for the coveted Prix Formentor, but, she says, an incident which happened during the judging daunted her for eight years, during which time she refused to show her work to anyone. She was told by a friend that Italian fiction writer and critic Alberto Moravia, who was one of the judges for the award, held her book up contemptuously and dismissed it as "an example of British decadence."

Tennant continued writing through the end of the decade, completing two novels, but refused to show them to anyone. She says they are "bad naturalist" novels, and she stuffed them away in drawers. She and Yorke were divorced, and in 1966 Tennant obtained a position as features editor with *Vogue*. She remarried and her second child, Daisy Cockburn, was born 5 February 1969. Tennant says that her new father-in-law, Claud Cockburn, a well-known British political writer in the 1930s, was influential in shaping her political views.

Still living in Chelsea, Tennant began reading science fiction and met two prominent science-fiction writers, J. G. Ballard and Michael Moorcock. She began to be drawn out of the realistic mode of writing into the world of the imagination and wrote

The Time of the Crack (1973), which her agent, A. P. Watt & Son, sent to Tom Maschler, the director of Jonathan Cape. It was accepted and is the first novel published under Tennant's real name. *The Time of the Crack* blends reality with imaginary, comic absurdity. Dubbed "allegorical sci-fi" by *The Encyclopedia of Science Fiction*, it combines Lewis Carroll technique with H. G. Wells material. Overnight, a huge crack, centering in the bed of the Thames River, splits London in two. London's population is decimated; people fall into the crack, drown, or are crushed in the rubble. Cheyne Walk in Chelsea, which is peopled with greedy property speculators, is flooded, and expensive homes lean precariously toward the bank of the river. Though dangerously near death, the speculators strive to reach the south side of the river in order to get there first and buy the property cheaply so that they can sell it at a huge profit to the homeless north side survivors. Baba, a blond, innocent, completely unliberated Playboy bunny, is the bewildered heroine, a counterpart to Alice in Wonderland, who embarks on a series of misadventures, as she wanders through London intent only on returning to the Playboy Club for a fresh set of ears and tail. A ludicrous, comical group

Emma Tennant

of people who were undergoing regression analysis at "the time of the crack" terrorize a hospital, their psychoanalysts placidly applauding this release of hostilities and leading these infantile adults away from the terrified, badly injured hospital patients. While all is chaos on the north side of the river, the south side appears to be thoroughly organized, with plenty of food and housing. Medea, a women's liberation prophetess who seems to have supernatural powers, summons surviving women to leave their menial household chores to join her on the south side of the river; but as the women are crossing they are captured by the capitalist property speculators and forced to work building a bridge to enable the men to cross the river first. The women eventually make it across to the "Promised Land" on the south side, but the property developers do not.

The novel received fairly good reviews. George Hill felt it was "too wild to be fully effective, but fun all the same." The *Times Literary Supplement* reviewer stated that "its merits far outweigh the minor faults," and added, "As a comic apocalypse this novel could hardly be bettered.... As a first novel ... it has a simplicity and enthusiasm that is often missing from the outputs of more professional writers of fiction." The novel was later published in paperback by Penguin.

Divorced from her second husband and married for a third time, Tennant gave birth to a third child, Rose Tennant Dempsey, on 10 March 1973. In 1973 she left Chelsea for the Ladbroke Grove area of London, which she says has the largest concentration of science-fiction writers in England. She began doing fiction reviews for *Listener* and completed *The Last of the Country House Murders* (1974), which has been called "ingenious and intelligent," "a powerful dystopia and a cunning parody of the . . . 'old' detective story."

The novel is set in the near future. There has been a revolution in Britain and most of the populace is starving in the countryside while a few rich tourists travel in well-protected coaches to shelter them from "the crowd." The government, feeling that tourism needs a good boost, has announced that Jules Tanner, "the only surviving example of the decadent pre-Revolutionary days" and owner of Woodiscombe Manor, the last country house in England, is to be murdered and the country house will become a grade one tourist attraction. Tanner is informed by the government that he can choose his own murderer, subject to the approval of a detective who will be appointed by the state. There are many people in Tanner's past, he realizes, who would be willing to murder him—people he cheated

Emma Tennant, age seventeen, photograph by Lenare

or lied to, people he disappointed or ruined. His long-dead father and David, a friend who died in prison after Jules betrayed him, appear to Jules as companions during his last days in the mansion. When Haines, the government detective, arrives and begins his preliminary investigation and selection of the murderer, Jules decides he would rather live an extra week and attempts to bribe Haines with an engagement ring set with a huge diamond. Jules's fiancée, Bessy, whom he jilted at the altar and sued for the return of this ring, appears at the house and is selected as one of two most likely murderers. The second candidate is Cedric, an old acting rival of Jules's who is the Leonardo da Vinci of the modern age and thus considered dangerous by the government. Cedric has discovered that "there was no universe at all. There was the sun; and Earth, of course, with its billions of inhabitants dreaming of the day when it would be possible to find space again. . . , settling, colonizing, and marking out a territory the very concept of which had vanished at home—and there was the moon, as the astronauts had proved. And there was nothing else!" When he hears the radio announcement of the upcoming murder of his old rival, he flies to the manor in a white helicopter to share with Jules one last joke against the government. He is a favorite with "the crowd"; as a master of impersonation, he changes from Borgart to Fagin to Hitler and convinces them to join him in a revolution, beginning with an attack on the country house at a prearranged signal.

Haines is a well-developed, comic character who dresses up as Lord Peter Wimsey to assume the role of detective: "He was the sort of man whom everyone dreaded. The State snooper, with a licence to carry arms." His elaborately worked out plans for the murder are completely bungled. Jules and Bessy, who are to marry just prior to Jules's murder, have a quarrel, and Bessy shoots Jules (who—unknown to her, is Cedric in disguise). Haines succumbs to the lure of the diamond and stands in at the wedding disguised as Jules, hoping to escape with Bessy and the diamond before the government realizes what has happened. But Jules appears at the wedding and signals "the crowd" to attack. Jules alone survives. Tourists are trampled; Haines and Bessy are crushed by "Cedric's army"; and Jules lives on in solitary splendor.

Reality and illusion are juxtaposed throughout the novel, with persecuted "ghosts" appearing first to Jules, then to Haines, and with the past being reenacted during the present. "Revolutions are made in drab landscapes by the evocation of past phantoms," suggested Stephen Clark in his *Times Literary Supplement* review. "To shatter the dead past, to make a new covenant with our creative powers: there, perhaps, an insight lies," he added, calling the novel a "minor, but elegant and sometimes moving satire."

Tennant's essay on women and the industrial revolution appeared in the anthology *Women on Women*, published by Sidgwick & Jackson in 1974, and in 1975 she started a literary magazine which she named *Bananas* (as in "I'm going bananas"). Aided by the British Arts Council, she devised a newspaper format combining fiction, poems, and original graphics, as well as some literary criticism. She edited the quarterly publication, which was sold at newsstands, giving it "a new look, like *Quarto* magazine," she says, and occasionally contributed an article or story. Colored red and black, its design was "repro-dada." *Bananas* brought Tennant into contact with many modern British writers, including Angela Carter, John Sladek, Tom Disch, J. G. Ballard, Beryl Bainbridge, and Martin Seymour-Smith. In 1978 John Ryle noted that the magazine did not yet "have any deep editorial coherence beyond the sum of its contributions. Its vindication as a magazine comes from eliciting and publishing

work that might not otherwise have seen the light; and its strength is that it represents not one but several lively tendencies."

In addition to editing *Bananas*, Tennant continued to write fiction. Her third novel, *Hotel de Dream*, was published in 1976 by Victor Gollancz Ltd., Cape having preferred not to publish it. Tennant is delighted to have met Liz Calder, an editor at Gollancz, as a result of switching publishers.

Hotel de Dream is an exploration of the power of dreams, blending reality and illusion. The dreams of the guests at Westringham Hotel begin to merge and get out of hand as they are dramatized by science-fiction devices. Mr. Poynter, an ineffectual, retired lieutenant colonel, dreams he is in his ideal city, where he is king. Miss Scranton, a spinster schoolteacher, dreams she is the leader of a group of Amazon women, while Miss Briggs, another spinster, dreams that the Queen leaves the country after asking Miss Briggs to assume the crown. Cecilia Houghton, an unwanted poor relation and writer of an adventure series, has allowed her two main characters in the series, Johnny and Melinda, to escape her, and they career through the novel plotting how to murder their creator. Poynter lusts after Cecilia Houghton, who appears in his city along with Miss Scranton and Miss Briggs. The dreams escape into the outside world, influencing the tides, and disgruntling the residents of London. Poynter's dream city disintegrates and a social reformer leads the crowd into revolution against Poynter.

Hotel de Dream received mixed reviews. The power of the imagination produces a dream of escape into "the grotesque . . . a trip of chaos and absurdity," said the *Times* reviewer, who noted some funny scenes but added that "the parable inside the fantasy about the condition of England today, lost between illusion and reality, is too far-fetched to be taken seriously or even noticed without being warned about it by the dustjacket." Despite such reviews, rights to the paperback version of *Hotel de Dream* were purchased by Penguin; it is soon to be republished by Picador (Pan Books), and it was runner-up in the *Guardian's* 1977 fiction contest.

In 1977 Tennant, who had herself explored feminine roles in *The Time of the Crack* and *Hotel de Dream*, reviewed Kate Millett's *Sita* in the *Times Literary Supplement*. Her review reveals disappointment in the book as well as in Millett. "What has come over Ms. Millett, brave civil rights champion and, as it's very easy to see from the book, a warm and intelligent person? Is this what happens to people when they have an unhappy love affair? Is this what she's trying to tell us? Or is it important for her that her followers, those women who are still trying desperately to hold the aircraft in the air, should understand that their goddess has feet of clay? Certainly she's chosen a dicey moment to tell us that she feels old and finished. . . ."

Tennant began writing *The Bad Sister*, her fourth novel, in 1977, and did not publish the summer edition of *Bananas* while engrossed in her writing and research. An anthology of *Bananas* articles, poetry, and stories appeared, however, bridging the gap between quarterly editions. Tennant made time to edit the anthology and to write a jubilant introduction to it: "Gloomy prophecies that a magazine of this type could only find a very limited readership proved false. Once *Bananas* was made available in newsagents and bookshops all over the country, people started to buy it." In a section of the anthology entitled "Women & Myth," Tennant's own short story, "Philomela," appears. A first-person narrative—a form which Tennant subsequently adopted in her next two novels—it treats the myth of Procne and Philomela.

In 1978 Tennant began writing fiction reviews for the *Guardian*. Tired of "two unpaid jobs—writing and editing a magazine," Tennant sold *Bananas* in July to Abigail Mosely, a poet. She continued to coedit *Bananas* for a short time but gave even that up in favor of devoting herself to full-time writing.

The Bad Sister, published in mid-1978 by Gollancz, takes place in the mountains of Scotland and London, and represents a break from her past writing in that she has moved away from satire to real life, adopting a journal format for a plot based on James Hogg's *The Private Memoirs and Confessions of a Justified Sinner* (1824). She did meticulous research, paralleling Hogg's story of a young man who brings about the deaths of his mother and brother with the story of Jane, who allegedly kills her father and sister. *The Bad Sister*'s structure is based on Hogg's structure, beginning with an editorial narrative, then presenting the journal of the assumed murderer, Jane Wild, and closing with an editor's note interpreting Jane's confessional journal. The editor's comments are dated 1986, and the journal begins well before the victims are murdered in 1976. Both murderers are presented as demonically possessed, although psychological disturbance is not ruled out as a contributing factor in the murders. The same satanic figure, Gil-martin, appears in both Tennant's book and Hogg's.

Tennant veers away from Hogg's story by inserting a consideration of the nature and role of women in society. Just down the street from Jane's flat, which she shares with her boyfriend, Tony, is a home for battered wives; next door to it is "the most successful lesbian nightclub in London, Paradise Island." Jane seems fascinated with "the women who had the foolishness not to stop themselves from being beaten up . . . and the women who want each other, whose breasts meet like soft pillows as they dance."

Jane appears normal to Tony, until one evening she leaves a party, going home and "decimating" her hair: "little spikes of straw stood on my head and it was quite rough when I ran my hands through it, like stroking a pig's back. For the first time since childhood I could see by looking straight ahead, instead of shaking my fringe to one side, a gesture which, over the years, had become apologetic and feminine, as if I had to admit it wasn't my right to contemplate the world." She assumes a second identity, calling this double Meg and wandering through the streets, a different size, in different clothes. She is under the spell of Meg: "I wondered, standing there, suspended in time, what Meg would do for me when I saw her. I could feel, now, that my shadows had been removed and that I was allowed to sample, for a while, the feeling of completeness. It was as if she had given me something else in place of the bad sister, something that made me as strong and round as the beginning of the world. For this feeling, I knew I would give her anything she asked. . . . My sisters had been nightmares. Meg would help me drive them away. . . . I knew Meg wanted to take, in return for this, everything I had: my salvation would be paid for in blood, but never hers: she was anti-Christ. . . ."

The Scottish poet Edwin Morgan said in his *Times Literary Supplement* review of *The Bad Sister* that Jane is searching for "an end to the 'double female self ' if she can kill her sister, and a gaining of the necessary 'male principle' if she can find Gilmartin. . . . She is really searching for a power that women are surmised to have had in pre-scientific times, lost, and now begin in various ways to set about retrieving." He also commented on the novel's "jagged, shifting, cinematic quality" and said that "To some, its concerns—feminism, witchcraft, 'wholeness'—will seem modish." Jacky Gillott found the novel more difficult to understand: "Vampirism, previous existences, departures from the body—all of which seem prompted by the notion of a profoundly conditioned division of the female psyche—play such a confusing part in the story that its fictional grip on the imagination is intermittently lost." Yet, she found "the writing and images . . . consistently striking."

The Bad Sister was later published in paperback by Avon, and sold about 70,000 copies in that edition. In 1979 it was published in a Picador edition by Pan Books. Tennant calls it her most "topical" book, feminism carried to the extreme: "Capitalism is paternalism, therefore I will murder my father." A dramatic version, which Tennant says is faithful to her novel, is scheduled to be produced on British television in spring 1983. The script was written by two old friends, Peter Wollen and Laura Mulvey, who together directed *The Riddles of the Sphinx*, an avant-garde feminist picture.

Saturday Night Reader, a large hardback anthology edited by Tennant, was published by W. H. Allen in 1979. It contains travel, horror, and adventure tales, as well as poetry and literary interviews. Most of the authors represented had also contributed to *Bananas*. Also in 1979, Tennant's editor at Gollancz, Liz Calder, took a job with Jonathan Cape, and Tennant, choosing to remain with Calder, submitted her next novel, *Wild Nights*, to Cape, who published it that year. She was delighted to return to Cape and feels it is especially exciting to belong to the Cape fiction list; Tom Maschler "wants to keep fiction alive," she says, "and it is stimulating to be in such company as William Styron and Doris Lessing, other Cape authors."

Emma Tennant calls *Wild Nights* a "fictional childhood memoir." It is "a strange, beautiful, child's vision of the world," full of magical adult maneuvering and the enchantments of the changing seasons. The book is dedicated "To Colin," Tennant's brother, and set in the Tennant's family home, a nineteenth-century "great monument to the Industrial Revolution," with "stone guns and flying buttresses of mid-nineteenth-century capitalism." The child's imagination is both fantastic and fanciful. To her, Aunt Zita, her father's visiting sister, is a powerful woman who can perform supernatural, witchlike feats. She upsets the household—father is delighted with Aunt Zita's visit, mother upset by it, the child enchanted. When evening settles in, it brings "a new darkness to the house, a darkness that came only with Aunt Zita." Once again, illusion and reality are interwoven throughout the novel, so that where Aunt Zita's storytelling stops and the child's wistful imagination begins is difficult to distinguish:

> "Shall we go to the ball?" said Aunt Zita. When she said this, her room began to fill with the people who always came with us on these occasions—and I knew she was in her most excited mood, at her most determined to pull back the past, to string herself with light, and sparkling goblets, and the fire festivals where she used to dance.
> The people who were coming into the

Tennant's family home in Scotland, which served as the setting for Wild Nights

room would have astonished my parents. . . .
The wind always shrieked as we rose above
the house and headed for the ravine, and the
cleuchs filled with heather that burned grey
in strips in winter . . . Aunt Zita held me as we
passed over the village. We never looked behind us, at the house where the ghostly maids
had put out their phantom lights . . .

Relatives, long-dead, come alive to the child
when Aunt Zita visits, haunting her father and
mother. Aunt Zita's annual visits are always at the
end of summer, and the child believes that she
brings the north wind with her. Without the wind,
her aunt is helpless. Witchlike Aunt Zita's visit is
interrupted with the arrival of Aunt Thelma, her
mother's sister and a devout Christian, who usually
visits at a different time. Her arrival cancels Zita's
powers.

Each year the family leaves the north for the
warmer air of the south, going to stay with Uncle
Rainbow and the woman who looks after him, Letty.
Because the visits were always timed in the spring,
the child believes Uncle Rainbow and Letty create it.
But her father yearns for the north, and the family
returns to Scotland, where the "dark came down in
the evenings as if it never would give way to spring."

Wild Nights, which was inspired by the writings
of Bruno Schulz, a Polish author shot in Warsaw in
1940, was one of Elaine Feinstein's favorites in the
1979 *Times* book-of-the-year column: "Of the English novels I have read this year, Emma Tennant's
child's eye vision in *Wild Nights* . . . [has] remained
with me most vividly." Jacky Gillott's recap of 1979
books stated that *Wild Nights* was "ultimately unsatisfactory as a novel," but "the sustained imaginative effort of this book is considerable. Indeed I
would say that hers was the most original book
among those by women writers." The *Sunday Telegraph* called Tennant "one of the most original writers to emerge in recent years," with *Wild Nights*
marking "her coming-of-age as a rare fantasist who
writes like a witch."

Tennant next began work on *Alice fell* (1980),
tackling the myth of Persephone and "the fall,"
placing it in the context of England in the late 1950s
and the 1960s. Like *The Time of the Crack* and *The Last
of the Country House Murders*, the novel deals once
again with the question of survival. Alice Paxton's
birth upsets the routine of The Old Man's house.
Her father feels no kinship with her; it is as though
she emerged from the sea, an abandoned infant
with a note pinned to her chest. In the original
myth, Persephone is the child of Demeter, the earth
mother, and Zeus. Zeus gives Persephone to Hades,

and she descends, or falls, into the underworld. Her
mother mournfully searches for her until finally
Zeus has pity on such sorrow and allows Persephone
to return to Demeter. Hades, however, gives her a
charm to ensure she will spend a third of every year
with him.

In Tennant's updated version of this myth,
Alice runs off to Soho and lives with a pimp, doing
everything "that was written in the book of the underworld," while her mother searches the London
streets for her. The story of the eventual location of
Alice and her return to the family home is entwined
with political troubles of Britain during the late
1950s and the 1960s. The old order is crumbling,
while it ignores the upstart new, just as The Old
Man refused to acknowledge Alice's existence.

Critical reception of *Alice fell* was mixed. While
John Nicolson found the book "a disappointment,"
Bernard Levin called it "a very strange and very
beautiful book." Carol Rubens, discussing the allegorical aspects of the novel, stated: "As archetypes, her characters have a limited choice of
actions." Yet she felt that the characters and family
structure were "credible" and that the novel was
written with a "delicate comic sense." While she
found the symbolism "over-obvious and rather
simplistic," she called *Alice fell* "stronger, less whimsical stuff than the predecessor it most resembles,
Wild Nights. . . . The prose itself is beautifully measured and graceful. . . ."

Obviously fascinated with mythology, Tennant laughingly discusses "the muse" which is so
worshipfully invoked by male poets. It would be
quite one thing, she says, to be a man and have this
lovely creature come and stay at one's side, and it is
quite another for a female author to live with this
muse, who is a "rather demanding, nasty woman."
She discusses writer's block in *Hotel de Dream*, revealing, perhaps, some of her own failed remedies
at overpowering this crippling malady: "it could last
for weeks, and . . . no amount of literary laxatives
had the slightest effect on it, whether ingested in the
form of the all-night reading of crime novels, or the
short sharp jabs of gardening manuals."

Yet Tennant seems able to overcome any writer's block she may encounter for she continues her
writing output. In 1980 she completed a children's
story, *The Search for Treasure Island*, which was published in 1981. Early in 1981 she switched from
prose fiction to playwriting and completed two
comedies, "The Children's Room" and "Holiday
Lets," which are being considered for production.
Her novel in progress, "Answer July," which she,
appropriately, began writing in July, takes its title

from the opening line of an Emily Dickinson poem (as does *Wild Nights*).

Tennant has been influenced most recently by the literature of South American and East European writers. She finds them "much more imaginative" than English and American writers and is striving to equal their literary creativity in the English language. She plans to continue novel writing and is sufficiently interested in playwriting that she may well direct further efforts to both genres. Tennant spends summers in her Dorset cottage in the heart of Wiltshire, Thomas Hardy country. He was one of her favorite authors, and it is easy, she says, to envision Tess sorrowfully trudging through "Wessex" vainly awaiting Angel Clare. Although most of her writing is done in her London home, Tennant does some work in the country, in between swimming in her backyard pool and caring for her children. Divorced again, she shares the cottage with

Tim Owens, a writer whose short stories appeared in both the *Bananas* and *Saturday Night Reader* anthologies.

Tennant is an exciting, original writer who deals with the issues of feminism and the quest for life's meaning in innovative, imaginative ways. If she succeeds in infusing her next novels with a stronger story line than her later novels have achieved, the combination of beautiful imagery and sensitive originality will be powerful and should ensure her a place among the leading writers of the decade.

Other:

Bananas [anthology], edited by Tennant (London: Quartet, 1977);
Saturday Night Reader, edited by Tennant (London: W. H. Allen, 1979).

Rosemary Tonks
(1932-)

Michelle Poirier and Jay L. Halio
University of Delaware

BOOKS: *On Wooden Wings: The Adventures of Webster* (London: Murray, 1948);
Wild Sea Goose (London: Murray, 1951);
Notes on Cafés and Bedrooms (London: Putnam's, 1963);
Opium Fogs (London: Putnam's, 1963);
Emir (London: Adam Books, 1963);
Iliad of Broken Sentences (London: Bodley Head, 1967);
The Bloater (London: Bodley Head, 1968);
Businessmen as Lovers (London: Bodley Head, 1969); republished as *Love Among the Operators* (Boston: Gambit, 1970);
The Way Out of Berkeley Square (London: Bodley Head, 1970; Boston: Gambit, 1971);
The Halt During the Chase (London: Bodley Head, 1972; New York: Harper & Row, 1973).

To be fully urban at a time when others are intrinsically, even fiercely, suburban is an accomplishment. Rosemary Tonks, who has seen herself as a modern Baudelaire, has written contemporary poems and novels that have established her

in the eyes of many as "the poet of the modern metropolis."

Writing novels in a highly personal style— more as a poet than a novelist, especially in her early fiction—Tonks has not received her full due of critical attention and favor, although her grasp of the English language and her sense of the city (London) are brilliant. Her novels tend to be a kind of fictional autobiography in which she not only plays the leading role but one or two supporting ones as well. She includes incidents and experiences directly from her past, often with only a thin fictional veil to disguise them. Some critics feel that this is a fault, that Tonks has not sufficiently distanced herself from her characters; others, that her directness and spontaneity are fresh and original, making for a lively, distinct fictional world. Whatever the verdict, Tonks's poems and novels are the story of her life up to 1972, when her last book was published.

Rosemary D. Boswell Tonks was born in 1932 in England. Her father had just died of blackwater fever in Africa (hence Rosemary "for remembrance"), and she spent her early childhood in baby homes and boarding schools. At the age of nine she began to invent things: cameras with drawings of her friends already "developed" inside them; airplanes that dropped two or three parachutes at carefully spaced intervals; and many other gadgets that revealed an already active imagination. Later, at Wentworth, in her early teens she began writing poetry. Although she was at the top of her class year after year, she was dissatisfied with the curriculum. She resented the absence of worthwhile lessons and considered the tasks assigned to her asinine. She contented herself, therefore, with her own amusements that included "gang warfare. Heavy fighting in the cellars with taking of prisoners." At sixteen she was expelled. Tonks likes to think it was for general frivolity, but officially it was for stealing tomatoes. When asked why it surprised her, she replied: "I don't know. It never occurs to you you'll be rejected." That same year she published her first book, one for children called *On Wooden Wings: The Adventures of Webster* (1948).

Having no roots anywhere else, Tonks convinced her mother to rent a flat for the two of them in London, where her real education began. She discovered libraries but was disappointed that there was nothing very good in them. She began writing stories for the BBC and received in return "rapturous letters and 10 to 12 guineas each." At nineteen she married her husband, Micky, a civil engineer, and a few years later they went off to Karachi, Pakistan, together, where she began to write poetry seriously. Her progress was halted, however, when she contracted typhoid fever and had to return to England. Back in Karachi soon afterward, she then contracted polio and for months she was paralyzed from the neck down but continued writing poetry, an epic in free verse that has not been published. Again she returned to England, but finding it full of relatives—and "in illness you want to be alone"—she went off by herself to Paris, since her husband had to remain in Karachi. Aspects of these experiences are well recorded in her last two novels, and she has written about her stay in Paris in an essay, "On being down, but not quite out, in Paris." In this essay she describes her encounter with what she later believed was the ghost of Baudelaire. It was evening and she was coming back across Pointe Marie from the right bank "when I saw a man from the nineteenth century. . . . He wore a stove-pipe hat, pale waistcoat, frock coat, narrow trousers, pale gloves, and he looked at me as he passed. I was shaking with fright, and had to prop myself up against a dirty wall." It occurred to her that she may have seen an actor returning from a fancy dress party, but twice after-

Rosemary Tonks

ward, when she crept back to the bridge at exactly the same time, she had a similar experience.

After recuperating fully from the polio attack, Tonks returned to London. There, in 1963, she published her first volume of poetry, *Notes on Cafés and Bedrooms*, to which there was a mixed critical reaction. One critic said that the poems were sometimes direct and comprehensible enough, "but after reading most of them, I was fit for nothing. . . . I emerged feeling as if I had been eaten to death by apocalyptic ducks." He found her poems stark, daring, sensuous, and totally humorless, while another critic saw in them "a brash, bouncy quality." Despite differences of opinion on the mood of the poems—and on their physical effects on readers—there was consensus on her literary techniques and content. Usually eschewing regular rhyme or meter, the poems in the volume concentrate upon city life and often manage to combine coherently the different flavors of metropolitan boredom, excitement, evil, and malaise, as in these lines from "Escape":

It is among the bins and dormitories of cities
Where the busker wins his bread

By turning music on a spit, and the heavens
Have the dirt of the great sky upon their
                                                  sides,

That one goes to gourmandize upon Escape!
Where alleys are so narrow that the Fates
Like meatporters can scarcely pass
With their awkward burden in muslin ban-
                                                  dages,
And carry off the rabble safely to their
                                                  graves. . . .

As Norman Craig remarked and many others
agreed, the images and metaphors in her poems
"dance maniacally through the ruin of syntax,
sometimes bumping head on . . . in loops and swirls
and rosy fogs of language." Extremely sensitive to
criticism of her poetry, Tonks expressed her fear in
"Poet and Iceberg":

No powerful and gloomy city,
Which has rid itself of vermin,
Will admit to keeping
One of these disreputable pets. . . .

Despite her sensitivity to criticism of her
poetry, or perhaps as an inverse reaction to it,
Tonks seemed little concerned by the response, or
lack of it, to her first two novels, both published in
the same year as her poems. She began writing
fiction for money and seems to hold her novels in
some contempt, calling them and those of others
"mud." This is the more curious since her fiction is
quite clearly an extension of her poetry. Another
curiosity: while she regards *Emir* (1963) as "the best
prose work I have written," it is not listed along with
her other works, including the two children's books,
in the front matter of her subsequent publications.

While it is not immediately evident which
novel she wrote first, *Opium Fogs* (1963), the first
one published, relates directly to Tonks's experiences upon returning to England after recuperating from polio. It is about a bizarre group of
Londoners—artists, ne'er-do-wells, "continental
Englishmen," and others—who seem to spend most
of their energies finding new and better ways to
torment each other and themselves. Into this society
reemerges Gabriella, who had left England, married, "a moody little beauty of twenty-two," some
eighteen months before and spent ten of them
paralyzed in India. For Gerard, her former lover,
she was "the only woman with whom I could ever
have lived, and for whom there was any reason to
live." Gerard is determined to win her back but only

briefly succeeds. After a month's pursuit in cold,
grimy London, culminating in a few hours of wild,
impassioned lovemaking in an old Victorian house,
Gabriella abandons Gerard at last. Overcome by
self-recrimination, she nevertheless accurately
sums up the situation thus: "I am not even an extension of his personality—but an escape route; a new
drug which melts his brains." Recognizing Gerard's
self-destructiveness and the "transforming madness" they share—which in six months' time will
leave them nothing but "marvellous wreckage"—
she concludes: "What it amounts to is this: I would
rather occupy five hours of his life on which he
looks back with regret, than try to build a future on
the quicksands of that temperament. For this reason alone, what I have done is morally wrong."

As before, Gabriella appears to choose "boredom, monotony, and middle-class morality," in
Gerard's view. The novel, in fact, retains a strong
undercurrent of moral criticism, often perversely
expressed but there nonetheless. The novel's outstanding attributes, however, are its highly
metaphorical style (which has led critics to view the
novel as a prose poem); its rapid shifts of attitudes,
ideas, perspectives, as well as situations; and its rendition of sharp, personal encounters conveyed
through dialogue (indicated by double quotes)
studded with thoughts uttered to oneself (indicated
by single quotes). The latter are not interior
monologues; they have a much more direct and
incisive effect, however artificial or occasionally
stilted they may appear. (This device is used again in
Emir but dropped in her later novels, when Tonks
adopts a first-person narrative technique.) Above
all, *Opium Fogs* captures the backbiting, egocentric
mode of life that links Tonks's vision of London
society in the 1960s with the appropriate counterpart in Baudelaire's Paris.

Like *Opium Fogs*, the action of *Emir* moves
through a very limited amount of scenery, which
floats in and out of the consciousness of a particular
individual, in this case a twenty-two-year-old
poetess named Houda Lawrence. Like Gabriella,
she is pursued by an admirer, a middle-aged aesthete and intellectual named Eugene, who wants to
be her lover. Although Houda despises him, especially after he wrecks her room looking for her
address when she is on holiday in the country,
Eugene is convinced that her attacks against him are
merely inverted compliments and therefore persists
in his attentions. If Eugene had "caught her in a
passing mood of disgust, and was determined, with
every trick at his disposal, to hold her there for life,"
nevertheless he has his attractions. "To get

drunk—on someone else's soul. Eugene, you have instructed me in the most fabulous of apetites," Houda says to herself. The conflict between the two is finally resolved only when Houda shows Eugene her poems, which appall him.

Tonks uses her protagonist's consciousness to voice what are probably her own views. For example, Houda sees "castes separated by the pronunciation of a word," and she thinks "Cézanne's agony made the public learn its lesson all too well, for now they will buy any stupidity with a frame around it." Again, her portrait of London and its inhabitants is similar to the one in *Opium Fogs*, and her style is almost identical in both books. What is different is that the female protagonist, Houda, is quite unlike Gabriella. She is someone who could never choose bourgeois existence but as a poet rejects it entirely. "Yes, chaos is fearful," she says. "But order is much worse because it is boring." Gabriella, Gerard, and Houda thus reveal what may be different, often contradictory, aspects of Tonks's own complex view of life at this time.

Although critics may fault Tonks for poor syntax and shallow plot, they usually give her credit for having a biting wit, a light tone, and delightful characters. Tonks, however, has said that she wishes people would stop regarding her as light-minded because in reality she is deadly serious. "But I don't believe in weighing down the reader with a ton of suet so I begin a novel lightly as the only way to convey information." In the same interview she said of her verse: "I'm really trying to make a new music out of natural speech. I can't otherwise cope with large thoughts. No one else is trying to do this so far as I know, though my direct literary forebears, Baudelaire and Rimbaud, were both poets of the modern metropolis. A poet's job is to excite, to send the senses reeling." Much the same could be said of Tonks's novels.

Tonks's ancestors include the biographer James Boswell, whom she rejected because "he went off to England and Ireland thus classifying himself as a horrible Scot." On her mother's side she is descended from the Italian composer Verdi and has registered under this name in Italian hotels because then the receptionists "come out from behind their desks and sing little arias to me." On the centenary of Baudelaire's death in 1967, when her second book of poems was about to come out, she went to visit the Frenchman's grave in Montparnasse cemetery. There she lay down on his life-sized effigy and found she was the same height. She shares other similarities with him. Both had a youth with only occasional flashes of sun and both lived in the

tropics. She used to see herself as the albatross of Baudelaire's poem, "encumbered on the ground with the same wings which enabled her to fly."

It is an apt reference: her second volume of poetry, *Iliad of Broken Sentences* (1967), never really took off, and the critics largely ignored it. Like the first, it is a thin volume whose verse criticizes contemporary authors of "mud" novels, the hotel-, discotheque-, and café-haunting literati, as in these lines:

> All this sitting about in cafés to calm down
> Simply wears me out. And their idea of liter-
>   ature!
> The idiotic cut of the stanzas; the novels, full
>   up, gross. . . .

As the London *Times* critic wrote, "Miss Tonks is creating a style, very calculatedly exotic and dramatic. . . . this is not loose writing." Indeed, at its best the verse has a unique toughness and sharp wit, although at its worst it is an indecisive distraction.

While her poems often went through many drafts—literally scores of them—her novels were usually written quickly. Her third novel, *The Bloater* (1968), was completed in four weeks, and it is probably her most successful one, at least as far as the public is concerned. Tonks is at her wittiest and most sensuous in the novel. As A. W. Murray commented in the London *Times*, "None of the jokes seem planted, all natural regeneration, pages stuffed with insight and observation. . . ." The protagonist of *The Bloater*, Min, is pursued by a determined would-be lover, here a gargantuan baritone whom she repeatedly but not always successfully tries to fend off. Unlike Houda, free-spirited Min is married. Her husband is mentioned only a few times: once in the beginning ("George is the man I am married to"); occasionally in the middle; and again at the end, when Min says to him: "I'm terribly sorry, I'm afraid I may have ruined your life." The remainder of his time George presumably spends going to and from the British Museum, where he is officially "Keeper of unprinted books," or otherwise engaging in one of the two or three lives he leads once he is away from the house. The plot is resolved (unclimactically) when Min falls in love with her musicologist friend, Billy. She is amazed with herself when they, "two diehard metropolitans," take an afternoon off and walk under the trees in Hampstead and discover how they feel toward each other. *The Bloater* ends with Min and Billy falling more and more in love and planning a Roman holiday.

The Bloater is written in the style of the diary Tonks kept at the time. "It is written directly, yet in a way that is glancing and impersonal: that is, ideal for confidences," as one critic recognized, taking the words directly from the novel. It definitely shows a firmer grasp of novelistic techniques without a corresponding wholesale sacrifice of the wit, originality, and zestfulness that characterize her earlier work.

Businessmen as Lovers (1969), Tonks's next book, is a holiday novel in every sense and reveals the author in a still lighter, gayer mood: its pages are almost literally bathed in the warm Mediterranean sunlight on an island off the coast of Italy. Two women, Caroline and Mimi, set out for Livone with Caroline's children, later to be joined by the children's father, Killi; Mimi's lover, Beetle; and a variety of other colorful, zany, British holiday-makers. Almost plotless, the novel is narrated in the first-person by Mimi, who describes the antics of this motley assortment of characters along with her own shenanigans. Wit and cleverness abound, but, colored by the joy of Mimi's deepening love for Beetle, they lack the tendentiousness of Tonks's earlier novels and poems. Even the comic grotesquerie of Dr. Oskar Purzelbaum, the butt of several practical jokes, is more generously portrayed than his counterpart in *Opium Fogs*, Dr. Bodo Swingler.

This novel, like her next one, *The Way Out of Berkeley Square* (1970), clearly justified the description of Tonks as "a novelist who writes short, wayward, but brilliant books, in which the wit steals on you gradually like a spark creeping among bracken roots before the sudden blaze." But Tonks was not pleased when her editor complimented her on *The Way out of Berkeley Square*; she replied, "It just proves the English like their porridge." While she was doubtless reflecting her prejudice in favor of poetry, some professional critics did not like the novel either, probably for the wrong reasons.

The female protagonist, Arabella, is held in thrall, not by one but by three men: her terribly spoiled, self-indulgent father; her twenty-year-old, rebellious brother, Michael; and a middle-aged, attractive businessman she calls her Wolf. The opening sentence announces the basic situation, as Arabella proclaims: "I'm thirty, and I'm stuck." How she eventually finds a way to get unstuck the ensuing 207 pages reveal, and they are not without the mixture of real agony and farce that Tonks by now has become adept at rendering. Although there are glimpses of bohemian life, like the poet Leo's—he lives in Hampstead and is one of several of Tonks's surrogates in this novel—the main focus is the upper-middle-class London society of successful stockbrokers and their bitchy wives. Among the more moving portraits is that of young Michael, who has fled to Karachi to escape his domineering father, writes poetry, and contracts polio in the terribly severe heat.

In *The Halt During the Chase* (1972), Tonks's last published novel, the heroine, Sophie, is Arabella a year older and in altered circumstances, both filial and amatory. She also demonstrates a deepening spiritual consciousness. Instead of a domineering father for whom she keeps house, Sophie has a lively, humorous mother with whom she does not live but still must look after. Among the other dramatis personae are Rudi Horder, a wealthy antiques dealer, and his two sons: Philip, a successful, clever, and handsome bureaucrat, who is Sophie's lover; and Guy, like Michael in *The Way Out of Berkeley Square*, a rebellious and tormented young man, whose sojourn in Paris on the Ile St. Louis, closely resembles Tonks's at the same age. (He also tells of meeting Baudelaire's ghost.) Although at

Dust jacket for Tonks's 1972 novel, her last before she became a born-again Christian and burned her work in progress

first much in love with Philip, Sophie realizes one evening when they spend the night in a hotel that Philip's devotion is and always will be shallow, that he has no intention of truly wedding her. The shock of this revelation is, however, salubrious, and her recovery is aided by her recent studies in mysticism, the counsel of a clairevoyant in Brighton, and a holiday in Normandy at a house inhabited by a charming French family to which her friend, Princess Melika, sends her. There, despite Philip's pursuit, Sophie awakens to a full consciousness of herself and freedom. At last she understands what the lectures on mysticism she was attending with Guy had taught: ". . . that it was your job to develop yourself, as the primary purpose of life; the chase is inward." While this knowledge confirmed the "natural tendency" of her mind, she had suppressed it as "selfish" up to then. She understands, too, that she must henceforward avoid "the company of those who limited you and themselves." Philip would stop her development just as she would his. The novel ends in the living room of the wise old Princess Melika who, despite her increasing poverty, gaily celebrates with Sophie the advent of her new life.

The Halt During the Chase is the most firmly plotted and carefully structured of all Rosemary Tonks's novels and reveals a maturity of style and purpose, prefigured in her previous work, but here most fully achieved. The pursuit, the chase, with which all of her novels deal, has now turned inward and, like Sophie, Tonks seemed to have found new freedom and new purpose. Fortunately, the poetry and the wit are not absent, and she still peppers her prose with sharply-defined images that are equally notable for their economy of language, as in this description of the landscape around St. Emilion: "There was a weak blue fire in the sky. The grey stakes of the fences ate ice from the wind." Throughout the novel expressions of genuine feeling, humor, and pointed repartee recur along with the emerging, clearly delineated quest in which Sophie is engaged.

With this obvious success under her belt, Tonks began her *chef d'oeuvre*, a long novel on which she spent over five years writing and which had grown to her longest sustained piece of fiction (90,000 words) before she abandoned it—and all literature—forever. For during the last decade, Tonks was on another significant quest as well. She has become a born-again Christian and as such has found poetry, fiction, essays entirely irrelevant to the Truth she has sought. As testimony to her conviction, doubtless forged with no little pain, she burned the manuscript of the major novel she had been working on, withdrew her poems from new anthologies, and withdrew from writers' directories. Her renunciation, in brief, is total, and she now lives only to propagate the Word, as it is revealed in the Christian Bible.

Other:
"On being down, but not quite out, in Paris," (London) *Times*, 12 May 1976.

Interviews:
Terry Coleman, "Bloater, Billy, and Min," *Guardian*, 27 June 1968;
Coleman, "Rosemary for Remembrance," *Guardian*, 24 October 1970;
William Foster, "A Poet of the Modern Metropolis," *Scotsman*, 21 November 1970.

Rose Tremain

(2 August 1943-   )

Simon Edwards
Roehampton Institute

BOOKS: *Freedom for Women* (New York: Ballentine, 1971);

Stalin (New York: Ballentine, 1974);

Sadler's Birthday (London: Macdonald & Janes, 1976; New York: St. Martin's, 1976);

Letter to Sister Benedicta (London: Macdonald & Janes, 1978; New York: St. Martin's, 1979).

Rose Tremain is the author of two short novels, both remarkable exercises in imaginative identification with aging characters, the mystery of whose lives appears to elude them, until, at the end, they mark a quiet triumph for some fundamentally human capacity for both acceptance and transformation. She is also an accomplished writer of radio drama who recently has begun work for television.

Rose Tremain

A third novel, *The Cupboard*, is scheduled for publication in 1982.

Rose Tremain was born in 1943 to Keith Nicholas Thompson, a writer, and his wife, Viola. She received a diploma in literature in 1962 from the Sorbonne and graduated with a B.A. in English Studies at the University of East Anglia in 1967, where she met and took classes with novelist Angus Wilson. After working for two years as an elementary school teacher and for two years as an editor at British Printing Corporation Publications, she began writing full time. Separated from her husband of seven years in 1978, she now lives with her two children in Suffolk. She does not regard her life as an interesting or significant one, and wonders what it would be like if she were not a writer. Such a disarmingly modest admission may partly account for the special quality of extended compassion for the otherwise unlikely protagonists of her fiction. She describes them herself as, in some respects, "alien territory."

Her first publications were two pieces of popular history: an illustrated account of the women's suffrage movement, *Freedom for Women* (1971), and a biography, *Stalin* (1974). Both of these are hitherto available only in the U. S. Her first novel, *Sadler's Birthday*, appeared in 1976. It is the story of an elderly retired butler who, after years of uncomplainingly efficient service, has inherited the home of his former childless employees, Col. and Mrs. Bassett.

It is a novel of distances and repressions in human relations, but gradually Sadler's fitful memories well up inside him and spread outwards as though to fill the deserted echoing rooms of the East Anglian mansion, where he now lives alone and virtually disregarded. They are not only his memories but include those of his mother (he is an illegitimate only child) and his employers. If indeed the novel is slightly flawed it is through the absence of any controlling perspective between these different elements. Sadler's life spans almost the whole century, but it has been a marginal one, lived in the interstices of others. Even access to books and music at an earlier employer's has to be abandoned be-

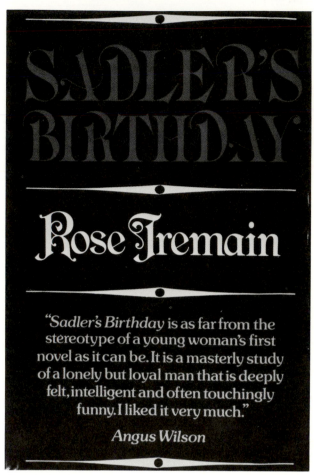

Dust jacket for the American edition of Tremain's first novel, about a retired butler who inherits his former employers' home

fession from both just before their deaths), he appears to be himself about to die. He returns to his old bedroom, shut up for years, and discovers it in a state of total neglect enabling him to make some comparable spiritual discovery. The "little central cell around which his life had arranged itself, he had let die," he reflects, and he is thus not ready for death yet. This is not quite a final stocktaking, and we are left on a note of resumed hope and subdued optimism. The absence of any clearly articulated strong feeling creates a rather chilling atmosphere not unlike that met in certain poems by Philip Larkin. Rose Tremain also acknowledges a debt to V. S. Naipaul, the Trinidadian novelist, and the note of internal exile so insistently sounded in his work seems to be heard both here and in the next novel.

Letter to Sister Benedicta (1978) solves the problem of unified point of view by taking the form of an intermittent letter-journal written by the fat, middle-aged, materially prosperous Ruby Constad to an old teacher of hers, a nun in India, where she was born and educated. Sister Benedicta may well be dead, but it is a measure of Ruby's aloneness that the sister is her only suitable addressee. The daughter of an army colonel, Ruby rejected the cold formality of her family and married an ambitious young Jewish solicitor, Leon, who is now a divorce lawyer of international repute. He has just been admitted to a hospital after a stroke induced by learning the totality of their children's rejection of them, which only gradually emerges from Ruby's "letter." Their daughter, Alexandra, has begun a lesbian affair at art college, and Noel, who it was hoped would follow his father into the law, is last heard of bumming around Europe. The ultimate turn of the screw is Alexandra's admission that she and her brother have been lovers, paradoxical evidence of the closeness of the family (although Ruby does not see it as such) as well as of the depth of their complicity against their parents. Ruby's empty life is lived now on a narrow axis between the private clinic where she visits her silent husband, resisting the temptation to accuse him of the family's troubles; Brompton Oratory, where she is incapable of prayer; and Harrods Department Store. These sites mark out her social world. Sister Benedicta is addressed as an image of illusory wholeness and peace. Round her memory Ruby tentatively reconstructs her life and marriage, Leon's adulteries, and her own single, but tender, excursion into infidelity.

Like *Sadler's Birthday* it is a meditation on a very specific case of lovelessness and failure, even as Ruby reveals a thwarted capacity for love, surprising the reader by the range of her compassion, not

cause of his mother's delicate position in service as the mother of a bastard. His most potent memory is that of a young cockney boy, Tom, who was evacuated to the house during the war and for whom he took responsibility largely through the inertia of the colonel and his wife. These were five years of love, spent largely in a fascinated watching of the boy, but also eventually including a physical relationship. Less through guilt at his own homosexuality than through Tom's insouciant failure to reciprocate his affection, Sadler finds it difficult to recover the full significance of this experience or even adequately recall it. This is, however, the result of a general forgetfulness in which all memories are fragile, and it is for its presentation of such a state of mind that the novel is so remarkable. At the end, just at the point where Sadler appears to have recognized that his condition of lovelessness and failure was shared by his employers (he remembers moments of unexpectedly intimate con-

merely for her children but for some of their unlikely friends. It is indeed one of the latter, a casual acquaintance of Noel's, who unwittingly inspires her decision at the end of the novel to overturn her restricted life and, after her husband's death, to return to India. This recovery of moral energy is another image of renewed possibility, a quiet acclamation that the inhibitions of aging are more illusory than real.

Such is the range of incidental characters introduced in the course of each novel's account of its central character that one suspects Rose Tremain has the capacity for a more expansive mode of fiction. As writer-in-residence at the University of Essex, 1980-1981, she completed what she describes as a long novel. Again it focuses on a single character, another elderly one, but its secondary theme is war: "which war must I fight in, and which oppose?" This theme suggests a greater intellectual depth too. If it is successful in its attempt to relate "private" and public warfare, it should prove a distinctive contribution to that tradition of the liberal humanist novel in which she has already produced exciting work.

Like many novelists she finds the experience of working for radio and television an exhilarating one creatively. It not merely affects the plays themselves, but it is a cooperative enterprise lending support to the often rather isolated activity of writing fiction. She sees her work in these media as not only sharing the novel's concern with love and lovelessness but also, perhaps, enabling her to develop more fully a comic detachment necessary to counter the occasionally restricting tendencies of that remarkable sensitivity which characterizes her two novels to date.

Television Scripts:
Halleluiah, Mary Plum, BBC TV2, 1979;
Findings on a Late Afternoon, BBC TV1, 1981;
A Room for the Winter, BBC TV1, 1981.

Radio Scripts:
The Wisest Fool, BBC Radio 4, 1976;
Blossom, BBC Radio 4, 1977;
Dark Green, BBC Radio 4, 1977;
Don't Be Cruel, BBC Radio 4, 1978;
Learnings, BBC Radio 4, 1978;
Down the Hill, BBC Radio 4, 1979;
Half Time, BBC Radio 4, 1979.

William Trevor
(24 May 1928-   )

Jay L. Halio
University of Delaware
and
Paul Binding

SELECTED BOOKS: *A Standard of Behaviour* (London: Hutchinson, 1958);
The Old Boys (London: Bodley Head, 1964; New York: Viking, 1964);
The Boarding House (London: Bodley Head, 1965; New York: Viking, 1965);
The Love Department (London: Bodley Head, 1966; New York: Viking, 1967);
The Day We Got Drunk on Cake (London: Bodley Head, 1967; New York: Viking, 1968);
The Girl (London: French, 1968);
Mrs. Eckdorf in O'Neill's Hotel (London: Bodley Head, 1969; New York: Viking, 1970);
The Old Boys [play] (London: Poynter, 1971);

Miss Gomez and the Brethren (London: Bodley Head, 1971);
A Night with Mrs. da Tonka (London: French, 1972);
The Ballroom of Romance (London: Bodley Head, 1972; New York: Viking, 1972);
Going Home (London: French, 1972);
Elizabeth Alone (London: Bodley Head, 1973; New York: Viking, 1974);
Marriages (London: French, 1974);
Angels at the Ritz (London: Bodley Head, 1975; New York: Viking, 1976);
The Children of Dynmouth (London: Bodley Head, 1976; New York: Viking, 1977);
Old School Ties (London: Lemon Tree Press, 1976);

Lovers of Their Time and Other Stories (London: Bodley Head, 1978; New York: Viking, 1978);
Other People's Worlds (London: Bodley Head, 1980; New York: Viking, 1981);
Beyond the Pale (London: Bodley Head, 1981).

William Trevor has established a solid reputation both in Britain and America as an exceptionally sensitive, morally concerned writer whose forte appears to be rendering comic pathos, whether in his novels or in his short stories. Although born in Ireland, he has lived for many years in England, where his fiction is more frequently set than in his native land. Perhaps his Protestant background gave him a comparatively easy access to English society. The country that he has really made his own, however, is the rarely mapped one of the socially displaced—not tramps or hobos or prostitutes, though these may appear in Trevor's novels and stories, as much as those who move through life fundamentally alone and cultureless, ill-versed in either their own or their larger society's make-up. Often his people are victims of their own half-understood fantasies, obsessive attachments to unreciprocating others, to animals or objects. His vision of the loneliness of "other people's worlds" does not lead him, however, to literary evocations of solipsism in forms that match the state—as in Beckett, for instance—but to a very English novel form of social observation. His first highly successful novel, *The Old Boys*, owes something in its controlled, stylized dialogue to Ivy Compton-Burnett, with whom he also shares a sense of evil immanent beneath polite surfaces. In his short stories, his debt is clearly to James Joyce, with whom he has often very favorably been compared.

He was born William Trevor Cox in Mitchelstown, County Cork, Ireland. His father, James William Cox, was a bank manager, and his mother's maiden name was Gertrude Davison. He was educated at thirteen different Irish provincial schools before attending St. Columba's College, Dublin, from 1942 to 1946, after which he went on to Trinity College, Dublin. In *Old School Ties* (1976), Trevor recalls his early years as a schoolboy, beginning with the convent school in Youghal where he was twice-over a minority—as one of a handful of boys amongst many girls, and as a Protestant. But it was a happy time: "When I look back on that convent in Youghal," he writes, "I experience a wave of happiness." He was then just six. Later, in Miss Willoughby's schoolroom in Skibbereen he first learned that "the world is not an easy-going place," for Miss Willoughby was stern as well as young—an

William Trevor

evangelical Methodist, in short. On a return visit years afterwards, Trevor sought refuge from her haunting presence in the bar of Eldon's Hotel, for only there, "in spectral form or otherwise," was he sure it could not be felt.

His "obsession" with schools and school life began, he says, with his sister's small library of schoolgirls' stories, which he loved to read. Years later he still obsessively bought copies of *The Girl* every Thursday, until that "excellent" publication ceased—"certainly a sign of the decadence that was to come." For long periods of his childhood he attended no school at all but was left to "wander the streets of provincial Irish towns untaught for months on end." Occasionally, he and his brother were tutored by a failed Christian brother or a farmer's daughter who had qualified through the intermediate certificate examination. Their tutors were found the way their mother found her maids, Trevor says, by knocking on farmhouse doors.

His first boarding school was the Tate School in Wexford. Though the girls did not actually board there, it was coeducational and designed for "poor Protestants" (as opposed to Anglo-Irish). Withdrawn in the middle of term for reasons he does not state (the new headmaster had also abruptly left), Trevor continued in and out of schools. At thirteen, he attended Sandford Park School, Dublin, as one of ten boarders. He had "no knowledge of French, Latin, or Geometry, and precious little of anything else," including most organized sports. However, under A. D. Cordoner, the headmaster, cricket was the thing, and after two terms he took young William in hand. Earlier, Trevor had earned a place in the "under-14 Rugby" side and had suffered a broken collarbone in a match against Belvedere College. Cricket was something else again: a hard ball obviously aimed to kill the batsman. But if the bowler did not get him, Trevor recalls, the boredom most certainly did. Nevertheless, Cordoner was relentless, and for boarding students this meant cricket practice every Saturday and Sunday afternoon during summer term unless (like Trevor and a friend) a boy escaped over the wall to the local cinema.

In 1942 Trevor left Sandford Park for St. Columba's and managed finally to escape the threat of cricket, but only by pretending an interest in a (to him) less lethal form of athletics. The school was situated high up in the mountains of Dublin. In his last term, he was made a prefect—a distinction he had declined earlier, saying to the headmaster, "I enjoy the ranks, sir." Reminded of his faltering sense of duty (the headmaster gave him a copy of Ian Hay's *The Housemaster*), and aware that his parents had been notified, Trevor finally accepted, and his life was transformed. "I was, as it were, knighted." Privileges multiplied along with responsibilities. Shortly afterwards, he matriculated at Trinity College, Dublin, where, in 1950, he took his B.A. in history. He was too young for World War II service, and in any case Ireland was a neutral country. In fact, until he was twenty-two, he never left Ireland at all. For several years he worked as a schoolmaster (after a year as a nearly impoverished tutor). At first he taught history at a school in Armagh, Northern Ireland, from 1950 to 1952; later he taught art at Rugby in England (1952-1956) and at Taunton (1956-1960). His memories of a schoolmaster's life are recounted in a later chapter of *Old School Ties*. He had left Ireland mainly for economic reasons: very little work was available, even for qualified teachers. During this period, he also worked as a sculptor, and in 1952 he won the Irish section of the Unknown Political Prisoner Award. Gradually, he says, he came to find his sculpture lacking in humanity, a quality that was going into the stories he began writing. Conversely, while abounding in a tender regard for variegated

humanity, his fiction possesses certain sculptural qualities: precision, an almost obsessive attention to proportions, and a tendency in group studies to lavish particular care on the central figure to whom all others in different ways relate; for example, Mrs. Eckdorf in the novel that bears her name, or Julia in *Other People's Worlds*.

On 26 August 1952 Trevor married Jane Ryan, and they have two sons, Patrick and Dominic. After his attempts at sculpting and schoolmastering, Trevor worked in London as an advertising copywriter at Notley's with Gavin Ewart, Peter Porter, and Edward Lucie-Smith from 1960 to 1965. It was not a happy existence, but his prose style was doubtless honed as he prepared copy. His first novel, *A Standard of Behaviour*, appeared in 1958. Although "a very creditable performance," as one reviewer called it," it is not a distinguished piece of work, and subsequent reviewers have tended to forget its existence, especially since it is usually not listed among Trevor's books on the card pages of his later novels. The narrator is a young man living in London eking out a living by tutoring students while he works toward an advanced degree, having barely made it through his first one. He has a room in a pleasant house owned by a Mrs. Lamont, whose two man-crazy daughters, Peggy and April, are part of the larger circle of friends and hangers-on who lead a bohemian, largely reprobate life. At one point the narrator meets up with Archer, a school acquaintance, who later steals his fiancee, Virginia, whom he had himself stolen from another man. At the end, Virginia leaves Archer, who hangs himself (though not, she insists, because of her desertion). A chance meeting, news of her second marriage, and further conversation finally extinguish the torch the narrator has been carrying for her all the while, completing the pall of gloom that has settled over all the characters who are either dead, in jail, or essentially alone at the end.

It was not until *The Old Boys* (1964) that Trevor's fiction attracted any considerable attention, and it is from this novel that his writing career may properly be said to have been launched. It won the Hawthornden Prize for 1964, and in the same year Trevor took the *Transatlantic Review*'s second prize in a short story competition. But even in the disregarded first novel with its ironic title, *A Standard of Behaviour*, we can see the characters and themes that will continue to interest Trevor throughout his career so far: misfits and charlatans, lost love, the gloom of loneliness and alienation.

The Old Boys centers on the Old Boys' Association of a minor English public school and the question of who shall become its next president. Behind the strained formalities of the old men's dealings with each other lie the hostilities, eccentricities, and asocial feelings of half a century earlier: Trevor exhibits here his characteristic interest in the rituals people devise to protect themselves from naked reality—private rituals and public ones—and the spurious gods people erect to give themselves strength. *The Old Boys* is haunted by the figure of a now long-dead housemaster at the school the Old Boys attended. He is H. L. Dowse, clearly a vain, perverted, self-drunk individual but one whose deeds and sayings are treasured, particularly by his one-time favorite Jaraby, as if they were Holy Writ: "You will learn to take punishment and maybe in time to distribute it. You will learn to win and to lose, to smile on misfortune with the same equanimity as you smile on triumph. The goodness that is in you will be carried to the surface and fanned to a flame, the evil will be faced fairly and squarely; you will recognize it and make your peace with it. We shall display the chinks in your armour and you will learn how best to defend yourself." These cliches, unpleasant where they are not merely banal and ridiculous, have survived among the Old Boys for many decades.

The Old Boys also demonstrates Trevor's feeling for the indignities of the human body, some brought about by disease but more often simply by age. In all of his later work appear the infirm, the incapacitated, those rendered ugly and sexually hors de combat merely through time. Meanwhile, Trevor was encouraged by the success of his novel to turn it first into a television drama and then into a stage play. Sir Michael Redgrave starred in the latter, which was performed in 1971, to mixed reviews. The reviewer in *Plays and Players*, for example, found the plot much too intricate and complex in what had been, for television, a taut hour-long drama. Trevor has maintained an active interest in both forms of drama—television and the stage—for which he has produced a number of successful scripts.

Each of the novels that followed *The Old Boys* presents an outpost of society filled with eccentrics. *The Boarding House* (1965) portrays the small, loose-knit community of lodgers of the strange William Wagner Bird, who has chosen them because they seem to him people no one would ever miss. Mr. Bird dies, and the ill-assorted lodgers are left to cope with one another without his presence. His principal heirs are two longstanding residents of the house: Studdy, "an unfulfilled blackmailer," and Nurse Clock, who rides a motorized bike. The pros-

pect of money brings these two unlikely conspirators and former enemies together, as they plan to evict the boarders Mr. Bird had assembled and to fill the house with the truly old, whom they expect to find easier to exploit. Predictably, the alliance collapses, and Nurse Clock is about to blackmail Studdy when one of the residents, Mr. Obd, burns the house down in an imagined vengeance on Mr. Bird. Critics saw in this novel an advance over his *The Old Boys*. As one of them said, it is "a satisfactory exploration on a larger scale of his own distorted world, written with beautiful control and showing a marvellous facility for macabre invention."

The Love Department (1966) moves to suburban Wimbledon and Putney and the activities of a sexual pervert, Septimus Tuam, who is strangely attractive to women. As a reviewer noted, Trevor presents himself in this novel with a more challenging problem than he had confronted up to now: "to investigate, not the ludicrous egoisms of the old and the adrift, but the death of marriage and the failure of love in the contemporary world." The innocent hero, Edward, leaves the monastery that has sheltered him and applies for a job in the "Love Department" of a national magazine. Supervising the department is Lady Dolores Bourhardie, who sends Edward to hunt out and destroy the wicked Septimus Tuam who seduces women and wrecks homes. In the process of developing this plot, Trevor also explores the marriage of Eve and James Bolsover through a series of sketches, often comic. But the comic tone veils the tragic aspects of James's spiritual condition as he watches his marriage disintegrate. At the end, Edward accidentally causes Tuam's death, and his mission is completed (Lady Dolores had told him he was "put on earth for that reason alone"). In the telling of the novel, matter and manner become almost identified with each other, but because something important has been lost or reduced, as one critic said, the manner "strikes us as in some measure unattractive."

Mrs. Eckdorf in O'Neill's Hotel (1969) is a more ambitious novel than either of these and explores more thoroughly than its immediate predecessors the notion of concentric worlds, which would seem mutually exclusive were it not that mutual exclusivity is impossible in life. A thrice-married woman hears a story about a Dublin hotel that has come down in the world to a morally and socially dubious status. She decides to visit and investigate the past drama of which she has heard such intriguing morsels of gossip. Perhaps this is too deliberate and contrived a device; yet the effect of outsiders upon a community of tangled relations is made to have,

Dust jacket for Trevor's second novel, winner of the 1964 Hawthornden Prize

successfully, a metaphoric significance that takes us beyond the barren and rudderless lives within the hotel. *Miss Gomez and the Brethren* (1971) makes use of a similar situation, the relation between a rootless woman and a religious society.

Trevor had by this time long since given up his work in advertising and devoted himself entirely to his writing, thanks to the success of *The Old Boys*. He was now living out of London in the countryside in Devon in a little village near Honiton, where he still lives. He began collecting his short stories, and a volume of them, *The Day We Got Drunk on Cake*, was published in 1967; others would follow at intervals over the next decade or so. His novels were getting excellent reviews from novelist-critics like Auberon Waugh, who found *Miss Gomez and the Brethren* "completely riveting—as good as *The Old Boys* and better than anything he has written since. . . . the treatment of the pointlessness and madness of urban life is utterly compelling." Earlier, Barry Cole, a novelist and poet, had found in *Mrs. Eckdorf in O'Neill's Hotel* an almost "perfect merger" be-

tween form and content, language and theme—a rarity in contemporary fiction. He said: "William Trevor has created a dotty, twilight, ultimately inconsequential world which is enhanced by a quiet but persistently nudging tone: he uses the *right* language for what he wants to say." As early as 1964, reviewers had commented upon this aspect of Trevor's writing, as for example in the *Times Literary Supplement*'s review of *The Old Boys*: "Mr. Trevor has written a book in which no phrase seems superfluous or wrong. It is as perfect in every part as it perfectly executes its theme." Trevor's style as well as his subject matter had become his trademark, a very enviable one.

Elizabeth Alone (1973), his sixth novel, marks a deepening of Trevor's insights, and while, no less than its predecessors, it is concerned with the loneliness of the human condition, with the problems of those who know their lives are peripheral to the public world, it is less fixed on the bizarre, the obscurely colorful. Its central character is a woman in early middle age, divorced, mother of three daughters. Elizabeth Aidallberry has to go into the hospital for a hysterectomy, and here she comes into contact with three other women whose frustrated lives mirror her own. This period, at once of retreat and fuller knowledge of the intricacies of others' hearts and minds, constitutes a watershed in Elizabeth's life. The novel was very well received. The reviewer in the *Times Literary Supplement*, for example, remarked on how well Trevor handled the "human comedy instead of merely manipulating comic human beings." Noting that "the territory and the methods of this enormously talented and entertaining writer" were unlikely to change, he singled out an aspect of Trevor's "world of people whose very ordinariness is their oddity."

Meanwhile, Trevor's stage and television career was flourishing. In the same year that *Elizabeth Alone* was published, three of his plays were produced in London: *A Perfect Relationship*, *The Fifty-seventh Saturday*, and *Marriages*. Three television plays were also performed: *Access to the Children*, *The General's Day*, and *Miss Farnshaw's Story*; in addition, Trevor adapted a Thomas Hardy story for television (*An Imaginative Woman*). In the previous year, 1972, *O Fat Woman* and *The Schoolroom* had been televised, and subsequently he had at least one television play and/or stage play performed every year. Speaking of his growing career as a dramatist for television a few years earlier, Trevor said that he enjoyed developing his television plays from his short stories: "What interests me in turning the story into a play is changing the characters around and getting to know them. You can go into the thing in greater depth. . . ."

In 1972 a second collection of his short stories, *The Ballroom of Romance*, appeared, and in 1975 another collection, *Angels at the Ritz* was published. Many had appeared earlier in magazines and journals, and a few had been made into television dramas. An American novelist living in England, Paul Theroux, commented on *The Ballroom of Romance*: he noted that the thread running through the stories set in England or Ireland "is of brittle or urgent femininity thwarted by rather boorish maleness. . . . Eleanor in 'Nice Day at School' and Bridie in the title story cling to an idea of love and romance while understanding that they will have to face a life with louts. Mavie tries hard to please Mr. McCarthy in 'The Forty-seventh Saturday,' but he remains a visitor, almost a client, and will not let her love shake him out of the routine of his fantasy. . . ." Robert Nye, another novelist and a poet, recognized Trevor's achievement in *Angels at the Ritz* as that of "a poet of brief fictions. Each of his stories is like a

poem, an incident, an experience, drawn out to just the length it will tolerably sustain. . . . His stories have more shape than those of any other contemporary practitioner . . . on either side of the Atlantic." Some critics had come to think of Trevor's work in the short story as superior to his achievement as a novelist, and comparisons began to be made to James Joyce. Although a few critics were at first skeptical, they became persuaded that Trevor's *Angels at the Ritz* was perhaps the best collection of short fiction since *Dubliners* (1914).

Despite his success with other forms, Trevor continued writing novels, and in 1976 *The Children of Dynmouth* appeared to generally high critical acclaim. (In many respects, it may well be Trevor's most accomplished, subtle, and individualistic novel.) It is set in a small, pretty, but slightly fly-blown resort on the Dorset coast and is dominated by an adolescent, Timothy Gedge. Smiling and cheery, a near-albino, he is possessed of a malign prurience which dictates almost all his actions. No one can like him; yet because he is a misfit, an outcast and an oddity, no one can dismiss him with the severity he almost deserves. The plot revolves around his determination to play the part of a murderess in a fete; for this role he requires clothes and props, all of which he has coveted in the homes of Dynmouth people. In order to obtain them, he whispers blackmails to the owners, for his habit of loafing about and peering into others' homes has brought him great knowledge of murky secrets.

Timothy Gedge is monstrous; his mind, at once agile and slow, is frightening to contemplate. But Trevor does not present him without compassion, without also casting disturbing shadows on the society which feeds his fantasies, and on those who in their darker selves are kin to him and yet shut him out with polite disdain. Commenting on Trevor's use of the traditional form of the novel and comparing him to other contemporary British novelists like Iris Murdoch and V. S. Naipaul, the American novelist Joyce Carol Oates has said that these writers are all "experimentalists" in a special sense. "They are far less concerned with formal virtuosity than their American counterparts, and far more explicitly concerned with the moral dimensions of their art. . . . they are more readable and . . . they are more entertaining." How just an appraisal this is may, of course, be debated (Miss Oates would herself fall into the category she describes); nevertheless, it points to an aspect of Trevor's fiction that is unquestionably important.

Although he just missed the Booker Prize for *The Children of Dynmouth*, Trevor received the Royal

Society of Literature Award, the Whitbread Award, and the Allied Irish Banks Award in 1976. On 9 November 1977, "in recognition of his valuable services to literature," he was made a Commander, Order of the British Empire, and presented with the appropriate badge at a ceremony in London. Lord Donaldson of Kingsbridge, minister of state, Department of Education and Science, with responsibility for the arts, made the presentation in the presence of Paul Keating, Ambassador from Ireland to the Court of St. James. Less than two years later Trevor received another significant award for his work. On 22 May 1979, it was announced that he, along with Cyril Cusack, the actor; Kieran More, the film producer; Brian Inglis, the author and narrator; and Sister Mary Bernardine, founder of a hostel for destitute women in London's East End, had received the Irish Community Award to "applaud noteworthy community effort and individual achievement by Irish people living in Britain."

By now Ireland, however, was almost as bewildering to Trevor as England had once been, and it is therefore not surprising that more and more of his stories are set in Ireland. One of the most moving stories in his next collection, *Lovers of Their Time* (1978), is called simply "Attracta" and is about an elderly Protestant schoolteacher in a village near Cork. When she hears of a particularly brutal outrage committed by terrorists in Belfast, she thinks back to the murder of her own parents and to the people who killed them but who later, atoning for their crime, became among her best friends. She has never told the story to her pupils, but now she feels compelled to do so, little thinking that her lesson of how human nature can change for the better will cost her a forced retirement. For her pupils cannot take in the story or its moral—not while they see televised every day the violence that shatters Ulster—and their parents cannot condone her use of the classroom for this purpose. The atrocities of the past and their impact upon lives in the present provide a theme Trevor uses in other stories, like "Matilda's England" and "Torridge" (another Old Boys story). Trevor never permits his moral comment to appear overtly—he is "too much of an artist for that," as Derek Mahon has said, "but a severe if compassionate judgement, handed down more in sorrow than in anger, is implicit in everything he writes."

In 1980 *Other People's Worlds* appeared, Trevor's most recent novel to date (another collection of stories, *Beyond the Pale*, was published in October 1981). Perhaps Timothy Gedge's imaginative fixation on a murderess suggested the more prominent part given to a similar *idée fixe* in this novel. Francis, the actor who becomes the second husband of Julia Ferndale, the central character, takes a part in a television play based upon the famous Constance Kent case. The details of the murder work on his psychotic mind. This is a darker novel than *The Children of Dynmouth* where Timothy Gedge stands redeemed through the pathos of his position, through the hopelessness of the narrow life that awaits him in adulthood. Francis is a liar, a trader on others' sympathy, a deliberate seeker after depravity, a thief; and though each of his crimes is explained to himself in terms of the pity he feels the world should bestow on him, did it know his sufferings, in the end it is as an *âme damnée* that we see him. This is possibly because of the sympathy with which Trevor regards his victims, above all Julia herself, kindly, quietist, utterly incapable of guessing at the lurid contours of her second husband's world. For Julia the novel ends on a note of hope; to appreciate evil is to confront life, and after confrontation comes another and deeper peace.

Both of Trevor's latest novels suggest a greater adventurousness in exploring human motives and states of being than the earlier, more circumscribed fictions would have suggested. While all of his writing life he has produced short stories—dark epiphanies within trapped social milieux—in *The Children of Dynmouth* and *Other People's Worlds* his grasp of form, of interrelationships, of how to control varieties of moods and mental conditions within a satisfactory unifying structure, is wholly novelistic. For the purposes of television, he prefers adapting his stories rather than novels, which is understandable, given the media involved. But he still has a high regard for the novel. It is "much more of a real thing than we've ever allowed for," he has said in an interview. "The one-to-one business of the novel: you know, between two people, not between one person and a theatreful, or between one person and nine million people on television. That is what a novel is, and if you like that you're going to go on liking it in spite of television or anything else."

Trevor calls himself an instinctive writer and a "secretive" writer who does not find it necessary to be in frequent touch with other writers. He has seen no movement developing among contemporary British novelists and has never regarded himself as part of any. He does not discuss his work in advance because it always changes as he writes. Among the novelists he enjoys and feels an affinity with are George Eliot, Jane Austen, the Brontës, and especially Dickens and Hardy among nineteenth-century writers, and P. G. Wodehouse, Joyce Cary, and E. M. Forster in the twentieth century. Among playwrights he admires Chekhov and Turgenev. He admits some similarity between his writing and Ivy Compton-Burnett's in *The Old Boys*, since both used an old-fashioned style, but notes the "enormous differences" in their attitudes toward people.

His style has been influenced more than anything else by his Irish background, especially in Cork, where "people did speak rather differently, rather slow and rather careful," and observes that Irish critics did not notice his style as much as English reviewers. He has no fear of "drying up" as a writer, though he began rather late to publish his work (he was thirty); he retains his profound curiosity about people, about how they work, and about the possibilities of various technical aspects of composition. He tends to see novelists as falling into two major groups: "There are those who write out of curiosity, curiosity about situations and people, and those who tend to be much more autobiographical; they tend to be much more involved with themselves." Although in the end, if a good novel is produced, it all amounts to much the same thing, William Trevor is without doubt a novelist of the first type—and of the first order. He has never been tempted to become a "writer in residence" at a university—"One wants to write, not to talk about it," he says—yet he recognizes the value in talking with students about their writing and believes he would find this work enjoyable. At present, however, he is fully occupied with writing fiction and drama—the Abbey Theatre in Dublin has recently produced one of his plays—and teaching may have to await a later opportunity.

Interviews:

"William Trevor," in *The Writer's Place: Interviews on the Literary Situation in Contemporary Britain*, edited by Peter Firchow (Minneapolis: University of Minnesota Press, 1974), pp. 304-312;

Mark Ralph-Bowman, "William Trevor," *Transatlantic Review*, 53/54 (1976): 5-12;

Tim Heald, "Beneath the mask of gentility," *Times* (London), 18 June 1980, p. 13.

References:

Julian Gitzen, "The Truth-Tellers of William Trevor," *Critique*, 21 (1979): 59-72;

Mark Mortimer, "William Trevor in Dublin," *Études Irlandaises* (Lille), 4 (1975), 77-85;

Janet Watts, "William Trevor's Little Irk," *Observer* (London), 11 June 1980.

Elizabeth Troop
(September 1931-   )

Simon Edwards
Roehampton Institute

SELECTED NOVELS: *A Fine Country* (London: Faber & Faber, 1969);
Woolworth Madonna (London: Duckworth, 1976);
Slipping Away (London: Granada Publishing, 1979);
Darling Daughters (London: Granada Publishing, 1981; New York: St. Martin's, 1981).

Elizabeth Troop's first novel, *A Fine Country*, was published in 1969, but it was not until *Woolworth Madonna* (1976) that she began to attract critical attention. Since then she has enjoyed an especially fruitful phase in her career as a writer of both fiction and of radio drama and features. Two novels have followed; *Slipping Away* (1979) and *Darling Daughters* (1981), the latter published in both England and the United States. She has also written eleven radio plays during the last five years (including adaptations of her novels), and is currently at work on a new novel provisionally entitled "Losing It."

She was born in Blackpool, Lancashire, in 1931 and her childhood there, during the Depression and the war, obviously forms the basis of her most recent novel, *Darling Daughters*. From this novel it would seem that, as an only child of a disintegrating marriage, she acquired an almost precocious awareness of the corrosive snobberies of bourgeois and petit-bourgeois life, the unbridgeable cultural and social gaps created by differences in class and education, combining to reinforce the repressions and tensions of family life. Such themes inform, in different ways, each of her novels. Similarly a growing dependence on her mother, who very early in the marriage began to drift apart from her husband, though ill-prepared for an independent life, seems to have provided Elizabeth Troop with a sharply critical understanding of the contradictory experience of growing up female in contemporary English society.

A whole set of factors may be seen as contributing to her wide grasp of the complexity of class formations, and that subtle rendering of the nuances of class consciousness and behavior which characterizes her fiction. This latter quality, it should be emphasized, is never a mere recording, but rather a contribution, however tentative, to the possibility of increased understanding and change. In her own words: "Writing is a political act, though not, of course, a direct one."

Blackpool is the largest holiday resort serving a predominantly working-class area of Britain. As such it is a prime site for the encounter between the dubious gentility of landladies, hotel owners, and the proprietors of other small businesses, pockets of "retired people," and the values and manners of the working classes who both create it and for whom it provides. Elizabeth Troop met all these elements while her mother worked in various hotel jobs. Her

Elizabeth Troop

father belonged to a relatively respectable and educated family and his marriage to a much younger and largely uneducated working-class girl, Elizabeth Troop's mother, may have been in part a gesture of political idealism. He had been a Labour party agent in Sowerby Bridge, Yorkshire. After the formation of the National Government in 1931 (an event Elizabeth Troop wryly celebrates in her radio play *Year of the Great Betrayal*, 1979), he continued as an unsuccessful ILP candidate for Blackpool. A sense of lost political causes and the failure of working-class radicalism continues to haunt the novels, a sense which may be intensified and given particular personal point by her father's gradual drift into alcoholism and unemployment and his consequent estrangement from his wife and daughter.

As she and her mother drifted in and out of various rented rooms and hotels, the addition of economic uncertainty and emotional upheaval disrupted her schooling, despite her academic promise. Unsurprisingly she had left school by the end of the war to help her mother run a small boardinghouse. In 1947 they left Blackpool for London. Her mother continued to work in hotels, managing service flats, and finally as a housekeeper to a dentist, where Elizabeth acted as receptionist. Although she now attended Regent Street Polytechnic and, briefly, St. Martin's School of Art, she had no real opportunity for full-time study, but she describes herself as reading avidly throughout this period. From managing the philosophy and psychology department of Foyle's bookshop, a position she took in 1950, she went to work in the university bookshop, before joining Pitman's publishers as a production assistant. It was there she met the Canadian journalist, Robert Troop, whom she married in 1957. For two years they lived in Toronto, Canada, where she had two sons, before returning to Hampstead, London. She began writing in the 1960s, a period when her husband published three novels (*Sound of Vinegar*, *The Hammering*, and *Bobesco*). Meanwhile she worked largely at home, as a publisher's reader while looking after her children.

A Fine Country appeared in 1969. It is an ambitious, but also an uneven and untidy first novel. An account of an awakening that is also a moment of disintegration, the novel interweaves fragmentary recollections of critical events in the heroine Sylvia's past. These frequently seem to her to have been inadequately perceived at the time and often the result of mere subjection to different kinds of experience, especially the either bewildering or

Dust jacket for Troop's first novel about the fragmentation of a woman's psyche

psychologically aggressive behavior of a number of men, including ex-lovers. It is the turn of her husband, George Cass, a successful businessman, to be bewildered by her now, and the novel is scrupulous, if not altogether successful, in imagining other points of consciousness, other interpretations of Sylvia's acts, at least in the present. The main action begins with Sylvia's admission to a mental hospital, following a self-inflicted Dostoevskian scandal when she advertises in the *Times* for a suicide partner. She receives over three hundred replies and is briefly the subject of press and television coverage. The novel ends with Sylvia leading the inmates of the hospital in a riot, starting a fire while a television documentary crew attempts to make a film about mental health. The crew includes an old friend of Sylvia's, Maggie, whose successful career and polished presence contrast as starkly with Sylvia's ragged personality, as does the Swedish *au pair*, Berit, with whom George begins a refreshingly unintimate affair, in his wife's absence.

In leading the riot Sylvia appears to have

identified with Rosa Luxemburg and her role in the abortive Spartacist uprising in Germany in 1919. This is the culmination of her more generalized guilt and unease about the dominance of bourgeois power and values, not merely in her own life, but wherever they are present in the bland forms of cultural reproduction and simulated concern effected by the mass media and television in particular. For Sylvia this guilt is intensified by what she regards as a renunciation of her own origins, so complete she can hardly recollect the shadowy figure of her socialist father—a circumstance related to a larger absence of any adequate authority in the overall conception and structure of Sylvia's personality and the novel alike.

Such a summary of plot and character can hardly capture the jagged texture of this densely allusive novel. It is full of fragments of Sylvia's reading, her memories of childhood and an adolescence spent in the bohemian milieu of 1950s London. (Indeed the novel treats more the experience of this decade than it does the "liberationist" culture of the 1960s. This is the more remarkable in that one senses that lying behind the work are a number of the assumptions of the radical "politicized" psychiatry of R. D. Laing, whose influence was then at its height.) The short, stabbing sentences of the prose suggest an immediacy of feeling and perception defying proper comprehension. They are symptoms of breakdown and the hopelessness of Sylvia's attempt to act on her own behalf, to escape from passive acquiescence in the female role of the class in which she finds herself.

Formally the novel probably owes more to writers like Beckett and Burroughs than any native tradition. Its frank presentation of the raw edges of emotional experience is the first example in Elizabeth Troop's work of a recurrent debt to American novelists like Saul Bellow and Philip Roth, whose work she admires. Another influence may be the work of the "confessional" poets. The heroine shares her name with Sylvia Plath who committed suicide in 1963 and whose poetry articulates some related themes. Reference is made to Robert Lowell as the author of "the saddest line in poetry." (John Berryman is referred to in a later novel, *Slipping Away*.) Indeed these references may be related to certain weaknesses in the novel, since there is a tendency to treat Sylvia's condition as a merely existential one, perhaps better suited to the possibilities of poetry.

There is little real exploration of the connections between political and psychological dimensions. George Cass is presented with obvious sympathy, yet he hardly provides an adequate alternative and balancing center of consciousness, signally lacking the political frame of reference which Sylvia herself can hardly articulate. Such a frame is fleetingly suggested by the character of the Indian psychiatrist Desai who, after attempting to treat Sylvia, returns to his own country reflecting that there is "no choice between the balance in need between Sylvia, and a child with a distended empty belly." Finally the novel expresses a "modernist" skepticism about the whole notion of self-discovery (other than as self-destruction) and the making of a coherent personality: "The futile personal pursuit. The Platonic she." Yet its very form leaves the reader unsure whether the novel does not endorse what the psychiatrist Desai takes to be Sylvia's self-indulgence.

Some of the best writing captures the pretentious absurdities of Sylvia's ex-lovers in a rather more coherent mode of irony (in particular a grotesquely pompous disciple of Wilhelm Reich), and these passages look forward to aspects of Elizabeth Troop's later achievement. Her next novel, "Send-Up," remains unpublished, although it forms the basis of a later radio play with the same title (1977). Thus there is a break before the appearance of *Woolworth Madonna*, which was universally well received, some critics believing it to be her first novel. Something of a tour de force, it captures succinctly some of the contradictory elements within contemporary English fiction; both that continuing claim to practice a realistic mode of social observation and concern with the promise and difficulty of describing new areas of experience, together with the exercise of individual, especially female, sensibility. Although there is continuity with certain themes and preoccupations of *A Fine Country*, this novel's strength derives from its alertness to important changes in social life and consciousness in the England of the 1970s. It reflects that process of *lumpen*-ization in certain sections of the English working class which is a product of postwar affluence and the subsequent period of economic recession. Its juxtaposition of the perspectives of a working-class housewife and a middle-class "radical chic" journalist illuminates the marginalization of politics that is involved in the reduction of issues of class struggle, economic and social transformation, to the status of "social problems." It deals boldly with the sense of powerlessness at various levels of experience while seeking access to the power that accompanies successful articulation. If that description makes the novel sound diagrammatic, any reading of it will suggest that the

urgency of its human commitment far outweighs its ironic treatment of formal problems. In this it seems closer to the work of novelists like John Berger and Doris Lessing than the more elaborate distancings of Iris Murdoch and John Fowles, with whose fiction it has some devices in common.

Woolworth Madonna is about a nameless working-class woman, living in shabby, rented property in South London, together with her husband, Terry, and their three children, Irene, Warren, and Carole. Undereducated and discontented, the "heroine" develops an obsession for the orchestral conductor Jan Mrozek, whom she first sees on television. In pursuit of her "hero" she is picked up outside the festival hall by a young journalist, Edward, who, pleading homelessness, maneuvers his way into living in their spare room on the pretext of writing a newspaper feature on the life of her family and their incipient move to a high-rise flat. Just separated from his own wife and children, he finds himself developing, in spite of his merely "sociological" curiosity, a romantic absorption in the life of the heroine; a relationship which paradoxically complements her passion for Mrozek. The reality of his concern shows itself in his ability to relate to the educationally backward youngest daughter Carole. He also knows that his relationship is an exploitative one, typical of the rewards journalism can create out of the plight of others. It is a temporary, sentimental refuge from both his own failed marriage and the frigid respectability of his materially prosperous and culturally advantaged background. A complex of painful paradoxes is activated at the end of the novel when his mother dies of cancer, and he realizes that the money he spends weekly on kennels for the pet dachshunds which outlive her is equivalent to his adopted family's housekeeping.

Nevertheless it is also a real, if troubled, engagement, which stands, in part, for the novelist's own ambivalence toward her material, her presumption in attempting to articulate the inarticulate. He reflects, "I contain them in my mind, and certainly in my heart. I breathe silently as I stand in the periphery of their being." The increasing sexual bond between Edward and the heroine leads to an act of violent consummation. It is as though at the moment of maximum closeness to her he finds he can only turn her back into an object. Similarly for her this act resembles all those moments of possible happiness throughout the novel which are measured against more perfect but elusive images of revelation. Edward turns out to be the only real and accessible face of her dream of Mrozek and inevitably disappoints her. Indeed music, as elsewhere in the novels, has an important symbolic role: both inhumanly transcendent and immeasurably touching as a source of human communion, the kind of significance it has in, say, the poetry of W. H. Auden. Edward is not a wholly convincing figure; he is too much a fictive device for revealing the distortions and betrayals of conventional narrative. While necessary to the novel, his role is easily outweighed by the rendering of the heroine's con-

sciousness and experience of ordinary, oppressive realities, together with those shifts of imagination and fantasy by which she copes with them.

Slipping Away (1979) is something of a disappointment after this achievement. It returns to the milieu of the troubled bourgeois marriage. In this case it transports failed film director Howard; his wife, Claudia; and their son, Sam, to a Tuscan farmhouse holiday. Here they are joined by a homosexual American scriptwriter, Tom Vermeer,

I

I hate.

    I have loved, in my time, people, objects, the smell of new books, the music of Mahler and Mozart, whisky and ice in a clean glass - but at the moment such things are alien to me. I tell myself it is a stage I am going through, that I am seeing the world in a distorting mirror, and that they are all still there, waiting for me to resume my interest. I hope they have not disappeared for ever. They are not dependent on my particular attention, I know that. They have other eyes, ears and noses to respond to their charms.

    Meanwhile I carry on as if still human. I eat, wash, dress. I type my works, I visit the hospital.

    The old women in the geriatric ward are laid out like waxworks. They have the white permed hair and the colourful nightwear of the new poor. Cajoled into a semblance of life by the cheerful nurses, they are propped into chairs at the end of their beds. One or two gaze at the bright consumer models in the weekly magazines; all vivacity and bared smiles. They scan articles on orgasm and troilism, or recipes for Osso Bucco and Devilled Shrimp. Their mouths drool, their dentures slip. They cry out, like peremptory children, to be taken down the hall.

    Eva, my mother, is among this brigade. The only dark head among the white flowers. With the stubbornness she has always shown to nature and time, she has refused to go even grey.

    A young doctor stops me on the way in.

    "Eva is breathing a little better today. When did the attack start?"

    I am tempted to say 'back in nineteen thirty nine - before you were even thought of.' But I refrain. I like his use of 'Eva', it makes her seem a girl again. She looks a girl, in the over-large hospital gown, in the big bed.

First page of the typescript for Darling Daughters

to work on an adaptation of Thomas Mann's *Tonio Kröger*, which, it is hoped, will restore Howard's artistic career. The novel opens with Claudia reflecting on the outward journey, "Would I like to die with this selection?" It ends with a car crash in which the whole family party is crushed to death on impact with a juggernaut lorry. This is interpreted as an apotheosis of the new, commercialized Europe into whose values the characters have been incorporated. It is set in part against their puzzlement at the behavior of the Italian peasantry whom they encounter, but this is only one of the sources of a vague unease permeating their relationship. The novel marks, perhaps, a return to a more English form of fiction, a variation on themes in the early E. M. Forster. A disastrous dinner party of undercooked rabbit reads like a parody of Mrs. Ramsay's famous *boeuf-en-daube* in Virginia Woolf's *To the Lighthouse*. The writing is assured, with a more controlled comic insight into middle-class mores than in either *A Fine Country* or those parts of *Woolworth Madonna* dealing with Edward's life. Its attempt at a more savage irony is softened by the continuing concern with the female perspective in Claudia, and the gentle ineffectiveness of the aging Howard. Their violent end seems, in the light of this, somewhat gratuitous. The sympathetic rendering of the son, Sam, his combination of tolerance and earnest criticism of his parents, suggests that they have more virtues than the novel is prepared to concede.

With *Darling Daughters* (1981) Elizabeth Troop returns to her real strength, a precise and confident interior narrative. The frankly autobiographical material, outlined earlier, is given the kind of distancing frame that Edward's narration provided for *Woolworth Madonna*. In this case the heroine/narrator is made, at the beginning and end of the novel, the author of a television dramatization of her own early life. Her problems with the production suggest unanswered questions about continuity and loss, responsibility and relevance, on the part of a writer making her experience an object for display. The central bulk of the novel is, however, the recreation of the life of both mother, Ellie, and daughter, Sarah, up to their departure from Blackpool. The prose is richly textured by a combination of affectionate intimacy and barbed criticism and manages brilliantly to suggest the conditions and ideological practices (the role of women, popular culture, cinema, and Gothic romance) by which the heroine is complexly created. It goes well beyond the autobiographical origins of its subject. Economically it creates a range of characters, who, though always seen in relation to Sarah, and even transformed by her in fantasy and her childish attempts to write fiction, are given a tragi-comic existence of their own. They are neither "done" as "characters," nor are they mere projections of Sarah's. She always sees how she is seen, but without any sense of superiority. The "loner" child is inextricably related to other "loners." Thus the novel avoids that "special pleading" which Raymond Williams has suggested is a danger of the autobiographical genre, and Sarah's failure to identify with Jane Eyre, in her childhood reading of the novel, neatly suggests one of the ways in which this fault is avoided.

The ease and clarity of the narration of complex experience mark a new stage in the development of Elizabeth Troop's fiction. If her achievement to date is a modest one, and the novels have not yet acquired that further dimension of political insight and understanding that they have consistently promised, there seems no reason why they should not go on eventually to incorporate those elements in ways that are less oblique. Her prolific output for radio suggests that she is not short of creative ambition. It has included drama, stories, work for children, and documentary features on Flaubert, Georges Sand, James Agee, and Samuel Bamford, the nineteenth-century radical.

Other:

"The Rise and Fall of Bulky Baby, Guerilla," in *Winter's Tales*, edited by James Wright (London: Macmillan, 1976), pp. 73-89;

"In Memoriam Brian Rosenfeld," in *New Stories 4*, edited by Elaine Feinstein and Fay Weldon (London: Hutchinson/Arts Council, 1979), pp. 70-77.

Frank Tuohy

(2 May 1925-   )

Lindsey Tucker

BOOKS: *The Animal Game* (London: Macmillan, 1957; New York: Scribners, 1957);
The Warm Nights of January (London: Macmillan, 1960);
The Admiral and the Nuns with Other Stories (London: Macmillan, 1962; New York: Scribners, 1962);
The Ice Saints (London: Macmillan, 1964; New York: Scribners, 1964);
Fingers in the Door and Other Stories (London: Macmillan, 1970; New York: Scribners, 1970);
Portugal (London: Thames & Hudson, 1968; New York: Viking, 1970);
Yeats (London & New York: Macmillan, 1976);
Live Bait and Other Stories (London: Macmillan, 1978; New York: Holt, Rinehart & Winston, 1978).

Frank Tuohy

Although Frank Tuohy is relatively little known in the United States, he is critically recognized as one of the finest of England's fiction writers. Author of three novels and three collections of short stories, he became a biographer of some skill with his study of W. B. Yeats. As a master of style and a keen observer of social situations, he has been ranked with writers like Angus Wilson, Muriel Spark, and Iris Murdoch. He is particularly noted for his treatment of the expatriate, and his years of living outside England—in Finland, Poland, Brazil, Japan, and the United States—have given his fiction a unique stamp.

Frank Tuohy was born in Uckfield, Sussex, where his father, Patrick Gerald Tuohy, was a doctor. Irish, originally from Cork, and distantly related to James Joyce, his father was from a family who had, in the later part of the nineteenth century, become members of the British professional class. His mother, Dorothy Annandale, was of Scottish descent, her father having been a paper manufacturer. Her religious background was Presbyterian; Patrick Tuohy was Irish. This mixture in terms of nationality and religion apparently left its mark on Tuohy who observes, "from their different backgrounds . . . both my parents had a strong Puritan tendency, which I suppose myself to have inherited." In any event, Patrick Gerald Tuohy met Dorothy Annandale during World War I, and they were married much later.

John Francis Tuohy was born with a congenital heart defect which made much of his childhood a time of illness. (He was not cured until 1960 when he underwent successful surgery.) Nevertheless, Tuohy was sent to a rugged preparatory school at the age of thirteen and survived its rigors despite his heart. He left Stowe School in 1943 and, because he could not go into the armed services, he entered Cambridge where he did his degree in philosophy and English. It was during these Cambridge years that he decided to become a writer. During the 1940s, Tuohy produced a number of short stories which were, unfortunately, lost by "a well-known literary figure," as Tuohy puts it.

There seemed little point in remaining in England after the war. "England in the late forties was not a hopeful place," Tuohy observes. Consequently, after taking a B.A. with first-class honors

736

from Kings College, Cambridge, in 1946, he served as a guest lecturer at Turku University in Finland during 1947 and 1948. Then, in 1950, he left for South America. He secured a position as Professor of English Language and Literature at the University of São Paulo and settled in to write and teach. This move was to prove important to his writing, for two novels grew out of his six years' stay in Brazil— *The Animal Game* (1957) and *The Warm Nights of January* (1960).

The Animal Game, set in Rio de Janeiro, opens with a powerful metaphor that establishes the theme of the book. Celina Fonseca, the central female character, aristocratic, beautiful, but also self-destructive, stops along a roadside where people are gathered for reasons not yet apparent to her or us. Suddenly, however, the reason is made horrifyingly evident: because of a railway strike, some pigs have been left for two days inside a truck, and now, hungry and desperate, they have begun to devour each other. Their screams have drawn this audience whose ironic bemusement is conditioned not by the horror of the devouring but by their knowledge that the pigs will be poisoned by their own cannibalism. This is a novel about desperate, cannibalistic people; but it is also a novel about people who watch the cannibalistic act and are unable or unwilling to do anything to stop the devouring. Besides Celina and her father Dr. Oswaldo, poet, dilettante, politician; her alcoholic American stepmother; and her rebel brother Jango; there is a rather pathetic Canadian couple, the Newtons; and an Englishman, Robin Morris, newly arrived on the scene. Sensitive, decorous, Robin finds himself caught up in the lives of Celina and the other suffering characters.

All action in the novel is futile or painful. Celina is dominated by her European lover, Cowan, whose aura of culture and sophistication disguises his predatory and consuming nature. Celina herself is closely identified with the sterility of her own country which she describes as "the most boring continent in the world. Everything looks all right but tastes flat. Everyone wants money, but only in order to be respectable and dull." Only Jango, who makes up in ardor what he lacks in intelligence, is willing to die for an ideal.

Robin, in love with Celina but put off by her involvement with the egotistical Cowan, keeps himself safe with casual sex while he ponders "the enormous possibilities of human passion." This awareness is intensified through his relationships with several others, especially his servant Esposita and her Negro lover; the Canadian Newton; and his mentally disturbed Brazilian wife. Esposita and her lover have, for Robin, an honesty and a reality about their passion that the febrile and decorous members of the British colony seem incapable of. Newton's wife Mercedes also possesses this kind of passion, but it manifests itself in a violent pathos, possibly the result of the fact that Newton, like Morris, would prefer to put the most civilized dressing on things.

All the characters turn at some time or other to Robin, but he fails them all. When Celina reaches out to him, attracted to him as he is to her, he cannot unbend to help because his own need for self-protection is too strong. When Newton, desperate to contain the horrific public outbursts of his wife, tries to reveal his marital troubles to Robin, he is met with a coldness which is almost an active cruelty. Robin's most humiliating and dangerous encounter is with the pathetic Mercedes, for whom he summons a taxi that will take her off to an asylum. All that Robin seems capable of managing is the observation that "everything that appears simple and clear in human relations is always a little damaged and wrong."

Tuohy is particularly skilled at depicting the subtleties of attitudes and behavior of the Europeans and contrasting them with the primal energies that seem so much a part of the Brazilian setting. In one scene, for example, Robin and Newton, seated on a bus, witness an argument between a drunk and a man whose prostitute lover has been the object of insult. Everyone is caught up in the drama and takes to the street to engage in "the obligatory rites," which Robin and Newton can only watch from the bus window. When it is all over, the drunk lies unconscious and bleeding in the gutter.

Compelling as such scenes are, however, they do not seem to be sustained by the novel's action. Both Celina and Robin are acute observers of human foibles, but Celina surrenders her own vitality to ape the supposed vitality of European civilization, while Robin's sensitivity leads him to revulsion and withdrawal. Ultimately their sensitivity only serves to make them filters for the passions of others. They fail to become centers of their own worlds but inhabit an emotional buffer zone between the worlds of others.

The Animal Game was critically well received. Most highly praised was Tuohy's style, its brilliance, its economy, its concentrated quality. The *Saturday Review* stated: "his art is so pervasive, the serious intentions underlying it so evident, his powers of observation so keen, and the quality of his writing so excellent, that it would seem almost churlish to ask for anything more." The *Spectator*, while reviewing

Tuohy's second novel in 1960, referred to *The Animal Game* as "the best novel to appear in 1957." The only negative criticism—and this was to be heard again in reference to later works—was that Tuohy had not committed himself to a strong point of view. Commenting on this point, Tuohy has said, "perhaps our present society provides no easy resting point between subjectivity and detachment."

In any case, detachment seemed to mark his position in regard to his next novel, *The Warm Nights of January*. Written in Paris after his stay in Brazil had ended, the book was, according to its author, "too special in background . . . to be readily comprehensible." Nevertheless, *The Warm Nights of January* is, in fact, a very comprehensible and in some ways more satisfying novel.

The reason for the book's vitality and more sustained action may be Tuohy's fuller development of his protagonist, Bella Magnard. Bella is a French expatriate artist living in Rio de Janeiro who, because of her "equipoise, her native talent for arranging her own life," draws to her an odd assortment of characters—Europeans and Brazilians whose passions are played out against a sultry summer during the weeks between Christmas and Carnival. Especially important in her life is her black Brazilian lover, Hadriano, with whom she shares a volatile and complex relationship; a parasitic Russian lesbian named Alix; a sister-in-law, Lucille, who uses Bella's apartment for her assignations; a young Frenchman named Eduard; and the emotionally disturbed Mario, an ambassador's son. To these weak and acquisitive hangers-on Bella gives money, lodging, sometimes even sex, while she keeps her "gallic poise" and manages her life. Her taste for food and drink, her love of the sea, her acceptance of her sexual role with Hadriano are set in a delicate, sometimes precarious balance.

The book opens with Bella's entering the sea; she will enter the sea later in the story with more profound consequences. But the sea is representative of both creative and destructive forces in her life. Wyndham Lewis, in his review of *The Warm Nights of January* in the April 1960 issue of *London Magazine*, remarks that there is not much plot, that the book is one in which a situation is examined but that at the end of the novel, the situation "is still much the same as at the beginning." This statement is not accurate, however, if we see the situation as one that involves not linear but rather cyclical action and resolution. Bella, who is told she will "go through darkness," does just that, and this is a story of her initiation.

To that end, conflicts of all kinds—racial, sex-ual, homosexual—which grow in intensity and climax at the time of Carnival, are skillfully revealed. The balance of Bella's life is reestablished after Carnival when she can reconcile herself to her life's meanings. ("I can be contented as long as I have the shore in the morning, fresh food from the street-market and Hadriano.") Yet the reconciliation she finds is not a facile one. She is no simple hedonist, and her calm winter days have been purchased at a sacrifice.

Tuohy is especially skillful at capturing the struggle of the expatriate consciousness to achieve an equilibrium between the pull of European sensibilities and the lure of the primitive energies personified by Hadriano and acted out during the days of Carnival. However, the depiction of these conflicting energies is never melodramatic, and Tuohy presents all the numerous clashes with an economy of style that is impressive.

As in all his work, the land serves as the real antagonist, and in *The Warm Nights of January* Tuohy captures the effect of the land and its powerful energies in a number of interesting scenes, one of which occurs during Carnival at a voodoo ceremony. Beyond the town, where light is drowned in darkness and sound is dominated by the drums, Hadriano takes on "the look of something sacrificial," as he becomes a "primitive innocent," possessed by older gods. Bella watches this transformation: "The drums were working against her like electric drills. Her sympathy was flooding out to where no more sympathy could go, beating vainly against a blank wall of alienation."

Critical reception to *The Warm Nights of January* was generally positive. (Ironically the book was rejected by Scribners, Tuohy's American publishers, because of its interracial affair.) Its author was described in general as original, a careful stylist, one of the best writers of his generation. The *Spectator* called the novel a "rigorously worked *étude* on a limited subject." Wyndham Lewis spoke of Tuohy as "capable of sudden direct statements that sum up, almost baldly, his meaning in a sentence. . . . There are few English novelists of his generation to equal him."

Meanwhile, Tuohy had moved on to a post as visiting professor at Jagiellonian University, Krakow, Poland, where he lived from 1958-1960. This residency was to provide him with a setting for his third novel. First, however, his initial collection of short stories appeared in 1962.

The Admiral and the Nuns was a collection of a dozen stories which were, like his novels, drawn from his experiences in Brazil and Poland as well as

England. The title story received the Katherine Mansfield Prize for 1960. Set in Brazil, it involves, as we come to expect in Tuohy's work, a number of expatriates, in particular, Stefan and Barbara Woroszylski. Barbara, a rather pathetic and unappealing Englishwoman whose Kensington background, admiral father, and convent upbringing do not prepare her for life in the interior of Brazil, is the central character around whom the narrator—an Englishman who offers Barbara the semblance of hope for the reestablishment of her identity—revolves. Her husband, Stefan, a technician on a state industrial development project in the interior, is described as a "talented destroyer," a man who hunts wild dogs that stalk his place but allows himself only one kill a night. Patron of the Bar Metro, to which he introduces the narrator, he also seeks some affirmation of his existence through the Englishman. The action culminates at the coronation ball, held at the British Embassy, during which Stefan's inclinations for alcohol and women become too uncomfortable a reality for us as well as for Barbara and the narrator, who is relegated to a role of salving Barbara's hurts. Yet there is something compelling, if not appealing, in the plight of Stefan whose peasant code has its integrity, while Barbara, for whom neither navy, Kensington, nor Catholicism provides much of a code, remains "hopelessly, slothfully inadequate." Beneath Stefan's disgrace at the British Club, we understand the ineffectuality and pretentiousness of the British upper middle class. Stefan is seen as a victim of attitudes personified by his wife, whose values have blinded her both to her real obligations and to her real failings. The English narrator is the figure we encounter so often in Tuohy's fiction—the male sojourner, sensitive, sympathetic yet emotionally distanced, ultimately uninvolved, and always moving on.

Another compelling story, again set in Brazil, is "A Survivor in Salvador." Here Tuohy's sense of place, his extraordinary ability to depict the plight of the expatriate, is much in evidence. His protagonist, a Polish "prince," amateur painter and refugee from the holocaust, finds Brazil his last stop on a seemingly downward journey through countries not his own. Accustomed to living by his wits, he is, nonetheless, forced to construct desperate strategies for survival as he finds himself alone in an interior Brazilian city with a packet of cocaine to deliver and no contact. When all attempts to make a profitable connection fail, the packet becomes an intolerable burden possessing an almost magical malevolence. Only a dusky prostitute serves as a

holding force against his gradual mental and physical deterioration. In the summer heat, which intensifies with his desperation, he moves on into the lower parts of the city where the other poor and despairing go. His descent is a fall into newer knowledge of himself, however. Tuohy is at his best as he depicts the atmosphere of this alien city. His detail, always sparse and selective, is highly appropriate, and his characters and our insight into them come alive in a line.

In "Private Lives," another story set in Brazil, Tuohy examines the petty affairs and passions that dominate and often destroy the foreigner in an alien landscape. This story focuses on a relationship between a Brazilian consul and a British foreign officer as they explore their sexual fantasies in terms of the offerings of seedy South American night life. Their nocturnal meanderings are the backdrop for their great cultural differences as well as their respective emotional impoverishment. Again, Tuohy catches the dark side of the city as it mirrors the dark side of the human personality, yet he does so without resorting to heavy handedness or self-consciousness. His image of the "Zone" where women, behind slatted grilles that resemble cages, wait for their customers, makes its own statement on the animal within and without.

Some stories in the collection are set in Poland. One, "The Matchmakers," evokes the haunting effects of World War II over communist Poland, where a countess and a music critic encounter the daughter of an English diplomat. The critic and the English woman meet for the purpose of mating two cocker spaniels. The encounter stirs the interest of the critic, but his hopes for some rapprochement are destroyed when he hears of the girl's engagement to a German. All matings, animal and human, all encounters, are irreparably damaged by the war, which seems to have left all survivors to exist in some sterile, mutated state. In "The Dark Years," the presence of the Communist Party, the bleakness of existence under its regime, is even more pronounced. The title is ironic, for the dark years have been replaced by something even darker—an atmosphere of suspicion, boredom, meaningless sex. Halina, who carries the "dark years" with her always, imagines (romantically) that her professor husband is in difficulties with the Party, while he is in fact before a disciplinary committee because of an indiscreet love affair with a student. The dreariness of postwar Poland is seen in a more violent context in "The Palace of Culture," a nightclub which provides the only social life for a village and also acts as a control. Without this context, activity becomes violent as three of the nightclub's patrons seek out the only alternative to its sterile amusements—drinking bouts by the river beside a peasant village. However, one of these bouts leads to the pointless deaths of the village Party member and his nephew.

Stories with an English setting are perhaps the least satisfying, for Tuohy's strength lies in his skillful detailing of exotic places, and this ingredient is absent in *The Admiral and the Nuns*. Stories like "At Home with the Colonel," in which a lonely old man rattles around his country house, confusedly pondering his alienation from a lesbian daughter and her malevolent friend, or "A Young Girl," a story of a seventeen-year-old girl subjected to humiliation by her artist lover, underscore the isolation and sterility of the human condition.

Reviews of *The Admiral and the Nuns* were unanimous in their recognition of Tuohy's skill. A few critics felt that some of the stories were inadequately developed or lacked emotional commitment. Michelle Murray, for example, stated in *Commonweal* that they displayed "the posture of a casual visitor" who gets momentarily drawn into the pattern of things but then escapes.

What emerged from Tuohy's stay in Poland was what may be his finest novel. Winner of two awards—the Geoffrey Faber Memorial Prize and the James Tait Black Memorial Prize for 1964—*The Ice Saints* is a novel about postwar Poland and also a complex exploration of the confrontation between western consciousness and that of eastern Europe. The novel's central character is Rose Nicholson, a young Englishwoman who journeys to Poland not simply to visit her sister who has married a Polish Communist professor, but to inform the family of a legacy left to their son, Tadeusz. Her desire is to bring her nephew to England for a taste of western freedom. During her visit, Rose's sensitivity does not prevent her from committing serious blunders as her assumptions about differences between West and East are undermined. By the time she leaves the country, she is sadder, perhaps, but hardly as wise.

It is obvious that Tuohy is not interested in a foreigner's view of Communist Poland, nor is he simply reinforcing western assumptions about the deficiencies of a postwar communist country. Dreary as the country is with its grey landscapes, shabby and overcrowded apartments, seething trains, monotonous diet, suspicious bureaucrats, hidden microphones, it is Rose who proves to be subversive, for all her good intentions. While Tuohy blurs the lines between West and East, he sharpens our awareness of other realities and unmasks not only the folly of good intentions but the

Westerner's blindness and intolerance.

The title of the work refers to St. Pancras, St. Servace, and St. Boniface, in whose time—the somber, rainsoaked raw days of April and May—the story takes place. Again, Tuohy's real protagonist seems to be the land itself, whose reality is written by the characters that live against its bleakness.

One compelling character is Witek Rudowski, Rose's Polish brother-in-law. Presented to us as the rumpled, forlorn, pathetic, second-rate scholar who is unloved by his wife and ridiculed by his colleagues, his mediocrity seems extravagant. As a professor of English philology, his one obsession is to become head of his department—a post for which he is a likely candidate only because of his party connections. To Rose, he is, of course, the enemy, the narrow-minded party technocrat who holds her sister in miserable poverty and emotional deprivation and who is willing to deny his son the opportunity for a brighter future outside the country. He even attempts to seduce Rose in a scene that is both painful and funny. Yet one of Tuohy's important accomplishments in this novel is his ability to make this opportunistic and unappealing conformist into a hero of sorts. Rose must view him as either threatening or ridiculous to justify her actions, but the only victory she really gains over him occurs in the instance when she can get him to admit his misery, and that is a small victory indeed. But it is through Witek that we see a different cold war—the one that exists in English middle-class families. Through Witek, Rose and the reader are exposed to the darker side of the family's relationships. The emotional impoverishment of Rose's family, her domineering Catholic mother's dislike for the older, plainer Janet, is revealed as a major reason for Janet's marriage to Witek and an explanation for her inability to act on behalf of her son.

One of Rose's most interesting lessons—significant because it is essentially a visual one—occurs during a walk along a polluted stream with her nephew. While she chatters animatedly of London, freedom, private bedrooms, she fails to notice that Tadeusz has led her to a block of concrete on which there is a small bronze plaque. Obligingly he translates: "There were fifty-eight shot here. The others in Biala Gora were taken to the camps." Rose recognizes that the walk has not been innocent and that propaganda seems to be the only way in which they communicate. Nevertheless, there is a truth to be told here and it is spoken by the plaque and the quiet boy who tries in vain to translate its message into English.

In the end, the figure of Witek forces the

reader to reevaluate his world. The victory in the book seems to belong to him. Not only is his attempted seduction a kind of affirmation, but his struggles to survive are real. And he does keep his son.

As previously mentioned, Tuohy blurs the lines. Technically he accomplishes this blurring of positive and negative through interesting blendings of imagery. One striking example is the May Day parade which is itself a blending of political and religious, a mix of contention and celebration. In the parade, one girl marches with light brown hair that is "blonde-streaked as though it had been tumbled in fresh pollen." Pictures of Gomulka, Marx, and Lenin, fluttering in the wind against the balcony, distend and shrink and seem "to smirk or to pull long faces at the crowds"; flags that have lost their brightness due to the inevitable rain shower become "the colour of an old nosebleed."

The reception of *The Ice Saints* was, in general, strongly favorable and, while some found it depressing, many thought the novel his best. *Encounter* described his narrative as "an immensely swift succession of little billiard-ball collisions," and the *New*

Statesman said, "the pleasure of his technical mastery never flags."

After his stay at Waseda University in Tokyo, Tuohy returned to England. Settling in Bath, he wrote a number of stories, mostly with English settings, which were collected in *Fingers in the Door* (1970). The stories in this collection, like Tuohy's earlier short fiction, are noteworthy for their small, epiphanic moments in the lives of suburban professional people and deal with social pretensions and isolated, emotionally impoverished lives and personalities. The title story is typical. It involves a socially pretentious Surrey family. The mother is a former typist whose snobbery has "laid her life waste"; the father is a real estate agent; the couple is taking their vapid sixteen-year-old daughter to a London matinee for her birthday. It is when the father catches his fingers in the door of the passenger car that the woman's condescension toward him and her social ambitions become etched in all their malignancy. To the mother, pain is not an acceptable condition in this first-class British carriage. Intent not only on silencing her husband's cries of pain but also on forgiving those who might

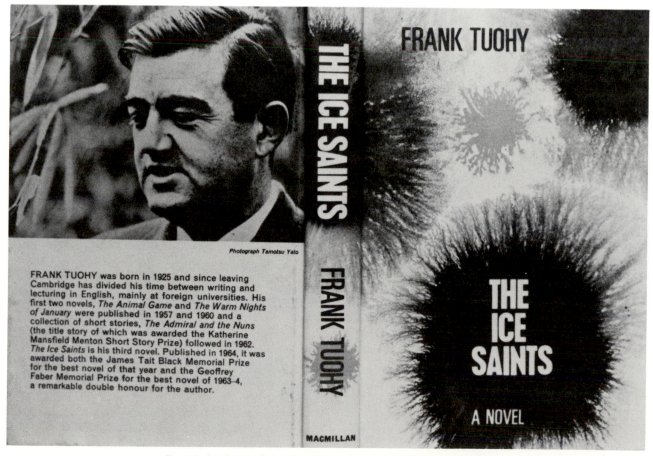

Dust jacket for Tuohy's prizewinning novel about postwar Poland

have prevented the accident, the wife not only faults him for this present embarrassment but is intent on reviewing past ones as well.

It is this kind of pain that is encountered by character after character. In "The License" a sensitive adolescent named Peter, who has recently lost his mother, fends off the patronizing offerings of icy comfort administered by a dutiful aunt who is more interested in her brother's affair with his housekeeper than she is in her nephew's pain. Peter's father, a surgeon who has taken to drinking too much, has no way of reaching his son either, except through the driving lessons he has promised him. Peter's mastery over the clutch is a small victory in comparison to the efforts required of him to face the truth about his father and the housekeeper. Peter does cope, but his own emotional stultification does not seem truly exorcized.

"A Floral Tribute" also concerns itself with isolation, pain, and the repression of emotion as a family makes funeral arrangements for a dead father. Since all reject any dependence on supporting ritual, none seems to have any way of dealing with the death. Abjuring any floral tributes, the widow and daughter-in-law turn to role playing, in which they "flower a little." Only the son, who was born too late for the wars and therefore knows nothing of death, finds no role for himself. He can only puzzle over his mother's inability to weep while he keeps his own feelings at bay and finally finds himself "ransacking his memory for a real corpse." His only true communication with his father seems to be in his death. The only real emotion expressed is their horrified reaction to one extravagant floral tribute sent by acquaintances better equipped to confront the reality of death in an emotional way.

Two hospital stories offer further comment, if not illumination, on the pervasive sense of isolation Tuohy depicts. "A Special Relationship" describes the disillusionment of Roland, a "kind of innocent," who, upon recovery from chest surgery and in a gesture of appreciation, takes his nurse out to dinner. Throughout the long and torturous evening he experiences a dislike of the woman whose lower-class affinities become a source of embarrassment to both. Any "special relationship" is seen to be illusory. In "A Reprieve," a retired colonial police captain, seriously ill with cancer, is to be sent to recuperate at the home of his spinster sister and her lesbian friend. "Home" for Captain Peacock is not in this hostile atmosphere but in Cyprus. If he cannot return to Cyprus, he prefers to die. Neither alternative is available to him this time, for he is granted a week's "reprieve."

"The Trap" is one of the most uncomfortable stories in the collection. It depicts a reserved professor, recently returned from a teaching post in Poland, who finds himself the prey of a female student who has followed him to England. Miss Rodzinska is unattractive ("she had a face that hard work and poor diet had driven quickly from prettiness into pathos"). She is priggish, intolerant, and bullying. While aware of the difficulties of her plight, aware also of the "historical debts" that seem implicit in the very existence of a country such as Poland, the professor nonetheless finds himself unwilling to be the agent of redress. His rejection is phrased in cliche-ridden language that offers scant comfort and is emphasized by his loss of the expensive present she has brought him. His most brutal act occurs when he pushes her into a train and watches as it moves away while she makes "half-blind movements, like an animal searching incredulously round the walls of its trap."

"A War of Liberation," a story of another isolated female, Miss Featherstone, again illustrates the small ways in which people damage one another. Miss Featherstone has planned for her two adopted daughters to continue in her path and become teachers, but the war and the need for freedom that inevitably beckon to young people take their toll. The war brings to her Surrey village the men who marry them and take them away. Rejected, left behind in an earlier time, Miss Featherstone calls on the mother of the narrator, a boy of sixteen, seeking comfort. Coldly, though innocently, the boy turns the spinster away only to discover later that she has taken her own life.

Critics were complimentary about this collection on the whole, but one interesting point was made by Knightly Shorter of the *New Leader* who observed in the stories "a powerful undercurrent of misogyny. . . . Women are seen as a sexual threat, an embarrassing nuisance, a dykish joke, or at best an alien form of life. . . ." A number of critics remarked on the stories' pessimism; *Saturday Review* called them "too insistent." But C. P. Snow called Tuohy "a master of the short story, one of the best now writing in English."

From 1964 to 1967 Tuohy was Visiting Professor at Waseda University in Tokyo, and out of this experience came a number of short stories that were later collected in *Live Bait* (1978). Japan was perhaps a factor in sharpening Tuohy's interest in William Butler Yeats, for he not only became friends with Professor Shotoara Oshima, author of *Yeats in Japan*, but also found keen interest in Yeats among many other colleagues there as well. However, it was at the request of his publisher that he became interested in writing a Yeats biography. (Macmillan owned the rights to Yeats's works in Britain and the United States.) When he consented to undertake the work on Yeats, he was opposed by both F. S. L. Lyons, the authorized biographer, and Yeats's son, Michael Butler. However, Tuohy went ahead, using the materials then available.

Tuohy's interest in Yeats was not new; he had written on "Leda and the Swan" for his B.A. at Cambridge. Furthermore, his own background added another factor: "I was interested in finding out about the Irish background for personal reasons—my own family being about 100 years in England but still aware of barriers and differences. . . . I also thought of the period as being the last one where writers interacted and disputed about writing itself—not the academic study of writing or literary theory."

It is this interaction among writers—from George Russell, William Morris, Oscar Wilde, John Millington Synge, Ezra Pound, and countless others, as well as from political figures like Lady Gregory, Maud Gonne, J. F. Taylor—that makes Yeats's world, as treated in Tuohy's book, so fascinating; indeed, the charisma of these people, captured so well by Tuohy, almost overshadows Yeats himself, especially in the first half of the book. In fact, it is Yeats's own father, Jack B., whose talent, wit, and overpowering personality dominate the early portions of it.

Tuohy's descriptive abilities also give life to such groups as the Irish Republican Brotherhood, the Abbey Theatre, and the Order of the Golden Dawn. In fact, it was because of the need to place Yeats in the context of nineteenth-century Irish politics (which also influenced his interest in the occult and the theater) that so much detailing of outside material was essential. John Wain, in his review of *Yeats* (1976) for the *Observer Review*, noted Tuohy's attention to background and personalities and the effect it has of almost diminishing the presence of Yeats. Yet, as he points out, "as the book goes on, the unflinching presentation of detail becomes more and more impressive. . . . Tuohy wins the reader's confidence, progressively, by the completeness and strength of his portraiture."

What makes this biography particularly attractive is Tuohy's ability—perhaps that of the good novelist—to treat Yeats's interest in the occult with honesty, compassion, and a touch of humor while resisting the popular prejudices about the poet and the mires into which some scholarship seems to sink. In fact, while Tuohy discusses a number of poems,

there is little criticism or explication which does not involve biographical contexts.

Critical reception of *Yeats* was enthusiastic. Elizabeth Jennings, writing in the *Daily Telegraph*, stated that "this book is something far more important than yet another critical thesis: it throws light on the external and internal events of Yeats's life with great sensitivity and care." Malcolm Brown in *Hibernia* called it "an important event in literary history, since it constitutes the first great breach in the academic monopoly of Yeatsian studies in nearly forty years." Derek Mahon in the *New Statesman* observed that it was "greatly to Mr. Tuohy's credit that he has managed to make the poet almost likeable."

In 1978, his most recent collection of short stories appeared. This collection, *Live Bait*, contained a dozen stories that were not unlike those of his earlier collection, *The Admiral and the Nuns*, and, as in the case of the earlier work, the emphasis is on isolation, the problems of class, the plight of the exile. The title story, the longest, and one of the most effective, returns to the subject Tuohy had treated before—the plight of the sensitive adolescent encountering an adult world of pettiness, snobbery, sexuality, and callousness. The "live bait" with which the unattractive yet appealing twelve-year-old Andrew will catch the big pike does not endure much more pain than the boy himself. Snubbed by his only friend, sexually threatened by the slightly mad major, attacked and criticized by the formidable Rowena with all her clumsiness and upper-class pretentions, caught in the still-mystifying relationship between his mother and her lover, Andrew learns about hierarchies and their subtle brutalizing.

A number of the better stories in the collection have their setting in Japan. "The Broken Bridge," for example, is a subtle exploration of Japanese and American relationships featuring an American professor who works with Japanese students in drama. A lover of Kabuki, successful in reaching some level of rapport with his students and colleagues, he is still ignorant and insensitive enough to cause the suicide of one of his students when he forces the students to act in a homosexual interpretation of Arthur Miller's *A View from the Bridge*. In "A Summer Pilgrim," western insensitivity and its destructive aftermath are again depicted, as an aging poet, visited by a female former Japanese student, humiliates his visitor with sexual overtures while his domineering and insensitive wife feeds her a luncheon that causes her to become ill. In "Nocturne with Neon Lights," Tuohy gives us another picture of hell in the form of the seamy side of a foreign city. In this story, an Englishman, left on his own in Tokyo when his wife returns to England, finds his fantasy of freedom and an Edenic existence complete with geisha becoming a nightmare as he loses himself in a city whose inhabitants seem to mirror his own exploitative nature.

There are also a few stories with a Polish setting. Tuohy's interest in hierarchies and the subtleties of politics in a communist university are the subjects of "The Candidate." The protagonist, a visiting professor at a Polish university, is called upon to help in the selection of new students where there are four hundred candidates competing for twenty positions. Unable to escape into his status as a foreigner, the professor faces problems of party pressures and gets caught up in a struggle that results, ironically, in the rejection of the party favorite due to a case of mistaken identity (she happens to be the best qualified candidate) and in the selection of one of the worst.

A comic, even exuberant story, "The Potlatch of Esmeralda" tells of a Brazilian woman who lives in Paris and who lavishes attention and material comforts on an unemployed Spaniard named Vicente. Another refugee figure, Esmeralda survives Vicente's callous exploitation and rejection by drawing on practices of her culture. When Vicente is to marry another, she embarks on a South American ritual that involves potlatch, the ceremonial distribution of one's wealth, for the purpose of dominating her peers and restoring her sense of pride. Her moment of triumph occurs when she attends the wedding to find Vicente resplendent in the clothes she has provided and when she can point out that fact to his bride.

Some critics found these stories well crafted. The *New Statesman* complained of the narrowness of some while suggesting that Tuohy's strength "lies in the way he captures the unusual viewpoint of the expatriate." The *New York Times Book Review* spoke of Tuohy's cruelly compassionate eye for social flounderings," adding "the predicaments in which he sticks his characters are horribly believable."

About his work, Tuohy has said: "Most of what I write seems to start off with the interaction between two cultures, modes of behavior, ways of living, etc. Sometimes the confrontation is between a foreigner and an alien environment, sometimes between groups in that environment itself. For me, the sense of displacement, loss, anxiety which happens to people derives from the world outside them, in their relationships with that world."

It is perhaps Tuohy's rather somber view of the human condition, the very special material he chooses for subject matter, and the delicacy and precision of his writing that make him more of a critical than a popular success. Nevertheless, he is recognized as a writer of consummate skill; what his work perhaps lacks is an emotional force equal to his technical abilities.

Tuohy continues primarily to divide his time between England and periods of residence in France, Greece, and Portugal. (He is fluent in both French and Portuguese.) He has served as writer-in-residence at Purdue University, and is presently at Texas A & M University.

Play:
The Japanese Student, 1973.

Auberon Waugh

(11 November 1939-)

Joan Grumman
Santa Barbara City College
and
Anne Kowalewski

BOOKS: *The Foxglove Saga* (London: Chapman & Hall, 1960; New York: Simon & Schuster, 1961);

Path of Dalliance (London: Chapman & Hall, 1963; New York: Simon & Schuster, 1964);

Who Are the Violets Now? (London: Chapman & Hall, 1965; New York: Simon & Schuster, 1966);

Consider the Lilies (London: Joseph, 1968; Boston: Little, Brown, 1969);

Biafra: Britain's Shame, by Waugh and Suzanna Cronjé (London: Joseph, 1969);

A Bed of Flowers; or As You Like It (London: Joseph, 1972);

Country Topics (London: Joseph, 1974);

Four Crowded Years: The Diaries of Auberon Waugh, 1972-76, edited by N. R. Galli (London: Deutsch, 1976);

In the Lion's Den (London: Joseph, 1978);

Auberon Waugh's Yearbook: A News Summary and Press Digest of 1980 (London: Pan, 1981);

The Last Word: An Eyewitness Account of the Thorpe Trial (London: Joseph, 1981).

Auberon Waugh

Auberon Waugh has his own place in British letters. Certainly his work shows the influence of his father, Evelyn Waugh (however much he tends to deny it and however much he avoids discussing the similarities in their work), for they lived in the same world and have drawn from similar sources. Both are satirists, but Auberon Waugh has chosen to concentrate his efforts on nonfiction as well as the novel.

In a time when news headlines are stranger than fiction, when the novelist's fantasies cannot keep up with the statements of presumably responsible world leaders, when the daily television report is a kaleidoscope of horror, inhumanity, and every form of arbitrariness, the satirist need hardly do more than report actual statements and events. Thus (aside from the financial need to support a family), Auberon Waugh has in the past decade turned to nonfiction. It gives him the opportunity for immediate comment on the world around him without the demands of the longer process of writ-

ing fiction. But Waugh incorporates what he has learned as a novelist: presentation of character, the use of wit, and the careful choice of language—particularly the devices of overstatement and irony. For Waugh, as for many other writers of our time, the strands of fiction and nonfiction feed into each other.

Auberon Alexander Waugh was born in Dulverton, Somerset, England, on 11 November 1939. He was the second child of seven and the oldest son of novelist Evelyn Waugh and Laura Herbert Waugh. His early education was at Old Hallows, a Roman Catholic preparatory school of approximately one hundred boys, located in Somerset. His secondary education was at Downside School in Somerset, a Roman Catholic public school.

After attending Downside, Waugh became a

national service officer in the Royal Horse Guards and served in Cyprus. In 1958 during an armed exercise, a Browning machine gun went berserk, riddling Waugh with several bullets. He lost a lung, his spleen, several ribs, and a finger, losses which still cause him acute pain. It was during his recuperation which lasted nine months that Waugh wrote his first novel, *The Foxglove Saga* (1960), drawing on his school and military experiences.

Following his recuperation from the National Service accident, Waugh enrolled at Oxford in 1959 but failed his preliminaries and left after the first year. He then began his professional writing career as a journalist working for the *Daily Telegraph* in London.

He married Teresa Onslow in July 1961, and they have four children: Sophie, Alex, Daisy, and Nat. The family live in Evelyn Waugh's rambling nineteenth-century manor house in Combe Florey, Taunton, Somerset, and spend summers in their home in Montmaur, Aude, France.

Waugh employs the satirist's mode in his novels as well as in his essays and journalism. He aims his satire at all of contemporary society: at people, at causes, at social and political institutions, and particularly at hypocrisy. His sharp pen will cut down anything or anyone, although he himself does not think he is a self-appointed devil's advocate or even a person with extreme opinions but rather a "middle-of-the-road egg." But critical and popular assessment of his work from his novels to his *Private Eye* column runs counter to this self-assessment; he is very often described as snobbish and extremely right wing.

Thematically, his novels cover the range of contemporary society as it relates specifically to his own experience. Thus, his novels look carefully and caustically at the family and marriage, school, the university, journalism, the church, political organizations and causes, and contemporary social experiments. Waugh holds up all of contemporary society to a mirror and finds it wanting. At times he is humorous, even warm, but his general mode is acerbic and dark. His large themes are certainly ones that preoccupy major modern novelists, but in Waugh they are unevenly handled; there is a failure in conception at times, or a concentration on plot and action over character and motivation. The endings of his novels often move too hurriedly to a conclusion—again concentrating on events over other aspects of the novel. But there are many memorable scenes and characters in Waugh's novels; he is particularly good at defining minor characters through idiosyncrasies.

Though Waugh's first novel, *The Foxglove Saga*, was written before he entered Oxford, it was not published until 1960; he was too shy a teenager to show it to anyone. But when he was recuperating from an automobile accident in 1960, he reread it and decided to have it published. It was an immediate success, and Auberon Waugh was hailed as a born writer. The novel's hero, Martin Foxglove, is one of nature's darlings who is continually nurtured by his powerful and pious mother, Lady Foxglove. No matter what direction Martin is encouraged to take, he continues to be drawn toward the novel's antagonist, Kenneth Stoat. Stoat embodies all the world's ugliness—even his parents want to disown him. But as often happens, the antagonist proves to be the more interesting character; Waugh gets inside the character of this unpopular, unkempt, and unlucky boy who longs to be like and is eventually disgusted with Foxglove. The novel follows their adventures through a school run by monks, the British Army, a brush with London life, and a rest home. Religion, schools, family relationships, the military, and hospitals are held up to scrutiny and found wanting. There are genuinely comic moments in this novel, along with interesting considerations of the various institutions depicted.

The Foxglove Saga was well received, but critics accused Waugh of trying to pattern his writing after his father's, citing *Brideshead Revisited* (1945) and the similarity between Sebastian Flyte and Martin Foxglove, and the similarity of the ideas of both novels. It is true that both novels deal with themes of class and religion, but there are differences of treatment and scope. Auberon Waugh draws on a tradition of English wit as well as experiences shared with his father. But he is of a different generation, born at the beginning of a devastating war and reaching adulthood in an age of chaotic change.

His second novel, *Path of Dalliance* (1963), though largely accepted by critics, was not as popular as his first. The similarity of style, story line, and social commentary in the two works may account for this reaction. The novel satirizes aspects of the intellectual life at Oxford seen through the eyes of Jamey Sligger, a provincial, sexually unaware, yet decadent undergraduate. According to Waugh, this book is autobiographical. As in his first novel, he satirizes social problems with less maliciousness than in his later work. His commentary ranges over areas of concern to students: nuclear disarmament (through a fraternity song, "Your Face Will Be Fleshless); state abortion (through the experience of an expelled pregnant student); attempts to fight apartheid, neo-colonialism, and fascism (through sponsoring an art exhibit to raise funds to combat them); and the unethical behavior of the clergy at the "new" Oxford (through Brother Rapey Rawley's clandestine tattletale club, "The Rapists," who report on their classmates' activities).

By 1964 Waugh was working as a special writer for the International Publishing Corporation in London, but he continued to write novels. His third, *Who Are the Violets Now?* (1965), is his least favorite novel. Yet it deals with several important themes: the arbitrariness of modern existence, religion, hypocrisy, sexual permissiveness, racism, and fascism. As in the other novels, there are sparkling moments and memorable minor characters—Toe-mass Gray, the black American would-be poet and activist; Mr. Besant, the peace leader who is discovered to be a Nazi war criminal. Yet too much seems to be contrived at the end of this book; the rush of events and the immediacy that are effective in journalism are less so in the novel.

Waugh's fourth and favorite novel, *Consider the Lilies* (1968), takes a pointed look at the contemporary Church of England clergyman who finds a widespread lack of interest in religion. Nicholas Trumpeter, a young clergyman, reflects antireligious sentiments when he describes his theological college's overdose of religious inculcation as an experience which "stretches credulity and encourages cynicism." He sees his role as a means of adding to other people's happiness and finally becomes chaplain at Kaptain Sunshine Holiday Camp, directing Ecumenical Fun Sessions. The unity of the point of view aids this novel. Waugh makes Trumpeter real to the reader who, whether he agrees with his attitudes and behavior or not, has some insight into the conditions of his life and its demands. Again there are memorable minor characters: Mr. Boissaens, the eccentric landowner; Mrs. Morelli, a gossipy old-age pensioner; Gillian, the clergyman's hypochondriac wife; and Mr. Tuck, the rural dean whose prime concern seems to be with the animals that belong to members of his congregation.

Waugh's novels become increasingly biting; his satirical social comments become more direct, as they would in journalism, and less embedded in character situation. His journalistic experiences most likely influenced the course of his changing style. In any case, his literary reputation for giving offense increased during the late 1960s. He worked as the chief political correspondent for the *Spectator* from 1967 to 1970 and visited Biafra in that capacity. He was thoroughly disillusioned by what he saw there and what he learned of British indifference.

The experience gave rise to his first nonfiction book, which he wrote with Suzanne Cronjé: *Biafra: Britain's Shame* (1969). The book portrays this young country's struggle to preserve its independence, but it is also an indictment of the role Britain played in the Nigeria-Biafra war. In clear, direct, and forceful critical prose (characteristic of his style at its best), Waugh concludes that "the British people, and above all the British intelligentsia, had ceased to have any interest or concern in the conduct of our foreign affairs. Having lost an Empire—after a tolerably good grace—the British people had abdicated from all responsibility on world affairs, leaving it to a handful of men about whose competence, reliability or simple human decency they were totally indifferent." Although not a commercial success, the book raised the consciousness of the British public about a situation that had thus far been ignored.

In the next few years, Waugh devoted most of his time to journalism. In addition to being a columnist for the *News of the World* and *The Sun* (1969 to 1970) and the *Times* (1970), he worked with the *Spectator* until 1973. His latest novel was also published during this period. In *A Bed of Flowers; or As You Like It* (1972), he revises the characters in Shakespeare's play, giving them personalities in the revolutionary 1960s and early 1970s. Waugh wrote this novel as a study of the political and moral implications of "dropping out." The main character, Brother John, also known as the Duke, heads a large international conglomerate with his brother, Frederick, but decides to leave it and settle in a commune in Glastonbury, Somerset. The members of the commune spend their time in discussions about the quest for the Holy Grail, London politics, and the Nigeria-Biafra war. The novel is clearly an attempt to look at British society in the early 1970s and to question Britain's imperialism. Commercially it was not a success; critics called Waugh's attack too heavy-handed. He admits the failure of this novel: the impatience of the journalist for direct statement overcame the more subtle claims on the novelist.

Since 1973, Waugh has worked as the fiction reviewer for the London *Evening Standard* and as a columnist for *Private Eye*, the *New Statesman*, and *Books and Bookmen* in London, as well as for the New York publication *Esquire*. His brutal literary and political columns in these publications have earned him the reputation of the "rudest man in Fleet Street." Anthony Shrimsley, the editor of *Now!* magazine, has called Waugh "a liar motivated by malice, who doesn't deserve either to be employed as a journalist or to share the company of decent

"The Life and Times of Grigorii Rasputin" by Alex de Jonge (Collins £9.95) (368 pp illus)

"Whatever Rasputin's influence may have been, it was rumour, not the fact, that counted." Previous biographies have certainly taken Mr de Jonge's conclusion at its face value. Grigorii Rasputin remains a creature of rumour and legend in most people's minds. His presence in St Petersburgh and at Tsarskoe Selo helped destroy the Romanov dynasty in two ways: the scandal of a peasant at court alienated the Tsar and Tsarina from the rest of the Imperial family and the nobility; rumours forced by these people, and by politicians in the Duma, not to mention the Imperial General Staff, that there was a pro-German faction at court trying to make separate peace with the Germans, so that the Imperial family became a scapegoat, rather than a rallying point, in times of distress.

Mr de Jonge's book does not convince me that Rasputin's murder somehow sparked off the Revolution, or that the Revolution would have been any less likely if the wretched man had survived his assassination on December 16 1916. He was a symbol of the dynasty's collapse, rather than an important cause of it. If he had not turned up, the wretched Tsarina would certainly have found some other faith healer for her sickly heir — Russia was full of them — and they would all have ended up in the cellar at Ekaterinburg just the same. Rasputin's story is a fascinating one, but it truly belongs to the world of Dracula and Frankenstein rather than to what we in England mean by history.

But so does much of Russia's genuine history, and Rasputin did, of course, exist. It is tempting to fall back into poetic whimsy accepting, as Felix Yusupov (one of the assassins did) the opinion of a French occultist, delivered shortly before his own death and Rasputin's own murder:

"Cabbalistically speaking Rasputin is a vessel like Pandora's box, which contains all the vices, crimes and filth of the Russian people. Should the vessel be broken we will see its dreadful contents spill themselves across Russia."

First page of the manuscript for a book review by Waugh

people." Yet many of Waugh's fellow journalists approve of him. He has twice received the British Press Award Commendation as Critic of the Year, and he was chosen Columnist of the Year by Granada's "What the Papers Say." Politicians number among his readers. Former Prime Minister James Callaghan once said he never missed a Waugh column (adding quickly that he disagreed with him, of course). Waugh is a force in British journalism not easily ignored if not always admired.

In addition to his journalism, Waugh has published five nonfiction books since 1974. *Country Topics*, a collection of essays written for the *Evening Standard*, appeared in 1974; much of it is in the bucolic mode and set in pastoral Britain and France. The subject matter covers a variety of topics such as his children and their snail collection, which eventually goes to Le Fat, a local character at Montmaur, and the suggestion that village churches should be used to house retired civil servants. The book is illustrated with caricatures of Waugh and his family as well as of their residences in Britain and France. Overall the tone is gentle and witty with an occasional serious comment, as when in the essay "Pity and the Poor French Rich" he draws an analogy between the old wars of religion in France and present conditions in Northern Ireland.

In 1976, he published *Four Crowded Years: The Diaries of Auberon Waugh, 1972-76*, which had appeared first as his *Private Eye* column. Arranged chronologically, the entries are sometimes harsh, even vicious; others are humorous but with the critical edge Waugh is noted for, as when he describes the spacemen meeting in space and shaking hands in a location roughly over Bognor Regis. There are respectful entries when he writes of men he admires, like P. G. Wodehouse and the late Duke of Norfolk; but the diaries are full of cutting references to feminism, minority groups, the working class, and public figures from the political as well as the entertainment world.

Another collection of essays, this time from the *New Statesman*, 1973 to 1975, was published in 1978. (In 1975 Waugh had returned to the *Spectator*.) *In the Lion's Den* shows Waugh's usual wide range of topics: an English Catholic's faith, the death of a goldfish named Marigold, the recent election results, and the attempted kidnapping of Princess Anne and her husband. In two essays he writes movingly of two writers he admires, B. S. Johnson and P. G. Wodehouse. Of the latter he says: "What Wodehouse has done is to distil for all time a form of pure comedy in more or less abstract guise, without any social application, let alone

political commitment; with no bitterness, cruelty, sex, rancour or any other impure purpose which comedy may serve." Waugh's critics might wish that he emulated Wodehouse more in his writing; this collection contains more of the vicious, biting wit Waugh's readers have come to expect.

Auberon Waugh's Yearbook: A News Summary and Press Digest of 1980 (1981) recounts events that made the daily headlines during that year. It underscores the precariousness of the times we live in and gives the reader an opportunity to reflect on the good and bad news of the year. Waugh plans to continue writing these news digests.

His most recent book, *The Last Word: An Eyewitness Account of the Jeremy Thorpe Trial* (1981), deals with a case which occupied the British press for several months. Jeremy Thorpe, former leader of the Liberal Party and a public figure for over twenty years, was charged with conspiracy to murder Norman Scott, a male model, who claimed to have had a homosexual relationship with Thorpe. Waugh's account, in which dramatic and rhetorical techniques are used to good effect, has been called a classic of trial literature. It lists the principals in the case as a cast of characters; one notable example refers to Scott's dog who was shot by one of the conspirators: "Rinka. A murdered Great Dane. Did not give evidence. The judge had no comment about this animal." Among the variety of rhetorical devices in this account are irony, in the way Waugh discusses the verdict and our expectations of people in public life, and exaggeration and overstatement, when he calls the book his atonement for entertaining the preposterous idea that such a man as Thorpe could be guilty. His line-by-line interpretive commentary on the judge's summary intersperses reportage with analysis.

Waugh's notoriety and his success stem from his journalism and his essays rather than from his fiction. He has said that he receives more satisfaction from journalism because of the nearly instantaneous response; perhaps this is a further reason why he is not pursuing novel-writing at present. Yet although he does not feel he has made much impact as a novelist, he hopes to write more novels in the future. When asked about the direction of the novel and of novelists today, he comments on the difficulty of making a living as a novelist, yet criticizes those novelists who write what the masses demand, hoping for profit rather than concerning themselves with the art of writing. Waugh believes that novel writing will become the virtual monopoly of housewives and academics. He does not think that academics' backgrounds necessarily provide "a healthy nursery" for novel writing. Housewives, he feels, can and do write admirable novels, but these he finds limited to Gothic fantasy which bears little relationship to the society in which they live; minute studies of their own social world; or egotistical manifestos and studies in self-absorption.

If as a novelist Auberon Waugh fails to achieve what his father did, he will be remembered for highly opinionated, usually vicious, literary and political columns and for the acuteness of his observation and delineation of the Biafra question and the Thorpe trial. He will, no doubt, continue to write searchingly about contemporary society in his columns and essays. And he promises to write more novels. Since he is in mid-career, he should be able to keep that promise. His closeness to the news should give him ideas for future novels. Waugh has always had a sense of a body of fiction—note the

paralleling of his life experience and the attempt to link his novels by employing flower titles: foxglove, primrose (implied), violets, lilies, and a bed of flowers which are, in turn, linked with either Shakespeare's plays or the Bible. Further possibilities for fiction open before Waugh's fertile imagination, his critical views, and his pen honed by constant column writing. We will hear from Waugh the novelist again almost as certainly as we will hear from Waugh the journalist.

References:

Neal Acherson, "Beyond Discussion," *London Review of Books*, 3 April 1980;

Rhoda Koenig, "A Handful of Mud," *Esquire* (December 1980): 86-92;

Geoffrey Moorehouse, "At Home with the Fogey of Combe Florey," *Guardian*, 16 February 1980.

Fay Weldon

(22 September 1931-   )

Harriet Blodgett
University of California, Davis

BOOKS: *The Fat Woman's Joke* (London: MacGibbon & Kee, 1967); republished as . . . *And the Wife Ran Away* (New York: McKay, 1968);

Down Among the Women (London: Heinemann, 1971; New York: St. Martin's, 1972);

Words of Advice [play] (London & New York: French, 1974);

Female Friends (London: Heinemann, 1975; New York: St. Martin's, 1975);

Remember Me (London: Hodder & Stoughton, 1976; New York: Random House, 1976);

Words of Advice [novel] (New York: Random House, 1977); republished as *Little Sisters* (London: Hodder & Stoughton, 1978);

Praxis (London: Hodder & Stoughton, 1979; New York: Summit, 1979);

Puffball (London: Hodder & Stoughton, 1980; New York: Summit, 1980);

Watching Me, Watching You (London: Hodder & Stoughton, 1981; New York: Summit, 1981);

The President's Child (London: Hodder & Stoughton, 1982).

Fay Weldon, who is also a successful stage, radio, and television playwright, established her

reputation as a novelist by writing tart, intelligent, and often comic fictions about the lives and natures of women. A satirist with a sharp sense of the ridiculous, adept at wry humor and witty prose, she has the feminist urge to improve women's attitudes towards themselves and their sisters and an imagination fertile in finding unusual embodiments for her independent attitudes and unsentimental values.

Born in the village of Alvechurch in Worcestershire, Weldon was to continue a family tradition with her writing. Her father, Frank Thornton Birkinshaw, was a physician, but her mother, Margaret Jepson Birkinshaw, published two light novels in the 1930s under her maiden name. Better-known authors, Weldon's grandfather, Edgar Jepson, a turn-of-the century editor of *Vanity Fair*, was a prolific writer of best-seller romances of adventure until the 1930s; her uncle, Selwyn Jepson, of mystery-thriller novels and films, radio and television plays, until the 1970s. During early childhood, Weldon emigrated to New Zealand with her parents, where she later attended Girls' High School in Christchurch. From the time she was six, when her parents were divorced, she lived with her mother and sister, seeing her father only during summer holidays—a circumstance reflected in her books in the preponderance of daughters reared by mothers alone. Upon her mother's receiving a small legacy, just sufficient for fare, Weldon returned to England, at age fourteen, to live in London: by her account, a period of "hardship and deprivation" in her life. It was also an intensification of living in a household of women, now with her grandmother as well as her mother and sister, besides attending a convent school, Hampstead High School in London—all of which made her feel that "the world was composed of women." She later theorized that experiencing so female a milieu since childhood had made her forever independent of the need for male approbation, hence able to write more openly and honestly. Her environment no doubt also contributed to the diminished role men play in her books. In 1949 she entered St. Andrew's University in Scotland, on a scholarship, and by 1952 had earned her M.A. in economics and psychology.

By 1955 she had borne her first son, Nicholas, and was to know the hardship of supporting him by herself. The unwed mother would also be a recurrent figure in her novels. Weldon has said, "I am all of them [my characters] to some degree," in that she

Fay Weldon

has herself known the frustrations, helplessness, feelings of compromise and desperation she has depicted in them. But even more specifically, she has pointed out that one unwed mother, twenty-year-old Scarlet of her novel *Down Among the Women* (1971), is partly "a portrait of me when I was younger, a mess, . . . totally and completely," and that like Scarlet she too had a bout with psychoanalysis (though during her own thirties). Other of her own experiences would become her characters' too. By the 1950s Weldon had already tried writing novels, but in desultory fashion and only to accumulate rejection slips for them. With no particular professional ambitions as yet, in another period of "odd jobs and hard times," she drifted first into writing propaganda for the Foreign Office, then into doing market research and answering problem letters for the London *Daily Mirror*, and, finally, into composing advertising copy. She worked her way up to more prestigious firms and continued in advertising until the 1970s. Meanwhile, she remained close to her family. When her sister died of cancer in 1969, leaving three children, Weldon assisted her mother in rearing them.

In 1960 she had married Ronald Weldon, a London antique dealer, to whom she would bear three sons (Daniel, in 1963; Thomas, in 1970; and Samuel, in 1977). The Weldons settled in Primrose Hill, a conventional North London suburb, where they would live for some fifteen years. Weldon combined domesticity successfully with her ever-expanding writing career, which really began only in the mid-1960s. Her marriage, she felt, had finally given a focus to a life "messed up hopelessly until I met my husband." Ever the woman to make her own decisions about feminist issues, she would later refuse to wear a wedding ring, regarding such banding as a symbolic insult to women; but she would delight in the title "Mrs.," declare herself in many ways conventionally female, and refuse to subscribe to the notion that it would be a better world for women without men. Without them, she would much later insist, "one misses the richness of life. . . . the vibes that men radiate . . . make them essential." In the 1960s, so conventional did she seem as devoted wife and mother, despite her career, that she was invited to participate in a David Frost debate in 1971, on the assumption that she would mock the radical agitators who were currently in the English news for denouncing the Miss World contest as a flesh market. Instead she disrupted the program by hailing their efforts. Even had the Frost researchers troubled to read her first—and feminist—novel, already published by then, before inviting her to speak, they could not have predicted her stand. In another characteristic anecdote, while working in the 1970s on a program about rape which brought her in contact with some of the women's movement's more ardent spokeswomen, she decided that they were "without doubt very dedicated women," who, had they been men, would "all have been rapists."

Already one of the most successful advertising copywriters in England, by the late 1960s Weldon was also well advanced in her career as script (and later scenario) writer and playwright that would continue up to the present. Her one-act "Permanence" was part of a multi-act play on the theme of married life, *Mixed Doubles*, which included other such distinguished contributors as Harold Pinter and was produced in London at the Comedy Theatre in 1969. There would later be seven other one-acts, and longer plays as well. And there would be radio plays, such as *Spider* (1972), which won the Writer's Guild Award for Best Radio Play in 1973; and *Polaris* (1977), which won the Giles Cooper Award for Best Radio Play in 1978. For the BBC and English commercial networks, she would write more than fifty television plays (plus films) on a wide range of subjects; for American television, a film on migrant workers. In 1971 and 1972 she wrote two episodes for the *Upstairs, Downstairs* series, the first of which, "On Trial," won the SFTA Award for Best Series. More recently, her five-part dramatization of *Pride and Prejudice* (1980) has been praised for its fidelity to Jane Austen's manner and perceptions.

Television writing proved to be Weldon's entry into fiction. Her first novel, the serio-comic *Fat Woman's Joke* (1967), was originally written as a television play (*The Fat Woman's Tale*, Granada, 1966) and then overextended into a novel. But it is a skillful, if minor work, whose humor critics admired and which introduces some of Weldon's typical themes and methods. Middle-aged, tubby Esther (who will triumph without losing a pound) has left her paunchy husband Alan in the aftermath of their ill-advised crash diet to regain something of their youthful selves. While he continues to philander with his slim, young secretary Susan, Esther retreats to a dingy basement apartment, where she gorges herself and testily parades her marital woes before the younger friend, Phyllis, who has sought her out. Although Esther's mother, eighteen-year-old son, and Susan also visit this ironic Job to urge her back to her husband, Esther assents only after he enters his plea too. Meanwhile, she has had somewhat of a rebirth of personality while vegetating under-

ground, imaged by the sprouting of a potted plant—Weldon often reinforces themes with symbolic objects and names, traditional analogies and myths. Esther's too omniscient reminiscence of the past month is told for her by a narrator, and dialogue, as always in Weldon's novels, preponderates. The narrator rather awkwardly interleaves in Esther's tale a separate account of the love lives of Susan's roommate and Susan, who finally prefers the son to his father.

Stout and aging in a world where youthful looks count, Esther conveys Weldon's fervent resentment of the devaluation of woman to a brainless, sexual object, a pretty and docile doll. Phyllis readily betrays her absent friend to sleep with Alan and be praised for fitting that category because she finds her self-respect (like most women) only in men's desire for her; like husband-stalking Susan, she has no sense of loyalty to women. No Weldon novel will tolerate such lack of sisterhood. Esther, whose sexuality has waned and in whom a more valid basis for self-respect is struggling to emerge, has seen (like Weldon) that it is a "fearful thing to be a woman in a man's world accepting masculine values" when "their opinion of womankind is . . . conditioned by fear, resentment and natural feelings of inferiority." But acknowledging women's woes while denying the right to self-indulgence over them is the distinguishing trait of a Weldon novel. Weldon will have no basking in self-pity, as Esther tries to do, or putting all the blame on men; women share in ruining lives, including their own. The domestic squabbles of Esther and Alan are designed to expose both sides of the story. Whether Esther, like the reader, recognizes all the ways in which she has denied Alan's needs, trammeled her energies, and reduced her marriage to gourmet meals is not entirely clear; later Weldon heroines will be more explicit about their blameworthiness. What Esther does recognize clearly is that she needs her marriage—one of "those human organizations that stand between us and chaos." The marriages Weldon depicts are usually, if not invariably, failures in communion of spirit even when they occasionally succeed as sexual outlets, but Weldon does not scorn marriage in her novels. Life is so imperfect, we need whatever defenses against chaos we can find. Her heroines are to find a variety of them.

When she wrote *The Fat Woman's Joke*, Weldon claimed to have no knowledge of a women's movement. By the time of her more elaborately structured second novel, the satiric yet compassionate *Down Among the Women*, she evidently did. A meditation on contemporary womanhood and an illustration of it, through glimpses into the lives of the semi-autobiographical Scarlet, her family, and her four girl friends, this book is told at the beginning, end, and occasionally in between by a first-person, reminiscent narrator, who elsewhere lapses into third person. The "I" is Scarlet's friend Jocelyn, who serves as a persona for Weldon (and has been given her Foreign Office experience). *Down Among the Women* takes its title from the refrain starting most of the chapters which is the theme song of devastating introductory passages of commentary on the female condition. Enlivened by pointed jokes, anecdotes, and cross-patter as well—Weldon is always uninhibited about the form of the novel—these illusion-breaking, but clever, chapter introductions convey her feministic themes more effectively than her narrative, where the main story of Scarlet and her family is encumbered by Scarlet's too sketchily portrayed friends. We meet them, and Scarlet's stepmother, Susan, still "down among the girls," rather than the women, and yet to learn that the great enemy is not just men, but existence, which tends to chaos and cancer. They are "down" because they are the preliberation females of the 1950s, still subjugated to subordinate roles and general inconsequence. But "down" is also both a lament for women, who have only a "brief dance in the sun" before going "down into the darkness" of domestic stupor, and a tart reprimand to them for living "at floor level" and looking upward only "to dust the tops of the windows. We have only ourselves to blame." However, the narrator optimistically (if ironically) envisions a brave new woman evolving, and Weldon shows such evolution working its way through three generations of Scarlet's family.

Most impressive is Scarlet's mother, feisty, middle-aged Wanda, an ex-communist and a feminist before her time, who was independent enough to leave her artist-husband, Kim, (during Scarlet's childhood) for prostituting his talent, even if it meant poverty. Wanda explicitly pities, rather than hates men, like the narrator, who finds the male creature "not so much wicked as frail" and depicts him accordingly. Kim, to Scarlet's distress (she wants her father for herself), marries her peer Susan, whom pregnant Scarlet, to comic effect, bilks of her lying-in quarters. Reared by Wanda to believe in sexual freedom, untidy Scarlet, to Wanda's chagrin, produces a bastard daughter, Byzantia, and still in search of a father (though now more for Byzantia), marries an impotent old man, whom she later divorces. Scarlet and her friends constitute the youth of the 1950s discovering rebellion against the strictures of the past, if not against their need of men. Not so Byzantia, who becomes the nihilistic young woman developed by the 1960s, a self-assured radical intent on tearing down "the old order" of women by the 1970s. Byzantia cannot fancy seeing success in terms of men, the "symptom . . . of a fearful disease from which you all suffered," not that she can name the disease. Weldon finds glib Byzantia frightening in her single-mindedness. Freedom is not so simple as Byzantia assumes—inspiration for Weldon's next book. Critics admired this novel for its witty lines and richly varied comic effects. Since they also thought it discerning and clever in its version of the female condition, they began hailing Weldon as a valuable addition to the feminist cadre.

In 1974 Weldon saw the one-act *Words of Advice*, her second play on marital life, performed and the next year published her substantial, better-focused third novel, *Female Friends*, the story of fortyish Chloe and her longtime friends, Marjorie and Grace. This novel is told sometimes from Chloe's first-person point-of-view, more often from a narrator's third-person one, or in the form of terse, play-script dialogue. The narrator and Chloe oftentimes merge, but whereas the narrator always conveys Weldon's attitudes, Chloe only develops assent to them. Covering only two days in the present, when Chloe resolves her marital crisis, *Friends* simultaneously recaptures a more eventful past (individual and joint) which began for the three women in Ulden in 1940. The three friends may have exasperated and backbitten each other since then, but they have also "clung together for comfort." Although "our loyalties are to men, not to each other," and therefore sisterhood may be hard to come by (as minor relationships in the novel show), these three friends attest to the possibility of the female community which forms out of distress and to which men are inconsequential. That all three have slept with artist Patrick Bates, Grace and Chloe even borne his children, scarcely ripples their friendship. Having gravitated together because they sensed each other's emotional needs as children, they remain each other's mutual support as adults; and Weldon urges even more such alliances. Her friends quite rightly urge Chloe to leave her contemptuous, bullying husband Oliver, a hack film writer, but she reassures herself that she is better off than the childless spinster Marjorie and hedonistic divorcee Grace and clings to her demeaning marriage.

Actually, Chloe is worse off. Weldon flatters neither her egotistical male figures here, nor their friendships: temporary camaraderie for bouts of drinking and sex or alliances for self-profit. At the heyday of their marriage, Oliver loves Chloe "as much as he loves himself—and what more than this can any woman ask of any man?" Since Weldon calls attention to names, the reader may notice that Oliver Rodure easily rearranges into Oliver Ordure and Patrick Bates (who drives his wife Midge to suicide) into Patrick Beast. Chloe, however, reverberates as the name of Demeter, goddess of the young green crops—Chloe is rearing not only her own two children, but the three offspring of Midge's and Grace's failed lives. Having already cost Chloe her college degree and jealously stopped publication of her first novel, Oliver now caps his liaison with their au pair by inviting Chloe to participate too, in order to accuse her of lesbianism. Yet Weldon remains careful about allotting blame. Chloe's friends have explicitly been responsible for men's deaths, and Chloe herself pushed Francoise into Oliver's bed—most important: Chloe knows that she lets Oliver exploit her and domineer.

The central thematic issue of women's control over their lives Chloe resolves to change—"women live by necessity, not choice." Weldon grants the powerful reality that women are shackled by fears and dependencies forged by maternal indoctrination. Chloe may chafe at maternal training in patient acceptance of suffering "for the children's sake" and female subordination (her widowed mother, Gwyneth, a barmaid, and Grace's mother, Esther, an Ulden housewife, are exemplary martyrs). But Chloe has been so well-conditioned that she subscribes to such ways nonetheless. The powerless, Weldon also sees, lose their nerve; after a deprived childhood and a submissive adulthood, Chloe dares not challenge fate: to her, asking for trouble. It also remains true that women are at the mercy of physical nature: their active hormones, their cancer-prone reproductive systems. And incalculable chance, or fate beyond individual control, creates its own level of necessity. The train on which Chloe and Marjorie first met stopped in Ulden by mistake; its cargo of evacuee children (such as Marjorie) was intended for elsewhere. However, Weldon insists that women must eschew the spineless habit of giving fate the credit or (as is Chloe's habit) the blame for their lives, since fate merely creates opportunities, not the directions they will take. Women are responsible for what happens to them, not in blame now, but in obligation to self-respect; they must assert choice over necessity. Gwyneth counseled "understand, for-

give, endure"—but "what kind of lesson is that for daughters?"

Chloe finally leaves Oliver. With five children to rear, she is not free, but she is freed of her husband's and her mother's negative influence; she has attained freedom of choice, which state Weldon wisely accounts victory enough. The blessing Chloe retains from Gwyneth and Esther is another defense against chaos: love of children and a sense of "maternal warmth. . . . It seeps down through the generations, fertilising the ground, preparing it for more kindnesses." With good reason *Female Friends* was very favorably reviewed, earning particular praise for its terse prose, controlled tone, and avoidance of feminist tendentiousness in favor of believable, sharply realized characters and situations. As one reviewer said, the "real triumph of *Female Friends* is the gritty replication of the gross texture of everyday life, placed in perspective and made universal."

In summer 1976 the Weldon family moved to

Dust jacket for Weldon's 1975 novel about the web of relationships in which three women are entangled

a substantial country house near Shepton Mallet, Somerset. The move was to prove, in time, more agreeable to Ronald Weldon, whose business flourished in Somerset, than to Fay, who would discover that she sorely missed her own friends and the London ambience. In 1976 Weldon's play *Moving House* was produced, and she started what were to be some four years of work on her adaptation of *Pride and Prejudice*. She also published another novel, whose moral values perhaps reflect Austen's influence. In any case, the strength of the mother-child bond, prominent in *Friends*, recurs as a motivation for the uncanny events of this skillful fourth novel, *Remember Me*, on human identity and the roles which shape it.

The unhappy ghost of Jarvis's first wife, middle-aged Madeleine, killed in an auto crash early in the book, refuses to rest until her teenage daughter, Hilary, is out of the clutches of her unloving stepmother, Lily. (Madeleine haunts the more kindly Margot until she undertakes to mother Hilary.) Lily herself finally decides that "To have a husband is nothing. To be a wife is nothing. Sex is an idle pastime. To be a mother is all that counts"—sentiments not necessarily Weldon's, but a fair rendition of many women's sense of identity, and not without Weldon's approval. If Madeleine's ghostly presence precipitates an identity crisis for mean-spirited Lily, proud to be an architect's wife when she was once just a New Zealand butcher's daughter, more centrally it shatters and restores middle-aged Margot, the doctor's wife, whose ego is quivering for appreciation outside her roles as devoted wife and mother. Weldon sensibly has no quarrel with such feminine roles; her quarrel is only with letting roles become absolutes. Her narrator (now clearly distanced from the characters and prone to evaluating them) deliberately presents the characters and repeatedly has the characters see themselves in terms of their roles in relation to others, even young Hilary, who identifies herself as "daughter of a dead mother, child of a lost father . . . [and] Lily's obligation." We know ourselves and are shaped by roles, past and present. But we must be wary of letting a role replace a self, distinct from any role it enters on. Although Madeleine so resents being "stripped of my identity" as Jarvis's lawful wife that her life is corroded, she will recognize (too late) that she must change and be just "myself. Neither daughter nor wife, but myself." We have, moreover, Weldon reminds us, our moral identity to consider.

The incredible return of a ghost is rendered

highly probable through a novel filled with mundane domestic details rather than sensational incidents. (The precise observation of daily life includes a new fictional device: line-by-numbered-line analyses of the obfuscations with which family conversations disguise actual motives.) Furthermore, the pervasive theme "we are all part of one another" does much to explain Madeleine's continued presence. A psychic link with the dead, forged by guilt, might well let them prey on our minds. Margot knows that sixteen years ago she slept once with Jarvis, even if he, most insultingly, has forgotten the incident. During the course of the action, Margot acknowledges her long suppressed awareness that her son, Laurence, is the fruit of that brief encounter and therefore should be reared with Hilary as her brother. More importantly, in a further development of oneness, she also acknowledges her guilt before Madeleine, whom she once "wronged": Madeleine was part of her in being "my sister, after all."

But even sisterhood is not the summit of oneness. Weldon insists, as never before, not only that "All things have meaning," but that we all participate in a "greater humanity," a family of humankind whose days are numbered and should be more kindly spent towards one another: the parting advice of Madeleine's spirit to "my sisters . . . and my brothers too." Emotionally matured by her experiences, Margot reaffirms her domestic roles, eased by having faced not only her own sufferings but "the damage that I did" to more than sisters. Even Lily rediscovers her long-stifled humanity, and Jarvis manages some penitence for his past philandering. As a satirist, Weldon still does not spare her characters exposure of their pretensions, hypocrisies, and self-indulgences, but she is less willing to turn an epigram at their expense now, and this novel lacks anyone approaching a villain. Even Renee (a minor character) is portrayed more sympathetically than is Weldon's wont with lesbians. Greater charity is not just a plea in this novel, but a practice. The responses of reviewers, of mixed minds about this book, were captured by the *Times Literary Supplement* reviewer, who concluded her list of objections with the admission that she found herself reading it "with an avidity way beyond the call of duty." The most frequent criticism was of authorial intrusions, primer-style question-and-answer dialogue, and role typing. But it was balanced by praise for solid construction, shrewdness, and authenticity.

Weldon discarded mellowing of attitude and

domestication of fantasy for her next novel, *Little Sisters*, published in England in 1978. (It appeared in America in 1977 as *Words of Advice*, a title reused from her earlier, but unconnected, play.) This fifth fiction, with its thinly developed characters, improbably exaggerated situations, and abrupt reversals, is a satiric, modern fairy tale, not a realistic novel. It mocks the shoddy parvenus and aspirants to wealth and glamour of the 1970s and the illusion-ridden, sensation-seeking folk of the 1960s, when the enemy was "forced back by peace and love and a little help from hallucinogens." Cautioning against the glittering promises of wealth and luck in fairy tales, Weldon subverts them with wicked wit, but she uses the psychological wisdom and moral certainty they embody to develop her maturation theme, coupled here with a characteristically Weldon plea for greater sisterhood.

The principal learners who fall from innocence into experience are the hefty, nineteen-year-old maiden Elsa, social-climbing mistress of middle-aged Victor, the antique dealer who is her "prince among men"; and Gemma, both wicked witch and wise old crone. Bastard daughter of an errant mother and now the beautiful, but hysterically paralyzed wife of an elderly millionaire, Hamish, Gemma has had Victor bring Elsa for a weekend at her nouveau-riche castle outside London because she is scheming for Elsa to conceive a child for her by Hamish and is prepared to keep her locked in the tower until she does.

Within this frame story, Gemma tells Elsa a monitory tale, in both first and third person, occupying half the novel, of her own initiation to worldly wisdom in London ten years earlier. Gemma's subjectively distorted account is modeled on the brothers Grimm tale of the cannibalistic robber bridegroom—a cautionary tale for women and most unflattering to men, though Gemma turns it against women, who are blind in their faith, in their own sexuality, and in their romantic delusions; and Weldon turns it against Gemma, who does not see her own lack of sisterhood.

Gemma's beloved boss Leon (lion) Fox, designer of erotic jewelry, proved to be not the prince charming she saw, but a predatory bisexual aesthete, "wounding, piercing with his you-know-what." Gemma cared neither about the ugly woman he murdered, after cutting off her ring finger, nor about rivalry with her friend Marion, since "girlfriends must fall when boyfriends push. That's one of the laws of nature." As Gemma tells it, Leon raped her and cut off her finger bearing two of his rings, and she became paralyzed by a fall; actually

she lost her finger in an elevator door and her mobility when she married Hamish. If Gemma's tale, as a character remarks, sounds overly "phallic," mad Leon did dismember his male lover, an event long preying on Gemma's psyche. More significantly, Gemma has chosen a fantasy which projects male fear of the destructive female, as much as female fear of the threatening male. She is herself both a male and a female menace. Gemma (the jewel) of the two rings, diamond and ruby, is repeatedly called Snow White and Rose Red, in allusion to the two devoted "little sisters" of fairy-tale fame, and having gone so far as to express a redemptive impulse to help another woman, she suddenly transcends herself and sets Elsa free to "run for me and all of us"; whereupon, Gemma once again can walk.

Since Victor has already returned to his wife and daughter (who have had their own incredible sexual escapades) and a visiting lesbian has been routed, normalcy of a sort has been restored to this stylized fictional world. Reviewers rightly were not favorably impressed, finding the book cliche-ridden in language and situation, unconvincing as reality (except for minor characters), and ineffectual as fantasy. However inaccurate, the puzzled decision of the *Time* reviewer that it "hasn't an idea in its head" pointed up the novel's failure to integrate a profusion of ideas on sexual and familial relations, psychological injuries, social pretensions, and cultural fads.

In 1978 Weldon not only had *Mr. Director*, her play on scientism in the welfare state, produced, but also published her ambitious sixth novel, *Praxis*, nominated for the prestigious Booker Prize. A grimmer book than her preceding ones, it was written under more trying circumstances. While living in Somerset and writing it, Weldon feared she might die of a current pregnancy, complicated by placenta praevia (misattached placenta). Although intellectually certain that she would carry safely, she was emotionally far less secure and thought of *Praxis* as her last testament.

The narrator quickly explains the strange name of the title character as meaning "turning point, culmination, action; orgasm; some said the Goddess herself"; whereas her sister Hypatia's name comes from "a learned woman; stoned to death by an irate crowd for teaching mathematics when she should have stayed modestly at home." The outlandish names their Jewish father, Ben, gave them, "out of a culture so far gone as to be meaningless," are changed by their Christian mother Lucy into a more prosaic Patricia and Hilda.

Yet the spirit of the goddess persists. Pat-Praxis Duveen (divine), an entirely individualized character, is also an ironic, great goddess declined into modern woman, but with her cult resurgent in the women's movement's own Eleusinian mysteries. Hilda-Hypatia, the thinker, is her own woman, as an ambitious and half-mad intellectual who uses her mind to protect herself from reality and becomes a successful, antifeminist career-woman. But she is also implicitly a distorting aspect of Praxis's nature. She has stood Praxis, the doer, on her head "metaphorically, often enough, until I doubted the truth of my own perceptions."

The symbolic suggestiveness enriches the themes of women's need to regain a sense of female importance and cohesiveness ("It does not take a man to make a woman cry") and the courage to act by conviction instead of sheltering behind men, respectability, and nature: truths of whose importance the women's movement convinces Praxis. Blind Nature remains the great enemy, decayer of female flesh and perverter of values; "Nature our Friend is an argument used, quite understandably, by men," Nature being "no more than our disposition, as laid down by evolutionary forces, in order to best procreate the species."

Praxis's story, told in retrospect, begins in Brighton with her traumatic childhood in the 1920s and ends in London in the present, spanning a period of change in some women's, if not men's, attitudes toward womanhood. Ben beats Lucy and abandons her to madness and institutionalization. Praxis's unwashed college boyfriend Willie exploits her to gain his degree at the expense of hers (as in *Female Friend*), but then Praxis doubts her self-worth and still assumes that catching a man is the goal of life. Yet she outgrows being Willie's servant and then suburban doll-wife to Philip, abandons him and her prim children to snatch her girl friend's man, and when finally herself betrayed in turn, becomes a zealous convert to, even a heroine of, the women's movement. Nonetheless, like narrator Jocelyn of *Down Among the Women*, she retains reservations about the New Young Woman: "Heartless, soulless, mindless—free!" True, a careless young Amazon has painfully bruised Praxis's foot, but Weldon still feels that hard experience has given her older women a humanity their more privileged descendants lack. The women's movement educates her but proves no panacea for Praxis, who has yet to come to personal terms with her sense of a meaningless life.

The novel alternates between Praxis's first- and third-person accounts, the latter being the voice of her writing personality, on whose veracity she sometimes comments. Like most Weldon narrators, Praxis inclines towards Weldon's recurrent sentiments and characteristic voice: deft ironic understatement and wry appraisals. She has also shared Weldon's copywriting experience. Writing her story while confined to her room with injuries and imprisoned in despair and self-doubt, Praxis has been recently released from two years in jail for smothering the mongoloid infant of her foster-daughter (an opportunity for Weldon to explore right-to-life attitudes). Playing Oedipus, the swollen-footed woman (who once slept with her own father) is searching out the truth of her past, looking for "the root of my pain and yours" to see if it is inherent in existence or something foisted on women. (It is both and more.) Recollection proves to be a cathartic act of vision which finally frees her from her isolation and returns her to faith "in some kind of force which turns the wheels of action and reaction, and gives meaning and purpose to our lives." But reaffirmation comes only after Praxis (a true Weldon heroine) has fully accepted responsibility for the course of her life and can say, "I did it all myself" when asked 'what have they done to you?' at the hospital. If we cannot change circumstances, we can modify our attitudes and consequent behavior, and Praxis, who courted pain throughout her life, by now sees her share in exacerbating her ordeals.

Praxis is Weldon's best novel to date, with the most fully realized female character, who succeeds in unifying a crowded plot and cast. The control of tone, and in Praxis's past, of atmosphere, is impressive. Social comedy is subdued, largely embedded in minor characters; earnestness prevails. Although there was some objection to occasional obscurities and simplifications and needless extension of Praxis into Anywoman, reviewers admired this book. They praised its energetic narration, polished style, and "personal and idiosyncrataic" version of woman's plight, happy that Praxis had "all the exasperating contradictions of a real woman."

In 1979 *Action Replay*, Weldon's drama on sexual incompatibility and warfare, was produced, and in 1980 her seventh novel, *Puffball*, was published. It reflects her dangerous pregnancy in Somerset (as does her 1978 short story "Angel, All Innocence"). But it was completed when she had already removed herself and her children to a terraced house in Kentish Town, North London, in summer 1979. Now living not far from the neighborhood where she had grown up, she would henceforth commute on weekends to Somerset. That country life had palled on her is evident enough in her novel, though there the pregnant wife remains the country mouse whom the husband visits on weekends. *Puffball* shares with *Remember Me* and with Weldon's 1978 radio play about nuclear submarine crews, *Polaris*, which incorporates telepathy and thought transference, Weldon's fascination with the weird. As she had done, her characters live in the shadow of numinous Glastonbury Tor, a region in the occult tradition and, to Weldon, imbued with an elemental power whose energy people may try to harness to their own ends, as does her villain Mabs with manipulative malice. The novel takes its title from a recurrent image: the swelling mushroom which usually resembles a pregnant abdomen, but sometimes the human brain, and therefore is an apt symbol for the book's central conflict between mind and biological mechanism. Satire is muted, and the story entirely positive.

Twenty-eight-year-old Liffey, who persuades her advertising agency husband to move to an isolated Somerset cottage by agreeing to the pregnancy she has always feared, becomes, at first, unsuspecting prey of witchlike neighbor Mabs, whose powerful concoctions give Mabs's husband, Tucker, entry into Liffey's bed, then threaten her pregnancy and life—occasions for much suspense. But the baby (it is Richard's) is safely born, despite placenta praevia, and Richard, who has philandered away his weekdays in London and deserted his wife for infidelity, returns and is accepted back for the child's sake. Not only has a healthy baby been born, but, as a result of pregnancy, marital disillusionments, financial problems, and local ordeals, a more mature and expansive Liffey has been reborn. Even Richard, who rejected the adult responsibilities of fatherhood and fidelity, shows signs of growth, accepting what he assumes is Tucker's child rather than lose Liffey. (Before allowing publication of this book, Weldon rewrote her male characters so that they would not be ciphers.)

The simple story proceeds chronologically through fifteen months of present time, told by an omniscient narrator clearly distanced from characters who are no more complex than the formal structure. Complexity belongs to the thematic structure instead. Although Nature here is no longer the decayer of female bodies but the creator of new life, biological and spiritual, a major theme is still the tyranny of the biological functions that control our bodies, of the chemistry that dictates so much of our behavior. Weldon's Darwinian definition of Nature remains unchanged—"the chance summation of evolutionary events"—and so blind is

Nature that her narrator would like to see its very name toppled to its "Zature" so that we will stop confusing it with God. "Nature works by waste. . . . Auntie Evolution, Mother Nature—bitches both!," fumes the narrator. Nonetheless, Weldon effects a reconciliation with the burden of subjection to natural process.

It requires the right kind of woman. Not chthonic, lunar Mabs, who revels in pregnancy as a tranquilizer and abuses her children once born, sends Tucker to Liffey out of general nastiness, then attacks her out of jealousy because she herself apparently cannot conceive again. (As soon as Mabs does conceive, she becomes harmless.) The mere breeder betrays her human nature. The vernal and sun goddess Liffey, appropriately named for her feminine fertility of both body and spirit (even if Weldon was not consciously thinking of *Finnegans Wake*), is the necessary woman. She, like her child, reflects another natural possibility, "a life-force, a determination in the individual of the species, as distinct from the group, not to . . . be wasted." Capable of fulfilling her nature as the human being Nature chanced to evolve, Liffey discovers the desire to feel herself "part of nature's process: to subdue the individual to some greater whole." Nor does Weldon mock her; like Praxis, Liffey has found a meaningful "force." That life is more than body chemistry is amply evident from Weldon's ironic use of extended, clinically precise descriptions of physiological processes, from menarche through ejaculation and conception to parturition: the "inside" story accompanying outer events.

Puzzled by this book, missing the comic writer, and sensing a softening of attitude, reviewers objected above all to such an "intrusion" of physiological data. But they failed to see the integral role and narrative value of the factual passages, which give *Puffball* a resonance its slim story otherwise lacks. If the impersonal functioning of a Nature beyond our control is manifest in Weldon's biology lectures, so too is Nature's orderliness and purposefulness, in contrast to the confusions and dishonesties in the outer events of the narrative. Nor can Weldon resist some explicit praise for Nature's works in the form of highly specialized cells "enabling their owner to read, and write, and reason in a way entirely surplus to its survival." Nature proves something to marvel at too, an attitude which may be irrelevant to Nature's mechanical processes but is pertinent to our existence and Weldon's fiction. She consistently says, by our attitudes we control the quality of our lives; mind has its way of mastering matter as well as fate—let women take heed.

The critics who wondered if *Puffball* showed a writer in transition, preparing to abandon the newer woman for an older feminine myth, probably overlooked the high valuation Weldon places on motherhood throughout her fiction, where it rivals sisterhood, self-responsibility, and self-determination as her positive standards for women. Always inspired by indignation at female suffering, Weldon has never been a feminist party liner, but rather a sometime affiliate, reserving the right to decide for herself what matters in female lives. It saves her from glibness and tendentiousness and allows her to depict different kinds of women persuasively, though it is true that her characters tend to be, or become, agents for her own perceptions. Her independence of mind manifests itself increasingly in her fiction, along with more polished technique and (except for *Little Sister*) mellowing of tone: less reliance on satiric barbs and comic effects, more on thoughtfulness. Her inventiveness is unfailing; although her books may repeat themes and, in minor ways, situations, each is a fresh act of imagination, not only unlike its predecessors, but unusual in itself. *Watching Me, Watching You* (1981), a collection of all her short stories to date, was followed in 1982 by *The President's Child*. A novel which has been described as a "feminist thriller," it presents a woman who advances from the Australian outback, to Washington high life (of the less reputable sort), to a home and career in London—only to have political intrigue and murderous conspiracy suddenly intrude on her private life.

Weldon has a large popular following both in Britain and the United States, and her novels are abundantly reviewed. Though sometimes faulted for bias and shallow characterization (especially of men), they have been admired for their astringent and terse prose, vitality, originality, authenticity, and moral conviction. Fellow novelist John Braine has called Weldon a "natural novelist"; Anita Brookner in the London *Times Literary Supplement* in 1980 reappraised all Weldon's fiction to estimate her as "one of the most astute and distinctive women writing fiction today."

Plays:

Permanence (in *Mixed Doubles: An Entertainment on Marriage*), London, Comedy Theatre, 9 April 1969;

Words of Advice, Richmond, Orange Tree Theatre, 1 March 1974;

Moving House, Farnham, Redgrave Theatre, 9 June 1976;

Mr. Director, Richmond, Orange Tree Theatre, 24 March 1978;

Action Replay, Birmingham Repertory Studio Theatre, 22 February 1979.

Interviews:

Melvin Maddocks, "Mothers and Masochists," *Time*, 101 (26 February 1973): 91;

Angela Neustatter, "Earth Mother Truths," *Manchester Guardian Daily*, 20 February 1979, p. 24;

John Heilpern, "Facts of Female Life," *London Observer Magazine* (18 February 1979): 36-37;

Elisabeth Dunn, "Among the Women," *London Telegraph Sunday Magazine*, 16 December 1979, pp. 55, 58, 61, 64;

Pauline Peters, "The Fay Behind Puffball," *London Sunday Times*, 17 February 1980, p. 36.

References:

Martin Amis, "Prose Is the Leading Lady," *New York Times Book Review* (2 October 1977): 13, 52;

Anita Brookner, "The Return of the Earth Mother," (London) *Times Literary Supplement*, 22 February 1980, p. 202;

Agate Nesaule Krouse, "Feminism and Art in Fay Weldon's Novels," *Critique*, 22, no. 2 (1978): 5-20;

Anthea Zeman, *Presumptuous Girls: Women and Their World in the Serious Woman's Novel* (London: Weidenfeld & Nicolson, 1977), pp. 64-65.

Paul West

(23 February 1930-   )

Brian McLaughlin
Pennsylvania State University

SELECTED BOOKS: *The Growth of the Novel* (Toronto: Canadian Broadcasting Corporation, 1959);

The Spellbound Horses (Toronto: Ryerson, 1959);

Byron and the Spoiler's Art (London: Chatto & Windus, 1960; New York: St. Martin's Press, 1960);

A Quality of Mercy (London: Chatto & Windus, 1961);

The Modern Novel (London: Hutchinson, 1963; New York: Hillary House, 1965).

I, Said the Sparrow (London: Hutchinson, 1963);

The Snow Leopard (London: Hutchinson, 1964; New York: Harcourt, Brace & World, 1965);

Robert Penn Warren (Minneapolis: University of Minnesota Press, 1964; London: Oxford University Press, 1965);

Tenement of Clay (London: Hutchinson, 1965; New York: Harper & Row, 1965);

Alley Jaggers (London: Hutchinson, 1966; New York: Harper & Row, 1966);

The Wine of Absurdity (University Park: Pennsylvania State University Press, 1966);

Words for a Deaf Daughter (London: Gollancz, 1969; New York: Harper & Row, 1970);

I'm Expecting to Live Quite Soon (New York: Harper & Row, 1970; London: Gollancz, 1971);

Caliban's Filibuster (Garden City: Doubleday, 1971);

Bela Lugosi's White Christmas (London: Gollancz, 1972; New York: Harper & Row, 1972);

Colonel Mint (New York: Dutton, 1972; London: Calder & Boyars, 1973);

Gala (New York: Harper & Row, 1976);

The Very Rich Hours of Count Von Stauffenberg (New

Paul West

York: Harper & Row 1980; London: Sidgwick & Jackson, 1981).

Reviewers have been unanimous in proclaiming Paul West a writer whose sheer energy and acrobatic intelligence demand attention. West has performed in many different arenas—as critic, theoretician, poet, and novelist—and in each he has probed the limits of his art. Yet it is as a fiction writer that he seems most happy, for there he can demonstrate at one and the same time the strength of the critic and the grace of the poet. However, despite years of critical praise, a series of awards (including a Guggenheim Fellowship in 1962, the Aga Khan Prize in 1974, a National Endowment for the Arts Fellowship in 1979, and most recently, the 1981 literature prize of the Pennsylvania Governor's Award for Excellence in the Arts), and a body of work that spans genre and nationality, West's writings have not gained the full attention they deserve. With intelligent consideration and lively reading, his novels can illuminate the debate over the form and nature of the modern novel and the relevance of contemporary fiction. In his concern with the nature of fiction and the need to experiment, West carries on the investigations pioneered in the first half of this century and joins company with contemporary experimentalists such as Juan Goytisola, Gabriel Garcia Marquez, and William Gass. In a British context, he can be seen as working out the implications of Virginia Woolf's and Samuel Beckett's fictional innovations. Moreover, with their concern about the implications of modern discoveries in astronomy, physics, and the other sciences, West's novels offer one way out of the impasse suggested by the "two cultures" dichotomy. Yet for all the apparatus of the avant-garde and the postmodernists' refusal to avoid the difficult in favor of the easily digestible, West's novels tell us directly about ourselves: not just what we discover simply by living, but how living *is* discovery.

Discovery can take time or can involve sudden revelation. Most of us, for instance, have been surprised at a skill suddenly mastered after years of fruitless endeavor. Paul West tells how after twenty-five years he learned to swim: "All of a sudden," he laughs, "I realized that I hadn't drowned!" His surprise comes not at being able to swim but in not having drowned! More fundamentally, this remark points to the sense of precariousness that runs through West's work; the willingness to experiment, to discover, engenders uneasinessness as well as delight and can become the basis of a book.

The relationship between autobiography and fiction in West's writings, however, is not simple. His early autobiography, *I, Said The Sparrow* (1963), contains avowedly fictional elements (particularly with regard to the shifting of chronology). Moreover, the two works dealing with his deaf daughter, Mandy, *Words for a Deaf Daughter* (1969) and *Gala* (1976), move from the implications of his daughter's condition in the first book to an "auto-fiction" in the second.

In *I, Said The Sparrow* West reflects on his childhood in the Derbyshire village of Eckington and gives a detailed portrait of a close-knit, northern mining community and of his relationships with his parents. His mother, Mildred Noden West, emerges as a strong, disciplined, yet loving woman, with high hopes for her children. Besides running the household, she gave piano lessons in the evenings and encouraged in Paul and his sister, Sheila, a respect for disciplined learning and, finally, for art. While Mildred, the daughter of a local butcher, came from a respectable family, her husband's parents were decidedly lower class. This fact is important, both in the portrait West gives us of his father, Alfred, engineer's fitter at the local ironworks, and for the disquiet Paul felt when his opportunities for education removed him from the working-class community. It is this sense of necessary, yet painful, removal which provides the book's force and possibly the author's motivation for writing it. Yet the book is no *Sons and Lovers*: West is careful not to exaggerate his mother's artistic or social pretensions or to present his father as brutish. The book is filled with affectionate descriptions of the minutiae of village life, yet there is a dark underside to all this. The loss of an eye in World War I not only cut short Alfred West's hopes of training to be an accountant; his wartime experience obviously colored his life and the life of his son. He emerges in the book as a complicated, sensitive man and as a deft craftsman.

Not surprisingly, *I, Said the Sparrow* provides a host of details which turn up in West's later work, from the attic in which both young Paul and later Alley Jaggers construct gliders, to more significant hints of something not quite right with the universe, a subject which concerns much of West's fiction. For instance, when Paul describes his household reading material, we note a particularly fertile source and an essentially Westian reflex, linking a view of the human predicament with scientific speculation: "One book, *Covenants With Death*, had originally had a warning seal on it: not for the timid, it read; and inside, originally sealing the last dozen pages or so, had been another, of similar import. This was a book of war atrocities, recorded in the most frightful photographs I have ever seen. From the grinning hanged to the tongueless, eyeless and garotted: photographic Goya sponsored by an English popular newspaper. To look at this book was like going into another world: it stunned, suspended me, just as my first look at water beneath a microscope had stunned." Despite the warning, young West looked at this book, and he kept on looking: we find descriptions of these atrocities, and often of the photographs, in many of his novels, particularly in *Colonel Mint* (1972) and in *The Very Rich Hours of Count Von Stauffenberg* (1980).

After graduating with a B.A. from the University of Birmingham in 1950 and studying for two years at Oxford, West received his M.A. from Columbia University, New York, in 1953. He then served as a flight lieutenant in the R.A.F. from 1954 to 1957. Later, he taught English, comparative literature, and creative writing, first at the Memorial University, Newfoundland, St. John's (1957-1962), and then at Pennsylvania State University, where he has been ever since. West is almost as energetic a literary critic as he is a novelist, producing a steady stream of critical works. The most acclaimed of these is probably *Byron and The Spoiler's Art* (1960); the most controversial is his encyclopedic two-volume study, *The Modern Novel* (1963). Both works display the depth and range of his concern with the triumphantly inventive power of great literature that characterize all of West's criticism. This inventive power, moreover, is what West has championed in articles and interviews as the special province of the modern novel.

The context for this inventiveness, for this "elasticity of consciousness" (as West calls it in the interview appended to *Caliban's Filibuster*, 1971), is never "academic" but derives from a radical ontology. If academic debate perhaps has sharpened the theoretical aspects of his viewpoint, the crucial impetus seems nevertheless to have come from West's own experience. Thus the period in New York (1952-1953), when, he says, "I grew up," and his time in the Air Force provided rich material for later work. In several interviews, West confesses that his first ambition was to be an aeronautical engineer, and he records his boyhood romance with aircraft in *I, Said The Sparrow*. The airplane is perhaps *the* vehicle in his fiction: many of the most powerful scenes in *Stauffenberg* take place in aircraft; the action of *Gala* is framed by a transatlantic flight, and one of the most exhilarating sections of that book deals with the trip of the narrator, Deulius, and his daughter, Milk, to the Smithsonian's aircraft collection at Silver Hill, Maryland.

Caliban's Filibuster is staged during a flight across the International Dateline to Japan, and the book is replete with aircraft images.

A Quality of Mercy (1961), West's first novel, displays all of the gaucherie that often results from a writer's still trying to find his own voice. The novel deals with the destructive and eventually fatal emotional struggles of old Camden Smeaton, his ferocious sister, Merula, and her frustrated daughter, Brenda, who live in a house in the Connecticut woods. The spark which finally explodes their tensions is provided by the arrival of a newlywed couple, the Fishers, and the book has a somewhat gory ending. While the book has obvious weaknesses, it also has many powerful passages and evokes genuine pathos in the account of how Camden's young wife died.

West no longer includes *A Quality of Mercy* in his list of works, but he is proud of his second work of fiction, *Tenement of Clay* (1965), set in New York City. In *World Authors*, he writes: "Manhattan was a miracle, like the black hole of Calcutta topped by undreaming obelisks, and I felt at home there—still do—more than anywhere else." Although West wrote the novel in Canada, *Tenement of Clay* is filled with the hustle and bustle of the lower depths of Manhattan, where Papa Nick maintains a refuge for tramps and where his alternate narrator, the midget Pee Wee Lazarus, plies his trade as a wrestler and pornographer. The novel mainly deals with the relationship between two men: Nick, playboy turned penitential almsgiver, and the needy, possibly crazed final recipient of Nick's misdirected charity, Lacland. Two other characters, Lazarus, and Nick's mistress, Venetia, drift in and out of the novel, offering a counterpoint of comment and a perspective on the actions of the main protagonists. Both Nick and Lazarus are unreliable narrators, though, and critics have found it difficult to arrive at a final conclusion concerning the novel's meaning. The Christian problem of caritas lies at the core of the novel: should we try to help our fellow man? Can we help him? In giving alms without the consideration of heavenly reward, whom are we helping? For the most part, these questions remain unanswerable.

Despite the religious nature of the novel, West was strongly influenced by Samuel Beckett, who supplies one of the epigraphs for the book: "If there were only darkness, all would be clear. It is because there is not only darkness but also light that our situation becomes inexplicable." Indeed, in the character of Lacland and the subject of vagrancy and in the use West makes of the houses as tenements of consciousness, the novel is often reminiscent of *Watt* (1953). Its hallucinatory quality may also be traced to Beckett's influence, as can much of the sardonic wit which sparkles through the book.

Such borrowings notwithstanding, West has found his own voice here, and it is in this novel that we first find his insistence on seeing human problems against a cosmological background. Thus Nick, tortured by his inability to stay with Venetia and ignore the tramps, changes a traditional lover's complaint into a medical question. Instead of "Why does my heart pain me so?" he asks, "Why does the heart speed up at night?"

With the *Alley Jaggers* trilogy—*Alley Jaggers* (1966), *I'm Expecting to Live Quite Soon* (1970), *Bela Lugosi's White Christmas* (1972)—the rich creative imagination, the exuberance of character, and the sheer sweep of ideas all come together for the first time in West's fiction. The three novels deal with the career of Alley Jaggers, a plasterer in Shalethorpe, England, who develops from local scatterbrain to a strangely innocent rapist and murderer. Alley's cheerful unconventionality is seen as the only sane defense against a maniacally conventional world, and the first sublimations of his frustrations—building gliders and finally a strange totemic sculpture—seem harmless enough. However, his temporary flights of fantasy finally lead to an explosion of violence, and Alley is incarcerated. *I'm Expecting to Live Quite Soon* takes up the career of his wife, Dot, as she comes to terms with her situation and moves towards not only independence, but liberation. Finally, in *Bela Lugosi's White Christmas*, Alley is in prison, sparring with his psychiatrists, and exerting such a hold on one, Withington, that the doctor helps him escape. During his brief flight, Alley goes on an anarchic spree, digging up the local graveyard with a hijacked bulldozer, sexually assaulting a herd of cows, and having sex with Withington's wife, whom he meets at a hippie colony; in short, he behaves like Frankenstein's monster with a sense of deranged humor. Other characters—principally Alley's mother, Withington, Dot's final lover, and the West Indian bus conductor Jimsmith Williams—are each given different degrees of prominence throughout the trilogy. The greatest change undoubtedly takes place in West's presentation of Dot, who is a mere shadow in the first book compared to the vital, wonderfully earthy woman she becomes in *I'm Expecting to Live Quite Soon*.

Moreover, despite many connections between the three novels, each has its own concerns and each shows a development in style, moving from a rather strained realism (which critics complained about) in the first to a defiant antirealism in the last, where

the author reminds the reader several times that this is only a fiction and where the two main characters, Alley and Withington, are reduced to AJ and With, a symbol and a grammatical character, respectively. Two main interdependent themes unite these books and, indeed, emerge from them to inform West's succeeding work: namely, the independence of ideas and their real existence almost as objects, and a protest against too rigorous categorization of creation. As West said in the interview with George Plimpton appended to *Caliban's Filibuster*: "I've felt a long time that whatever you imagine exists. Whatever anybody imagines has been added to the sum of creation. It's not a matter of whether or not it reproduces or replicates what is visible to everybody else." In the same interview, he defines his protagonist in the following way: "Alley Jaggers, that Promethean spacehead of mine whose main desire is to get the universe—the earth, at any rate—back to the plasticity it might have had as an idea in the mind of God. Before things acquired fixed natures: tigers their stripes, water vapor the ability to form as, say, cumulus cloud, and man his multipurpose mouth. Alley Jaggers finds life's compartments infuriating, so he reconceives it in imagination—the faculty we were given for the express purpose of flying in the face of the First Cause."

Each book met with high praise, the reviewers applauding the linguistic inventiveness which West displayed throughout the trilogy and singling out the first novel for its "Rabelaisian" qualities. Some critics, such as John Lucas and Roderick Cook, did qualify their praise with reservations concerning the lack of psychological realism. Lucas argued that the novels lack "any really precise or deep enquiry into human psychology or any steady look at social realities" and maintained that "the novels in the sequence become steadily more attenuated in their inventiveness." Although *Bela Lugosi's White Christmas* does show signs of strain—for instance, the narrator protests a bit too much that this is only a fiction—there is a wider issue here and a view of fiction that West has argued for in several essays, such as "Enigmas Of Imagination: Woolf's Orlando Through the Looking Glass." While not ignoring the social aspects of reality, West parts company from most other twentieth-century English novelists in their apparent presumption that society *is* reality.

Underpinning West's cosmological rather than sociological emphasis is undoubtedly the experience of having a daughter born deaf and with possible brain damage. *Words For a Deaf Daughter* deals with this experience: with Mandy's progress up until her eight birthday and with her parents' reactions to her disability. The force which powers the book is West's need to see the world as his daughter sees it in order to communicate with her and his need as a writer to find words to record such a universe for her and for us. Above all, he asks how we explain the existence of someone with Mandy's condition. In an effort to do all this, the writer imaginatively ransacks the universe to find parallels to his daughter's condition, concluding: "—you're still as incoherent as daily light, as vulnerable as uranium 235, and have an atom where an atom shouldn't be."

Words For a Deaf Daughter crackles with essential human drama; we never feel that even questions about minutiae of physics are in any way indulgently esoteric, and West's conclusions seem both starkly horrifying and strangely jubilant. We get the feeling that he and Mandy have found the universe out. The combination of considerations concerning the human condition and cosmological speculation, which seems to have been a reflex action in some other of West's writings, meets its happiest employment in this work. Furthermore, the verbal extravagances and sometimes frantic wit encouraged by West's stress on the worth of the creative imagination are well justified. The critics certainly seemed to think so: the book has received almost unanimous praise and is probably West's best known work.

West examines the issue of the creative imagination confronting a gratuitous universe in three other novels: *Caliban's Filibuster*, *Colonel Mint* (1972), and *Gala*. The first of these, written between *Words For a Deaf Daughter* and *Bela Lugosi's White Christmas*, uses a diversity of scientific patterns (principally the spectrum) and a host of cultural archetypes (such as the trinity) and takes Cal, a failed novelist turned commercial screenwriter, on a flight across the International Dateline to Japan. During the flight, Cal kills time by constructing three narratives in which he and his two companions, the producer Sammy Zeuss and McAndrew the actor, are transformed into various exotic characters. The tales, featuring Malchios, Maleth, and Malkari and dealing with Wealth, Genius, and Magic, respectively, are densely allusive and continually puzzling. West's scientific knowledge is given full play here (later, in 1975, he received an award from the National Endowment for the Humanities for special studies in science), and the reader may have to struggle to keep up. The final tale takes place on some antipodean island and is, for all its hallucinogenic qualities, finally rather old-fashionedly naturalistic; moreover, its picture of human cruelty (displayed here by an aboriginal tribe), makes Edgar Allan Poe's *The Narrative of Arthur Gordon Pym* (1838) seem positively benign. The book works best when viewed as a bold experiment requiring active involvement by the reader. Indeed, the number of American readers who reacted favorably to the novel must have reinforced West's often-stated hope to win "a readier, less hidebound response" to his fiction in the United States than he felt he could expect in England. Echoing several other very favorable reviews, Frederick Busch called *Caliban's Filibuster* "something like a master craftsman's masterpiece."

The question of which patterns we should impose on the universe in order to respect both the scope of our imaginations and the cosmological flux reappears again in *Gala*. In this fictional sequel to *Words for a Deaf Daughter*, Mandy and West appear again, this time transformed into Michaela, nicknamed "Milk," and Wight Deulius, novelist and amateur astronomer. The fiction's main action, once more framed by a flight, concerns the pair's construction of a model of the Milky Way in Deulius's basement. Apart from the star charts and the progress through the Milky Way heralded by the chapter headings, the reader is also guided by a pattern based on genetic code symbols, each paragraph beginning with either G, C, A, or U. The significance of this arrangement West explains at the beginning of part 2, after he has decided to abandon a random ordering in favor of a strict sequence in the genetic chain (he supplies a chart). Although this would seem to be rather intrusively artificial, West writes smoothly enough so that it is doubtful whether most readers notice the rigid patterning until they are apprised of it halfway through the text. Like the laws of genetics, the novel's style is behind everything but visible almost nowhere. Although West's use of such arcana is fascinating, the novel perhaps lacks the drama of the speculations found in *Words for a Deaf Daughter*, except for one passage in which Deulius imagines what Milk *would* say if she could understand the principles behind the games they are playing. If a problem of focus exists here, it comes from a disruptive tension at the center of the novel, as both Milk and Deulius vie for the reader's attention. We are too often forced to ask: Whose gala is this? In one of the many favorable reviews which greeted the novel, Walton Beacham in the *Nation* touches on this problem: "What West discovers at the end of *Gala* is that he, not Milk, has flown beyond the sun

Can a human being hide? Not like a god,
at any rate. You skulk within the shade
of your various selves, though doomed to
one esophagus, one brain stem, one ration
of three-score years and ten (plus any
bonus from prosthetic surgery). Speak in
tongues you may, but with one tongue only.
Your only biding place is arithmetical: you
will always have thoughts than — pass
unrecorded, even by yourself, and so, over a
lifetime, you build up into an incalculable
sum. You will know yourself only through
samples, factors, preponderances, of value of
ore in rock, and this is how
others have to know you too. A man's mail
is't addressed to all of him. A human is a
brawling tribe; and of the million, say,
who compose him, the last one's never
known, not even after death, nor even
before it by the executioner who's handcuffed
you behind and stuffed a soft rubber bell

(first page of Gala, holograph)

Page from the manuscript for Gala

and like Pi [his mistress] must travel to infinity before he can close the open end of an indefinite number. *Gala* convinces us of that, and in doing so turns the story into Deulius's, not Milk's. And yet it is Milk who speaks for us all metaphorically, and West knows this even if he can't write the story without making it his own."

Of course, a person's imagination does not operate in a vacuum; to this extent the social contexts of much British fiction are justified. Again, to grant such autonomy to ideas is to invite trouble, as appears in Alley's career. In *Colonel Mint*, West examines the problem the creative imagination (and hence heterogeneous ideas) poses for a society which, to survive, must maintain the fiction of a rationally ordered universe. The conflict arises when astronaut Mint sees, or thinks he sees, that most unclassifiable of ideas, an angel. This situation allows West to indulge in many delightfully witty sallies against society's urge to squash all contradictions. The pretensions of psychiatry, a favorite theme of West's, also comes in for some witty ridicule. As in the trilogy, psychiatrists, in their naive handling of sex as the key to understanding personality, mistake the primitive for the true. As a result, sex becomes monstrous, even bestial, and it is no accident that the scenes of copulation between Mint and his calculating seducer, Connie Langoustine, take place in a room whose walls are covered with photographs which resemble those in *Covenants With Death*. Many reviewers were revolted by the display of violence here, Patricia Meyer Spacks in the *Hudson Review* even going so far as to complain of "the detectable relish with which sadism is elaborated." Others praised the novel's grim satire as evidence of West's courageous belief in the adequacy of the form to deal with such grotesqueness. Diane Johnson summed up this point of view—and highlighted the book's deeper concern with the threat society feels from unclassifiable ideas—when she concluded: "The most affirmative thing about this book, as about West's other books, is his faith in the novel as an art form, as a dignified production of the human mind, capable of rendering, in its infinite variety, social comment, philosophic statement, comedy, pain, all of which West can do—impressively. 'Meaning is the most explosive thing there is. Like angels,' Lew R. says. Here is a novel that means."

The problems which a truly imaginative individual faces in coping with the hostility of society and with the indifference of the universe have, in fact, provided West with a great scope for humor, pathos, and even rage. He also follows Beckett in his use of freakish characters through which to view the world. Thus we move from the midget Lazarus, to mad Alley, to disabled Mandy and the rest, all mentally or socially imprisoned. None of them ever quite escapes.

At the risk of appearing too neat, we can detect a logical progression of this process in West's latest novel, *The Very Rich Hours Of Count Von Stauffenberg* (1980). West took almost three years to write this book, partly because of the amount of historical research it required. In a *Preliminary* to the text, West tells us of the project's genesis and the way he came to decide on the novel's form. After detailing his boyhood memories of the war and of the coincidence of both his father and Stauffenberg losing an eye in battle, West says: "Soon I was devouring books about the bomb plot against Hitler, some grand, some shoddy, many of them giving details the others omitted, and almost all of them contradicting one another until I felt that some of what I was reading was fiction already and that a fictional attempt of my own—say an historical impersonation—might go. Long after I had been engaged in the actual writing, I turned up some books of hours in a library, and the idea came of giving this particular German nobleman his own book of hours, after the fashion of *The Very Rich Hours of the Duc du Berry* and (my favorite) *King Rene's Book of Love*. I gave him everybody else's hours to add to his own, crammed into a thirty-six-hour pass from Outre-Tombe, the most dismal suburb of the heart."

Beneath the brilliantly detailed and vivid portrayal of the corruption of Nazi Germany lies the novel's main theme: the interaction of personal trauma and public trauma. Here humanity is seen *as* its ideas, with all the extravagances of beauty and horror, of glory and pathos that this conception of humanity implies. The novel is packed with the cosmological, literary, historical, and religious speculations which punctuated West's earlier work. All the major characters, from Stauffenberg to Leber the socialist leader, to the soldiery, and even to Nina von Stauffenberg, are caught in a sea of contending codes which finally drowns them. In the last section of the book, when we read of the reprisals against the conspirators, we feel that civilization is being swept away. And yet the novel is intensely personal: Stauffenberg emerges through all his wrongheadedness and fatal bumbling as a man with a center, with a core of integrity which it is painful to watch being torn down by the world's batterings.

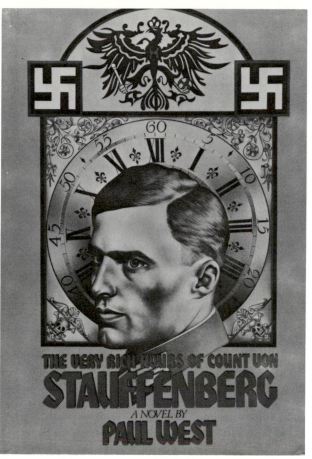

Dust jacket for West's fictional book of hours by a nobleman in Nazi Germany

Stauffenberg is perhaps the only work of West's to have achieved the same unanimity of critical acclaim accorded his *Words For A Deaf Daughter*. Herbert Leibowitz of *Parnassus* reflected a general view when he commented: "A bravura performance . . . the moral questions resonate inside the skull long after the first page. The historical impersonation is uncannily accurate and persuasive, no doubt because the writing is so artful: precise, nuanced, richly allusive; unflinching as it looks at the butchery, supple and affecting as it looks at married love, children, or friendship."

From *Tenement of Clay* to *Stauffenberg*, then, we are faced with an exciting yet uncompromising view of life. West is not alone in his testaments of doubt and parodies of vain hopes. He is singular in his acceptance of a gratuitous universe as perhaps the only challenge great enough for man's imagination. In this sense, West is essentially a stylist, a shaper, someone who takes the flux and channels it. He is

like a designer of fountains, who must persuade the water to contradict its downward urge and, in doing so, evince its beauty and our understanding of nature while still allowing the stream to remain limpidly free and various in its shapes. It is difficult to predict the course of West's future work; we can expect continually changing forms to appear in his novels and can look forward to more examinations of the interaction between the creative imagination and the spinning universe. The novelist himself, in a recent, unpublished interview says: "Anyone who wades around will hit on a structure—for example, spiral galaxies or the chambered nautilus. I am a compulsive exotic and a structural opportunist. I have no idea what structures I will choose next—although I do feel that they will probably be from nature rather than from society. For instance, right now I am interested in Stefan's Quintet, five galaxies which we group together but which, in fact, contain one renegade galaxy which does not belong with the other four at all."

Whether fiction, as produced by West and like-minded others, is not to be just a realistic recording of events but rather an essential contribution to those happenings will depend on the outcome of the debate now taking place concerning the nature and form of the modern novel. In the *New York Review of Books*, lamenting both the empty irrelevancy of much contemporary fiction and the dry intellectualism of the "Serious Novel," Gore Vidal concludes: "In any case, write what you know will always be excellent advice for those who ought not to write at all. Write what you think, what you imagine, what you suspect: that is the only way out of the dead end of the Serious Novel which so many ambitious people want to write and no one on earth—or even on campus—wants to read." In their intelligence and sweep of imagination, West's writings may offer a satisfactory way out.

Other:

Byron: A Collection of Critical Essays, edited by West (Englewood Cliffs, N. J.: Prentice-Hall, 1963).

Selected Periodical Publications:

"Symposium: The Writer's Situation II," *New American Review 10* (1970): 214-220;

"Adam's Alembic, or Imagination versus mc^2," *New Literary History*, 2 (1970): 523-539;

"Sheer Fiction: Mind and the Fabulist's Mirage," *New Literary History*, 7 (1975-1976): 549-561;

"Enigmas of the Imagination: Woolf's *Orlando*

Through the Looking Glass," *Southern Review*, new series 13 (1977): 438-455;
"Field Day for a Boy Soldier," *Iowa Review*, 10 (Spring 1979): 22-33.

Reference:
Frederick Busch, "The Friction of Fiction: A *Ulysses*

Omnirandum," *Chicago Review*, 26, no. 4 (1975): 5-17.

Papers:
The largest collection of Paul West's manuscripts is at Pennsylvania State University Library, University Park, Pennsylvania.

Raymond Williams
(31 August 1921-)

René J. A. Weis
University College, London

BOOKS: *Reading and Criticism* (London: Muller, 1950);
Drama from Ibsen to Eliot (London: Chatto & Windus, 1952; New York: Oxford University Press, 1953); revised as *Drama from Ibsen to Brecht* (London: Chatto & Windus, 1968; New York: Oxford University Press, 1969);
Drama in Performance (London: Muller, 1954; Chester Springs, Pa.: Dufour, 1961; revised edition, London: Watts, 1968; revised and extended edition, London: Penguin, 1972);
Preface to Film, by Williams and Michael Orrom (London: Film Drama, 1954);
Culture and Society, 1780-1950 (London: Chatto & Windus, 1958; New York: Columbia University Press, 1958);
Border Country (London: Chatto & Windus, 1960; New York: Horizon Press, 1962);
The Long Revolution (London: Chatto & Windus, 1961; New York: Columbia University Press, 1961);
Communications (Harmondsworth, U.K.: Penguin, 1962; London: Chatto & Windus, 1966; revised edition, New York: Barnes & Noble, 1967);
Second Generation (London: Chatto & Windus, 1964; New York: Horizon Press, 1965);
Modern Tragedy (London: Chatto & Windus, 1966; Stanford: Stanford University Press, 1966);
The English Novel from Dickens to Lawrence (London: Chatto & Windus, 1970; New York: Oxford University Press, 1970);
George Orwell (London: Collins, 1971; New York: Viking, 1971);
The Country and the City (London: Chatto & Windus,

Raymond Williams

1973; New York: Oxford University Press, 1974);
Television: Technology and Cultural Form (London: Fontana, 1974; New York: Schocken Books, 1975);

Keywords: A Vocabulary of Culture of Society (London: Fontana, 1976; New York: Oxford University Press, 1976);

Marxism and Literature (Oxford: Oxford University Press, 1977);

The Volunteers (London: Methuen, 1978);

The Fight for Manod (London: Chatto & Windus, 1979).

For the past thirty years Raymond Williams has been a major figure in the world of English letters. It is for his sociological criticism of literature that he is best known to intellectual circles and the universities. Because of a rare combination of right-of-center Marxism and a moral passion akin to that of F. R. Leavis, Williams's massive interdisciplinary output has commanded the respect of both the New Left and the traditional liberal literary establishment. It is not always realized that Williams is also a practicing novelist. He was writing novels before criticism, and he himself maintains that the writing of fiction will go on for longer than the analytical essays. Williams attaches great importance to his novels and has consistently denied that they occupy a secondary position in his literary work. While granting that the disproportion between his critical output and his fiction (a ratio of five to one) may wrongly indicate that he himself has devoted less attention to his novels, he has also stressed that he finds the writing of fiction, unlike criticism, a slow and painful process, involving detailed and lengthy rewriting. Critical recognition for Williams's novels has been sporadic and various, and to date there is no real consensus about their position in the tradition of English fiction. Dennis Potter in the *New Left Review*, for example, hyperbolically praised *Border Country* (1960), Williams's first published novel, while D. A. N. Jones in the *Times Literary Supplement* severely censured *The Volunteers* (1978) for "lacking in the traditional skills of fiction." Neither is a fair estimate of Williams's fiction as a whole, which defies traditional literary categorization and expectation. Notwithstanding clear affinities with earlier works, the novels stand remarkably apart by virtue of their unique subject matter. Finally, it must be acknowledged that in spite of only a cautious, "polite" interest in Williams's fiction by professional critics, the novels have commanded a considerable popular audience.

Raymond Henry Williams was born on 31 August 1921 at Pandy (near Abergavenny in Wales), where his father worked as a railway signalman. In 1932 he won a county scholarship to the King Henry VIII Grammar School at Abergavenny,

from which he proceeded to Trinity College, Cambridge, in 1939. He joined the student branch of the Communist party at Cambridge, and from 1941 to 1945 he served in the Guards Armoured Division, landing in Normandy and participating in the Arnhem and Ardennes operations. He married Joyce Mary Dalling in 1942, and a daughter was born to them in 1944. Released from military service in 1945, Williams returned to Cambridge, from which he graduated with a degree in English in 1946. The same year, for financial reasons, he turned down a senior scholarship at Trinity College and instead took up an appointment at the Extra-Mural Delegacy of Oxford University in East Sussex. By then he had become firmly committed to left-wing intellectual radicalism, although he did not renew his membership in the Communist party. Together with Wolf Mankowitz and Henry Collins, Williams launched the journal *Politics and Letters* (1946-1947), which he described as "left of the Labour Party, but at a distance from the Communist Party." The decisive influence on this venture and on the tone of the journal was F. R. Leavis, whose cultural radicalism (but not his elitism) Williams found "immensely attractive." It was in 1947 that he started the novel that was eventually published as *Border Country*.

Border Country is the first novel in Williams's Welsh trilogy, which also includes *Second Generation* (1964) and *The Fight for Manod* (1979). From its first draft as "Brynllwyd" (1947-1949), it went through a series of seven rewritings as "Village on the Border" (1951-1952), "Border Village" (1954), and finally *Border Country* (1957-1958), before it was published in 1960. During the same period, Williams produced three unpublished novels ("Ridyear," 1948; "Adamson," 1950; "The Grasshoppers," 1951), an unpublished play ("King Macbeth," 1957), and major critical studies such as *Drama from Ibsen to Eliot* (1952), *Culture and Society* (1958), and *The Long Revolution* (1961).

Border Country, which is in two parts, has a double plot in which past alternates with present. It starts in the present with Matthew Price, a university lecturer in economics, returning from London to his native Welsh border village after his father has suffered a heart attack. The present narrative ostensibly portrays Matthew in the role of temporary caretaker during his father's disability. When his father, who is a railway signalman, is recovering, Matthew departs for London but is stopped on the border by the news that his father's condition has worsened because of a stroke. He returns for the second time, and his father dies. With this present, the novel simultaneously unfolds the past of the older generation and Matthew's growing up. Most of the action is centered in this past chronological narrative which stretches from the Matthew's birth to the General Strike (in which his father, Harry, and his father's friend Morgan Rosser in particular take part), and ends with Matthew leaving for university in England.

The overriding concern of *Border Country* is the conflict between alienation and reintegration. Matthew Price is unwillingly alienated from his origins through education, which not only takes him away from his geographical home, but also lends a direct class emphasis to the inevitable, natural rift between a grown-up son and his father. Matthew's return to Wales therefore symbolically becomes an attempt to bridge that gap which emerges between him and his home, as well as forming part of his ongoing struggle to reconcile his own past and present. In conversation with Morgan Rosser, the former militant trade unionist who has turned small-time entrepreneur, Matthew says: "But a father is more than a person, he's in fact a society, the thing you grow up into. For us, perhaps, that is the way to put it. We have been moved and grown into a different society. We keep the relationship, but don't take over the work. We have, you might say, a personal father, but no social father. What they offer us, where we go, we reject." The same point is taken up later, with equal explicitness, when Matthew meets Phil Watkins, the father of a former acquaintance:

> "He's a worker, isn't he?"
> "Aye, keeping me at it." It came through quite suddenly: a father and son in the same line of work!

The relationship between father and son, it appears, can be complete only if the emotional and physical bond is compounded by a social fealty: a personal father *and* a social father. The equal importance in the novel of the social father to the personal father devolves from Williams's firmly held convictions about the impossibility of separating personality from class. To do so, he would argue, is to pander to the defunct idealism of nineteenth-century fiction. A key question raised by the novel is, therefore, how Matthew can become the guardian, not only of his real father, but also of his social father, ultimately the working class. He could, like Peter in *Second Generation*, opt for his father's work, but in the end he does not, and, in an ambiguous sense, the novel generates a context in which such a choice is ultimately impossible. Mat-

thew's way back, spiritually, lies not through direct action but through his research, which deals with "population movements in Wales during the Industrial Revolution." While in *Border Country* he becomes increasingly aware of the inadequacy of a purely intellectual commitment as a release from the guilt of deserting class and family, the book his research produces eventually does attract attention. In *The Fight for Manod* Matthew is told that "Just because it was a book on population movement it wasn't only . . . the statistics. You had the statistics, but you turned them back into people. . . . A human movement. The flow of actual men and their families into the mining valleys."

The "actual men and their families" also form the most important component of *Border Country*. Although Williams has repeatedly distanced himself from the topical concerns of "bourgeois" fiction, the fact remains that his novel's most successful moments are those dealing with personal relationships and experiences. The early married life of Harry and Ellen Price, their friendship with Morgan Rosser, the tensions between the men during the General Strike, the adjustments between Harry and Morgan when Morgan shifts his allegiance to business, are all powerful and beautifully realized; and as Matthew leaves home for university in England, Williams offers an exquisite vignette of the mingled emotions of nostalgia and excitement when Matthew scurries through the railway compartment to catch a last glimpse of home before settling down for the journey, opposite a British Rail map of Wales. It is only when Matthew, as the novel's controlling consciousness, explicates the implications of his actions that a sense of intrusive didacticism mars the flow of the fiction. An example is his setting of the signals in the novel's present. At first the passage conveys a sense of felt life and identifiable experience, almost Proustian in its effect and context. But it is not allowed to stand and suggest. The signalman is embarrassed, and the discomfiture is explained at once in terms of the class difference between the university lecturer and the workman. Matthew feels that "He had no right, after all, to come playing at a man's work." It is almost as if Williams were afraid that the point would be missed and therefore spells it out.

When *Border Country* was published, it was immediately perceived as an autobiographical work. Williams has argued that this assumption is misleading on the grounds that the most obvious parallel between the novel and life, the father figure, has been separated out in the fiction into Harry Price and Morgan Rosser. Even so, the novel is undoubtedly replete with autobiographical details, such as its location, the victimizing of the stationmaster after the General Strike, Harry's passion for beekeeping, and above all, the figure of Matthew Price. There is more of Williams in the Matthew Price of *Border Country* than in any one of his other fictional characters. Not only is Price as a whole modelled on Williams, but the details also fit: like Williams, Price leaves Wales for England on a university scholarship, and he also has two first names: Will in the past, and Matthew in the present, while Williams was Jim at home and became Raymond at the university. Whereas Matthew attempts to reintegrate himself in his local community through researching and exposing its sufferings at the hands of nineteenth-century capitalism, Williams's life has been devoted to academic pamphleteering of the most respectable kind against social injustice and the class structure in Britain. Williams and Matthew also share a sense of guilt about their partial compromises with the establishment, which, in a different context, are an issue again in the next novel.

In terms of literary tradition, Williams's mentor in *Border Country* is undoubtedly D. H. Lawrence. After an initial hostility in his early Cambridge days to Lawrence as an alleged right-winger, Williams has since been an ardent admirer of Lawrence's novels as working-class fiction of a kind; and there is no mistaking his debt in *Border Country*—in the early marriage of Harry and Ellen, or in the christening of Matthew—to *Sons and Lovers*, which Williams, against Leavis, reappraised over *Women in Love* (because Lawrence's later novels develop away from "full social relationships"). That there may be a more specific reason for Williams's leaning toward Lawrence in *Border Country* is suggested by a revealing comment on Lawrence in Williams's *Culture and Society*, which is contemporary with the novel. There he writes: "the early chapters of *Sons and Lovers* are at once a marvellous recreation of this close, active, contained family life, and also in general terms an indictment of the pressures of industrialism. Almost all that he learned in this way was by contrasts, and this element of contrast was reinforced by the accident that he lived on a kind of frontier, within sight of industrial and of agricultural England." Williams clearly senses an affinity between Lawrence and himself with regard to origin, social critique, and the ambiguity in the predicament of the self-exile, socially poised between two cultures. The influence of Lawrence, and *Sons and Lovers* in particular, is even more marked in the next novel, *Second Generation*.

Second Generation, unlike *Border Country*, took only two years to complete (1960-1962) and was published in 1964. During this period, Williams had moved from Sussex to Oxford, and then on to Cambridge, where in 1961 he was made a fellow of Jesus College. The story of *Second Generation* is set in Oxford (though the name of the town is not given) and deals with the parallel and interacting lives of two generations. The older generation are two Welsh emigre working-class couples, Harold and Kate Owen, and Harold's brother, Gwyn, with his wife, Myra. Harold's son, Peter, is a research student in sociology at the university, and since early childhood he and Beth, Myra's daughter from a first marriage, have been unofficially engaged. In the course of the novel Williams traces the widening rift between Kate and Harold and, parallel with it, the alienation of Peter from Beth. While Harold and Kate are militantly dedicated to the same ideal of social equity, he on the shop floor of a car factory and she on Labour party committees, Kate drifts into an affair with Arthur Dean, a cynical, noncommitted Oxford don with left-wing sympathies. Similarly her son, Peter, temporarily deserts Beth for a previous girlfriend, Rose, whom he meets again at the house of his thesis supervisor, Robert Lane. The novel ends on an uneasy note of harmony, with Kate reunited with Harold and Peter marrying Beth.

Dust jacket for Williams's first novel, which consciously parallels D. H. Lawrence's Sons and Lovers

Williams has described *Second Generation* as "a true present," whereas *Border Country* was "the present, including and trying to focus an immediate past." To the extent that the first novel hinges on a counterpointing of past with present in the consciousness of one character, this statement is correct. A similar effect is, however, achieved in the second novel through the parallel narrative which compares and contrasts the movements and motives of the older with the younger generation. Furthermore, although the settings of the novels are superficially very different, an explicit link between them is established in the history, past and present, of the parent generation who have moved from the Welsh border country near Gwenton to a university city, where frontiers also exist but without being defined on a map. The first sentence of the novel sets the key: "If you stand, today, in Between Towns Road, you can see either way: west to the spires and towers of the cathedral and colleges; east to the yards and sheds of the motor works. You see different worlds, but there is no frontier between them; there is only the movement and traffic of a single city." Williams could not miss the irony that in moving from Sussex to Oxford and then to Cambridge, he was reentering another kind of border country, the division in the two ancient university cities between town and gown; and border land, for Williams, is not necessarily tied to geography (as is evident from his comment on Lawrence's Nottingham). That it should be Oxford rather than Cambridge which becomes the prototype for the city in *Second Generation* is because "town" in Cambridge means the old middle-class market town, whereas at Oxford, since World War II, "town" has included heavy industry. The social matrix which carries the action of *Second Generation* is not therefore essentially different from the setting of the first work in the trilogy. Unlike *Border Country*, however, *Second Generation* gives full scope to a working-class environment with scenes on the shop floor of the factory, union meetings, and strike committees.

The alienating class-crossing process in the novel is not triggered through personal initiative (such as Kate's mixed admiration for Arthur Dean), but is seen as rooted ultimately in a past social division between Harold and his wife. Kate, we are told, "had started with more advantages than Harold. Her father was a teacher, and her future was to be in education." As it is, she marries a trade unionist, and, after failing to mold him in her image (through private evening lessons), she transfers her ambitions to Peter. Williams's debt to Lawrence's *Sons and Lovers* here is self-evident: like Gertrude Cop-

pard, Kate is her husband's superior in class and culture, and, like Mrs. Morel, she attempts to live out her dreams by proxy, through her son. While lacking the intensity of the bond between Gertrude and Paul Morel, Kate's relationship with Peter becomes one of social and negative moral identity. It is in keeping with the novel's structuring of its two alienated characters in a series of parallels and contrasts on every level that Peter's involvement with Rose and Beth should be modelled on the Paul-Miriam-Clara triangle in *Sons and Lovers*, with Beth as Miriam and Rose as Clara; and when Beth and Peter finally do meet in a moment of self-assertive sexual freedom, Williams consciously confers on it a sanction of true Lawrentian oneness: "Peter touched and knew her whole body, and she held him close to her, knowing him again as they touched. Slowly, as they moved, came a new feeling, that seemed in the warmth, an actual change in their bodies, a change of tissue and substance so that they felt quite newly alive, newly capable of life. They responded, wondering, to this transformation, and again it seemed a deep recognition. The known features were blurred and their separateness lost, yet in the change they were more deeply known. The touch between them was warm and moving, and yet reached beyond them, to a felt consummation, that would again flow and continue, beyond itself, into sleep and into life."

If *Second Generation* does have a central theme, it is the nature of commitment. No dilemma arises for Harold or any member of his brother's family: they know where they stand, and, in that respect, they are absolute. It is the outsiders, Kate and Peter, who have to make choices, and for Peter the choice ultimately means joining his father on the assembly line. By virtue of his position as a trainee academic, Peter invites comparison with Matthew Price and, by implication, with Williams himself. When Peter apologizes for his university education with "You have to beat the system before you're in any position to reject it," the reader is reminded of Williams's own ambiguous position as a socialist don in one of Britain's elite universities. This suspicion of authorial guilt projected, as in *Border Country*, on a fictional character is confirmed by at least two directly self-referential passages. When Robert Lane reveals that, during the war, he participated in the advance on Brussels, the private irony is missed if the reader does not know that Williams himself took part in that action. The clue is not essential, but it does indicate Williams's doubts as conveyed through Lane about the legitimacy of any kind of commitment (like his own, for example) other than grass root. Lane, in the novel, knows what he should do, but he does not act on it: he watches the Christmas-strike demonstration, but does not join of his own accord. More direct and bitter is the implicit comparison between Williams and Wall, the novel's shop-floor manager at the car factory. Wall is described by Harold as a "scholarship boy" whose father was a "railwayman." When asked whether it matters, he replies: "It's the usual route. He's gone where his education's taken him. Into the company's pocket." As well as articulating a sense of guilt, this particular incident also functions by way of justification, in that Williams, unlike Wall, has decidedly not become a henchman of the establishment. The ambiguity is taken further in Peter's choice of factory work over the academy. The action is undertaken in good faith, but Harold suspects—rightly, it will emerge—that the decision is ultimately gestural. In the end, therefore, a sense of capitulation prevails, not only within the fiction, but also in Williams, when he implies that the intellectual cannot return to grass roots. The only course available, however unsatisfactory, is to carry over the same struggle to a more abstract level, as Matthew Price does in *Border Country*.

Second Generation is far from flawless and has rightly attracted less attention than *Border Country*. It is overly schematic, and, even on its own terms, it must be regarded a partial failure: the factory scenes are unintentionally lifeless, while the atmosphere of the college common room is perfectly realized, indicating that the author is more comfortable with the university than with a working-class environment. The language of the novel often falls flat and is hardly ever evocative. Where it does succeed, however, is in the poignant depiction of the emotional struggle between Beth and Peter and, to some extent, in the meetings of Kate with Arthur Dean. A wholly fair description of the novel was given in the *Times Literary Supplement* when the reviewer complained that "It is difficult to know how to assess a novel that is so admirably serious in its intentions, yet often solemnly clumsy in the way those intentions are carried out." The reviewer then deplored the characters' "interminable conversations about their emotions and actions very much in the spirit of a discussion group."

The Fight for Manod (1979), which completes the Welsh trilogy, was started in 1965, at the same time as *The Country and the City* (1973), with which it shares thematic concerns, as Williams acknowledged. Like *Border Country*, *The Fight for Manod* took a long time to complete, and for six years (1970-1976) Williams worked on it concurrently with *The*

Volunteers (1978). The major event in Williams's professional life during this period was his appointment as a professor of drama at Cambridge.

At the center of *The Fight of Manod* is a rural, depopulated area of Welsh border land about to be revitalized by a government project. Robert Lane, now working for the government in the Department of the Environment, invites Matthew Price and Peter Owen to serve as consultants to the project. They are to report on the "human factor"—the impact that the planned transformations would have on the local inhabitants. Matthew accordingly moves to Manod for a year and is joined eventually by Peter. Peter's intuitive suspicions about the project are partly confirmed when Matthew clashes with the local magnate John Dance. It finally emerges that the project is nothing less than a capitalist conspiracy by supranational Anglo-Belgian corporations in league with the local land speculators. At the decisive board meeting with the government minister toward the end of the novel, Peter storms out in disgust, taking his story to the press, and Matthew suffers a heart attack.

Although *The Fight for Manod* ostensibly concludes what *Border Country* and *Second Generation* had begun, it is a radically different novel from either of its predecessors. Admittedly characters are carried over from them, and the location is similar to *Border Country*, but the emphasis has shifted from class alienation to a direct confrontation with an invisible but all-powerful ogre, capitalism *tout court*. Peter and Matthew are impotent in the face of international market forces and, in a grimly ironic sense, become stooges of the government, as the humane cosmetics on an inhuman program of exploitation. In spite of the novel's thematic polarization of the rural and urban-industrial capitalism, the temptation to lapse into pastoral nostalgia is resisted. *The Fight for Manod* has been called Williams's most "Welsh" novel. It certainly is his most Hardyesque work, and like Hardy at his best, Williams's rural community remains realistic, un-idealized. Whatever pastoral undertones there are in the novel are carefully controlled; and a distinct sense of moral pollution prevails at Manod, as is inevitable in a community which is willing to betray itself through opportunism.

The Fight for Manod is a strange, almost nightmarish, evocation of what happens when the connections between economic figures and human beings are ignored. As Matthew explains to his wife Susan: "The companies. And then the distance, the everyday obviousness of the distance, between the lane in Manod, all the immediate problems of Gwen and Ivor and Trevor and Gethin and the others: the distance from them to this register of companies, but at the same time the relations are so solid, so registered. The transactions reach right down to them. Not just as a force from outside but as a force they've engaged with, are now part of. Yet still a force that cares nothing about them, that's just driving its own way."

Unlike the first two parts of the trilogy, *The Fight for Manod* is virtually devoid of autobiographical references, with the possible exception that capitalism takes on a distinctly European flavor in the cross-Channel corporations. One may wish to speculate whether this characteristic indicates that Williams at the time shared the traditional British Labour bias against the European Economic Community (he was himself a member of the Labour party from 1961 to 1966), but ultimately there is no need to localize the threat geographically. It is in its social, economic impact that the exploitation of Manod hits, and in this respect it is essentially of a kind with the class structure in the earlier works.

The Fight for Manod suffers from several of the same vices as its predecessors, and particularly in its over-explicitness. When Lane says to Peter that "Manod would simply have been dead," Peter replies, "You mean the project you call Manod, not the actual place." Similarly, Peter is authorially "placed" when Beth knows him to be "a systematic opportunist, the man with no feeling, no connection. . . . This wasn't the active, vigorous, connecting man everyone else seemed to know. It was a dreadful nullity." Clearly Williams is summing up in this last work of the trilogy. But it is hard to see that perfunctory authorial writing of this nature (which Lawrence called "immoral") is defensible on any grounds, the more so since it is evident that Williams's powers as a novelist are unabated: the concluding paragraph of *The Fight for Manod*, with Matthew and Susan about to embark on a new life, home in Wales, is Williams's best piece of prose to date. It is as evocative, mellow, and serene as the finale of a late Dickens novel, and its echo of *Paradise Lost* XII, when Adam and Eve are on the threshold of history, confers on Matthew and Susan the quiet dignity of those who, though they have been defeated in the eyes of the world, have won in their hearts. As Williams wrote in *Drama from Ibsen to Eliot*, it is the fight that matters, not the outcome.

Williams started *The Volunteers* (1978) in 1970 (the same year that he started his Fontana Modern Masters volume on Orwell, published in 1971). It is easily the weakest of his works of fiction. Its plot, set in the near future, revolves around the shooting at St. Fagans (near Cardiff) of a right-wing government minister, Buxton, whose order to troops to break up a strike results in the death of one of the workers. The incident hits the headlines; and Lewis Redfern, a consultant analyst for a supranational news agency called Insatel, investigates. Through a series of improbable deductions derived primarily from reading a left-wing pamphlet about the strike, Redfern unearths an international conspiracy network which operates through infiltration of the powers that be in order to undermine them from within. It emerges that the controlling mind behind the plot in the local Welsh-British context is a former charismatic Labour politician who, with the help of his action cell of inscrutable young people, manages to "turn" Redfern by appealing to Redfern's left-wing past.

When *The Volunteers* appeared, the publisher's blurb described it as a "political thriller." Williams himself stated that his intention was to write a political novel set in the late 1980s, but he would not concede that the book was a "thriller." The novel, however, undeniably does generate a certain suspense as to whodunit, although in this respect, it is not essentially different from *The Fight for Manod* with its ingredients of mystery and sleuthing. Nor could it be argued that *The Volunteers* is far more overtly political than any of the preceding works. Its politics admittedly are on a larger scale in that, through a ramification of secret societies, they ultimately involve the whole of Europe and America. But the immediate focus of the novel remains local and British; and Redfern's reflections in St. Fagans (a lovely open-air museum of rural Wales) invite comparison with *Border Country*, as do the strike scenes with *Second Generation*. A further link between *The Volunteers* and Williams's preceding fiction is in the character of its first-person narrator. Like Peter Owen's, Redfern's past history is one of left-wing radicalism which brings him a term in jail, hence his qualification, paradoxically, as a researcher of the political underground for Insatel. The novel leaves one in no doubt that Redfern's compromise with the state is a treacherous act of bad faith, and his willingness to turn, or be turned, is viewed as a redeeming feature, however ambiguous the superior claims of the underground cell are made to appear. If Williams's mentors in the Welsh trilogy can, with some confidence, be named as Lawrence and, to a lesser extent, Hardy, Orwell would have to be credited with providing the decisive trigger for *The Volunteers*. It would not be an overstatement to claim that *The Volunteers* is Williams's *Nineteen Eighty-Four*, although this comparison should be qualified by noting that Williams had already explored Orwellian material in *Koba* (written in 1959), his unproduced play about the replacing of a right-wing regime by an equally repressive Stalinist state. But if Orwell to a certain extent determined, or affirmed, Williams's nightmare vision of repression and rebellion in a totalitarian society (the government in *The Volunteers* is a national government), the novel's laconic style is an unsuccessful attempt at imitating Raymond Chandler. The debt to Chandler, and the character of Marlowe in particular, is in evidence not merely in Redfern's supposed toughness, his compassion for the socially deprived, his name dropping, and his enforced celibacy, but most immediately in paratactic passages like the following: "We finished lunch: I walked her back; I told her I would be in again, in a day or two, for a can. As I walked away I felt sick." Chandler has been imitated by many, and equalled by none; certainly not by Williams in *The Volunteers*. Yet these lines must range among the better ones in a novel where the style generally is seriously defective and cursory. A sample is offered by Redfern's relating his investigation's lack of progress: "I decided to concentrate on Evans coming back. I would have liked to talk to Bill Chaney, and of course to Lucy again. But I was in this crunch anyway, having to face Evans, and I needed much more than I had. I had still had no reply from my inquiry in the States. . . ."

It is easy to see that such lines or others like them (for example, Redfern's comment on Buxton's television performance: "He was talking the usual crap but I sat up") provided reasons for the *Times Literary Supplement* reviewer to state that the novel is lacking in the traditional skills of fiction. One is left wondering how much of the work's perfunctory writing is a consequence of the dramatic cuts (one fifth of the entire novel) Williams was required to make by his publisher. But even if it is granted that the economics of fiction marketing may have affected the language and structure of the work, the fact remains that the novel which is ultimately presented to the reader is unsatisfactory on every level.

In an essay entitled "Realism and the Contemporary Novel" (included in *The Long Revolution*, 1961), Williams wrote: "The experience of isolation, of alienation, and of self-exile is an important part of the contemporary structure of feeling, and any contemporary realist novel would have come to real terms with it. . . . The truly creative effort of our time is the struggle for relationships, of a whole kind, and it is possible to see this as both personal and social: the practical learning of *extending* relationships." The shared emphasis here on relationships, their social context, and the role of the alienated exile, epitomizes the thematic concerns of Williams's novels, to which should be added the qualification that the matrix is invariably a class struggle viewed from a socialist perspective. Williams is not interested in spiritual exile such as Stephen Dedalus's in Joyce's *A Portrait of the Artist as a Young Man*, nor for that matter in what ultimately alienates Paul Morel in *Sons and Lovers*: a personal inadequacy in relationships and a sense of artistic vocation. The most abstract description of Williams's novels to date would be that they form a body of socialist fiction written from within the bourgeois milieu of middle-class intelligentsia. Hence, his alienated characters are socially conscious middle-class figures trying to recuperate their identities in a working-class community. In this they ultimately fail: Matthew Price cannot reestablish contact with his past, Peter's egotistical radicalism is destructive, and when both Peter and Matthew try to fight the system from within in *The Fight for Manod*, their impotence vindicates the irony of that novel's title. As such, Williams's best work, the Welsh trilogy, must be regarded as a deeply pessimistic statement about the individual's lack of freedom, particularly when seen, as it is increasingly, in a wider context: whereas the "enemy" is still identifiable in *Border Country* and *Second Generation*, in *The Fight for Manod* the "enemy" becomes, as in *The Volunteers*, a conspiracy of huge capital, spread like an invisible giant spider's net. But when Williams shifts from class confrontation in a localized recognizable context to an almost apocalyptic setting in which the individual battles capitalism, as in *The Volunteers*, he fails. The difference between *The Fight for Manod* and *The Volunteers* suggests that Williams himself was dissatisfied with the turn his work was taking. It is no accident that, before completion (two years after *The Volunteers*), *The Fight for Manod* had reverted to a local setting; and Williams's next novel (already started in 1971) will, he says, unfold "somewhere between *Border Country* and *Second Generation*."

The key work in Williams's fiction to date is *The Fight for Manod*. While in many ways it is inferior to *Border Country*, it remains his most complex novel in its precarious poise between the local "grass roots" and the wider concerns of a socialist consciousness. Williams has said that his major fiction project for the future is a huge, historically panoramic work with a distinct Welsh working-class flavor. This plan confirms his shift in the direction of commitment evident in *The Fight for Manod*, and it will be interesting to see whether he can find an adequate formula to accommodate what he himself views as his most ambitious novel yet.

It is too early to advance any definite assessment of William's overall fictional output. What can be asserted confidently, however, is that Williams as a novelist has tried, with varying success, to write nondogmatic socialist fiction, with a distinct theoretical basis in Marxist dialectics. That Williams in his novels is instinctively stronger on personal relationships is a tribute to his freedom of mind and sensibility, although it has to be admitted that, at times, the feeling structure does become functional to the social issues, as in the cursory, almost heartless, account of Beth's pregnancy in *The Fight for Manod*. Williams's major failing as a novelist, however, remains his suspicion of the inadequacy of language to communicate freely in fiction, hence the jarring over-explicitness in much of his writing.

Television Scripts:
A Letter from the Country, BBC 2, 1966;
Public Inquiry, BBC 1, 1967.

Other:
May Day Manifesto, edited by Williams (Harmondsworth, U.K.: Penguin, 1968);
The Pelican Book of English Prose: From 1780 to the Present Day, edited, with an introduction, by Williams (Harmondsworth, U.K.: Penguin, 1969; Baltimore: Penguin, 1970);
D. H. Lawrence on Education, edited by Williams and Joyce Williams (Harmondsworth, U.K.: Penguin, 1973);
George Orwell: A Collection of Critical Essays, edited by Williams (Englewood Cliffs, N.J.: Prentice-Hall, 1974);
Charles Dickens, *Dombey and Son*, edited by P. Fairclough, with an introduction by Williams (Harmondsworth, U.K.: Penguin, 1970);
English Drama: Forms and Development, edited by Williams and M. Axton (Cambridge: Cambridge University Press, 1977).

Periodical Publications:
"Contemporary Drama and Social Change in Britain," *Revue des Langues Vivantes*, 42 (1976): 624-631;
"Utopia and Science Fiction," *Science Fiction Studies*, 5 (1978) 203-214.

Interviews:
Raymond Williams: Politics and Letters (London: New Left Books, 1979).

References:
Dennis Potter, "Unknown Territory," *New Left Review* (1961): 63-65;
J. P. Ward, *Raymond Williams*, Writers of Wales series (Mystic, Conn.: Verry, 1981).

A. N. Wilson
(27 October 1950-   )

Alan Hollinghurst

BOOKS: *The Sweets of Pimlico* (London: Secker & Warburg, 1977);
Unguarded Hours (London: Secker & Warburg, 1978);
Kindly Light (London: Secker & Warburg, 1979);
The Healing Art (London: Secker & Warburg, 1980);
The Laird of Abbotsford: A View of Sir Walter Scott (London & New York: Oxford University Press, 1980);
Who Was Oswald Fish? (London: Secker & Warburg, 1981).

A. N. Wilson's novels have enjoyed immediate critical success in Britain, and he has worked rapidly to consolidate his reputation with a series of books which combine high comedy with increasingly serious and complex interpretations of British life in the 1970s. While a knowledge of the details of his satirical targets—particular figures in academic and religious and political life, fads of all kinds—will enrich a reading of his novels, these works are by no means limited in relevance to the era of which they form, in the most serious sense, a criticism. Like the early comedies of Evelyn Waugh, they are books which create a symbolic sense of an aimless younger generation and of a hierarchic society in which increasingly troubling patterns of behavior are discerned, substantiated by the discovery of other generations and a search for meaning in explorations into the past.

Andrew Norman Wilson was born in Stone, Staffordshire, to Norman and Jean Dorothy Crowder Wilson; he is the youngest of three children. His father's father was a pottery owner, and his father was for a while a managing director of Wedgwoods but retired at the beginning of the 1960s. Wilson was educated first by Dominican nuns before attending preparatory school in Great Malvern, where he spent a very unhappy seven years. In 1964 he went to Rugby School and in 1969 to New College, Oxford, where he read English under the tuition of John Bayley and Christopher Tolkien, choosing Course Two, which concentrates on Old and Middle English and linguistics. He won the Chancellor's Essay Prize in 1971, and on 29 May of that year he married Katherine Duncan-Jones, daughter of E. E. Duncan-Jones and Fellow in En-

A. N. Wilson

glish of Somerville College, Oxford. They now have two daughters. Wilson took Final Honour Schools in 1972.

Though he had been writing "sub-Rose Macaulay novels"—one of them being about nuns—for some time, his career as a writer did not flourish immediately. Being interested in other arts, he had until going to the university thought of himself as a painter and had won a place at Saint Martin's College of Art (which he did not take up). After completing his studies he undertook free-lance teaching for New College and for Edward Greene's tutorial agency, which he continued until 1975. In October 1973 he went to St. Stephen's House to read theology and train for the priesthood, but abandoned the course after a year.

The Sweets of Pimlico (1977) was written while Wilson was a master at Merchant Taylor's School, Northwood, Middlesex, a position he held for five terms beginning in January 1975. It is a short and original novel, and though its dedication to Iris Murdoch and John Bayley made many critics suggest it was Murdochian, the influence is in fact slight. At the center of the novel lies the relationship between Evelyn Tradescant, daughter of a retired ambassador, and Baron Theo Gormann, an elderly German whose history is never fully explained. He picks Evelyn up in Kensington Gardens, and within a short space of time a bond of some intensity develops between them to the point that they become mutually dependent and their relations move to the very brink of the sexual. Though there is much that Evelyn never discovers about Gormann, there is much that she does discover in parallel and in different modes. At the start she fills her time with a passion for beetles, and coleoptery becomes a working metaphor for her analysis of society, one which is both satirical and sociological: "The Whirligig Beetles, *Gyrini natatores*, she recalled, swim about in crowds, in endless circles and gyrations on the surface of still water. How one distinguished their sex, she rather forgot." This uncertainty of sexual orientation is typical of Wilson's novels, and it is in finding out more about such vagaries that Evelyn, drawn into Gormann's world, goes beyond her scientific attitude to a more complex and shaded apprehension of life. Gormann's world, centering on a memorable indoor swimming pool, is really a demimonde of people whose connection to each other only slowly becomes known to Evelyn, and much of it is homosexual. Her brother Jeremy has had relations with "Pimlico" Price, a gay sweets manufacturer whom Gormann supports and who is jealous of the old man's attention to the girl.

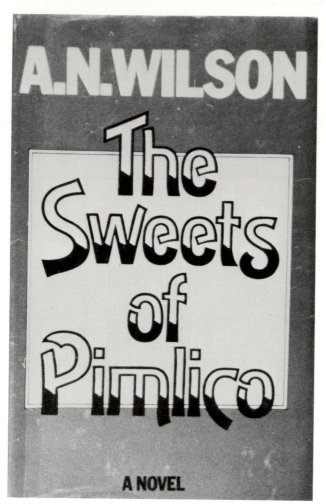

Dust jacket for Wilson's first novel, winner of the John Llewelyn Rhys Memorial Prize

When Jeremy (something of a fantasy-figure of erotic attractiveness) stays with Evelyn, they have sex, and this incest is the extremest instance in Wilson's novels of an idea of sexuality so liberal that it borders at times on the gratuitous. It does, however, contribute to a further dimension of the complex plotting in which Jeremy's behavior, as well as his failure to sit Finals at Oxford, offends his parents (who are evoked in sharp Austenesque cameos).

As in later novels, Wilson here contrives the catastrophe first in a manner which is farcical (when Jeremy posts letters to his parents, his sister, and his boyfriend in the wrong envelopes), and second in a sad and ironic coda in which Gormann dies and Evelyn, with a passivity which becomes typical of Wilson's characters, accepts "Pimlico" Price's offer of marriage. Gormann's death is hastened by an explosion at the National Gallery where a newly attributed Veronese is on show; its title is thought to

be *Danger*, which Evelyn recognizes as not without relevance to her own situation. This double use of an allegorical subject in art is perhaps the most Murdochian feature of the novel, reminiscent of the deployment of Bronzino's *Venus, Cupid, Folly and Time* in *The Nice and the Good* (1968). The explosive, incendiary climax is a device of plot that recurs in later work—but more important is the profounder fascination with relationships involving masks: the essential mutual privacy of Gormann and Evelyn which makes sex impossible, and the extent to which characters wear masks that they have chosen as defense ("Pimlico's" pretence of vigorous heterosexuality) or that are expected of them by society and of course by the satirical novelist.

In his next two novels Wilson changed the emphasis, putting personal relationships in the background and concentrating on characters who, though surprising, do not diminish their comic effect by revelations of inner seriousness. *Unguarded Hours* (1978) and *Kindly Light* (1979) have the same protagonist, Norman Shotover, and much of the same cast. Norman is a passive innocent somewhat recalling Paul Pennyfeather in Evelyn Waugh's *Decline and Fall* (1928), and the two books can be seen as an exercise in the satirical mode of early Waugh. Drifting after leaving university, Norman has no experience of life or vocation, and when he loses his job with a firm of London solicitors (very conventional and obsessed with titles), he goes to stay with relatives in the provincial cathedral town of Selchester. Also staying in the same household is Mr. Skegg, an *episcopus vagans* whose interest in titles, illusory and magnificent, is greater even than that of the legal profession. Wilson's fascination with *episcopi vagantes*, who claim direct succession of authority from the apostles and who can create further bishops in their turn, was fed by reading Peter F. Anson's *Bishops at Large* (1964), an absorbing and tellingly illustrated account of their beliefs and practices. Skegg is an alcoholic who gets Norman drunk and then ordains him with a host of titles. Alongside this parodic version of the church Norman is exposed to the real church, satirized in the trendiness of Ron Hope, the demotic Dean of Selchester with his determination to bring the church into fuller contact with modern social issues, and in the dotty transsexual obscurity of a seminary which Norman attends.

Norman's innocence is both a liability as he unguardedly allows things to happen to him and a form of protection: he is immune to ideas and largely unruffled by the disasters which befall him and which culminate in his replacing Ron Hope in a hang-gliding jump from the cathedral roof. He is unneurotic and surprisingly sexually straightforward. Even so, the machinery of the novel turns on moments of shock, in which sexual acts involving unexpected people or practices are stumbled on by others. These things illustrate the frailty of expectations and the changeability and ambivalence of human nature, in contrast to Norman's normality in his relationship with the Dean's daughter, Cleopatra, where love is unemphatically allowed to vindicate his ordinariness and "awkward gentility."

Having been given up for dead at the end of *Unguarded Hours*, Norman is rediscovered in *Kindly Light* in the ludicrous Catholic Institute of Alfonso (a close relation of its more famous acronym) trying unsuccessfully to escape from its clutches. Though many of the characters of *Unguarded Hours* recur, they are subjected to a more farcical and bizarre story and are refracted through a sketchier and funnier manner in *Kindly Light*. The plot is highly complicated and becomes a kind of unspoken metaphor for the plotting of Norman and of Father Cassidy of the C.I.A. and for the labyrinthine confusions of the lives they lead. Though there are still Waugh-like vignettes, as in the exasperatingly funny figure of Lubbock, forever disappearing and returning, the feel of the book is more modern, like that of Lindsay Anderson's film *O Lucky Man!*, paranoid, zany, and alienated. Norman comes to understand that "The notion of human freedom was a totally artificial one which we try to impress on our existence in order to give ourselves dignity." He from one direction and the C.I.A. From another attempt to construe the facts of a life over which neither has control, and the use of religion as a cover for these misconstructions is an important part of Wilson's message. "In many ways, religion was so obviously an admirable and necessary thing. And yet it never seemed to make anyone any better. The reverse was often the case."

This view of religion as an illusion or a confidence-trick willingly accepted by religious people is uncharitably adapted to the medical profession in *The Healing Art* (1980). From 1976 Wilson had been a lecturer in English at St. Hugh's College, Oxford, and from January 1977 until the summer of 1980 he was also a lecturer at New College, Oxford, which provides a satirical setting and ingredient in this fourth novel. The register of the book, however, is quite different from its two predecessors, and its central concerns are not satirical but the most intimate personal questions and relationships. Its initial device—in which the X-rays of two women suffering from cancer are confused—is potentially

farcical, but it promotes farce subverted by the gravity of its issues. Pamela Cowper is an Oxford don, told that she is about to die, who undertakes a last journey to America to visit the man with whom she has had the longest, most masked relationship. There she meets her friend's lover, a young girl called Billy with whom she too has an affair: again bisexuality is a central device of plot. Throughout Pamela is in perfect health. Dorothy Higgs is a working-class woman, told that she is cured, who is in fact rapidly dying of bone cancer. Wilson tests himself in this novel not so much by the seriousness of the fictional treatment as by the range of society and styles he chooses to cover; the novel is a curious blend of Murdochian tragi-comedy and almost libellously satirical elements, a blend in which the psychologically credible and realistic rub shoulders with subjects less certainly achieved and at times blatantly *in*credible. Pamela Cowper is far more convincing as a character than the somewhat condescendingly drawn Dorothy Higgs, and the concluding envoi, in which the characters are sent off to their interdependent futures, rides oddly on the tail of a gratuitous satirical climax in which Pamela's friend's Oxford college is gutted by fire. Even so, there is a new density of human interest in the novel; characters who again are wearers of masks and cultivate the unstated in relationships are exposed to passion in a way Wilson had not attempted before. This is particularly interesting in the friendship of Pamela and her priest Hereward Stickley, whom she ultimately marries.

The Healing Art is prefaced by a quotation from a manuscript in "the Pottle library," which Wilson had invented in *Unguarded Hours*; in *Who Was Oswald Fish?* (1981), several characters from earlier novels make appearances, and Jeremy Tradescant (who has now come out) makes a substantial one. The effect of this reappearance is in some respects to unify the fictional world and to give it a sense of reality and a shadowy coherence beyond the confines of the particular book. But this novel expands not only laterally but downwards, like *The Sweets of Pimlico* exploring relationships and dependencies between different generations and the debts and responsibilities inherited or neglected from the past. Oswald Fish was a late Victorian architect and designer whose only masterpiece, St. Aidan's, Purgstall Heath, Birmingham, is threatened with demolition. Fanny Williams, a vivaciously vocal boutique owner, saves it by having an affair with the council solicitor—but her children destroy the lives of all the adulterous adults whom they know, and her own gutting of the church for an exhibition of

Fish's metalwork brings about the collapse of the whole structure. The resurrection of Fish from obscurity reflects at the level of his art and also of his life: his now elderly daughter finds and reads his journal (in itself the finest thing Wilson has written, partly on account of the dramatic distancing and modulation of voice demanded by the task), which establishes, through the details of Fish's own adulteries, complex blood-relations among many of the principal characters. In this many-faceted study of responsibility, the genealogical labyrinth gives a rich, multilayered and at times Dickensian feel to the narrative; it also constitutes a device for distancing Wilson's modern world from the Victorian one from which it sprang and for turning a disillusioned eye on the sense of the potential for happiness and innocence which is characteristic of Dickens's work. Despite passages as funny as any Wilson has written, the tone of the book is increasingly sinister and unhappy. The end of innocence and the implications of the behavior of adults on future generations are developed as nastily as possible, and Fanny's nine-year-old twins, who start out as satirical illustrations of an unthinkingly liberal education, develop a malevolence which destroys the confused, ordinary world of their mother and her friends. The novel marks a substantial step in Wilson's career: it creates a craven new world in terms at once passionate and intellectually agile.

A.N. Wilson's novels have enjoyed an extremely warm reception. *The Sweets of Pimlico* won the John Llewelyn Rhys Prize in 1978, and in 1981 *The Healing Art* won the Southern Arts Association Literature Prize, the Arts Council Fiction Prize, and the Somerset Maugham Prize.

Colin Wilson
(26 June 1931-)

John A. Weigel
Miami University

SELECTED BOOKS: *The Outsider* (London: Gollancz, 1956; Boston: Houghton Mifflin, 1956);

Religion and the Rebel (London: Gollancz, 1957); Boston: Houghton Mifflin, 1957);

The Age of Defeat (London: Gollancz, 1959); republished as *The Stature of Man* (Boston: Houghton Mifflin, 1959);

Ritual in the Dark (London: Gollancz, 1960; Boston: Houghton Mifflin, 1960);

Encyclopaedia of Murder, by Wilson and Patricia Pitman (London: Barker, 1961; New York: Putnam's, 1962);

Adrift in Soho (London: Gollancz, 1961; Boston: Houghton Mifflin, 1961);

The World of Violence (London: Gollancz, 1963); republished as *The Violent World of Hugh Greene* (Boston: Houghton Mifflin, 1963);

Man Without a Shadow: The Diary of an Existentialist (London: Barker, 1963); republished as *The Sex Diary of Gerard Sorme* (New York: Dial, 1963);

Origins of the Sexual Impulse (London: Barker, 1963; New York: Putnam's, 1963);

Necessary Doubt (London: Barker, 1964; New York: Simon & Schuster, 1964);

Introduction to the New Existentialism (London: Hutchinson, 1966; Boston: Houghton Mifflin, 1967);

The Glass Cage: An Unconventional Detective Story (London: Barker, 1966; New York: Random House, 1967);

The Mind Parasites (London: Barker, 1967; Sauk City, Wis.: Arkham House, 1967);

A Casebook of Murder (London: Frewin, 1969; New York: Cowles, 1970);

The Philosopher's Stone (London: Barker, 1969; New York: Crown, 1971);

Voyage to a Beginning (New York: Crown, 1969; London: Cecil & Amelia Woolf, 1969);

The God of the Labyrinth (London: Hart-Davis, 1970); republished as *The Hedonists* (New York: New American Library, 1971);

Lingard (New York: Crown, 1970); republished as *The Killer* (London: New English Library, 1970);

The Black Room (London: Weidenfeld & Nicolson, 1971);

Order of Assassins (London: Hart-Davis, 1972);
New Pathways in Psychology (London: Gollancz, 1972;
    New York: Taplinger, 1972);
The Schoolgirl Murder Case (London: Hart-Davis,
    MacGibbon, 1974; New York: Crown, 1974);
The Space Vampires (London: Hart-Davis, McGib-
    bon, 1976; New York: Random House, 1976).

Colin Wilson's first book, *The Outsider* (1956),
was almost instantly an international best-seller. It
quickly became one of the most controversial items
in recent literary history. Wilson's significance still
depends to a large extent upon what one thinks of
this book, its sequels, and avatars in the way of
essays, biographies, critiques of literature and
music, dramas, encyclopedias, and many novels.

Wilson's inclusion here primarily as a novelist
is justified in his own terms. He firmly believes that
fiction is an appropriate vehicle for exploring
philosophical concerns. In 1958, in "Beyond the
Outsider," published in *Declaration* (1958), the
young author wrote that if he "were to prescribe a
rule that all future philosophers would have to obey
it would be this: that no idea shall be expressed that
cannot be expressed in terms of human beings in a
novel."

Wilson was born on 26 June 1931, in Leicester,
England. Aware at an early age of what he called in
his autobiography (*Voyage to a Beginning*, 1969) the
"vegetable mediocrity" of his working-class
background, he chose greatness, feeling that his
choice was limited to that or nothing. He wasted
little time in getting started. Leiceister offered basic
schooling, books, and movies. After age sixteen Wilson was on his own. He knew he was different from
others, dared even to think of himself as a genius in
order to bolster his courage. After a series of menial
jobs and a short time in the Royal Air Force, a
marital disaster, and other evidences of his own
outsiderism, Wilson settled in London, and during
the years 1954 and 1955 determinedly educated
himself. Much was made later, after the publication
of his first book, of his study habits. For months he
slept on Hampstead Heath in a sleeping bag and
spent his days reading in the British Museum. The
Wilson legend was beginning to take shape.

Strongly motivated to do something important and increasingly informed by his prodigious if
erratic reading (including mystics such as St. John
of the Cross, Jan van Ruysbroeck, Giovanni Scupoli,
and Jakob Böhme), Wilson began to write the book
that became *The Outsider*. He was confident of the

Colin Wilson

value of his book, judging it "the most important book of its generation." And indeed for some time after its publication in May 1956 many others agreed with him. Rave reviews by important critics, some of whom later recanted, and enthusiastic promotion by the publisher, Victor Gollancz, made the work an instant best-seller. Wilson became famous, and along with John Osborne, whose play *Look Back in Anger* had opened the same month in London, and several other young rebels, he was placed among England's "angry young men." (The label was more or less repudiated promptly by the young men, but it became a popular and correct name for the newness in the air.)

What then happened to young Wilson was what he calls in his autobiography "a grotesque parody of success." Although he had in his reckless enthusiasm appointed himself the "heir of Eliot and Joyce" and unabashedly indentified himself with Nietzsche, Nijinsky, and Shaw, he had, he admits, never foreseen "being treated like a film star, an intellectual prodigy, a boy wonder." The reaction soon set in, however, and a half year after its publication *The Outsider* was reconsidered. "It was the general opinion among English intellectuals," Wilson dispassionately notes, "that *The Outsider* had been a craze that had died a natural death, and that I should now be returned to the obscurity from which I had accidentally emerged."

Depressed but not defeated by the backlash, Wilson in 1957 left London and moved to a cottage in Cornwall, where he began to solve the "success problem" by getting back to work. He wrote another book, a kind of sequel to *The Outsider*, called *Religion and the Rebel*, published in October 1957. Then the massacre began. Philip Toynbee, who had originally praised Wilson's first book by comparing its author to Sartre, was evidently anxious to redeem his faux pas and called the second work "a rubbish bin." Perry Miller wrote: "To call these essays sophomoric is to dignify them." The American press joined in the manhunt, and Wilson's publisher advised him to stop writing and to take a regular job, at least for a year or two.

Wilson refused to consider such a retreat, despite the fact that his play, *The Death of God*, had been rejected the same year by the Royal Court Theatre. His contemporaries, the other so-called "angry young men," were also being rejected. Kenneth Allsop describes them as they appeared to hostile critics: "This peasant army (all the group, I think, grew up in provincial industrial towns) have had the temerity to clump into the academic closes where the trainee priests are learning their catechism from

A. J. Ayer and Bertrand Russell, and break in with a loud boy's whistle. 'Throw your logical positivism out of the window and stick up your hands,' they shouted. They have irritated and offended the orthodoxy."

Happily enough, during the ensuing years Wilson worked all the harder at offending the orthodoxy. His third volume in the *Outsider* series appeared in 1959. *The Age of Defeat* (published in the United States as *The Stature of Man*) was reviewed rather politely. Apparently Wilson "was here to stay," the *Times* reviewer sighed. The young writer agreed and began at once to show how serious he was about enduring. His first novel, *Ritual in the Dark*, appeared in 1960, and the Wilson production line got underway with about two books a year—on subjects diverse enough to verify his genius, or, as the hostile hinted, to underwrite his dilettantism.

Soon after the publication in 1956 of *The Outsider*, its author was invited to lecture at Cambridge University. For a week after the visit, so the story goes, all Cambridge debated the proposition: Colin Wilson—bloody fool or great writer? There was no formal decision, and the debate, on a reduced scale, still continues although Wilson's industriousness has won him a grudging respect from most of his former detractors. Also, changes in the philosophical climate have redefined Wilson's significance as a thinker who has persistently opposed pessimism and the existentialism of Jean-Paul Sartre. Sartre had warned cheerful human beings that their cheerfulness was bad faith. The evidence clearly pointed to a discrepancy between the way things are and the way things could be. People were asked to consider this evidence seriously, to come to terms with absurdity. All optimism was fraudulent insofar as it made things seem better than they are. Wilson's ideas dominate whatever genre he frankly exploits for its idea-conveying potential. His many novels and fablelike fantasies are for him devices for promoting his commitments. Predictably many of his writings have been misunderstood and discounted for the wrong reasons—and sometimes praised for equally wrong ones.

The Outsider, which is still probably the most famous of Wilson's books, despite the assaults it has rather badly weathered, contains most of his virtues and most of his faults. *The Outsider* is an enthusiastic synopticon of an earnest youth's eclectic and extensive reading. As an autodidact Wilson did not hesitate to copy passages directly from his notes into his work-in-progress, sometimes inaccurately, sometimes without properly crediting his sources. A host of characters from literature, life, and history are made to bear witness to a thesis which is constantly altered—at least in details—as the result of the accumulating testimony.

Wilson's thesis posits a common difference in a small group of people which makes the members of the group outsiders to those not in the group and often outsiders to one another. Capitalizing the name of the category, he specifies the ways in which

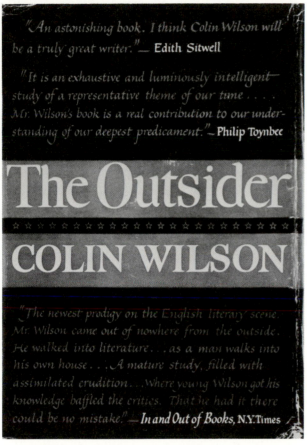

Dust jacket for the American edition of Wilson's first book, which he called "the most important book of its generation"

the Outsider manifests his difference. An Outsider, for example, knows he is sick partly because he lives in a sick society. (The society, however, lacks awareness of its sickness.)

Wilson's reading was esoteric, eclectic, and extensive. He found many books that had been overlooked, he believed, by his elders: a novel by Henri Barbusse about a man who lived in a hole in the wall; H. G. Wells's autobiography, *Mind at the End of Its Tether*, a chronicle of increasing despair; Sartre's novel, *Nausea*; Albert Camus's *The Stranger*; Evan Stroude's *Secret Life*; and Herman Hesse's *Demian* and *Siddhartha*, to start with. As he went on reading he accumulated testimony from such dis-

parate "thinkers" as T. E. Lawrence, Vincent van Gogh, and Waslaw Nijinsky. Everywhere he found a paradox. The Outsider possessed an inner source of power, but he was not happy, and frequently he failed in reaching his real goal. The Outsider's power was also his source of weakness. The Outsider, Wilson theorized, *must* believe in the relevance of his insights and his sensibilities; yet those very insights and sensibilities tell him that his insights and sensibilities are probably irrelevant. Because the Outsider has greater awareness and sensitivity he is capable of ecstasy and despair. Unfortunately, however, because of his special awareness he is incapable of the ordinary evasions that help the mass of men survive their quiet desperation. Apparently intellect alone is not enough.

Wilson wholly endorsed the advice of William Blake: "Go and develop the visionary faculty." In addition to Blake, Wilson endorsed the teachings of George Fox and his resistance to those who regarded his visions as evidence of insanity. Outsiders, however, can end up as Insiders because of too much and too early success. Wilson cites in this category D. H. Lawrence, Charles Dickens, Bernard Shaw, and Rainer Maria Rilke. Ironically, says Wilson, none of them reached ultimate self-realization simply because they did not need to struggle long and hard enough.

Among the Outsiders that interested Wilson in his search for understanding were famous suicides. Apparently, in Wilson's view, those who kill themselves care enough to act, to do something about their despair. Murder is also an act of the will, and in some cases is an intensely creative act, as Wilson tries to demonstrate in much of his fiction.

It is not surprising that Wilson became interested in the ideas of George Gurdjieff, an eccentric philosopher who believed that the planets are alive. Wilson credits him with finding the first ideal *Existensphilosophie*. Those persons capable of being awakened into a fuller existence must not be allowed to be lulled into security and mediocrity. A kind of elitism begins to show its equivocal head at this point. Not all men can be awakened—perhaps only five percent, the truly gifted or potentially gifted. Wilson, finding himself temporarily left of this particular center or right of the same center, is uncomfortable at times in identifying with a minority. If Outsiders were in the majority they would not, of course, be on the outside. Morons are also a minority, however, and are potential demagogues.

Obviously Wilson needed time to resolve such problems, or at least to face them. After the success and subsequent failure of his first book Wilson saw ahead of him the need to study religion, psychology, more literature and philosophy—in fact practically everything, including witchcraft. His second philosophical work, which followed hard on the now slightly run-down heels of *The Outsider*, was an attempt to resolve and fill out. *Religion and the Rebel* examines the decline of Western Civilization—with capital letters—and proposes certain remedies. Authorities cited include Ludwig Wittenstein, Alfred North Whitehead, Sören Kierkegaard, Vilfredo Pareto among innovators, and the old guard such as John Henry Newman, Blaise Pascal, and Emanuel Swedenborg. Nobody was too big or too profound for the young Wilson to wrestle with, and he certainly felt he won every match. Inevitably he generalized hastily, made special pleas and annoyed many specialists whose areas he was invading or who had never heard of most of these authorities.

Incredible as it now seems, in 1956 Kingsley Amis admitted in his review of *The Outsider* that he had never heard of Sartre, Camus, Nietzsche, Hesse, van Gogh—and Hemingway! How much more hostile were the ignorant when Wilson began to publish novels overlaid with his learning *and* "pugnacious ignorance."

In 1960 his first novel, designed to support his determination, appeared. Of the many works by Wilson *Ritual in the Dark* is in some ways still the most ambitious book. As an attempt to invoke the dark mystery, he claims for it an intricate and solemn genesis as it went through several major revisions before being published. Wilson has claimed that his first novel is to *The Egyptian Book of the Dead* what Joyce's *Ulysses* is to the *Odyssey*. Be that as it may, the novel is carefully structured to reveal its purposiveness. The authorial point of view, never present as first person, is nevertheless divided between several young Outsiders: Gerard Sorme, a writer; Austin Nunne, a dilettante and murderer; and Oliver Glasp, a painter. Secondary characters include a German psychiatrist, a Scottish detective, and an aged priest. Final significances, however, are filtered through Gerard Sorme: ultimately only he remains a reliable witness.

The story exploits a search for who-did-the-murders without ever trying for either mystery or tension. No one is surprised when Austin is identified as the killer of four women. The interest focuses on why he kills rather than on whom or when. Gerard Sorme partially succeeds in justifying Austin's killing four prostitutes by stabbing them brutally. Even murder is a creative act when done by a superior person, for the act releases a sense of power. Gerard confesses to having some of the same

impulses at times. "I belong among the Enemies," he tells his murderer-friend: "certain men whose business is to keep the world in a turmoil—the Napoleons, Hitlers, Genghis Khans."

Finally Gerard sees Austin as truly insane—not "supersane"—and no longer condones the killings, telling himself that such killing is "a complete negation of all our impulses. It means we've got no future." Wilson, however, unlike his Gerard, remains very much interested in murder, and the subject comes up frequently in his writings. Specific works include an *Encyclopaedia of Murder* in 1961 (with Patricia Pitman), a second novel on the subject called *The World of Violence* in 1963 (*The Violent World of Hugh Greene* in the United States), *A Casebook of Murder* in 1969, another novel called *The Killer* in 1970 (*Lingard* in the United States), and *Order of Assassins* in 1972, a psychological analysis of killers as Outsiders—to name only the most substantial works on the subject.

Wilson's output has remained prodigious for many years, as if the prodigy cherished the root meaning of the label derived from *prodigium*: omen and/or monster. In the survey of his later work which follows here, emphasis and selectivity are not necessarily his, for he has often considered rather small items in his canon as of special significance. Indeed, he has never disowned any of his creations, so that any selective discussion does injustice to his fervor and dedication. One suspects that he has written much more than he has published. One knows that some of his projects have been aborted by reluctant publishers. The "case," however, of Colin Wilson still remains very much in his own idiom which is at the service of his commitment to defeat defeatism.

The novels that followed *Ritual in the Dark* vary in themes and techniques from one of the first "beat" stories, *Adrift in Soho* (1961), to speculative projections into the future and psychological thrillers. Published in 1963, *Man Without a Shadow* (American title, *The Sex Diary of Gerard Sorme*) purports to be the intimate confession of the central character from *Ritual in the Dark*. The work was attacked as pornographic, but as the author claims, it "owes more to Gabriel Marcel's *Metaphysical Journal* than to Frank Harris." In the fictitious diary Gerard defends the mad Austin more precisely than he did in the earlier novel, where he had finally decided Austin was not justified. Now, however, he has decided that "Austin was dimly, vaguely trying to follow his own deepest nature to some unheard-of form of self-expression." Identifying the "sexual force" as "the nearest thing to magic—to the supernatural—that human beings ever experience," the diarist justifies the intensity of his own sex drive. He then proceeds to illustrate his sexuality so vividly that the book had to be cleared in court before it could be sold in England—after which, of course, it sold fairly well.

Critical reception of *Man Without a Shadow* followed the usual pattern of ambivalence, vituperation, and adulation. One critic, Stanley Kauffmann in the *New Republic*, hazarded a guess that "Colin Wilson is a spoof and that Kingsley Amis, Malcolm Muggeridge, and Peter Ustinov go away together on occasional weekends and compose a Colin Wilson book." A few years later Wilson himself, perhaps rationalizing, admitted that he viewed the work as "a volume of tongue-in-cheek pornography and diabolism . . . which embodies, in fictional form, the ideas expounded in my phenomenological study, *Origins of the Sexual Impulse*." *Origins of the Sexual Impulse* is the fifth volume, published in 1963, in the so-called Outsider cycle. In it Wilson draws heavily upon Edmund Husserl and Gestalt psychologists for his "facts."

Another work of fiction also published in 1963 testifies to Wilson's excitement at that time about his own intuitions. *The World of Violence* (American title, *The Violent World of Hugh Greene*) is a slow-paced story told in the first person by a narrator who often stops to philosophize about the significance of his education and other experiences. In the tradition of the Bildungsroman, the work is concerned with identifying the most significant variables in the hero's growth and in fixing the sources of his mature convictions and strange habits. Like his creator, Hugh Greene is a prodigy, self-taught and eager for knowledge. As a child he begins to question the value of ordinary experience as an index to knowledge. As he moves from "The Outer Dark" to "The Inner Dark" (subtitles for the two parts of the novel), Hugh relates to various kinds of violence and experiments personally with brutality. After a series of "vastations" he attacks the meaning of existence and his own Outsiderism, much as Wilson himself had done by studying in the British Museum Reading Room. There he reads "straight through" Berkeley, Hume, Kant, Hegel, William James, Husserl, and others—all in three months!

Critical opinion of this novel tended to follow the usual pattern: Bad but also good, or passionate but illiterate, or well-meaning but hopeless. Indeed, the violent world that Hugh was trying to understand resembles the novel itself—not easy to solve. In the last sentence of the novel the searcher concludes that "the contradictions of the bundle of responses called a human being can never be resolved as simply as the contradictions of philosophy."

Nevertheless, Wilson goes on trying, sometimes introducing the very contradictions he loves to wrestle with—often unsuccessfully. Wilson's fifth novel, *Necessary Doubt* (1964), takes its title from Paul Tillich's theology. The main character, Professor Zweig, is an "existential theologian," so there are plenty of problems to deal with, including the nature of God as well as of man. The plot revolves about a manhunt for the son of a famous surgeon. The surgeon's recent suicide has aroused suspicions. Zweig knows the family and undertakes the responsibility. He can identify emotionally with the hunted, and paradoxically the hunter in this novel feels more guilt than the hunted. Eventually Zweig is joined in the hunt by two friends, an eccentric mystic and a detective. When they find the surgeon's son they also encounter moral complexities, for the man is not clearly and unequivocally "guilty." The killer believes sincerely that he has benefited his victims by encouraging them, with the help of pills, to kill themselves. So Zweig finally arranges for the killer's escape, defending his decision, explaining that the man is a visionary rather than a criminal—a typical Wilson distinction, and one that is all too familiar among supporters of supermen theories: special people with special powers should be given special privileges.

Within the covers of the novel the doubts work well, however, for they are the proper stuff of fiction. As one reviewer concluded: "the whole odd mixture of miscellaneous erudition and casual flim-flam does somehow add up. Partly this is because of the audacity of it all, the sheer cheek. Partly it is because of Mr. Wilson's persistence in search of significance, even here. But basically it is because he continues to try to find out what is really important in life."

Encouraged by such half-understanding at least, Wilson continued to write fiction while pondering and reworking his philosophy in nonfiction. The novels that follow *Necessary Doubt* include an "unconventional detective story," *The Glass Cage* (1966); a Lovecraft imitation, *The Mind Parasites* (1967); another parable qua novel, *The Philosopher's Stone* (1969); another "crime novel," *The Killer* (1970); another adventure of Gerard Sorme in *The God of the Labyrinth* (1970); an advanced piece of speculative fiction called *The Black Room* (1971); a novel which was planned as the first of a series and is exactly what the title promises, *The Schoolgirl Murder Case* (1974); and another science-speculative piece of fiction, *The Space Vampires* (1976).

Wilson's novels are not ordinary story books. They are sometimes repetitious, even naively plotted. Their *ideas* are worth some attention, although once one grasps the concept of "mind parasites" and "black rooms," there is little difficulty in perceiving what each work is trying to say. Wilson's admiration of the "Lovecraft tradition" has been an important aspect of his speculative fiction. Lovecraft's 1926 essay, "Supernatural Horror in Literature," claims that his kind of fiction encourages extending the narrow boundaries of ordinary science by exploiting the fear of the unknown. Wilson's novel *The Mind Parasites* projects a conflict many years from now with the Tsathogguans, wily microscopic parasites that menace civilization by infecting the best minds of the age. It is meant to frighten the reader, and perhaps it does frighten some; yet Wilson admits that at least the opening pages of "flaccid prose" did not "come off," adding: "but what the hell. I'd rather get on with another book than tinker about with it."

In "another book," *The Philosopher's Stone*, Wilson speculates about breaking barriers in human consciousness by inserting a bit of special metal in the frontal lobe of the brain to stimulate the imagination. The conclusion is pretentious: "Man should possess an infinite appetite for life. It should be self-evident to him, all the time, that life is superb, glorious, endlessly rich, infinitely desirable." Yet both novels are enthusiastically humanistic and optimistic in their messages.

The Black Room is perhaps Wilson's most intense projection of his conviction that human consciousness is still slumbering and that it needs real awakening. Wilson's quest is not for the noble primitive who got lost in the past but for a new self which must be radically discovered and then perfected. A "black room" is a device for cutting off information from the outside. In a lightproof and soundproof room an individual is outside the outside by being truly inside. In such a room—metaphor for cutoff state—a person either survives because he is strong enough to keep his awareness alive by himself or eventually capitulates to the blackness and the silence and "loses his mind." The idea of a black room begins as a metaphor, develops into a device for brainwashing, and ends up in Wilson's novel as a crisis experience in which "danger and difficulty unite the whole being."

The Space Vampires refines the mind-parasite metaphor and adds humanoids and various trappings of outer space. It builds into an exciting and more nearly conventional thriller as plot dominates

didacticism without sacrificing philosophical intent. Wilson has always seen an affinity between crime and creativity, and between detecting crime and saving souls. Psychic visions and occult phenomena are facts to him as they are for many readers, who may, however, ultimately confuse their facts with fantasies once useful as escape mechanisms. (What happens to reality when it becomes more fantastic than fiction has been the concern of many contemporary storytellers, some of whom have given up on inventing new stories.)

In *The Schoolgirl Murder Case*, for example, a novel meant to be popular and readable, Wilson throws away chances at suspense in the interests of his kind of truth. The suspect has been under suspicion all along and no one is surprised at the ending. One may be surprised, however, at the combining of magic and brothel and the fact that the detective is more of a clergyman, finally, than one could have predicted. After he has solved the crime, which revealed, in passing, that this is a bad world, he still insists it is a good one.

To sum up Wilson's significance is not easy, for his urgency to communicate can quickly change any genre into a vehicle for his ideas, and the critic often evaluates genre rather than ideas, according to Wilson's most often voiced complaint. He is not a *great* novelist, not a *great* dramatist, not a *great* literary critic, music critic, or philosopher—as he has hoped. He is, however, remarkably earnest, versatile, and informed, and nearest greatness when he speaks as a "new existentialist." In 1966 he published a readable volume modestly called *Introduction to the New Existentialism* with the emphasis on the *newness* of his ideas. In this work he outlines the case for his claim of having broken with the dead-end, old, and pessimistic existentialism of Sartre and others. Again and again Wilson objects to accepting an empty and meaningless universe. Stressing the evidence that consciousness is intentional, he rejects Sartre's gloomy conclusion that such intentionality is only apparent and thus bad faith. In a 1967 essay, "Existential Psychology: A Novelist's Approach," Wilson explores the metaphor of a debilitating robot in human beings that cuts off creativity. And finally his interest in Abraham Maslow's ideas motivated him to write a book called, less modestly, *New Pathways in Psychology* (1972), in which he exhorts mankind to increase and intensify awareness until all who are able see the "third world" as a *real* place. Wilson insists that this higher reality is "there all the time, like China or the moon. . . . It is fundamentally a world of pure *meaning*."

The thirst for more and more knowledge must

perforce always outrun research. Wilson has sought the byways as well as the highways to satisfy his hydrophytic thirst, evaluating and re-evaluating the special powers of others, such as mystics, occultists, and assorted dreamers and visionaries. As a self-styled existential critic he digs for the effect on him of the work of others, rejecting as inadequate many sacred works of the orthodox canons. His own canon is long and complicated, and this essay neglects necessarily many nuances. Colin Wilson, however, has earned his place in history—whether literary history or the history of ideas is still moot only because at this time historians in general disagree with him that there is no difference. Literature is the handmaiden of ideas for Wilson. To misunderstand that point is to try him in the wrong court for crimes he never intended to commit. Meanwhile, Colin Wilson is still hard at work: essays on philosophers, more speculative fiction, and works on the occult are in progress.

Other:

"Beyond the Outsider," in *Declaration*, edited by Tom Maschler (New York: Dutton, 1958; London: MacGibbon & Kee, 1958),pp. 13-41;

"Existential Psychology: A Novelist's Approach," in *Challenges of Humanistic Psychology*, edited by James F. T. Bugental (New York: McGraw-Hill, 1967), pp.69-78.

References:

Sidney R. Campion, *The World of Colin Wilson* (London: Muller, 1962);

R. H. W. Dillard, "Toward an Existential Realism: The Novels of Colin Wilson," *Hollins Critic*, 4 (October 1967): 1-12;

John A. Weigel, *Colin Wilson* (Boston: Twayne, 1975).

Appendix I:
"You've Never Had It So Good"
Gusted by "Winds of Change":
British Fiction in the 1950s, 1960s, and After

"You've Never Had It So Good"
Gusted by "Winds of Change":
British Fiction in the 1950s, 1960s, and After

John Fletcher
University of East Anglia

To start with an inescapable historical truism: the political and economic background against which British novels since 1945 have been written is one of almost continuous national decline. The United Kingdom emerged from World War II as a virtual equal partner of the victorious alliance which had defeated Nazi Germany and Japan; it was economically shaken, perhaps, but still rich, with its overseas empire more or less intact. Little over twenty years later—well before the oil crisis and the onset of worldwide economic recession—Britain had sunk to the rank of a minor power politically, with a failing and inefficient economy which made her one of the poorer countries of the industrialized world. As historians Alan Sked and Chris Cook argued in *Postwar Britain: A Political History* (1979), until 1963 Britain was still a world power, if no longer a superpower; but since 1963, major economic problems have increasingly beset the British, undermining the prestige of their government, with the result that the United Kingdom has lost confidence at home and authority abroad. As these historians point out, the 1950s were the critical decade, particularly so far as economic decision making was concerned: "Tory Chancellors [of the Exchequer] in the 1950s . . . developed confused and inaccurate ideas regarding the way in which the economy worked," they allege, and these errors laid the foundations for the catastrophic decline registered in the later 1960s and in the 1970s. Nevertheless, for several years all went well, even extremely well; a boom got under way which made the austerity of the immediate postwar period a bad memory only. Elizabeth David, the well-known authority on fine cookery, wrote in *A Book of Mediterranean Food* (1955): "in 1950 . . . almost every essential ingredient of good cooking was either rationed or unobtainable, [but] it was stimulating to think about [it] to escape from the deadly boredom of queuing and the frustration of buying the weekly rations; to read about real food cooked with wine and olive oil, eggs and butter and cream, and dishes richly flavoured with onions, garlic, herbs, and brightly coloured southern vegetables." Such products were, as she implies, virtually unobtainable in Britain for several years after the cessation of hostilities in Europe. Austerity having been brought to an end, the Conservative regime was able, for over a decade, to convince voters that its enlightened policies were solely responsible for the situation which allowed Prime Minister Macmillan to say, quite truthfully, in one of those slogans which he had the rare gift of coining, "You've never had it so good."

It was all fundamentally spurious, of course, because falling commodity prices in world markets, and, in particular, grossly underpriced energy supplies, made better times possible. Nevertheless, while the last shreds of Britain's imperial might were being gusted away by those famous "winds of change" Macmillan also spoke about, the living standards of ordinary people improved beyond all recognition. In 1956, for example, only eight percent of British households had a refrigerator, while in 1978 the proportion had risen to ninety percent. As Pat Healy wrote in the *Times* on 6 December 1979, "in the early 1950s, nearly half the population lived in terraced homes, which tended to be the oldest property . . . . By 1978, more than half the population lived either in semi-detached houses or flats or maisonettes . . . and only four percent did not have the use of a bath or shower." So, side by side with steady national decline, the man or woman in the street was experiencing ever-increasing prosperity. By 1970, hunger and squalor, so widespread in the 1930s, were virtually eradicated from British life, largely because a significant proportion of the nation's real product had been transferred from property-derived incomes to wages and salaries; moreover, the traditionally better-remunerated middle and professional classes acquiesced in a gradual diminution of the gap between their incomes and those of the manual and unskilled sections of the work force. An expressive indicator of this change is the manner in which rickets, the classic children's disease wherever malnutrition and lack of sunshine occur together, is now unknown to the average British family doctor.

This then, is the background against which British fiction has been written in the last few decades. In this essay I should like to concentrate on the most fertile years, artistically speaking; these were the later 1950s and the 1960s. Politically they may have been disastrous, but aesthetically they were successful indeed, perhaps because, unlike the situation now, they were full of hope. As author Joan Bakewell has said (in a 3 April 1980 *Listener* essay entitled "Complete and Generous Education?"): "The Fifties were heady days of high idealism. We lived on a postwar tide of optimism that the world would become a better place for more people." In filling out what Bernard Bergonzi called a "historical footnote" in his 1970 survey of contemporary British fiction, *The Situation of the Novel*, I should like to sort out some of the sociological implications of novels like *Lucky Jim* and to look for the underlying trends and unspoken assumptions of the society in which the British writer lives and works.

The initial time limits lie, broadly speaking, between two political quotations. The first is an entry in George Orwell's last notebook: writing in March-April 1949, he alluded scathingly to "the essential hypocrisy of the British labour movement" and commented that "for a left-wing party in power, its most serious antagonist is always its own past propaganda." The second is a fragment of later left-wing propaganda, the Labour Party's manifesto for the 1964 general election (which, of course, it won, though just barely): "Labour is ready. Poised to swing its plans into instant operation. Impatient to apply the New Thinking that will end the chaos and sterility. . . . Restless with positive remedies for the problems the Tories have criminally neglected."

It is now clear that under the Conservatives, in the years which fall between these two quotations, Britain had lost an empire but not yet found a role, whereas at home, according to Sked and Cook, "Tory economic complacency ensured that the necessary economic growth would never be generated, [for] not enough money was channelled into key industries." Ironically, the new Labour leader, Harold Wilson, while consciously ushering in a new era, was motivated by equally conservative instincts. The historians' verdict is damning: "He too was determined to uphold the sterling system and the value of the pound, with the result that all the mistakes of the 1950s were repeated in the 1960s. After 1963-4 things were never the same again; but, in another sense, they were never really different." In spite of the brave words of the 1964 Labour man-

ifesto, therefore, nothing much in British policy was altered, although the world around the British Isles was changing as steadily as were the seas which washed its shores. In the thirteen years ("thirteen wasted years," opposition propagandists maintained) of Tory rule from 1951, when Atlee's postwar Labour administration was finally defeated, to 1964, when the Conservatives lost in their turn to Labour, most of the major British novels of the post-1945 era were published. Let us look more closely, then, at the literary production of those "Tory years," winds-of-change years, the years of "you've never had it so good."

In Britain, a profoundly conservative nation, it is often the case that "plus ça change, plus c'est la même chose." For instance, it is astonishing now to reread Leslie A. Fiedler's influential essay of 1958, "Class War in British Literature." Fiedler is an astute and perceptive critic, but he was misled, by the sound and the fury of the time, to posit a radical schism in the world of British letters, between those from E. M. Forster to W. H. Auden, on the one hand, who all "came to tea with Virginia Woolf," and the postwar writers on the other, scholarship boys and rebellious girls, "who are," he claims, "resolved to break at last out of a world of taste which has been . . . too long confined to the circumference of a tea table." These writers, the notorious "angry young men," felt trapped in their class in an age of transition. They reacted, Fiedler said, by flaunting a "New Philistinism" and a "secular Puritanism"; they had inherited, and indeed espoused, "a world where graciousness [had] followed the last servant out the door."

That essay was published, of course, well over twenty years ago. The Kingsley Amis whom Fiedler praised for his accurate rendering of "a classless, grim world" now talks very differently. Or does he? The young university teacher who in 1954 pilloried cultural pretentiousness in *Lucky Jim* is after all the same man who in a recent interview was quoted as saying that "you can't share real culture equally and deeply over a whole society" and that "there aren't enough brains to go round, really." Reproached with having moved to the right as he grew older, Amis claimed that he has stayed in the center and that other people have lurched to the left. He maintains that the invasion of Hungary in 1956 brought home to him what communism was: "it then," he says, "became article one of my programme, resistance to Soviet power," which he felt to be as great a menace at home, through "a lot of people on the left," as it was abroad. This anticommunist Amis is not, however, so very remote from the novelist who, in *Take a Girl Like You* (1960), could write, what to Bernard Bergonzi reads (correctly) like, "a prolonged proleptic elegy for [the heroine's] lost virginity, itself a symbol for traditional pieties." Behind the ambivalence, even "moral incoherence" of *Take a Girl Like You*, there is, Bergonzi claims, a sharp sense of regret, on Amis's part, that "the ideals of provincial rectitude give a last faint flicker before being lost for ever in the swinging scene" of the later 1960s. This is, though—morally and aesthetically speaking—a profoundly conservative attitude; for despite appearances Amis has not, essentially, changed.

Another novelist who was much praised twenty or so years ago for having created a "hero of our time" like Amis's "Lucky" Jim Dixon was John Braine, author of *Room at the Top* (1957). Braine's character Joe Lampton is probably the last of a long line of "parvenu" heroes inaugurated with splendid brio a century and a half ago by Stendhal's Julien Sorel. Indeed, Joe Lampton is in some ways more characteristic of this type than he is of postwar British heroes. He makes good, as indeed Thackeray's Becky Sharp does, by means which are more than somewhat morally dubious; but unlike Becky he is not punished for his sins. When his mistress dies in appalling suffering, Joe's dormant conscience comes to life. "Nobody blames you, love," says a woman friend in order to comfort him. "Oh my God," he replies a shade mawkishly, "that's the trouble." Still, despite this momentary stirring of feelings finer than those he usually goes in for, he survives: the successful sequel, *Life at the Top* (1962), catches up with him, quite unreformed "after ten years amid the fleshpots."

More elegiac even than Amis in *Take a Girl Like You* is Keith Waterhouse in his novel of 1959, *Billy Liar*, a delicate, allusive, sad comedy which both is redolent of the 1950s in Britain and sums them up. The book's uneasy attitude toward sexual liberation and its still largely deferential (if privately disrespectful) manner toward those in authority are clearly transitional: a halfway house, perhaps, between the conformity of the 1930s and the permissiveness of the later 1960s which were just around the corner. The spectacle of the young hero plying his completely noninflammable fiancee with "passion pills" (that is, supposed aphrodisiacs) is funny, of course, but it is also rather nervous on Waterhouse's part. After all, girls could—and did—get pregnant, and there was no abortion legislation on the statute book in those days. So the pregnant heroines of 1950s novels either marry their seducer, as in *Room at the Top* and Stan

Barstow's *A Kind of Loving* (1960), or they go to a back-street abortionist with sometimes appalling consequences, as in *Ordeal by Shame* (a forgotten novel of 1951 by Sarah Prentiss, which, in vaguely Lawrentian terms, attacks contemporary repressive attitudes in Britain toward abortion), or they decide to keep the child, as in the movie version (1960) of Alan Sillitoe's *Saturday Night and Sunday Morning* (1958).

Barstow's *A Kind of Loving* is a deeply revealing book which is well-nigh unreadable today. It is soaked (the term is not too strong) in adolescent sexual guilt which is in no way "distanced" by the author. The following passage is depressingly characteristic: ". . . . because if it depended on what she [his mother] told me—or the Old Feller [his father] for that matter—I'd still be thinking you got babies by saving Co-op Cheques and that there isn't any difference between men and women except women grow their hair longer and don't have to shave. And then I get to thinking what a funny business it all is, this sex and blokes going mad over women and doing all sorts of daft things because of them." What makes this such painful reading is that the hero is about to see his sweetheart unclothed for the first time, and he is terrified. Waterhouse would handle such a moment tenderly, if a shade wryly. Barstow, as this passage shows, transmits it raw. That does not necessarily mean that it is authentic; or if it is, the authenticity is of a rather trivial kind.

Another famous title of the 1950s was *Saturday Night and Sunday Morning* by Alan Sillitoe. It began as a collection of short stories centered on the doings of its working-class hero, Arthur Seaton, and its episodic nature is reflected in the two parts of the book: "Saturday Night," which concentrates mainly on Arthur's bachelor life, and "Sunday Morning," when he is "going steady," as the expression had it, with Doreen, the archetypal "nice girl" whom he will eventually, willy-nilly, marry. Though not a fully unified work of art Sillitoe's novel nevertheless surpasses Barstow's by a wide margin so far as authenticity is concerned. In fact, in its precise and accurate depiction of working-class situations, characters, and locales, it reminds the reader to some extent of Zola. The book was a success overnight for other reasons than its undeniable authenticity: Arthur Seaton was seen, albeit erroneously, as a sort of working-class "angry young man." In fact, he is simply acting out the anarchistic hedonism of his class. He has no basic quarrel with his lot, provided he continues earning good wages to spend on drink and women. "It's a good life and a good world, all said and done," he muses at the end, adding significantly, "if you don't weaken." But he is no rebel. He is politically indifferent, culturally philistine, and he is agnostic about religion and morality. If he is attractive—and he certainly is—this is because he appeals to much the same sympathies as do the heroes of the Spanish picaresque, his spiritual fathers.

In retrospect, then, it is hard to see what the literary fuss of the 1950s was all about. Books like *Lucky Jim*, *Room at the Top*, *A Kind of Loving*, and *Saturday Night and Sunday Morning* undoubtedly represented a refreshing new note of realism, as if—to adopt Leslie Fiedler's expression—the Woolfs' tea party were really and truly over. But after an interval of more than twenty years, one can only be surprised at how very calm the millpond must have been if the throwing of such pebbles could have caused such ripples. But then we must remember that British society had not yet undergone the traumatizing shocks it was to experience later on. After all, when a bank rate of four percent was thought to be astronomically high—as it was in Butler's time as Chancellor of the Exchequer—little wonder that disrespectful writers (not only novelists, of course, but playwrights like John Osborne, whose *Look Back in Anger* was the theatrical bombshell of 1956) could provoke so much uproar.

Nevertheless, these books—even those from which (as Iris Murdoch would say) there emanates only "a special and limited sense of the past"—do reflect the changing times, particularly as regards new attitudes toward sex and marriage. As Joan Bakewell puts it, "In my day, D. H. Lawrence was our god. . . . We acted out, as worshippers should, the precepts of Lawrence's dark flame—a burning honesty towards one's inner self. The consequence was as much sexual freedom as our inhibited backgrounds would allow us." There was also a new attitude toward material affluence accepted no longer as a privilege but demanded as a right. Those "advancing armies of new pink houses," for instance, "flowing over the fields like red ink on green blotting paper," in *Saturday Night and Sunday Morning*, were a few of the 300,000 per year which Harold Macmillan was building to fulfill a Tory electoral pledge and, incidentally, to lay the foundations for his own election to the premiership a little later. And ultimately frivolous (like *Lucky Jim* or *Saturday Night and Sunday Morning*) or ponderously earnest (like *Room at the Top* and *A Kind of Loving*) though such novels were, they did open up the way for more ambitious and artistically complex novelists like Iris Murdoch or Muriel Spark to build a reputation; indeed, it was shortly after 1964, the

date which represents such a clear break in British political history, that Iris Murdoch published her most daring novel—daring, that is, in terms of the frank delineation of the sexual deviations of some of her characters—a novel which somehow epitomizes the 1960s: *The Time of the Angels* (1966). And the way opened up by Amis, Sillitoe, and the others was soon to be followed, too, by novelists of the next generation, like Margaret Drabble, Malcolm Bradbury, and David Lodge, who thanks to the endeavors of their predecessors, were able to take certain things for granted. For instance, this delightfully cool account by Margaret Drabble (in *The Garrick Year*, 1964) of a long-deferred seduction could not have been written in quite this tone ten years before: " 'You feel like a sparrow,' he said, 'you're all bones.' 'I'm not bones,' I said, and he pushed me back on to the pillow. We struggled there for a little, and after a while I began to think that I really might as well give in: there was after all everything on the side of submission, and nothing to be gained by resistance except a purely technical chastity. . . . So I let him get on with it, and I wish to God that I could say that I enjoyed it. At the end I looked around limply for my handkerchief: then, not finding it, blew my nose loudly on the corner of the sheet."

Had Stan Barstow tackled this scene, he would have made it stormy with guilt; Kingsley Amis would have done an elegant and sophisticated piece of mild bawdy; and Alan Sillitoe would not have even bothered. But unlike these precursors, Margaret Drabble (born in 1939) was still only a child when the Labour Party swept to victory in 1945. That makes all the difference. As someone who grew up with the welfare state, who had no memories of prewar times and only childish ones of war, she is (like other outstanding novelists of the post-1960 era such as Beryl Bainbridge and Angela Carter) free of the attitudes which writers of the previous generation felt compelled to strike. The last sentences of her novel *The Garrick Year* are characteristic of her manner: "One just has to keep on and to pretend, for the sake of the children, not to notice. Otherwise one might just as well stay at home." The tone here is neither aggressive nor humble, neither guilt-ridden nor amoral. The world is what it is, neither more nor less, and true wisdom consists, Drabble suggests, in accepting, stoically although not humorlessly, things as they are. We are a long way indeed from anger, but neither are we back at the Woolfs' tea table.

This last point can be further illustrated—bringing us up to date, as it were—by a look at a very

British literary controversy in which I recently took part. The circumstances were these. The cultural channel of the British Broadcasting Corporation's radio services—Radio 3—held a short-story competition with a first prize of £ 1,000. It was won by Sean Virgo, a thirty-nine-year-old author of some four volumes of verse and a couple of books of short stories. The winning entry—"Interact"—was broadcast on Radio 3 and published in the *Listener*, which revealed that there had been 7,500 entries in all to the competition. This is how Virgo's perhaps minor, but entirely exemplary story begins:

> He had sufficient money to live free for a year and meant to do so. She had the small car her mother had left her and a degree in fine arts, brand-new. He had the family's summer cottage in North Wales and memories of his last visit there. . . . They met at Chatsworth, she alone, he with three friends. She had been sketching from the wood's edge and was sharing her lunch with a pair of jays. . . . She joined them on the three o'clock tour of the house and drove him back to London in her car.
>
> So, in their own style, they were married.

The neutral tone of these opening sentences has not really prepared us for this last bland statement, but there is more to follow:

> They were generous with each other's bodies. Both of them were unashamedly curious and in their discoveries they were friends together exploring a secret estate. Learning him, she came to know herself with his eyes; by her he was initiated into the promptings and confusions of a school dormitory.

Striking as this is, it could (except perhaps for the comic note heard in the last sentence) have been written for a magazine like *Nova* or *Cosmopolitan*, as a "sophisticated" tale of contemporary life and love. But the reader is still not allowed to relax, because the next sentences read:

> He wove for her an immodest blouse of white bryony vines, and she wore it across the fields with berries shining around her breasts. He stood beside her where they bathed in the valley stream, and as she combed her hair back she used his high white manhood *as a towel rail.*

I italicize those last few words because—to use

a musical expression—the prose modulates to a different key at that point. So far, Virgo has given us what we might be forgiven for taking as a rather earnest rewrite of *Lady Chatterley's Lover* (1928) for *Playboy* magazine. But—much in the style of Swift's treacherous (because unsignposted) shifts of stress in his ironical prose—Virgo changes direction, at the point I have indicated, and the alert reader senses that someone is being made a fool of. It cannot be the reader himself, since he is paid the compliment of being able to respond to the difference of tone. It must be the couple in the story, who are behaving in a silly way. Now we realize what was meant precisely by the phrase *"in their own style*, they were married" (again, I italicize). That "style" is the style of the so-called permissive age. That this style is being viewed with some degree of detachment, to say the least, is clear from a later sentence, which dryly summarizes how this idyllic summer came to an end (again, italics mine):

> *So, in their own style, they were divorced.* . . . She drove him into Llangollen and said goodbye at the bus station. She turned the car around and they waved to each other across the high street. The little car disappeared behind a milk tanker, and he bought a newspaper before he settled down to wait for the London bus.

What a "cool"—to use the word both in its usual and in its contemporary colloquial senses—what a cool parting, the reader reflects, between lovers who have lived as D. H. Lawrence's Connie and Mellors would have given their eyeteeth to have been allowed to live! How different is the situation which Sean Virgo describes ("They had nothing to distract them from each other, no family to perform for, no social role.") from that which forces Lady Chatterley to live apart from the man she loves and whose child stirs within her. No children get conceived in *this* rural retreat, the reader notices; the girl, like all sensible young women nowadays, takes good care of that.

No sooner had the story been read on the air than the critics started to attack it. It was stylish, yes (they conceded), but vapid and sentimental, and unworthy of any prize, let alone the top one in a numerically large entry. Disappointed contestants vented their spleen on the selectors while disinterested noncontenders wrote in to the *Listener* to say that the story was flawlessly written but "without a corpuscle of blood, passion, life; just written for the sake of writing, as mannered as an art deco fashion drawing" (unfair to art deco, but let that pass). A Mr. Deramore scorned the "feeble" plot, as he saw it, and the "vague characterization"; this correspondent was particularly annoyed that the hero and heroine were never named—as if "he" and "she" were not, by now, pretty commonplace as "names" for characters in contemporary fiction. It was, he went on, "trivial and boring," unworthy of the tradition of short stories in the English language—as if understatement were not one of the great qualities cultivated by practitioners as diverse as D. H. Lawrence, V. S. Pritchett, and John Updike, so that in this respect, at least, Sean Virgo finds himself in excellent company. It was typical, Mr. Deramore concluded, of the way, in the contemporary arts, "the gewgaw" is valued more highly than the gem.

I could not remain silent and wrote to say that it is to the credit of modern writing and evidence of its continuing robust health that readers and listeners could get it so wrong. One letter writer had taken particular exception to a reference to Passchendaele, the 1917 battlefield where, as a German general once put it, the British army broke its teeth, suffering appalling casualties in order to gain a few kilometers of muddy ground. This is how the reference comes up; the hero is reminiscing about an incident that took place when he was eight:

> "A tramp shared his bread and cheese with me under a hedge and we watched them harvesting the wheat. He told me about fighting in the trenches at Passchendaele."
>
> She said: "Passchendaele...."
>
> "Yes, it is too beautiful a name to forget," he said.

Phil Smith commented on this passage that Virgo's "sugary idyll" had "sweetened everything it touched upon." My riposte to this was that he had completely misread the passage. The reference to a British military disaster suggests to me, with the economy which is held to be the mark of a good short story, just how callow, and shallow, the "he" of this tale of our times is. For him, obviously, Passchendaele means "passion dale," a place like the one in which he is energetically making love to a fine-arts graduate. But it was "passion dale" in a different sense of the word "passion" for the grandfathers of this young man and woman: it was the place where they, and their friends, died by the tens of thousands. All this is suggested, but not stated, in the story; but, as I have said, understatement is

supposed to be a particular merit of this art form. Fortunately, another correspondent came to my support and asserted, rightly, that "Interact" was faithful to the *genre*.

Much in this fine story, I argued, performed the same function vis-a-vis D. H. Lawrence's novel *Lady Chatterley's Lover* as T. S. Eliot's sardonic enjambement of "and" does with the Oliver Goldsmith quotation in *The Waste Land* ("When lovely woman stoops to folly and . . . ."). Eliot is saying in his poem that for the bright young things of the 1920s the suicidal despair of Goldsmith's *abbandonata* is reduced to the weary smoothing down of hair and placing of a record on the gramophone. He is not poking fun at Goldsmith; he is using his lines as ironic commentary. So is Sean Virgo vis-a-vis D. H. Lawrence. His laconic ending, quoted above, is a discreet but pointed commentary on how far British society has moved—especially in its attitudes toward sexual morality—since that great English novelist wrote (without irony) "John Thomas says goodnight to Lady Jane, a little droopingly, but with a hopeful heart."

The irony, of course, lies in the fact that Lawrence's novel had to wait until 1960—by which time it was, sadly but revealingly, almost out of date—before it could be freely published in England. As Philip Larkin, one of the great writers who came to prominence in the 1950s, wrote in the 13 June 1980 *Times Literary Supplement*: "*Lady Chatterley's Lover* . . . unwittingly installed Lawrence as something like the patron saint of the permissive society, a canonization he would certainly have viewed with the utmost repugnance." But he was forced to endure this posthumous role as the standard bearer of the new morality, or rather immorality; if *Lady Chatterley's Lover* had not existed it would have had to have been invented. But perhaps fortunately, this silly misappropriation of a past masterpiece did not survive the oil crisis. As younger novelists like Christopher Priest and Ian McEwan show, we live in an altogether grimmer and harsher world now. The miniskirt, like the flapper, is a relic and reminder of an era when frivolity was possible, even de rigueur. In his quiet but effective way, Sean Virgo undercuts with satire the platitudes and commonplaces which attempted to render such frivolity respectable, and so strikes a note which is profoundly characteristic of the novels, written during the Macmillan years and after, with which *British Novelists Since 1960* deals.

Appendix II:
Books for Further Reading

Books for Further Reading

This is a selective list of studies concerning contemporary British fiction and aspects of the modern novel in English. Additional information may be obtained from the annual bibliographies of *PMLA* or the special issues of *Modern Fiction Studies*. The most recently published bibliography of criticism on twentieth-century British novelists is that by Paul Schlueter and Jane Schlueter, *The English Novel: Twentieth Century Criticism: Volume II, Twentieth Century Novelists* (Chicago, Athens, Ohio & London: Swallow Press / Ohio University Press, 1982), which covers the criticism from 1900 to 1975.

Allen, Walter. *The Modern Novel in Britain and the United States*. New York: Dutton, 1964.

Astbury, Raymond, ed. *The Writer in the Market Place*. London: Clive Bingley, 1969.

Bergonzi, Bernard. *Situation of the Novel*. London: Macmillan, 1970.

Bergonzi, ed. *The Twentieth Century*. London: Sphere, 1970.

Blair, John G. *The Confidence Man in Modern Fiction: A Rogue's Gallery with Six Portraits*. New York: Barnes & Noble, 1979.

Booth, Wayne. *The Rhetoric of Fiction*. Chicago: University of Chicago Press, 1961.

Brace, Gerald Warner. *The Stuff of Fiction*. New York: Norton, 1969.

Bradbury, Malcolm and David Palmer, eds. *The Contemporary English Novel*. London: Arnold, 1979; New York: Holmes & Meier, 1980.

Bradbury, ed. *The Novel Today*. Manchester: Manchester University Press, 1977; Totowa, N.J.: Rowen & Littlefield, 1977.

Bradbury, ed. *Possibilities: Essays in the State of the Novel*. London & New York: Oxford University Press, 1973.

Burgess, Anthony. *The Novel Now: A Guide to Contemporary Fiction*. London: Faber & Faber, 1967; New York: Norton, 1967.

Calderwood, James L. and Harold E. Toliver, eds. *Perspectives in Fiction*. New York & London: Oxford University Press, 1968.

Cope, Jackson I. and Geoffrey Green, eds. *Novel vs. Fiction: The Contemporary Reformation*. Norman, Okla.: Pilgrim Books, 1981.

Crosland, Margaret. *Beyond the Lighthouse: English Women Novelists in the Twentieth Century*. London: Constable, 1981.

Federman, Raymond, ed. *Surfiction: Fiction Now ... and Tomorrow*. Chicago: Swallow Press, 1975.

Firchow, Peter. *The Writer's Place: Interviews on the Literary Situation in Contemporary Britain*. Minneapolis: University of Minnesota Press, 1974.

Fletcher, John. *Novel and Reader*. London & Boston: Boyars, 1980.

Forster, E. M. *Aspects of the Novel*. London: Arnold, 1927.

Friedman, Norman. *Form and Meaning in Fiction*. Athens, Ga.: University of Georgia Press, 1975.

Gass, William H. *Fiction and the Figure of Life*. New York: Knopf, 1970.

Gindin, James. *Post-War British Fiction: New Accents and Attitudes*. Berkeley & Los Angeles: University of California Press, 1962.

Glicksberg, Charles I. *The Sexual Revolution in Modern English Literature*. The Hague: Martinus Nijhoff, 1973.

Gray, Nigel. *The Silent Majority: A Study of the Working Class in Post-War British Fiction*. London: Vision, 1973.

Gregor, Ian and Brian Nichols. *The Moral and the Story*. London: Faber & Faber, 1962.

Gunn, James. *Alternate Worlds: The Illustrated History of Science Fiction*. Englewood Cliffs, N.J.: Prentice-Hall, 1975.

Hale, Nancy. *The Realities of Fiction*. Boston: Little, Brown, 1962.

Hall, James. *The Lunatic Giant in the Drawing Room: The British and American Novel Since 1930*. Bloomington: Indiana University Press, 1968.

Harvey, W. J. *Character and the Novel*. Ithaca, N.Y.: Cornell University Press, 1965.

Hazell, Stephen, ed. *The English Novel: Developments in Criticism Since Henry James*. London: Macmillan, 1978.

Jameson, Storm. *Parthian Words*. London: Collins & Havrill, 1970.

Kaplan, Sydney Janet. *Feminine Consciousness in the Modern British Novel*. Urbana: University of Illinois Press, 1975.

Kermode, Frank. *The Sense of an Ending: Studies in the Theory of Fiction*. New York: Oxford University Press, 1967.

Klaus, H. Gustav, ed. *The Socialist Novel in Britain: Towards a Recovery of a Tradition*. Brighton: Harvester, 1982.

Lewald, H. Ernest, ed. *The Cry of Home: Cultural Nationalism and the Modern Writer*. Knoxville: University of Tennessee Press, 1972.

Lindsay, J. *After the Thirties: The Novel in Britain and Its Future*. London: Lawrence & Wishart, 1956.

Lodge, David. *The Language of Fiction: Essays in Criticism and Verbal Analysis of the English Novel*. New York: Columbia University Press, 1966.

Lodge. *The Novelist at the Crossroads and Other Essays on Fiction and Criticism*. Ithaca, N.Y.: Cornell University Press, 1971.

Madden, David. *A Primer of the Novel: For Readers and Writers*. Metuchen, N.J. & London: Scarecrow Press, 1980.

McEwan, Neil. *The Survival of the Novel: British Fiction in the Late Twentieth Century*. London: Macmillan, 1981.

Miles, Rosaline. *The Fiction of Sex*. New York: Barnes & Noble, 1976.

Morris, Robert K. *Old Lines, New Forces: Essays on the Contemporary English Novel, 1960-1970*. Rutherford, N.J.: Fairleigh Dickinson Press, 1976.

O'Connor, William Van. *The New University Wits and the Ends of Modernism*. Carbondale: Southern Illinois University Press, 1963.

Parinder, Peter. *Science Fiction: Its Criticism and Teaching*. London & New York: Methuen, 1980.

Reed, John R. *Old School Ties: The Public Schools in English Literature*. Syracuse: Syracuse University Press, 1964.

Rose, Mark. *Alien Encounters: Anatomy of Science Fiction*. Cambridge, Mass.: Harvard University Press, 1981.

Ross, Stephen D. *Literature and Philosophy: An Analysis of the Philosophical Novel*. New York: Appleton-Century Crofts, 1969.

Scholes, Robert and Robert Kellogg. *The Nature of Narrative*. New York: Oxford University Press, 1966.

Shapiro, C. *Contemporary British Novelists*. Carbondale, Ill.: University of Southern Illinois, 1965.

Smith, David J. *Socialist Propaganda in the 20th-Century British Novel*. Totowa, N.J.: Rowman & Littlefield, 1978.

Spilka, Mark, ed. *Towards a Poetics of Fiction*. Bloomington & London: University of Indiana Press, 1977.

Stevenson. *Yesterday and After*. Vol. XI, *The History of the English Novel*, edited by Ernest Baker. New York: Barnes & Noble, 1967.

Sutherland, John. *Fiction and the Fiction Industry*. London: Athlone Press, 1978.

Swinden, Patrick. *Unofficial Selves: Character in the Novel from Dickens to the Present Day*. London & New York: Barnes & Noble, 1973.

Toliver, Harold. *Animate Illusions: Explorations of Narrative Structure*. Lincoln: University of Nebraska Press, 1974.

Warrick, Patricia S. *The Cybernetic Imagination in Science Fiction*. Cambridge, Mass. & London: MIT Press, 1980.

West, Paul. *The Modern Novel*. London: Hutchinson, 1963.

Wicker, Brian. *The Story-Shaped World: Fiction and Metaphysics*. London: Athlone, 1975.

Wilson, Colin. *The Craft of the Novel*. London: Gollancz, 1975.

Contributors

Elizabeth Allen...*London, England*
Paul Binding ....*London, England*
Harriet Blodgett...*University of California, Davis*
Mary Rose Callaghan..*Dublin, Ireland*
Linda Canon ....*University of Delaware*
Catherine Wells Cole...*Leatherhead, Surrey*
Cairns Craig ....*University of Edinburgh*
Simon Edwards..*Roehampton Institute*
Anne Fisher...*University of Delaware*
John Fletcher...*University of East Anglia*
Philip Flynn...*University of Delaware*
Kathleen Fullbrook ....*Tavistock, England*
Bill Grantham..*Sheffield, England*
Colin Greenland ....*North East London Polytechnic*
Joan Grumman ....*Santa Barbara City College*
Patricia Boyle Haberstroh ....*La Salle College*
Jay L. Halio ....*University of Delaware*
Sheila G. Hearn ....*University of Edinburgh*
Gordon Henderson ....*Newark, Delaware*
Alan Hollinghurst ....*London, England*
Dennis Jackson...*University of Delaware*
Fleda Brown Jackson ....*University of Arkansas*
John P. Kent ....*West Chester State College*
Anne Kowalewski ....*Wilmington, Delaware*
Georgia L. Lambert...*London, England*
Jane Langton...*Lincoln, Massachusetts*
Morton P. Levitt...*Temple University*
Margaret B. Lewis ....*Durham, England*
Peter Lewis...*University of Durham*
Judith Mackrell...*Oxford University*
Susan Matthews ....*St. Anne's College, Oxford*
Brian McLaughlin ....*Pennsylvania State University*
Glenda Norquay..*University of Edinburgh*
Malcolm Page ....*Simon Fraser University*
Michelle Poirier...*University of Delaware*
Catherine Smith ....*Atlanta, Georgia*
Elizabeth Holly Snyder ....*University of Delaware*
June Sturrock...*Simon Fraser University*
Lindsey Tucker...*Newark, Delaware*
Teresa Valbuena...*Newark, Delaware*
Judith Vincent..*College of Ripon & York*
John A. Weigel ....*Oxford, Ohio*
Amanda M. Weir...*Swarthmore, Pennsylvania*
Rene J. A. Weis...*University College, London*
Gerard Werson ....*London, England*

Cumulative Index

Dictionary of Literary Biography, Volumes 1-14
Dictionary of Literary Biography Yearbook, 1980, 1981
Dictionary of Literary Biography Documentary Series, Volumes 1-3

Cumulative Index

DLB before number: *Dictionary of Literary Biography*, Volumes 1-14
Y before number: *Dictionary of Literary Biography Yearbook*, 1980, 1981
DS before number: *Dictionary of Literary Biography Documentary Series*, Volumes 1-3

A

Abbott, Jacob 1803-1879 ....DLB1

Adamic, Louis 1898-1951 ....DLB9

Adams, Henry 1838-1918 ....DLB12

Ade, George 1866-1944...............................DLB11

Adeler, Max (see Clark, Charles Heber)

Agassiz, Jean Louis Rodolphe 1807-1873
....DLB1

Agee, James 1909-1955 ....DLB2

Aiken, Conrad 1889-1973 ....DLB9

Albee, Edward 1928- DLB7

Alcott, Amos Bronson 1799-1888 ....DLB1

Alcott, Louisa May 1832-1888.......................DLB1

Alcott, William Andrus 1798-1859 ....DLB1

Aldiss, Brian W. 1925- DLB14

Algren, Nelson 1909-1981.............................DLB9

Alldritt, Keith 1935- DLB14

Allen, Hervey 1889-1949...............................DLB9

Josiah Allen's Wife (see Holly, Marietta)

Allston, Washington 1779-1843 ....DLB1

Alvarez, A. 1929- DLB14

Amis, Martin 1949- DLB14

Ammons, A. R. 1926- DLB5

Anderson, Margaret 1886-1973 ....DLB4

Anderson, Maxwell 1888-1959.....................DLB7

Anderson, Poul 1926- DLB8

Anderson, Robert 1917- DLB7

Anderson, Sherwood 1876-1941
....DLB4, 9; DS1

Anthony, Piers 1934- DLB8

Archer, William 1856-1924 ....DLB10

Arden, John 1930- DLB13

Arnow, Harriette Simpson 1908- DLB6

Arp, Bill (see Smith, Charles Henry)

Arthur, Timothy Shay 1809-1885................DLB3

Asch, Nathan 1902-1964 ....DLB4

Ashbery, John 1927- DLB5; Y81

Ashton, Winifred (see Dane, Clemence)

Asimov, Isaac 1920- DLB8

Atherton, Gertrude 1857-1948 ....DLB9

Auchincloss, Louis 1917- DLB2; Y80

Auden, W. H. 1907-1973 ....DLB10

Austin, Mary 1868-1934 ....DLB9

Ayckbourn, Alan 1939- DLB13

B

Bacon, Delia 1811-1859.................................DLB1

Bagnold, Enid 1889-1981 ....DLB13

Bailey, Paul 1937- DLB14

Bainbridge, Beryl 1933- DLB14

Bald, Wambly 1902- DLB4

Baldwin, James 1924- DLB2, 7

Baldwin, Joseph Glover 1815-1864
....DLB3, 11

Ballard, J. G. 1930- DLB14

Bancroft, George 1800-1891 ....DLB1

Bangs, John Kendrick 1862-1922 ....DLB11

Banville, John 1945- DLB14

Baraka, Amiri 1934-...............................DLB5, 7

Barker, A. L. 1918- DLB14

Barker, Harley Granville 1877-1946
....DLB10

Barker, Howard 1946- DLB13

Barks, Coleman 1937- DLB5

Barnes, Djuna 1892-1982................DLB4, 9

Barnes, Margaret Ayer 1886-1967................DLB9

Barnes, Peter 1931- DLB13

Barney, Natalie 1876-1972................DLB4

Barrie, James M. 1860-1937................DLB10

Barry, Philip 1896-1949 ....DLB7

Barstow, Stan 1928- DLB14

Barth, John 1930- DLB2

Barthelme, Donald 1931- DLB2; Y80

Bartlett, John 1820-1905................DLB1

Bartol, Cyrus Augustus 1813-1900................DLB1

Bass, T. J. 1932- Y81

Bassler, Thomas Joseph (see T. J. Bass)

Baumbach, Jonathan 1933- Y80

Bawden, Nina 1925- DLB14

Bax, Clifford 1886-1962................DLB10

Beach, Sylvia 1887-1962................DLB4

Beagle, Peter S. 1939- Y80

Beal, M. F. 1937- Y81

Beckett, Samuel 1906- DLB13

Beecher, Catharine Esther 1800-1878
................DLB1

Beecher, Henry Ward 1813-1887 ....DLB3

Behan, Brendan 1923-1964 ....DLB13

Behrman, S. N. 1893-1973................DLB7

Belasco, David 1853-1931................DLB7

Belitt, Ben 1911- DLB5

Bell, Marvin 1937- DLB5

Bellamy, Edward 1850-1898 ....DLB12

Bellow, Saul 1915- DLB2; DS3

Benchley, Robert 1889-1945................DLB11

Benedictus, David 1938- DLB14

Benedikt, Michael 1935- DLB5

Benét, Stephen Vincent 1898-1943
................DLB4

Benjamin, Park 1809-1864................DLB3

Bennett, Arnold 1867-1931................DLB10

Berg, Stephen 1934- DLB5

Berger, John 1926- DLB14

Berger, Thomas 1924- DLB2; Y80

Berrigan, Daniel 1921- DLB5

Berrigan, Ted 1934- DLB5

Berry, Wendell 1934- DLB5, 6

Bester, Alfred 1913- DLB8

Bierce, Ambrose 1842-1914? DLB11, 12

Biggle, Lloyd, Jr. 1923- DLB8

Biglow, Hosea (see Lowell, James Russell)

Billings, Josh (see Shaw, Henry Wheeler)

Bird, William 1888-1963 ....DLB4

Bishop, Elizabeth 1911-1979................DLB5

Bishop, John Peale 1892-1944................DLB4, 9

Blackburn, Paul 1926-1971 ....Y81

Blackwood, Caroline 1931- DLB14

Bledsoe, Albert Taylor 1809-1877................DLB3

Blish, James 1921-1975 ....DLB8

Bly, Robert 1926- DLB5

Bodenheim, Maxwell 1892-1954................DLB9

Boer, Charles 1939- DLB5

Bogarde, Dirk 1921- DLB14

Bolt, Robert 1924- DLB13

Bond, Edward 1934- DLB13

Botta, Anne C. Lynch 1815-1891 ....DLB3

Bottomley, Gordon 1874-1948................DLB10

Boucher, Anthony 1911-1968................DLB8

Bourjaily, Vance 1922- DLB2

Bova, Ben 1932- Y81

Bowen, Francis 1811-1890 ....DLB1

Bowen, John 1924- DLB13

Bowers, Edgar 1924- DLB5

Bowles, Paul 1910- DLB5, 6

Boyd, James 1888-1944 ....DLB9

Boyd, John 1919- DLB8

Boyd, Thomas 1898-1935 ....DLB9

Boyesen, Hjalmar Hjorth 1848-1895..........DLB12

Boyle, Kay 1902- DLB4, 9

Brackett, Leigh 1915-1978 ....DLB8

Brackenridge, Hugh Henry 1748-1816
....DLB11

Bradbury, Malcolm 1932- DLB14

Bradbury, Ray 1920- DLB2, 8

Bradley, Marion Zimmer 1930- DLB8

Bradley, William Aspenwall 1878-1939
....DLB4

Bragg, Melvyn 1939- DLB14

Brautigan, Richard 1935- DLB2, 5; Y80

Brenton, Howard 1942- DLB13

Bridie, James 1888-1951 ....DLB10

Briggs, Charles Frederick 1804-1877
....DLB3

Brighouse, Harold 1882-1958....................DLB10

Brisbane, Albert 1809-1890.......................DLB3

Bromfield, Louis 1896-1956 ....DLB4, 9

Brooke-Rose, Christine 1926- DLB14

Brooks, Charles Timothy 1813-1883 ....DLB1

Brooks, Gwendolyn 1917- DLB5

Brooks, Jeremy 1926- DLB14

Brophy, Brigid 1929- DLB14

Brother Antoninus (see Everson, William)

Brougham, John 1810-1880.......................DLB11

Broughton, James 1913- DLB5

Brown, Bob 1886-1959.............................DLB4

Brown, Christy 1932-1981.........................DLB14

Brown, Dee 1908- Y80

Brown, Fredric 1906-1972 ....DLB8

Brown, George Mackay 1921- DLB14

Brown, William Wells 1813-1884................DLB3

Browne, Charles Farrar 1834-1867 ....DLB11

Browne, Wynyard 1911-1964.....................DLB13

Brownson, Orestes Augustus 1803-1876......DLB1

Bryant, William Cullen 1794-1878................DLB3

Buck, Pearl S. 1892-1973 ....DLB9

Buckley, William F., Jr. 1925- Y80

Budrys, A. J. 1931- DLB8

Buechner, Frederick 1926- Y80

Bukowski, Charles 1920- DLB5

Bullins, Ed 1935- DLB7

Bumpus, Jerry 1937- Y81

Burgess, Anthony 1917- DLB14

Burgess, Gelett 1866-1951..........................DLB11

Burnett, W. R. 1899- DLB9

Burns, Alan 1929- DLB14

Burroughs, Edgar Rice 1875-1950 ....DLB8

Burroughs, William Seward 1914-
....DLB2, 8; Y81

Burroway, Janet 1936- DLB6

Busch, Frederick 1941- DLB6

Byatt, A. S. 1936- DLB14

Byrne, John Keyes (see Leonard, Hugh)

C

Cabell, James Branch 1879-1958 ....DLB9

Cable, George Washington 1844-1925
....DLB12

Cahan, Abraham 1860-1951 ....DLB9

Caldwell, Erskine 1903- DLB9

Calhoun, John C. 1782-1850........................DLB3

Calisher, Hortense 1911- DLB2

Calmer, Edgar 1907- DLB4

Calvert, George Henry 1803-1889................DLB1

Campbell, John W., Jr. 1910-1971................DLB8

Cannan, Gilbert 1884-1955 ....DLB10

Cannell, Kathleen 1891-1974......................DLB4

Cantwell, Robert 1908-1978 ....DLB9

Capote, Truman 1924- DLB2; Y80

Carroll, Gladys Hasty 1904- DLB9

Carroll, Paul Vincent 1900-1968.................DLB10

Carruth, Hayden 1921- DLB5

Carter, Angela 1940- DLB14

Carter, Lin 1930- Y81

Caruthers, William Alexander 1802-1846
....DLB3

Casey, Juanita 1925- DLB14

Casey, Michael 1947- DLB5

Cassill, R. V. 1919- DLB6

Cather, Willa 1873-1947.....................DLB9; DS1

Caute, David 1936- DLB14

Chambers, Charles Haddon 1860-1921
....DLB10

Channing, Edward Tyrrell 1790-1856
....DLB1

Channing, William Ellery 1780-1842
....DLB1

Channing, William Ellery, II 1817-1901
....DLB1

Channing, William Henry 1810-1884
....DLB1

Chappell, Fred 1936- DLB6

Charles, Gerda 1914- DLB14

Chayefsky, Paddy 1923-1981 ....DLB7; Y81

Cheever, John 1912-1982.....................DLB2; Y80

Cheney, Ednah Dow (Littlehale) 1824-1904
....DLB1

Cherryh, C. J. 1942- Y80

Chesnutt, Charles Waddell 1858-1932
....DLB12

Chesterton, G. K. 1874-1936.....................DLB10

Child, Francis James 1825-1896.................DLB1

Child, Lydia Maria 1802-1880 ....DLB1

Childress, Alice 1920- DLB7

Chivers, Thomas Holley 1809-1858
....DLB3

Chopin, Kate 1851-1904.....................DLB12

Christie, Agatha 1890-1976.................DLB13

Churchill, Caryl 1938- DLB13

Ciardi, John 1916- DLB5

Clark, Charles Heber 1841-1915 ....DLB11

Clark, Eleanor 1913- DLB6

Clark, Lewis Gaylord 1808-1873.................DLB3

Clark, Walter Van Tilburg 1909-1971.........DLB9

Clarke, Austin 1896-1974.....................DLB10

Clarke, James Freeman 1810-1888
....DLB1

Clemens, Samuel Langhorne 1835-1910
....DLB11, 12

Clement, Hal 1922- DLB8

Clifton, Lucille 1936- DLB5

Coates, Robert M. 1897-1973
....DLB4, 9

Cobb, Irvin S. 1876-1944 ....DLB11

Cole, Barry 1936- DLB14

Colegate, Isabel 1931- DLB14

Coleman, Emily Holmes 1899-1974
....DLB4

Colwin, Laurie 1944- Y80

Connell, Evan S., Jr. 1924- DLB2; Y81

Connelly, Marc 1890- DLB7; Y80

Conrad, Joseph 1857-1924.....................DLB10

Conroy, Jack 1899- Y81

Conroy, Pat 1945- DLB6

Conway, Moncure Daniel 1832-1907
....DLB1

Cooke, John Esten 1830-1886.....................DLB3

Cooke, Philip Pendleton 1816-1850
....DLB3

Cooke, Rose Terry 1827-1892 ....DLB12

Cooper, Giles 1918-1966 ....DLB13

Cooper, James Fenimore 1789-1851
....DLB3

Coover, Robert 1932- DLB2; Y81

Corman, Cid 1924- DLB5

Corn, Alfred 1943- Y80

Corrington, John William 1932- DLB6

Corso, Gregory 1930- DLB5

Costain, Thomas B. 1885-1965 ....DLB9

Coward, Noel 1899-1973 ....DLB10

Cowley, Malcolm 1898- DLB4; Y81

Coxe, Louis 1918- DLB5

Cozzens, James Gould 1903-1979
...............DLB9; DS2

Craddock, Charles Egbert (see Murfree, Mary N.)

Cranch, Christopher Pearse 1813-1892
...............DLB1

Crane, Hart 1899-1932 ....DLB4

Crane, Stephen 1871-1900 ....DLB12

Crayon, Geoffrey (see Irving, Washington)

Creeley, Robert 1926- DLB5

Cregan, David 1931- DLB13

Crews, Harry 1935- DLB6

Crichton, Michael 1942- Y81

Cristofer, Michael 1946- DLB7

Crockett, David 1786-1836 ....DLB3, 11

Crosby, Caresse 1892-1970 and Crosby,
Harry 1898-1929 ....DLB4

Crothers, Rachel 1878-1958 ....DLB7

Crowley, Mart 1935- DLB7

Croy, Homer 1883-1965 ....DLB4

Cullen, Countee 1903-1946 ....DLB4

Cummings, E. E. 1894-1962 ....DLB4

Cummings, Ray 1887-1957 ....DLB8

Cunningham, J. V. 1911- DLB5

Cuomo, George 1929- Y80

Cuppy, Will 1884-1949 ....DLB11

Curtis, George William 1824-1892
...............DLB1

D

Dall, Caroline Wells (Healey) 1822-1912
...............DLB1

Daly, T. A. 1871-1948 ....DLB11

D'Alton, Louis 1900-1951 ....DLB10

Dana, Charles A. 1819-1897 ....DLB3

Dana, Richard Henry, Jr. 1815-1882
...............DLB1

Dane, Clemence 1887-1965 ....DLB10

Davidson, Avram 1923- DLB8

Davidson, Lionel 1922- DLB14

Daviot, Gordon 1896-1952 ....DLB10

Davis, Charles A. 1795-1867 ....DLB11

Davis, Clyde Brion 1894-1962 ....DLB9

Davis, H. L. 1894-1960 ....DLB9

Davis, Margaret Thomson 1926- DLB14

Davis, Ossie 1917- DLB7

Davis, Richard Harding 1864-1916
...............DLB12

Davison, Peter 1928- DLB5

Day, Clarence 1874-1935 ....DLB11

Deal, Borden 1922- DLB6

De Bow, James D. B. 1820-1867 ....DLB3

de Camp, L. Sprague 1907- DLB8

De Forest, John William 1826-1906
...............DLB12

de Graff, Robert 1895-1981 ....Y81

Delaney, Shelagh 1939- DLB13

Delany, Samuel R. 1942- DLB8

Delbanco, Nicholas 1942- DLB6

DeLillo, Don 1936- DLB6

Dell, Floyd 1887-1969 ....DLB9

del Rey, Lester 1915- DLB8

Dennis, Nigel 1912- DLB13

Derby, George Horatio 1823-1861 ....DLB11

Derleth, August 1909-1971 ....DLB9

DeVoto, Bernard 1897-1955 ....DLB9

De Vries, Peter 1910- DLB6

Dick, Philip K. 1928- DLB8

Dickey, James 1923- DLB5

Dickey, William 1928- DLB5

Dickinson, Emily 1830-1886.......................DLB1

Dickson, Gordon R. 1923- DLB8

Didion, Joan 1934- DLB2; Y81

Di Donato, Pietro 1911- DLB9

Dillard, Annie 1945- Y80

Dillard, R. H. W. 1937- DLB5

Diogenes, Jr. (see Brougham, John)

DiPrima, Diane 1934- DLB5

Disch, Thomas M. 1940- DLB8

Dix, Dorothea Lynde 1802-1887..................DLB1

Doctorow, E. L. 1931- DLB2; Y80

Doesticks, Q. K. Philander, P. B. (see Thomson, Mortimer)

Donnelly, Ignatius 1831-1901 ....DLB12

Donleavy, J. P. 1926- DLB6

Doolittle, Hilda 1886-1961 ....DLB4

Dorn, Edward 1929- DLB5

Dos Passos, John 1896-1970
.........................DLB4, 9; DS1

Douglass, Frederick 1817?-1895 ....DLB1

Downing, J., Major (See Davis, Charles A.)

Downing , Major Jack (see Smith, Seba)

Drabble, Margaret 1939- DLB14

Dreiser, Theodore 1871-1945
.........................DLB9, 12; DS1

Drinkwater, John 1882-1937......................DLB10

Duffy, Maureen 1933- DLB14

Dugan, Alan 1923- DLB5

Dukes, Ashley 1885-1959 ....DLB10

Duncan, Robert 1919- DLB5

Duncan, Ronald 1914-1982.......................DLB13

Dunne, Finley Peter 1867-1936 ....DLB11

Dunne, John Gregory 1932- Y80

Dunning, Ralph Cheever 1878-1930
.........................DLB4

Plunkett, Edward John Moreton Drax,
Lord Dunsany 1878-1957 ....DLB10

Duyckinck, Evert A. 1816-1878 ....DLB3

Duyckinck, George L. 1823-1863.................DLB3

Dwight, John Sullivan 1813-1893 ....DLB1

Dyer, Charles 1928- DLB13

E

Eastlake, William 1917- DLB6

Edgar, David 1948- DLB13

Edmonds, Walter D. 1903- DLB9

Effinger, George Alec 1947- DLB8

Eggleston, Edward 1837-1902....................DLB12

Eigner, Larry 1927- DLB5

Elder, Lonne, III 1931- DLB7

Eliot, T. S. 1888-1965.............................DLB7, 10

Elkin, Stanley 1930- DLB2; Y80

Elliott, Janice 1931- DLB14

Elliott, William 1788-1863 ....DLB3

Ellison, Harlan 1934- DLB8

Ellison, Ralph 1914- DLB2

Emerson, Ralph Waldo 1803-1882
.........................DLB1

Erskine, John 1879-1951 ....DLB9

Ervine, St. John Greer 1883-1971
.........................DLB10

Eshleman, Clayton 1935- DLB5

Everett, Edward 1794-1865.........................DLB1

Everson, William 1912- DLB5

Exley, Frederick 1929- Y81

F

Farmer, Philip José 1918- DLB8

Farrell, J. G. 1935-1979.............................DLB14

Farrell, James T. 1904-1979
.........................DLB4, 9; DS2

Fast, Howard 1914- DLB9

Faulkner, William 1897-1962 ....DLB9, 11; DS2

Faust, Irvin 1924- DLB2; Y80

Fearing, Kenneth 1902-1961 ....DLB9

Federman, Raymond 1928- Y80

Feiffer, Jules 1929- DLB7

Feinstein, Elaine 1930- DLB14

Felton, Cornelius Conway 1807-1862 ....DLB1

Ferber, Edna 1885-1968 ....DLB9

Ferlinghetti, Lawrence 1920?- DLB5

Field, Rachel 1894-1942 ....DLB9

Fields, James Thomas 1817-1881 ....DLB1

Figes, Eva 1932- DLB14

Finney, Jack 1911- DLB8

Finney, Walter Braden (see Finney, Jack)

Fisher, Dorothy Canfield 1879-1958 ....DLB9

Fisher, Vardis 1895-1968 ....DLB9

Fitch, William Clyde 1865-1909 ....DLB7

Fitzgerald, F. Scott 1896-1940 ....DLB4, 9; Y81; DS1

Fitzgerald, Penelope 1916- DLB14

Fitzgerald, Robert 1910- Y80

Flanagan, Thomas 1923- Y80

Flanner, Janet 1892-1978 ....DLB4

Flavin, Martin 1883-1967 ....DLB9

Flecker, James Elroy 1884-1915 ....DLB10

Fletcher, John Gould 1886-1950 ....DLB4

Follen, Eliza Lee (Cabot) 1787-1860 ....DLB1

Follett, Ken 1949- Y81

Foote, Shelby 1916- DLB2

Forché, Carolyn 1950- DLB5

Ford, Charles Henri 1913- DLB4

Ford, Corey 1902-1969 ....DLB11

Ford, Jesse Hill 1928- DLB6

Fornés, María Irene 1930- DLB7

Foster, Michael 1904-1956 ....DLB9

Fowles, John 1926- DLB14

Fox, John, Jr. 1862 or 1863-1919 ....DLB9

Fox, William Price 1926- DLB2; Y81

Fraenkel, Michael 1896-1957 ....DLB4

France, Richard 1938- DLB7

Francis, Convers 1795-1863 ....DLB1

Frank, Waldo 1889-1967 ....DLB9

Frantz, Ralph Jules 1902- DLB4

Frayn, Michael 1933- DLB13, 14

Frederic, Harold 1856-1898 ....DLB12

Freeman, Mary Wilkins 1852-1930 ....DLB12

Friedman, Bruce Jay 1930- DLB2

Friel, Brian 1929- DLB13

Friend, Krebs 1895?-1967? DLB4

Frothingham, Octavius Brooks 1822-1895 ....DLB1

Fry, Christopher 1907- DLB13

Fuchs, Daniel 1909- DLB9

Fuller, Henry Blake 1857-1929 ....DLB12

Fuller, Sarah Margaret, Marchesa D'Ossoli 1810-1850 ....DLB1

Furness, William Henry 1802-1896 ....DLB1

G

Gaddis, William 1922- DLB2

Gaines, Ernest J. 1933- DLB2; Y80

Gale, Zona 1874-1938 ....DLB9

Gallico, Paul 1897-1976 ....DLB9

Galsworthy, John 1867-1933 ....DLB10

Galvin, Brendan 1938- DLB5

Gardam, Jane 1928- DLB14

Gardner, John 1933-1982 ....DLB2

Garland, Hamlin 1860-1940.......................DLB12

Garrett, George 1929- DLB2, 5

Garrison, William Lloyd 1805-1879

....DLB1

Gass, William 1924- DLB2

Geddes, Virgil 1897- DLB4

Gelber, Jack 1932- DLB7

Gems, Pam 1925- DLB13

Gernsback, Hugo 1884-1967.......................DLB8

Gerrold, David 1944- DLB8

Geston, Mark S. 1946- DLB8

Gibson, William 1914- DLB7

Gillespie, A. Lincoln, Jr. 1895-1950

....DLB4

Gilliam, Florence DLB4

Gilliatt, Penelope 1932- DLB14

Gillott, Jacky 1939-1980 ....DLB14

Gilman, Caroline H. 1794-1888

....DLB3

Gilroy, Frank D. 1925- DLB7

Ginsberg, Allen 1926- DLB5

Giovanni, Nikki 1943- DLB5

Glasgow, Ellen 1873-1945 ....DLB9, 12

Glaspell, Susan 1882-1948.........................DLB7, 9

Glass, Montague 1877-1934 ....DLB11

Glück, Louise 1943- DLB5

Godwin, Gail 1937- DLB6

Godwin, Parke 1816-1904 ....DLB3

Gold, Herbert 1924- DLB2; Y81

Gold, Michael 1893-1967...........................DLB9

Goldberg, Dick 1947- DLB7

Goodrich, Samuel Griswold 1793-1860

....DLB1

Gordon, Caroline 1895-1981

....DLB4, 9; Y81

Gordon, Giles 1940- DLB14

Gordon, Mary 1949- DLB6; Y81

Gordone, Charles 1925- DLB7

Goyen, William 1915- DLB2

Grau, Shirley Ann 1929- DLB2

Gray, Asa 1810-1888 ....DLB1

Gray, Simon 1936- DLB13

Grayson, William J. 1788-1863

....DLB3

Greeley, Horace 1811-1872..........................DLB3

Green, Julien 1900- DLB4

Green, Paul 1894-1981.....................DLB7, 9; Y81

Greene, Asa 1789-1838 ....DLB11

Greene, Graham 1904- DLB13

Greenough, Horatio 1805-1852

....DLB1

Greenwood, Walter 1903-1974

....DLB10

Greer, Ben 1948- DLB6

Persse, Isabella Augusta,
        Lady Gregory 1852-1932 ....DLB10

Grey, Zane 1872-1939 ....DLB9

Griffiths, Trevor 1935- DLB13

Griswold, Rufus 1815-1857 ....DLB3

Gross, Milt 1895-1953................................DLB11

Grubb, Davis 1919-1980...............................DLB6

Guare, John 1938- DLB7

Guest, Barbara 1920- DLB5

Guiterman, Arthur 1871-1943 ....DLB11

Gunn, James E. 1923- DLB8

Guthrie, A. B., Jr. 1901- DLB6

Guthrie, Ramon 1896-1973.........................DLB4

Gwynne, Erskine 1898-1948........................DLB4

H

H. D. (see Doolittle, Hilda)

Haines, John 1924- DLB5

Haldeman, Joe 1943- DLB8

Hale, Edward Everett 1822-1909
....DLB1

Hale, Nancy 1908- Y80

Hale, Sara Josepha (Buell) 1788-1879
....DLB1

Haliburton, Thomas Chandler 1796-1865
....DLB11

Hall, Donald 1928- DLB5

Halleck, Fitz-Greene 1790-1867
....DLB3

Halper, Albert 1904- DLB9

Hamilton, Cicely 1872-1952 ....DLB10

Hamilton, Edmond 1904-1977
....DLB8

Hamilton, Patrick 1904-1962 ....DLB10

Hamner, Earl 1923- DLB6

Hampton, Christopher 1946- DLB13

Hankin, St. John 1869-1909
....DLB10

Hanley, Clifford 1922- DLB14

Hannah, Barry 1942- DLB6

Hansberry, Lorraine 1930-1965
....DLB7

Hardwick, Elizabeth 1916- DLB6

Hare, David 1947- DLB13

Hargrove, Marion 1919- DLB11

Harness, Charles L. 1915- DLB8

Harris, George Washington 1814-1869
....DLB3, 11

Harris, Joel Chandler 1848-1908
....DLB11

Harris, Mark 1922- DLB2; Y80

Harrison, Harry 1925- DLB8

Hart, Moss 1904-1961 ....DLB7

Harte, Bret 1836-1902.........................DLB12

Harwood, Ronald 1934- DLB13

Hawkes, John 1925- DLB2; Y80

Hawthorne, Nathaniel 1804-1864
....DLB1

Hay, John 1838-1905.................................DLB12

Hayden, Robert 1913-1980 ....DLB5

Hayne, Paul Hamilton 1830-1886
....DLB3

Hearn, Lafcadio 1850-1904.................DLB12

Heath, Catherine 1924- DLB14

Hecht, Anthony 1923- DLB5

Hecht, Ben 1894-1964.........................DLB7, 9

Hecker, Isaac Thomas 1819-1888
....DLB1

Hedge, Frederic Henry 1805-1890
....DLB1

Heinlein, Robert A. 1907- DLB8

Heller, Joseph 1923- DLB2; Y80

Hellman, Lillian 1906- DLB7

Hemingway, Ernest 1899-1961
.............................DLB4, 9; Y81; DS1

Henderson, Zenna 1917- DLB8

Hentz, Caroline Lee 1800-1856
....DLB3

Herbert, Alan Patrick 1890-1971
....DLB10

Herbert, Frank 1920- DLB8

Herbert, Henry William 1807-1858
....DLB3

Herbst, Josephine 1892-1969
....DLB9

Hergesheimer, Joseph 1880-1954
....DLB9

Herrick, Robert 1868-1938
....DLB9, 12

Herrmann, John 1900-1959
....DLB4

Hersey, John 1914- DLB6

Heyen, William 1940- DLB5

Heyward, Dorothy 1890-1961 and
Heyward, DuBose 1885-1940.............DLB7

Heyward, DuBose 1885-1940
....DLB9

Higgins, Aidan 1927- DLB14

Higgins, George V. 1939- DLB2; Y81

Higginson, Thomas Wentworth 1822-1911
....DLB1

Hildreth, Richard 1807-1865 ....DLB1

Hill, Susan 1942- DLB14

Himes, Chester 1909- DLB2

Hoagland, Edward 1932- DLB6

Hochman, Sandra 1936- DLB5

Hodgman, Helen 1945- DLB14

Hoffenstein, Samuel 1890-1947
....DLB11

Hoffman, Charles Fenno 1806-1884
....DLB3

Hoffman, Daniel 1923- DLB5

Hogan, Desmond 1950- DLB14

Holbrook, David 1923- DLB14

Hollander, John 1929- DLB5

Holley, Marietta 1836-1926 ....DLB11

Holmes, Oliver Wendell 1809-1894
....DLB1

Home, William Douglas 1912- DLB13

Honig, Edwin 1919- DLB5

Hooper, Johnson Jones 1815-1862
....DLB3, 11

Horovitz, Israel 1939- DLB7

Hough, Emerson 1857-1923 ....DLB9

Houghton, Stanley 1881-1913 ....DLB10

Housman, Laurence 1865-1959 ....DLB10

Howard, Richard 1929- DLB5

Howard, Sidney 1891-1939 ....DLB7

Howe, E. W. 1853-1937 ....DLB12

Howe, Julia Ward 1819-1910 ....DLB1

Howells, William Dean 1837-1920
....DLB12

Hoyem, Andrew 1935- DLB5

Hubbard, Kin 1868-1930 ....DLB11

Hughes, David 1930- DLB14

Hughes, Langston 1902-1967
....DLB4, 7

Hugo, Richard 1923-1982 ....DLB5

Humphrey, William 1924- DLB6

Hunter, Jim 1939- DLB14

Hunter, N. C. 1908-1971 ....DLB10

I

Ignatow, David 1914- DLB5

Imbs, Bravig 1904-1946 ....DLB4

Inge, William 1913-1973 ....DLB7

Ingraham, Joseph Holt 1809-1860
....DLB3

Irving, John 1942- DLB6

Irving, Washington 1783-1859
....DLB3, 11

J

Jackson, Shirley 1919-1965 ....DLB6

Jacob, Piers Anthony Dillingham (see Anthony, Piers)

Jacobson, Dan 1929- DLB14

James, Henry 1843-1916 ....DLB12

Jellicoe, Ann 1927- DLB13

Jenkins, Robin 1912- DLB14

Jenkins, William Fitzgerald (see Leinster, Murray)

Jerome, Jerome K. 1859-1927
....DLB10

Jewett, Sarah Orne 1849-1909
....DLB12

Johnson, B. S. 1933-1973 ....DLB14

Johnson, Diane 1934- Y80

Johnson, Samuel 1822-1882 ....DLB1

Johnston, Denis 1901- DLB10

Johnston, Jennifer 1930- DLB14

Johnston, Mary 1870-1936 ....DLB9

Jolas, Eugene 1894-1952 ....DLB4

Jones, Henry Arthur 1851-1929
....DLB10

Jones, James 1921-1977 ....DLB2

Jones, LeRoi (see Baraka, Amiri)

Jones, Major Joseph (see Thompson, William Tappan)

Jones, Preston 1936-1979 ....DLB7

Jong, Erica 1942- DLB2, 5

Josephson, Matthew 1899-1978
....DLB4

Josipovici, Gabriel 1940- DLB14

Joyce, James 1882-1941 ....DLB10

Judd, Sylvester 1813-1853 ....DLB1

K

Kanin, Garson 1912- DLB7

Kantor, Mackinlay 1904-1977 ....DLB9

Kaufman, George S. 1889-1961 ....DLB7

Keane, John B. 1928- DLB13

Keeffe, Barrie 1945- DLB13

Kelley, Edith Summers 1884-1956
....DLB9

Kelly, George 1887-1974 ....DLB7

Kelly, Robert 1935- DLB5

Kennedy, John Pendleton 1795-1870
....DLB3

Kennedy, X. J. 1929- DLB5

Kerouac, Jack 1922-1969 ....DLB2; DS3

Kerr, Orpheus C. (see Newell, Robert Henry)

Kesey, Ken 1935- DLB2

Kiley, Jed 1889-1962 ....DLB4

King, Clarence 1842-1901 ....DLB12

King, Grace 1852-1932................................DLB12

King, Stephen 1947- Y80

Kingsley, Sidney 1906- DLB7

Kingston, Maxine Hong 1940- Y80

Kinnell, Galway 1927- DLB5

Kirkland, Caroline 1801-1864.....................DLB3

Kirkland, Joseph 1830-1893........................DLB12

Kizer, Carolyn 1925- DLB5

Klappert, Peter 1942- DLB5

Klass, Philip (see Tenn, William)

Knickerbocker, Diedrick (see Irving, Washington)

Knight, Damon 1922- DLB8

Knoblock, Edward 1874-1945 ....DLB10

Knowles, John 1926- DLB6

Kober, Arthur 1900-1975.............................DLB11

Koch, Kenneth 1925- DLB5

Komroff, Manuel 1890-1974........................DLB4

Kopit, Arthur 1937- DLB7

Kops, Bernard 1926?...................................DLB13

Kornbluth, C. M. 1923-1958 ....DLB8

Kosinski, Jerzy 1933- DLB2

Kraf, Elaine 1946- Y81

Kreymborg, Alfred 1883-1966......................DLB4

Kumin, Maxine 1925- DLB5

Kuttner, Henry 1915-1958............................DLB8

L

La Farge, Oliver 1901-1963 ....DLB9

Lafferty, R. A. 1914- DLB8

L'Amour, Louis 1908?- Y80

Lane, Charles 1800-1870..............................DLB1

Laney, Al 1896- DLB4

Lanham, Edwin 1904-1979 ....DLB4

Lardner, Ring 1885-1933 ....DLB11

Laumer, Keith 1925- DLB8

Lawrence, D. H. 1885-1930.........................DLB10

Lea, Tom 1907- DLB6

Lee, Don L. (see Haki R. Madhubuti)

Lee, Harper 1926- DLB6

Le Gallienne, Richard 1866-1947

....DLB4

Legare, Hugh Swinton 1797-1843

....DLB3

Legare, James M. 1823-1859......................DLB3

Le Guin, Ursula K. 1929- DLB8

Leiber, Fritz 1910- DLB8

Leinster, Murray 1896-1975....................DLB8

Leitch, Maurice 1933- DLB14

Leland, Charles G. 1824-1903...................DLB11

Leonard, Hugh 1926- DLB13

Levertov, Denise 1923- DLB5

Levin, Meyer 1905-1981

....DLB9; Y81

Levine, Philip 1928- DLB5

Levy, Benn Wolfe 1900-1973

....Y81; DLB13

Lewis, Charles B. 1842-1924.....................DLB11

Lewis, Henry Clay 1825-1850.....................DLB3

Lewis, Sinclair 1885-1951....................DLB9; DS1

Lewisohn, Ludwig 1882-1955..................DLB4, 9

Liebling, A. J. 1904-1963.......................DLB4

Linebarger, Paul Myron Anthony (see Smith, Cordwainer)

Littlewood, Joan 1914- DLB13

Lively, Penelope 1933- DLB14

Livings, Henry 1929- DLB13

Locke, David Ross 1833-1888.....................DLB11

Lockridge, Ross, Jr. 1914-1948...................Y80

Lodge, David 1935- DLB14

Loeb, Harold 1891-1974.........................DLB4

Logan, John 1923- DLB5

London, Jack 1876-1916.......................DLB8, 12

Longfellow, Henry Wadsworth 1807-1882

....DLB1

Longfellow, Samuel 1819-1892

....DLB1

Longstreet, Augustus Baldwin 1790-1870

....DLB3, 11

Lonsdale, Frederick 1881-1954..................DLB10

Loos, Anita 1893-1981......................DLB11; Y81

Lopate, Phillip 1943- Y80

Lovingood, Sut (see Harris, George Washington)

Lowell, James Russell 1819-1891

....DLB1, 11

Lowell, Robert 1917-1977.......................DLB5

Lowenfels, Walter 1897-1976....................DLB4

Loy, Mina 1882-1966...........................DLB4

Luke, Peter 1919- DLB13

Lurie, Alison 1926- DLB2

Lytle, Andrew 1902- DLB6

M

MacArthur, Charles 1895-1956...................DLB7

MacDonald, John D. 1916- DLB8

MacInnes, Colin 1914-1976......................DLB14

Macken, Walter 1915-1967......................DLB13

MacLean, Katherine Anne 1925- DLB8

MacLeish, Archibald 1892-1982 ....DLB4, 7

Macleod, Norman 1906- DLB4

MacNamara, Brinsley 1890-1963

....DLB10

MacNeice, Louis 1907-1963 ....DLB10

Madden, David 1933- DLB6

Madhubuti, Haki R. 1942- DLB5

Mailer, Norman 1923- DLB2; Y80; DS3

Malamud, Bernard 1914- DLB2; Y80

Malzberg, Barry N. 1939- DLB8

Mamet, David 1947- DLB7

Manfred, Frederick 1912- DLB6

Mangan, Sherry 1904-1961.......................DLB4

Mann, Horace 1796-1859.............................DLB1

Mano, D. Keith 1942- DLB6

March, William 1893-1954 ....DLB9

Marcus, Frank 1928- DLB13

Markfield, Wallace 1926- DLB2

Marquand, John P. 1893-1960
....DLB9

Marquis, Don 1878-1937 ....DLB11

Marsh, George Perkins 1801-1882
....DLB1

Marsh, James 1794-1842 ....DLB1

Martin, Abe (see Hubbard, Kin)

Martyn, Edward 1859-1923..........................DLB10

Masefield, John 1878-1967.........................DLB10

Matheson, Richard 1926- DLB8

Mathews, Cornelius 1817-1889 ....DLB3

Matthews, Jack 1925- DLB6

Matthews, William 1942- DLB5

Matthiessen, Peter 1927- DLB6

Maugham, W. Somerset 1874-1965
....DLB10

Mavor, Elizabeth 1927- DLB14

Mavor, Osborne Henry (see Bridie, James)

Maxwell, William 1908- Y80

Mayer, O. B. 1818-1891 ....DLB3

McAlmon, Robert 1896-1956........................DLB4

McCaffrey, Anne 1926- DLB8

McCarthy, Cormac 1933- DLB6

McCarthy, Mary 1912- DLB2; Y81

McCoy, Horace 1897-1955 ....DLB9

McCullers, Carson 1917-1967 ....DLB2, 7

McEwan, Ian 1948- DLB14

McGahern, John 1934- DLB14

McGinley, Phyllis 1905-1978 ....DLB11

McGuane, Thomas 1939- DLB2; Y80

McIlvanney, William 1936- DLB14

McKay, Claude 1889-1948 ....DLB4

McMurtry, Larry 1936- DLB2; Y80

McNally, Terrence 1939- DLB7

Medoff, Mark 1940- DLB7

Meek, Alexander Beaufort 1814-1865
....DLB3

Meinke, Peter 1932- DLB5

Melville, Herman 1819-1891........................DLB3

Mencken, H. L. 1880-1956.........................DLB11

Mercer, David 1928-1980 ....DLB13

Meredith, William 1919- DLB5

Merrill, James 1926- DLB5

Merton, Thomas 1915-1968 ....Y81

Merwin, W. S. 1927- DLB5

Mewshaw, Michael 1943- Y80

Michener, James A. 1907?- DLB6

Middleton, Stanley 1919- DLB14

Millar, Kenneth 1915- DLB2

Miller, Arthur 1915- DLB7

Miller, Caroline 1903- DLB9

Miller, Henry 1891-1980
....DLB4, 9; Y80

Miller, Jason 1939- DLB7

Miller, Walter M., Jr. 1923- DLB8

Millhauser, Steven 1943- DLB2

Milne, A. A. 1882-1956 ....DLB10

Mitchell, Donald Grant 1822-1908
....DLB1

Mitchell, Julian 1935- DLB14

Mitchell, Langdon 1862-1935 ....DLB7

Mitchell, Margaret 1900-1949 ....DLB9

Monkhouse, Allan 1858-1936 ....DLB10

Montgomery, Marion 1925- DLB6

Moody, William Vaughn 1869-1910
....DLB7

Moorcock, Michael 1939- DLB14

Moore, Catherine L. 1911- DLB8

Moore, George 1852-1933..........................DLB10

Moore, Ward 1903-1978 ....DLB8

Morgan, Berry 1919- DLB6

Morley, Christopher 1890-1957
................................DLB9

Morris, Willie 1934- Y80

Morris, Wright 1910- DLB2; Y81

Morrison, Toni 1931- DLB6; Y81

Mortimer, John 1923- DLB13

Mosley, Nicholas 1923- DLB14

Moss, Arthur 1889-1969.............DLB4

Moss, Howard 1922- DLB5

Motley, John Lothrop 1814-1877
................................DLB1

Muir, Helen 1937- DLB14

Murdoch, Iris 1919- DLB14

Murfree, Mary N. 1850-1922.......DLB12

Murray, Gilbert 1866-1957.........DLB10

N

Nabokov, Vladimir 1899-1977
.................DLB2; Y80; DS3

Nasby, Petroleum Vesuvius (see Locke, David Ross)

Nash, Ogden 1902-1971.............DLB11

Nathan, Robert 1894- DLB9

Naughton, Bill 1910- DLB13

Neagoe, Peter 1881-1960 ....DLB4

Neal, John 1793-1876...............DLB1

Neal, Joseph C. 1807-1847.........DLB11

Neihardt, John G. 1881-1973.......DLB9

Nemerov, Howard 1920- DLB5, 6

Newcomb, Charles King 1820-1894
................................DLB1

Newell, Robert Henry 1836-1901
...............................DLB11

Newman, Frances 1883-1928 ....Y80

Nichols, Mary Sargeant (Neal)
Gove 1810-1884 ....DLB1

Nichols, Peter 1927- DLB13

Niggli, Josefina 1910- Y80

Nims, John Frederick 1913- DLB5

Nin, Anais 1903-1977...............DLB2, 4

Niven, Larry 1938- DLB8

Nolan, William F. 1928- DLB8

Noland, C. F. M. 1810?-1858........DLB11

Noone, John 1936- DLB14

Nordhoff, Charles 1887-1947
................................DLB9

Norris, Charles G. 1881-1945 ......DLB9

Norris, Frank 1870-1902 ....DLB12

Norton, Alice Mary (see Norton, Andre)

Norton, Andre 1912- DLB8

Norton, Andrews 1786-1853
................................DLB1

Norton, Charles Eliot 1827-1908
................................DLB1

Nourse, Alan E. 1928- DLB8

Nye, Bill 1850-1896 ....DLB11

Nye, Robert 1939- DLB14

O

Oates, Joyce Carol 1938- DLB2, 5; Y81

O'Brien, Edna 1932- DLB14

O'Brien, Tim 1946- Y80

O'Casey, Sean 1880-1964 ....DLB10

O'Connor, Flannery 1925-1964
........................DLB2; Y80

Odets, Clifford 1906-1963...........DLB7

O'Faolain, Julia 1932- DLB14

O'Hara, Frank 1926-1966 ....DLB5

O'Hara, John 1905-1970.......DLB9; DS2

O. Henry (see Porter, William S.)

Oliver, Chad 1928- DLB8

Oliver, Mary 1935- DLB5

Olsen, Tillie 1912 or 1913- Y80

Olson, Charles 1910-1970 ....DLB5

O'Neill, Eugene 1888-1953 ....DLB7

Oppen, George 1908- DLB5

Oppenheimer, Joel 1930- DLB5

Orlovitz, Gil 1918-1973 ....DLB2, 5

Orton, Joe 1933-1967 ....DLB13

Osborne, John 1929- DLB13

Owen, Guy 1925- DLB5

P

Pack, Robert 1929- DLB5

Padgett, Ron 1942- DLB5

Page, Thomas Nelson 1853-1922
....DLB12

Palfrey, John Gorham 1796-1881
....DLB1

Pangborn, Edgar 1909-1976 ....DLB8

Panshin, Alexei 1940- DLB8

Parker, Dorothy 1893-1967 ....DLB11

Parker, Theodore 1810-1860 ....DLB1

Parkman, Francis, Jr. 1823-1893
....DLB1

Pastan, Linda 1932- DLB5

Patrick, John 1906- DLB7

Paul, Elliot 1891-1958 ....DLB4

Paulding, James Kirke 1778-1860
....DLB3

Peabody, Elizabeth Palmer 1804-1894
....DLB1

Percy, Walker 1916- DLB2; Y80

Perelman, S. J. 1904-1979 ....DLB11

Peterkin, Julia 1880-1961 ....DLB9

Phillips, David Graham 1867-1911
....DLB9, 12

Phillips, Jayne Anne 1952- Y80

Phillips, Stephen 1864-1915 ....DLB10

Phillpotts, Eden 1862-1960 ....DLB10

Phoenix, John (see Derby, George Horatio)

Pinckney, Josephine 1895-1957
....DLB6

Pinero, Arthur Wing 1855-1934
....DLB10

Pinter, Harold 1930- DLB13

Piper, H. Beam 1904-1964 ....DLB8

Plath, Sylvia 1932-1963 ....DLB5, 6

Plumly, Stanley 1939- DLB5

Plunkett, James 1920- DLB14

Poe, Edgar Allan 1809-1849 ....DLB3

Pohl, Frederik 1919- DLB8

Poliakoff, Stephen 1952- DLB13

Poole, Ernest 1880-1950 ....DLB9

Porter, Eleanor H. 1868-1920
....DLB9

Porter, Katherine Anne 1890-1980
....DLB4, 9; Y80

Porter, William S. 1862-1910 ....DLB12

Porter, William T. 1809-1858 ....DLB3

Portis, Charles 1933- DLB6

Pound, Ezra 1885-1972 ....DLB4

Pownall, David 1938- DLB14

Prescott, William Hickling 1796-1859
....DLB1

Price, Reynolds 1933- DLB2

Price, Richard 1949- Y81

Priest, Christopher 1943- DLB14

Priestley, J. B. 1894- DLB10

Purdy, James 1923- DLB2

Putnam, George Palmer 1814-1872
....DLB3

Putnam, Samuel 1892-1950 ....DLB4

Puzo, Mario 1920- DLB6

Pym, Barbara 1913-1980 ....DLB14

Pynchon, Thomas 1937- DLB2

Q

Quad, M. (see Lewis, Charles B.)

Quin, Ann 1936-1973.................................DLB14

R

Rabe, David 1940- DLB7

Raphael, Frederic 1931- DLB14

Rattigan, Terence 1911-1977.....................DLB13

Rawlings, Marjorie Kinnan 1896-1953
....DLB9

Ray, David 1932- DLB5

Read, Piers Paul 1941- DLB14

Reed, Ishmael 1938- DLB2, 5

Reed, Sampson 1800-1880 ....DLB1

Remington, Frederic 1861-1909 ....DLB12

Reynolds, Mack 1917- DLB8

Rice, Elmer 1892-1967 ....DLB4, 7

Rich, Adrienne 1929- DLB5

Richardson, Jack 1935- DLB7

Richter, Conrad 1890-1968 ....DLB9

Riddell, John (see Ford, Corey)

Ripley, George 1802-1880..........................DLB1

Ritchie, Anna Mowatt 1819-1870
....DLB3

Robbins, Tom 1936- Y80

Roberts, Elizabeth Madox 1881-1941
....DLB9

Roberts, Kenneth 1885-1957......................DLB9

Robinson, Lennox 1886-1958 ....DLB10

Roethke, Theodore 1908-1963 ....DLB5

Rogers, Will 1879-1935 ....DLB11

Roiphe, Anne 1935- Y80

Rölvaag, O. E. 1876-1931 ....DLB9

Root, Waverley 1903- DLB4

Rosenthal, M. L. 1917- DLB5

Ross, Leonard Q. (see Rosten, Leo)

Rossner, Judith 1935- DLB6

Rosten, Leo 1908- DLB11

Roth, Philip 1933- DLB2

Rothenberg, Jerome 1931- DLB5

Rubens, Bernice 1928- DLB14

Rudkin, David 1956- DLB13

Runyon, Damon 1880-1946 ....DLB11

Russ, Joanna 1937- DLB8

S

Saberhagen, Fred 1930- DLB8

Sackler, Howard 1929- DLB7

Sage, Robert 1899-1962..............................DLB4

Salemson, Harold J. 1910- DLB4

Salinger, J. D. 1919- DLB2

Sanborn, Franklin Benjamin 1831-1917
....DLB1

Sandoz, Mari 1896-1966.............................DLB9

Sargent, Pamela 1948- DLB8

Saroyan, William 1908-1981
....DLB7, 9; Y81

Sarton, May 1912- Y81

Saunders, James 1925- DLB13

Sayers, Dorothy L. 1893-1957....................DLB10

Schmitz, James H. 1911- DLB8

Schulberg, Budd 1914- DLB6; Y81

Schuyler, James 1923- DLB5

Scott, Evelyn 1893-1963 ....DLB9

Scott, Paul 1920-1978 ....DLB14

Seabrook, William 1886-1945.....................DLB4

Sedgwick, Catharine Maria 1789-1867
....DLB1

Selby, Hubert, Jr. 1928- DLB2

Settle, Mary Lee 1918- DLB6

Sexton, Anne 1928-1974 ....DLB5

Shaffer, Anthony 1926- DLB13

Shaffer, Peter 1926- DLB13

Shairp, Mordaunt 1887-1939 ....DLB10

Sharpe, Tom 1928- DLB14

Shaw, Bernard 1856-1950 ....DLB10

Shaw, Henry Wheeler 1818-1885

....DLB11

Shaw, Irwin 1913- DLB6

Shaw, Robert 1927-1978 ....DLB13, 14

Sheckley, Robert 1928- DLB8

Sheed, Wilfred 1930- DLB6

Sheldon, Alice B. (see Tiptree, James, Jr.)

Sheldon, Edward 1886-1946 ....DLB7

Shepard, Sam 1943- DLB7

Sherriff, R. C. 1896-1975 ....DLB10

Sherwood, Robert 1896-1955 ....DLB7

Shiels, George 1886-1949 ....DLB10

Shillaber, Benjamin Penhallow 1814-1890

....DLB1, 11

Shirer, William L. 1904- DLB4

Shulman, Max 1919- DLB11

Shute, Henry A. 1856-1943 ....DLB9

Shuttle, Penelope 1947- DLB14

Sigourney, Lydia Howard (Huntley) 1791-1865

....DLB1

Sillitoe, Alan 1928- DLB14

Silverberg, Robert 1935- DLB8

Simak, Clifford D. 1904- DLB8

Simms, William Gilmore 1806-1870

....DLB3

Simon, Neil 1927- DLB7

Simpson, Louis 1923- DLB5

Simpson, N. F. 1919- DLB13

Sinclair, Andrew 1935- DLB14

Sinclair, Upton 1878-1968 ....DLB9

Singer, Isaac Bashevis 1904- DLB6

Singmaster, Elsie 1879-1958 ....DLB9

Sissman, L. E. 1928-1976 ....DLB5

Slavitt, David 1935- DLB5, 6

Slick, Sam (see Haliburton, Thomas Chandler)

Smith, Carol Sturm 1938- Y81

Smith, Charles Henry 1826-1903

....DLB11

Smith, Cordwainer 1913-1966 ....DLB8

Smith, Dave 1942- DLB5

Smith, Dodie 1896- DLB10

Smith, E. E. 1890-1965 ....DLB8

Smith, Elizabeth Oakes (Prince) 1806-1893

....DLB1

Smith, George O. 1911- DLB8

Smith, H. Allen 1907-1976 ....DLB11

Smith, Seba 1792-1868 ....DLB1, 11

Smith, William Jay 1918- DLB5

Snodgrass, W. D. 1926- DLB5

Snyder, Gary 1930- DLB5

Solano, Solita 1888-1975 ....DLB4

Sontag, Susan 1933- DLB2

Sorrentino, Gilbert 1929- DLB5; Y80

Southern, Terry 1924- DLB2

Sparks, Jared 1789-1866 ....DLB1

Spencer, Elizabeth 1921- DLB6

Spicer, Jack 1925-1965 ....DLB5

Spielberg, Peter 1929- Y81

Spinrad, Norman 1940- DLB8

Squibob (see Derby, George Horatio)

Stafford, Jean 1915-1979 ....DLB2

Stafford, William 1914- DLB5

Stallings, Laurence 1894-1968

....DLB7, 9

Stanford, Ann 1916- DLB5

Starkweather, David 1935- DLB7

Steadman, Mark 1930- DLB6

Stearns, Harold E. 1891-1943 ....DLB4

Steele, Max 1922- Y80

Stegner, Wallace 1909- DLB9

Stein, Gertrude 1874-1946.......................DLB4

Stein, Leo 1872-1947 ....DLB4

Steinbeck, John 1902-1968
....DLB7, 9; DS2

Stephens, Ann 1813-1886 ....DLB3

Stewart, Donald Ogden 1894-1980
....DLB4, 11

Stewart, George R. 1895-1980 ....DLB8

Still, James 1906- DLB9

Stoddard, Richard Henry 1825-1903
....DLB3

Stoppard, Tom 1937- DLB13

Storey, Anthony 1928- DLB14

Storey, David 1933- DLB13, 14

Story, William Wetmore 1819-1895
....DLB1

Stowe, Harriet Beecher 1811-1896
....DLB1, 12

Strand, Mark 1934- DLB5

Streeter, Edward 1891-1976.......................DLB11

Stribling, T. S. 1881-1965...........................DLB9

Strother, David Hunter 1816-1888
....DLB3

Stuart, Jesse 1907- DLB9

Stubbs, Harry Clement (see Hal Clement)

Sturgeon, Theodore 1918- DLB8

Styron, William 1925- DLB2; Y80

Suckow, Ruth 1892-1960..............................DLB9

Suggs, Simon (see Hooper, Johnson Jones)

Sukenick, Ronald 1932- Y81

Sullivan, Frank 1892-1976..........................DLB11

Summers, Hollis 1916- DLB6

Sutro, Alfred 1863-1933.............................DLB10

Swados, Harvey 1920-1972 ....DLB2

Swenson, May 1919- DLB5

Synge, John Millington 1871-1909
....DLB10

T

Tarkington, Booth 1869-1946.......................DLB9

Tate, Allen 1896-1979.................................DLB4

Tate, James 1943- DLB5

Taylor, Bayard 1825-1878..........................DLB3

Taylor, Henry 1942- DLB5

Taylor, Peter 1917- Y81

Tenn, William 1919- DLB8

Tennant, Emma 1937- DLB14

Terhune, Albert Payson 1872-1942
....DLB9

Terry, Megan 1932- DLB7

Terson, Peter 1932- DLB13

Theroux, Paul 1941- DLB2

Thoma, Richard 1902- DLB4

Thomas, Dylan 1914-1953 ....DLB13

Thomas, John 1900-1932 ....DLB4

Thompson, John R. 1823-1873
....DLB3

Thompson, William Tappan 1812-1882
....DLB3, 11

Thomson, Mortimer 1831-1875
....DLB11

Thoreau, Henry David 1817-1862
....DLB1

Thorpe, Thomas Bangs 1815-1878
....DLB3, 11

Thurber, James 1894-1961 ....DLB4, 11

Ticknor, George 1791-1871 ....DLB1

Timrod, Henry 1828-1867 ....DLB3

Tiptree, James, Jr. 1915- DLB8

Titus, Edward William 1870-1952
....DLB4

Toklas, Alice B. 1877-1967 ....DLB4

Tonks, Rosemary 1932- DLB14

Toole, John Kennedy 1937-1969
....Y81

Traven, B. 1882? or 1890?-1969....................DLB9

Travers, Ben 1886-1980..............................DLB10

Tremain, Rose 1943- DLB14

Trevor, William 1928- DLB14

Troop, Elizabeth 1931- DLB14

Tucker, George 1775-1861 ....DLB3

Tucker, Nathaniel Beverley 1784-1851
....DLB3

Tuohy, Frank 1925- DLB14

Twain, Mark (see Clemens, Samuel Langhorne)

Tyler, Anne 1941- DLB6

U

Upchurch, Boyd B. (see Boyd, John)

Updike, John 1932- DLB2, 5; Y80; DS3

Ustinov, Peter 1921- DLB13

V

Vail, Laurence 1891-1968 ....DLB4

Vance, Jack 1916?- DLB8

van Druten, John 1901-1957.......................DLB10

Van Duyn, Mona 1921- DLB5

van Itallie, Jean-Claude 1936- DLB7

Vane, Sutton 1888-1963 ....DLB10

Van Vechten, Carl 1880-1964
....DLB4, 9

van Vogt, A. E. 1912- DLB8

Varley, John 1947- Y81

Very, Jones 1813-1880 ....DLB1

Vidal, Gore 1925- DLB6

Viereck, Peter 1916- DLB5

Vonnegut, Kurt 1922-
....DLB2, 8; Y80; DS3

W

Wagoner, David 1926- DLB5

Wakoski, Diane 1937- DLB5

Walcott, Derek 1930- Y81

Walker, Alice 1944- DLB6

Wallant, Edward Lewis 1926-1962
....DLB2

Walsh, Ernest 1895-1926.............................DLB4

Wambaugh, Joseph 1937- DLB6

Ward, Artemus (see Browne, Charles Farrar)

Ward, Douglas Turner 1930- DLB7

Ware, William 1797-1852.............................DLB1

Warner, Susan B. 1819-1885 ....DLB3

Warren, Robert Penn 1905-
....DLB2; Y80

Wasson, David Atwood 1823-1887
....DLB1

Waterhouse, Keith 1929- DLB13

Waugh, Auberon 1939- DLB14

Webster, Noah 1758-1843 ....DLB1

Weinbaum, Stanley Grauman 1902-1935
....DLB8

Weiss, John 1818-1879 ....DLB1

Weiss, Theodore 1916- DLB5

Weldon, Fay 1931- DLB14

Wells, Carolyn 1862-1942.........................DLB11

Welty, Eudora 1909- DLB2

Wescott, Glenway 1901- DLB4, 9

Wesker, Arnold 1932- DLB13

West, Jessamyn 1902- DLB6

West, Nathanael 1903-1940
....DLB4, 9

West, Paul 1930- DLB14

Wharton, Edith 1862-1937 ....DLB4, 9, 12

Wharton, William 1920s?- Y80

Wheeler, Charles Stearns 1816-1843
....DLB1

Wheeler, Monroe 1900- DLB4

Whetstone, Colonel Pete (see Noland, C. F. M.)

Whipple, Edwin Percy 1819-1886
....DLB1

Whitcher, Frances Miriam 1814-1852 ....DLB11

White, E. B. 1899- DLB11

White, William Allen 1868-1944
....DLB9

White, William Anthony Parker (see Boucher, Anthony)

Whitehead, James 1936- Y81

Whiting, John 1917-1963 ....DLB13

Whitlock, Brand 1869-1934 ....DLB12

Whitman, Sarah Helen (Power) 1803-1878
....DLB1

Whitman, Walt 1819-1892........................DLB3

Whittemore, Reed 1919- DLB5

Whittier, John Greenleaf 1807-1892
....DLB1

Wilbur, Richard 1921- DLB5

Wild, Peter 1940- DLB5

Wilde, Oscar 1854-1900 ....DLB10

Wilde, Richard Henry 1789-1847
....DLB3

Wilder, Thornton 1897-1975
....DLB4, 7, 9

Wilhelm, Kate 1928- DLB8

Willard, Nancy 1936- DLB5

Williams, C. K. 1936- DLB5

Williams, Emlyn 1905- DLB10

Williams, Heathcote 1941- DLB13

Williams, Joan 1928- DLB6

Williams, John A. 1925- DLB2

Williams, John E. 1922- DLB6

Williams, Jonathan 1929- DLB5

Williams, Raymond 1921- DLB14

Williams, Tennessee 1911- DLB7

Williams, William Carlos 1883-1963
....DLB4

Williams, Wirt 1921- DLB6

Williamson, Jack 1908- DLB8

Willingham, Calder, Jr. 1922- DLB2

Willis, Nathaniel Parker 1806-1867
....DLB3

Wilson, A. N. 1950- DLB14

Wilson, Colin 1931- DLB14

Wilson, Harry Leon 1867-1939
....DLB9

Wilson, Lanford 1937- DLB7

Wilson, Margaret 1882-1973 ....DLB9

Windham, Donald 1920- DLB6

Wister, Owen 1860-1938 ....DLB9

Woiwode, Larry 1941- DLB6

Wolfe, Gene 1931- DLB8

Wolfe, Thomas 1900-1938
....DLB9; DS2

Wood, Charles 1932-1980 ....DLB13

Woolson, Constance Fenimore 1840-1894
....DLB12

Worcester, Joseph Emerson 1784-1865
....DLB1

Wright, Harold Bell 1872-1944 ....DLB9

Wright, James 1927-1980..........................DLB5

Wright, Richard 1908-1960..........................DS2

Wylie, Elinor 1885-1928 ....DLB9

Wylie, Philip 1902-1971..........................DLB9

Y

Yates, Richard 1926- DLB2; Y81

Yeats, William Butler 1865-1939 ....DLB10

Young, Stark 1881-1963..............................DLB9

Z

Zangwill, Israel 1864-1926 ....DLB10

Zebrowski, George 1945- DLB8

Zelazny, Roger 1937- DLB8

Zimmer, Paul 1934- DLB5

Zindel, Paul 1936- DLB7

Zukofsky, Louis 1904-1978
....DLB5